# UNIVERSITY OF KANSAS PUBLICATIONS

Library Series, 28

# A BIBLIOGRAPHY OF
# 17TH CENTURY GERMAN IMPRINTS
# IN DENMARK
# AND THE DUCHIES OF
# SCHLESWIG-HOLSTEIN

By

## P. M. MITCHELL

Volume 2

UNIVERSITY OF KANSAS LIBRARIES

1969

1668  BADENHAUPT, HERMANN

Choragium Melicum, bestehend in VII. Büchern, als Violin 1. &. 2., Cant.
1. &. 2., Bass. Vocal., Bass. Instrum. vel Violon und Basso Continuo,
worinn XL. Danck-und Lob-, Communion-und Buß-, Fest-und Sontags-
Musicken, mit 1.2.3. Vocal-, und 2.3. Instrumental Stimmen, samt dem
General Basso pro Organis. Glückstadt, 1674.

4to.                                                                                        *

*Moller* I, 27. Formerly in Hamburg Staatsbibliothek.

1669  BERCKENDAL, JOHANNES

Dritte Abbildung | Anthonette Bourignons/ | Darauß zu sehen daß Sie |
Wie länger wie ärger/ wie älter wie | schrumpflicher/ und abscheu- |
licher wird. | Auß ihrem grossen Buch von 87. Bo- | gen (von ihr
betrieglich/ unter dem Titul Ge- | zeugnisse der Warheit vorgestellet)
getreulich | zusammen gezogen/ und allen Wahrheit lieben- | den
Christen/ zum Abscheu ihrer Kä- | tzerey mit getheilet. | durch | Johann
Berckendall/ | Zum Vortrab | von folgender | Gezeugniß der Lügen
Anthonette | Bourignons | [ornaments] | [rule] | Jm Jahr Christi/ 1674

8vo. [6], 26 pp.; A-B⁸.                                                                    CKB

1670  BRÄMER, CHRISTIAN

Frey Städte der Sünder | Bey HochAnsehnlicher Leich-Begängnüß |
. . . | H. M. Hieronymi | Buecks/ | . . . | Von | M. Christian Brämer
Lubec. | [rule] | Kopenhagen/ Gedruckt durch Matthias Jürgenssen/
1674.

4to. [6], 168, [4] pp.; (a)⁴, A-X⁴ Y².                                                     CKB

Title and text within borders of type ornaments. On Y1r-Y2r, poem by
"Poliander."

1671  BRANDT, FRIEDRICH

Ein guter Wechsel: | Welt und Unruhe verlohren; | . . . | Johann-
Friederich | Brandten/ | Philosophiæ & Juris Studiosi, | . . . | Jn
Dänischer Sprache vorgetragen; Nachmals auch/ | auf Begehren/ ins
Teutsche übersetzet/ | Von | Friederich Brandt/ | Predigern zu Svenning
bej Glorup. | [woodcut: coffin] | [rule] | Kopenhagen/ Gedruckt bey
Matthias Jürgensen 1674.

4to. A-F⁴.                                                                                 CKB

1672  BRANDT, FRIEDRICH

Die allerlieblichste | Wild-Bahn; | Das ist: | Der heilige Ehestand. | An

dem hochzeitlichen Freunden-Fest/ | Des Wolgebornen Herrn | Herrn
Vincentz Joachim | von Hahnen/ | . . . | Und | Der Wolgebornen Jung-
frauen/ | Jungfr. Jda Hedewig | Rumorinn. | . . . | gezeiget und ent-
worffen/ von | Friedrich Brandt/ | Predigern zu Schwenning bei
Glorup. | . . . | [rule] | Kopenhagen/ Gedruckt im Jahr 1674.

4to. χ⁴.                                                                                                CKB

1673  BURCHARD, GEORG HEINRICH

Christliche Gründliche | Anmerckungen/ | über | die groben und
mehrentheils Gotteslästerlichen | Jrthümer und Lehren/ | Welche ge-
funden werden in den Schrifften | der | Anthoniæ Bourignon | Und |
insonderheit in dem Buch derselben | welches sie | Bezeugnüß der War-
heit | benennet/ | Zur schüldigen rettung der Ehren GOTTES | und
unsers Heylandes Jesu Christi, | Und | den Unwissenden zur nöthigen
Warnung | kurtz und deutlich zusammen gefasset | Durch | M. Georg.
Henr. Burchardum, | Predigern des Göttlichen Wortes am Thumb | in
Schleßwig | [ornament] | Gedruckt daselbst in der Fürstl. Druckerey |
[rule] | durch Johan Holwein im Jahr 1674.

4to.  Pp. [1-48], 1-144, 149-164; (a)-(f)⁴, A-V⁴.                              CKB

On pp. 161-164 Latin note to the reader by Antonius Possevinus, dated 3 May 1585.
Augmented edition: *Christliche Gründliche | Anmerckungen/ | . . . | Sampt
beygefügtem Judicio | H. D. Sebastiani Neumanni Gener. Super- | intend. der
Fürstenth. Schleßw. Holst. | [rule] | Hamburg bey Gottfried Schultzen. | Schleß-
wig gedruckt durch Johann Holwein/ | Jm Jahr 1674.* 8vo, [72], 240 pp.; a-d⁸, e⁴,
A-P⁸ (Tübingen UL).

1674  BURCHARD, MATTHIAS

A. & Ω. | Der betrübten und sterbenden Hertzen | bewehrtestes COR-
DIAL, | . . . | Hn. Claus von Alefeldt/ | Jhrer Königl. Majest. zu Denne-
marck/ | Norwegen/ &c. wolverdienten Obristen-Leutenants/ | . . . |
Haupt-Kirchen zum Kiel/ den 14. Maji, | Anno 1674. | Fürgestellet und
erkläret | durch | MATTHIAM BURCHARDUM, | Archidiaconum. |
[rule] | Kiel/ | Gedruckt durch Joachim Reuman/ Acad. Buchdr.

4to. 64, [4] pp.; A-H⁴ J².                                                                           CKB

On J 1-2, poem by D. G. Morhoff.

1675  BURCHARD, MATTHIAS

A. & Ω. | NUBILA. JUBILA. | Der Christen | Traurige Fasten/ und
fröliche Ostern/ | . . . | Fr. Emerentzia von Buchwaldt/ | gebohrnen von
der Wischen/ | . . . | Haupt-Kirchen zum Kiel/ mit vornehmen Ade-

lichen Traur-geleite | zu Jhrem Castro doloris geführet worden. | Fürge-
stellet | durch | MATTHIAM BURCHARDUM, | Archidiaconum
daselbst. | [rule] | Kiel/ gedruckt durch Joachim Reuman/ Acad.
Buchdr. [1674]

4to. 74 pp.; A-J⁴.                                                                          CKB

Last 2 pages incorrectly numbered 71 and 72.

1676  DENMARK. *Laws, statutes, etc.*

WJr Christian der Fünffte/ von | ... | ... 4. Januarij, Anno 1674.

Broadside.                                                                              KIEL UL

Decree that creditors should pay their debts according to the value of coins before
devaluation.

1677  DENMARK. *Laws, statutes, etc.*

WJR Christian der Fünffte/ von | ... | ... Glückstadt den 23. Martij,
Anno 1674.

Broadside.                                                                                 CNA

Decree issued jointly with Duke Christian Albrecht of Schleswig-Holstein, calling a
"Landtages Convocation" at Rendsburg 4 May.

1678  DENMARK. *Laws, statutes, etc.*

WJr Christian der Fünffte/ von | ...' | ... 9. Junij, Anno 1674

Broadside.                                                                              KIEL UL

Decree issued jointly with Duke Christian Albrecht of Schleswig-Holstein, regarding payment in installments of a tax on land.

1679  DENMARK. *Laws, statutes, etc.*

WJr Christian der Fünffte/ von | ... | ... 2. Augusti, Anno 1674.

Broadside.                                                                                 CKB

Decree issued jointly with Duke Christian Albrecht of Schleswig-Holstein, regarding a meeting of the courts at Rendsburg 15 September.

1680  DENMARK. *Laws, statutes, etc.*

WJR Christian der Fünffte/ von | ... | ... Glück- | stadt/ den 19.
Augusti, Anno 1674.

Broadside.                                                                           CNA; CKB

Decree issued jointly with Duke Christian Albrecht of Schleswig-Holstein, calling a
"Land Gerichts Tag" in Flensburg 16 October.

1681  DENMARK. *Laws, statutes, etc.*

WJR Christian der Fünffte/ von | . . . | . . . Glückstadt/ den 14. |
Decembris, Anno 1674

Broadside.                                                                                   CNA

Decree regarding a meeting of the "Ober-Amtgericht" at Glückstadt 18 February.

1682  DENMARK. *Laws, statutes, etc.*

WJR Christian der Fünffte/ von | . . . | . . . Glückstadt/ | den 14.
Decembris, Anno 1674.

Broadside.                                                                                   CNA

Decree, renewing a decree of Christian IV, regarding the inspection of church ac-
counts and schools.

1683  EPISTOLA | AMICI AD AMICUM | Die Oldenburgische | Succession
und darin gegen Gottorff | eröffnete Käyserliche Urtheil | betreffend. |
[rule] | Jm Jahr 1674

4to. 23, [1] pp.; A-C⁴.                                                                       CKB

1684  Die 44. | Extraordinaire | RELATION | von | Allerley Orten [1674]

8vo. Pp. 345-352.                                                                             SRL

Issued by Daniel Paulli, Copenhagen. At head of page: *Fol. 345*

1685  Extraordinaires | RELATIONES | von denen | Denkwürdigsten Sachen |
aus allerley Orten | eingekommen | Anno 1674 | im | JANUARIO |
Relata [woodcut: Mercury] refero

Small 4to. 1812 [i.e., 1824], [16] pp.; A-E⁴, F⁸, G-M⁴, N⁸, O-S⁴, T⁸, V-Z⁴, Aa⁴,
Bb⁸, Cc-Yy⁴, χ², Zz⁴, A3-Q3⁴, R3⁸, S3-X3⁴, Y3⁸, Z3-K4⁴, L4⁸, M4-V6⁴, X6-D8⁴, E8⁸,
F8-W8⁴, X8⁸, Y8-Z8⁴, A9⁸, B9-F9⁴, G9⁸, H9⁴, I9⁸, K9-Y9⁴, Z9⁸.                              CKB

Title within ornamental border. T-p from January serves as collective title for year.
First issue of each month with added title-page, with larger cut of Mercury. Issues
other than first of month with caption title, "Extraordinaires RELATIONES Aus
Allerley Orten" (Title varies). In all, 212 numbers. Pagination disregards leaf Yy,
repeats p. 1038, 1052, 1125-1132, and skips p. 1044, 1074, 1107-08, 1133-40, 1173-1180.
"W" used as signature except in alphabets 6 and 9. Inserted between pp. 152-153,
*Neue Zeitung aus Hummelburg.* . . . , separately entered (No. 1703). Leaf A9-1
with separate title: *Der Königl. Majestät | in Schweden | bey dem Käyserlichen
Hofe ietzo | anwesenden | Extraordin. Abgesandtens | Excellenz | Herrn Benedict |
Oxenstirns | . . . | Friedens-Vortrag | . . . . | . . . 1674.* In all, 8 leaves signed vari-
ously )( and A9; the item is Nr. 191 of the newspaper's series. No pagination indi-
cated, but item is inserted between p. 1612 and p. 1629. On Z9-1, separate title:
*Tractat de Marine, | oder | Vereinigungs-Puncten | über den | See-Handel und
Schiffahrt: | zwischen | Sr. Königl. Maj. | von Groß-Britannien/ | und | die Her-*

ren | *General-Staten* | *der vereinigten Niederlanden:* | ... | *Geschlossen in Londen* *den 1. Decemb. 1674.* | [rule] | *Kopenhaven* | *Bei Daniel Paulli Königl.* *Buchhändler.*

1686    (Gedicht auf Ernst Moritz Landwehr 12.5. 1674. von den Land-
        wehr'schen Tischgenossen). Kiel: Joachim Reumann, 1674.

Folio. χ¹.

Formerly in Kiel UL (LmC 30ª-59).

1687    GRÄSSEL, JACOB

Lobgesang über den Geburtstag Jesu Christi. Schleswig, 1674.

4to.

*Moller* II, 243.

1688    GREFFLINGER, GEORG

ETHICA | COMPLEMENTORIA | Das ist: | Complementir | Büch-
lein/ | Jn welchem enthalten/ eine | richtige Art/ wie man so wol mit
hohen | als niedrigen Standes- | Personen: bey | Geselschaften/ und
Frauenzim- | mer Hoff zierlich reden und | umbgehen solle. | Neulichst
wieder übersehen/ an vie- | len Orten gebessert und vermeh- | ret/ durch |
Georg Grefflingern/ | gekrönten Poeten/ und | Notar. Publ. | Mit ange-
fügtem Trenchir- | Büchlein/ | Auch züchtigen Tisch- und | Leber-
Reimen | [rule] | Kopenhagen/ Gedruckt bey Christian Wering |
Universit. Buchdr. Jm Jahr. 1674. Jn | Verlag Wolff Lamprecht.

12mo. Pp. 1-120, 120-215; A-J¹²; frontispiece, 23 plates.        CKB

The 2 pages numbered 120 (E12v and F1r) are a double chart. The *Trenchir-*
*Büchlein* and the *Tisch- und Leber-reime* (by Heinrich Schaeve) have separate title-
pages and may have been issued separately: page 103 (E4r): *Neues* | *Trenchier-* |
*Büchlein:* | *Anleitende/* | *Wie man rechter Art und* | *jetzigem Gebrauch/ nach*
*allerhand* | *Speisen ordentlich auff die Taffel* | *setzen/ zierlich zerschneiden und*
*vorlegen/* | *auch artlich wiederumb abhe-* | *ben solle.* | *Hiebevor an verschiedenen* |
*Orten herauß gegeben/ neulichst* | *aber mit Fleiß übersehen/ und mit schö-* | *nen*
*Kupffer-vorbildungen ans* | *Licht gebracht/* | *Durch* | *Andreas Kletten/ Cygn.* |
*Misn. & Iur. Stud.* | [ornament] | *Kopenhagen/* | *Druckts Christian Wehring Acad.*
*Buchdr.* | *Anno M DC LXXIV;* and page 168 (H12r): *Jungfer* | *Euphrosinen* |
*Von* | *Sittenbach* | *Züchtige* | *Tisch-und Le-* | *ber-Reime/* | *An jhre Gespilinnen.* |
[ornament] | *Kopenhagen/* | [rule] | *Gedruckt bey Christian Wehring 1674.* Plates
7 and 8 lacking from CKB copy.

1689    [HEINS, VALENTIN]

Ewigwährender | Calender | nebst | einer Verzeichnis aller | Jahr-Viehe-
und anderer | Märckten | welche von den Kaufleuten | und Krämern |

in | Dännemarck/ Norwägen/ | wie auch in Schweden/ Fin- | land und
anderswo | besucht werden; | Diesem ist annoch ein Wegweiser | und
sonst ein mehrers hin- | beigefügt.

12mo. 36 pp.; A-C⁶.                                                              CKB

Bound with Elias Piluland, *Neues | Müntz-Buchlein |* . . . 1674 (No. 1706).

**1690**  HESSELIUS, PETER

Hamburgischer | Palmen-baum | Vorgesezt | Und nach seinem | Alter-
thumb/ Wachsthumb | Und | Eigenthumb | Kürtzlich Beschrieben |
Von | M. Petro Hesselio | Pastorn zum Pesthoff. | [ornament] | Zu
Altona | [rule] | Gedruckt bey Victor de Löw/ Anno M. D.C. LXXIV.

4to. 15, [1] pp.; A-B⁴; 1 plate.                                                 CKB

Frontispiece: engraving of Hamburg.

**1691**  Immanuel | GOTT mit Uns | auf allen | rechtmässigen Wegen | das ist |
Reise-manual | in sich begreiffend | andächtige Gebete/ geistliche |
Lieder und inbrünstige Seufzerlein | in allerhand Noht und Anlie- | gen
zu gebrauchen. | 16 [symbol] 74. | Auf einiger Personen Begehren |
zusammen getragen | [rule] | Kopenhagen | Bei Daniel Paulli Königl.
Buchhändl. | Gedruckt bey Christian Wehring | Universit. Buchd.

12mo. [8], 131, [1] pp.; §⁴, A-L⁶.                                               CKB

Bastard-title: *Reise-Manual | und | Handels-Büchlein.* Verso of bastard-title: "Ap-
probatio," signed "Georg: Witzleben, D." and dated "Anno 1674."

**1692**  JENSEN, JOHANNES JACOB

Die Klagerede . . . tröstender Wittwen, Generalmaior Hans Ranzaus
Wittwe Doroth. Olg. Bluhmin . . . vorgestellt. Kiel, 1674.

Folio.                                                                            •

*OHM* I, 274.

**1693**  JESSEN, FRIEDRICH

Der Gerechten zukünfftiger Trost/ | . . . | Hn. Johannis Hansen/ | Dero
zu Schleßwig und Holstein Regieren- | den Hoch-Fürstlichen Durch-
leuchtigkeiten gewese- | nen vielbetrawten Amptschreibers auff Got-
torff. | . . . | Von | FRIDERICO JESSENIO, S.S. Theol. D. | & Past.
prim. daselbst. | [rule] | Kiel/ | Gedruckt durch Joachim Reuman/ Acad.
Buchdr. [1674]

4to. [8], 54, [14] pp.; )(⁴, A-H⁴ J².                                            CKB

On G4r, added title: *Letztes Ehren-Gedächtniß | . . . | von | Nachgesetzten*

*Freunden.* | [rule] | *Kiel/* | *Gedruckt durch Joachim Reumann/ Acad. Buchdr.*
On G4v-J2, verse by several hands.

1694  JESSEN, FRIEDRICH

Rechter EhrenPreiß | Aller | Recht-Gläubigen Christen/ | . . . | Herr
Hans Rantzow/ | General Majeur, | . . . | . . . in der Stadt Kiel mittelst
hochansehnli- | cher/ und Hoch-Adelicher Ehren-Begängnuß | bestäti-
get worden/ | . . . | von FRIDERICO JESSENIO, | S.S. Theol. D. &
Pastore daselbst. | [rule] | KJEL/ Gedruckt durch Joachim Reuman.
[1674]

4to. 79, [1] pp.; A-K⁴.                                                   CKB

1695  KENCKEL, STEPHAN

Der | Geistliche Wanderstab/ | . . . | Hr. Johann Preuß/ | . . . | von |
STEPHANO Kenckel/ der H. Schrifft | Doctore, Pastorn zu Tundern/
wie auch Probsten | daselbst und der Æmpter Tundern und | Lügum-
Closter. | [woodcut: coffin] | Kiel/ gedruckt durch Joachim Reuman/
Acad. Buchdr. [1674]

4to. [12], 66 pp.; A-K⁴ (K4 blank).                                       CKB

Pages 64-66 incorrectly numbered 54-56.

1696  KENCKEL, STEPHAN

Die | Gekrönte Trew/ | . . . | Frawen | Mette Mariæ/ | gebohrner
Preussin/ | . . . | Thomæ Dettleffs/ | . . . | . . . HaußEhr/ | . . . | Von
STEPHANO Kenckel/ der H. Schrifft Doctore, | Pastorn zu Tundern/
wie auch Probsten daselbst und der Æmpter | Tundern und Lügum-
Kloster. | [rule] | Schleßwig in der Fürstl. Druckerey gedruckt | durch
Johan Holwein. [1674]

4to. [6], 66, [68] pp.; A-R⁴ S².                                          CKB

Title within border of type ornaments. On K1r added title: *Klag-und Danck-
Rede* | *Bey Hochbetraurlich-frühzeitigen jedoch* | *seligen Hintritt* | . . . | *Von* |
*Johan. Christian de Bähr;* on L2r, added title: *Die verfinsterte Sonne* | *Oder* |
*Klag- und Trost-Schrifft* | . . . | *Von* | *Johanne Lundio* | . . . .; on N1r, added
title: *Traur-Ehren-und Trost-Seule/* | . . . . (verse by several hands); on O2r,
added Latin title: *TUMULUS* | *Mellitiss. Omniq. Virtutum Numero* | . . . .
(Memorials and verse by several hands).

1696A Der Königl. Majestät | in Schweden | bey dem Käyserlichen Hofe
ietzo | anwesenden | Extraordin. Abgesandtens | Excellenz | Herrn Bene-
dict | Oxenstirns | Grafens in Borsholm/ und | Wasen/ Freyherrn in
Morby/ | Herrn zu Lindholm/ etc. etc. | in geheimer Audienz münd-

lich- | abgelegter | Friedens-Vortrag. | [rule] | Nach dem zu Wien gedruktem Exemplar. | Den 19. 29. October/ 1674.

8vo. *A9⁸.                                                                    (CKB)

Issued with Daniel Paulli's *Extraordinaires Relationes*. In lower left-hand corner of title-page: "Num. 191."

1697    Kurtzes | Gebet-Büch- | lein/ | Doch | Auf vielerhand Fälle und An- | liegen gerichtet. | Plöen/ | [rule] | Gedruckt und verlegt durch Tobias | Schmiedt. Jm Jahr 1674.

12mo. 162, [6] pp.; a-g¹².                                                    SRL

1698    [MAJOR, JOHANN DANIEL]

[monogram] | Unvorgreiffliches Bedencken | von | Kunst-und Natura- | lien-Kammern | ins gemein | [figure, with motto] | [rule] | Kjel/ | Gedruckt durch Joachim Reuman/ Acad. Buchdr. [1674]

4to. A-E⁴.                                                                    CKB

1699    [MAJOR, JOHANN DANIEL]

Verbesserter Zustand | Der Weiland (Tit.) numehr-Seeligen Frauen/ | Fr. Dorothee Catharin | Hansen/ gebohrner Schachtinn/ | [woodcut: angel above monogram] | auff Deroselben/ in Schleßwig/ den 8ᵗᵉⁿ Mertz | 1674. angestellte Be-erdigung/ | schuld-willig entworffen. | [rule] | KJEL/ | Gedruckt durch Joach. Reuman/ Acad. Buchdr.

Folio. A² [B]².                                                               SHLB

1699A [MAJOR, JOHANN DANIEL]

[monogram] | Vorstellung etlicher | Kunst-und Natura- | lien-Kam- | mern/ | in Africa/ und an Gräntzen | Europæ | [figure, with motto] | [rule] | Kjel/ | Gedruckt durch Joachim Reuman/ Acad. Buchdr. [1674]

4to. A-D⁴.                                                                    CKB

1700    [MAJOR, JOHANN DANIEL]

[monogram] | Vorstellung etlicher | Kunst-und Natura- | lien-Kam- | mern/ | in America und Asia | [figure: angel with trumpets over motto: A/ solis/ ortu/ | usque ad/ OCCASUM/ | laudabile/ nomen/ DNI] | [rule] | Kjel/ | Gedruckt durch Joachim Reuman/ Acad. Buchdr. [1674]

4to. A-C⁴.                                                                    CKB

*Index Alphabeticus der Kunst- Naturalien- Schatz- und Antiquitäten-Kammern, in und außer Europa,* published later in Kiel, 4to. *Moller* II, 516.

1701  MARTINI, BENEDICT

SPECULUM SALOMONÆUM, | ostendens, | Mundum muliebrem
optimum. | . . . | Fr. Dorotheæ Catharinæ | gebohrner Schachtinnen/ |
Des HochEdlen/ Vesten und Hochgelahrten | Herrn MELCHIORIS
HANSEN/ | . . . | Hertzliebsten Ehe-Schatzes/ | . . . | Von | BENE-
DICTO MARTINI, Ecclesiæ Cathedralis | Slesvicensis Pastore. | [rule] |
Gedruckt durch Johann Holwein/ Fürstl. Buchdruckern | in Schleßwig/
An. 1674.

4to. 44, [36] pp.; A-K⁴.                                    GÖTTINGEN UL; CKB

On F3, separate title: *Ultimum Vale,* | . . . | *Amicis Kiliensibus.* | . . . ; on H1,
separate title: *Eutienisches Mitleiden/* | . . . | *Frauen Dorotheen Cathrienen* |
*Hansen/ gebohrner Schachtinn/* | . . . | *Schleßwig/* | *Gedruckt durch Johann*
*Holwein.* Verse by Christian v. Stökken, *et al.* On J1, separate title: *Letzte Ehren-*
*Pflicht/* | . . . *F. Dorotheæ Catharinæ* | *Gebohrnen Schachtin/* | . . . | *Schleßwig/* |
*Gedruckt durch Johann Holwein.* Verse by Joh. Volcmar Rötscher, *et al.* CKB
copy has only A-E⁴ F².

1702  MUSÆUS, SIMON HINRICH

Der gekrönete | FRJEDERJCH | in einem Freuden-Spiel | vorgestel-
let/ | Und | Dem Hochwürdigsten/ Durchläuchtig- | sten Fürsten und
Herrn/ | Hn. August | Friederich/ | Erwehlten Bischoff des Stiffts
Lübeck/ | Erben zu Norrwegen/ Hertzogen zu Schleßwig/ | Holstein/
Stormarn und der Dittmarschen/ Graffen | zu Oldenburg und Delmen-
horst. | Als Seiner Hoch-Fürstl. Durchl. Nahmens-Tag | den 14. Win-
termonaths dieses itzo lauffenden | 1674 Jahres einfiel | Jn tieffster
Demuth überreichet | von | Seiner Hoch-Fürstl. Durchl. | unterthänig-
sten Knecht | Simon Hinrich Musæus. | [rule] | KJEL/ Druckts
Joachim Reuman/ Acad. Buchd. 1674.

4to. A-E⁴ F².                                                    PRINCETON UL

1703  Neue Zeitung | aus | Hummelburg | allwo oberhalb Schweins- | fuhrt ein
Deich durchgebrochen/ und | eine frembde Art Passagierer | ankom-
men. | [rule] | Jm Jahr 1674

8vo. χ⁴.                                                             CKB

Issued by D. Paulli in Copenhagen in conjunction with his *Extraordinaires Rela-*
*tiones,* 1674 Nr. 17 (No. 1685).

1704  OLEARIUS, ADAM

Gottorffische | Kunst-Kammer/ | Worinnen | Allerhand ungemeine
Sachen/ So | theils die Natur/ theils künstliche Hände her- | vor
gebracht und bereitet. | Vor diesem | Aus allen vier Theilen der Welt |

zusammen getragen/ | Und | Vor einigen Jahren beschrieben/ | Auch mit behörigen Kupffern gezieret | Durch | Adam Olearium, Weil. Bibliothecarium | und Antiquarium auff der Fürstl. Resi- | dentz Gottorff. | Welchem zu Ende angefüget ist/ des itzt-gedachten seel. | Herrn Olearii Holsteinische Chronica. | Anjetzo aber übersehen/ und zum andern mal | gedruckt/ | [type ornaments] | Auff Gottfriedt Schultzens Kosten. 1674. | [rule] | Jn dessen Buchladen zu Schleßwig solche zu finden ist.

4to. [12], 80 pp.; a⁴ b², A-K⁴; 37 folding plates.                    CKB; (BM)

Leaf a1 is preliminary title engraving.

## 1705   [OLEARIUS, ADAM]

Kurtzer Begriff | Einer | Holsteinischen | CHRONIC | Oder | Summarische Beschreibung der denckwür- | digsten Geschichten/ so innerhalb 200. und mehr | Jahren/ nemblich von Anno 1448. biß | 1663. in den NordLanden/ sonderlich in | Holstein sich begeben. | Alles auß bekanten Geschicht-Schreibern/ so auff | der andern Seiten nahmhafftig | gemachet. | Auffs kürtzest zusammen getragen | durch | A. O. | [ornament] | Gedruckt im Jahr 1674.

4to. [4], 148, [8] pp.; π², a-t⁴, u², 1 plate.                    CKB, (YALE)

On verso of title-page list of *Autores Auß welchen dieses Büchlein zusammen getragen. Cf.* No. 1716.

## 1706   [PILULAND, ELIAS]

Neues | Müntz-Büchlein | begreiffend | I. Den Valeur der Dänischen Müntze. | II. Wie man Reichs-Thaler zu | Schlechte-Thaler/ und Schlechte-Thaler | zu Reichs-Thaler; item Corrant-Thaler zu | Reichs- und Schlechte-Thaler; auch | andere Sorten mehr reduciret. | III. Eine Caßier-Rechnung/ dadurch | zu erlernen/ wie viel Würffe außzugeben oder | zu entpfangen/ wann man von ein und an- | dern kleinen Geld-Sorten/ entweder was zu | bezahlen oder einzunehmen hat. | IV. Eine Interesse-Rechnung: was | Reichs-Corrant-und Schlechte-Thaler/ &c. | gegen 6. pro Cento/ Jährlich Rente | bringen. | V. Außländischer Müntzen Verglei- | chung mit der Dänischen. | [rule] | Kopenhaven | Bey Daniel Paulli/ Königl. Buchhändl. | Anno 1674.

12mo. 147, [1], 36 pp.; A-H⁶, [I]⁶, K-M⁶ N 1-2, Aa-Cc⁶.            CKB

CKB copy lacks leaf [I]4. On Aa1r, separate title, beginning new pagination 1-36: *Unterschiedlicher | Ellen- | auch anderer | Maaß- | und mehrerlei | Gewichts Vergleichung | ... | von | Elia Piluland.*

1707 RATENBURG, BRODER

Glückwünschungs Ehren-Gedicht/ | Auff das | Hochzeitliche Freuden-
Mahl | . . . | H. Friederich Jürgensen/ | . . . | Jungf. Catharina/ | . . . |
Herrn Stephani Kenckels/ | . . . | . . . Tochter | . . . | von | Brodero
Ratenburg. | [woodcut] | KJEL/ | Gedruckt durch Joachim Reumann/
Acad. Buchdr. [1674]

Folio. χ². 
                                                                        CKB

1708 RITTER, JOHANN BALTHASAR

Der | Unvergleichliche Adel | . . . | Herr Georg Brochenhus | Sigwards-
søn/ | . . . | Von | Johann Balthasar Ritter | . . . | [rule] | Kopenhagen/ |
Gedruckt bey Matthiam Jürg. Godicchen. 1674

4to. [2], 160 pp.; π1, A-V⁴; 1 folding plate. 
                                                                        CKB

Title and text within borders of type ornaments. Text, pp. 127 ff. in Danish.

1709 Schertz-Gedicht/ | Auff den Hochzeitlichen Ehren-Tag | Deß Wolge-
bohrnen Herrn/ | Hn. Moritz Rantzow/ | Erbe zu Nöhr und Grün-
wald. | . . . | Mit der | Wolgebohrnen Jungfer | Jungf. HEDEWJG/ |
Deß Wolgebohrnen Herrn | Herrn Kay von Ahlfeld/ | Erbherr auff
Aschau Eheleiblichen Jungf. Tochter | . . . | Von | Etlichen guten
Freunden. | [emblem] | KJEL/ | Gedruckt durch Joach. Reuman/ Acad.
Buchdr. [1674]

Folio. χ². 
                                                                        CKB

Signed by A. H.

1710 SCHLESWIG-HOLSTEIN-GOTTORFF. *Laws, statutes, etc.*

Artickuls Brieff | Des Hochwürdigsten/ Durch- | läuchtigsten Fürsten
und | Herrn/ | Herrn Christian | Albrechten/ | Erben zu Norwegen/
postulir- | ten Coadjutoris des Stiffts Lübeck/ | Hertzogen zu Schleßw:
Holstein/ Stormarn | und der Dithmarschen/ Graffen zu | Oldenburg
und Delmen- | horst/ &c. | [ornament] | Schleßwig | Gedruckt durch
Johann Holwein/ | [rule] | Jm Jahr 1674.

8vo. 96 pp.; A-F⁸. 
                                                                        CKB

1711 SCHLESWIG-HOLSTEIN-GOTTORFF. *Laws, statutes, etc.*

Des | Hochwürdigsten/ Durchleuchtigsten | Fürsten und Herrn/ | Herrn
Christian Albrechten/ | Erben zu Norwegen/ Postulirten Coad- |
jutoris des Stiffts Lübeck/ Hertzogen zu Schleßwig/ | Holstein/ Stor-
marn und der Dittmarschen | Grafen zu Oldenburg und Delmenhorst/ |
Gnädigst | elucidirte und erleuterte | Constitution | Von | Justificir-und

Zuschreibung der in der | Stadt Kiehl seynden | Begräbnussen und | Kirchen-Stühle/ | Zu Jedermans Wissenschaft | in offenen Druck gegeben. [1674]

4to. χ⁴.                                                 CNA

Signed at end: B. Niederstedt.

1712  SCHLESWIG-HOLSTEIN-GOTTORFF. *Laws, statutes, etc.*

Wir von Gottes Gnaden Christian Albrecht/ Erbe | zu Norwegen/ postulirter Coadjutor des Stiffts Lübeck/ Hertzog zu Schleßwig/ Holstein/ ... | ... | ... Gottorff 27. Juni An 1674

Broadside (2 sheets pasted together).                         CNA

A list of import and export duties for Eyderstätt, Dithmarschen, and Husum ("Licensrolle").

1713  SCHLESWIG-HOLSTEIN-GOTTORFF. *Laws, statutes, etc.*

WJr von Gottes Gnaden Christian Albrecht/ | Erbe zu Norwegen/ postulirter Coadjutor des Stiffts Lübeck/ Hertzog zu Schleßwig/ Holstein/ | ... | ... Gottorff/ den 27. Junii Anno 1674

Broadside (2 sheets pasted together).                         CNA

"Zollrolle" for Eyderstätt, Dithmarschen, and Husum.

1714  SCHMIDT VON EISENBERG, VALENTIN

Ardentissimum Eliæ Desiderium | ... | Herrn BONAVENTURÆ Rehefeld | ... | Von | VALENTINO Schmidt von Eisenberg/ ... | ... | [rule] | Schleßwig | Gedruckt bey Johan Holwein/ Anno 1674.

4to. 40, [6] pp.; A-E⁴ F1-3.                                    CKB

Title within ornamental border. On F1r, added title: *Glaubens Triumph/* | ... CKB copy defective: all after F3 lacking.

1715  Der Soldaten freche Hand/ | Wird gelähmt durch Liebes Band | Auff das | Hochzeitliche Freuden-Mahl | Deß Wolgebohrnen Herrn/ | Herrn Moritz Rantzow/ | ... | Mit der | Wolgebohrnen Jungfer | Jungf. Hedewig/ | ... | ANNO 1674. den 2. Martij | ... | von einem Neuen Soldaten auß Rensburg | [below:] Kjel/ Gedruckt durch Joachim Reuman/ Acad. Buchdr.

Broadside (35.2 x 25.2 cm).                                       CKB

1716  SOLINUS, CHRISTIAN

Holsteinische | Chronica/ | Aus | Des Herrn Christiani Solini, weyland | Predigern in der Königl. Stadt und Veste | Krempe in Holstein |

CHRONOLOGIA | Kürtzlich verfasset und zusammen | gezogen. | Welchen beygefügt ist | A. O. Kurtzer Begriff einer Holsteinischen | Chronike. | [ornament] | Gedruckt im Jahr 1674.

4to. 72, [4], [4], 148, [8] pp.; A-J⁴ K², a-t⁴ u²; 1 plate.                 CKB, (BM)

Printed with: *Kurtzer Begriff* | *Einer* | *Holsteinischen* | *CHRONIC* | . . . | *durch* | *A*[dam]. *O*[learius] | . . ., 1674 (No. 1704).

1717 [STÖCKEN, CHRISTIAN VON]

Eutienisches | MJTLEJDEN/ | . . . | F. Dorotheen Catrienen | Hansen/ gebohrner Schachtin | . . . | Schleßwig gedruckt durch Johan Holwein [1674]

4to. A⁴.                                                                 HERLUFSHOLM

1718 STORNING, HENRICH

Jesus Christus | Der Höchste Freund in der Noth. | . . . | Fr. Anna Powischen/ | . . . | von | Mag. HENRICO STORNING, | Pastore des Klosters. | [rule] | Kiel/ | Gedruckt durch Joachim Reuman/ Acad. Buchdr. [1674]

4to. [6], 80, [22] pp.; A-N⁴ O².                                              CKB

On L4, separate title: *Traur-und Klag-Reimen/* | . . . Verse by several hands.

1718A Tractat de Marine, | oder | Vereinigungs-Puncten | über den | See-Handel und Schiffahrt: | zwischen | Sr. Königl. Maj. | von Groß-Britannien/ | und | die Herren | General-Staten | der vereinigten Niederlanden: | Wornach beederseits Unter- | thanen in allen Landen und sonderli- | chen Theilen der Welt zu Wasser und | Lande sich richten und verhalten | sollen. | Geschlossen in Londen den 1. Decemb. | 1674 | [rule] | Kopenhaven | Bei Daniel Paulli Königl. Buchhändler.

8vo. Z9⁸.                                                                    CKB

Issued with Daniel Paulli's *Extraordinaire Relationes*.

1719 Vollständiges | Gesang-Buch/ | Darinnen | Nicht allein alle alte gewöhnliche | Kirchen-Gesänge zu finden/ sondern | auch mit vielen neuen geist-reichen/ und theils | vorhin nie in Druck gekommenen Lie- | dern vermehret: | Alle auff bekante Melodeien/ zu | männigliches/ absonderlich der | Einfältigen desto bessern Ge- | brauch/ eingerichtet. | Deme zu Ende beygefüget ist | Ein kurtzes/ aber auff vielerhand | Fälle und Anliegen | gerichtetes | Gebet-Büchlein. | [type ornaments] | HAMBURG/ | Jn Verlegung Heinrich Völckers. | [rule] | Plöen/ Gedruckt durch Tobias Schmiedt. | Jm Jahr 1674.

12mo. [8], 559, [25] pp.; )($^4$, A-Y$^{12}$, Z$^8$, Aa$^{12}$ Bb$^8$, 1 plate.     SRL

Bound with *Kurtzes | Gebet-Büch- | lein/ | . . . Ploen/ | . . . | . . . 1674.* (No. 1697).

1720   WILHELMI, JOHANNES CASPAR

Unverwelcklicher und unsterblicher Nachruhm der Gottseeligkeit und Auffrichtigkeit auf Generalmajor Hans Rantzau auf Puttbus. Kiel, 1674

4to.                                                                                        *

*OHM* I, 732.


## 1675


1721   [AMDERSEN, ANDREAS]

Der Tunderschen | Unsterblichen Sterblichkeit | Ander Theil/ | Das ist: | Etlicher der weyland vornehm und Namhafftesten | Herren und Matronen/ | So dann auch anderer zu und neben Tundern in | GOtt ruhenden | Jungen Personen | Grab-Schreiben/ | Dem Hertzog des Lebens/ der das Leben/ und ein | unvergängliches Wesen wieder ans Licht gebracht/ zu Eh- | ren/ den selig entschlaffenen zum gebührlichen Nachruhm/ den hinter- | bliebenen zu tröstlichem Gefallen/ und der unumbgänglichen Sterblich- | keit Erinnerung/ theils bey der Begräbniß/ theils nach demsel- | ben auffgesetzet und wolmeinentlich | übergeben. | [woodcut: skull and crossbones] | Schleßwig/ gedruckt durch Johan Holwein/ | [rule] | Jm Jahr 1675.

4to. [8], 187, [5] pp.; )($^4$, A-Aa$^4$; engraved frontispiece.     CKB

Same frontispiece as in part I (No. 546); date changed by hand to 1675.

1722   Andächtige Gebet Auff alle Tage in der Wochen/ Morgens und Abends zu sprechen. [Altona, 1675]

8vo. 256 pp.                                                                              *

*Cf.* P. T. Hoffmann in *Altonaische Zeitschrift* I (1931), p. 198.

1723   BRÄMER, CHRISTIAN

Himmels Bürger | Glückseeligkeit: | . . . | Fr. Augusta Maria | Eliesabeth von der Osten/ | gebohrnen von Winterfeld. | . . . | Von | M. Christian Brämer Lubec. | [rule] | Kopenhagen/ | Gedruckt bey Matthias Jürgenssen/ | Jm Jahr 1675.

Folio. [(a)$^2$], (b)$^2$, c1, B-L$^2$, M1, a-c$^2$, [d]$^2$. ([d]2 blank.)     CKB

Title within border of type ornaments.

1724 BRANDT, FRIEDRICH

Gläntzende Tauben-Flügel/ | das ist: | Ausführlicher Bericht/ | Von
dem Leben und Todt | Herrn | Friederich Taub- | manns/ | Weiland
hochberühmten/ | treüfleissigen und sehr beliebten | Professoris zu Wit-
tenberg/ | [emblem, with motto: "in conatv labor"] | Aufgesetzet von |
Friederich Brandt/ | Predigern zu Svenning bei Glorup. | [rule] | Kopen-
hagen/ | Bei Peter Haubold der Königl. Acad. | Buchhändler zufinden.
1675.

8vo. [16], 96 pp.; (*)$^8$, A-F$^8$.                                      BM

Title printed in red and black. Latin poem by Andreas Beyrholmius to Brandt,
(*)7v-(*)8v; Latin elegy by Daniel Heinsius, pp. 88-96.

1725 BÜTTNER, DANIEL

Traur-Gedicht/ | . . . | Hn. Matthias Claussen/ | Med. Doct. Derer zu
Schleßwig/ Holstein &c. | . . . | abstatten wollen | Daniel Büttner/ von
Minden auß Westphalen/ J.U.L. | & in Acad. Ger. Ex-Profess. | [wood-
cut: coffin] | Kiel/ Gedruckt durch Joach. Reuman/ Acad. Buchdr.
[1675]

4to. χ$^2$.                                                               CKB

Possibly printed on one sheet with D. G. Morhof, *Ode* . . . 1675 (No. 1762).

1726 BURCHARD, MATTHIAS

Tabula Smaragdina, | Oder | Der Christen | Glückselige Heil-und
Lebens-Taffel/ | . . . | Hn. Matthiæ Clausen/ | Weitberühmten Doctoris
Medicinæ und | . . . | Jn der HauptKirche St. Nicolai zum Kiel/ | Jn
einer Christlichen Leich-Predigt vorgestellet/ | und auff begehren zum
Druck übergeben | Dürch | MATTHIAM BURCHARDUM | Archi-
diaconum daselbst. | [rule] | KJEL/ | Gedruckt durch Joach. Reuman/
Acad. Buchdr. [1675]

4to. 86, [2] pp.; A-L$^4$ (L4 blank).                                     CKB

1727 BURCHARD, MATTHIAS

A. Ω. | Eines ist Noth. | . . . | Fr. Sophia Sültzbergerinnen/ | gebohrnen
von Stevens/ | . . . | Durch | MATTHIAM BURCHARDUM | Archi-
diaconum daselbst. | [rule] | Kiel/ | Gedruckt durch Joach. Reumann/
Acad. Buchdr. [1675]

4to. 79, [1] pp.; A-K$^4$.                                    GÖTTINGEN UL

1728 Christlicher Hochzeit-Wunsch/ | Als | Der Ehrenveste/ Fürnehme und
Wolgeachte | TRULS NISSEN, | Auff Jerndrup-Hoff Erbgesessen/ |

Bräutigamb: | Und | Die viel Ehr: und Tugendreiche Jungfrau/ |
CHRISTINE FABRICIEN | Braut/ | ... | Jhren Hochzeitlichen Ehren-
Tag den 8. Jun. 1675 in Jerndrup gehalten. | [below:] Schleßwig
gedruckt bey Johan Holwein.

Broadside (30.3 x 25.7 cm).                                          CKB

Signed by T. A. P.P.

1729    Cimbriens Trauer-Flohr | ... | Hn. MATTHIÆ | CLAVSEN/ | Der
        Medicin Doctorn ... | ... | Von | Nachgesetzten Freunden. | [rule] |
        Kiel/ | Gedruckt durch Joach. Reuman/ Acad. Buchdr. [1675]

        4to. χ².                                                         CKB

        Verse by Heinrich Johnsen & Bruno Hanenfeldt. *Cf.* No. 1752.

1730    DENMARK. *Laws, statutes, etc.*

        Wir Christian der Fünffte von | ... | ... Gottorff/ den 29. Martij, Anno
        1675

        Broadside.                                                      CNA

        Decree issued jointly with Duke Christian Albrecht of Schleswig-Holstein, calling a
        meeting of the "Landtag" in Kiel 6 May.

1731    DENMARK. *Laws, statutes, etc.*

        Wir Christian der Fünffte von | ... | ... Gottorff/ den 31. Martij 1675

        Broadside.                                                      CNA

        Decree issued jointly with Duke Christian Albrecht of Schleswig-Holstein, ordering
        prayers of thanksgiving on the birth of a son to King Christian.

1732    DENMARK. *Laws, statutes, etc.*

        WJr Christian der Fünffte/ von | ... | ... 6. Maij, Anno 1675.

        Broadside.                                                      CKB

        Decree, suppressing a publication by Major General Jan von der Wieck and D.
        Johann Kirchmann.

1733    DENMARK. *Laws, statutes, etc.*

        WJR Christian der Fünffte/ von | ... | ... Glückstadt/ den 10. Maij,
        Anno 1675

        Broadside.                                                      CNA

        Decree setting a limitation on the length of time old legal suits may be heard.

1734    DENMARK. *Laws, statutes, etc.*

        Wir Christian der Fünffte von | ... | ... Gottorff/ | den 15. Maij Anno
        1675.

        Broadside.                                                      CNA

Decree issued jointly with Duke Christian Albrecht of Schleswig-Holstein, regarding the sale of horses.

1734A DENMARK. *Laws, statutes, etc.*

Wir Christian der Fünffte von | Gottes Gnaden/ König zu Dennemarck/ Norwegen/ der | ... | ... Gottorff/ | den 16. Augusti, Anno 1675.

Broadside.                                                                    CKB

Decree issued jointly with Duke Christian Albrecht of Schleswig-Holstein, establishing 17, 24 September and 1 October as "Fast: Buß: und Bete-Tage."

1735    Extraordinaires | RELATIONES | vorstellende | Was mit vielerlei/ anderswo | gedruckten/ Novellen/ und schriftlichen | Zeitungen/ aus allerlei Orten/ | denckwürdigst eingekommen | Anno | 1675 [rule] | [D. Paulli's emblem] | [rule] | Kopenhagen | Bei Daniel Paulli Königl. Buchh. | an St. Marien-Kirch.

4to. Pp. 1-840, [1-16], 841-1776; A-E$^4$, F$^8$, G-O$^4$, P$^8$, Q$^4$, R$^8$, S-2F$^4$, 2G$^8$, 2H$^4$, 2J$^4$, 2K$^8$, 2L$^8$, 2M-5C$^4$, 5D$^8$, 5E-10A$^4$.                                    CKB

First issue of each month with separate title-page: *Extraordinaires RELATIONES aus allerley Orten* and large cut of Mercury. Other issues with caption title. Numerous "appendices" consecutively numbered with regular issues. In all, 215 numbers. Signatures include symbol "W." Between pp. 840-841 as gathering D5$^8$: *Manifest und angeführte Uhrsachen* (No. 1758).

1736    FRISCH, JOHANNES

Johan Frischen | Historischer Tagweiser | oder | Anweisung dessen was | sich in der Christen- | heit von Tag zu Tage | zugetragen hat | Erster Theil. | Darin die Begeben- | heiten des 1670. 1671. | 1672. und 1673. | Jahrs fürgestellet | Altona in Verlegung des Autoris 1675.

8vo. Pp. [1-8], 1-159, 158-161, 160-285, 284-320; $\pi^4$, A-K$^8$, $\chi^2$, L-S$^8$, $^2\chi$1, T-V$^8$.
                                            SALTYKOV-SCHCHEDRIN LIBRARY, LENINGRAD

Engraved title-page, signed J. Wichman, with battle scenes at head and foot of page.

1737    Gebet | Zu denen | Jn der Graffschafft Ran[tzau] | von der Hohen Obrigkeit bey gegen- | wärtigen Läufften angeordne- | ten/ täglichen | Bet-Stunden. | [rule] | Gedruckt in der Königl. Veste Glückstadt/ | durch Melchior Kochen/ Jm Jahr 1675.

4to. A-B$^4$.                                                              KIEL UL

1738    (Gedicht über Petrus Musaeus, prof. (1620-1674); von den Musaeus'schen Tischgenossen). Kiel: Joachim Reumann, 1675.

Folio. $\chi^2$.                                                                *

Formerly in Kiel UL (LmC 12-154).

**1739** GRÄSSEL, JACOB

Lob des Weingottes. [Schleswig?], 1675.

4to.                                                                            *

*OHM* II, 243.

**1740** HESSELIUS, PETER

Hertzfliessende Betrachtungen/ | Von dem | Elbe-Strom/ | Zur Danck-
barkeit gegen GOTT geschöpffet/ | darneben allen Schiff-Leuten zu
einer geistlichen Zeit- | Vertreibung vermacht; | Auch | Einem jeden
Christen in diesem Angst-Meer | zu gute auffgesetzet/ | Von | M.
PETRO HESSELIO, Pastorn | zum Pest-Hof. | Erster Theil. | [emblem,
with motto: "Solideo gloria"] | [rule] | Altona/ Gedruckt bey Victor de
Leeu, | in Verlegung des Autoris, Anno 1675.

4to. 24, 204, [16] pp. (A)-(C)$^4$, A-Dd$^4$, Ee$^2$; 25 plates.        CKB

Verse by several hands: (C)1-4.

**1741** Hochrühmliches Ehren-Gedächtniß/ | . . . | Frauen Metta Kielmannin |
von Kielmans-Eck/ | gebohrne von der Wisch. | . . . | . . . in der | Thum-
Kirchen zu Schleßwig beygesetzet worden. | Zu bezeugung schüldiger
Condolentz auffgerichtet | Von guten Freunden und Dienern.

4to. A-J$^4$.                                                          CKB

Title within ornamental border. Text within double rule border. Latin and Ger-
man verse by several hands. On J3, added title: *Schuldiges Denckmahl* | . . . | *D.
K.* CKB copy bound with Ben. Martini, *Der Gerechten und Frommen* . . . 1675
(No. 1760).

**1742** HORN, HILDEBRAND

Rede | Des Weiland | . . . | Herrn PETRI MUSÆI, | . . . | von | Hilde-
brand von Horn | [rule] | Kiel/ gedruckt durch Joachim Reumann/
Acad. Buchdr. | A. 1675

4to. χ$^2$.                                                     GÖTTINGEN UL

**1743** HORNBOSTEL, CHRISTIAN

Roht in Weiß | verkehrte | Sieges-Fahne | Nach Eroberung der berühm-
ten Stadt | Wißmar | Dem | Allerdurchleuchtigsten/ Großmächtigsten |
König und Herrn/ | Herrn | CHRISTJAN V. | Zu Dännemarck/ Nor-
wegen/ der Wenden | und Gothen | Erb-König/ | Hertzog zu Schleß-
wig/ Holstein/ Stormarn und der Dith- | marsen/ Graffen zu Oldenburg
und Delmenhorst/ etc. | Seinem Allergnädigsten König und Herrn | Jn
allertieffster Demuth und Unterthänigkeit Glückwünschend dargestel-

let | Von | S. K. M. | Allergehorsamstem und Unterthänigstem | Diener |
Christian. Hornbostelio Cello-Luneburg. S.S. T. St. | [rule] | Kopen-
hagen/ Gedruckt bey Matthias Jürgenssen/ 1675.

Folio. χ². CKB

1744  JESSEN, FRIEDRICH

Aller trewen Lehrer | Stand/ Ambt und Glantz/ | . . . | Herr PETRUS
MUSÆUS, | . . . | Von | FRIDERICO JESSENIO, SS. Theol. D. und
Past. P. an der Kirchen zu S. Nicolai in Kiel | [rule] | Kiel/ | Gedruckt
durch Joach. Reumann/ Acad. Buchdr. [1675]

4to. [8], 58, [6] pp.; a⁴, A-H⁴. GÖTTINGEN UL

On H2-4, verse by several hands. Appended, memorials and poetry in Latin and
German, with separate signatures. (Three) German titles separately entered (Nos.
1742, 1753 and 1754).

1745  JESSEN, FRIEDRICH

Das UNICUM ET OPTIMUM | . . . | Hn. JOACHIMI Kolblath/ |
. . . | Hn. Amptschreibers zu Trittau/ | . . . | von | FRIDERICO
JESSENIO, S.S. Theol. D. | und Pastoren der Kirchen S. Nicolai
daselbst. | [rule] | Kiel/ | Gedruckt durch Joach. Reuman/ Acad.
Buchdr. [1675]

4to. [8], 54 pp.; a⁴, A-G⁴. CKB

G4 lacking, probably blank.

1746  Jhrer Königl. Majestät | in Dennemarck | Glückliche Eroberung | Eines
starckbesetzten und wohlversehenen | Schwedischen | Kriegs-Schiffes/ |
Falck genandt/ | Wie auch der für unüberwindlich gehalte- | nen vesten
Schantz/ Wallfisch/ ja besorglich der | Stadt Wißmar selbst/ wie nicht
weniger/ Jhrer | Churfürstl. Durchl. zu Brandenburg Gewinnung deß |
vesten Schlosses Wolgast. | Samt vielen andern Schreib-und sonderlich |
aus Engeland meld-würdigen Dingen. | Vom 18. November/ 1675.

4to. )(⁴. SRL

1747  Klag-Gedichte | über | . . . | Herrn | H. MELCHIORIS | HANSEN, |
Vornehmen JCti, | . . . | . . . den 14. Martii An. 1675. bey hochansehn- |
licher und Volckreicher Versamlung in der ThumKirchen zu Schleß- |
wig | mit Christlichen Ceremonien beygesetzet | worden. | [woodcut:
coffin] | Schleßwig/ gedruckt durch Johan Holwein.

4to. H-J⁴ K². CKB

Poems by several hands. Printed with Benedict Martini, *Christlicher Leich-und
Trost-Sermon* (No. 1759).

1748  KLOTZ, STEPHAN

Erläuterter Catechismus; oder Einfältige Catechismus-Fragen und Antworten, aus dem Kleinen Catechismo Lutheri, zu Unterweisung der
Jugend und Einfältigen, abgefaßt. Glückstadt, 1675.

12mo.                                                                                                    *

*Moller* II, 421.

1749  Kurtzer und warhaffter | Bericht/ | Alles dessen/ was sich vom 26. Junij |
bis 15. Julij 1675. mit Jhrer regierenden | Hochfürstl. Durchl. | Herrn
Hertzog | Christian Albrechten | zu Schleßwig/ Holstein &c. und dero |
Ministris, in der Königl. Dennemärckischen | Vestung Rendsburg &c.
begeben.

4to. A-B⁴.                                                                                             CKB

Also with title: *Kurtzer/* | *Doch* | *Warhaffter Bericht/* | *Was* | *Zu Rendesburg*
*zwischē Jh.* | *Königl. Maj. zu Dennemarcken/* *&c. und* | *zu Schleßwig Hollstein/*
*&c. Mit regierenden Hoch-* | *Fürstl. Durchl. respectivè dero beygehabten Ministris* |
*vom 22. Junij biß den 15. Julij dieses 1675sten Jahrs* | *passiret.* | [ornament] | *Jm*
*Jahr* | [rule] | *M. DC. LXXV.* 16 pp.; A-B⁴.

1750  [LA MARTINIÈRE, P. M. DE]

Herrn Martiniere | Neue Reise | Jn die Nordischen Landschafften. | Das
ist: | Eine Beschreibung | Der Sitten/ Gebräuche/ Aberglauben/ Ge- |
bäuden/ und Kleidung der Norweger/ Lapländer/ Killo- | pen/ Boran-
dianer/ Siberianer/ Samojeden/ Zemblaner und Eißlander/ | Sampt
einem Bedencken über den Jrrthum unser Erdbeschreiber/ wo | nemlich
Grönland und Nova Zembla liegen/ und wie weit sie | sich erstrecken. |
Aus dem Englischen ins Deutsche übersetzet | Durch | Johann Langen |
[publisher's(?) emblem] | Hamburg/ | Jn Verlegung Johann Naumans
und Georg Wolffs/ Buchhändler. | [rule] | Gedruckt zu Glückstadt bey
Melchior Kochen/ Jm Jahr 1675.

4to. [8], 80 pp.; A-L⁴.                                                                                 CKB

1751  LAURENTII, NICOLAUS

Musicalischer Dialogus, bey Ordination zweyer Prediger zu Gardingen
abgesungen. Kiel, 1675.

Folio.                                                                                                   *

*Moller* I, 336.

1752  Letzte Ehren-Pflicht/ | . . . | Hn. Matthiæ Claussen/ | . . . | Auß
schuldiger Willigkeit erzeigt und erwiesen/ von Zween | Jnwendig

bekanten Freunden. | [rule] | KJEL/ | Gedruckt durch Joach. Reuman/ Acad. Buchdr. [1675]

4to. χ².                                           CKB

Verse by Andreas Ploman & Johan Thombsen. Possibly printed on one sheet with *Cimbriens Trauer-Flohr* ... (No. 1729).

1753   Letzte Pflicht | ... | Herrn PETRI MUSÆI | ... | von | der Frau Schultzen sämptlichen | Tischgenossen. | [woodcut: coffin] | Kiel/ gedruckt durch Joach. Reumann/ Acad. Buchdr. [1675]

4to. χ².                                    GÖTTINGEN UL

1754   Letzte Rede/ | aus dem Grabe | ... | Herrn PETRI MUSÆI, | ... | von der Fr. Waßmuthin sämbtlichen | Tischgenossen. | [rule] | Kiel/ gedruckt durch Joachim Reuman/ Acad. Buchdr. | A. 1675

4to. χ².                                    GÖTTINGEN UL

1755   [LIBRAMM, JOHANNES]

Letzte Ehren-Pflicht/ | ... | Hn: Matthias Clausen/ | ... | [skull and crossbones] | [rule] | KJEL/ | Gedruckt durch Joach. Reuman/ Acad. Buchdr. [1675]

4to. χ².                                    CKB

1756   LUBBERT, HEINRICH

Schrifft- und Vernunfft- | mäßiger Unterricht | Von der | Waffen-Cur/ | Wie dieselbe wider GOtt und | alle Vernunfft streite/ ein hauffen | abergläubische und unchristliche Possen | mit sich führe/ und auff nichtigen/ | falschen/ | ungereimten/ Zauberschen und unverant- | wortlichen Gründen bestehe/ | Zu GOttes Ehre und Unter- | richtung seines Nechsten wolmey- | nendlich auffgesetzet | Von | HENRIC. LUBBERTUS, | Pastor zu Böhlendorff. | [type ornaments] | Lübeck/ | Bey Ulrich Wettstein. | [rule] | Gedruckt zu Plöen/ | Durch Tobias Schmiedt/ 1675.

12mo. 192 pp.; A-H¹².                             CKB

1757   [MAJOR, JOHANN DANIEL]

[monogram] | Vorstellung etlicher | Kunst-und Natura- | lien-Kammern/ | in Jtalien | Zu Neapolis und Alt-Rom | [figure, with motto] | [rule] | Kjel/ | Gedruckt durch Joachim Reuman/ Acad. Buchdr. [1675]

4to. A-C⁴.                                    CKB

1758   MANIFEST | und angeführte | Uhrsachen/ | Worumb | Jhre Hochmög. den | Krieg gegen der Kron | Schweden declariren | lassen. | [rule] |

Nach der in dem Hage bey Jhr. | Hochm. ordinar Drücker gedruckten |
Exemplar verdeutschet/ | Jm Jahr 1675

8vo. D5⁸.                                                                                          CKB

Issued by D. Paulli in conjunction with his *Extraordinaires Relationes,* June 1675.
Inserted between pp. 840 and 841 of the newspaper, but with correct signature D5
(i.e., 5D).

**1759  MARTINI, BENEDICT**

Christlicher | Leich- und Trost-Sermon | . . . | H. Melchior Hansen/ |
Vornehmen JCti, | . . . | Von | BENEDICTO MARTINI, | Ecclesiæ
Cathedralis Slesvicensis Pastore | primario. | [skull and crossbones] |
Schleßwig | Jn der Fürstl. Druckerey gedruckt durch Johan Holwein/ |
[rule] | ANNO 1675.

4to. 34, [44] pp.; A-K⁴.                                                                          CKB

On F2r, added Latin title: *LACRYMÆ,* | *Quibus* | *Tumulos Insperatos* | *Viri* |
. . . ; on H1r, added title: *Klag-Gedichte* | *über* | . . . | *H. MELCHIORIS* | *HAN-*
*SEN* | . . . | *Schleßwig/ gedruckt durch Johan Holwein* (No. 1747), poems by sev-
eral hands; on K3r, added Latin title: *TRISTES ELEGI* | . . . .

**1760  MARTINI, BENEDICT**

Der | Gerechten und Frommen | Glückseligste Fahrt im Tode/ | . . . |
Frawen | Metta Kielmannin von KielmansEck/ | gebohrnen von der
Wischen/ | . . . | Von | BENEDICTO MARTINI, Ecclesiæ Cathedralis |
Slesvicensis Pastore. | [rule] | Gedruckt durch Johan Holwein/ Fürstl.
Buchdrucker in Schleßwig/ | ANNO 1675.

4to. [12], 56 pp.; )(⁴, )()(², A-G⁴.                                                              CKB

Title within woodcut frame. Text within double rule border. CKB copy bound
with: *Hochrühmliches Ehren-Gedächtnis/* | . . . . (No. 1741).

**1761  MOHR, JOHANN**

NOVA ARITHMETICA. | Das ist: | Ein Neues | [ornamental rule] |
Rechen-Buch/ | Nach Jtaliänisch kürtzster Art/ | Von vielen nütz-
lichen Kauffmans Regu- | len/ in allen Handelungen und Gewerben/
dien- | und gebräuchlich/ mit nöthigen Erinner-und An- | merckungen
abgefasset/ und auff unterschiedlicher | Städte Müntz/ Maaß und Ge-
wicht/ mit | Fleiß gerichtet. | Allen den jenigen/ so sich bey Gemein- |
oder auch Vornehmer Handelung begeben wollen/ | Jnsonderheit seinen
Rechenknaben zu gedeilichen | Auffnehmen in Druck gegeben | Von |
JOHANNE Mohren/ Hamburgensi, | der Mathematischen Künsten
Ergebenen/ und be- | stalten Rechenmeister an der Stadt-Schul | in

Husum. | [rule] | Gedruckt zu Schleßwig bey Johan Holwein/ | Jm
Jahr 1675. | Jn Verlegung des Autoris, und David Goldbeck in | Husum/
bey ihnen zu bekommen.

8vo. [10], 180, [2] pp.; A-M$^8$.                                      CKB

A 1696 edition listed in *Moller* I, 418, presumably identical with *Ein kurtz-abge-
faßtes Rechen-Buch,* 1696 (No. 2788).

1762  MORHOF, DANIEL GEORG

Ode/ | Auff | Den Tödtlichen Hintrit | Des Weiland WolEdlen/ Vesten
und | HochErfahrnen/ | Hn. Matthias Claussen/ | Der Artzney weit-
berühmten Doctoris und | HochFürstl. hochbetrauten Archiatri. | Auß
schuldigstem Mitleiden geschrieben | von | Daniel Georg Morhofen/
D. Pr. | [rule] | KJEL/ | Druckts Joachim Reuman/ 1675.

4to. χ$^2$.                                                            CKB

1763  M[ORHOF], D[ANIEL] G[EORG]

(Hochzeitsgedicht: Joh. Jos. Beck & Margareta Dickhof). Kiel:
Joachim Reumann, 1675.

Folio. χ$^2$.                                                          *

Formerly in Kiel UL (LmC 5-58).

1764  PAULLI, DANIEL

Triumph-Altar | Dem | Allerdurchleuchtigsten/ Großmächtigsten Mon-
archen | und überwinder | CHRISTIAN | dem Fünften | seinem aller-
gnädigsten Erb-König | bej Deroselben höchsterfreulichen Wiederkunft |
und glücklichem abgelegtem Feld-Zuge | nach Eroberung der Fäste
Wißmars | in allertiefster Demuht | gewiedmet | von | Daniel Paulli/
Simons Sohn. | [rule] | Anno 1675 den 24 Decembris.

Folio. χ$^2$.                                                          CKB

1765  RAM, STEPHAN

Aller Gottes Heiligen | für dem Herrn wehrt-gehaltener Todt/ | . . . |
Fr. Maria Arends/ | gebornen BRAUNJN/ | . . . | Von | M. STEPHANO
RAM, | an gedachter StadtKirchen Predigern. | [rule] | Gedruckt in der
Königl. Vestung Glückstadt/ durch | Melchior Kochen/ Jm Jahr 1675.

4to. 56 pp.; A-G$^4$.                                                  CKB

1766  RETORSIO DEFENSIVA | juncta Protestatione | Pro | JOHANNE
KIRCH- | MANNO J.U.D. | Fürstl. Holsteinischen Fisci, wie auch
Hoff- | und Landgerichts Advocato und Bürgermeistern der | Fürstl.

Residentz Stadt Schleßwig/ | Contra | Den Authorem des zu Gripps-
walde am 30. | Decembris Anno 1674. gedruckten und intitulirten |
Gründlichen Ohnpassionirten Gegenberichtes/ betreffend die zwi- |
schen dem Königl. Dennemärck. Rath an der Regierungs Cantz- | ley zu
Glückstadt Herrn Friderich Hans Gloxine. | Und dann | Dem gewesenen
Fürstl. Holsteinischen General Ma- | jeurn und KriegsRath Herrn Johan
von der Wieck/ a. th. | versirende Querellen. | [rule] | Gedruckt Anno
M. DC. LXXV. | 12. Januarij.

4to. )(⁴.                                                              CKB

1767 RICHARDUS, JACOB

(Klag und Trost Zeilen de Wilh. Schomaker consulis Tonnes filio).
Schleswig, 1675.

4to.                                                                     *

OHM I, 543.

1768 SCHULTZE, CORNELIUS

Geistliche Creutz-Artzeney . . . oder Leichpredigt über Peter Backsen.
Schleswig, 1675.

4to.                                                                     *

OHM I, 605.

1769 TAUBE, JACOB

Hertzens-Grund | JACOBI Tauben/ | Darin er | Gründliche Verant-
wortung | thut an Jedermann/ der Grund fordern möchte der | Hoff-
nung die in ihm ist. | Auch zugleich Absaget/ | Allen Jrrigen Lehren/
deren man ihn wegen | der Absonderung von den Versamblungen der
Evange- | lisch-Lutherischen Kirchen/ und deren öffentlichen Gottes-
dienst/ | und seiner Conversation mit unterschiedlichen Jrren- | den
Secten verdächtig gehalten/ | Durch eine öffentliche Predigt GOtt zu
Ehren/ der War- | heit zu Gute/ den Jrrenden zur Besserung/ seinem
eigen Gewissen zur | Ruhe/ und Wegnehmung alles bösen Scheins und
Arg- | wohns/ Gehalten an S. Matthiæ Tage in der Lutheri- | schen
Kirchen zu Altona/ | Und nunmehr auff Begehren vieler Frommen
Hertzen in Druck | befordert/ | Beydes auff Permission des Hn: General
Superintendenten, | Durch | JACOBUM Tauben/ gewesenen ordent-
lichen Pre- | diger der Evangelisch-Lutherischen Gemeine zu Arnheim |
in Gelderland. | [rule] | Jn Verlegung des Autoris, | Gedruckt zu Glück-
stadt durch Melchior Koch/ Kö- | nigl. Buchdrucker daselbst/ Anno
**1675.**

4to. [12], 68, [16] pp.; A⁴, (B)², B-J⁴ K², ²A-B⁴.                 HALLE UL

1770 Tröstliche auffmunterung | . . . | Hn. MATTHIÆ | CLAVSEN/ |
Medic. Doctoris . . . | . . . | Von | Nachbenahmten. | [woodcut: coffin] |
KJEL/ | Gedruckt durch Joach. Reuman/ Acad. Buchdr. [1675]

4to. A⁴.                                                                      CKB

Verse by several hands.

1771 Vermählungs-Gedächtnis | Dem Wol-Ehrwürdigen und Hochgelahr-
tem | Herrn | M. Heinrich Bornemann | Wolverdientem Præposito und
Haupt-Predigern | an Sanct Marien Kirche &c. | und | Der Tugend-
reichen und Gottliebenden | Fr. Anna Würgerinn | Des weiland Wol-
Ehrwürdigen/ und Andächtigen | M. Hironymo Buecks/ | Wolberuff-
enen Königl. Pastoris Primarii bei der Teutschen | Kirchen zu St. Petri
nachgelassene Wittibe | gestifftet | von dem | Dienstfertigstem. | [rule] |
Anno 1675 den 18 Octobris

4to. χ².                                                                      CKB

1772 Villedieu, *Mme*. de (Catharine H. Desjardins)

Der Grenadische Lusthoff der Frauen (transl. Jacob Villedsen Wulff).
Copenhagen 1675.

12mo.                                                                          *

*Cat. bibl. Just. Höeg,* 1695, p. 124; *Cat. lib. Moth,* 1705, 12mo, 294; *Cat. bibl.
Joannes Grammius,* 1748, 12mo, 854. Place of publication is possibly false.

1773 Vollständiges | Gesang-buch/ | Darinnen | Nicht allein die alte/
gewöhn- | liche Kirchen-Gesänge/ sondern | auch viel neue/ geist-reiche
und theils | vorhin nie in Druck gekommene | Lieder zubefinden: | Alle
auff bekandte Melodeien/ | zu männigliches/ absonderlich der | Ein-
fältigen desto bessern Ge- | brauch. | Deme zu Ende beygefüget ist ein
kur- | tzes/ aber auff vielerhand Fälle/ Zeiten | und Anliegen gerichtetes |
Gebet-Büchlein. | Zum zweyten mahl gedruckt/ | und nicht allein an
vielen Orten verbes- | sert/ sondern auch mit einer mercklichen An- |
zahl geistreicher/ mehrentheils neuen | Lieder/ und verschiedenen Ge- |
beten vermehret. | [rule] | Plöen/ | Gedruckt und verlegt von Tobias |
Schmiedt. Jm Jahr 1675.

12mo. [8], 600, [16], 211, [5] pp.; ):(⁴, A-Bb¹², Cc⁸, Dd-Mm¹².        HAB

On Dd1, separate title: *Kurtzes* | *Gebet-büch-* | *lein/* | *. . .* | *Plöen/* | *Gedruckt und
verlegt von Tobias* | *Schmiedt.* | *Jm Jahr 1675.*

1774 Wedderkopf, Gabriel

STATUA HONORIS | Die Christrühmliche EhrenSeule | . . . | Fr.
Catharina | Rantzauin | gebohrne von Qualen. | . . . | von | M.

GABRIELE Wedderkopff/ | . . . | Kiel/ gedruckt durch Joachim Reuman/ Acad. Buchdr. [1675]

4to. [10], 52 pp.; π1, )(⁴, A-F⁴ G², a-b⁴.                                    CKB

On a1, added title: *Klag-und Trost-Gedicht/ | . . . | Fr: CATHARINA | Rantzowin/ | . . . | Kiel/ | Gedruckt durch Joach. Reuman/ Acad. Buchdr.*

1775 WEGHORST, PAUL

Letzterer Abschied/ | . . . | Herrn Joachim Kohlbladt/ | . . . | von | Paul Weghorst | auß Kiehl | [woodcut: coffin] | [rule] | KJEL/ | Gedruckt durch Joach. Reumann/ Acad. Buchdr. [1675]

4to. χ².                                                                 KIEL UL

1776 WÖRGER, FRANZ

Fasciculus Concionum, oder außerlesene Zeitpredigten. Copenhagen, 1675.

4to.                                                                          *

*Moller* I, 745; *Cat. univ. designatio omnium Librorum qui hisce Nundinus* . . . (Autumn) 1675 (Groß).

# 1676

1777 Abriß und kürtze Beschreibung | der | Haupt-Vestung | Christian- Stadt/ | Und | Wie dieselbe durch J. K. M. von Denne- | marck den 15 Augusti mit Sturm ist er- | obert worden. [1676]

8vo. χ⁴.                                                                    CKB

Caption title. Below title: map of fortress.

1778 Accords-Puncta | Zwischen | Dero zu Dännemarck/ Norwegen/ &c. | Königl. Majest. Vice-Roy/ und Oeneralen [sic] | über die Nordische Armee/ &c. Jhrer Hohen Excell. | dem Hochgebohrnen Herrn | Herrn Vlrich Fridrich | Güldenlöven/ | Und dem Wol Edelgebornen Herrn | Johann Lilie/ Obrist | und Commendanten auff Wennersburg getrof- fen: | wie auch | Von der StadtLandes-Crohn [1676]

4to. χ².                                                                 KIEL UL

1779 Accords-Puncten | So zwischen | Denen hohen Alliirten an einer/ und | dem Königl. Schwedische Commendanten | in Carlsburg Hn. Obristen Mellen/ andern | theils/ getroffen worden.

8vo. χ⁴.                                                                     CUL

Caption title. Colophon: *Gedruckt bey Georg Göden/Kön. M. Buchdr. | den 8. Jannarij Anno 1676.*

1780    Allerunterthänigste | RELATION | an | Jhre Königl. Maj. | zu Dänne-
marck Norwä- | gen/ etc. | Welcher Gestalt | Dero Stadthalter und
General über die | Armee in Norwägen/ | des Herrn | Ulrich Fridrich
Gülden-Lewen | Hohe Excellence | die Stadt Oddewald/ wie auch | die
Stadt und Fästung Wennersburg | erobert/ | Samt dem Abriß von
gedachter Fästung | und Situation, in Kupfer gestochen. | [rule] |
Kopenhaven/ | Bei J.K.M. Buchhändler Daniel Paulli, | Anno 1676.

4to. )(⁴; 1 folding map.                                            CKB

1781    Allerunterthänigste | RELATION | An | Jhre Königliche Mayestät zu
Dännemarck/ | Norwägen/ &c. | Vom Commendanten Obrist-Lieuten-
ant | Georg Möller/ | Aus dem Casteel Helsingsburg | den 2. Novembr.
geschrieben. [1676]

4to. χ².                                                          KIEL UL

Caption title.

1782    Anhang | der | ORDINAIRE | Post-Zeitung | Aus allerley Orten. |
[type ornaments] Num. 3 [type ornaments] | N.B. Hier bey werden
außgegeben die zwischen dehnen hohen | Alliirten und der Vestung
Carlsburg getroffenen Ac- | cords-Puncten. | Kopenhagen/ | [rule] |
Gedruckt bey Georg Göden/ Kön. M. Buchdr. | den 8. Jannarij Anno
1676.

8vo. χ⁴.                                                           CKB

1783    AREND, BALTHASAR

Des Leibes und der Seelen Zustand . . . oder Leichpredigt über Ant.
Gunth. von Reinkingen aus Eccl. XII. Glückstadt, 1676.

4to.                                                                 *

*Moller* I, 20.

1784    AREND, CAI

Trost-Qvellen | Leidtragender Ehe-Hertzen/ | . . . | Fr: Margaretha
Waß- | merinn/ Gebohrnen Bruhnin/ | . . . | . . . Durch | CAJUM
Arend/ Königl. Schloß-Pastoren auff Dero | Glücksburg in der Veste
Glückstadt. | [rule] | Glückstadt/ Gedruckt durch Melchior Kochen/
im Jahr 1676.

4to. [8], 40, [32] pp.; A-F⁴, a-d⁴.                                 CKB

On leaf c1, added title: *Schuldigstes/ aber leider! Klagendes | Angedencken |
. . . | Glückstadt/ Gedruckt durch Melchior Kochen;* on leaf c3, added title: *Als |
Der HochEdle/ Gestrenge/ und Veste Herr/ | Herr Conrad Waßmer/ | . . . |*

*Johannes Müller/ Advoc.;* on leaf d2, added title: *Ehren-Krohn/* | . . . | *Von* | *Hanns Grotschilling/ N.P.C.* | *und Königl. Cancellisten.*

1785 ARNKIEL, TROELS

Die Seligkeit des reinen Hertzen . . . oder Leichpredigt über Cathar. Marg. gebohrner Stahlin, Casp. von Sallern Ehefrau. . . . Schleswig, 1676.

4to. *

*Moller* I, 22. Formerly in Kiel UL (Cat. theol. 16:15246).

1786 Außführliche | RELATION | Wegen Ubergabe des festen | Castels Lands-Crohnen/ | An Jhr. Königl. Majest. zu Denne- | marck und Nor- wegen/ etc. etc. | Vom 4. August | [rule] | Gedruckt im 1676sten Jahre

4to. $\chi^2$. CKB

1787 BEITIUS, MARTIN

Bethlemitische Hirten-Freude. Copenhagen, 1676.

4to. *

Jens Worm, *Forsøg til et Lexicon* I, 1771, p. 93.

1788 BINER, TIMOTHEUS HILARIUS

Sieben böse Geister welche zeißlicher Weise viel Menschen besitzen und auch sonderlich zu dieser Zeit ihre Wercken in den Kindern des Un- glaubens haben, aus dem gewöhnlichen Evangelio Dominico Oculi einfältig doch schriftmäßig vorgestellt im Jahr da man geschrieben. . . . Schleswig, 1676.

4to. *

*OHM* II, 63.

1789 BOLTEN, JOHANNES

Magisterium Perlarum . . . Leichpredigt über Margareta, D. Joh. Rhederi Ehefrau. . . . Glückstadt, 1676.

4to. *

*Moller* I, 55.

1790 BRÄMER, CHRISTIAN

Werckaußschliessende Gerechtigkeit/ | . . . | Fr. ANNA | Ziemers/ | . . . | . . . von | M. CHRISTIAN Brämer Lub. | [rule] | Kopenhagen/ auff Unkosten des leidtragenden Ehewirts/ | Gedruckt bey Nicolai Müllers nachgelassenen Wittwe. [1676]

4to. Pp. [1-8], 3-45, 45, 46, 46-120, [1-12]; A-R⁴ S²; 2 plates. CKB

Title and text within borders of type ornaments. On leaf R1r ff., poems by several hands. Plates precede t-p. One with portrait of Christian Cassube, the widower. The other with bastard title: *M. Christ. Brämers Leichpredigt über Chri-* | *stiani Cassubij 28. Jahr gewesene Eheliebste.*

1791    Copenhagensche | RELATION | Von dem | Was irgend in diesen Nor- | dischen Königreichen pas- | siret. | Num. 4. | Copenhagen/ | [rule] | Gedruckt bey Georg Göden/ Königl. Maj. | und Univ. Buchdr. den 2. Decembr. 1676.

8vo. χ⁴.                                                          CUL

1792    CRAMER, CHRISTIAN ANTON *and* CHRIST. ALB. SCHMIDT

Glückwünschender Schertz auff die hochzeitliche Festivität des Herrn Friedrich Hans Gloxinn und Maria Elisabeth . . . Cramer. Schleswig, 1676.

Folio.                                                                    *

Formerly in Kiel UL (LmC 8-18).

1793    CRUGER, STEPHAN

Klag-Gedicht | über den zwar frühzeitigen doch seeligen Hintritt | . . . | Fr. Marthæ Justinæ | gebohrnen Försterin/ | Des HochEhrwürdigen/ HochEdlen und Hochgelahrten | Herrn | SEBASTIANI Niemans/ | . . . | Ehelichen Hertzliebsten/ | . . . | Mitleidentlich auffgesetzet | Von | ST. CRUGERO Sch. Cath. ConR. | [rule] | Schleßwig gedruckt bey Johan Holwein. [1676]

4to. χ².                                                          CKB

1794    DENMARK. *Laws, statutes, etc.*

Königliche | Dännemarckische Kirchen- | CONSTITUTIO | in der Graffschafft Pinnen- | berg. | Anno 1662. den 19. Martij publiciret | [crown] | [rule] | Gedruckt in der Königl: Veste Glückstadt/ | durch Melchior Kochen/ Jm Jahr 1676

4to. [2], 10 pp., A⁴ B².                               CKB; KIEL UL

1795    DENMARK. *Laws, statutes, etc.*

WJR Christian der Fünffte/ von | . . . | . . . Kopenhagen den 28. Februarij, | Anno 1676.

Broadside.                                                                CNA

Decree confiscating property of Swedish subjects "in Unseren Reichen . . . insonderheit auch in Unserer Erb-unterthänigen Stadt Hamburg."

1796. DENMARK. *Laws, statutes, etc.*

WJR Christian der Fünffte/ von | . . . | . . . Glückstadt/ den 4. April,
Anno 1676.

Broadside.                                                                                              CNA

Decree issued jointly with Duke Christian Albrecht of Schleswig-Holstein, forbidding subjects to serve with foreign fleets.

1797 DENMARK. *Laws, statutes, etc.*

WJR Christian der Fünffte/ von | . . . | . . . Glückstadt/ den 11. Maij,
Anno 1676.

Broadside.                                                                                              CNA

Decree issued jointly with Duke Christian Albrecht of Schleswig-Holstein, setting
aside 2, 9, and 16 June as days of prayer.

1798 DENMARK. *Laws, statutes, etc.*

WJr Christian der Fünffte/ von | . . . | WJr Leopold von Gottes Gnaden/
Erwählter Römi- | scher . . . | . . . | . . . 8. Junij Anno 1676.

Broadside (three sheets pasted together).                                                               CKB

Decree of Emperor Leopold forbidding importation and use of certain French
manufactured wares, reissued by King Christian V and Duke Christian Albrecht of
Schleswig-Holstein.

1799 DENMARK. *Laws, statutes, etc.*

WJR Christian der Fünffte/ von | . . . | . . . Glückstadt/ den 21. Junij/
Anno 1676

Broadside.                                                                                              CNA

Decree ordering public thanksgiving (for a maritime victory) 2 July.

1800 DENMARK. *Laws, statutes, etc.*

WJr Christian der Fünffte/ von Gottes Gnaden/ König | . . . | . . . 16.
Decembr. Anno 1676.

Broadside.                                                                                              CKB

Decree forbidding subjects to enter foreign maritime service.

1801 Dero | Königlichen Majestät | zu Dennemarck Norwegen/ &c. | An |
Jhr. Hoch-Fürstliche | Durchl. zu Schleßwig Holstein | Abgelassene
Schreiben/ | Nebenst | Der darauff ergangenen Antwort/ die Sequestra-
tion | des Hertzogthums Schleßwig betreffend. [1676]

4to. A-F⁴, χ².                                                                                          CKB

Another edition: no title-page, A-F⁴. Lacks 2 pp. of "Beylage."

1802  (Erläuterter Catechismus). Glückstadt, 1676

12mo.                                                                      ✱

*Bibl. Ehrencron,* 1717, p. 41. Presumably a reprint of Stephan Klotz's book by same title (1666, 1670, 1675).

1803  Extract-Schreibens | Des Hn. General Admiral Trompen an Jhre | Königl. Maytt. dat. aufm Schiff CHRISTIANUS | QVINTUS den 5. Junii 1676. die andere gegen | die Schwedische Flotta erhaltene Vitoria | betreffend. | Saavelsom/ en udførlig | Extract aff Admiral Her Niels | Juels Skriffvelse iligemaade til hans Kongelige | Maytt. dat. hans Kongl. Maytt. Oorlogs Skib | Chur-Printzen den 9. Junii. | Kiøbenhaffn/ | [rule] | Tryct hos Jørgen Gøede Kongl. Maytt. Bogtr.

4to. $\chi^2$.                                                              CKB

1804  Extraordinaires | RELATIONES | vorstellende | was mit vielerlei anderswo | gedruckten Novellen/ und schriftlichen | Zeitungen/ aus allerlei Orten | denckwürdigst eingekommen | Anno | 1676.

4to. 1752 pp.; A1-C10⁴.                                                     CKB

First issue of each month with separate title-page. Other issues of the *Extra-ordinaires Relationes* with caption title. The several appendices are paginated, signed, and numbered like regular issues. 56 issues of *Extraordinaire Oeresundische Relation* similarly paginated, signed, and numbered like regular issues, but each with separate title-page (verso blank) and special numbering 1-56. In all, 217 numbers.

1805  FABRICIUS, TOBIAS

Christianorum Trophæum . . . oder Leich-Sermon über Magdalena [Goldbach] Herren Gregorii Krögers . . . Eheliebste. Altona: Victor de Loew, 1676

4to. [44] pp.                                                              ✱

*Moller* I, 167; *Stolberg* II, 87.

1806  FRÆRESEN, ERIC

Ehren-gedächtnüß und Traur-Seule | . . . | Hn. Daniel Sachsius, | . . . | Auffgesetzt von | Ericus Fræresen Ph. & M.D. | [woodcut] | [rule] | Altona/ Gedruckt bey Victor de Löw/ Anno 1676.

4to. $\chi^2$.                                                              CKB

1807  General Admiral | TROMPEN | RELATION.

4to. $\chi^2$.                                                              CKB

Caption title. At end: *Kopenhaven den 17. Junii 1676. Bey Daniel Paulli Königl. Buchhändl.*

1808   Greiffenfeldischer Inqvisitionis End Urtheil | Jn INQVISITIONS Sa- | chen/ des vorigen Reichs Cantzlers/ | . . .

Folio. χ².                                                                                                                     CKB

Caption title. Dated 26 May 1676.

1809   HAGER, CHRISTOPH ACHATIUS

CHRISTOPH: ACHATII | HAGERI | ARITHMETICA | MERCA-TORIA, | Oder | Wolbegründete Anweisung | zur | Rechen-Kunst. | Anno [printer's emblem] 1676. | Kopenhaven/ | Bey Daniel Pauli, Königl: Buchh: | an St: Marien Kirchhofe.

8vo. [4], 224 pp.; π², [A]⁸, B-O⁸.                                                                         CKB

Title in red and black. CKB copy is defective: pp. 1-16 missing. On second leaf, separate title page: *CHRISTOPHORI-ACHATII | HAGERI | ARITHMETICA | MERCATORIA, | Erster Theil/ | Jn welchem eine wolbegrün- | dete Anweisung der Rechen- | Kunst enthalten/ | . . . Anitzo mit Fleiß nach dem Hamburgischen | Exemplar übergesehen/ und der Lieben Jugend | zum Nutzen wiederum zum Druck verfertiget/ und | mit dem Zweyten Theil vermehret. | [ornament] | Kopenhaven/ | Bey Daniel Paulli Königl. Buchhändler.* Presumably a reissue with new title-page of a work originally published in two volumes by Georg Papen in Hamburg, 1654. Bound with *ARITHMETICA | MERCATORIA, | Ander Theil. | . . . Hamburg/ | [rule] | Gedruckt bey Georg Papen/ im Jahr 1654.*

1810   HAGER, CHRISTOPH ACHATIUS

ARITHMETICÆ | MERCATORIÆ, | Ander Theil. | Jn welchem eine wolbegrün- | dete Anweisung geschicht | von | Mehrerley Handlungs-Rechnungen/ | Interesse und Wechseln/ wie dieselben nach Lauff | und Gebrauch der Börse/ von Hamburg aus per Hoch- | und Nieder-Teutschland/ Franckreich/ Engelland/ Hi- | spanien und Jtalien/ etc. auch von dannen anhero | auff Hamburg coursiren. | Allen jungen Negotianten, Mercantisten | Agenten, Buchhaltern/ Cassirern und allen | Handelsbedienten sehr vorträglich. | Abgefasset und anjetzo zum Druck verfertiget | durch | CHRISTOPHORUM ACHATIUM Hagern | Francom. Misn. Bürgern/ Buchhaltern | und Arithmetic. E. in Ham-burg. | [ornament] | Kopenhaven/ | Bey DANIEL PAULI, Königl. Buchhändl. | an St. Marien Kirchhofe/ | Anno 1676.

8vo. 96 pp.; A-F⁸.                                                                                               CKB

1811   HECKLAWER, HANS CHRISTIAN

Letzte Ehren-Bezeugung . . . der Frauen Margareten Agneten geboren Soltowinnen, Herrn Hans Christian Hecklawers . . . gewesene Ehegelieb-teste. . . . Schleswig, 1676

Folio.                                                                            *

Formerly in Kiel UL (LmC 9-73).

1811A [Hornemeyer, Johann Theodor]

Das gülden Kleinod Pauli von der Liebe Christi Kostbarkeit, auß Phil.
III. 19. der Gemeine zu Beienfleht vorgestellet. Glückstadt, 1676.

8vo.                                                                              *

*Cat. bibl. Jo. Hadr. Bolten* (Hamburg, 1808), p. 74.

1812  Jebsen, Johannes

Der heimlich nachschleichende Todt/ | . . . | Fr. Catharinæ Jöns/ | . . . |
Von | M. JOHANNE Jebsen/ | Probst und Pastore zu Rendsburg. |
[woodcut: coffin] | [rule] | KJEL/ Gedruckt durch Joach. Reuman/
Acad. Buchdr. [1676]

4to. 42, [14] pp.; A-G⁴.                                                          CKB

On leaf F2, added title: *Christliche Klag- und Trost-Gedancken/ | . . . . | Von
Nachgesetzten Freunden;* on leaves F2-G4, verse by H. Hamerich and J. M. Eccard.

1813  Jhrer Königl. Majest. | zu Dännemarck/ Norwegen/ &c. | Admiralen |
Herrn Niels Juelen | außfürliche Relation | von | Eroberung | Der Jnsul
Gothland und | des Castels daselbsten/ | De dato den 2. Maji 1676. | auf |
Dem Königl. Orlogs-Schif Chur-Printz | vor Wißby geschrieben | [rule] |
Kopenhaven/ | Bei S.K.M. Buchhandler | Daniel Paulli.

4to. )(⁴.                                                                         CKB

1814  Knall und Fall | des erhöheten | und erniedrigten | Peter Schumachers/ |
sonst | Graffen Greiffen-Felds/ | und gewesenen Königl. Denne-
märckischen | Reichs-Cantzelers/ | Fürgestellet | Jm Jahr 1676. | Wer
stoltz ist/ den kan Gott demühtigen/ | Dan. 4. v. 34.

4to. χ⁴.                                                                          CKB

Verse.

1815  Kortholt, Christian

Christian Kortholten/ | Der H. Schrifft D. und | Prof. Prim. | Treu-
hertzige Warnung | Für dem an einigen Orten ein- | gerissenen gantz
unchristlichen | Kirchen-Fluch | sich zu hüten. | [rule] | KJEL/ |
Gedruckt durch Joach. Reumann/ | 1676.

8vo. 48 pp.; A-C⁸.                                                                Kiel UL

1816  Kortholt, Christian

Christian Kortholten/ | Der Heil. Schrifft D. und | Prof Primarii zum

Kiel/ | Theologisches Bedencken | von | Heimlichen | Leichbestatun-
gen. | [rule] | KJEL/ | Gedruckt durch Joachim Reuman/ | 1676.

8vo. 48 pp.; A-C$^8$.                                                                KIEL UL

1817 Kurtze | Beschreibung | der | Stadt | Lands-Cron | samt bejgefügtem |
Grundris | von | der Stadt und dem Casteel | in Kupfer gestochen. |
[rule] | Kopenhaven | Bei Daniel Paulli Königl. Buchhändler | 1676.

4to. )($^4$; map.                                                                   CKB

1818 Kurze | Beschreibung | Von | Der Haubt-Fästung | CHRISTIAN-
STAD | Jn | Blekingen | Nebst einem Abriß in Kupfer | [ornamental
rule] | Kopenhaven/ | Bei J. K. M. Buchhändler Daniel Paulli | Ao. 1676

4to. $\chi^2$.                                                                        CKB

The engraving is lacking in CKB copy.

1819 LUND, THOMAS

Christliche Leichpredigt | . . . | Herrn Peter Rivesells/ | Gewesenen
treufleissigen Curatoris der Lateini- | schen Schulen/ . . . | . . . | Durch |
THOMAM LUNDIUM, | Prediger zu S. Marien in Flensburg. |
[skull and crossbones] | Mors certa, hora incerta, | Ergo homo, memento
bene mori. | [rule] | Schleßwig gedruckt bey Johan Holwein/ An. 1676.

4to. 51, [9] pp.; A-G$^4$ H$^2$.                                                      CKB

1820 LUND, JOHANNES

Die | EZECHIELISCHE | Und | KENCKELISCHE | Augen-Lust/ |
Bey Volckreicher und ansehnlicher LeichBegängniß | . . . | Fr. ANNÆ, |
Des HochEhrwürdigen/ HochEdlen/ Vesten und Hochge- | lahrten
Herrn/ | Herrn STEPHANI KENCKELN, | . . . | Hertzallerliebsten
Ehegatten/ | . . . in der Tunderi- | schen StadtKirchen . . . | . . . | Von |
JOHANNE LUNDIO, | Predigern daselbst. | [rule] | Gedruckt zu
Schleßwig bey Johan Holwein/ An. 1676.

4to. A-N$^4$.                                                                        CKB

Title within ornamental woodcut frame. On H4, added Latin title: *Prosphonesis
Consolatoria | . . . | PROFESSORUM ALIQUOT | KILONIENSIUM | . . . .*; on
M2, added title: *Nachruhm | Der WolEdlen/ GroßEhr- und HochTugend-
reichen | Frauen/ | Fr. ANNÆ | . . . . | Von | Fr: Christiani, Sch. Sonderb:
Rectore. | . . . .* Verse by several hands.

1821 MARTINI, BENEDICT

Himlische | Warheit und Gewißheit | . . . | Fr. MARTHÆ JUSTINÆ |
NIEMANNINNEN | gebohrner Försterinnen/ | . . . | Vorgestellet von |

BENEDICTO MARTINI, Ecclesiæ Cathedralis Pastore primario. |
[rule] | Schleßwig/ gedruckt durch Johan Holwein ANNO 1676.

4to. 44 pp.; A-E⁴ F².                                                                    CKB

CKB copy bound with several occasional poems in Latin and German, separately
signed; two German items separately entered: *Trost-Lied* | ... | *Von M.M.R.P.P.* |
.... (No. 1847); *Klag-Gedicht* | ... | *ST. CRUGERO* ... | .... (No. 1793).

1822  Oeresundische | RELATION | Enthalten vielerley Merckwürdiges. |
von | Lands-Cron und vielen andern Orten mehr. | Jm Jahr 1676. den 18.
Novembr.

4to. χ².                                                                              KIEL UL

1823  Oeresundische | RELATION | von den Actionen | in | Norwägen. |
Anno 1676. den 29. Augusti

4to. χ².                                                                              KIEL UL
Caption title.

1824  [PETRAEUS, PETER], *editor*

Außerlesene | Geistliche Lieder/ | Auß unterschiedenen Gesangbüchern
zusammen | getragen | Und | Auff gnädigste Anordnung | Der Durch-
läuchtigsten Fürstinn und Frauen | Fr. Maria Elisabeth/ Gebohrnen
auß | Churfürstlichen Stamm zu Sachsen/ Erb-Princessin in der | Ober-
und NiderLaußnitz/ verwittweten Hertzogin zu Schleßwig Holstein/ |
Stormarn und der Dithmarschen/ Gräffin zu Oldenburg | und Delmen-
horst/ &c. | Zu beförderung des so wol öffentlichen Gottesdienstes in
dero | Hoff-Capelle/ als auch geheimen Andacht | außgefertiget. | [rule] |
Schleßwig | Jn der Fürstl. Druckerey gedruckt durch Johann Holwein. |
Anno 1676.

4to. [26], 687, [11]; 88, [12] pp.; )(-3)(⁴, 4)(1, A-Ssss⁴ Tttt 1; a-l⁴, ²)(⁴, ):(²
                                                                                       CKB

Title within woodcut frame; text within single rule borders. On leaf a1, separate
title-page: *Anhang/* | *Darinn enthalten* | *I.* | *Die Gebete/* | *Welche am Sontage/*
*Mitwochen* | *und den hohen Festen nach geendigter Predigt* | *in der Schloß Kirche*
*zu Husum verlesen* | *werden.* | *II.* | *Die Buß-Gebete in den täglichen Bet-* |
*Stunden üblich.* | *III.* | *Einige Gebete vor und nach der Beicht und* | *Communion*
*zu gebrauchen.* | *IV.* | *Die gewöhnliche Collecten.* | *Psalm XXVII. v. 7.8.* | *HERR*
*höre meine Stimme/ wenn ich ruffe/ sey mir gnädig/* | *und erhöre mich. Mein*
*Hertz hält dir für dein Wort:* | *Jhr solt mein Antlitz suchen; Darumb suche ich*
*auch* | *HERR dein Antlitz.* | [ornament] | *Schleßwig gedruckt durch Johan Hol-*
*wein/ 1675;* on leaf ²)(1, separate title: *Ein Gebet* | *Auff die heutige vielfältige* |
*KriegsNoth gerichtet.* Dedication is signed "M.P.P." "Vorrede" is signed "M.
PETRUS PETRÆUS, ... Hoffprediger," and is dated Husum, 27 October 1676.

1825 Petraeus, Peter

(Hochzeitsgedicht über H. Fried. Gloxin). Schleswig [1676].

4to. χ⁴. *

Formerly in Kiel UL (LmC 74-63).

1827 Relation | dessen/ | so zwischen beyden | Nordischen Cronen | Dänne-
marck und Schweden | in denen Hertzogthümern Bremen/ | Mecklen-
burg und Pommeren vorgefallen/ | samt theils anderer mit Jhrer Königl.
Majest. zu | Dännemarck Alliirter Potentaten Kriegs | Operationibus |
Von den 1. Junii 1675 biß den 1. Januarii 1676.

4to. A-C⁴. CKB

Verse.

1828 RELATION | Hvorledis | Christianstad af Hans Kongl. Mayest. | voris
allernaadigste Herre oc Arf- | ve Kongis Armee den 15. Aug. | med
Stormer Haand er | blefven indtagen. | RELATION | Wie | Christian-
stadt den 15. Aug. an Jhre | Königl. Maytt. unsern allergnä- | digsten
Erb-Könige und Herr/ | mit Sturm sey ubergangen. | [rule] | Kopen-
hagen/ gedruckt bey Georg Göden Kön. Maytt. | Buchdr. den 17.
Augusti [1676]

4to. χ². CKB

Text in Danish and German.

1829 RELATION | von der den 4. Decembris bey Londen in | Schonen
zwischen den Königl. Dännemarckischen | und Königl. Schwedischen
Arméen gehaltenen Bataille | de dato Lands-Crone den 5. Decembris
1676.

4to. )(⁴. CKB

Caption title.

1830 RELATION | Von der zwischen der Königl. | Dännemarckischen und
der Königl. | Schwedischen Armeen gehaltener Ba- | taile bey Lunden in
Schonen Mon- | tags am 4. Decembr. | 1676. | Copenhagen/ | [rule] |
Gedruckt bey Sehl. Georg Gödens/ Königl. Majest. | und Univers.
Buchdrucker Nachlebenden Witbe/ | den 7. Decembr. 1676.

8vo. χ⁴. CKB

1831 Relation | Welcher Gestalt der | Königliche Dännemärcki- | sche Gen-
eral Admiral Herr Cornelius | Tromp die Stadt Uysted nebst dem Fort
in | Schonen erobert | den 27. Junii Anno 1676 | VERA [ornament]

REFERO. | [rule] | Kopenhaven/ | Bey Daniel Paulli Königl. Buch-
Händler | den 29. Junii

4to. χ². CKB

1832 RELATION | Wie die Stadt Ydstæd nebst dem | dabey liegenden Fort
am nechst verwichenen Diensta- | ge den 27. Junii von Jhre Kön. Maj.
General Admiral | Herr Cornelius Tromp/ sey erobert worden;
Selbige | Stadt liegt 7. Meile von Malmøe und 8. | von Landskron. |
Udførlig RELATION | Hvorledis Ydsted udi Skaane/ med det derhos
liggen- | de Fort nestforleden Tißdag den 27. Junii af Hans Kongelige |
Maj. Gen. Adm. Herr Cornelius Tromp/ er bleffven ind- | tagen. Samme
Stad ligger 7. Mile fra Malmø oc | 8. fra Landskrone. | [rule] |
Kiøbenhafn/ | Trøckt hos Jørgen Gøede/ Kongl. Maytt. Bogtr. den 30.
Junii [1676]

4to. χ². CKB

Text in German and Danish.

1833 RIST, JOHANNES CASPAR

Versingender Tugend-Bach . . . Magdalena Crögerin geboren Goldbachin
bewundert und beklaget. Altona, 1676.

4to. *

*OHM* I, 554.

1834 RODATZI, CHRISTOPHER

PIORUM | . . . | Leich-Ehren-und Gedächtnis-Predigt | . . . | CHRISTI-
ANI | CASII, | . . . | Von | CHRISTOPHORO RODATZI, Pastore
primar. | bei der Haupt- und Collegial-Kirchen in der Bischöfflichen |
Residentz Euthin | [rule] | PLÖEN/ | Gedrukt durch Tobias Schmidt/
im 1676sten Jahr.

Folio. A-L², a-e². GÖTTINGEN UL

Other items issued on same occasion, and bound together with Rodatzi's sermon,
published in Lübeck.

1835 SCHELE, PETER

Bewillkommung | der Gläubigen Seelen im Himmel; | . . . | Fr. Wibke/
Magdlenen/ | . . . | Herren Christian Sellmers/ | . . . | von | PETRO
Schelen/ Archidiac. in Rens- | burg/ und des Consistorii daselbst
Beysitzern. | [rule] | KJEL/ | Gedruckt durch Joach. Reuman/ Acad.
Buchdr. [1676]

4to. 180 pp.; A-Y⁴, Z². CKB

1836 Schreiben | so zwischen | Jhrer Königl. Maj. | zu Dännemarck/ Norwe-
gen | und | Jhrer Fürstl. Durchl. | zu Schleßwig/ Holstein Gottorff/ |
Wegen der Seqvestration Jhrer Fürstl. | Durchl. Antheils in dem Her-
tzogthum | Schleßwig | gewechselt worden. [1676]

4to. π1 [=D4], A-C⁴, D⁴ (−D4).                                      CKB

1837 Seiner Hochfürstl. Durchl. zu Schleßwig- | Holstein/ Gottorff &c. |
Antwort Schreiben | Auf das | Königliche Dänische Mandat | Welches |
am 19. Decembris im Jahr 1676. | heraußgegeben worden. | Nebst andern
mehrern Kriegs-Handeln/ | Vom 9/19. Februarii 1677

4to. )(⁴.                                                          CKB

1838 Send-Schreiben | Eines Dennemärckischen von | Adel/ an seinen guten
Freund in | Deutschland/ | Des Fürstl. Schleßwig-Holstein-Gottorf-
fischen | Regierungs Præsidenten/ Johan Adolff Kielmans | von Kiel-
mansEck/ und seiner Dreyen Söh- | ne gefängliche Hafft betreffend. |
[rule] | Gedruckt im Jahr 1676

4to. [2], 24, [2]; A-C⁴ D².                                        CKB

Another edition: 24 pp., A-E⁴, presumably published outside Danish monarchy.

1839 SPECIFICATION | der Reiter und Dragoner Estandarten, | auch
Fahnen und Heerpaucken/ so die unserigen den 4. | Decembr. 1676. von
der Schwedischen Armée in vor- | gangener batallie erobert haben.

4to. χ².                                                           CKB

Caption title.

1840 STÖCKEN, CHRISTIAN VON

Das Eiserne | Teutsch-Land/ | Jn der | Löwen-Gruben | Des | Krieges/ |
Zum Buß-Gebeht | DANIELS, | Eifrig und ernstlich an- | gewiesen/ |
Durch | CHRISTIAN von Stökken/ | der H. Schrift D. Hof-Predigern
und | Superintendenten | [ornament] | [rule] | Plöen/ | Gedrukkt durch
Tobias Schmiedt/ | Jm 1676sten Jahre.

8vo. [8], 90 pp.; ):(⁴, A-E⁸ F⁴, χ¹.                 STADTBIBL. BRAUNSCHWEIG

1841 STÖCKEN, CHRISTIAN VON

Christian von Stökken/ | Der H. Schrift Doctorn | Heilige | Nacht-
mahls- | Musik/ | Auß des | Thomas von Kempen Andach- | ten vom
Sacrament/ | Jn Dreimahl Zwölf Lieder | verfaßet; | Welche sämtlich |
So wol nach bekañten/ alß auch ganz | neuen/ von Hn. Christian Floren/
Kunst- | berühmten Musico in Lünenburg/ sehr schön- | gesezzten Melo-
dien, | Bei dem Gebrauch des H. Abendmahls/ | auch sonst zur An-

dachts-übung/ könen gesun- | gen werden. | Erstes Zwölfe/ | Nebenst einer Vorrede/ warüm des | von Kempen IV Buch vom Sacra- | ment/ in gewiße Lieder übersezzet? | [rule] | PLÖEN/ | Gedrukt von Tobias Schmiedt/ | Jm 1676sten Jahre.

8vo. Pp. [1-16], 1-176, [1-16], 177-268, [1-12]; ):( $^8$, A-E $^8$, F $^4$, )( $^8$, G $^8$, M $^4$, $^2$):( $^8$, N-S $^8$.

CKB; TÜBINGEN UL

1842  STÖCKEN, CHRISTIAN VON

Das Hoch-Fürstlich | Eh-und Liebes-Bette | Des | Hochwürdigst-Durchleuchtigsten Fürsten und Herren/ | Herrn | [ornamental rule] | August-Friedrichs/ | Erwehlten Bischoffs des Stiffts Lübek/ Erbens zu Nor- | wegen/ Herzogens zu Schleßwig/ Holstein/ Stormarn und der | Ditmarschen/ Grafen zu Oldenburg und | Delmenhorst/ | Und | Der Durchleuchtigsten Fürstinnen und Frauen/ | Frauen | [ornamental rule] | Chrjstjnen/ | Vermählten Herzogiñen zu Schleßwig/ Holstein/ Stor- | marn und der Ditmarschen/ Gebohrnen Herzogiñen zu Sach- | sen/ | Jülich/ Clev und Berg/ Gräfiñen zu Oldenburg und | Delmen- | horst/ | Höchstgedacht Seiner Hochfürstlichen Durchl. | Höchstgeliebten Gemahlin | Bei der geschehenen Hoch-Fürstlichen Heimführung | auß untertähnigster Pflicht in dero Bischöfflichen | Hoff-Kirchen eingeseg- | net/ | Durch | CHRISTIAN von Stökken/ der H. Schrift D. | Hoff-Prediger und Superintendenten. | [rule] | PLÖEN/ | Gedrukt durch Tobias Schmiedten/ | Jm 1676 Jahre.

Folio. 40 pp.; [A] $^2$ B-K $^2$.

KIEL UL

1843  STOLTZ, BERNHARD

Beweißthumb des letzten Jahrs dieser Welt . . . 1676.

*

See No. 1513.

1844  Traur-Ruhm-und Lob-Rede/ | . . . | Herr Daniel Sachs/ | Der Heiligen Schrifft fürneh- | men Doctoris | [woodcut] | [rule] | Altona/ Gedruckt bey Victor de Löw/ Anno 1676.

4to. χ $^2$.

CKB

1845  Triumphirende | Sieges-Fahn | (Dem Höchsten sey gedanckt) | Durch tapfferen Triumph vnd verliehenen Sieg | zu Wasser und zu Land | Von | Dem Durchleuchtigsten/ Großmächtigsten | König und Herrn/ Herrn | CHRISTIAN | dem Fünfften/ | Zu Dännemarck Norwägen/ der Wenden und | Gothen König/ Herzog zu Schleswig etc. etc. etc. |

Unsern Allergnädigsten König und Herrn | Ritterlich erhalten | Und | Davon getragen. | [rule] | Kopenhagen/ | Gedruckt bey Daniel Eichhorn/ 1676.

4to. χ⁴.                                                                                     CKB

Verse.

1847   Trost-Lied | Auff | Der weyland TugendEdelsten Frauen | Fr. Martha Justina | Niemannin/ | gebohrnen Försterin | . . . | Dem hochbetrübten H. Witwer zu stärckung auffgesetzet | Von | M.M.R.P.P. | [skull and crossbones] | Schleßwig gedruckt bey Johan Holwein/ 1676.

4to. A⁴.                                                                                     CKB

Verse.

1848   Vollständiges | Gesang-Buch/ | Darinnen | Nicht allein die alte/ | gewöhnli- | che Kirchen-Gesänge/ sondern auch viel | neue/ geist-reiche und theils vorhin | nie in Druck gekommene Lieder | zubefinden: | Alle auff bekandte Melodeien/ zu män- | niglichs/ absonderlich der Einfälti- | gen desto bessern Gebrauch. | Deme zu Ende beygefüget ist ein kurtzes/ | aber auff vielerhand Fälle/ Zeiten und | Anliegen gerichtetes | Gebet-Büchlein. | Bey dem vorigen zweyten Drucke nicht | allein an vielen Orten verbessert/ sondern auch | mit einer mercklichen Anzahl geistreicher/ meh- | rentheils neuen Lieder/ und verschiedenen | Gebeten vermehret. | Jtzo zum dritten mahl auffgeleget. | [rule of type ornaments] | PLÖEN/ | Gedruckt und verlegt von Tobias | Schmiedt. | [rule] | Jm Jahr 1676.

8vo. [8], 629, [19], 224, [8] pp.; ):(⁴, A-Rr⁸, Ss⁴ Tt-Jii⁸, Kkk⁴.                HAB

On Tt1 separate title: *Kurtzes Gebet-Büchlein/ | Doch | Auff vielerhand Fälle und | Anliegen gerichtet. | . . . Jtzo zum Drittenmahl | auffgelegt | [ornament] | Plöen/ | Gedruckt und verlegt von Tobias | Schmiedt. | [rule] | Jm Jahr 1676.*

1849   WILDENHEIN, JOHANNES

Christliche Leichpredigt/ | . . . | Fr. Christinen/ | . . . | Herrn Marx Thomsen | Hertzgeliebtesten HaußEhren/ | . . . | Durch | Joh. Wildenhein/ Past. im Friderichsb. | [rule] | Schleßwig/ gedruckt durch Johan Holwein/ An. 1676.

4to. 80, [8] pp.; A-L⁴.                                                                      CKB

1850   WILLIUS, JOHANN VALENTIN

Der | Nordische Bezoar | oder | Das Wunder-würdige | Hirsch-Horn-Saltz | in leichten Reimen | aus | Natürlichen und Medicinischen | Gründen | vorgestellet | von | Johann. Valentin. Willius | [rule] | Anno [emblem of Daniel Paulli] 1676 | [rule] | Bej Daniel Paulli Königl. Buchhändler.

4to. A-B⁴.                                                              CKB

Colophon: *Kopenhaven/ | Gedruckt bey Matthias Jürgenssen 1676.*

1851  Zwey von | Jhrer Königl. Majestät zu Däne- | marck ergangene | Befehl-Brieffe/ | Die Abschaffung der Geschenck | und Gaben/ und dann die Einziehung | der Greiffen-Feldischen Güter | betreffend/ | Neben Jnhalt | Der an den König in Engeland von denen | im Haag versamlet-gewesten Bunds- | genossen entschlossenen | Antwort/ | Wegen Ausfertigung der Paß-Porten | nach Niemägen | Samt mehrern neuen Händeln. | Vom 18. April st. v. | 1676.

4to. )(⁴.                                                              CKB

## 1677

1852  AREND, CAI

Das hochbegnadete | Alter/ | . . . | Hn: Christoff Schauen- | burgs/ | Vicarij des Thumb-Capittuls zu Ham- | burg/ . . . | . . . | Von CAJO AREND/ Königl: Schloß-Pastorn | auff Dero Glücksburg in der Veste Glückstadt. | [rule] | Glückstadt/ Gedruckt durch Melchior Koch/ Jm Jahr 1677.

4to. [8], 40, [20] pp.; A-F⁴, a-b⁴ c².                               CKB

1853  ARNKIEL, TROELS

Die abwechselung | unsrer | Freud und Traurigkeit/ | . . . | Dorothe Hegelundin | gebohrner STAHLJN/ | Des WolEhrwürdigen/ Andächtigen und Wol- | gelahrten | Herrn PETRI Hegelund/ | Treufleissigen Pastoren der Kirchen zu Ries | gewesenen Hertzlieben Ehe-Frauen/ | . . . | Von | M. TROGILLO Arnkiel/ | Probsten und Pastoren zu Apenrade. | [skull and crossbones] | Schleßwig gedruckt bey Johan Holwein/ | [rule] | Jm Jahr 1677.

4to. 26, [18] pp.; A-E⁴ F².                                          CKB

On leaf E1r, added title: *Flores Funebres | . . . ,* followed by verse by several hands, in Latin and German.

1854  Außführliche | RELATION | von dem | See-Gefecht/ | zwischen | S. Königl. Majestät zu Dennemarck/ Norwegen | ADMJRAEN [sic] | Herrn Niels Juel/ Ritter/ &c. | und | Dero Königl. Majestät zu Schweden Admiralen | Herrn Erich Söeblat. | Am 1. Junii 1677. gehalten

4to. χ².                                                           KIEL UL

Caption title.

1855 Außführliche | Relation | von der zweyten | See-Batallie | so zwischen | Jhrer Königlichen Majestät | zu Dännemarck/ Norwägen | Admiralen | Herrn Niels Juelen/ Rittern/ etc. | und | Jhrer Königlichen Majestät | zu Schweden General-Admiralen/ | Herrn Heinrich Horn/ etc. | Jm Fahr-Wasser Zwischen Falsterboe und | Stefvens Anno 1677. Sontags den 1. Julii | gehalten worden. | [rule] | Kopenhaven/ | Zu finden bey Jhrer Königl. Majest. Buchhändler | Daniel Paulli | gedruckt den 8. Julii.

4to. A-B⁴. KIEL UL; CKB

CKB copy lacks B4.

1856 Außführliche | RELATION | Welchergestalt | Von Jhrer Königl. Maytt. zu Denne- | marck/ &c. Statthaltern und General | in Norwegen/ | Jhrer hohen Excellence/ | Hr. Ulrich Fride- | rich Güldenlewe/ | Die Stadt Marstrand | sampt den beiden Blockhäusern/ | auch dreyen festen Schantzen | Hedwigsholm, Gustav-burg und | Mahlpert, | Zugleich mit dem fast imprenablen Casteel | Carlstein | den 18. und 23. Julij dieses 1677. Jahrs glück- | lich erobert/ und unter allerhöchstgemelt Jhrer | Königl. Mt. Devotion gebracht | worden | De dato Marstrand den 24. Julij. | [rule] | Gedrucht zu Copenhagen bey Sehl. Georg Gödens/ | Königl. Mt. und Univ. Buchd. nachgelassener Witwen.

4to. χ⁴. CKB

1857 BECKER, DIEDRICH

Ehren-Gedächtniß | Oder | Begräbniß-Music, | Bey | Hochansehnlicher Bestattung | Des weiland HochEdlen und Gestrengen Hn: | Herrn FRIDERICO | Lenten/ | Jhro Königl: Mayest: zu Dennemarck Nor- | wegen Hochbetrauten Regierungs-und CantzeleyRaths | in Dero Für- stenthümern Schleßwig Hollstein/ etc. | ErbHerrn auff Sarlshausen/ | Gehalten in Glückstadt den 13. Decembr. 1677. | Von | Diedrich Becker/ | Bestalten Raths Violisten | in Hamburg. | [ornament] | [rule] | Glück- stadt/ Gedruckt bey Melchior Kochen.

4to. [A]², B-J². CKB

On B1r ff., music.

1858 BERGMANN, JOHANN FRIEDRICH

Vera Religio; das ist, Wahrer in Gottes Worte gegründeter, und Gotte wolgefälliger Gottesdienst, in einer Bußpredigt auß Deut. V. 2. seqq., zu Stralsund Anno 1677 vorgestellet. Plön, 1677.

4to. *

*Moller* II, 62; *Bibl. Breitenaviana,* I, 1747, p. 382 lists Plön, 1679.

1859  BIFIELD, NICHOLAS

Verheissungen | Oder | Ein Tractätlein/ wel- | ches zeigt wie ein
Gottsfürch- | tiger Christ sein Hertz auffmuntern und | sich selbsten
stärcken möge wider alles | Creutz/ Elend/ Jammer/ oder Versu- |
chung welche in diesem Leben ihn | überfallen können/ | Begreiffend
die meisten tröstlichen | Oerter der H. Bibel ordentlich zu- | sammen
getragen | Durch | N. Bifield/ Predigern deß | Wortes GOTtes zu
Jsleworth | in Middlesex. | Numehro aber auß dem Englischen | in
unsere Sprache übersetzt | Durch | J.N.J.S. | [rule] | KJEL/ | Jn
Verlegung Simon Beckensteins | und Christian Gerlachs/ 1677.

12mo. 168 pp.; A-G¹².                                              HALLE UL

1860  BOLTEN, JOHANNES

Grab | Zu Modin. I. Macc. XIII, | aus dem III. Artic. des Christ-
Apostolischen Glaubens/ | . . . | HERRN/ | JOHANNIS Rehdern/ |
J.U. berühmten Doctoris, | . . . | Von | JOHANNE BOLTEN Pastore |
im Vaterlande Wilster. | [rule] | Gedruckt in der Königlichen Vestung
Glückstadt/ | durch Melchior Kochen/ Jm Jahr 1677.

4to. 56, [24] pp.; A-K⁴ (K4 blank).                                CKB

On leaf J1, added title: *Die | lange im Leben vergeblich gesuchte/ und/ endlich
im Sterben einmahl noch gefundne/ | echte und rechte | Gesundheit | . . . | Hn:
Johannis Rheders/ | . . . | Von | M. Joachimo Ludovico Reimero/ Hamburg/ |
Prediger daselbst.*

1861  BURCHARD, GEORG HEINRICH

Nothwendige Wiederholete | Erzehlung | Dessen/ | Welches mit der
bekandten Schwermerinnen/ | Der | Antonia Bourignon | allhie in den
Landen der Fürstenthümer Schleß- | wig Holstein bißhieher vorge-
gangen/ | Nebenst klärlicher Erweisung/ daß die- | selbe in ihren
Schrifften/ wider alle Theile des Christ- | lichen Glaubens/ und die
allgemeinen Symbola der Kirchen: insonderheit wider die Ehre/ Person
und Ver- | dienst unsers HERRN Jesu Christi, ärgerlich und | Gottes-
lästerlich lehre: sampt kurzer gründlicher | Widerlegung solcher ihrer
Irrthümer/ | zusammen gefasset/ | Und deroselben/ so genantem Pro-
bierstein/ auch andern | Schrifften entgegen gesetzet/ | Durch | M.
Georg. Henr. Burchardum, | Predigern am Thumb in Schleßwig. | Mit
beygefügtem Jhr Königl. Mayest. zu Den- | nemarck Norw. &c. wider
derselben Lehre abgegebenem | Rescripto, und wider ihre Bücher ergan- |
gener Exsecution, | Auch Censura der Theologischen Facultät | Acad.

Kilon. | [ornament] | Schleßwig/ gedruckt durch Johan Holwein | [rule] | Jm Jahr 1677.

8vo. [56], 441, [7] pp.; a-c⁸, d⁴, A-Ee⁸.                                          CKB

1862   Copenhagensche | RELATION | Von dem | Was irgend in diesen Nordi- | schen Königreichen passiret. | . . . | Copenhagen/ | [rule] | Gedruckt bey Sehl. Georg Gödens/ Königl. Mayt. | und Univers. Buchdr. Nachgelassener Witwen/ | . . . 1677

8vo in 4's.                                                                       CKB

CKB has "Num. 49," 25 August 1677, "Num. 53," 8 September 1677, "Num. 54," 11 September 1677, "Num. 63," 13 October 1677. Each number consists of 4 unsigned leaves.

1862A DENMARK. *Laws, statutes, etc.*

Ordonnance | WOrnach Vnser Christian des | Fünften von Gottes Gnaden/ Königs zu Den- | nemarck . . . | . . . | . . . Artillerie Bediente zu Verpflegen. | . . . | . . . Copenhagen den 24. Januarii Anno 1677.

Broadside.                                                                        CKB

1862B DENMARK. *Laws, statutes, etc.*

Ordonnance | WOrnach Vnser Christian des | Fünften von Gottes Gnaden/ Königs zu Den- | nemarck/ . . . | . . . | . . . Cavallerie zu Verpflegen. | . . . | . . . Copenhagen den 24. Januarii Anno 1677.

Broadside.                                                                        CKB

1862C DENMARK. *Laws, statutes, etc.*

ORDONNANCE | WElcher Gestalt bey Vnser Chri- | stian des Fünfften von GOTtes Gnaden/ Königs zu Denne- | marck/ Norwegen . . . | . . . | . . . Milice, es mit Distribution der Verpflegungs Gelder soll | gehalten werden: | . . . | . . . Geben auff Vnserer Residence zu Copenhagen den 24. Januarij | Anno 1677. | Christian.
ORDONNANCE | WOrnach Vnser Christian des Fünf- | ten von Gottes Gnaden/ Königs zu Denne- | marck/ Norwegen/ . . . | . . . | . . . Infanterie zu verpflegen. | . . . | . . . Geben auf Vnserer Re- | sidence zu Copenhagen den 24. Januarij 1677. | Christian.

Broadside.                                                                       (CUL)

The two ordinances are printed on the left and right halves, respectively, of a single sheet. CKB has separate of second decree.

1862D DENMARK. *Laws, statutes, etc.*

March-Ordnung | NAch welcher es mit | den bey Vnser Christian des |

Fünften . . . | . . . | . . . Armee, | befindlichen Bagagie-Artillerie- und
Pro- | viant-Wagen ordinairement sol gehalten | werden.

4to.  $\chi^2$.                                                                                       CKB

Caption title. At end: . . . *Copenhagen den 26. Jan. Anno 1677.* | *Christian.*

1863   DENMARK. *Laws, statutes, etc.*

WJR Christian der Fünffte/ von | . . . | . . . Glückstadt . . . | . . . 18. Junij,
Anno 1677

Broadside.                                                                                            CNA

Decree ordering prayers that the queen may have a "glückliche Entbindung."

1863A  DENMARK. *Laws, statutes, etc.*

ORDONNANCE | WOrnach Vnser Christian des Fünf- | ten von
Gottes Gnaden/ Königs zu Denne- | marck/ . . . | . . . | . . . Dragoner zu
verpflegen. | . . . | . . . Copenhagen den 24. Januarij 1677.

Broadside.                                                                                            CKB

1863B  DENMARK. *Laws, statutes, etc.*

ORDONNANCE | WOrnach Vnser Christian des Fünff- | ten von
Gottes Gnaden/ Königs zu Dännemarck/ . . . | . . . Tragouner zu ver-
pflegen. | . . . | . . . Lands-Cron den 23. Julii Anno 1677.

Broadside.                                                                                            CKB

1864   DENMARK. *Laws, statutes, etc.*

WJr Christian der Fünfte/ von Gottes Gnaden/ König zu Den- |
nemarck . . . | . . . | . . . 22. Decembr. Anno. 1677.

Broadside.                                                                                            CKB

Decree forbidding mariners to leave the country "oder sich zu verstecken."

1865   Dero | Königlichen Majestät | zu Dennemarck Norwegen/ &c. | An |
Jhr. Hoch-Fürstliche | Durchl. zu Schleßwig Holstein | Abgelassene
Schreiben/ | Nebenst | Der darauff ergangenen Antwort/ die Sequestra-
tion | des Hertzogthums Schleßwig betreffend. [1677]

4to. A-F⁴, $\chi^2$.                                                                         CKB; KIEL UL

First decree, A2, dated 19 December 1676. Another edition, containing only two
decrees, of 19 December 1676 and 16 January 1677, A⁴ B1-3; another edition, A-F⁴
(Kiel UL).

1866   Des Dähnischen und Schwedischen Krieges Außgang/ | prognosticiret
von einem Dähnischen Astronomico, | im Jahr 1677.

Broadside.                                                                                            SRL

1867  Des zu Nimwegen | Extraordinari- Abgesandten | und | Gevollmächtig-
ten | Jh. Königl. Majest. | Jn Dennemarck Norwe- | gen/ etc. etc. |
übergebene | PRÆTENSIONES | und Anförderungen | An dem | König
und Reiche | Schweden/ etc. etc. | [rule] | Gedruckt im Jahr 1677.

4to. χ⁴.                                                                      CKB

1868  Ehren-und Schertz Gedicht am hochzeitlichen Tage des Herrn Georg
Henning Eckleff, wie derselbe sich verehliget mit Margarethe Dorothea
Kirchmannin. Schleswig, 1677.

Folio.                                                                          ✱

Formerly in Kiel UL (LmC 7-6; 7-7).

1868A Eigentliche | Relation | von dem | was vor der | Bokul-Schantze | pas-
sirt. | [rule] | Kopenhagen/ | Gedruckt Anno 1677.

4to. χ².                                                                       CUL

1869  Extraordinaire | Oeresundische | Relation | No. [figure] 4 | ANNO
1677 | Sambstag den 13. Januarii | [rule] | (Num. 7) G 1

12mo. Pp. 49-56; χ⁴.                                                   DEUTSCH-NIENHOF

Published in Copenhagen. *Berättelser om Sveriges Krig II* (1888-91), 202, lists issues of 28 July and 25 August 1677.

1870  Extraordinaire | Oeresundische | Relation | No. [figure] 42 | ANNO
1677 | Diengstag den 5. Junii | [rule] | (Num. 78) G4

12mo. Pp. 605-612; χ⁴.                                                 DEUTSCH-NIENHOF

1871  FINCK, ABEL, *and others*

(Trauergedichte über Eilhard Schacht). Schleswig: Joh. Holwein
(1677).

Folio. χ².                                                                      ✱

Formerly in Kiel UL (LmC 16-36).

1872  (Gedicht über Kasper March Professor von den March'schen Tischgenossen). Kiel: Joachim Reumann, [1677].

Broadside.                                                                       ✱

Formerly in Kiel UL (LmC 30ᵃ-66).

1873  GEUSS, JOH. PHIL. *and* ELIAS SCHRÖTER

(Trauergedichte über Eilhard Schacht). Schleswig: Joh. Holwein,
(1677).

Folio. $\chi^2$.                                                                    *

Formerly in Kiel UL (LmC 16-37).

1874   H. K.

(Trauergedicht über Henning Eckleff). Schleswig: Joh. Holwein, (ca. 1677).

Folio. $\chi^2$.                                                                    *

Formerly in Kiel UL (LmC 7-6).

1875   Handgriff | Von | Musqveten und | Picken/ | Wornach Jhro Königl: Mayt: | Infanterie, in dero Königreich Nor- | wegn Exercirt, und die Commando | Wörter/ über all gebraucht | werden sollen. | [ornament: seal] | Christiania/ | Gedruckt/ Jm Jahr 1677.

4to. A$^8$.                                                                        CKB

On A8v, dated, "Jn Anno 1675."

1876   Hoch-Fürstlicher Liebes-Schall in einem erfreulichen Gegen-Hall an der Fürstin Christinen Gebuhrts-Tage den 25sten des August-Monats im 1677sten Jahre. Plön: Tobias Schmidt, 1677.

Folio.                                                                             *

J. A. Bolten in Niemann's *Miscellaneen* II/2 (1800), 206.

1877   KOGEL, FRIEDRICH

Ehren-Zeilen/ | An | den Herrn | Andächtigen/ | über | Sr. Hochwol- würden/ | des Hn. SuperIntend. | zu Eutien | Himmelblaue Lilje/ | Mit dem Zunft-Spruch | Nach dem Hiñel zu! | Gestellet | Von | Fried- rich Kogel/ Käis. Gek. P. | und der Schulen zu Eutien ConR. | [rule] | PLOEN/ | Gedrukkt durch Tobias Schmiedten. [1677?]

4to. $\chi^2$.                                                                     HAB

Addressed to Christian von Stöcken. Includes a poem by his son Heinrich von Stöcken.

1878   KORTHOLT, CHRISTIAN

Christian Kortholten/ | der H. Schrifft D. und bey der | Hoch-Fürstl. Holstein. Universitet zum | Kiel Profess. Primar. | THAVMATO- | GRAPHIA, | Oder | Umbständliche Relation/ | was in der Weltberümb- ten Stadt | Hamburg mit einem | Glüenden Ei- | sernen Ringe | sich wundersames und merck- | würdiges zugetragen; | Samt angezeigtem Nutzen/ | wie man dessen wider die Atheisten/ Pa- | pisten/ und bey angefochtenen Perso- | nen sich zu bedienen habe. | [rule] | KJEL/ | Gedruckt und verlegt durch Joachim Reuman/ Acad. Buchdr. 1677.

8vo. 176 pp.; A-L⁸; folding plate.                                          CKB

In CKB copy folding plate, woodcut depicting ring, inserted both before title-page and between leaves B4 & B5. Attested by Otto Sperling and M. Herman v. Petkum, and dated Hamburg 26 Sept. 1677, on p. 176. Republished, 1699, n.p. (No. 2992).

1879    Kurtzer Bericht/ | Wie von den Schweden die | mit dehnen auff Hel- | singburg/ Christia- | nopel und Carlshaven gewesenen Kö- | nigl. Dänschen Commendanten getrof- | fene Accords-Puncten wieder allen | Kriegs-gebrauch violiret und | gebrochen worden. | [rule] | Kopen- | hagen/ | Gedruckt bey Sehl. Georg Gödens/ Königl. Maytt. | und Univers: Buchdr: Nachlebenden Witwe | den 10 April Anno 1677

4to. χ².                                                                    CKB

1880    LASSENIUS, JOHANNES

Hand-leitung | Zur | Seligkeit. | Darin der heil: Catechißmus | Lutheri, von Frag zu Frag/ nach sei- | nem Geistreichen Verstande erkläret/ und | mit Sprüchen der heil: Schrifft | beleget. | Sampt beygefügten Morgen- und | Abend-Buß-Beicht-Communion- | und anderen Gebeten | Für die Christliche Gemeinen in der | Graffschaft Ranzau. | Mit gnädigsten Gefallen der | Obrigkeit/ | Gestellet | Von dem Probst daselbst. | [rule] | Glückstadt/ Gedruckt durch Melchior | Kochen | [rule] | Jn Verlegung Georg Wolffs/ Buch- | händlers zu Hamburg in S. Johan- | nis Kirchen/ Jm Jahr 1677.

12mo. [12], 309, [1], 24 pp.; A-O¹² P⁶ (P6 blank).                          CKB

"Vorrede" is signed Johann-Lassenius. The final 24 pp. constitute: *Morgen-* | *und* | *Abend-Lied/* | *Sampt andächtigen* | *Gebeth- und Seufftzern/* | *Vor die Christliche* *Jugend* | *in der Graffschafft Rantzau.* (Added title on leaf O7.) *Cf.* No. 1648.

1881    Letzte Ehren-Bezeugung | . . . | Herrn FRIDERICO | JESSENIO, | . . . | von etlichen | Wollwollend- und Dienst-ergebenen Freunden. | [rule] | Kiel/ | Gedruckt durch Joach. Reuman/ Acad. Buchdr. [1677]

4to. A-E⁴.                                                              KIEL UL

Bound with, probably issued with: *Schuldiges Trost-und Ehren-Gedächtnüß/* | . . . | *Madrigalon/* | *von* | [monogram], n.p., n.d., A⁴ B1-3.

1882    Löw, JOHANN *and* ANDREAS BERGSTÆDT

Letztes Ehren-Gedächtnis | . . . | Fr. Sara Kollen/ | Gebohrnen Ro- landtin. | . . . | Althona/ Gedruckt bey Victor de Löw/ Anno 1677.

4to. χ⁴.                                                                KIEL UL

1883    MARTINI, BENEDICT

Leidender und abscheidender Christen | seliges | Trost-Küssen/ | . . . | Fr.

Margareten Agneten/ | geborner Soltowinnen/ | . . . | Herrn Hans
Christian Hecklauers JCti, | . . . | . . . Ehe-Schatzes/ | . . . | Von |
BENEDICTO MARTINI, Ecclesiæ Cathedra- | lis Slesvicensis Pastore
primario. | [rule] | Schleßwig gedruckt bey Johann Holwein/ An. 1677.

4to. [1], 21 pp., [4] leaves; [A]² B-G⁴.                                        CUL

Title within woodcut border; text within double rule borders.

1884   Nord-schwedische | Hexerey/ | oder | SIMIA DEI, | GOttes Affe. | Das
       ist: | Ausführliche Beschreibung der schändlichen | Verführungen des
       leidigen Satans/ darinnen zu sehen | GOttes erschröckliches Straff-
       Verhängen/ wegen greu- | licher Sünden-Mengen. | Jn einem Jammer-
       behertzigten Send-Schrei- | ben am Tag gegeben/ | [woodcut] | von |
       Theophilo Sincero/ an Christianum. . . . [1677]

       4to. A-H⁴.                                                              CKB

       Ascribed to Chr. Kortholt in *Bibliotheca Danica, Suppl. Bibl. Slesvico-Holsatico*, col.
       1014. Place of publication uncertain. Last line of print trimmed off title-page in
       CKB copy.

1886   SCHLESWIG-HOLSTEIN-GOTTORFF. *Laws, statutes, etc.*

       WJr von Gottes Gnaden Christian Al- | brecht/ Erbe zu Norwegen/
       postulirter Coadjutor des Stifts | . . . | . . . 1. Maij Anno 1677.

       Broadside.                                                              CKB

       Decree establishing 16-18 May as "Fast: Buß und Beht-Tage."

1887   SCHMIDT VON EISENBERG, JOHANNES

       Gottes | Todes-Regiment. | . . . | VALENTINI SCHMIDII von Eisen-
       berg/ | . . . | CHRISTIANI SCHMIDII von Eisenberg/ | . . . |
       GODOFRIDI SCHMIDII von Eisenberg/ | . . . | Von | M. Johanne
       Schmidt/ der Christl. Gemeine zu Biert . . . | . . . | [rule] | Schleßwig/
       gedruckt bey Johan Holwein/ An. 1677.

       4to. 78, [6] pp.; A-K⁴ L².                                        CKB; KIEL UL

       Kiel has copy with variant title-page.

1888   Schreiben | so zwischen | Jhrer Königl. Maj. | zu Dännemarck/ Nor-
       wegen | und | Jhrer Fürstl. Durchl. | zu Schleßwig/ Holstein Gottorff/ |
       Wegen der Seqvestration Jhrer Fürstl. | Durchl. Antheils in dem
       Hertzogthum | Schleßwig | gewechselt worden. [1677]

       4to. π1, A-D⁴.                                                         CKB

       D4 lacking, perhaps = π1. Another edition, π1, A-F⁴, no title page in CKB copy;

another edition with title: *Dero | Königlichen Majestät | . . . | Abgelassene Schreiben/ | . . .*, A-F⁴; χ².

1889 SEHESTED, JENS STEEN

Allerunterthänigster | Glück und Wilkoms-Wundsch | an | Den Groß-mächtigsten Erb- | König' und Herren | Herrn | CHRISTIAN | Der Fünffte/ | Zu Dännemarck und Norwegen etc. | über | den siegenden Success und glückliche Wiederkunfft | von Rügen/ | Meinem Aller-gnädigsten König und Herren | eignet dieses zu | Der allerunterthänigst gehorsahme | J. S. Sehestedt. | Hafn. den 8. Oct. An. 1677 | [rule] | Gedruckt in Kopenhagen

4to. )o(⁴. CKB

1890 STÖCKEN, CHRISTIAN VON

An die Durchläuchtigste Fürstin und Frau Maria Elisabeth . . . Söhn-und Sehnliche Dank-Zeilen. . . . Plön: Tobias Schmidt, 1677.

Folio. *

J. A. Bolten in Niemann's *Miscellaneen,* II/2 (1800), 206.

1891 STÖCKEN, CHRISTIAN VON

Der Friedens-Post im Norden bey der Taufe Friedrich Pohlen (Gott-friedi Pastor Schönewald Sohnleins). Plön, 1677

4to. *

*OHM* I, 659.

1892 STORNING, HINRICH

Jm Nahmen deß DreyEinigen GOttes | Die wahre und veste | Grund-lehre | Von der Ehelichen Keuschheit | Zwischen einem Manne und ei- | nem Weibe/ | Auß dem Heil. Wort des HERREN | dargethan | Von einem Diener JESu CHRJsti | HENRICO Storning. | [Latin quotation] | [rule] | KJEL/ | Jn Verlegung Simon Beckensteins und Christian | Gerlachs/ im Jahr 1677.

4to. [12], 52 pp.; )(⁴, )()(², A-F⁴ G². CKB

1893 STORNING, HINRICH

Planctus Ecclesiæ, oder Klage von wegen allerley in der Christlichen Kirchen eingerissenen Aberglaubens. Zum Unterricht der evangelischen Jugend in der Fremde. Plön, 1677

12mo. *

*Moller* I, 666; *Bibl. Kielmans-Egg.,* III, 1371; *Cat. Amthoriana,* 1722, p. 84. For-merly in Kiel UL.

1894 Vhrsachen/ | Welche Jhre. Königl. Mayt. als | Dominum directum & supremum des Für- | stenthumbs Schleßwig bewogen/ den | Fürstl. Gottorfischen Antheil zu | sequestriren. | [rule] | Gedruckt im Jahr 1677.

4to. χ⁴. CKB

Another edition, 4to, place of publication uncertain; another edition, 8vo, )(⁸; )(8 is blank.

1895 Vollständiges Gesang-Buch darinnen nicht allein die alte gewöhnliche KirchenGesänge sondern auch viele neue geist-reiche Lieder zu befinden ..., Plön, 1677

＊

*Bibl. Kielmans-Egg.*, I, 988. Fourth edition of Plön hymnal?

1896 WEDDERKOPF, GABRIEL

Heiliges Verlangen | der | Diener GOttes/ | ... | FRIDERICI JES-SENII, | ... | von | M. GABRIELE Wedderkopff/ | Prediger an S. Nicolai. | [rule] | KJEL/ | Gedruckt durch Joach. Reumann/ Acad. Buchd. 1677.

4to. [8], 48 pp.; πE⁴, A-F⁴. CKB

## 1678

1897 Accords-Puncten | so zwischen dem Königl. Dänschen Gene- | ral Major und Gouverneur Carl Heinrich von der | Osten/ und dem Königl. Schwedischen Feldmarschal | Lieutenant/ Baron Rutger von Aschen-bürg/ samt denen beeder- | seits zur Capitulation deputirten Commis-sarien/ die Stadt | und Fästung Christianstadt betreffend/ geschlossen | und vollenzogen worden. [1678]

4to. )(⁴. CKB

Caption title. Variant edition, with same caption title, 8vo, χ⁴.

1898 Accords-Puncten | der Stadt | Christianstadt; | Welche zwischen dem Königlichen | Feldmarschall Aschenberg und den Dähni- | schen General Major und Gouverneur von der | Osten/ sampt den beyderseits zu Capitulation | deputirten Commissarien den 4 Aug. 1678. | geschlossen und vollenzogen worden. | [woodcut of Christianstadt] | A. Die lange Brücke Brücke, B. der Fluß Hella Aa. C. Morast. | F. die beiden Raveline G. Stein-Damm. | Nach dem zu Copenhagen gedrückten | Exemplar. [1678]

8vo. χ⁴. SRL

Place of publication uncertain.

1899  APELLES, MATTHÆUS DE LOEW *and* CORNELIUS CÆSARIUS

Frühlings-Mayen, oder Geistliche Lieder meistentheils auff Symbola
Fürst-und Freyherrlicher Personen 1644. gerichtet. Kiel, 1678.

Folio.                                                                          *

*Moller* II, 517; *Goedeke*, 2 Aufl. III, 53; Lipenius, *Bibl. real. phil.* I, 596; *Thott* IV,
60; *Bibl. Breitenaviana,* 1747, p. 388.

1900  Außfürliche | RELATION | Von der | Attaque auff Rügen | De Dato
Wittau den 14. Septembris Anno | 1678.

4to.  $\chi^2$.                                                                  CKB

Caption title.

1901  BECKER, DIEDRICH

Traur-und Begräbnuß- | Music | Bey | Hochansehnlicher Christlicher
Leichbestättigung | Des | HochEdlen und Gestrengen Herrn/ | Herrn
Johann Helms/ | . . . | Zu Glückstadt in der Stadt-Kirchen gehalten |
Von | Diedrich Beckern/ | bestalten Raths Violisten in Hamburg. |
[woodcut: angel] | [rule] | Glückstadt/ Gedruckt durch Melchior
Kochen/ 1678.

4to.  $\pi^2$, A$^4$, B-J$^2$.                                                   CKB

On A1r ff., music.

1902  BERGSTÄDT, ANDREAS

Ehren-Gedächtnuß | . . . | Hn: JOHANN Helms/ | . . . | Zu bezeugung
nachtragender Liebe und | schuldigen Pflicht | Eylfertig übersandt |
Von | Andreas Bergstädten/ Advoc: | [woodcut: skull] | [rule] |
Gedruckt in der Königlichen Veste Glückstadt/ durch | Melchior
Kochen/ Jm Jahr 1678.

4to.  $\chi^4$.                                                                  CKB

1903  Beschreibung | der | Jnsul Rügen | nebst einer | RELATION | welcher
Gestalt die Königl. Dänsche Trouppen | am 12. Septembris/ und die
Chur-Brandenburgische | am 13. Dito Anno 1678. auf selbiger gelandet/
und | folgends alle darauf liegende Schantzen | erobert. | [rule]
[at bottom of title-page four Latin verses entitled "In recuperatam
RUGIAM" and containing a rebus giving date, 1678]

4to.  A$^4$.                                                                     CKB

At end: *Welcher Gestalt Chur-Brandenburg gelandet/ folget | nächstens.*

1904   BRÄMER, JOHANNES

Das | Zustossen Rohr | Und | Glümmend Tocht des | Glaubens/ |
Welches der HErr nicht | zubrechen noch außlöschen | wird/ | Den
Schwachen zum Trost und | den Starcken zur Erinnerung | gezeiget
von | Der zu Dennemarck und Norwegen | Königlichen Majestät |
Deutschem Hof-Prediger | Johannes Brämer/ | Lübeckern | CUM PRI-
VILEGIO. | [type ornaments] | Zum zweytenmahl gedruckt | Auff
Kosten Danielis Paulli, Königl. | Buchh. in Koppenhaven 1678 | [rule] |
Ratzeburg/ bey Niclos Nissen verfertiget.

12mo.  [2], 5-368, [52] pp.; π1, A¹²(−A1,2), B-R¹² S⁶; engraving.         HAB

Title in red and black. New issue of Frankfurt, 1670, edition. Not strictly an imprint of Denmark.

1905   BRANDT, FRIDERICH

Braut-Fackel zu Ehren dem Ehe-Paar Peter Brandt und Abel Maria von
Stöcken. . . . Copenhagen, 1678.

Folio.                                                    *

*Thott* V/1, 346.

1906   BÜLL, CHRISTIAN KAI *and* FRIEDRICH RUNGE

(Trauergedichte über Anna Büll). Kiel: Joachim Reumann, 1678.

4to. χ⁴.                                                  *

Formerly in Kiel UL (LmC 72-66).

1907   COPIA | Eines Schreibens aus Do- | bran vom 27. Novembr. worinnen
die | daselbst zwischen Jhr. Königl. Maj. zu Dennemarck- | Norwegen
und Churfürstl. Durchl. zu Brandenburg | gepflogene Consilia guten
Theils zu finden. | Aus dem Frantzös. Original in | Hochteutsch
übergesetzt/ zu Ende des | 1678. Jahres.

4to. A-B⁴.                                                CKB

Caption title. One of 4 editions with same title. The others were presumably issued
outside the monarchy: *a)* A⁴ B 1-2 (two columns to page); *b)* A-B⁴ (−B4); *c)* A-C⁴
(−C4).

1908   DENMARK. *Laws, statutes, etc.*

WJr Christian der Fünffte/ von | . . . | . . . 8. Jan. Anno 1678.

Broadside.                                                KIEL UL

Decree regarding coinage.

1909 DENMARK. *Laws, statutes, etc.*

WJR Christian der Fünffte/ von | . . . | . . . Glückstadt . . . 25.
Februarij, Anno 1678.

Broadside.                                                                                CNA

Decree regarding the value of certain foreign coins in circulation.

1910 DENMARK. *Laws, statutes, etc.*

WJR Christian der Fünffte/ von | . . . | . . . Glückstadt . . . 28. Martij,
Anno 1678

Broadside.                                                                                CNA

Decree ordering days of prayer 19 and 26 April and 3 May.

1910A DENMARK. *Laws, statutes, etc.*

Verordnung | Wornach der Kopff- und Viehe-Schatz in | den Städten
und Flecken der Fürstenthümber | Schleßwig/ Holstein zu zahlen.

4to. $\chi^2$.                                                                             CKB

Caption title. Signed at end: *Geben Copenhagen den 15.* | *Augusti, Anno 1678.* |
*Dero Königl. Maytt. zu Deñemarck/ Norweg.* | *Deputirte des General Commis-*
*sariats.* | *H. Wind. C. Sehestedt. H. von Stöcken.* | *P. Pederson Lerke.*

1911 DENMARK. *Laws, statutes, etc.*

WJR Christian der Fünffte/ von | . . . | . . . Glückstadt/ den 23. |
Decembr. Anno 1678

Broadside.                                                                                CNA

Decree calling a meeting of the "Ober-Ambtgericht" in Glückstadt 20 February.

1912 DIECKHOF, JOHANNES

Breviarium Arithmeticum, oder kurtzer Unterricht und Anleitung zum
Rechnen. Schleswig, 1678.

12mo.                                                                                      *

*Moller* I, 139.

1913 EBERS, JOHANN DANIEL

(Trauer und Ehren Gedicht auf den Hintritt Joachim von Buchwald auf
Pronstorf). Schleswig, 1678.

Folio.                                                                                     *

*OHM* I, 144.

1914 Extraordinaires | Oeresundische | RELATIONES | [figure: Mercury] | eingekommen | im | JANUARIO | Anno 1678

12mo. Pp. 19-22; $\chi^2$.                                    DEUTSCH-NIENHOF

Fragment.

1915 GROTSCHILLING, HANNS

Wolverdienter Ehren-Nachklang/ | Dem weyland | HochEdlen/ Gestrengen und Vesten Herrn/ | Herrn Johann Helm/ | ... | Von | Hanns Grotschilling/ Käyserl. Notario | und Königl. Cancellisten. | [rule] | Gedruckt in der Königlichen Veste Glückstadt/ durch | Melchior Kochen/ Jm Jahr 1678.

4to. $\chi^2$.                                                    CKB

1915A HELDVAD, NIELS

Kurtze und einfältige Beschreibung ...

Cf. No. 1638.

1916 Jhrer Königl. Majest. zu | Dännemarck/ Norwegen respective ge- | heimen Räthe und General Ad- | miral Lieutenants | Hn. Jens und Niels | Juelen | Allerunterthänigste Relationes von | Eroberung deß | Landes Rügen | De datis den 12 und 14 Septembr. | Anno 1678. | Sampt einem P.S. Von dem Königl. | Orlog Schiff die Drey Lewen genandt | de dato den 15. Sept. 1678. | [rule] | Copenhagen/ Gedruckt bey Sl. Georg Gödens/ Kön: | Maytt: und Univerfit [sic] Buchdr: Nachgelassener Witwen.

4to. $\chi^4$.                                                    CKB

1917 Jhrer Königl. Majestät zu | Dännemark, Norwegen, respective ge- | heimen | Räthe und General Admiral Lieu- | tenants | Herrn Jens und Niels Juelen | Allerunterthänigste Relationes | Von dem/ waß ferner auff dem Lande Rügen passiret ist/ | de datis den 14. 16. und 17. Septembr. 1678.

4to. $\chi^2$.                                                    CKB

1918 JÖNSEN, HEINRICH

Traur-Gedancken/ | ... | Herrn JOHANNIS | Helms/ | ... | Zu bezeugung hertzlichen und schuldigen | Mitleidens | geführt | Von | HENRICO | Jönsen. | [rule] | Glückstadt/ Druckts Melchior Koch. [1678]

4to. $\chi^2$.                                                    CKB

Presumably printed with N. Nothelffer, *Abdanckung* ... 1678 (No. 1928).

1919  KEGEL, PHILIPP

Zwölf geistliche Andachten. Ploen, 1678

8vo (oblong).                                                              *

*Bibl. Breitenaviana*, I, 1747, p. 385; *Cat. libr. Johannes Dauw*, 1723, 8vo, 1178.

1920  Kurtzer Bericht/ | Was bey dem | zu Coppenhagen am 13. Ja- | nuarij/
dieses 1678. Jahrs/ deß Abends in dem Königl. | damahls von brennen-
den Liechtern sehr hell gemachten Reut-Hauß/ | so wohl wegen
erhaltener Victorien, als auch insonderheit wegen | Jhrer Churfürstl.
Durchl. von Brandenburg glücklichen Erobe- | rung der Statt vnd
Vestung Stettin/ in Gegenwart beyder Königl. | Mayest. der Princessin/
Fürstlich-Gräfflich-vnd Adelichen | Frauen-Zimmers /wie nicht weniger
vornehmer Herren/ gehal- | tenen Auffzuge/ Ring-vnd Kopff-Rennen/
vor- | gegangen/ vnd zu sehen war. | Sub Dato Coppenhagen/ den 20.
Januarij/ 1678

4to. $\chi^2$.                                                            SRL

Place of publication uncertain.

1921  LASSENIUS, JOHANNES

Handleitung | Zur | [rule of type ornaments] | Seligkeit/ | Darin der
Heil. Cate- | chismus Lutheri, von Frag zu | Frag/ nach seinem Geist-
reichen | Verstande erkläret/ | Samt beigefügten Morgen und | Abend/
Buß-Beicht-Communion und | andern Gebeten; Auch etzlichen Gewis-
sens- | Fragen/ uñ kurtzem Fundament der Christl: | Religion, aus H.
Schrifft. | Zur Ehre Gottes und gemeinen Nutzen/ | in der Furcht des
HErrn außgefertiget | von | D. Johanne Lassenio. | [rule] | Zum Dritten-
mahl gedruckt | vor Daniel Paulli Kön. Buchhändl. | in Kopenhaven
Anno 1678. | Lübeck/ bey Seel: Schmalhertzens Erben.

12mo. [24], 286, [2], 141, [1], 22, [2] pp.; A-N$^{12}$, Aa-Gg$^{12}$ (−N12; Aa1, Gg12
blank).                                                                   HAB

Title printed in red and black. Title engraving on A1. Aa2, separate title:
*Morgen- | Und | Abend-Buß-Beicht- | Communion und andere | Zeit- und Noht |
Gebet.* Listed as a separate in Wilhelm Rabe, *Johannes Lassenius*, 1933, p. 182.

1923  LISTA | Derer unter Bornholm Anno 1678. zwischen | den 4. und 5.
Decembris gestrandeten und ge- | fangenen Schweden.

4to. )($^4$.                                                              CKB

Caption title. Another edition, )(4.

1924  LOHMANN, GEORG

Amor Dei trahens; . . . oder Leichpredigt über Henrich Hanibal von
Aichelberg. . . . Plön: Tobias Schmidt, 1678.

4to. 42 pp.                                                                          *

*Moller* I, 359; *Stolberg* I, 25.

1925  MEUSCHEN, JOACHIM CHRISTIAN

Anweisung zur Lesung der Heiligen Schrifft. Kiel, 1678

8vo.                                                                                 *

*Cat. lib. Lehmann,* II, 1741, p. 254.

1926  MÜLLER, CHRISTIAN RUDOLF

Abdanckungs-Rede/ | . . . | H: Friedrich Lenten/ | . . . | Durch |
Christianum Rudolphum Müller/ | Past: Neobr: | [woodcut: skull] |
[rule] | Gedruckt in der Königlichen Veste Glückstadt/ durch | Mel-
chior Kochen/ Jm Jahr 1678.

4to. A-F⁴.                                                                        CKB

Title and text within borders of type ornaments.

1927  Nimwegischer | Friedens-Currier | herbringend | Worauf die Anfoder-
ungen zwischen | beiderseits Chronen Dännemarck/ und | Schweden/
auch S. C. Durchl. von Bran- | denburg annoch bestehen/ nebst dersel-
ben | Beantwortungen. | Nemlich | 1. J.K.M. zu Dännemarck Anforde- |
rung an Schweden. | 2. der Chron Schweden Anforderung | an Dänne-
marck. | 3. Chur-Brandenburgs Anforderung | an Schweden. | 4. J. Kais.
M. Antwort auf die Schwe- | dische Anforderung. | 5. J.K.M. zu Dänne-
marck Antwort | auf der Schweden Anforderung. | 6. S.C.D. zu Branden-
burg Antwort | auf der Schweden Antwort. | 7. J.K.M. von Franckreich
Vortrag | an J.K.M. zu Dännemarck. | 8. J.K.M. zu Dännemarck Ant-
wort | auf des Königs von Franckreich beschehene | Anforderungen. |
[rule] | Anno 1678.

4to. )(⁸.                                                                         CKB

Presumably issued in conjunction with D. Paulli's *Extraordinaires Relationes,* 1678
(not preserved in CKB).

1928  NOTHELFFER, NICOLAUS

Abdanckung | Bey hochansehnlich Christlicher Leich-Bestattung | Deß |
HochEdlen und Gestrengen Herrn/ | Herrn Johann Helms/ | . . . | Von |
M. NICOLAO Nothelffer/ | Königl. Dennemärckischen Schloß-Pas-

torn. | [rule] | Gedruckt in der Königlichen Veste Glückstadt/ durch | Melchior Kochen/ Jm Jahr 1678.

4to. 32 pp.; A-D⁴.                                                              CKB

1929   Ohnvorgreiffliches | Feder-Gefechte | Uber | Die am 4. und 5. Decemb. 1678. Jahrs | unter Bornholm Schwedischer Seiten | erlittene Strandung/ &c. | Mit einigen | Pro- & Contra-Geführten | Jedoch | Ohnpräjudicirlichen Argumenten.

4to. χ⁴.                                                                         CKB

1930   PROJECT, | Welcher Gestalt Jhrer Königl. Majest. zu Dännemarck/ Norwägen General Admiral Lieutenant | Seine Excellentz Herr NIELS JUEL, Ritter/ etc. Ordre gegeben/ daß die Königliche Trouppen bey der Descente | auf der Jnsul Rügen an Wittow sich rangiret Anno 1678. den 12. Septembris.

Broadside (26 x 28.7 cm).                                                        CKB

1930A REICH, CHRISTOPHER

Helden-Ruhm | in den | Heroischen Verrichtungen | Deß | Weld berümbten See-Helden | Herren | NIELS JUEL | Herren zu Sæbygaard/ etc. | Ritter. | Dero Königlichen Majestät | zu Dennemarck und Norwegen/ etc. | hochbestalter | General Admiral Lieutenant/ | Admiralitets Rath/ | wie auch | General Gouverneur über | die Provintz | Gottland/ etc. | So von dem selben | in dem 1676sten wie auch im 1677sten Jahr vollenbracht: | fürgestellet von | Christophorus Reich | v.K.a.P. [1678]

Folio. π², A-H².                                                                 CKB

1931   RELATION | Was sich mit denen | auß Pommern nach Schweden | wollenden Schwedischen Völ- | ckern bey der Jnsul Born- | holm zugetragen. | [rule] | Copenhagen/ | Gedruckt bey Jhr: Königl: Maytt: und | Universit. Buchdr. Corfitz Luft. [1678]

8vo. χ⁴.                                                                          CKB

Another edition, 4to, χ², dated: *Kopenhagen den 14. Decemb. Anno 1678.*

1932   RÖTSCHER, JOHANNES VOLCMAR.

(Leichpredigt über Joh. XVIII. 9.) Kiel, 1678.

4to.                                                                                *

*Moller* II, 732.

1933   SCHULTZE, CORNELIUS

Christlicher Haußvatter, oder einfältige Anleitung, wie ein Haußvatter seine Kinder und Gesinde den Morgen-und Abendsegen, wie auch die Tischgebete Gottgefällig möge beten lehren; der Gemeine auf Nordmarsch in etlichen Predigten mitgetheilt. Schleswig, 1678.

8vo.                                                                              *

*Moller* I, 605; *Cat. lib. Lehmann* I, 1740, p. 92.

1934 SCHWARTZ, JOSUA

Drey | Außgesonderte | Krieges- Predigten. | I. | Von einigen ungemeinen Sünden/ alß | Ursachen des Krieges nun auch | in Schweden. | II. | Von dem Schoß/ den man dem überwinder/ | im Kriege zu geben schnldig [sic] ist. | III. | Von der Art des Krieges/ darin man mit gutem | Gewissen leben kan. | unter andern | Jn einem/ leider Gottes/ annoch wehrendem Bluttrieffenden Kriege/ | zu Lunden gehalten | Von | JOSUA Schwartzen/ der Heil. Schrifft Docto- | re und Professore, des Geistlichen Consistorii Assessore und | Deutschen Prediger daselbst. | Sampt einer Schutz-Rede/ darin der Author die ander Pre- | digt/ und seine daher entstandene Flucht nacher Copenhagen/ wieder das | ärgerniß/ welches Jhm der jetzige Malmogische Gouverneur und General-Lieut. | Herr Baron Georg Sperling, selbst darauß genommen hat/ mit Gottes | Wort vertheidigen thut. Anno 1678. | [rule] | Gedruckt zur Kopenhagen von Christian Wehring/ Acad. Buchdr. | zu finden aber bey Christian Gerhard Buchhandlern daselbst.

4to. Pp. [1-32], 1-24, 29-268; a-d⁴, A-Kk⁴.                                      CKB

1935 SPECIFICATION | Derer unter Bornholm gestrandeten | Schwedischen Trouppen soviel deren anhero | nach Copenhagen gekommen [1678]

4to. χ⁴.                                                                          CKB

Caption title

1936 STÖCKEN, CHRISTIAN VON

Der | [ornamental rule] | Stekken Arons/ | Wie er durch die Hand Mosis aus der | Stiffts-Hütten genom̄en/ und in seiner Blühte | der gantzen Gemeine Jsrael gezeiget worden/ | Jn einer/ | Den letzten Pfingst-Tag/ war der 21 des Mai-Monahts dieses | 1678 Jahres/ in der Bischöflichen Hof-Kirchen/ bei der Hoch- | Fürstlichen Residenz/ | Gehaltenen | Abschieds-Predigt/ | betrachtet/ | Nuhnmehr auch/ auf gnädigsten Befehl/ | herausgegeben | Durch | Christian von Stökken/ der Heil. Schrift D. dero Königl. | Majest. zu Dennemark/ Norwegen erneñter General-SuperInt. in deren Für- | stenthümern Schleswig/ Hollstein/ und incorporirten Landen/ Probsten | zu Renßburg und Segeberg/

auch Pfarrherrn gedachter Königl. Festung. | [ornamental rule] |
PLÖEN/ | Gedrukkt durch Tobias Schmidt/ im 1678sten Jahr.

Folio. 24, [12] pp.; A-J². CKB

On leaf G1, separate title: *VOTA,* | *Viro* | *MAGNIFICO, MAX. REVERENDO,*
*NOBILISSIMO,* | *EXCELLENTISSIMOQUE,* | *Domino,* | *DN.* | *CHRISTIA-* |
*NO von Stökken/* | . . . . There follow poems in Latin and German by several
hands.

1937  STÖCKEN, CHRISTIAN VON

TRAUR- und TROST- | Cypressen/ | Bey dem frühzeitigen/ doch
sanfft-seligem Absterben | Des weiland HochEdlen und Gestrengen
Herrn/ | Hn: Friederichs Lenten/ | . . . | Durch | Christian von Stök-
ken/ der H. Schrifft D. | Bischöflichen Hof-Predigern und SuperIn-
tendenten. | [rule] | Glückstadt/ Gedruckt durch Melchior Kochen/ Jm
Jahr 1678.

4to. A-D⁴. CKB

Contains poems by several hands. On B4r, added Latin title: *Beatissimis Manibus* |
. . . | *Joh. Müller,* | *Advoc.;* on D2, added Latin title: *Inscriptio lugubris* | . . . |
*FRIDERICI* | *LENTEN* | . . . | *Gerhard Hütteman Osnabrug: Westph:* | . . .

1938  STOLTZ, BERNHARD

Klag-Schrifft/ | Wie auch | Traur-und Trost-Music: | Uber den hoch-
seeligen Tödlichen Hintrit/ | Des weyland | HochEdlen/ Gestrengen/
und Vesten Herrn/ | Hn: JOHANNIS Helm/ | . . . | Von | Bernhardo
Stoltzen S.S. Theol. | [rule] | Gedruckt in der Königl: Veste Glück-
stadt/ | durch Melchior Kochen. [1678]

4to. χ⁴. CKB

Words and music.

1939  THOMAS À KEMPIS

Klahre | Andeutung/ | Und wahre | Anleitung | Zur | Nachfolge
Christi/ | Bei Verschmähung der weltlichen | Eitelkeiten/ | Und Uber-
stehung der wiedrigen | Begebenheiten/ | Jn Ansehung der göttlichen |
Süßigkeiten; | Aus des | Thomas von Kempen dreien | Büchern/ solcher
gestalt ausgeführet/ | Auch mit XXXVIII Andachts-Liedern/ und fast |
so viel-neuen Melodeien ausgezieret/ | Daß nunmehr von wahren Evan-
gelischen | Christen alles ohn Irrung gelesen/ ohn Hinderung | ver-
standen/ und zur Andachts-übung | nüzzlich kan gebrauchet werden/ |
Durch | Christian von Stökken/ D. d.Z. Jhrer | Hochfürstl. Durchl. des
Bischoffs zu Lübek | Hoff-Predigern und SuperIntend. | [rule] | Plöen/
Gedrukkt durch Tobias Schmidten/ | Jm 1678sten Jahre.

8vo. [16], 425, [17] pp.; )(<sup>8</sup>, A-Dd<sup>8</sup> Ee<sup>4</sup>, χ1.                              CKB

CKB copy is bound with von Stöcken's *Nachtmahls-Musik*, 1676 (No. 1841), and the volume has a handwritten dedication by von Stöcken to Princess Anna-Dorothea of Schleswig-Holstein.

1940    Umständliche | RELATION | Von der zwischen | Jhrer Königlichen Majestät | zu Dännemarck Norwegen | und | Jhrer Chur-Fürstl. Durchl. | zu Brandenburg | gehaltnen | Unterredung. | Nebenst einer | PROCLA-MATION | Jhrer | Königl. Majest. von Engelland/ | und andern Neuen Sachen. | Herausgegeben/ | Vom 13. 23. December/ 1678.

4to. )(<sup>4</sup>.                                                              SRL

Place of publication uncertain.


# 1679


1941    Abdruck | des Zwischen | Jhrer | Königl. Maj. | zu | Dennemarck/ Norwegen/ &c. | Und der Stadt | Hamburg | Am 1. Novembris Anno 1679. beschlossenen/ | und darauff den 3. Ejusdem von beyden Seiten | Ratificierten | Interims-Recesses. | [rule] | Gedrückt in demselben Jahre.

4to. χ<sup>4</sup> (15.8 x 11.7 cm).                                              CKB

Another edition: same title, χ<sup>4</sup> (15.5 x 12.1 cm); another edition, same title, χ<sup>4</sup> (15.8 x 11.9 cm); another edition (perhaps printed in Hamburg): *Interims-RECESS, | so | Jhre Königliche Majestät | zu Dännemarck/ Norwegen/ &c. | mit | Der Stadt Hamburg | Den. 1. Novembr. Anno 1679. zu Pin- | nenberg auffrichten und schliessen lassen,* )(<sup>4</sup>, (16.2 x 11.8 cm); another edition (perhaps Hamburg), title as the preceding, )(<sup>4</sup>, (16.5 x 11.9 cm).

1942    Allergnädigste Verordnung des Allerdurch- | läuchtigsten/ Großmächtigsten Königs und Herrn | Herrn Christian des Fünfften/ | Erb-Königs zu Dennemarck/ Norwegen/ der | Wenden und Gothen/ Hertzogs zu Schleswigs/ | Hollstein/ Stormarn und der Ditmarschen/ Grafen | zu Oldenburg und Delmenhorst/ u.s.w. | Wie es mit dem den 30 Novembris am ersten Advents- | Sontag angestellten allgemeinen Danck-Fest/ wegen des | allgemeinen in Dero Reichen nnd [sic] Landen wiedergebrachten | Friedens/ bey allen Kirchen/ in Städten und auff dem | Lande/ mit dem ordentlichen Gottes-Dienst zu | halten. | [rule] | Gedruckt in der Königlichen Vestung Glückstadt durch | Melchior Kochen/ Jm Jahr 1679.

4to. χ<sup>4</sup>.                                                               SRL

1943    BINER, TIMOTHEUS HILARIUS

Geistlicher Zucker/ | Welcher | Noth und Todt | versüssen kan. | Bey

Volckreicher beerdigung | Der weyland viel Ehr-und Tugendreichen |
Frauen | ANNA HANSES | . . . | Von: | Timotheo Hilario Binero, |
Pastore zu Bredstett. | [skull and crossbones] | Schleßwig gedruckt bey
Johan Holwein/ | [rule] | Jm Jahr 1679.

4to. A-D⁴.                                                                                              CKB

1944 BRÄMER, CHRISTIAN

Einfältige Catechismus-Fragen. Copenhagen, 1679.

12mo.                                                                                                        *

*Moller* I, 68; *Bibl. Kielmans-Egg.,* II, 1181.

1945 [BURCHARD, ANTON, CASPAR BURCHARD, *and* MATTHIAS BURCHARD]

Schuldigstes Thränen-Opfer/ | Jhrem | Hochgeehrten Seligen Herrn
Vater | Herrn Matthias | Burchardi | HauptPastorn der HauptKirchen
in Kiel | Bey dessen schmerzlichen Leichbestattung | abgestattet | Von |
Dreyen hinterbliebenen Söhnen [1679]

4to. χ².                                                                                                 CKB

Published with J. D. Major, *Seelige Todes-Betrachtung,* 1679 (No. 1973).

1946 Christliche Einfeltige | Anweisung | über | die heiligen Zehen Gebote |
Gottes/ | Zur übung eines Gottsähli- | gen Lebens und Wandels/ |
auffgesetzt | von | J.F. | Altona/ | [rule] | Gedrückt bey Victor de
Löw/ | Anno 1679.

12mo. [12], 204 pp.; π⁶, A-H¹² J⁶.                           STADTBIBL. BRAUNSCHWEIG

Author is Georg Frese, according to *Moller,* I, 190.

1947 COGEL, FRIEDRICH

[Des Uthinischen Stadt-Gedächtnisses von Friedrich Cogel. Ploen, 1679]

12mo. A-B¹² C⁸.                                                          EUTIN STADTBIBLIOTHEK

Eutin copy lacks title-page and C8.

1948 Copenhagensche | RELATION | Von dem | Was irgend in diesen
Nordi- | schen Königreichen passiret | . . . | [rule] | Copenhagen/ |
Gedruckt bey Jhr: Königl: Maytt: und | Universit Buchdr. Corfitz Luft.

8vo.                                                                                                         CKB

CKB has "Num. 2. Den 11. Januarij Anno 1679," "Num. 14. Den 10. Maij. Anno
1679," "Num. 16. Den 20. Maij. Anno 1679," "Num. 18. Den 3. Junij. Anno 1679,"
"Num. 26. Den 2. Augusti. Anno 1679." The first five comprise 4, the last, 2,
unsigned leaves each.

1949  COPIA | Jhrer König: Maj: | Zu Dennemarck Norwegen | Groß-
      Cantzlers | Herrn Grafen von Ahlefelds zu Lan- | geland und Rixingen/
      Hochgräfl. | Excell. Abgelassenen | Antwort Schreibens/ | An | Den
      Königl. Schwed. Feldmarschall/ | Herrn Graffen Königsmarcken/ | Sub
      dato Copenhagen | Anno M.DC.LXXIX.

      4to. χ⁴.                                                                   CKB

      Another edition, with caption title, )?(⁴.

1950  DEFENSIV-ALLIANCE, | Und Bündnüß/ | So zwischen | Jhr Königl.
      Maytt. | Zu Dennemarck/ Norwegen | Einen/ und | Jhr Königl. Maytt.
      zu | Schweden/ | Andern Theils/ | Durch dero zu Lund in Sconen
      zusam- | men geschickte gevolmächtigte | Extraord. Ambassadeurs |
      Den 27. Septemb. ANNO 1679. | aufgerichtet und geschlossen worden. |
      Auß dem Dänschen übergesezet.

      4to. A⁴.                                                                  CKB

1951  DENMARK. *Laws, statutes, etc.*

      Der | Königlichen Bedienten | Verbesserte und confirmirte | PRIVI-
      LEGIA. | Hafniæ die 11 Februarij, Anno | 1679 | [rule] | Gedruckt bey
      Königl. Maytt. und Universit. Buchdrucker | Corfitz Lufft.

      4to. )(⁴.                                                                  CKB

1952  DENMARK. *Laws, statutes, etc.*

      WJr Christian der Fünffte/ von | . . . | . . . 21. Octob. 1679

      Broadside.                                                                 CKB

      Decree issued jointly with Duke Christian Albrecht of Schleswig-Holstein, calling a
      "Land-Tag" in Flensburg 10 November.

1953  DENMARK. *Laws, statutes, etc.*

      WJr Christian der Fünffte/ von | . . . | . . . 28. Octobris 1679

      Broadside.                                                                 CKB

      Decree levying an additional tax on land.

1953A DENMARK. *Laws, statutes, etc.*

      ORDONNANCE | Wornach Vnser Christian des | Fünften von Gottes
      Gnaden/ Königs zu Dennemarck| . . . | Infanterie zu verflegen [sic] |
      . . . | . . . Glückstadt den 1. Novembr. 1679.

      Broadside.                                                                 CKB

1954  DETHARDING, GEORG

      Der | Unterwiesene | Krancken-Wärter | Jn 14 Capittel bestehend |

Darinnen dessen/ so bey | den Krancken umbgehet Gebühr | und Ampt abgebildet und fürge- | stellet wird | Von | Georg Dethardingen/ Stetin: | Pom: Medic: Doctore und Phy- | sico Stralsundensi | [ornament] | [rule] | KIEL/ | Gedruckt durch Joachim Reumann/ | Acad Buchdr. 1679

12mo. A-C$^{12}$ D$^6$.

KIEL UL

1955 Extraordinaires | RELATIONES | anzeigende | in denen aus allerlei Orten | was sich hin und wieder/ absonderlich | in Europa begeben/ und von dannen mit | unterschiedlichen gedruckten und schrift- | lichen Zeitungen eingekommen; | und | in denen Oeresundischen | das jenige mehrentheils/ was in den | Nordischen Königreichen/ und zuge- | hörigen Landen merckwürdiges | vorgefullen | ANNO 1679.

4to. 1506 [i.e., 1264], [180] pp.; A1-H1$^4$, H1-M1$^4$, [χ$^4$], N1-P1$^4$, [χ$^2$], Q1-W1$^4$, [χ$^2$], X1-Z1$^4$, A2-B2$^4$, [χ$^4$], C2$^4$, [χ$^4$], D2-E2$^4$, [χ$^4$], F2$^4$, [χ$^2$], G2-H2$^4$, [χ$^4$], I2-Q2$^4$, [χ$^2$], R2-Z2$^4$, [χ$^4$], A3-C3$^4$, [χ$^2$], D3-F3$^4$, [χ$^4$], G3-N3$^4$, [χ$^4$], O3-Q3$^4$, [χ$^4$], R3-T3$^4$, [χ$^4$], V3-Z3$^4$, [χ$^2$], A4-B4$^4$, [χ$^2$], C4-G4$^4$, G4$^4$, [χ$^4$], H4$^4$, [χ$^2$], I4$^4$, [χ$^4$], K4-Q4$^4$, [χ$^4$], R4-V4$^4$, [χ$^2$], W4$^4$, [χ$^4$], X4$^4$, [χ$^4$], Y4-Z4$^4$, Aa4$^4$, [χ$^4$], B5$^4$, [χ$^4$], B5-F5$^4$, [χ$^4$], G5-Z5$^4$, A6-Z6$^4$, A7-C7$^4$, C7-K7$^4$.

CKB

The unsigned leaves contain issues of the supplemental, unpaginated *Oeresundische | Relation | ....* (between pp. 436-437, *Relation | Von dem/ was zwischen zwey | Königl. Dänischen/ und fünff Königl. | Schwedischen Orlog-Schiffen im Gesichte | ....*). The recurrent "Appendix" is both signed and paginated, however. For each month there is a similar separate title page: January's is *Extraordinaires | RELA-TIONES | aus | allerlei Orten | eingesandt | im | JANUARIO | Anno* [woodcut of Mercury] *1679 | [rule] | Kopenhaven | Bei Daniel Paulli Königl. Buchhändl. | an St. Marien-Kirch.* Each issue other than at beginning of month has caption title: *Extraordinaires RELATIONES | RELATA* [woodcut: Mercury] *REFERO | aus allerlei Orten.* (Title varies; woodcut varies). In the several numbers of the news-paper, there is reference to reports in the appendices and the *Oeresundische Rela-tion.* The issue of January 14 refers to an appended "vollkommene Lista derer gefangenen Schweden auff Bornholm," which is, however, not included in CKB copy. The paginated issues of the newspaper are numbered (1)-158. "W" is used to sign leaves in alphabets 1 and 3-6. Repeated in pagination: pp. 389-392, 661-670, 773-792, 829-830, 914-915; omitted, 671-678, 733-762, 825-828, 833-870, 982-989, 1139-1318, 1321-1322, 1437-1446.

1956 Friedens Puncten | zwischen | Jhrer Königl. Maytt. Maytt. Maytt. | zu | Dennemarck/ Franck- | reich und Sweden. | [rule] | Gedruckt im Jahr 1679

4to. χ$^4$.

CKB; (BM)

1957 Friedens- | TRACTAT | zwischen | Seiner Königlichen Majestät | in Dännemarck und Norwägen/ &c. | an Einer | und | Seiner Königlichen Majestät | in Franckreich/ | wie auch | Seiner Königlichen Majestät | in

Schweden | an der andern Seite geschlossen | zu Fontainebleau den 2. Septembr. Anno 1679. | Nebst beygefügetem | Friedens-ARTICUL | zwischen höchstgedachter | Königl. Maj. zu Dännemarck | und Norwägen | mit | Sr. Hoch-Fürstl. Durchleuchtigkeit | zu Holstein-Gottorp | und | dem Niedersächsischen Kräyse. | [rule] | Aus dem Lateinischen verdeutschet/ Anno 1679.

4to. )?(⁸.                                                         CKB

Strongly resembles supplements to D. Paulli's *Extraordinaires Relationes*.

1958  Friedens | TRACTATEN, | So | Zwischen | Jhrer Königl. Majest. | zu Dännemarck und Norwegen | an einem/ | Und | Jhrer Königl. Majest. | und der Cron Schweden | am andern Theil | Zu Fontainebleau den 2. Septembr. und zu | Lund in Sconen den 26. Septembr. 1679 | aufgerichtet und geschlossen | sein.

4to. A-B⁴ C².                                                     CKB

Printed in double columns.

1959  Gebete und Texte | Welche/ | GOtt zur Ehre/ dem Lande zum nutzen/ | dem Könige/ und Unterthanen zu allem | Wohlergeben/ | Auff die drey allgemeine | Fast- und Bet-Tage | Seiner Königl: Maytt: unsers allergnä- | digsten Erb-Königs und Herrn | CHRISTIAN des Fünfften, | Aller Christlöblichstem Befehl nach/ hochfeier- | lich zu halten/ und zu erklären/ verordnet | worden. | Jn Dännemarck den 28. Martij/ 4. und 11. April. | Jn Norwegen den 9. 16. und 23. Maji; | ANNO [royal emblem] 1679 | Cum gratia & Privilegio Ser: Reg: Majest: | [rule] | Kopenhagen/ Gedruckt bey Jh. Königl. Maj. | und Universit. Buchdr. Corfitz Lufft.

8vo. A-B⁸.                                                        CKB

B7-8 lacking with no apparent loss of text.

1960  [Gensch von Breitenau, Christoph]

Vrsachen und Beschaffenheit | der | Streitigkeiten/ | zwischen | Jhrer Königl. Majest. zu Den- | nemarck/ Norwegen/ | und | Jhrer Fürstl. Durchleuchtigkeit | zu Schleßwig Holstein Gottorff/ | Nebenst einer Summarischen Anzeige des falschen/ | ungegründeten Berichts/ welcher von seiten | Holstein Gottorff deswegen bißhero | an das Licht kommen. | Auff Königl. Allergnädigsten Befehl. | [rule] | Gedruckt im Jahr 1679.

4to. 178, [2] pp.; A-X⁴, Y², Z⁴ (Z4 blank).                       CKB

*Cat. lib. Thomæ Bartholini* 1737, p. 25, lists an edition of 1696.

1961 GIESE, JOACHIM

JESUS/ | der Brunn des Lebens/ | . . . | H. MATTHIÆ | BURCH-ARDI, | Wohlverdienten Pastoris Primarii | der Christlichen Gemeine im Kiel. | . . . | Und auff Begehren ausgegeben | von | M. JOACHIMO Giesen/ | Pastore Prim. in Kiel. | [rule] | KJEL/ gedruckt durch Joachim Reuman/ Ac. Bdr. [1679]

4to. [2], 82 pp.; π1, A-K⁴, χ1. CKB

1962 GRANOVIUS, DANIEL

Dreyfaches geistliches Heilpfaster, oder Leichpredigt über Wilhelm Venninghausen, Bürgermeistern in Plön, auß Apoc. III. 5. Plön, 1679.

4to. *

*Moller* I, 216.

1963 HELD, BALTHASAR

Als | Der WollEhrwürdige/ Großachtbare/ | und Wolgelahrte | Herr MATTHIAS | BURCHARDUS, | . . . | Entwarff diß wenige woll-meinend | Balthasar Held/ L L. Studiosus. | [rule] | KJEL/ | Gedruckt durch Joachim Reuman/ Acad. Buchdr. [1679]

4to. χ². CKB

1964 Hochzeitliches Ehren-Gedicht | . . . | Herr Wolffgang Hennrich von Kalnein | . . . | Jungf. Anna Dorothea Munck/ | . . . | Gehorsamst offerirt von | M.M. |
[below:] Gedruckt/ Jm Jahr 1679 [Copenhagen]

Broadside. OSLO UL

1965 Jn JESU Namen. Amen! | Davidische | Buß-und Bete- | Glokke/ | Das ist: | Die sieben Bußpsalmen | in Teutsche Lieder | auff bekante Weisen ge- | setzet. | [ornaments] | [rule] | Kopenhagen/ | Gedruckt bey Sel. Daniel Eichhorns | Nachgelassene Witwe, | Jm Jahr 1679

12mo. A-C¹². (C12 blank). CKB

1966 INSTRUMENTUM | wegen des | Hertzogs zu Holstein Gottorff | RESTITUTION, | und | Absonderlicher Articul | Wegen einiger As-signationen und daherrüh- | renden Foderungen. | [rule] | Gedruckt im Jahr 1679.

4to. χ². CKB

1967 KORTHOLT, CHRISTIAN

Christian Kortholten/ | der H. Schrifft D. und bey | der Kielischen Universitet Pro- | fess. | Primar. | Theologische | Zu Befoderung der Gottsee- | ligkeit angesehene | Tractätlein | [ornament: leaves & flowers] | Kiel/ | Gedruckt und verlegt durch Joachim Reuman/ | Acad. Buchdr. 1679

8vo. [15], 543, [1] pp.; a⁸, A-Ll⁸.                                    CKB; (BM)

*Moller* III, 374, lists tracts separately: *Schwere Bürde des Predigampts . . . ; Theophili Sinceri wolgemeinter Vorschlag . . . , 12mo.*

1968    KORTHOLT, CHRISTIAN

Vorbereitung | zur Ewigkeit/ | Oder | Gründliche | Anweisung/ | Wie ein Mensch recht glau- | ben/ Christlich leben/ und seelig | sterben solle; | Gesteller [sic] | von | Christian Kortholten/ | der H. Schrifft D. und Profess. | Primar. bey der HochFürstl. | Holsteinischen Universitet | zum Kiel | [rule] | KJEL/ | Gedruckt und verlegt durch Joachim | Reuman/ Acad. Buchdr. 1679.

8vo. [16], 408 pp.; *⁸, A-Bb⁸ Cc⁴.                                     HAB

1969    Kurtze | DEDUCTION | und Antwort | Auff die Bischöffliche Mün- | ster- | sche zu Newhauß den 18. Julij dieses Jahrs | publicirte Avoca- | torien/ Worinnen der ohnpartheylichen | Welt klärlich vor Augen gestellet wird/ mit was Fueg und Recht | die von dem negst verstorbenen Herrn Bischoffen zu Münster/ | Jhrer Königl. Mayest. zu Dennemarck Norwegen etc. überlas- | sene Völcker in höchstbemeldt Jhr. Königl. Mayest. Diensten würcklich getreten/ hingegen mit was Ohnbilligkeit und Ohn- | fueg dieselbe von dem jetzigen Herrn Bischoffen zu Mün- | ster | und Paderborn avociret werden wollen. | Von vorbemeldten gesambten Officirern und Soldatesque | zur nöhtigen Rettung ihres guten Leumuths und Repu- | tation an den Tag gegeben. | [ornament] | [rule] | Gedruckt im Jahr 1679.

4to. A-B⁴.                                                                  CKB

1970    [LANGE, PAUL, PETER LANGE *and* BALTHASAR OTTO LANGE]

Als | Der Wolwürdige/ WolEdle/ und | Hochgelahrte | Herr PAULUS | Sperling/ | . . . | beygesetzet ward/ | . . . | Dessen hinterlassene Höchst- Betrübte | NEPOTES. | [rule] | KJEL/ | Gedruckt durch Joachim Reuman/ Acad. Buchdr. [1679]

4to. χ².                                                                     CKB

Verse. CKB copy bound with three Latin pamphlets published on same occasion.

1971    LAURENTII, BERNHARD

Letzte Ehrenbezeugung des Herrn Andreas Cramern . . . bey dessen Leich-Deduction abgefaßet. Schleswig, 1679.

                                                                              *

Formerly in Kiel UL (LmC 6-87).

1972 LISTA | Von | Jhrer Königl: Majest: zu | Dennemarck/ Norwegen/ |
Flotte/ | Sowohl von dero einigen Orlogs- | Schiffen und Fahrzeug alß
dero Unterthanen Defensi- | ions-Schiffen/ so dieß 1679 Jahr in Aller-
hogstgemelt Jh- | rer Königl: Mayest: Kriegs Diensten gebrauchet wer- |
den sollen/ welche mit allem Fleiß equippiret und | frühe zeitig in die
See gehen | werden. | [rule] | Gedruckt in Copenhagen/ im Jahr 1679.

4to. χ². CKB

1973 MAJOR, JOHANN DANIEL

Ehren-denckmahl/ | welches | Dem Seeligen (Tit:) Herren/ | Hn. Paul
Sperling/ | S.S. Theol. D. und Prof. wie auch Fürstl. | Holsteinischem
Præposito, | Dessen Leichbegängnüß in Kiel den 7. Maj. 1679. | bestättiget
wurde/ | aus Collegialischer Liebe/ und hertzlicher Pflicht | gestifftet |
Johann Daniel Major, D. | [woodcut: angel, over motto:] | Der Ge-
rechten | Seelen sind in | GOttes Hand | &c. &c. | [rule] | Kjel/ |
Gedruckt durch Joachim Reumann/ Acad. Buchdr.

Folio. χ². CKB

1974 MAJOR, JOHANN DANIEL

Großer Reichthum zusammen gebracht auß den meisten Schätzen der
Welt, oder Poetischer Interims-Discurs von Kunst und Naturalien-Kam-
mern, einem dergleichen Dinge wolerfahrnen guten Freunde zugeeignet.
Kiel, 1679.

Folio. *

*Moller* II, 516.

1975 [MAJOR, JOHANN DANIEL]

Seelige Todes-Betrachtung/ | allem irrdischen Glück und Weißheit |
vorgezogen/ in dem Exempel | Des weiland Wol-Ehrwürdigen/ Groß- |
Achtbaren/ und Hochgelahrten | Herren Matthiæ | Burchardi, | ge-
wesenen wolverdienten Haupt-Pastoris | bey der Kirchen zu St. Nicolai
in Kiel: | Als nehmlich sein in Gott entseelter Cörper | in öffentlichem
Traur-Proceß | den 9. Septembr. 1679. | daselbst beygesetzet wurde.

4to. *⁴. CKB

1976 Des | Nordischen Kriegs | Anderer Theil: | Das ist: | Ausführliche Vor-
stellung | aller Merk- und Denkwürdiger | Kriegs-Handlungen Und
Schlachten/ | welche sich von Anfang des 1677 | Jahrs/ bis auf gegen-
wärtige Zeit zwi- | schen denen Nordischen Kronen | und Potentaten
ereig- | net. | [ornament] | [rule] | Gedruckt im Jahr Christi/ | 1679

12mo. 441, [3] pp.; a-s$^{12}$ t$^6$.                                        CKB

CKB's copy of *Des Nordischen Krieges Erster Theil* bears imprint Nürnberg, 1679. This "Anderer Theil" appears to have been printed by Daniel Paulli.

1977   Anno 1679.... | [rule] | Oeresundische | Relation | [rule] | Sambstag den 18. Januarii

12mo. Pp. 65-72; χ$^4$.                                        DEUTSCH-NIENHOF

Caption title.

1978   PETERSEN, NICOLAUS

Danckschüldiges Ehrengedächtniß | ... | H: JOHANNES Bircken-busch/ | ... | Von | M. NICOLAUS PETERSEN, | Pastor zu Elmes-horn. | [rule] | Gedruckt in der Königl. Vestung Glückstadt/ durch | Melchior Kochen/ Jm Jahr 1679.

4to. χ$^2$.                                                            CKB

Contains only 4 verses in German on verso of t-p. On verso of second leaf, blank area, bounded by the words: "Hie Schawe | Der Welt | ihr Ei- | telkeit!"

1979   Propositio | So wegen Jhro Königl. | Mayest. zu Dennemarck Nor- | gen/ denen Hamburgischen Deputirten den | 26. Septembr: 1679. in Pinnen-berg | geschehen. | [rule] | Gedruckt in der Königl. Vestung Glück-stadt/ durch | Melchior Kochen/ Königl. bestalter Buchdrucker

4to. χ$^4$.                                                        KIEL UL; SHLB

1980   PROPOSITION | So den 26. Sept: 1679. den | Herren Hamburgischen Deputirten | Nahmentlich/ | Burgermeister Schultz/ | Syndico Schrein-ing/ | Rahts-Herrn Schafshausen/ und Wör- | denhofen/ und Secret: Schrödern/ | Von dem | Herrn Groß-Cantzler/ | Reichs-Marschalck uud [sic] | Ober-Jägermeister | in des Ambtmanns-Hause zum Pinne-berg | gethan worden. | [rule] | Gedruckt in der Königl. Vestung Glück-stadt/ durch | Melchior Kochen/ Königl. bestalter Buchdrucker.

4to. χ$^4$.                                                        CKB; (BM)

Another edition, with added line "Nach der Copye," χ$^4$; another edition, variant title, n.p. "Gedruckt in selbigem Jahre," χ$^4$; another edition, variant caption title, χ$^2$, (16.3 x 11.4 cm), colophon: *Nach dem Glückstädtischen Exemplar gedrucket bey Melchior Kochen/ | bestalten Königl. Buchdrucker;* another edition, variant caption title, same colophon as in preceding copy, (16 x 11.8 cm).

1981   REFUTATION | Und | Klärliche Wiederlegung | Auff die | Von Bischöflicher Münsteri- | scher Seiten außgegebene so genante | Anzeig und Remonstration, | Worin deutlich dargethan wird/ wie un- | fueg- und wiederrechtlich nicht allein die Avocatoria ge- | gen die von dem

nechst-verstorbenen Hrn. Bischoffen zu | Münster hochsel. Gedächtnis
Jhr Königl. Majestät zu | Dennemarck-Norwegen überlassene Völcker
gepublici- | ret/ sondern auch/ wie unförmlich und ohne Grund Rech- |
tens Sie die darauf außgelassene Deduction beantwor- | tet/ aus ein und
andern falschen præsuppositis zu ihrem | Intent dienenden illationes
angezogen/ und die Extracte | aus denen gewechselten Schreiben derge-
stalt heraus ge- | suchet/ damit nur die eigentliche Beschaffenheit der
Sa- | chen invertiret/ und der unparteyische Leser dadurch con- | fus
gemacht werde/ und dann endlich/ wie wenig sie | die obgemeldte
Völcker eines unzuläßigen | Außtrits zu beschuldigeu [sic] befugt |
gewesen | [rule] | Gedruckt im Jahr 1679.

4to. A-K⁴.                                                          CKB

On D4, separate title: *Anzeig* | *und* | *REMONSTRA-* | *TION,* | *Wie wenig und*
*übel die Nahmens einiger* | . . . | *Gedruckt im Jahr 1679.*

1982  [REICH, JOHANN LUDWIG]

(Trauergedichte über Jakob Christoph Reich). Schleswig: Joh. Holwein
(1679).

Folio. $\chi^2$.                                                          *

Formerly in Kiel UL (LmC 15-26).

1983  REICH, JOHANN LUDWIG, CHRISTIAN ANTON CRAMER *and* CHRISTIAN ALB.
SCHMID

Schuldige letzte Ehrenbezeigung Andreas Cramer. Schleswig, 1679.

Folio.                                                              *

*OHM* II, 154.

1984  REINCKING, THEODOR

Betrachtungen von der Bethe- Leidens- und Sterbe-Kunst. Glückstadt,
1679

12mo.                                                              *

*Bibl. Schroedter,* 1724, p. 694. Previously published 1665. (No. 1282).

1985  RELATION | Von dem/ was zwischen zwey | Königl. Dänischen/
und fünff Königl. | Schwedischen Orlog-Schiffen im Gesichte | der
Jnsul Bornholm/ ohnfern Rönne/ | vorgefallen/ Anno 1679.

4to. $\chi^4$.                                                          CKB

Caption title. Issued in conjunction with D. Paulli's *Extraordinaires Relationes* of
10 May 1679 (No. 1955).

1986 Revidirter | Französischer | SYNCRETISMUS | oder | vier und zwantzig | ARTICKELEN, | Welche den Ministris | von der R.P.R. | zu Pariß | Durch die Geistliche Herren | Deputirte von Seiten Jh. K. Maj. | wegen Vereinigung der Catholischen | und Evangelischen Religionen | vorgetragen sind. | Gedruckt | Anno 1679

4to. χ⁴.                                                                                CKB

Issued in conjunction with D. Paulli's *Extraordinaires Relationes*, 31 May 1679 (No. 1955).

1987 Schuldige Pflicht | Bey | Volckreicher Beerdigung | . . . | Hn. MAT-THIÆ | BURCHARDI, | Wolverdienten Haupt-Pastorn bey der | Kirchen zu St. Nicolai in Kiel/ | abgestattet | in | höchster Eil | von | R.N. | der Heil. Schrifft Beflissenen | [rule] | KJEL/ | Gedruckt durch Joachim Reumann/ Acad. Buchdr. [1679]

4to.  χ².                                                                               CKB

1988 Schwedischer | Völcker | [type ornaments] | Schiff-Bruch/ | [type ornaments] | Bey | Der/ zur Kron Dennemarck gehörigen | Jnsul | Born-holm. | Samt angeführten Ursachen/ warum erwehnte Völ- | cker/ so viel deren mit Mühe und Gefahr gerettet/ von we- | gen Jhrer Königl. Majest. zu Dennemarck/ Norwe- | gen. &c. für Kriegs Gefangene ange-nom̃en/ | und gehalten werden. | [rule] | Jm Jahr 1679.

4to. [2], 78 pp.; A-K⁴.                                                                CKB

1988A SCHWESINGER VON CRONHELM, ANDREAS

Richtiger Consistorial-und Kirchen Dienst; | . . . | Herrn JOHANNIS Bir- | ckenbusches/ | . . . | Durch | ANDREAM Schwesingern von Cronhelm/ . . . | . . . | [rule] | Gedruckt in der Königlichen Vestung Glückstadt/ durch | Melchior Kochen/ Jm Jahr 1679.

4to. 40 pp.; A-E⁴.                                                                     CKB

On pp. 29 ff., *Abdanckung* | . . . | *von* | *MATTHIAS Bornholdt/* | . . .

1989 SOTHMANN, JOHANN

(Predigt über Anna Catharina Clausen). Schleswig, 1679.

4to.                                                                                    *

*Thott* V/2, 562.

1990 Stilstand/ | so von | Jhrer Königl. Maytt. zu | Dennemarck | und | Jhrer Königl. Maytt. zu | Schweden | Extraordinair Ambassadeuren durch | fleißige Unterhan- | delung des Chur-Sächsischen Mediatoris Herrn | Baron | Gerßdorff den 30. Augusti 1679. zu Londen in | Schonen ge-

schlossen. | [rule] | Gedruckt bey Jhrer Königl. Maytt. und Universit.
Buckdr. | Corfitz Lufft.

4to. χ².                                                              CKB

1991   STÖCKEN, CHRISTIAN VON

Was ists? oder Caßisches Ehrengedächtniß, zum Nachruhme Christ.
Cassi, Bischöflichen Lübeckischen Geheimen Rahts, in einer Leichab-
danckung aufgerichtet. . . . Glückstadt, 1679.

12mo.                                                                  *

*Moller* I, 659; *Verzeichnis Voss,* 1743, p. 169; *Bibl. Muhliana,* 1735, p. 605. Originally published as appendix (printed in Lübeck, 1677) to sermon by Christopher
Rodatzi, Plön 1676 (No. 1834).

1992   Die Thränende Thalia | . . . | Hn. Christian Kortholten | . . . | Hertz-
geliebtes Töchterlein | Jfr. Dorothea Elisabeth | . . . | Gesampte
Tischgenossen. |
[below] KJEL/ Gedruckt durch Joachim Reuman/ Acad. Buchdr.
[1679]

Broadside.                                                          KIEL UL

1993   Das verenderte LABORATORIUM. | Auff | Den Hochzeitlichen Ehren-
Tag | Des | WolEhrenvesten/ VorAchtbahren und Kunst- | Wol-er-
fahrnen | Herrn Christopher ROSTIUS, | der Officin höchst-Geflissen-
sten/ | Mit der | GroßEhr-und Tugendbegabten | Jungfer Anna-Maria |
Brethauers/ | . . . | Von einem guten Freunde | wohnend | Dort Gegem
[sic] Mühlen-Thor. | [woodcut: angels] | [rule] | Gedruckt in der
Königlichen Veste Glückstadt/ durch | Melchior Kochen/ Jm Jahr 1679.

Folio. χ².                                                            CKB

Verse.

## 1680

1994   Die abgefallene Frühlings-Blume | oder | Trost-Schrifft | . . . | Hn.
Heinrich Suhmen/ | . . . | Hertzliebsten Jf. Töchterleins | Jf. ANNA
CATHARINA, | So am 28. Febr. dieses 1680sten Jahres . . . | . . . | von |
Nachfolgenden mitleydenden Freunden | auffgesetzet. | [rule] | Ge-
druckt/ Jm Jahr 1680.

4to. χ².                                                              CKB

Verse by Andreas Gödeke and Henricus Riese.

1995   ACTA | Jn | Sachen | Der | Herren Gebrüdern/ | Frey-Herren | Von |

Kielmanns-Egg/ | Klägeren/ | Gegen und wieder | Sehl. Ægidij Hen-
nings Wittibe | Beklagtin | [ornament] | [ornamental rule] | Gedruckt
im Jahr Christi/ 1680.

Folio. [20], 144, [12] pp.; π1, A-D², E1, F-Z⁴, Aa-Cc².                     CKB

1996   BORCH, OLE

OLAI BORRICHII | Metallische | Probier-Kunst | deutlich und kurtz
beschrie- | ben. | Verteutscht | durch | Georgium Kus. | [rule] | [publish-
er's emblem] | [rule] | Kopenhaven/ | Bei Daniel Paulli, Kön. Buch-
händl. | Anno 1680.

8vo. Pp. 1-64, 67-74; A-D⁸ E⁴.                                            CKB; (BM)

1997   BRÄMER, CHRISTIAN

Redlicher Christ/ | . . . | Herrn | D. SIMO- | NIS PAULLI, | . . . | Jn der
Teutschen St. Petri Kirchen zu Kopenhagen den 10 Maji | 1680. fürge-
stellet/ und auff Begehren zum Druck | übergeben worden | von | M.
CHRISTIAN Brämer/ Lübec. | [ornamental rule] | PLOEN/ | Ge-
druckt durch Tobias Schmidt.

4to. [6], 68 pp.; )(⁴ (−)(4), A-H⁴ J².                                      CKB

1998   BRUHN, C.

Letzte Ehren-Bezeigung | . . . | Jf. Maria Elisabeth | Niederstättin/ | . . . |
C. Bruhn. S. Thol. [sic] Studioso. | [rule] | Schleßwig gedruckt bey
Johan Holwein. | Jm Jahr 1680.

Folio. χ².                                                                 SHLB

1999   BÜTNER, DANIEL

(Glückwünschender Zuruff in nupt. Hans Blume). Kiel, 1680.

Folio.                                                                        *

*OHM* II, 132.

2000   DENMARK. *Laws, statutes, etc.*

WJR Christian der Fünffte/ von | . . . | . . . Glückstadt/ den 3ten Junij, |
Anno 1680.

Broadside.                                                                CNA; CKB

Decree issued jointly with Duke Christian Albrecht of Schleswig-Holstein, calling a
meeting of the "Quartal-Gericht" at Rendsburg 2 August.

2001   DENMARK. *Laws, statutes, etc.*

WJR Christian der Fünffte/ von | . . . | . . . Glückstadt den 8. Junij 1680.

Broadside. CNA

Decree against breaking the sabbath by "Kauffen und Verkauffen."

2002 DENMARK. *Laws, statutes, etc.*

WJR Christian der Fünffte/ von | . . . | . . . Glückstadt/ den 22. Junij, |
Anno 1680.

Broadside. CNA

Decree, issued jointly with Duke Christian Albrecht of Schleswig-Holstein, calling a
"Land-Gerichts-Tag" in Flensburg 20 September.

2003 DENMARK. *Laws, statutes, etc.*

WJR Christian der Fünffte/ von | . . . | . . . Glückstadt/ den 16. Augusti.
Anno 1680

Broadside. CNA

Decree regarding quarantine of travellers who do not have a (medical) "Attestatum
der Obrigkeit."

2004 DENMARK. *Laws, statutes, etc.*

Wir Christian der Fünffte | . . . | . . . Gottorff/ den 12. Nov. Anno 1680

Broadside. CNA

Decree issued jointly with Duke Christian Albrecht of Schleswig-Holstein, forbidding entry of gypsies and vagabonds into the Duchies.

2005 GIESE, JOACHIM

Hiobs uñ aller gläubigen Kinder GOttes | Trotz und Trost/ | in | Noth
und Tod/ | . . . | Herrn JOHANNIS PHI- | LIPPI Roßmanns/ | . . . |
durch | M. JOACHIMUM Giese. Pastorem | Primarium bey St. Nicolai
im Kiel. | [rule] | KJEL/ | Gedruckt durch Joachim Reuman/ Acad.
Buchdr. [1680]

4to. Pp. [1-4], 1-88, 97-120; π², A-O⁴. CKB

2006 GIESE, JOACHIM

Christliche Danckseule, mit zugehörigen Bildern und Ueberschriften,
Gott zu Ehren, und zum Andencken seiner Wohlthaten, an dem wegen
des Friedens angestelltem Dancktage (Dom. II. Epiph.), aus dem gewöhnlichen Evangelio Joh. II., aufgerichtet. Kiel, 1680.

4to. *

*Moller* I, 210; *Bibl. Muhliana,* 1735, p. 519; *Bibl. Kirchof* I, 1746, p. 148.

2007 GRANOVIUS, DANIEL

Επιταφιον oder Sterb-Gedächtniß . . . oder Leichpredigt über Joh.
Clausen. . . . Plön, 1680

4to.                                                                          *

OHM I, 216; *Bibl. Breitenaviana* V, 1747, p. 424.

2008 Hochzeitliches Ehren-Gedicht . . . | [Albert Schrotering & Monica Num-
mels] | . . . | Altona/ Gedruckt bey Victor de Löw, Anno 1680.

Folio. χ².                                                                    *

Title from *Borchling-Claussen*, Nr. 3622. Formerly in Hamburg UL.

2009 Holtz-Ordnung | Jn | Unsern Hertzogthümern | Schleßwig-Holstein. |
Copenhagen d. I Septembr. Ao. 1680. | [monogram] | [double rule] |
Copenhagen/ Gedruckt in dero Königl. Majests. und | Universitäts
privileg. Buchdruckerey.

4to. )(⁴.                                                                     CKB

2010 HÜLSEMANN, CASPAR PETRUS

Die | Väterliche | Hertzens-Wunde | Des WolEdlen/ Vesten und Hoch-
gelahrten | Herrn | H. BURCKHARDI | Niederstädten/ | . . . | durch
den | frühzeitigen Todt | seiner eintzigen/ Hertzgeliebten Jungfer
Tochter/ | . . . | Jf. Maria Elisabeth | Niederstädtin/ | vermittelst einer
eilfertigen | Trost-Schrifft | gelindert | Durch | M. Casp. Petr. Hülse-
mann/ | Prediger zu St. Jacobi. | [skull and crossbones] | Schleßwig
gedruckt durch Johan Holwein. | [rule] | Anno 1680.

Folio. B-D⁴.                                                                  CKB

Another edition, in 4to, appeared in Hamburg, dated 26 Januarii 1680.

2011 Klag- und Trost-Schrifften/ | an | D. Johann Daniel Majorn/ | und
dessen HertzEheliebste/ | Fr. Margreth-Elisabeth/ | gebohrne Pin-
cierinn/ | Wegen schmertzlichen und früh-zeitigen Verlustes | Dero
Zwey seeligen lieben Kinder/ | gerichtet von | Guten Gönnern und
Freunden/ | den 17. Decembris 1680. | [rule] | Kjel/ | Gedruckt bey
Joachim Reumann/ Acad. Buchdr.

4to. 16 pp.; A-B⁴.                                                            CKB

On A3 added title: *Abdanckung | Jn einer hochansehnlichen | Versamlung/ |
. . . | Zwey hertzgeliebte Kinderlein | . . . | Von M. JOACHIMO Giesen/
Pastore | Primario daselbst.*

2012 KLUG, CHRISTIAN

Die im Zorn-feuer Gottes | Auffgehende | Gnaden-Sonne. | Auß dem auffgegebenen Spruch | HOS. XI. vers. 8. 9. | Bey | Volckreicher und ansehnlicher Versamlung/ in der | Haupt-Kirchen zu St. Nicolai in Hamburg/ am 20. No- | vembris (war der Mittwoch nach dem 22. Sontag | Trinitatis) des 1679. Jahres/ in einer | damahlig gehaltenen | Prob-Predigt | Abgebildet/ und numehro umb gewisser ursachen | willen/ so wie sie damahls in kürtze der zeit abgefasset | worden/ dem Günstigen Leser zur beliebenden | anschauung im Druck vorgestellet/ | von | M. CHRISTIANO Klug. | [rule] | Altona/ Gedruckt bey Victor de Löw. Anno 1680.

4to. 27, [1] pp.; A-C⁴ D². CKB

2013  [KORTHOLT, CHRISTIAN]

Trost-Zeilen | . . . | Jf. Maria Elisabeth | Niederstädtin/ | . . . | [woodcut: coffin] | Schleßwig gedruckt bey Johan Holwein/ | Anno 1680.

Folio. $\chi^2$. SHLB

2014  Kurtzer Bericht | Welchergestalt Jhre Königl. Hoheit | Princesse | Vlrica Eleonora | zu | Dennemarck/ Norwegen | Den 1. Maji dieses 1680. Jahrs Jhren | Außzug auß Copenhagen | gehalten.

8vo. $\chi^2$. CKB

Caption title.

2015  [LANGERHANS, NICOLAUS]

Trost-Schrifft | . . . | Maria Elisabeth | Niederstättinnen/ | . . . | [orna-ment with coffin] | [rule] | Schleßwig/ gedruckt bey Johan Holwein/ An. 1680.

Folio. A⁴. SHLB

2016  MATRAS, DANIEL

Dan. Matras | ITALIANISCHE | GRAMMA- | TICA, | [printer's mark] | Cum S. R. M. Privilegio. | [rule] | Kopenhagen/ | Zu finden bey Daniel Paulli Königl. | Buchhändler. [1680?]

8vo. 140, [4] pp.; A-I⁸. (I8 blank). CKB

2017  MOLLER, JOHANNES

Das in Freude verkehrte Leid in nuptiis Joh. Holstii . . . Elisabethæ, Carstani Thomsen . . . filiæ. Schleswig, 1680

4to.                                                                                              *

*OHM* I, 430-1.

2018 MOLLER, JOHANNES

Der göttliche Uhrsprung des heiligen Ehestandes, in nuptiis, Andr.
Hoieri ... Annæ Christinæ, Georgii Zimmermanni ... filiæ. Schleswig,
1680.

Folio.                                                                           *

*OHM* I, 430-1.

2019 MORHOF, DANIEL GEORG

Madrigalón | ... | Maria Elisabeth/ | ... | Andreæ Olken/ | ... |
Verlobten Hertzliebsten Braut. | ... | Burkhard Niderstetten/ | ... |
Maria Elisabeth Niderstettin/ | gebohrner Olearrin/ | Eintzigen Jungfer
Tochter/ | ... | Von | Daniel Georg Morhofen. D. Pr. | [rule] | KJEL/
Gedruckt durch Joachim Reumann Acad. Buchdr. [1680]

Folio. )(⁴.                                                                      SHLB

2020 NIEMANN, SEBASTIAN

Christliche | Fried-und Freuden- | Predigt/ | Nach geschlossenen und
wider erlangten Frie- | den an dem von Dero Regierenden HochFürstl.
Durchl. zu | Schleßwig/ Holstein gnädigst verordneten | Danck-Fest |
Den 2. Sontag nach Epiphan. als den 18. Jan. | 1680. über das ordent-
liche Sontags Evangelium Joh. 2. | v.1. seqq. in der HochFürstl. Schloß-
Kirchen zu Gottorff Gott zu Eh- | ren in gegenwart unterschiedlicher
HochFürstl. Personen | und anderer Zuhörer gehalten/ | Nunmehr aber
in Druck gegeben | Von | Sebastian Niemann. D. | OberHoffPred. und
General- | Superintendenten. | [woodcut] | Schleßwig | Jn der Fürstl.
Druckerey gedruckt durch Johan Holwein | [rule] | Jm Jahr 1680.

4to. 40 pp.; A-E⁴.                                                               CKB

2021 [NIEMANN, SEBASTIAN, *editor*]

Außerlesene | Geistreiche | Gebete und Seuffzerlein/ | Von einigen
andächtigen und Gottliebenden | Hertzen aus unterschiedenen Bet-
Büchern | zusammen getragen/ | Nunmehr aber GOtt zu Ehren/ dem
Nechsten zu | Nutze und zu täglicher übung und erbauung ihres ei-
genen | Christenthumbs zum Druck befördert. | [ornament] | Schleß-
wig/ | Gedruckt durch Johan Holwein/ Fürstl. Buch- | drucker und
Formschneider/ | [rule] | Jm Jahr 1680.

4to. [8], 1088, [20] pp.; )(⁴, A-Zzzzzz⁴, Aaaaaaa². GÖTTINGEN UL

2022 NOTHELFER, NICOLAUS

Lob-Rede zum Gedächtniß Hugonis Lenten, Königl. Dän. Regierungs-
Rahts. Glückstadt, 1680.

4to.

*Moller* II, 591.

2023 OLEARIUS, PHILIP CHRISTIAN

Traur-Schrifft | . . . | Jf. Maria Elisabeth | Niederstättin/ | . . . | Philip
Christian Oleario. | [woodcut: coffin] | Schleßwig gedruckt durch Johan
Holwein. [1680]

Folio. $\chi^2$. SHLB

2024 RAM, STEPHAN

Wolgemeinte Warnung an die Evangelische Stadtgemeine in Glückstatt,
das Pabsthum zu meiden. Glückstadt, 1680.

4to.

*Moller* I, 519.

2025 RECKEL, SIMON

Das GOTT gelassenes | Mutter Hertz | . . . | Hn. JOHANNIS |
ADOLPHI Uthermarcken | . . . | Von | Simone Rechelio, | Archi-
Diacono daselbst [i.e., Husum] | [skull & crossbones] | . . . | [rule] |
Schleßwig/ gedruckt durch Johan Holwein/ An. 1680

4to. 38, [30] pp.; A-H⁴ J². CKB

F1r, added title: *Schuldiges Ehren-Gedächtniß* | *. . . Hn. JOHANNI* | *ADOLPHI*
*Uthermarcken,* separately entered as No. 2036.

2026 RELATION | Was bei dem | von | Jhr. Königl. Maytt. zu Den- |
nemarck/ Norwegen/ etc. | Angeordneten | CARROUSEL | Jn Gegen-
wart der Königl. Familie auch ande- | rer hohen Personen und vieler
Vornehmen | Herren | Auff der Königl. Reitbahne vorgegangen in |
Copenhagen den 21. April. An. 1680. | [rule] | Gedruckt bey Sl. Corfitz
Lufften/ Königl. Maytt. und | Acad. Buchdr. Nachgelassener Witwen.

4to. $\pi$1[=B2], A⁴ B² (−B2). CKB

2027 Relation | was bey | Jhrer Königl. Hoheit | PRINCESSE | ULRICA |
ELEONORA | zu | Dännemarck/ Norwägen/ etc. | Ankunft und
Abfahrt in Helsignör | paßiret/ | auch wie | Sie zu Helsingburg
entfangen worden. | Geschehen den 3. und 4. May | Anno 1680.

4to. $\chi^2$. CKB

2028 Relation | welcher Gestalt | Jhre Königl. Hoheit | PRINCESSE |
ULRICA | ELEONORA | Zu Dännemarck/ Norwägen/ &c. | Als |
Königl. Schwedische | Braut/ | Aus | Der Königl. Residenz-Stadt

Kopenhaven | sehr prächtig und überaus herrlich abge- | führet wor-
den/ | So | geschehen den 1 May Anno 1680

4to. $\chi^2$.                                                              CKB

2029  ROSMANN, JOHANN ADOLF

(Trauergedicht über Ursula Rosmann, geb. Faust). Kiel: Joachim
Reumann, (1680).

4to. $\chi^2$.                                                              *

Formerly in Kiel UL (LmC 79-62).

2030  SCHLESWIG-HOLSTEIN-GOTTORFF. *Laws, statutes, etc.*

Christian Albrecht von Gottes | Gnaden/ Erbe zu Norwegen/ postulirter
Coadjutor des Stiffts | Lübeck/ Hertzog zu Schleßwig/ Holstein/ . . . |
. . . | . . . Gottorff/ den 18. Januarij Anno 1680.

Broadside.                                                              CNA

Decree forbidding "unziemliche discourse . . . Rede und Plaudereyen" regarding
public affairs.

2031  SCHLESWIG-HOLSTEIN-GOTTORFF. *Laws, statutes, etc.*

TAXA der Gerichts-Sportulen

Broadside.                                                              KIEL UL

Issued by Duke Christian Albrecht, dated at Gottorff 9 November 1680. Countersigned by B. Niederstett.

2032  SCHLESWIG-HOLSTEIN-GOTTORFF. *Laws, statutes, etc.*

Christian Albrecht von Gottes | Gnaden/ Erbe zu Norwegen/ postu-
lirter Coadjutor des | . . . | . . . Gottorff/ den 22. Maij Anno 1680.

Broadside.                                                              CNA

Decree forbidding "unziemliche Discourse . . . Rede und Plaudereyen."

2033  SCHLESWIG-HOLSTEIN-GOTTORFF. *Laws, statutes, etc.*

Wir von Gottes Gnaden Christian | Albrecht/ Erbe zu Norwegen/
postulirter Coadjutor des Stiffts Lübeck/ | . . . | . . . Gottorff den 6. Sept.
Ao. 1680.

Broadside.                                                              CNA

Decree regarding quarantine of travellers without certificates that they are free of
contagion.

2034  SCHLESWIG-HOLSTEIN-GOTTORFF. *Laws, statutes, etc.*

Wir Christian Albrecht von | Gottes Gnaden/ Erbe zu Norwegen/ postulirter Coadjutor | . . . | . . . 4. Octobr. An. 1680.

Broadside. KIEL UL

Decree requiring annual reports, on stamped paper, from certain officials.

2036 Schuldiges Ehren-Gedächtniß | . . . | Hn. JOHANNIS | ADOLPHI Uthermarcken | . . . | Schleßwig gedruckt bey Johan Holwein/ Jm Jahr 1680.

4to. F-H⁴ J². CKB

German and Latin verse by several hands. Printed with Simon Rechel, *Das Gott gelassenes* | *Mutter Hertz* | . . . 1680 (No. 2025).

2037 [STÖCKEN, CHRISTIAN VON]

Andächtiges | Buß-Gebeht/ | Welches | Auf allergnädigsten Befehl | Sr. Königl. Majest. zu Den- | nemarck/ Norwegen/ der Wenden | und Gohten/ u.s.w. | Unsers allergnädigsten Königs | und Herrn/ | Jn den Königl. Kirchen dero | Fürstentühmer/ Schleßwig/ Hollstein/ | und incorporirten Landen/ auch in | dero Herrschaft Pinnenberg/ | Nach gewissen Sontags-Wochen-und Beht- | Tags-Predigten zu gebrauchen; | Um dem erzürnten GOTT vom Him- | mel/ bei Einreissung gefährlicher Krank- | heiten/ und der in Teutschland grassirenden Seu- | chen/ bei Zeiten in seine Zorn-Ruhte zu fallen/ | und denselben/ üm Abwendnng [sic] dieser wol- | verdienten Land-Strafen/ weh-und | demütigst anzurufen. | [ornamental rule] | Rensburg/ Gedrukkt durch Tobias Schmiedt/ | Jm 1680sten Jahr.

8vo. A-B⁸. CKB

2038 STÖCKEN, CHRISTIAN VON

OPERA SACRA | de pace recuperata, | Heilige | Freud-und Friedens-Werke | Uber den/ durch Gottes sonderbahre Gnade/ erlangten | Nord-ischen Frieden/ | Auf dem | Von Seiner Königl. Majest. zu Dennemark | Norwegen/ unserm allergnädigsten König und | Herrn/ | Jn Dero Reichen/ Fürstentühmern und Landen/ | allergnädigst-angestelltem all-gemeinen | Dank-Fried-und Freuden-Fest/ | Welches war der 30 des Winter-Monahts/ oder der I. | Advents-Sontag des verstrichenen 1679sten Jahrs/ | Jn der Stadt-Kirchen zu Rendesburg aus dem ordent- | lichen Evangelio vorgestellet/ | und mit einem | sonderlichem Sing-Spiel | vermehret; | Nunmehr auch auf vielfältiges Begehren heraus gegeben/ | und mit einiger Vorrede | von den Kunst-Werken/ die man sonst OPERA nennet/ | versehen/ durch | CHRJSTJAN von Stökken/ D. |

Dero Kön. Majest. zu Dennemark/ Norwegen &c. verordneten General- │ SuperIntendenten in dero Fürstentühmern Schleßwig Holstein/ │ und deren incorporirten Landen; auch Probsten │ zu Rendesburg und Sege-berg. │ [ornamental rule] │ Gedrukt zu PLOEN/ durch Tobias Schmidt/ im 1680sten Jahre.

4to. 42, [4] pp., pp. 11-24; A-E$^4$ F$^2$, b-c$^4$.             CKB

On leaf F2, German poem to Stöcken by Gregorius Michael "Probst zu Flensburg." Leaf b1 with separate title: *Dem Allerdurchleuchtigst-* │ *Großmächtigsten* │ *König und Herrn/* │ *Herrn* │ *Christian* │ *dem Fünften/* │ . . . │ *Seinem allergnädigsten* │ *König* │ *und* │ *Herrn/* │ *Aller-untertähnigst-* │ *gewidmete* │ *FRIEDENS- und FREUDENS-* │ *MUSIC.*

2039    STÖCKEN, CHRISTIAN VON

Der Seelen-Perlen │ . . . │ Margareten von Elßwig/ │ . . . │ Durch │ CHRISTIAN von Stökken/ D. │ . . . │ Gedrukt zu PLOEN/ durch Tobias Schmidt/ im 1680sten Jahre.

4to. [2] pp., pp. 7-56; A$^2$, B-G$^4$.            KIEL UL

2040    STÖCKEN, CHRISTIAN VON

Der von Gott gesegneten │ Krohn und Helm/ │ . . . │ Fr. Annen Sophien/ │ von Kronhelm/ gebohrnen Walterin/ │ . . . │ Durch │ CHRISTIAN von Stökken/ D. │ . . . │ Rensburg/ Gedrukkt durch Tobias Schmidt. [1680]

4to. 96, [16] pp.; [A]$^4$ B-N$^4$ [O]$^4$.            CKB

Pp. 87-96, "Abdankung" by Matthaeus Bornholdt. N1, separate title: *Aufgehengter Ehren-Helm* │ . . . │ *von* │ *Unterschiedlichen Gönnern* │ *und Freunden.* O1, separate title: *Als* │ . . . │ *Frau Anna Sophia* │ . . . │ *P. Lange/ Secretar.* │ *der Stadt Jtzehoe.* O3, separate title: *Klägliche Abschieds-Rede* │ . . . │ *von* │ *HERMANNO Müllern/* │ . . . .

2041    STÖCKEN, CHRISTIAN VON, *editor*

Christian von Stökken/ D. │ Kleines Holsteinisches │ Gesang-Buch │ Darinn außerlesene │ Alt und neue Gesänge/ │ Von den Alten zwar die gewöhnlichsten/ │ Und von den Neuen die nöhtigsten/ │ Von Beeden die nüzzlichsten; │ Durchgehends aber also verbeßert/ │ daß die Alten darinn geduppelt/ nach ihrer │ vorigen und izz-üblichen Poetischen Reim-Art; die │ Neuen dabei mit vielen vermehrt zu finden/ so noch │ nie gedruk-ket worden: │ In guter Ordnung/ unter gewißen Haupt-und │ sonder-bahren Titeln/ nicht so sehr zusãmen-als │ außgesucht; üm zuversuchen/ ob auf solche │ Art anzurichten │ Ein vollständiges Gesang-Buch │ Dem auch beigefügt ein geist-und sinnreiches │ Gebeht-Buch. │ Mit König-

licher Majest. zu Dennemark | Norwegen/ auch Cuhrfürstl. Durchl. zu
Sachsen Freiheiten. | [rule] | RENSBURG/ | Gedrukkt bei Tobias
Schmidt/ im 1680sten Jahr.

12mo. [24], 1084, [24] pp., pp. 1085-[1217], [1-7]; A-Zz¹², )()()(², Aaa-Fff¹²,
Ggg1-10.                                                                                          HAB

Pagination incorrect after p. 1099 (2000-3017). On Bbb1r, separate title: *Heilige* |
*Beht-Andacht/ . . .* | *Rensburg/ Gedrukkt durch Tobias Schmidt/* | *im 1681sten*
*Jahr.*

2042  Theriaca Caelestis oder Himmels Theriac. Von Josepho Quercentano . . .
erstlich erfunden. Nachgehendts von Friderico Greiffio . . . zu Tübingen
verfertiget . . . Jetzo aber Auff gutfinden der Herren Medicorum dieser
Statt Hamburg von Josia Kalden Pharmacopaeo und Chymico daselbsten
wiederum auffgelegt und dispensiret worden. Altona, Gedruckt bei
Victor de Löw, 1680.

16mo. 28 pp.                                                                                       *

See P. T. Hoffmann in *Altonaische Zeitschrift,* II, 1932, p. 175 ff.

2043  Vnpartheyliche Er- | wegung/ | dessen/ so itziger Zeit zwischen | Jhr.
Königl. Majest. zu Dennemarck- | Norwegen/ und Jhr. Hoch-Fürstl. |
Durchl. zu Schleßwig/ Holstein- | Gottorff streitig ist. [c. 1680]

4to. A-D⁴ E².                                                                                      CKB

2044  WEDDERKOPF, GABRIEL

Das schöne Regenten-Bild/ | . . . | Herrn GEORGII | Sültzbergers/ |
. . . | von | M. GABRIELE Wedderkopff/ | Prediger der Kirchen St.
Nicolai im Kiel. | [rule] | KJEL/ | Gedruckt durch Joachim Reuman/
Acad. Buchdr. [1680]

4to. [4], 68 pp.; π², A-H⁴ J².                                                                     CKB

2045  WEDDERKOPF, GABRIEL

(Trost-Schrift an Joh. Dan. Major über das Absterben zweyer Kinder).
Kiel, 1680.

4to.                                                                                               *

*OHM* I, 713.

2046  WOLF, CHRISTIAN SIGISMUND

Sacrum exequiate oder Trostgedichte über den Tod der Maria Elisabeth
Niederstettin. Schleswig, 1680.

                                                                                                  *

*Stolberg* III, 205. Formerly in Kiel UL (LmC 13-19/23).

## 1681

2047 ARNKIEL, TROELS

Theologische Betrachtung | Des grossen schreckhafften | COMETEN, |
Bey | Außgang des Alten/ und Ein- | gang des Neuen Jahrs/ zu aller
Menschen höch- | ster Verwunderung/ 1680. und 1681. | erschienen. |
Der Gemeine Gottes zu Apenrade/ durch Zwo | Buß-Predigten | Jetzo
allen Gottliebenden Seelen/ durch den Druck | Zur | Erweckung hertz-
licher Reu und Busse/ über die angedro- | hete Sünden-Straffe des höchst-
erzürneten | Gottes | Vorgetragen/ | Von | M. TROGILLO Arnkiel/
Probsten und | Pastoren daselbst. | [ornament] | Schleßwig gedruckt bey
Johan Holwein/ Jm Jahr 1681

4to. [4], 58 pp.; A-H⁴.                                              CKB

H4 lacking, probably blank.

2048 BRUHN, CHRISTIAN

(Trauergedicht über M.E. Niederstädt, geb. Olearius . . . ). Schleswig:
Joh. Holwein, 1681.

Folio. χ².                                                             ✳

Formerly in Kiel UL (LmC 13-32). Possibly identical with No. 1998.

2049 I. N. J. C. | Catechißmus | Kleinigkeiten/ | Oder: | Anleitungen | zu
demselben. | — Maxima pendent | E minimis. — | Am kleinen Nagel
hängt oft eine gros- | se Last. | Mehr wirst verstehen/ wo du diß ver- |
standen hast. | [ornament] | PLOEN/ | Gedruckt durch Tobias
Schmidt. | Jm Jahr 1681.

12mo. [8], 62, [2] pp.; A-C¹² (C12 blank).                GREIFSWALD UL

2050 CHRISTIANI, FRIEDRICH

Das Leben der Seelen im Tode/ | . . . | [ornamental rule] | Frau Eleo-
nora/ | [ornamental rule] | Verwittibte Hertzogin zu Schleßwig Hol-
stein/ | . . . | fürgestellet/ Von | FRIDERICO CHRISTIANI, | Sch.
Sunderb. Rect. | [ornamental rule] | Gedruckt zu Plöen/ | Durch Tobias
Schmidt/ 1681

4to. [2], 50 pp.; π1, A-F⁴ G1.                                       CKB

2051 DENMARK. *Laws, statutes, etc.*

Wir Christian der Fünffte/ von Gottes Gnaden/ | . . . | . . . 5. Januarij.
Anno 1681.

Broadside.                                                            CKB

Decree issued jointly with Duke Christian Albrecht of Schleswig-Holstein, requiring travellers to have proof that they come from "mit gemelter contagion nicht inficirten Orte."

2052  DENMARK. *Laws, statutes, etc.*

Wir Christian der Fünffte | ... | ... 12. Febr: Anno 1681.

Broadside.                                                                                       CKB

Decree issued jointly with Duke Christian Albrecht of Schleswig-Holstein, limiting the export of wood.

2053  DENMARK. *Laws, statutes, etc.*

Wir Christian der Fünffte/ von Gottes Gnaden/ | ... | ... Gottorff/ den 12. Februarij Anno 1681

Broadside.                                                                                       CNA

Decree issued jointly with Duke Christian Albrecht of Schleswig-Holstein, against recruitment for foreign military service.

2054  DENMARK. *Laws, statutes, etc.*

WJR Christian der Fünffte/ von | ... | ... Glückstadt den 14. Februarij/ Anno 1681.

Broadside.                                                                                       CNA

Decree forbidding clergymen to give trial sermons or to leave their parishes without royal permission.

2055  DENMARK. *Laws, statutes, etc.*

Wir Christian der Fünffte | ... | ... 21. Maij Anno 1681.

Broadside.                                                                                       CKB

Decree issued jointly with Duke Christian Albrecht of Schleswig-Holstein, about a meeting of the "Landgericht" at Schleswig 5 July.

2056  DENMARK. *Laws, statutes, etc.*

Wir Christian der Fünffte/ von Gottes Gnaden/ | ... | ... 12. Julii 1681.

Broadside.                                                                                       CKB

Decree issued jointly with Duke Christian Albrecht of Schleswig-Holstein, regarding a "Landgericht" to be held in Kiel 6 September.

2057  DENMARK. *Laws, statutes, etc.*

WJR Christian der Fünffte/ von | ... | ... Glückstadt/ den 24. Octobr: Anno 1681

Broadside.                                                                                       CNA

Decree issued jointly with Duke Christian Albrecht of Schleswig-Holstein, ordering improvement of the highway between Lübeck and Hamburg.

2058  DENMARK. *Laws, statutes, etc.*

WJR Christian der Fünffte/ von | . . . | . . . Glückstadt/ den 24. Octobr. Anno 1681

Broadside.                                                                              CNA

Decree issued jointly with Duke Christian Albrecht of Schleswig-Holstein, ordering commerce not to avoid the highway passing through Oldesloe.

2059  DENMARK. *Laws, statutes, etc.*

WJr Christian der Fünfte/ von Gottes Gnaden/ König zu | . . . | . . . 28. Octobris Anno 1681.

Broadside.                                                                              CKB

Decree levying a new tax on land.

2060  E. E. Raths der Stadt | KJEHL/ | Kleider- | und andere | Ordnung | Wornach sich dero Bürgere | und andere ihrer jurisdiction | unterwürf- fige Einwohner mit de- | nen Jhrigen zu achten. | [rule] | KJEL/ | Gedruckt durch Joachim Reumann/ Acad. Buchdr. | Jm Jahr 1681

4to. A-B⁴.                                                                       KIEL UL

2061  EXTRAORDINAIRE | RELATION | [Copenhagen 31 January 1681]

12mo. χ⁴.                                                                DEUTSCH-NIENHOF

Caption title. Reprints "Königliche Verordnung . . . wegen des Rangs" of 31 De- cember 1680.

2062  FABRICIUS, PETER

Der Christen | Wissen und Sehnen | . . . | Herrn | D. JOËLIS Langelott/ | . . . | Durch | PETRUM FABRICIUM, | Pastorem zu S. Miehaëlis. [sic] | [skull and crossbones] | Schleßwig/ gedruckt bey Johan Holwein. | [rule] | Jm Jahr 1681.

4to. 54, [26] pp.; A-K⁴.                                                         CKB

On leaf G4r, added title-page in Latin: *MEMORIÆ,* | *VIRI* | . . . . Thereafter, verse in Latin and German by several hands.

2063  GIESE, JOACHIM

Das Stadt-Recht | Der Bürger GOTTES | Jn der Kirchen/ | Auß dem erwehleten Sprüchlein der Epistel an die | Römer/ am 14. Cap. v. 7.8.9. | . . . | Hn. JOHANNIS | von Lengerken/ | . . . | von | M. JOACHIMO

Giesen/ | Pastore Primario in Kiel. | [rule] | KIEL/ Gedruckt durch
Joachim Reuman/ Acad. Buchdr. [1681]

4to. [4], 96 pp.; π², A-M⁴.                                                  CKB

2064   HELD, CHRISTIAN

נצחון הנוצרי | Victoria Christiana contra Judæos, | Das ist/ |
Klarer Beweiß | Aus der heiligen Göttlichen Schrifft | des alten Testa-
ments/ | I. Von dem wahren dreyeinigen GOtt: | II. Von dem einigen
rechten Messia Christo Jesu; | Wie daß derselbe hat | (1) Gott und
Mensch seyn müssen; | (2) Ein Erlöser und Heyland des Menschlichen
Geschlechts; | und | (3) Solches durch Leiden und Sterben für der
Welt | Sünde: | (4) Daß die bestimpte Zeit solches Messiä längst müsse
ver- | flossen seyn. | Mit einem APPENDIX, daß noch eine grosse Be-
kehrung der Juden | zur letzten Zeit verheissen sey. | Nach Anleitung
Herrn D. Wasmuthi, | vorgestellet und zum Druck befördert/ | Zu Uber-
zeugung und Reitzung seiner Brüder nach dem Fleisch/ | Von | CHRIS-
TIANO HELD, vormahls im Judenthumb gewese- | nen Rabbi, nun
aber/ durch Gnade des Allerhöchsten/ von ein und | zwantzig Jahren
hero beständigen Christ. | [rule] | Luc. Cap.22 v. 32. Wenn du der
wahleins bekehret wirst/ | so stärcke auch deine Brüder | [rule] | Kiel/
Gedruckt durch Joachim Reuman/ Acad. Buchdr. A. 1681

4to. 63, [1] pp.; A-H⁴.                                               TÜBINGEN UL

2064A  KRAHE, CHRISTOPHER

Biblisches EPITAPHIUM, | Des Propheten Danielis und aller | treuer
Lehrer/ | . . . | Hn. VALENTINO | Schmidt von Eisenberg/ | Alten
Hochverdienten Pastori der Stadt- | Kirchen zu Hadersleben/ Seniori
des Ehrwürdigen | . . . | So geschehen Anno 1681 den 22 Novemb. . . . |
. . . von | M. CHRISTOPHORO KRAHE, | Königl. Dännemarckischen
Kirchen-Probst der Stadt | und des Ampts Hadersleben/ Schloß-Predi-
gern/ und | des Königl. Consistorii Directorn. | [rule] | Schleßwig/
gedruckt bey Johann Holweins Erben.

4to. 104 pp.; A-N⁴.                                                          CKB

Title within woodcut frame. On pp. 97-104, verse by several hands, in Latin, German, and Hebrew.

2065   KRÜKK, JOHANNES

Klag-Schrift | über das unverhoffte/ doch höchstseelige | Absterben |
Des weyland Wol-Ehrenvesten/ Großachtbaren und | Wolweisen Herrn |
Hn. Niels Lorentzen/ | Wohlverdienten Rathsverwandten/ auch | für-

nehmen Kauff- und Handelsmanns | In Flensburg/ | . . . | Von |
Johannes Krükken. | [rule] | Kopenhagen/ den 5. Julii Anno 1681.

4to. 3 leaves.                                                          CKB

Bound with Thomas Lundius, *Christliche Leichpredigt,* 1681 (No. 2066).

2066   LUNDIUS, THOMAS

Christliche Leichpredigt | . . . | Herrn Niels Lorentzen | Rathsverwand-
ten hieselbst | . . . | Durch | THOMAM LUNDIUM | Prediger zu S.
Marien in Flensburg. | [woodcut] | Schleßwig gedruckt bey Johan Hol-
wein/ | [rule] | Jm Jahr 1681.

4to. 42 pp.; A-E⁴ F1.                                                   CKB

Bound with Johannes Krükk, *Klag-Schrift* . . . (No. 2065).

2067   MORHOF, DANIEL GEORG

Letzte Pflicht dem Hn. Joel Langelott bei dessen Leichbestattung erwiesen. Kiel, 1681.

Folio.                                                                   ∗

*OHM* III, 474. Formerly in Kiel UL (LmC 11-18).

2068   MÜLLER, HENRIK

CATALOGUS, | Aller | Jn Europa | befindlichen | Hohen Schulen/ |
Sampt unterlauffenden kurtzen Bericht/ an wel- | chen Wasser-Strömen/
und in welchen Ländern dieselbe | zu suchen/ und anzutreffen/ nebst
beygefügter vermeldung/ wann/ und | zu welchen Zeiten die Academien
gestifftet und eingeführet/ | und welche Potentaten derselben Uhr-
hebere | gewesen. | Männiglich/ sonderlich/ denen Freyen Künsten
ergebenen | Gemüthern/ zu Nutzen/ mit Fleiß zusammen getragen/
zum | Druck befordert/ und ans Liecht gegeben/ | Von | Henrico
Müllero, | vom Kiel/ aus Holstein. | [ornament] | Schleßwig gedruckt
durch Johan Holwein/ | Jm Jahr 1681.

4to. [4], 16 pp.; π², A-B⁴.                                             KIEL UL

2069   [MÜLLER, HENRIK]

CATALOGUS | Der vornehmsten Städte und | Plätze/ | Jn denen bey-
den weitberühmten Her- | tzogthümern/ | Schleßwig und Holstein.
[c. 1681]

4to. χ².                                                                CKB

Caption title. Place of publication uncertain.

2070 Nɪᴄᴏʟᴀɪ, Nɪᴄᴏʟᴀᴜs

(Traurode über Bern. Oldermann). Schleswig, 1681.

Folio.                                                                          *

*OHM* I, 461.

2071 Nᴏᴛʜᴇʟꜰꜰᴇʀ, Nɪᴄᴏʟᴀᴜs

Trost-und Leich-Predigt/ | . . . | Hn. Johann Schwerd- | fegern/ | . . . |
Gehalten | Von | M. NICOLAO Nothelffern/ | Königl. Schloß-
Predigern hieselbst. | [rule] | Glückstadt/ | Gedruckt bey sel. Melchior
Kochs nachgelassener Wittwen/ | Jm Jahr 1681.

4to. [4], 42, [38] pp.; π², A-K⁴.                                     CKB

On G3 ff.: *Abdanckungs-Rede/ | Vor der Leich-Begängniß/ | Gehalten | von |
JOHANN: Müllern/ Juris Practico | Jn Glükkstadt.*

2072 Rühmliches Ehren-Lob | . . . | Herren JUSTUS THEO- | DORUS
VOLCMARUS | . . . | Als derselbe Anno 1681. den 17. Martii | auff der
hochlöblichen Universität zum Kiel nach abge- | legter Inaugural-
Disputation, beeder Rechten Li- | centiatus öffenlich proclamiret wor-
den/ | Glückwünschend außgeruffen | von | Nachgesetzten. | [rule] |
KJEL/ | Gedruckt durch Joachim Reumann/ Acad. Buchdr.

4to. χ².                                                              Kɪᴇʟ UL

2073 Sᴄʜʟᴇsᴡɪɢ-Hᴏʟsᴛᴇɪɴ-Gᴏᴛᴛᴏʀꜰꜰ. *Laws, statutes, etc.*
WJr von GOttes Gnaden Christian Albrecht/ Erbe | zu Norwegen/
postulirter Coadjutor des Stiffts Lübeck/ Hertzog zu Schleßwig . . . | . . . |
. . . 5. April Anno 1681.

Broadside.                                                           Kɪᴇʟ UL

Decree regarding stamped paper.

2074 Sᴄʜʟᴇsᴡɪɢ-Hᴏʟsᴛᴇɪɴ-Gᴏᴛᴛᴏʀꜰꜰ. *Laws, statutes, etc.*

Wir Christian Albrecht von | Gottes Gnaden/ Erbe zu Norwegen/
postulirter Coadjutor | . . . | . . . Gottorff/ den 2. Junij An. 1681

Broadside.                                                           CNA

Decree forbidding sale of agricultural products outside market places (as a measure
against rising prices).

2075 Sᴄʜᴜᴍᴀɴɴ, Jᴏʜᴀɴɴᴇs

Plötzliche Todes-Fälle | . . . | N. Koesfeld | . . . | Von | JOHANNE
Schumann/ P. | [rule of type ornaments] | PLOEN/ Gedruckt durch
Tobias Schmidt. [1681]

4to. 31, [5] pp.; A-D⁴ E².                                           CKB

2076  STÖCKEN, CHRISTIAN VON

Geistliche Wallfahrt zum rechten Heilbrunnen, bey denen durch Gottes
Gnade nicht weit von Bramstedt im Königlichen Amte Segeberg neu-
lich entsprungenen Gesundbrunnen, in Gegenwart etlicher tausend
Menschen in einer im freien Felde gehaltenen Predigt vorgestellet, und
auf vieler Herzen inständiges Begehren, mit dem dabey verordneten
Gebet und einer gründlichen Nachricht davon zum Druck übergeben
durch Christ. von Stökken, der Heiligen Schrift Dr. G. S. und Königlichen Probsten des Amts Segeberg. Rendsburg, 1681

16mo.                                                          *

J. F. Suersen, *Über die Mineralquellen bei Bramstedt im Holsteinischen.* Hamburg, 1810, pp. viii f.; *Moller* I, 660; *Thott* III/2, 545; *Bibl. Schroedter*, 1724, p.
798; *Cat. lib. Joh. Meyer*, 1721, 21mo, Nr. 195, gives date 1684. The book presumably contained separate title: *Gründliche Nachrichten wegen des Gesund-
brunnens zu Bramstedt, vom 7ten des Heumonats, im 1681sten Jahre zum Druck
übergeben durch Christian von Stöcken, der heiligen Schrift Doctor und Königlichen Probsten des Amtes Segeberg. Cf.* Suersen, p. 3.

2077  STÖCKEN, CHRISTIAN VON

Christian von Stökken/ D | Holsteinisches | Gesang-Buch/ | Darinn
außerlesene | Alt und neue Gesänge/ | Zwar | Von den Alten die gewöhn-
lichsten/ | Von den Neuen die nöhtigsten/ | Von Beeden die nüzzlich-
sten; | Durchgehends aber also | verbeßert/ daß die Alten darinn ge- |
duppelt/ nach ihrer vorigen und izz-übli- | chen Poetischen Reim-Art;
die Neuen | dabei mit vielen vermehrt zu finden/ | so noch nie gedruk-
ket wor- | den: | Jn guter Ordnung/ unter ge- | wißen Haupt- und son-
derbahren | Titlen/ nicht so sehr zusammen- als auß | gesucht/ und in
dieser zweiten Außferti- | gung mit mehr als hundert vermehret; | üm zu
versuchen/ ob auff sol- | che Art anzurichten | Ein vollständiges Gesang- |
Buch; | Mit einer Anweisung zum völligem | Gebeht-Buch. | [rule] |
RENSBURG/ | Gedrukkt im 1681sten Jahr.

12mo. [34], 1067, [25] pp.; a¹² b1-5, B-Zz¹², Aaa1-4, )(², engraving of author and
engraved preliminary title-page printed on one sheet and folded in.  GÖTTINGEN UL

CKB also has later issue, with final gathering )(¹². Leaf )( bears separate title:
*Nachrichtliche Anzeige | Was/ nebenst den alten und be- | kañten/ für gute neue
Gesänge aus | dem | Holsteinischem | Gesang-Buch/ Unter dem schlagen der Or- |
gel/ an den Soñtagen/ und sonst | . . . . ;* on leaf )(9 ff.: *Den Raum der noch-
übrigen Blätter zu füllen/ sind hier folgende Gesänge gesezzet/ Die in der ersten
Ausfertigung nicht zu finden.*

2078  STÖCKEN, CHRISTIAN VON

Der Jährliche | Schleßwig-Holsteinische | Fast-Buß-und | Beht-Tag/ |

Welcher | Auf allergnädigsten Befehl | Des Allerdurchl. Groß-Mächtig-
sten | Königs und Herrn/ | Herrn | Christian des Fünften | Erbkönigs zu
Dennemark/ Norwegen/ | der Wenden und Gohten/ Herzogs zu |
Schleßwig/ Holstein/ Stormarn und | der Ditmarsen/ Grafen zu |
Oldenb. | und Delmenhorst. | u.s.w. | Unsers Allergnädigsten Kö- | nigs
und Herrn/ | Jn Dero Fürstentühmern Schleßwig/ | Holstein/ auch
incorporirten Landen und der | Herrschaft Pinnenberg/ den Mittwochen
vor dem Beht- | Sontag/ wird sein in diesem 1681sten Jahr der 4. des |
Mai-Mon. höchst-feierlich mit Fasten/ Bußen | und Behten sol gehalten
werden. | Mit beigefügten Texten/ Collecten/ Gebeht- | und Gesängen
aus dem Holsteinischen | Gesang-Buch. | [rule] | RENSBURG/ |
Drukkts Tobias Schmidt.

8vo. )(⁸.                                                                    CKB

2079  STÖCKEN, CHRISTIAN VON

Christian von Stökken/ D. | Kleines Holsteinisches | Gesang-Buch |
Darinn außerlesene | Alt und neue Gesänge/ | Von den Alten zwar die
gewöhnlichsten/ | Und von den Neuen die nöhtigsten/ | Von Beeden die
nüzzlichsten; | Durchgehends aber also verbeßert/ | daß die Alten darinn
geduppelt/ nach ihrer | vorigen und izz-üblichen Poetischen Reim-Art;
die | Neuen dabei mit vielen vermehret zu finden/ so noch | nie gedruk-
ket worden: | In guter Ordnung/ unter gewißen Haupt-und | sonder-
bahren Titeln/ nicht so sehr zusamen-als | außgesucht; üm zuversuchen/
ob auf solche | Art anzurichten | Ein vollständiges Gesang-Buch; | Dem
auch beigefügt ein geist- und sinnreiches | Gebeht-Buch. | Mit König-
licher Majest. zu Dennemark/ | Norwegen/ auch Cuhrfürstl. Durchl. |
zu Sachsen Freiheiten. | [rule] | RENSBURG/ | Gedrukkt bei Tobias
Schmidt/ im 1681sten Jahr.

12mo. [24], 1084, [24] pp., pp. 1085-3017 [i.e., 1217], [3] pp.; A-Zz¹², )()()(²,
Aaa-Fff¹², Ggg⁸ [−Ggg8].                                                     CKB

Leaf Bbb1 has separate title-page: *Heilige | Beht-Andacht/ | Bestehend | In | Zeit-
und Standes- | Buß-und Tugend- | Krank-und Sterbens- | Andachten/ | . . . |
Rensburg/ | Gedrukkt durch Tobias Schmidt/ | Im 1681sten Jahr.* CKB copy from
Hjelmstjerne collection has engraving of v. Stöcken, facing engraved bastard title-
page with short title, "Holsteinisches Gesangbuch." SHLB has variant signed π1,
B-Zz¹², )()()(1-2, Aaa2-12; without prayer book.

2080  [STÖCKEN, CHRISTIAN VON]

Die vernünfftige lautere | Milch | Des | Heiligen | Catechismi/ | Wie
dieselbe | Den Kindern GOttes/ | durch Frag und Antwort/ | kan
eingeflösset werden; | Mehrentheils auß den Worten | des Catechismi

herauß gezogen/ mit | beigefügten Kern-Sprüchen aus der | Schrifft
erwiesen/ und der heilsamen Leh- | re-Begierigen zum Dienst | auffge-
sezzet. | Anizzo auf inständiges Begehren/ zum | dritten mahl herauß
gegeben. | [rule] | Rensburg/ | Gedrukt durch Tobias Schmidt/ | Jm
1681sten Jahr.

12mo. 120 pp.; A-E¹².                                                CKB

Handwritten in CKB copy: "von Stökkens Catechismus." The dedication (to
Jesus Christ) is signed "Der Christliche VerfaSser." On p. 120, dated *Rensburg
den 10. des Winter-Monats/ am Tage des grossen Luthers im 1680sten Jahre.*

2081   [Storning, Hinrich]

Der schöne Glantz Gottes, auß dem Nordischen Evangelischen Zion, zur
Verfinsterung des also genandten Römisch-Catholischen Nordsterns,
zuförderst auf dessen Gebet-und Gesangbuch gerichtet. [Plön] 1681.

12mo.                                                           *

*Moller* I, 666.

2082   [Storning, Hinrich]

Kurtze Entdeckung der verkrochenen Papistischen Lehre; samt einer
Protestation von solchen Streitsachen, gegen den Herren seinen Gott.
[Plön?] 1681.

12mo.                                                           *

*Moller* I, 666.

2083   Stubbe, Jacob

Parvus mundus, die kleine Welt, samt derselben kurtzen Anatomischen
Beschreibung, nach allen ihren Theilen auß bewehrten Autoribus zusam-
mengetragen. Schleswig, 1681

8vo.                                                              *

*Moller* I, 668. Formerly in Preussische Staatsbibliothek.

2084   Wernicke, Christian

(Gedicht über Johann Stephan Schippel). Kiel: Joachim Reumann,
1681.

4to. χ².                                                        *

Formerly in Kiel UL (LmC 80-17).

2085   Wexel-Recht | Von | Dennemarck und Norwegen. | Mit den Wexeln
       wollen wir hinführe solcher Gestalt | gehalten haben; weil . . .

4to. χ².                                                                    CKB

Caption title. At end, dated "Copenhagen 16. April/ Anno 1681."

2086  Zeitvertreibende und erlustigende Wahrsagungen. Copenhagen bey
      Daniel Paulli [1681]

      12mo.                                                                 *

      *Cat. univ. designatio omnium Librorum, qvi hisce Nundinus* . . . Spring, 1681
      (Groß). Possibly published in Frankfurt.


# 1682

2087  Berahtschlagung | APOLLI- | NIS | und | der Musen | im | PAR-
      NASSO | über das | Holsteinische Gesangbuch | [rule] | Gedruckt zu
      Romanopoli | [handwritten in CKB copy: 1682]

      12mo. 48 pp.; A-B¹².                                                  CKB

      Author presumably Nic. Winterberg or Magnus Gärtner.

2089  DENMARK. *Laws, statutes, etc.*

      WJR Christian der Fünffte/ von | . . . | . . . Glückstadt/ den 20sten April/
      Anno 1682

      Broadside.                                                           CNA

      Decree ordering a day of fasting and prayer 17 May.

2090  DENMARK. *Laws, statutes, etc.*

      WJr Christian der Fünffte/ von | . . . | . . . 12. Julij, Anno 1682.

      Broadside.                                                           CKB

      Decree issued jointly with Duke Christian Albrecht of Schleswig-Holstein, regard-
      ing a meeting of the courts at Rendsburg 4 September.

2091  DENMARK. *Laws, statutes, etc.*

      WJR Christian der Fünffte/ von | . . . | . . . Glückstadt den 14. Augusti
      1682.

      Broadside.                                                           CNA

      Decree forbidding "Kauffen und Verkauffen" on the sabbath in Pinneberg.

2092  DENMARK. *Laws, statutes, etc.*

      WJR Christian der Fünffte/ von | . . . | . . . Glückstadt/ den 13. Sept.
      Anno 1682.

      Broadside.                                                           CNA

Decree issued jointly with Duke Christian Albrecht of Schleswig-Holstein, calling a "Landgerichts-Tag" in Flensburg 2 November.

2093  DENMARK. *Laws, statutes, etc.*

WJR Christian der Fünffte/ von | ... | ... Glückstadt/ | den 23. Octob. Anno 1682.

Broadside.                                                          CNA

Decree regarding treatment of a disease of horses and cattle.

2094  DENMARK. *Laws, statutes, etc.*

WJr Christian der Fünffte/ von | ... | ... 27. Octob. Anno 1682.

Broadside.                                                       KIEL UL

Decree regarding payments for baptisms and weddings held at home.

2095  DENMARK. *Laws, statutes, etc.*

WJr Christian der Fünfte/ von Gottes | ... | ... 4. Novembr. Anno 1682.

Broadside.                                                          CKB

Decree levying a tax on land.

2096  FRIESE, JOHANN CHRISTIAN

(Trauergedicht über Maria Friese). Kiel: Joachim Reumann, 1682.

4to. χ².                                                              *

Formerly in Kiel UL (LmC 74-31).

2097  FÖRTSCH, JOHANN PHILIPP

Concert auß Phil. III. 14., in einem vierfachen Contrapunct und Canone infinito versetzet, und auf die Leichbegängniß Fr. Mariæ Elisabethæ Niederstädtinn gerichtet. Schleswig, 1682.

Folio.                                                               *

*Moller* II, 199.

2098  GIESE, JOACHIM

Der | Christliche | Freyer | und | Eheman/ | unterrichtet auß dem Worte GOttes/ | Wie er nemlich einen guten Ehe-Fund | glücklich auffsuchen/ und Christge- | bührlich halten solle. | Nach dem Sprüchlein Salo-monis/ | genommen | Auß seinen Sprichwörtern | am 18. Cap. v. 22. | Wer eine EheFraw findet/ der findet | was gutes/ und kan guter dinge | seyn im HERRN. | Und also vorgestellet | Von | M. Joachimo Giesen/

Pastore | Primario im Kiel. | [rule] | KJEL/ | Gedruckt und verlegt durch Joachim Reumann/ | Acad. Buchdr. im Jahr 1682.

8vo. [2], 271, [17] pp.; π1, A-S⁸ (S8 blank).        Wittenberg College Library

2099   Glückwünschende Ehrenzeilen/ | [Matthias Mutzenbecher & Maria Catherina Eck] | . . . | KJEL/ gedruckt bey Joachim Reumann/ Acad. Buchdr. [1682]

4to. A⁴.                                                                              CKB

Title from *Borchling-Claussen,* Nr. 3631. Formerly in Hamburg UL.

2100   Glückwünschende Ode welche als Herr Simon Heinrich Musäus nach Beruffung zum Professore juris . . . bey der Holsteinischen Universität zu Kiehl . . . solenniter eingeführt wurde, bey einer Nacht-Music . . . abgestellet worden . . . Studiosis daselbst. Kiel, 1682.

Folio.                                                                                  *

Formerly in Kiel UL (LmC 12).

2101   Die grosse in der kleinen Welt, oder Entwurff der Eigenschafften des Menschlichen Lebens. Kiel, 1682.

Folio.                                                                                  *

*Bibl. Kielmans-Egg.,* III, 74.

2102   Hamerich, Henrich

Abdanckungs-Rede/ | Bey Hochansehnlicher Leich-Bestetigung | . . . | Fr. Margareta von Stökken/ | Gebohrner Graviñ/ | . . . | Von | HENR. Hamerich/ | Rect. der Renßburgischen Schulen. | [rule] | Glückstadt/ Gedruckt bey Reinhard Janßen/ 1682.

4to. 38 pp.; a-b⁴, c², d-e⁴, f1.                                                    CKB

2103   Kortholt, Christian

Christian Kortholten/ | der H. Schr. D. und Prof. Pr. | Send-Schreiben/ | Worin die verleumbderische Auff- | lage/ ob solte auff der HochFürstl. Hol- | stein-Kielischen Universität die Polygamie oder Viel- | Weiberey öffentlich gebilliget und behauptet werden/ | gründlich abgeleinet und hintertrieben wird. | [rule] | Kjel/ | Gedruckt durch Joachim Reuman/ Acad. Buchdr. | c I ɔ I ɔ c LXXXII

4to. 35, [1] pp.; A-D⁴ E².                                                          CKB; (BM)

2104   Kortholt, Christian

Weiblicher | Tugend-Spiegel/ | fürgestellt | von | Christian Kortholten/ | der H. Schrifft D. und Profess. | Prim. bey der Kielischen Uni- | versität. | [rule] | KJEL/ | Gedruckt bey Joachim Reumañ/ Acad. Buchdr. | 1682

8vo. [4], 58 pp.; $\pi^2$, A-C$^8$ D 1-5.                                          CKB

All after D5 lacking, with no apparent loss of text.

2105  LAURENTIUS, ÆGIDIUS

Zwo Ehren-Seulen | . . . | Herrn | Hanß Nissens/ | . . . | von | ÆGIDIO LAURENTII, | Der Christlichen Gemeinde daselbst | Pastore. | [rule] | KJEL/ | Gedruckt durch Joachim Reumann/ der Acad. | Buchdruckern/ Anno 1682.

4to. 84 pp.; A-K$^4$, L$^2$.                                                       CKB

Pp. 69 ff., "Abdanckungs-Rede" by Tycho Th. Tychsen.

2106  MAJOR, JOHANN DANIEL

Himlische Beschauung der Göttlichen allergrößesten und herlichsten Kunstkammer der gantzen Welt, von zweyen nunmehr hocherleuchteten Seelen, Adamo Oleario, und deßen ihm nachgefolgten Tochter, Fr. Maria Elisabetha Niederstädtinn, vorgenommen, in Versen entworfen. Kiel, 1682.

Folio.                                                                              *

*Moller* I, 463; II, 516.

2107  MORHOF, DANIEL GEORG

Daniel Georg Morhofen | Teutsche | Gedichte | [rule] | Kjel/ | Gedruckt uñ verlegt durch Joachim Reuman/ | Acad. Buchdr. im Jahr 1682

8vo. [8], 471, [1] pp.; )($^4$, A-Ff$^8$ Gg$^4$.                                    CKB

2108  MORHOF, DANIEL GEORG

Daniel Georg Morhofen | Unterricht | Von | Der Teutschen Spra- | che und Poesie/ deren Uhr- | sprung/ Fortgang und | Lehrsätzen. | Wobey auch von der reimenden Poe- | terey der Außländer mit mehren ge- | handelt wird. | [rule] KIEL/ | Gedruckt und verlegt durch Joachim Reumann/ | Acad. Buchdr. im Jahr 1682.

8vo. [8], 807, [1] pp.; )($^4$, a-ddd$^8$ eee$^4$.                                  CKB; (BM)

2109  MORHOF, DANIEL GEORG

Florum sparsio ad tumulum incomparabilis matronæ Mariæ Elisabeth Niederstatten, natæ Oleariæ. Sonnet an den höchstbetrübten Wittwer. 1682.

Folio.                                                                                          *

*OHM* III, 474.

2110   MORHOF, DANIEL GEORG

Glückwünschender Zuruff womit Nicol. Martini, wie ihm den 6. Apr.
das Prorectorat beygelegt aufwarten wollen, des Acad. Secretarii Tischgenossen. (Kiel), 1682.

Folio.                                                                                          *

*OHM* III, 474.

2111   OPORINUS, CONRAD

Der Tod in Christsehnliche und hertzliche Todes-Lust, oder Leichpredigt
über Anna Todinn. . . . Kiel, 1682.

4to.                                                                                          *

Contains Joh. Bachmann, *Leich-Lob-und Danck Rede*, . . . *Moller* I, 472.

2112   Relation aus dem Parnasso, betreffent das Holsteinische Gesangbuch.
Glückstadt, 1682

4to.                                                                                          *

*Cat. lib. Cosmi Bornemann*, 1694, 4to, 250; *Bibl. Ehrencron*, 1717, p. 183; *Cat.
lib. Laur. Arhusii*, 4to, 81.

2112A  ROLLA des Tonnen-Baken-und Kapen-Geldes. | . . . | [below:] Gegeben
in der Stadt Tönningen den 4 December/ Anno 1682.

Broadside.                                                                               CKB

2113   Schertz-Gedicht | Up dat vörnehme Pummel-Fest | . . . | Herr Mathies |
Mutzenbecher | . . . | Jungfer Marie | Catharina Ecken/ | . . . | [Kiel:
Joachim Reumann, 1682]

4to. B⁴ C².                                                                               *

Title from *Borchling-Claussen*, Nr. 3632. Formerly in Hamburg UL.

2114   SCHLAPRITZ, HIERONYMUS

Kleine | Reiß-und Hauß- | APOTHECK | Darinnen zu finden viel
Herrliche/ und | auff solche Art noch niemahln Elaberirte Chi- | mische
Essentien/ mit welcher viele gefährliche | Kranckheiten mit kleiner Dosi,
subtiler mas- | sen und wenigen Tröpflein/ gantz sicher/ | lieblich und
anmuthig von Männiglichen | selbst Curiret werden können. | Jnsonder-
heit befinden sich sehr herrliche/ so wohl | Curativa als Præservativa vor
die leidige/ hin | und wieder im Schwang gehende Pest. | Alles selbst
Elaboriret, und aus Christlicher Lie- | be/ dem Nechsten zum besten mit

getheilet| durch | Hieronymum Schlapritz, Chimicum, med: | & Chirur-
giæ Practicum, Operatorem, | Oculisten Stein-und Bruch- | schneidern. |
Hamburg in Verlegung des Autoris. | [rule] | Gedrückt zu Altona bey
die Witwe von | Victor de Leeu 1682

8vo. A-G⁸; title engraving.                                        KIEL UL

2114A SCHLESWIG-HOLSTEIN-GOTTORFF. *Laws, statutes, etc.*

Vnser von Gottes Gnaden Christian Albrechten/ | Erbens zu Norwegen/
postulirten Coadjutoris des Stiffts Lübeck/ Hertzogens zu Schleßwig/
Holstein/ | ... | ... Gottorff/ den 26. Martii, An. 1682.

Broadside.                                                          CKB

Decree regarding the payment of monthly taxes.

2115 SCHLESWIG-HOLSTEIN-GOTTORFF. *Laws, statutes, etc.*

WJr von GOttes Gnaden Christian Albrecht/ Erbe zu | Norwegen/
postulirter Coadjutor des Stiffts Lübeck/ Hertzog zu Schleßwig/ | ... |
... 5. April Anno 1682

Broadside.                                                          KIEL UL

Decree taxing stamped paper.

2116 SCHLESWIG-HOLSTEIN-GOTTORFF. *Laws, statutes, etc.*

Von Gottes Gnaden Wir Christian Albrecht/ | Erbe zu Norwegen/
postulirter Coadjutor des Stiffts Lü- | beck/ ... | ... | ... [7. Aprilis
Anno 1682]

Folio. χ².                                                          KIEL UL

Decree regarding bookkeeping and annual statements by certain officials.

2116A SCHLESWIG-HOLSTEIN-GOTTORFF. *Laws, statutes, etc.*

Wir von Gottes Gnaden Christian Albrecht/ Erbe | zu Norwegen/
postulirter Coadjutor des Stiffts Lübeck/ Hertzog zu Schleßwig/ Hol-
stein/ | ... | ... Gottorff den [blank] An. 1682.

Broadside.                                                          CKB

Decree requiring adherence to the "Zoll- und Licent-Rolle" of 1674.

2117 Schreiben | Eines Freundes an Seinen | Freund/ | über die so genante |
Relation aus dem | Parnasso, | Betreffend | Das Hollsteinische Gesang-
buch. | [rule] | Glükstadt/ | Gedrukt durch Reinhard Janßen/ | Jm
1682sten Jahr.

4to. [8], 22 pp.; )(⁴, A-C⁴.                                        CKB

C4 lacking, probably blank. Written in CKB copy: "Udg. med Fortale af Heinr. von Stöcken."

**2117A** SCHWESINGER VON CRONHELM, ANDREAS

Heftigster Trübsahl kräftigste Labsahl/ | ... | ... Frau | Margaretha/ Geborne Gravin/ | Des HochEhrwürdigen/ HochEdlen und | hochgelehrten Herrn/ | Herrn Christian von Stökken/ | ... | Von | Andreas Schwesinger von Cronenhelm/ | ... | [rule] | Glückstadt/ gedruckt bey Reinhard Janßen/ Königl. Buchdr. 1682.

4to. [5], 19 pp.; $\pi^2$, A-B$^4$ C$^2$. CKB

**2118** Der | Stadt Schleßwig | Schiff-Brücken | Ordnung/ Revidiret Anno 1682

4to. A-B$^4$. CKB

Colophon: (under arms of Schleswig): *Schleßwig | Gedruckt bey Johan Holwein | Jm Jahr 1682.*

**2119** STÖCKEN, CHRISTIAN VON

Erläuterter Adventsgesang: Nun komm der Heiden Heiland. Glückstadt, 1682.

8vo. *

*Moller* I, 660.

**2120** STRUVE, REIMAR

Die verborgene Propheten-Traur | ... | Fr. Margarethen Dorotheen/ | ... | M. NICOLAI Nothelffers/ | ... Eh-Liebsten/ | ... | Von | M. REIMARO Struven/ | Stadt-Pastoren | [rule] | Glückstadt/ gedruckt bey Reinhard Janßen/ 1682.

4to. 72 pp.; A-J$^4$. CKB

Pp. 49 ff., "Abdanckungs-Rede" by Balthasar Ernst Semper.

**2121** TÄNTZER, JOHANN

Der | DIANEN | Hohe und Niedere Jagtgeheimnüß/ | Darinnen | Die gantze Jagt-Wissenschafft | Außführlich zubefinden/ | Und zwar | Jn diesem Ersten Theil/ | Wie die Wälder und Höltzungen müssen versehen seyn/ | Daß allerhand Jagt-Lusten darinnen können vorgestellet werden; | dann von den Thieren/ ihrer Eigenschaft/ von deren Jugend an/ | biß ins Alter/ welche in Teutschland und den an- | gräntzenden Reichen zu befinden. | Nach welchen/ | Das übrige in noch unterschiedlichen Theilen folget/ | Mit grosser Arbeit inventiret und beschrieben | von | Johann Täntzern. | Und auff seine selbst-eigene

Unkosten heraus gegeben/ | Am Tage Bartholmæ Anno 1682. | [orna-
ment] | [ornamental rule] | KOPPENHAGEN/ | Gedruckt bey Conrad
Hartwig Neuhoff.

4to. 140 pp.; )(⁴, B-P⁴. CKB; (BM)

Numerous engravings in text. Pagination includes 10 plates. Engraved preliminary
title: *Der Dianen | Hohe vnd Niedere | Iagtgeheimbniß.* CKB copy bound with
"Ander Theil," Copenhagen: Schmedtgen 1686 (No. 2286).

2122 Vollständiges Gesang-Buch. Plön, 1682.

Oblong 8vo. •

*Bibl. Breitenaviana,* 1747, I, p. 389. Fifth edition of Plön hymnal? *Cf.* No. 1895.

2123 WILDENHEIN, JOHANN

Lehr und | Trost-Schrifft | ... | Fr. Maria Elisabeth | Niederstettin | ... |
Von | Joh. Wildenhein/ Past. in Fridrichsberg. | [woodcut: coffin] |
Schleßwig/ gedruckt bey Johan Holwein. | [rule] | Anno c I ɔ I ɔ c
LXXXII.

Folio. 33, [3] pp.; A-J². SHLB

## 1683

2125 Altonaische RELATION | No. 66 [woodcut: crowned female figure on
lion] 1683.

8vo. Pp. 521-528. SWEDISH NATIONAL ARCHIVES

Caption title. At head of page, "Vom 16 Augustij. Fol. 521." Swedish National
Archives have also No. 68 (23 August), 70 (30 August), 72 (6 September), 74 (13
September), 76 (20 September), 80 (4 October), 82 (11 October), 84 (18 October),
86 (25 October), 88 (1 November), 94 (22 November), 96 (29 November), 98 (6
December), 100 (13 December), 102 (20 December), 104 (27 December; pp. 825-
832). Each issue 8 pp. Nr. 32 (19 April 1683)-104 (27 December 1683) formerly in
Marienstift-Gymnasium, Stettin. *Cf.* G. Kowalewski in *Zschr. f. Bücherfreunde,*
N.F. V/2 (1914), 357.

2126 ARNKIEL, TROELS

Gülden-Horn/ | 1639. bey Tundern gefunden/ | Aus dem darunter
verborgnem | Heidenthumb | Vnsrer Vorfahren Cimbrischer Nation/ |
Als eine denckwürdige Antiquität/ | und höher als Gold geschätztes
Monument | ihrer Heidnischen Abgöttereien | erklärt/ | Und wieder die
anderswoher gesuchte Erklä- | runge verthäidiget/ | Allen Antiquität-
liebenden zur Nachricht/ | von | M. TROGILLO Arnkiel/ | Probsten

und Pastoren | zu Apenrade. | [rule] | KJEL/ | Gedruckt und Verlegt durch Joachim Reumann/ 1683.

4to. [12], 208 pp.; A-Dd⁴, Ee²; 1 folding plate. CKB

2127 BECK, JOHANN JOSEPH

Beraubte Kron | ... | Fr. Christina gebohrne Hennings/ | ... | Hr. Paul Kohlblatten/ | gewesenen Eheliebsten | ... | von | Johann Joseph Beckh. Poeta Coronato | ... | KJEL/ | Gedruckt bey Joachim Reumann/ Acad. Buchdr. [1683]

4to. χ⁴. KIEL UL

2127A CLAUSEN, ADOLF

Klag-Trost-und Danckrede/ | ... | Catharine Clausen/ | ... | Von | Adolff Clausen | [skull & crossbones] | [Schleswig] Anno 1683

4to. t-p, pp. 35-44. KIEL UL

Part of another publication.

2128 DAMPIERRE, JACQUES SERCUEIL DE

Frantzösischer Haupt-Schlüssel. Copenhagen, 1683.

12mo. *

*Catal. libr. 19 May 1690*, p. 110; *Fort. Chr. Cassuben*, 1693, Indb. 12mo, 131; Ehrencron-Müller, *Forfatterlexikon*, II, 315 lists unlocated editions of 1672 and 1682.

2129 DENMARK. *Laws, statutes, etc.*

Des | Aller-Durchläuchtigsten | Großmächtigsten Königs und | HERRN/ | Herrn Christian | Des Fünften | Von GOttes Gnaden/ Königs zu | Dännemarck/ Norwegen/ der Wenden und Go- | then/ Hertzogs zu Schleßwig/ Hollstein/ Stormarn | und der Ditmarschen/ Grafens zu Oldenburg und Delmenhorst. | Articuls-Brief. | Und | Kriegs-Gerichts- | Instruction | Belangende | Den Krieg zu Lande/ | Worauf alle und jede/ Uns mit Kriegs-Pflicht | Verwante und zu Lande Dienende/ schwehren/ und | darnach in allen Puncten sich schuldiger Gebühr bezeigen sollen. | Mit Königlichem Privilegio. | [rule] | KOPEN-HAGEN/ | Gedruckt von Joachim Schmedtgen Jm Jahr 1683.

4to. 126, [2] pp.; A-Q⁴. CKB

Another edition: 8vo; 138, [6] pp.; A-J⁸ (J8 blank). See also No. 2130.

2130 DENMARK. *Laws, statutes, etc.*

Des | Aller-Durchläuchtigsten/ | Großmächtigsten Königs und | HERRN/ | Herrn Christian | Des Fünften | Von GOttes Gnaden/

Königs zu | Dännemarck/ Norwegen/ der Wenden und | Gothen/ Hert-
zogs zu Schleßwig/ Hollstein Stor- | marn und der Dithmarschen/
Grafens zu | Oldenburg und Delmenhorst | Articuls-Brief | Und | Kriegs-
Gerichts- | Instruction | Belangende | Den Krieg zu Lande/ | Worauf
alle und jede/ Uns mit Kriegs- | pflicht Verwante und zu Lande Die-
nende/ schwehren/ | und darnach in allen Puncten sich schuldi- | ger
Gebühr bezeigen sollen. | [rule] | Christianiæ | Gedruckt von Michel
Thomsen im Jahr 1683.

8vo. 138, [6] pp.; A-J⁸ (J8 blank).                                          CKB

See also No. 2129.

2131    DENMARK. *Laws, statutes, etc.*

Königliches Patent wegen Einziehung des Fürstenthumbs Schleswig
den 30te Maji 1683

4to.                                                                                    *

*Cat. lib. Slange,* [c. 1737] p. 57.

2132    DENMARK. *Laws, statutes, etc.*

ORDONNANCE | . . . | Cavallerie zu Verpflegen . . .

Broadside.                                                                           CKB

Dated 24 July 1683.

2133    DENMARK. *Laws, statutes, etc.*

ORDONNANCE | Wornach unser Christian des Fünf- | te von Gottes
Gnaden/ Königs zu Dennemarck | . . . | Jnfanterie zu verpflegen.

Broadside.                                                                           CUL

Dated 24 July 1683.

2134    DENMARK. *Laws, statutes, etc.*

WJr Christian der Fünffte/ von | . . . | . . . 7. April Anno 1683.

Broadside.                                                                           CKB

Decree establishing three "Fast-Buß-und Beht-Tage."

2135    DENMARK. *Laws, statutes, etc.*

WJr Christian der Fünfte/ von Gottes Gnaden/ | . . . | . . . Copenhagen
den 5. May Anno 1683

Broadside.                                                                           CNA

Decree ordering men and horses in Duchies to military service.

2136  DENMARK. *Laws, statutes, etc.*

WJR Christian | der Fünfte/ von GOttes | Gnaden/ König zu Denne-
marck/ | . . .

Folio. χ².                                                                                              CNA

Decree regarding billeting of officers and cavalrymen. At end: "Rendsburg/ den 7.
Augusti; Anno 1683." Another version, mentioning "Officerer/ Reuter oder Dra-
gouner," signed at end: Christian.

2137  DENMARK. *Laws, statutes, etc.*

WJR Christian der Fünffte/ von | . . . | . . . Rendeßburg den 7. Aug:
Anno 1683.

Broadside.                                                                                         CNA

Decree regarding the billeting of officers and soldiers.

2138  DENMARK. *Laws, statutes, etc.*

Wir Christian der Fünffte/ von Gottes Gna- | den/ . . . | . . . | . . . Gottorff
den 24 | Septembris Anno 1683

Broadside.                                                                                         CNA

Decree issued jointly with Duke Christian Albrecht of Schleswig-Holstein, ordering
a day of thanksgiving 14 October for a victory over the "Erbfeind Christlichen
Nahmens" (i.e., the Turks).

2139  Europäische Relation. [Altona], 1683.

8vo.                                                                                                    *

Nr. 32 (20 April 1683)-108 (25 December 1683) formerly in Marienstift-Gymnasium, Stettin. *Cf.* G. Kowalewski in *Zschr. f. Bücherfreunde*, N.F. V/2 (1914), 364
ff. See note to No. 1665.

2140  FRIIS, LAURIDS

Der herrlich-gekrönte und wolbelohnte Kampff | . . . | Fr. Catharina
Clausen | gebohrnen Steenbechin | . . . | Von | M. LAURENTIUS
FRISIUS, Dienern des Göttlichen | Wortes zu Brede im Ampte Lügum
Kloster | [skull & crossbones] | Schleßwig/ gedruckt durch Johan Hol-
wein An. 1683.

4to. 32 pp.; A-D⁴.                                                                            KIEL UL

2141  [GENSCH VON BREITENAU, CHRISTOPH]

Nachricht/ | Von Jhrer Königl. Mayest: zu Denne- | marck/ Norwegen
&c. &c. | Wider | Des Hn: Hertzogen zu Schleßwig- | Holstein- Got-

torff &c. &c. | Fürstl: Durchl: | Annoch habenden rechtmässigen Be-
schwerden | und Ansprüchen. | [ornament] | Jm Jahr 1683

4to. [2], 92, [2] pp.; A-M⁴ (M4 blank).                                     CKB

Published in Glückstadt or Altona. Another edition: same title, [2], 92 pp.; A-M⁴,
different ornament on t-p; another edition, 1684 (No. 2190A).

2142   GIESE, JOACHIM

Der Gläubigen Paß und Geleits-Brieff | in das ewige Leben/ | . . . | Fr.
CHRISTINÆ | gebohrnen Henningsen/ | Des WolEdlen/ Gestrengen
und Vesten | Herrn Paul Kohlblatten/ | Erbherrns auff Spotterup/ |
Eheliebsten/ | . . . | von | M. JOACHIMO Giesen/ Pastore Primario | an
St. Nicolai im Kiel. | [rule] | Daselbst gedruckt bey Joachim Reumann/
Acad. Buchdr. [1683]

4to. [4], 100 pp.; π², A-M⁴ N².                                             CKB

2143   GIESE, JOACHIM

Der Himmels-Gefliessenen | Verlangete und Erlangete | Beforderung
zum Himmel/ | Auß der Epistel S. Pauli an die Phillpper [sic] am I.
Capittel/ | . . . | Herrn JOHANNIS | ADOLPHI Roßmans/ | . . . | von |
M. JOACHIMO Giesen/ Pastore Primario | an St. Nicolai im Kiel. |
[rule] | Daselbst gedruckt bey Joachim Reumann/ Acad. Buchdr. [1683]

4to. 118 pp.; A-P⁴.                                                         CKB

P4 lacking, probably blank.

2144   GIESE, JOACHIM

Der Todt der Gerechten. | . . . | Jungfr. Margaretha | Sehestettin/ | . . . |
von | M. JOACHIMO Giesen/ | Pastore Primario daselbst. | [rule] |
KJEL/ | Gedruckt bey Joachim Reuman/ Acad. Buchdr. [1683]

4to. [4], 124, [8] pp.; π², A-Q⁴ R².                                        CKB

2145   Hoch-Fürstliche | Schleßewig-Holsteinsche | erneuerte | Verordnunge. |
Wie es hinfüro bey allen Hafen- und Zoll- | stetten an der Eider und
Hever mit Abfertigung | der Ein und Außgehenden Güter und | Schiffen
gehalten wer- | den soll. | [vignette] | [rule] | Jm Jahr 1683

4to. A-B⁴.                                                          KIEL UL

Place of publication uncertain. Dated at Hamburg 20 April 1683.

2146   HOLST, JOHANNES

Menschliches Lebens | Kürtze und Mühseligkeit | bey Beerdigung | Der
Weiland Groß Ehr-und viel Tugent- | reichen Matronen | Fr. MAR-

GARETÆ IESSEN | . . . | durch | Iohannem Holst Predigern zu | S. Nicol. in Flenßburg. | [rule] | Zu Altona Gedrückt/ bey der Wittwen von Victor | de Leu Anno 1683.

4to. [2], 48 pp.; π1, A-F⁴; 3 plates.                                        CKB

Plates are emblems, explained in verse on p. 1. On p. 33, added title: *Rühmlicher Nachklang | womit/ Der Selig Verstorbenen/* . . . . On pp. 34-48, verse by several hands.

2148  KORTHOLT, CHRISTIAN

Christian Kortholten/ D. | Güldene | Glaubens-Kette. | [rule] | KJEL/ | Gedruckt und verlegt durch Joachim Reu- | mann/ Jm Jahr 1683.

8vo. 64 pp.; A-D⁸.                                                           CKB

2149  [KORTHOLT, CHRISTIAN]

Der Theologischen | Facultet | bey der HochFürstl. Holstei- | nischen Christian-Albrechts | Universitet zum Kiel | Beantwortung | einiger | Fragen/ | das unlängst in Hamburg | vom leidigen Satan | Besessene Mägdlein | betreffend. | [rule] | KJEL/ | Gedruckt bey Joachim Reu- mañ/ | Acad. Buchdr. 1683

12mo. 42, [6] pp.; A-B¹² (B 10-12 blank).                                    HAB

2150  KRAMER, MAURITIUS

Heilige Andachten, bestehend in etlichen geistlichen Liedern. Glück- stadt, 1683.

8vo.                                                                         *

*Moller* I, 114; *Bibl. Kirchhof,* 1746, p. 117; *Bibl. Ehrencron,* 1717, Lib. theol. 8vo, Nr. 20.

2151  Kurtzer Bericht | von | Jhrer Königl. Hoheit/ | Prince | GEORGEN | Ankunfft | Jn Engeland/ | und | Wie Dieselbe dorten empfangen wor- den. | de dato Londen den 20. Julii 1683 | [rule] | Gedruckt in Copen- hagen den 3. Augusti

4to. χ².                                                                     CKB

2152  LASSÆUS, BERNHARD

Schuldige | Dienst-Bezeugung | Welche | Am Hochzeitlichen Ehe-und Ehren-Feste | Des WolEdlen/ Vest und WolMannhafften auch | Wolge- lahrten Herrn | Hn. HEINONIS GER- | HARDI RIGE, | . . . | Und | . . . | Jungf. MARINÆ THOMSEN, | . . . | Jn Tundern den 19. Julii des

1683. Jahrs | Geleistet/ | Von | BERNHARDO LASSÆO. | [rule] | Schleßwig gedruckt bey Johan Holwein.

4to. $\chi^2$.                                                                          CKB

Verse.

2153  LUCAE, FRIEDRICH

Das | Besänftigte Trähnen Auge | Der | Allerdurchläuchtigsten/ Groß-mächtigsten | Fürstin und Frauen/ Frauen | [ornamental rule] | Char-lotten Amelien/ | Königinn zu Dennemarck/ Norwegen/ der Wenden | und Gothen/ Hertzogin zu Schleßwig; Gebohrnen Landgräfin | zu Hessen/ auch Hertzogin zu Holstein/ Stormarn und der Dith- | marschen/ Fürstin zu Hersfeld; Gräfin zu Oldenburg und Del- | men-horst/ Catzenellnbogen/ Dietz/ Ziegenhayn; Nidda | und Schawen-burg. | Auf Veranlassung | Des tödtlichen jedoch Höchstseeligen | Hintritts | Der weyland | Durchläuchtigsten Fürstin und Frawen/ | Frawen | [ornamental rule] | Hedwig Sophien/ | Gebohrner aus Chur-Fürstlichem Stamm der | Marckgrafen zu Brandenburg; Jn Preussen/ zu Magdeburg/ | Gülich/ Cleve/ Berg/ Stettin/ Pommern Hertzogin; Landgräfin | zu Hessen; Fürstin zu Halberstadt/ Minden und Hers-feld; | Gräfin zu CatzenEllnbogen/ Dietz/ Ziegenhayn/ Nidda/ | Schaumburg/ der Marck und Ravensberg; | Frawen zu Ravenstein. | Jn einer unterthänigsten Trost-Schrift | entworffen | Von | Friedrich Lucæ/ | Prediger des Heiligen Evangelii | in Cassel. | [rule] | Gedruckt in der Königl. Vestung Glückstadt/ | durch Reinhard Janßen/ 1683.

Folio. A-K².                                                                          CKB

2154  MAJOR, JOHANN DANIEL

Ehren-Gedächtnüß/ | zu schuldigem Christlichen Ruhm | der weyland- | Wol-würdig-Andächtig- | und Wolgebohrnen Jungfrau/ | Jf. Mar-garetha | See-städtinn/ | Conventualinn des HochAdelichen | Jung-frauen-Klosters Jtzehoe/ | als welche im Kiel den 18ten Tag Monaths | Januarii/ im Jahr Christi 1683. | in Gott seelig entschlaffen/ | und den 1. Martii darauff/ | in grosser Versamlung der Leid-tragenden | daselbst beygesetzet worden: [Kiel]

4to. 16 pp.; A-B⁴.                                                                    CKB

2155  [MAJOR, JOHANN DANIEL]

[stars] | Tugend/ gutter Nachruhm/ und Ewigkeit/ | an dem exempel der | weiland Wol-Edlen/ numehr Hoch-seeligen Frauen/ | Fr. Christina Kohlblathin/ | [ornament: angel on circle with motto: Mensch | wiltu

seelig werden/ | so mache dir | mit GOTT | den Himmel hier | auff | Erden.] | in einem dreyfachen Sonnet | allem irrdischen Wesen entgegen gesetzet | in Kiel/ den 16 Decembris/ A. 1683. | als an Deroselben Beerdigungs-Tage. | [stars].

Folio. $\chi^2$.                                                                     CKB

Verse.

2156   MARTINI, BENEDICT

Heilsame Gedancken | Vom Menschlichen Leben. | . . . | Fr. Margareten/ | gebohrnen Jügertinnen/ | Des weiland Wolwürdigen/ Hoch-Edlen und | Gestrengen | Herrn BALTHASARIS GLOXINII, | . . . | Von | BENEDICTO MARTINI, Ecclesiæ Cathedralis | Slesvicensis Pastore. | [rule] | Schleßwig gedruckt durch Johan Holwein/ Fürstl. Buchdrucker | daselbst. | Jm Jahr 1683.

4to. 47, [1] pp.; A-F⁴.                                                              CKB

2157   NICOLAI, NICOLAUS

Das Ehrwürdige Alter | . . . | Fr. Margareten/ | gebohrnen Jügertin/ | . . . | Herrn Balthasar Gloxinen | . . . | hinterlassenen Fr. Wittiben/ | In der ThumKirchen zu Schleßwig den 25. Febr. des 1683sten Jahrs | . . . | Von | Nicolao Nicolai. | [woodcut: coffin] | Schleßwig gedruckt bey Johan Holwein.

Folio. $\chi^2$.                                                                     SHLB

2158   NICOLAI, NICOLAUS

(Traur Ode auf Sophia Magdal. Doroth. Pechlin Absterben). Schleswig: Joh. Holwein, 1683.

Folio. $\chi^2$.                                                                       *

*OHM* I, 461. Formerly in Kiel UL (LmC 14-31).

2159   Nordischer [Merkur] [woodcut: Mercury]. [Altona], 1683.

8vo.                                                                                  *

Numbers 32 (20 April) through 104 (28 Dec.) formerly in Marienstift-Gymnasium, Stettin. *Cf.* G. Kowalewski, in *Zschr. f. Bücherfreunde* N.F. V/2 (1914), 356.

2160   RIST, JOHANN CASPAR

Richterliches Grabmahl | . . . | Hr. Gregorii Crögers | . . . | von | J. C. Rist. | [rule] | Altona Gedrückt/ bey der Witwen von Victor de Leeu | Anno 1683

4to. $\chi^2$.                                                                        CKB

2161 RIST, JOHANN CASPAR

Todten Fakkel | . . . | Hr. Gregorii Crögers | . . . | von | Joh: Casp: Rist
Wed: Past. | [rule] | Altona Gedrückt/ bey der Witwen von Victor de
Leeu. | Anno 1683.

4to. A-B⁴. CKB

2162 SCHLESWIG-HOLSTEIN-GOTTORFF. *Laws, statutes, etc.*

Des | Hoch-Fürstl. Hauses | Schleßwig-Hollstein- | Gottorp/ | Jn | Denen
Erbtheilungs/ Unions, | Defensions, auch anderen Recessen, Lehen- |
Briefen/ Friedens-Instrumenten, und | Verträgen/ | Begründete gerecht-
same | Uff | Gnädigstem Befehl | Dem Druck untergeben | [rule] | Jm
Jahr MDCLXXXIII.

4to. A-P⁴ Q². CKB

Another edition: [30], 92, [2] pp.; π1, A-C⁴, D², ²A-L⁴, M². (Altenhof; CKB).

2163 SCHMID, JOACHIM

Christliche Einweyhungspredigt, bey der von Hertzog Joh. Adolphen zu
Holstein-Plön, am andern Advents-Sontage Anno 1683., angestellten Ein-
weyhung der neuerbauten Kirche zu Kurou, auß Matth. XXI. 1. sq.,
gehalten. Plön, 1683.

4to. ✳

*Moller* I, 594.

2164 SCHMID, JOACHIM

Das von Gott erleuchtete scharfsehende Glaubensauge . . . Leichpredigt
über Henr. Ern. von Kram. . . . Plön, 1683.

4to. ✳

*Moller* I, 594; *Bibl. Breitenaviana* V, p. 423.

2165 Schuldiges | Lob- und Danck- | Opffer | Wegen der grossen Siege/ die |
GOtt in kurtzverwichener Zeit seinen Christen | wieder die Türcken
gegeben hat. [1683?]

χ² (16.1 x 13.2 cm). CKB

Caption title.

2166 STEMANN, JUST VALENTIN

Der Höchst-beklagte Abschied/ | . . . | Fr. Christina gebohrne Hen-
nings/ | . . . | H. Paul Kohlblatten/ | gewesenen Eheliebsten | . . . | von |

... | J. V. Steman/ | [rule] | KJEL/ | Gedruckt bey Joachim Reumann/
Acad. Buchdr. [1683]

4to. χ².                                                        KIEL UL

2167 STÖCKEN, CHRISTIAN VON

Der älteste Weinacht- | Gesang/ | Ein Kindelein so lö- | belich/ | Nach
seinem eigentlichen | Wortverstande/ | Schriftmässig erläutert | Durch |
Christian von Stökken/ D. | Sr. Königl. Majest. zu Dennemark/ | Nor-
wegen/ Verordneten Kirchen-Raht | und General-Superint. | [rule] |
Gedrukkt zu Glükkstadt durch | Reinhard Janßen/ im 1683sten Jahre.

8vo. [4] pp., pp. 89-180; π², G-L⁸ M⁶.          STADTBIBLIOTHEK LÜBECK

2168 STÖCKEN, CHRISTIAN VON

Erläuterter Passionsgesang: Ach wir armen Sünder. Glückstadt, 1683

8vo.                                                              *

*Moller* I, 660.

2169 THEILE, JOHANN

Letzter Abschied | ... | Fr. Christinen gebohrnen Hennings/ | ... |
Herrn Paul Kohlbladten/ | ... | entworffen von | Johan Theilen/ C. M. |
... [1683]

4to. χ².                                                        KIEL UL

2170 Trauer-und Trost-Gedicht | ... | Fr. Christinen Kolblathin | gebohrnen
Henningin/ | ... | von | Etlichen Mitleidenden Freunden. | [rule] |
KJEL/ | Druckts Joachim Reumann/ 1683.

4to. χ⁴.                                                        KIEL UL

2171 WALTHER, ANTON HEIMREICH

Dithmarsische | Chronick/ | Darinn | Nebenst der Landes Beschreibung |
Die Geschichte/ | So sich vor erlangeter/ bey gehabter | und nach
verlohrener Freyheit des | Dithmarscher Landes | begeben/ | Jn drey
Büchere/ | Aus allerley glaubwürdigen gedruck- | ten und geschriebenen
Nachrichtungen | ordentlich verfasset worden | Durch | M. Antonium
HeimReich Walthern/ | Pastoren auff dem Nordstrandischen | Mohre. |
Gleich wie der Spiegel uns gar artig zeigen kan | Was wol und übel
steht/ so zeigen die Geschichten | Daß man sich mit bedacht nach andere
sol richtē/ | Was übel meiden/ was wol stehet/ fangen an. | Schleß-
wig | Gedruckt durch Johan Holwein/ | Impensis Autoris. | Anno
MDCLXXXIII.

12mo. [16], 308, [12] pp.; )(⁸, A-N¹² O⁴.                          CKB

2172  WALTHER, ANTON HEIMREICH

Schleßwigische | Kirchen Historie/ | Darinn | Die abschaffung der
Heid- | nischen Abgötterey/ und einführung | der in der Römischen
Kirchen üblichen | Christlichen Religion, | Auch stifftung des Schleß-
wigi- | schen Bißthums und desselben | Bischöffe Leben/ | Und die end-
lich vorgenommene Refor- | mation, und nach derselben sich eräugnete |
Ketzereyen neben anderen im Schleß- | wigischen Hertzogthum | vorge-
fallenen Kirchen Händelen/ | Aus glaubwürdigen Schriften und Nach- |
richtungen | ist verfasset und zusammen gezogen | Durch | M. Antonium
Heimreich Walthern/ | P. auf dem Mohre im NordStrande. | [asterisks] |
Schleßwig gedruckt bey Johan Holwein/ | Jm Jahr 1683.

12mo. [14], 260, [26] pp.; A-M¹², N⁶ (N6 blank).                           CKB

2173  WEISSER, PHILIPP

JESUS/ | Aller Christen gewisser Hertzens-Trost/ | . . . | Fr. Elisabeth
Anna | Gebohrne von Kröchern/ | . . . | von Worgewitz/ | . . . | Von |
PHILIPPO Weißer/ des Glücksburg. Con- | sistorij & Ministerij Seniore,
und der Christl. Gemeine | zu Neukirchen in Angeln Pastore. | [rule of
type ornaments] | PLOEN/ Gedruckt durch Tobias Schmidt. [1683]

4to. [4], 67, [13] pp.; A⁴ (A2 + )o(²), B-J⁴, )(⁴.                         CKB

On page 49, separate title: *Trost-Schreiben* | . . . | *Von* | *Henningo Petersen,*
*Fürstl. Holsteini-* | *schen Probst und Hoff-Predigern zu Glücksburg.* Leaves )( 1-4:
*Hoch-Adeliche Leich* | *und Beysetzung* | . . . | *Fr. Elisabeth Anna* | *von Worgewitz* |
. . . | *PLOEN/ Gedruckt durch Tobias Schmidt.*

# 1684

2176  Altonaische RELATION | No. 3 [woodcut: crowned female figure on
lion] 1684

8vo. Pp. 17-24.                                        SWEDISH NATIONAL ARCHIVES

Caption title. At head of page, "Vom 7. Januarij. Fol: 17." Swedish National
Archives have also No. 4 (10 January), 8 (24 January), 10 (31 January), 14 (14
February), 18 (28 February), 20 (6 March), 22 (13 March), 24 (20 March), 26 (27
March), 28 (3 April), 30 (10 April), 32 (17 April), 34 (24 April), 36 (1 May), 38
(8 May), 42 (22 May), 44 (29 May), 46 (5 June), 50 (19 June). Each issue 8 pp.
Nr. 1 (1 January 1684)-22 (13 March 1684) formerly in Marienstift-Gymnasium,
Stettin. *Cf.* G. Kowalewski in *Zschr. f. Bücherfreunde,* N.F. V/2 (1914), 357 ff.

2177  ANDREÆ, JOHANNES CHRISTOPHERUS

Letzte Schmertzens-Thränen über dem Grabe Mich. Petzolt. . . . Kiel,
1684.

Folio.                                                                                  *

*OHM* I, 19.

2178  ARNKIEL, TROELS

Catechismus Lehre, in 3. Theile unterschieden, vor angehende zuneh-
mende und geübte Catechismus-Schüler. Schleswig, 1684.

12mo.                                                                                   *

*Moller* I, 23.

2179  BOJE, MICHAEL

Schuldiges Lob und Nachruhm | . . . | Fr: Margaretha Johanna |
Geborne Rhederinn/ | Des | WollEdlen/ Vest-und Hochgelahrten
Herren/ | Herren | JOHANNIS MATTHIÆ | Sommern/ J. U. D. |
. . . . | Auffgesetzet | Von | MICHAEL BOJEN, | Wilst. Archi-Diac. in
patr. | [rule] | Gedruckt in der Königl. Vestung [Glückstadt] [1684]

Folio. χ².                                                           CKB

CKB copy trimmed with slight loss of text. Bound with Boje's *Stand-und Lob-
Rede* about the deceased (No. 2180).

2180  BOJE, MICHAEL

Stand-und Lob-Rede/ | . . . | Fr. Doct. Margaretha | Johanna Som-
merin/ | gebohrne Rhederin/ | . . . | Von | MICHAEL BOJEN, Wilstr. |
Archi-Diac. in patr. | [rule] | Glückstadt/ gedruckt durch Reinhard
Janßen/ 1684.

4to. 23, [1] pp.; A-C⁴.                                              CKB

2181  BOLDICH, ERNST CHRISTIAN

Christliche | Entdeckung | Calvinischer | Betrieglichkeit/ | Nebst gründ-
licher Widerlegung | Calvinischer Jrrthümer. | Welche enthalten und
verstecket | sind in dem so genandten Ausführli- | chem Bericht und
dessen Anhang/ nebst bey- | gehenden Schrifften von der Calvini- |
nischen Friedbietung. | Zu steuer der Warheit/ zu Rettung der | Ehre
Christi/ und zur Warnung der Ein- | fältigen/ nach der Regel deß
Göttlichen | Worts/ verfasset/ | Und der rechtglaubigen Evangelischen
Kir- | chen zum Nutzen in Druck gegeben | von | M. Ernesto Christiano
Boldichio, | Dienern am Worte GOttes der Teut- | schen Gemeine zu
Helsingör in | Dennemarck. | [rule] | Gedruckt im 1684sten Heyl-Jahr

8vo. [12], 636 pp.; )(⁶, A-Qq⁸ Rr⁶.                               CKB

Place of publication uncertain.

2182  BURCHARD, PETER ANTON

(Schertzgedicht auf das Hochzeitliche Fest des EtatsRaths Eliæ Hübsch
und Elisabeth Jansin.) Copenhagen, 1684.

Folio.                                                                        *

*OHM* I, 82.

2183  DENMARK. *Laws, statutes, etc.*

(Gebethe und Texte auff die 3 allgemeinen Fast-und Beth-Tage).
Copenhagen, 1684.

8vo.                                                                          *

*Bibl. Mejeriana,* 1701, 8vo Nr. 1100.

2184  DENMARK. *Laws, statutes, etc.*

Königl. Kirchen- | Gebeht/ | Welches auf allergnädigsten | Befehl | Des
Aller Durchleuchtigsten/ Groß- | mächtigsten Königs und Herrn/ | Hn:
Christian | des Fünften/ Erb-Königs zu | Dännemarck/ Norwegen/ der
Wenden | und Gohten/ Herzogs zu Schleßwig/ | Hollstein/ Stormarn
und der Ditmar- | schen/ Grafen zu Oldenburg und Del- | menhorst/
u.s.w. | Jm ganzen Fürstentuhm Schleßwig | ohn Unterscheid | allemahl
nach der Predigt | zu gebrauchen. | [ornament] | [rule] | Glükkstadt/ |
Gedrukkt bei Reinhard Janßen | im 1684sten Jahr.

4to. ):(⁶.                                                                  CKB

CKB copy interleaved and with extensive notations on additional blank pages.

2185  DENMARK. *Laws, statutes, etc.*

Königl. Dänisches | MANDAT | Das Hertzogthumb Schleßwig |
betreffendt.

4to. )(1-2.                                                                 CKB

Caption title. Signed, *Rensburg den 30. May. Anno 1684.*

2186  DENMARK. *Laws, statutes, etc.*

Verordnung/ | Wie es mit Administration | der Justitz in dem Hertzog- |
thum Schleßwig hinführo ge- | halten werden solle. | Copenhagen den
15. Novembr. 1684. | [monogram] | [rule] | Gedruckt bey Johan Philip
Bockenhoffer/ Jhr Königl. Maj. | und Univers. Buchdrucker.

4to. χ⁴.                                                                    CKB

2187  DENMARK. *Laws, statutes, etc.*

WJR Christian der Fünffte/ von | . . . | . . . Glückstadt/ den 25. Martij,
Anno 1684.

Broadside.                                                                                                        CNA

Decree ordering days of prayer 18 and 25 April and 2 May.

2187A DENMARK. *Laws, statutes, etc.*

WJR Christian der Fünffte/ von | GOttes Gnaden/ König zu Dänne-
marck/ Norwegen/ der Wenden | . . . | . . . | Renßburg den 30sten Maij
Anno 1684.

Broadside.                                                                                                        CKB

Decree against Duke Christian Albrecht of Schleswig-Holstein, withdrawing the
Duchy of Schleswig from his sovereignty.

2188 DENMARK. *Laws, statutes, etc.*

WJr Christian der Fünfte von Got- | tes . . . | . . . | 11. Novembr. Anno
1684

Broadside.                                                                                                        CKB

Decree against "Fressen und Sauffen" at weddings, christenings, and other
gatherings.

2189 Eid | Und | OBLIGATION | der Prediger im Hertzogthum | Schleßwig-
Holstein | [double rule] | Schleßwig/ | Gedruckt bey sel. Johann Hol-
weins Erben. [1684?]

4to.  )(⁴.                                                                                                        CKB

Another edition without place or publisher, A⁴.

2190 Europäische Relation. [Altona], 1684.

                                                                                                                 *

Nr. 1 (1 January 1684)-22 (14 March 1684), formerly in Marienstift-Gymnasium,
Stettin. *Cf.* G. Kowalewski in *Zschr. f. Bücherfreunde* N.F. V/2 (1914), 364 ff.

2190A [GENSCH VON BREITENAU, CHRISTOPH]

Nachricht/ | Von Jhrer Königlichen Majestät | zu Dennemarck/ Nor-
wegen/ &c. &c. | Wider | Deß Herrn Herzogen zu Schleßwig-Holstein- |
Gottorff/ &c. &c. Fürstl. Durchl. | Annoch habenden rechtmässigen
Beschwerden | und Ansprüchen. | Jm Jahr 1684.

4to. 86, [2] pp.; A-L⁴ (L4 blank).                                                                                CKB

Pp. 53 ff., "Anhang." Two other editions published 1683 (No. 2141).

2191 Gründliche und Nähere | Nachricht | Der zwischen | Sᵉ. Königl. Maje-
stät | zu Deñemarck/ Norwegen/ | Und | Sᵉ. Hochfürstl. Durchl. | zu
Schleßwig/ Holstein/ | Gottorp. | Obschwebenden Jrrungen. | [orna-
ment] | Gedruckt im Jahr 1684

4to. A-F⁴ G² (G2 blank).                                    KIEL UL; CKB

Place of publication uncertain. Another edition: π1, A-H⁴, J1.

2192  HAMERICH, HENRICH

Klag-und Ehren-Rede/ | so | Bei Christlicher Leich-Bestatung | Des
weiland Hoch-Ehrwürdigen/ Hoch-Edlen | und Hochgelehrten | Herren
CHRISTIANI | von Stökken/ | . . . | H. Hamerich/ | S.R.R. | [rule] |
Glückstadt/ gedruckt durch Reinhard Janßen/ 1684.

4to. a-c⁴ d².                                                        CKB

Printed with Cai Arend, *Drey schöne Amaranten*, 1685 (No. 2213), as catchword
on last page of Arend's work indicates. CKB's copy of the double work is
unseparated.

2193  HOYER, ANDREAS

(Predigt über Georg Reichen). Copenhagen, 1684.

4to.                                                                    ✱

*Thott* V/2, 576.

2194  KINGO, THOMAS

D. Thomas Kingos | Fiorten | Morgen-oc | Aften-Sange | [ornamental
rule] | Vierzehen Geistreiche | Gesänge/ | Oder | Morgen und Abend- |
Opffer/ Deß Edlen und Hochwürdigen Bischofs | Hn. D. Thomas
Kingos/ | Superintendent des Stifts Fühnen. | Auf Anregung und viel-
fältiges Begehren hoher und | Gott-liebender Seelen auß dem Dähn-
ischen | übergesetzet von | Friederich Brandt/ | Pastorn in Nieköping
und Probsten des Süder- | Theils Falstern. | [rule] | Zukauf bey Johan
Just Erythropilum Bibl [1684]

8vo. [4], 163, [1] pp.; a⁸ b², A-J⁸ K².                    KAREN BRAHE

Title printed in red and black. Leaf A2 incorrectly signed B2. Approbatio on a1v
dated 2 Sept. 1684 (and signed by Joh. Lassenius). Latin poems to Brandt by Kingo,
Christian Kortholt, D. G. Morhof, Nicolaus Brandt, A. C. Kragh, Claudius Heicke,
Simon Petræus (Aarhus), Abraham Solomon, and others, p. 1 ff. Latin address to
the reader, pp. 7-13. Additional Latin poems by Hermann Erdmann, Christopher
Balzlou and Jacob Bircherod, pp. 14-15. Brandt's Latin preface to reader dated 11
Oct. 1684, p. 16. Danish facing German text, pp. 18-19 ff.

2195  KORTHOLT, CHRISTIAN

Christian Kortholten/ | Der H. Schrifft D. und bey | der Kielischen
Universitet Pro- | fess. Primar. | Theologische | Zu Befoderung der
Gottsee- | ligkeit angesehene | Tractätlein. | [ornament: leaves and

flowers] | Kiel/ | Gedruckt und verlegt durch Joachim Reumann/ |
Acad. Buchdr. 1684

8vo. [16], 543, [1] pp.; a⁸, A-Ll⁸.                                    CKB

Exact reprint of 1679 edition (No. 1967). Also republished in Kiel in 1704.

2195A KORTHOLT, CHRISTIAN
Historia des Lebens-Lauffs Jesu Christi. I-II. Theil. Kiel, 1684.

                                                                        *

N. C. N. Lassen, *Fortegnelse over Aarhuus Cathedralskoles Bibliothek*, IV, (1858),
p. 52.

2196 [KORTHOLT, CHRISTIAN]

Kurtzer Unterricht von geistlichen Versuchungen und Anfechtungen,
absonderlich böser lästerlichen Gedancken. 1684.

8vo.                                                                    *

*Moller* III, 375.

2198 LASSENIUS, JOHANNES

Beseüffzete Nichtigkeit | Alß | Die Ehren-Gebeine | Der Weiland Hoch-
wolgebornen Frauen | Frauen | Margaretha Catharina | Jhr. Excellentz |
Des Hochwolgebornen Herrn | Herrn | Michael Viben/ | . . . | JO-
HANNE LASSENIO. | Der H. Schrifft Doctore, Prof. P. Ordin. Collegii
Consistorial. Assessore | und gedachter Kirchen Pastore. | [rule] |
Copenhagen/ Gedruckt bey Jhr. K. M. und Univ. Buchdr. Joh. Phil.
Bockenhoffer/ 1684.

4to. [8], 200 pp.; ):(⁴, A-Bb⁴; 2 plates.                              CKB

On pp. 169-178, Latin "Programmus" by Christian Noldius; on pp. 181-188, German poems by N. L. Eßmarch and Friederich Weigbers; on p. 189 ff. letters ascribed
to Paulinus, Bishop of Nola, and to St. Jerome. Engraved initials on title-page. Engravings in text.

2199 MARTINI, BENEDICT

Der von Gott ewig wolbelohnte Lehrer, oder Leichpredigt über D.
Sebast. Niemann, . . . Schleswig, 1684.

Folio.                                                                  *

*Moller* I, 383.

2201 NEGOTIA DOME- | STICA. | Daß ist/ | Gründliche Vberwei- | sung/ |
Daß die zwischen Jhre Königl. Maytt. in Denne- | marcken/ und die zu
Schleßwig Holstein Got- | torp Regierende Hoch-Fürstl. Durchl. | jetzt

schwebende Mißhelligkeiten keines weges | vor den Unions-Außträgen/ unter be- | nennung der Negotiorum do- | mesticorum können gezo- | gen werden. | Auff gnädigstem Befehl zum Druck ge- | geben. | [ornamental rule] | Anno 1684.

4to. 16 pp.; A-B⁴ (16 x 10.7 cm).                                    CKB

Place of publication uncertain. Another edition: same title, 16 pp., A-B⁴ (16.1 x 10.4 cm).

2202    Ein | Neu Tractat/ | Von | Schifbrüchigen Gütern | Auff Dänisch Wrack genandt/ | Aus | Alten Dänischen Loubüchern | zusammen getragen/ und in rechte | Ordnung gebracht | durch | Erich Krabben. | [rule] | Kopenhagen/ | Gedruckt durch Conrad Hartwig Neuhoff [1684]

4to. [2] pp., pp. 105-140; π1, O-R⁴ S².                              CKB

Offprint of pp. 103-140 of *Kong* | *VALDEMARS* | *Den Andens* | *Jysk Low-Bog/* | *udsat paa Tysk* | *aff* | *Herr Erick Krabbe* | *Aar 1557.* | *Oc nu efter et 127. Aars forløb befodret* | *til Trycken* | *aff* | *Peder Hansen Resen:* | *Med en Fortale* | *om* | *bemeldte Jydske Lowbog.* | *[rule]* | *Kiøbenhafn/ Tryckt hos Conrad Hartwig Neuhof/* | *Aar 1684;* 4to; [68], 140 pp.; π², a² b-h⁴ i², A-R⁴ S², 1 plate, 4 folding plates; German text on A1 through S2.

2203    Nordischer [Merkur]. [Altona], 1684.

8vo.                                                                       *

Numbers 1 (1 Jan.) through 18 (4 March) formerly in Marienstift-Gymnasium, Stettin. *Cf.* G. Kowalewski in *Zschr. f. Bücherfreunde* N.F. V/2 (1914), 356.

2204    NOTHELFFER, NICOLAUS

Ruhm-und Klag-Rede/ | . . . | Hn. Friedrich Hanns | Gloxin/ | . . . | Durch | M. NICOLAUS Nothelffern/ | Königl. Dennemarckischen Schloß-Predigern. | [rule] | Glückstadt/ gedruckt durch Reinhard Janßen/ | Jm 1684sten Jahre

4to. [2], 61, [1] pp.; π1, A-H⁴.                                    KIEL UL

H4 lacking.

2205    RIES, JOHANNES

Die beglückte Fischerey | Welche scherzend | An dem Hochzeitlichen Freuden-Fest | . . . | Hr. Friderich Boysen/ | . . . | Jfr. Marina Fischers | . . . 28. Augusti 1684 . . . | . . . | Johannes Ries. | [ornamental rule] | KOPENHAGEN/ | Gedruckt bey Christian Wering Acad. Buchdrucker.

4to. χ².                                                              CKB

2206    RÖTSCHER, JOHANNES VOLCMAR

Gnädige Fürsorge Gottes | . . . | Fr. Dorotheen | . . . | Hn. BENEDICTI

MARTINI, | . . . | . . . von | M. Johanne Volcmaro Rötschern/ Archid. | . . . | [rule] | Schleßwig/ gedruckt bey sehl. Johañ Holweins Erben. [1684]

4to. A-H⁴.                                                           CKB

Title within ornamental frame. H4 lacking.

2207  [STÖCKEN, CHRISTIAN VON *and* CHRISTIAN KORTHOLT]

Bedencken | Zwener vornehmer | THEOLOGORUM | Uber | Die/ denen Schleßwigschen Landständen/ Bedien- | ten/ Unterthanen und Eingesessenen/ ange- | mutete Eidesleistung [1684]

4to. A-B⁴.                                                           CKB

2208  [STÖCKEN, CHRISTIAN VON]

Die vernünftige lautere Milch des Heiligen Catechismi. Glückstadt, 1684.

12mo.                                                                 *

*Moller* I, 659. *Bibl. Muhliana*, 1735, p. 59 and *Bibl. Mejeriana*, 1701, 12mo Nr. 488, both list a "Glückstädtischer Catechismus," 1684. *Bibl. Muhliana*, p. 59, also ascribes a *Vernüftige lautere Lehre des Heiligen Catechismi*, Glückstadt, 1684, to Severinus Walther Schlüter. All entries presumably refer to Glückstadt, 1684, edition of Stöcken's catechism.

2209  STÖCKEN, CHRISTIAN VON

Die zweite Heiraht/ | Abrahams des Geehrten | . . . | Hn. CAJUS Arend/ | . . . | Fr. Magdalenen Guden/ | Gebohrnen von Schönfeldin/ | . . . | Durch | Christian von Stökken/ | . . . | Glükstadt/ gedruckt durch Reinhard Janßen/ 1684.

4to. 16 pp.; A-B⁴.                                                   CKB

2210  STORNING, HINRICH

Eigentlicher Verstandt der Worte Christi vom Heiligen Abendmahle, der lieben Einfalt sonnenklar dargethan. Plön, 1684.

12mo.                                                                 *

*Moller* I, 666; *Bibl. Kielmans-Egg.*, II, 1190; *Bibl. Muhliana*, 1735, p. 150; *Cat. Rasmus*, 1754, p. 53.

2210A  [ULCKEN, ANDREAS]

Abgenötigte | Beantwortung | Der | Schrifft/ | welche unter der | RVBRIC | Nachricht | Von Jhrer Königl. Maytt. zu Denne- | marck, Norwegen/ | wieder | Des Herrn Hertzogen zu Schleßwig Hollstein |

Gottorp | Fürstl. Durchl. | Annoch habenden Rechtmäßigen Be-
schwerden | und Ansprüchen. | Ans Licht gegeben/ | Uff gnädigstem
Befehl/ Dero zu Schleswig Hollstein | Gottorp Regierenden Hochfürstl.
Durchl. abgefasset/ | und zum Druck befordert. | Jm Jahr 1684.

4to. [2], 92, [36] pp.; π1, A-L⁴ M⁴ (−M4), a-d⁴ e², χ1.                CKB; Drült

Leaves a1 ff. contain "Beylagen." Published in Kiel.


## 1685


2211   Vom 1 Januarij. Fol: I | Altonaische RELATION. | No. I [woodcut:
       crowned female figure on lion] 1685

8vo. 8 pp.                                                                  SRL

Caption title. SRL has also Nr. 5 (pp. 33-40) 15 Jan.; 7 (pp. 49-56) 22 Jan.; 11 (pp.
81-88) 5 Feb.; 12 (89-96) 9 Feb.; 26 (201-208) 30 March; 29 (225-234) 9 April; 63
(497-504) 6 August; 65 (513-520) 13 August; 67 (529-536) 20 August; 70 (553-560)
31 August; 72 (569-576) 7 Sept.; 74 (585-592) 14 Sept.; 76 (601-608) 21 Sept.; 77
(609-616) 24 Sept.; 79 (625-632) 1 October; 82 (649-656) 12 Oct.; 86 (681-688) 26
Oct.; 94 (745-752) 23 Nov.


2212   Anmerckungen/ | über die/ | An Seiten Jhr. Fürstl. Durchl. | H. Hertzog
       Christian Albrecht | zu Schleßwig Holstein/ | Unlängst in Druck
       gekommene unbegründete | Beantwortung | Der | Nachricht/ | Welche/
       für etlicher Zeit/ wegen Jhr. Königl. | Maytt. zu Dennemarck/ Nor-
       wegen &c. wieder hochge- | dachte Jhre Fürstl. Durchl. habender Be-
       schwerden | und Ansprüche publiciret | worden. | Auff Königl. Aller-
       gnädigsten Befehl. | [rule] | Jm Jahr 1685

4to. 101, [3] pp.; A-N⁴ (N4 blank).                                          CKB


2213   AREND, CAI

Drey schöne Amaranten | Oder | Liebes-und Gedächtnuß-Blümlein/ |
Mit welchen zum unverwelcklichem Angedenken | Des weiland Hoch-
WolEhrwürdigen/ HochEdlen | und Hochgelahrten Herren/ | Herrn
Christian von Stökken/ | . . . | CAJUS AREND/ Königl: Probst im
Süder- | Ditmarschen und Pastor zu Meldorff. | [rule] | Glückstadt/
gedruckt durch Reinhard Janßen/ | Jm 1685sten Jahr.

4to. [4], 52 pp.; [A]², B-G⁴ H².                                             CKB

Appended (and printed with above item, as catchword indicates) H. Hamerich,
*Klag-und Ehren-Rede/* | . . . | *Herren Christiani* | *von Stökken/* | . . . 1684. (No.
2192). See Plate VII.

2215  BORNHOLT, MATTHIAS

(Leichpredigt über Wolber Hudemann, geb. Alardus,† 1678, 29 Maj)
Glückstadt: R. Janßen, 1685

4to. 40 pp.                                                                                          *

H. Bruhn, *Jb. Ver. Dith. Landeskunde* V (1925), 95; *Stolberg* IV/2, 813.

2216  BORNHOLT, MATTHIAS

(Leichpredigt über M. Joh. Hudemann, Königl. Superintendenten in
Holstein, aus Gen. XXXII. 10.). Glückstadt: R. Janssen, 1685.

4to. 40 pp.                                                                                          *

*Moller* I, 59; *Stolberg* II, 384.

2217  BRANDT, FRIEDRICH

(Leichrede über Margaretha Maria Schwartzinn, Könl. Hofmeisterinn).
Copenhagen, 1685.

Folio.                                                                                              *

*Moller* I, 65.

2218  [CLAUSSØN, PETER]

TOPOGRAPHIA NORWEGIÆ. | Das ist | Eigentliche Beschreibung |
des | Königreichs | Norwegen/ | Darinnen von desselben natürlicher
Gelegenheit/ | Grösse und Gräntzen/ richtiger Abtheilung und ent-
halte- | nen Landschafften/ Aemptern/ Gebieten und Vogteyen/ |
Pfarren/ Städten/ Schlössern/ Lad-und Zoll-Städ- | ten/ Gebirgen/
Wälden/ Thälen/ Bergwercken/ Jagd und | Weidewerck/ Vogelfang/
und andern Bequemligkeiten | und Nützungen: Jmgleichen von den
Jnsulen/ Sunden/ | Meerströmen/ Meerhafen/ frischen Seen/ Flüssen
und | reichen Fischereyen/ sampt denen von alters her zuge- | hörigen
Landen/ Jsland/ Feröe/ Grönland: Wie auch | von der Jnwohner Her-
kunfft/ Natur/ Sitten/ Gewohn- | heiten/ Religion/ Gerichten/ und
gehabten Regenten | und Königen eigentlicher und ausführlicher Be- |
richt zu finden ist. | Aus dem Dänischen ins Teutsch übersetzet/ | ver-
bessert und vermehret. | von | C.S.K.H.D. | [rule] | Gedruckt im Jahr
1685.

4to. [12], 173, [11] pp.; )(⁴, b², A-Z⁴.                                      CKB; (BM)

Dedication signed by translator, Christoph Steinkuhl.

2219  DENMARK. *Laws, statutes, etc.*

Der Königl. Majest. zu Dänne- | marck Norwegen/ in dero Hertzog- |

thum Schleßwig. | Anno 1685. auf den 17 Junii | Verordnete | Fast- Buß-
und Bet-Tags | Texte. | Mit den Collecten Gebet und | Gesängen/ | So
alsdann zugebrauchen seyn. | [royal monogram of Christian V] | Schleß-
wig/ gedruckt bey sehl. Johann | Holweins Erben.

8vo. χ⁸.                                                                                    CKB

CKB copy bound with Josua Schwartz, *Sciagraphia Concionis* | . . . | *Anno 1685.*
*die 17 Junii* | . . . | *SLESWIGÆ,* | . . . .

2220   DENMARK. *Laws, statutes, etc.*

Verordnung/ | Wegen | Des gestempelten Papiers/ | Publiciret Anno
1667. | [double rule] | Gedruckt in der Königl. Stadt Schleßwig/ | Anno
1685.

4to. χ⁴.                                                                                   KIEL UL

2221   DENMARK. *Laws, statutes, etc.*

WJR Christian der Fünffte/ von | . . . | . . . Glückstadt den 2ten April.
Anno 1685

Broadside.                                                                                  CNA

Decree ordering mourning at the death of the queen-mother, Sophia Amalia.

2221A  DENMARK. *Laws, statutes, etc.*

Wir Christian der Fünffte/ | von GOttes Gnaden/ König zu Dänne-
marck/ | . . . | . . . Gottorff den 12 Maii | Anno 1685.

Broadside.                                                                                  CKB

Decree regarding attendance at the "Ober-Ampt-Gericht" at Gottorff Castle 10 June.

2222   DENMARK. *Laws, statutes, etc.*

WJR Christian der Fünffte/ von | . . . | . . . Glückstadt/ den 25. | Maij,
Anno 1685.

Broadside.                                                                                  CNA

Decree ordering a day of prayer 17 June.

2223   DENMARK. *Laws, statutes, etc.*

WJR Christian der Fünffte/ von | . . . | . . . Glückstadt . . . | . . . 14ten
Septembris, Anno 1685

Broadside.                                                                                  CNA

Decree ordering thanksgiving 27 September for a victory over the Turks.

2224　Denmark. *Laws, statutes, etc.*

WJR Christian der Fünffte/ von | . . . | . . . Glückstadt . . . 19ten |
Octobris, Anno 1685.

Broadside.                                                                                                   CNA

Decree regarding the importation of certain coins.

2225　F. D. M. D.

Hochzeitsgedicht über Kaspar March und M. Oelgard Fuchs. Kiel:
Joachim Reumann, 1685.

                                                                                                           *

Formerly in Kiel UL (LmC 12-10).

2226　Hamerich, Henrich

Abdankung/ | Oder | Schuldige Klag-und Ehren-Rede. | . . . | Herrn
ANDREÆ | Thomsen/ | . . . | von | HENRICO Hamerich/ | Sch.
Rendesb. Rect. | [double rule] | SCHLESWJG/ | Gedrukt bei sehl.
Johann Holweins Erben. [1685]

4to. [2], 26 pp.; A-C⁴ D².                                                                                  CKB

2227　Holst, Johannes

Rechter Witwen | Tugend-Cron | Und | Gnaden-Lohn/ | . . . | Fr:
Luciæ Meinkin/ | . . . | Durch | JOHANNEM Holsten/ | Prediger des
göttlichen Wortes daselbsten. | [rule] | Schleßwig/ gedruckt bey Sel.
Johann Holweins Erben. [1685]

4to. [2], 42 pp.; A-E⁴ F².                                                                                  CKB

2228　Jhre Königl. Mayest. | Sophiæ Amaliæ/ | . . . | Leich-Procession, | So |
Den 26. Martii Anno 1685. geschehen.

4to. χ².                                                                                                    CKB

Presumably an offprint.

2229　Kingo, Thomas

Vierzehen | Geistreiche Gesänge/ | Oder | Morgen- | Und | Abend-
Opffer/ | Deß | Edlen und Hochwürdigen Bischoffs/ | Herrn | D.
Thomas Kingos/ | Superintendenten deß | Stiffts Fühnen. | Auff An-
regung und vielfältiges | Begehren hoher und Gott-liebender | Seelen auß
dem Dähnischen | übergesetzt | Von | Friederich Brandt/ | Pastorn in
Niecöping/ und | Probsten deß Süder- | theils Falstern. | [ornament] |
Coppenhagen/ | Bey Daniel Paulli seel. Wittib. | Gedruckt zu Franck-
furt/ | Bey Johann Georg Drullmann/ | Jm Jahr 1685

12mo. [14], 81, [1] pp.; a⁶ b1, A-C¹² D⁶ (−D6).                                    CKB

Title printed in red and black. On a1v, "Approbatio" in verse, dtd. "Haffniæ d. 2. Sept. 1684" and signed by Joh. Lassenius. Dedication (in Latin) to King Christian and Queen Charlotta Amalia. On leaves a3, a4, and b1, verse by several hands, in Latin. Contains 14 hymns, with musical notation. Strictly speaking not a German imprint of Denmark.

2230    Kurtze Information | in Sachen/ zwischen | Jhr. Königl. Maytt. | zu Dennemarck/ Norwegen &c. | Einen/ | H. Hertzog Christian Albrecht | zu Schleßwig/ Holstein &c. | Andern | und dem löblichen Dom-Capitul | des Stiffts Lübeck/ | Dritten Theils. | Die Coadjutor-Wahl/ am besagtem Stiffte/ | betreffend. | Auff Königl. Allergnädigsten Befehl. | [rule] | Anno 1685

4to. 24 pp.; A-C⁴ D1.                                                              CKB

2231    Kurtzer | Unterricht/ | Von der | Frantzösischen | Sprache. | [vignette] | [rule] | Gedruckt bey K. M. und Univ. Buchd. | Johan Philip Bockenhof-fer. | Jm Jahr 1685.

12mo. 95, [1] pp.; A-D¹² (−D12).                                                   CKB

*Cat. lib. Reenberg,* 1736, p. 137, and *Cat. lib. Joh. Lassenii,* 1693, 8vo, Nr. 1579, list an edition of 1689.

2232    LASSENIUS, JOHANNES

Versüssete Bitterkeit | Im | Leben/ Lieben und Leiden | Angewiesen von dem Apostel I. Corinth. X. v. 13. | Und | Zu allgemeinem Trost in allerhand | Geistlichen und Leiblichen Anfechtungen | Als | Die Wei-land/ mit reiner GOttes-Furcht/ und Edler | Tugend-Begabte | Jungfer | Sophie Charlotte | Weigbers/ | . . . | von | JOHANNE LASSENIO, | Der H. Schrifft D: Prof: Publ: Ordin. Colleg. Consistorial: Assess: | und Past: daselbst. | [rule] | Copenhagen/ Gedruckt bey Jhr. K. M. und | Universit. Buchdr. Joh. Philip | Bockenhoffer/ im Jahr 1685.

4to. [8], 376 pp.; )(⁴, A-Aaa⁴; engraved preliminary title-page; 2 plates.        CKB

Engraved preliminary title: *Ehren Stein | Zum | Unsterbliche Gedächtnis | Der Weiland | Mit | Reiner Gottes-Furcht | und Edler Tugent becronte | Jungfer | Sophien Charlotten | Weigbers. | gewidmet | von | D Johan Lassenio.* Page numbers trimmed off after p. 344. Engraved initials on title-page. Engravings in text. On Aaa1 ff., German poems by J.C.W. and J. Dr.

2233    Der leidtragende Rosenstok | über den frühzeitigen/ doch säligen | Abschied | . . . | Herrn Kristians von | Stökken/ | . . . | Höchstpreis-würdigen Deutschgesinten Genossenschaft Mit- | Ertzschreinhalters/ unter dem Zunftnahmen | Des Andächtigen/ | u. a. m. | Jm Ertzschreine

höchstgedachter Genossenschaft | vorgestellet durch etliche Derselben |
Mitglieder. | [rule] | Glükstadt/ gedrukt durch Reinhard Janßen/ | Jm
1685sten Jahr.

4to. χ⁴. CKB

Verse by Filip von Zesen and others.

2234 MAJOR, JOHANN DANIEL

Hochzeit-frage, Ob zu heurathen . . . bey Vermählung D. Casp. Marchen
und Marg. Oelgart Fuchsinn. Kiel, 1685.

Folio. *

*OHM* II, 517. Formerly in Kiel UL (LmC 12-10).

2235 MAJOR, JOHANN DANIEL

Redendes Todten-Gebeine . . . Leichen Memoriæ Annæ Margaretæ Hen-
ningiæ, natalibus Mauritiæ. . . . Kiel, 1685.

Folio. *

*OHM* II, 517.

2236 MOLLER, JOHANNES

Thränen und Trost . . . bey dem . . . Abschiede Olai Mölleri 40. jährigen
Predigers zu S. Nicolai in Flensburg. . . . Schleswig, 1685.

4to. *

*OHM* I, 430-1.

2237 MONIGO, JOHANN HEINRICH VON

REVOCATION, | Oder | Vom Jrthum Päbstlicher Fin- | sternüß entsag-
ter und nunmehro durch Anregung | des Heiligen Geistes zur Luther-
ischen wahren Evangeli- | schen Religion und Glaubens-Licht/ bekehr-
ter | Ernstlicher | Wieder-Ruf/ | Von mir gestellet | Johann Heinrich
von Monigo/ | Aus der Heil. Röm. Reichs Käyserl. befreyeten Kauff
und | Handels-Stadt Augspurg gebürtig. | Da er sich von der Römisch-
Catholischen Evangeli- | schen in GOttes Wort und Augspurgischer
Confession verfasten | Lehre begeben/ auch zu Leipzig von der gantzen
Gemeine in der St. Thomas-Kirchen/ den 20. Sontag nach Trinitatis
verwichenen 1678sten | Jahres öffentlich dargestellet/ und mit inbrün-
stiger Hertzens-Andacht | oberwehnten Päbstl. Greuel/ in welchem er
von Kindheit an/ als | ein verirtes Schaff gestecket/ entsaget: Auch biß
an sein | seliges Ende beständig zu verharren | gedencket. | Jtzo aber zu
mehrer Anzeugung seiner Beständigkeit in der Evan- | gelischen Lehre/

in Truck gegeben dieses 1685ste Jahr. | [rule] | Kopenhagen/ Gedruckt bey Johann Jacob Bornheinrichen.

4to. A-B⁴.                                                              CKB

2238  MORHOF, DANIEL GEORG

(Auf Herrn Casp. Marchen und Marg. Oelgard Fuchs glückliche Vermählung). Kiel, [1685].

Folio.                                                                    *

*OHM* III, 474. Formerly in Kiel UL (LmC 12-11).

2239  [NORMAN, JOHANNES FRIEDRICH]

Kurtze/ doch warhafftige | Beschreibung | Der | Silber und anderer Bergwercke | in Norwegen/ so viel derselben An. 1649. | im Königreiche bekandt gewesen. | Durch einen Liebhaber der Bergwerck an Tag gebracht. | Anjetzo aber | Auff begehren wieder neu auffgelegt und mit allen denen | Gruben/ welche von selbiger Zeit an ferners | gefunden worden/ vermehret. | [royal monogram] | [rule] | Gedruckt bey Jhro Königl. Mayest. und Univers. Buchdrucker/ | Johann Philip Bockenhoffer/ Jm Jahr 1685

4to. A-B⁴.                                                              CUL

2240  PETERSEN, JOHANN WILHELM

Ein Christliches | Glaubens- | Bekäntniß/ | Aus dem unmittelbahrem Worte | Gottes hergenommen/ | und | Der Jugend zum besten auff- | gesetzt | Von | Johann Wilhelm Petersen/ | Hoff-Prediger/ und des Bischofftuhms | Lübeck Superintendens | [ornamental rule] | PLOEN/ | Druckts und verlegts Tobias Schmidt/ | im 1685sten Jahr.

8vo. 38, [2] pp.; A-B⁸, C⁴ (C4 blank).                                  HAB

2241  PETERSEN, JOHANN WILHELM *and* CHRISTIAN KORTHOLT

J. N. JESU! | Spruch-Cate- | chismus/ | Aus dem Catechismo des sel. Lutheri | in Fragen vorgestellet/ | Die mit den unmittelbahren Sprüchen | der heiligen Schrifft | beantwortet werden; | Auff gnädigsten Befehl | Des | Hochwürdigsten/ und Durchläuchtigsten | Fürsten/ und Herrn/ | Herrn August Friedrich/ | Erwehlten Bischoffs zu Lübeck/ Erben | zu Norwegen/ Hertzogen zu Schleßwig- | Hollstein/ &c. | Der Kirchen Gottes zum Besten herauß gegeben/ | Von | Johann Wilhelm Petersen/ Jhro Hochf. | Durchl. Beicht-Vater/ Hoff-Prediger/ | und des Stiffts Lübeck Superintend. | Samt einer Vorrede | Hn: Christiani Kortholt/ der H. Schrifft | D. und Prof. Primar. auff der Universität |

KJEL | [rule] | Plöen/ Gedruckt und verlegt durch Tobias Schmidt/ | Jm Jahr Christi 1685

8vo. [72], 176, 63, [1] pp.; )o( − 4)o($^8$, 5)o($^4$, A-L$^8$, a-d$^8$.                    HAB

On a1r, separate title: *Ein | Kleiner Auszug | Aus | dem großen | Catechismo/ Für | Der Jugend.* Cat. bibl. Konigsmanni, 1729, p. 105 lists an edition: Ploen, 1691, 12mo. Cf. *Jöcher-Rotermund, V*, 1994.

2242  PRIVILEGIEN | und | Freyheiten/ | So | Jhre Königl. Maj. zu Denne- | marck/ Norwegen/ | allen frembden/ so wohl von der Evangelischen/ | alß Refor- | mirten Religion, welche sich in dero Reichen häuslich niederlassen/ | und den jenigen/ so in Copenhagen Wüste Plätze be- bawen las- | sen/ allergnädigst ertheilet/ Sampt einer Anord- | nung wegen Hauß-Häur und bebawung | der Wüsten Plätze | Hafniæ die 11. April Anno 1685.

4to. χ$^2$.                                                                       CKB; CUL

Caption title.

2242A RACHEL, SAMUEL

Ausführlich in der | Theologie und denen Rechten | Wohl-begründetes | Bedencken/ | über zwo | Haupt-Fragen/ | I. | Ob die gewaltsame Occu- pirung deß Hertzog- | thums Schleßwig/ welche den 30. May Anno 1684. | vorgenommen/ Jure belli, oder sonsten/ könne | justificiret und behauptet werden? | II. | Was von der Eydesleistung/ so Dero zu Schleß- | wig-Holstein Regierenden Hoch-Fürstl. Durchl. Be- | dienten und Unterthanen/ nach beschehener | Occupation daselbst/ abgenöthi- get/ | zu halten sey? | Auf Gnädigsten Befehl zum Druck | gegeben | Anno 1685.

4to. [2], 70 pp.; A-J$^4$.                                                           CKB

Kiel UL lists Samuel Rachel as author. Place of publication uncertain.

2243  RECKEL, SIMON

Grosse Freudigkeit im Tode/ | . . . | BRODERO BOISEN, | J.U.D. Wollverdient-gewesenen Burgermeistern der | Stadt Husum/ | ... | ... 21 Aprilis, Anno 1685 . . . | . . . | Außgefertiget von | SIMONE RECHELIO, | Der Christl. Gemeine daselbst dienendem | Haupt- Pastore | [ornament] | SCHLESWJG/ | Gedruckt bey Sel. Johann Hol- weins Erben.

Folio. [6], 34 pp.; A-E$^4$.                                                         CKB

2244  RECKEL, SIMON

Der von GOTT erlassener | und willig-gefolgter Diener JEsu/ | . . . |

Herrn M. MARTINI | HÖLMERS, | . . . [von] | SIMON RECHE-
LIUS, | . . . | SCHLESWIG/ | Gedruckt bey sel. Johann Holweins
Erben. [1685]

Folio. [8], 36 pp.; A-C⁴, [D]⁴, E-G². CUL

CUL copy lacks D1 and D4. D2-3 incorrectly paginated. On pp. 33-36, verse by
several hands.

2245 [SPERLING, OTTO]

Des Woll-Ehrwürdigen und Hochgelahr- | ten Herrn/ | Hrn. M.
PETRI | HESSELII. | Sel. Pastoris zum Pesthoff | Lebens-Lauff/ | . . . |
Kurtz gefasset und auffgesetzet zum | Gedächtniß | von | seinem guten
Freunde. [1685]

4to. 24 pp.; A-C⁴. CKB

Written by Otto Sperling and published in Altona 1685, according to *Moller* II, 854.

2246 STÖCKEN, HINRICH VON

Heilige Todten-Wunder/ | . . . | ANDREAS Thomsen/ | . . . von |
Hinrich von Stökken/ Designirten | Königl. Probsten und Haupt-
Pastoren daselbst [i.e., Rendsburg] | . . . | Schleßwig/ gedrukt bei sehl.
Johann Holweins Erben A. 1685

4to. [4], 35, [1] pp.; A-E⁴. CKB

2247 STÖCKEN, HINRICH VON *and* FRIEDRICH GERHARD VON STÖCKEN

Söhn-und Sehnliche Trähnen | . . . | Herrn Christian von | Stökken/ |
. . . | Von | Dessen nachgelassenen beiden ältesten Söhnen. | [rule] |
Glükkstadt/ gedrukkt durch Reinhard Janßen. [1685]

4to. χ⁴. CKB

Verse.

2248 Der verblühte | und | Annoch blühende | Christen-Stokk/ | . . . | Herr
Christian von | Stökken/ D. | . . . | Aus schuldigster Condolenz ent-
worffen | Von | Nachgesezzten Feunden [sic]. | [rule] | Glükkstadt/
gedrukkt durch Reinhard Janßen. [1685]

4to. χ⁴. CKB

2249 Die von | Jhrer Königlichen Mayt. | zu Dennemarck/ Norwegen/ |
Denen | Von der Reformirten Religion | allergnädigst ertheilte | PRIVI-
LEGIEN | de dato Kopenhagen den 3 Januarii Anno 1685. | [mono-

gram] | [rule] | Gedruckt bey Jh. Kön. Maytt. und Univ. Buchdrucker/ |
Johan Philip Bockenhoffer.

4to. $\chi^2$.                                                                                                     CKB

2250  WASMUTH, MATTHIAS

Beste Mittel zur Bekehrung der Juden; das ist: Kurtzer und klarer
Beweiß aus der Heiligen Schrift A. T., I. von dem wahren Dreyeinigen
Gotte, II. von dem einigen wahren Messia, Jesu Christo, wie daß derselbe,
auch nach dem Alten Testamente, I. Gott und Mensch seyn müsse, 2.
ein Erlöser und Heiland des Menschlichen Geschlechtes, und 3. solches
durch Leiden und Sterben vor der Welt Sünde; 4. daß die von Gott
bestimmte Zeit solches wahren Messiæ schon mehr als dreymahl sey
verflossen: samt einem Anhange von der in der Schrift vorher verkun-
digte, und noch bevorstehenden, grossen Bekehrung der Juden zur
letzten Zeit. Kiel, 1685.

4to.                                                                                                                *

*Moller* III, 640; *Thott* I/2, 246; *Bibl. Kielmans-Egg.*, I, 545. Formerly in Preussische
Staatsbibliothek. Republished 1694 in Frankfurt & Leipzig.

2251  WEDDERKOPF, GABRIEL

Der Gläubigen siegreiche-Osteren/ | . . . | Fr. ANNA MAR- | GA-
RETHA Hennings/ | gebohrne Mauritzin. | . . . | durch | M. Gabrielem
Wedderkopf, | Predigern an S. Nicolai im Kiel. | [rule] | KJEL/
Gedruckt bey Joachim Reumann/ Acad. Buchdr. | Anno 1685

4to. [8], 83, [1] pp.; )( 4, A-K4 L2.                                                   CKB

2252  WERNER, CHRISTIAN

Jhrer Königl. Mayt. | Zu | Dennemarck/ Norwegen | Factoren | Christian
Werners | Wohlgemeinter Vortrag | An | Alle Liebhabere | der gemeinen
Wohlfarth. | [rule] | Copenhagen/ | Gedruckt bey Jh. Königl. Mayt. und
Univers. Buchdr. | Johan Philip Bockenhoffer/ Jm Jahr 1685.

Folio. $\chi^2$.                                                                                              CKB

2253  WITTE, JOHANNES

Trifolium sacrum, oder drey erbauliche Predigten . . . in der Kirche zum
Hagen gehalten: Samt Wolfg. Phil. Leiken, Past. zu St. Cath. am
Gillenbeke, Leichpredigt über den Autorem auß 2. Tim. IV, 18 und
seinem Lebenslauf. Ploen, 1685

4to.                                                                                                                *

*Moller* II, 1007; I, 338; *Bibl. Kielmans-Egg.*, III, 613.

# 1686

2254 Vom 25. Januarij Fol. 49 | Altonaische RELATION. | Nr. 7 [woodcut: crowned female figure on lion] 1686

8vo. Pp. 49-56.                                                          SRL

Caption title. SRL has also Nr. 9 (pp. 65-72) 1 Febr.; 15 (113-120) 22 Febr.; 17 (129-136) 1 March; 19 (145-152) 8 March; 21 (161-168) 15 March; 23 (177-184) 22 March; 25 (193-200) 29 March; 26 (201-208) 1 April; 39 (236-212) 20 May; 41 ("121", 322, "223", 324-328) 31 May; 43 (337-343, "244") 7 June; 47 (369-376) 21 June; 49 (385-392) 28 June; 53 (417-424) 12 July; 60 (473-480) 5 August; 63 (497-504) 16 Aug.; 84 (665-672) 22 Nov.; 86 (681-688) 29 Nov. Publication continued in 1687.

2255 [BAGGER, HANS]

Gebet und Texte/ | Welche Gott zu Ehren/ | An dem Extraordinaire allgemeinen | Fast- und Bet-Tag/ | Seiner Königl. Mayst. Unsers Allergnädig- | sten Erb-Königs und Herrn/ | Christian des Fünfften/ | Aller-christlöblichsten Befehl nach/ in Dän- | nemarck und Norwegen Jährlich/ am vierten | Freytag nach Ostern/ in diesem | Jahr aber | Jn Dännemarck den 7. May. | Jn Norwegen den 15. Junii. | Hochfeyerlich sollen gebrauchet/ und erklä- | ret werden. | Anno [crown] 1686. | Cum gratia & privilegio Ser. Reg. Majest. | [rule] | Copenhagen/ Gedruckt bey J. Phil. Bockenhoffer/ | Königl. Mayest. und Universit. Buchdrucker.

8vo. A⁸ B².                                                              CKB

2256 BEECK, GEORG *and* P. A. BURCHARD

(Trauergedichte über Detlev Ruhe). Schleswig: Joh. Holweins Erben, 1686.

Folio. χ².                                                                *

Formerly in Kiel UL (LmC 15-129).

2257 BURCHARD, GEORG HINRICH

Derer Boten Gottes/ | Das ist: | Treuer Lehrer und Prediger/ Ehre und Lehre/ | Aus den Worten des Propheten Malachiæam 2 cap. v. 5/6/7. | Bey Volckreicher Leichbestätigung | Des weiland Hoch-Woll-Ehrwürdi- | gen/ Hoch- | Achtbahren und Hoch-Wollgelahrten Herrn/ | Hn. BENEDICTI MARTINI, | ... | Vorgestellet | Von | M. GEORG. HENR. BURCHARDO. | [rule] | SCHLESWJG/ | Gedruckt bey Johann Holweins Erben/ 1686.

4to. [4], 48 pp.; π², A-F⁴.                                               CKB

Title within ornamental woodcut border.

2258 CLAUSSEN, CHRISTIAN ALBRECHT

(Trauergedicht über Anna Weidenkopf, geb. Brockes). Schleswig: Joh. Holweins Erben, (1686).

Broadside.                                                                    *

Formerly in Kiel UL (LmC 18-57).

2259 CONTINUATION | Des unlängst im Druck herauß gegebenen | War-hafften | Berichts/ | Waß sich in dem Hamburgischen | Wesen zuge-tragen/ vom 5 biß den 14 Septemb. | Anno 1686. als an welchem Tage Jhre Königl. | Mayestät dero Armee wiederumb aus | einander/ und in ihre vorige Qvar- | tier gehen lassen. | [rule] | Kopenhagen/ Gedruckt bey Jh. Königl. Maj. und Univ. | Buchdrucker Johan Philipp Bockenhoffer.

4to. χ⁴.                                                                    CKB

Another edition, A⁴; another edition, A-B⁴; another edition, A⁴ B².

2260 DENMARK. *Laws, statutes, etc.*

Wir Christian der Fünffte/ | von GOttes Gnaden/ König zu Dänne-marck/ | ... | ... Gottorff den 3 Februarii Anno 1686.

Broadside.                                                                    CKB

Decree regarding the payment of postage and the treatment of "verdächtige Pacquetten."

2261 DENMARK. *Laws, statutes, etc.*

WJR Christian der Fünfte/ von Got- | tes Gnaden/ ... | ... | ... Copenhagen den 16. Martii Anno 1686

Broadside.                                                                    CNA

Decree levying an extraordinary tax on land.

2262 DENMARK. *Laws, statutes, etc.*

WJR Christian der Fünffte/ von | ... | ... Glückstadt/ den 8ten Aprilis, Anno 1686.

Broadside.                                                                    CNA

Decree ordering a day of prayer 7 May.

2263 DENMARK. *Laws, statutes, etc.*

WJR Christian der Fünffte/ von | ... | ... Glückstadt/ den 5. Sept. 1686

Broadside.                                                                    CNA

Decree ordering a day of thanksgiving 12 September, on occasion of a victory over the Turks in Hungary.

2264   DENMARK. *Laws, statutes, etc.*

Wir Christian der Fünffte/ | … | … 24. Septembris, Anno 1686.

Broadside.                                                              KIEL UL

Decree regarding grain to be provided the army.

2265   DENMARK. *Laws, statutes, etc.*

Wir Christian der Fünffte/ | … | … Gottorff/ den 20. Novemb. Anno 1686

Broadside.                                                              CNA

Decree calling a meeting of the courts at Gottorff 30 March 1687.

2265A  Endliche | DECLARATION | So | Jhr. Königl. Majestät zu | Denne-marck/ Norwegen/ etc. | Denen | Chur-Brandenburgischen/ Fürst- | lichen Braunschweig-Lüneburgischen und | Hessen-Casselschen Minis-tris, bey dero Aufbruch auß | Gottorff/ der Hamburgischen Jrrungen hal- | ben/ unter dero Hand und Siegel | zustellen lassen. | Mit beyge-fügten zwey Hamburgischen Schrei- | ben/ worauff sich höchstged. Jhr. Königl. Majestät | Declaration beziehet/ | De datis den 6 und 16 Octo-bris 1686 | Lit. A & B.

4to. )(⁴.                                                               CKB

Another edition: )(⁴, new setting with different types; another edition, with short-ened title (all words after "zustellen lassen" deleted), and without the Hamburg letter. χ².

2266   Fleiss der Gottseligkeit, bestehend in vier Theilen heiliger Andachten. Plön, 1686.

12mo.                                                                    *

*Thott* I/2, 666; *Cat. lib. Chr. Brämer*, 1701, 12mo Nr. 180; *Fortegnelse A. Gulden-sparre*, 1696, 12mo Nr. 55. Author may be Joachim Schmidt.

2267   Freyens und Freuens Worte/ | … | Hrn. Andreas Evertzen | Beyer-holms/ | … | Catharina Rabens | … | Jens Raben/ Ivari F. [1686]

Folio. χ².                                                              OSLO UL

2268   GIESE, JOACHIM

Tauf-Sermon, bey der Tauffe eines Mohren gehalten. Kiel, 1686.

                                                                        *

*Moller* I, 210.

2269 HENNINGS, ERICH

(Gedicht auf Anton Burchard). Kiel: Joachim Reumann (1686?).

4to. χ². *

Formerly in Kiel UL (LmC 72-81).

2270 Jhrer | Königlichen Majestät | zu Dennemarck/ Norwegen/ | etc. etc. | Rechtmässige | Beschwerden | und Ansprüche | wieder | Des Herrn Hertzogen zu Schleß- | wig-Holstein-Gottorff &c &c. | Fürstl. Durchl. | [ornamental rule] | Gedruckt im Jahr 1686

4to. 86 pp.; A-L⁴. CKB

L4 lacking, probably blank.

2271 KORTHOLT, HEINRICH CHRISTIAN

(Gedicht auf Anton Burchard). Kiel: Joachim Reumann, (1686?). 

4to. χ². *

Formerly in Kiel UL (LmC 72-81).

2272 LASSENIUS, JOHANNES

D. Joh. Lassenii | Morgen- | Und | Abend-Buß-Beicht | Communion und an- | dere Zeit-und Noht | Gebete. | [rule] | Copenhagen/ | Verlegtens Christian Hauboldt | und | Johann M. Liebe | Der Königl. Univers. Buchhändtlere. | Anno 1686.

12mo. Pp. [1-2], 3-96; π1 (=Bb1?), Bb2-12, Cc-Ee¹². CKB

CKB copy has pp. 3-82 of Thomas Kingo, *Vierzehn Geistreiche Gesänge* . . . (No. 2229) inserted between title-page and Bb2.

2273 LASSENIUS, JOHANNES

Lob-singende | Andacht/ | Darin des teuren Mannes | GOTTES | D. MARTIN LUTHERS | Und anderer Christlichen Lehrer | Alte und Neue Lieder | mit fleiß zusammen gebracht | und auserlesen/ | zu behuff | Eines Kirchen | Gesang-buchs | Für die Teutsche Gemeine zu | St. Petri in Copenhagen. | Mit Kön. M. allergnedigsten Privilegio. | Samt einem kleinen | Gebet-Büchlein/ | auch Vorrede und Censur | H. Johannis LassenI | der H. Schrifft Doctoris, Prof. P. | und Predigers daselbst. | [rule] | Copenhagen/ 1686. | Jn Verlegung | Christian Hau-bolds und | Johann M. Liebe. | der Königl. Univers. Buchhändler.

12mo. [12], 586, [14], 108 pp.; a⁶, A-V¹², W¹², X-Ee¹², Ff⁶. HAB

On Bb1, separate title: *D. Joh Lassenii | Morgen- | Und | Abend-Buß-Beicht | Communion und an- | dere Zeit-und Noht | Gebete. | [rule] | Copenhagen/ |*

*Verlegtens Christian Hauboldt | und | Johann M. Liebe | Der Königl. Univers.*
*Buchhändtlere. Anno 1686.* At end: *Gedruckt bey J. P. Bockenhoffer/ Kön |*
*Maytt. und Univers. Buchdr.*

2274  ORDONNANCE | Wornach | Wir Christian | Der | Fünffte/ | Von
Gottes Gnaden/ König zu | Dännemarck Norwegen/ der Wenden und
Gohten/ | Hertzog zu Schleßwig/ Hollstein/ Stormarn und der Dit- |
marschen/ Graff zu Oldenburg/ und Dellmenhorst/ aller | gnädigst
wollen/ unsere Dragoner/ so lange selbe in | den Hollsteinischen
Aembtern einqvartiret/ Ver- | pfleget werden sollen.

4to. )(⁴.                                                            CNA; Lund UL

Caption title. Dated at end 30 November 1686.

2275  [Paulli, Jacob Henrik]

Wolbegründete | DEFENSIONS- | Schrifft | Wieder Bürgermeistere
und Raht | der Stadt | Hamburg/ | Auch ihren Fiscalem | ANDREAS
Bötger/ | und Andere/ | Von welchen intus zu Ende-Benanter/ und |
einige Hamburgische Bürger/ | wegen eines | Stadt-Verraths/ | Jn ihren
den 19. Novembr. publicirten und öffentlich affi- | girten Placat, über
gegebenen Klag-Libellen, und sonsten | fälschlich beschüldiget worden. |
[rule] | Glückstadt/ Jm Jahr 1686.

4to. 47, [1] pp.; A-F⁴.                                               CKB

CKB also has copy with "Fiscalem" corrected to "Fiscalen" on t-p, and two
"Corrigenda" listed at end of text on p. 47. CKB also has the revised issue with
imprint: *Zu finden bey Christian Reimers/ in der Königs- | strassen/ Jn Altona/*
*1686.*

2276  [Paulli, Jacob Henrik]

Abgenötigte | DECLARATION | Wegen des außgeschrienen | Ver-
raths/ | So einigen Persohnen/ welche mit Mir Ends- | benandten wegen
Sachen die Stadt Hamburg angehend | communication gepflogen/
fälschlich auffgebürdet | wird. | [rule] | Jm Jahr 1686

4to. χ⁴.                                                             CKB

2277  Pfister, Christoph

Kleine Hauß-und Feld-Apotheck. Plön, 1686.

8vo.                                                                    *

*Moller* II, 644; *Thott* III/2, 526.

2278  Schumann, Johannes

Eine unter Gottes Willen | willige Seele. | . . . | BERTRAM | von

RANTZOW, | . . . | Johannes Schumann/ | Past. zu Plöen/ | [rule of type ornaments] | PLÖEN/ Gedruckt durch Tobias Schmidt. [1686]

Folio. [8], 40, [12] pp.; )($^2$, )( )($^2$, A-N$^2$.                              CKB

On L2r, added title: *Klag- und Trost-Gedichte*/ | . . . Verse by several hands.

2279 STÖCKEN, CHRISTIAN VON

Tritaunischer Antritt und Abschied. Schleswig, 1686

4to.                                                                              *

*Georgi* IV, 145.

2280 STÖCKEN, HINRICH VON

Heilige Todten-Kammer/ | . . . | Herr Rotger Neve | . . . | Von | Hinrich von Stökken/ Königl. Probsten/ | . . . | PLOEN/ Gedrukkt durch Tobias Schmidt. [1686]

4to. 32 pp.; A-D$^4$.                                                              CKB

2281 STÖCKEN, HINRICH VON

Die grosse Hertzensangst eines ietzt Sterbenden, wie man sich derselben, noch vor dem Sterben, entschütten, und desto frölicher und seliger sterben kan. Plön, 1686.

4to.                                                                              *

*Moller* I, 661.

2282 STÖCKEN, HINRICH VON

Predigt über Sophia Elisabeth Neve. Plön, 1686.

4to.                                                                              *

*Thott* V/2, 562; *Bibl. Blockiana*, 1773, p. 43.

2283 STORNING, HINRIK

Obersouverainität des Herrn Jesu Christi/ als das allein zulängliche Mittel alle Ketzer . . . Kirchen zu vereinigen. Plön, 1686.

12mo.                                                                             *

*Bibl. Kielmans-Egg.* I, 1129; *Cat. lib. Lehmann* I, 1740, p. 164; *Moller* I, 666 lists place of publication as Hamburg. Possibly identical with *Der auf das einige Wort des Evangelii wieder erstandene Unbekante* listed in *Georgi,* Suppl. I, 356.

2284 STRICKER, PAUL

Ernstliche Schatz Gedanken auf das Hochzeitsfest Henr. Christ. Esmarchs . . . und Christinæ Lüders. Schleswig, 1686.

4to.                                                                              *

*OHM* I, 667.

2285    Summarische | Wiederlegung | Einer | Hamburgischen | Jn | öffentlichen
Druck spargirten so genanten/ | in jure & facto wohlbegründeten |
REMONSTRATION, | Was es mit der von | Jhr. Königl. Mayt. zu
Den- | nemarck/ Norwegen &c. prætendirten Hul- | digung der Stadt
Hamburg für eine Bewandtnüs ha- | be/ darinnen solcher Remonstration
entgegen gesetzet und klährlich | dargethan wird/ daß Jhr. Königl.
Mayt. zu Dennemarck/ Norwe- | gen &c. besagte Stadt die Huldigung zu
leisten schuldig/ und Jhr. | Königl. Mayt. mit guten Fug/ auch jetzo/
nach Anno 1679. errich- | tetem Pinnenbergischen Interims-Recess, von
der Stadt Ham- | burg dieselbe fodern/ solche auch der Stadt an ihrem
Wohl- | stande und Handtlung nicht schädtlich/ son- | dern nützlich
sey. | Auff Königl. Allergnädigste Verordnung herausgeben/ | und zum
Druck befordert. | [rule] | Im Septembr. 1686.

4to. 22, [2] pp.; A-C⁴ (C4 blank).                                        CKB

2286    Täntzer, Johann

Der | DIANEN | Hohe und Niedere | Jagt | Geheimnüß | Ander Theil/ |
Darinnen | Abermahln viel nützliche und sehr nöhtige | Jagt Wissen-
schafften | Gründlich und außführlich zubefinden/ | Welche auch | Mit
unterschiedenen Kupfer-Stücken erklähret | werden. | Mit grosser Arbeit
beschrieben und viel darinn | neu inventiret | Durch | Johann Täntzern. |
Jn Verlegung des Autoris und bey Jhm zufinden. | [ornamental rule] |
Kopenhagen/ | Gedruckt | Bey Jhr: Königl.: Hoh: Bucht: Joachim
Schmedtgen/ | Anno 1686.

Folio. [2], 136 pp. (including 22 plates numbered as 30 pages), [4] pp.; [A²]-Ee²;
engraved preliminary title-page.                                          CKB

Engraved preliminary title: Der | DIANEN | Iagtgeheimnuß. | Ander Theil. Title
printed in red and black. Plates numbered in the pagination with one number per
format leaf, whether single, double, or folding.

2287    Traur-Cypressen | . . . | Hn. Johann Michael | Wincklers/ | . . . | Von |
Nachgesetzten guten Freunden. | [skull & crossbones] | [rule] | Glück-
stadt/ | Druckts Reinhard Janßen/ Jm Jahr 1686

4to. χ⁴.                                                                   CKB

Verse by Petrus Lang and J. D. Tribbe.

2287A   Traur-Ode/ | . . . | Fr: Annen gebohrnen Brocksin. | . . . | Herrn
Eberhard Weidenkopfs/ | . . . | Hinterlassene Frau Wittiben. | . . . | Auf
Begehren geschrieben | Von | Einem wollbekanten Freunde. | [woodcut:
coffin] | [rule] | SCHLESWJG/ | Gedruckt bey Sel. Johann Holweins
Erben. [1686]

Folio. χ².                                                                 SHLB

2288   T<small>RENCKNER</small>, J<small>OHANN</small> H<small>EINRICH</small>

Liebes-Flammende | JEsus Rubinen/ | Jn dem Blutigen | Schauspiele |
Seiner Creutzigung. | Jn einer kleinen Musicalischen Opera nebenst |
etlichen nach bekanten Kirchen-Melodeyen gesetz- | ten Arien oder
Gesängen vorgestellet | von | Johann Heinrich Trencknern/ | Freiberg.
Misn. Phil. Stud. | [ornament] | Kopenhagen/ | Druckts Johan Jacob
Bornheinrich/ | Jm Jahr 1686

8vo.  π⁴, A-C⁸ D⁴.                                                                              CKB

D4 lacking, probably blank.

2289   T<small>RIBBE</small>, J<small>OHANN</small> D<small>ANIEL</small>

Die besternete Winckel-oder Eckseule | des Jtzehöischen Raht-Hauses/ |
. . . | Herr Johann Michael | Winckler/ J. Ctus, | . . . | Jn einer schlechten
Leichen-und | Abdanckungs-Rede vorstellete | Johann-Daniel Tribbe/ |
. . . | Glückstadt/ gedruckt bey Reinhard Janßen/ | Jm Jahr 1686.

4to.  22 pp.; A-C⁴.                                                                             CKB

C4 lacking, probably blank.

2290   Warhafftiger Bericht/ | Wie es mit ietzigem | Hamburgischen Wesen |
bewandt/ | Und was sich dabey/ vom 19 Augusti an | biß den 4ten
Septembris, 1686 | zugetragen.

4to.  A⁴ B² (B2 incorrectly signed B3).                                                         CKB

*Another edition: identical title-page, A-B⁴; another edition: same title, Kopen-*
*hagen/ Gedruckt bey Jh. Königl. Mayt. und Univ. | Buchdrucker Johan Philipp*
*Bockenhoffer, 4 leaves; another edition: title adds: . . . als an welchem Tage |*
*Jhre Königliche Maytt. Dero Armee wiederumb auß- | einander/ und in ihre vorige*
*Quartier gehen | lassen. | . . . | Nach dem Copenhagischen Exemplar | [rule] |*
*Gedruckt bey Jhrer Königlichen Mayst. und Univ. | Buchdrucker Johan Philipp*
*Bockenhover, A-B⁴ (—B4).*

2291   W<small>ASMUTH</small>, M<small>ATTHIAS</small>

MATTHIÆ Waßmuths/ D. und Prof. | auff der Hochfürstl. CHRI-
STIAN-ALBRECHTischen Univers. Kiel/ | New Astronomischer |
Haupt-Schlüssel | Aller Zeiten der Welt | So wol der Vergangenen als
Künfftigen: | Wodurch | Ein Jeder/ so nur ein wenig die Rechenkunst
gelernet/ ohn | alle Astronomische Tabellen oder Wissenschaft/ gar
leicht und geschwind | außm Kopff rechnen/ und beweißlich darthun
kan/ | Zu jeder auffgegebenen Zeit | da sich was zugetragen/ | Das wahre
Alter der Welt: | Als | . . . | Zur abermaligen gewissen Probe | des Neuen
Astro-Chronologischen Wercks/ und darauß | herfliessender Fundamen-
talen höchstverlangter | Zeit-und Fest-Vereinigung | oder Calender-

Reformation. | [rule] | KJEL/ | Jm rechten Jahr der Geburt unsers
Heylands 1686. | Der Welt 5827. | Gedruckt durch Joachim Reumann/
Acad. Buchdr.

Folio. A². KIEL UL

Kiel copy defective, all after A2 lacking.

2292 Wiederauffgelegte | PRIVILEGIA | Oder Freyheiten/ | Welche Dero
zu Dennemack [sic] | Norwegen &c. Königl. Majest. höstsel: | und
rühmlichsten Angedenckens &c. | Der Portugisischen Nation Hebrä-
ischer | Religion, auch ihren Adhærenten und Familien, So | in der Veste
Glückstadt anitzo wohnen und in künfftig kommen | möchten/ Aller-
gnädigst hat mitgetheilet und gegeben | den 19. Junij Anno 1630. | Wobey
Derer zu Dennemarck/ Norwegen etc. | Königl. Königl. Majest. Majest
Allerglorwürdigsten | Andenckens allergnädigst ertheilte Confirmation
de Anno 1648 | Declaration von Anno 1651. Prolongation auff zehen
Jahr/ | de Anno 1655. Anderweitige Declaration von Anno 1657. |
Erweiterte Prolongation auff noch Fünff und Zwantzig Jahr | von Anno
1664. Und der itzo Regierenden Königl. Majest. | Confirmation wie auch
Declaration de Anno 1670. Auch | Extensio Privilegij de Anno 1882 [sic]
Und Declaration von | Anno 1684. Auch erweiterte Prolongation auff
noch | Fünff und Zwantzig Jahr in Anno 1686. | gefüget. | Præsent: dem
Herrn Præsidenten Nicolaus Starck | den 29. Junij. | Publicat in Curia
coram Senatu Glückstadt den 30 | Junij Anno 1686. | [rule] | Gedruckt
bey Reinhard Janßen.

4to. A-D⁴. CKB

2293 Wohlgegründete Be- | haubtung | Der | Schleßwig Holl- | stein Gottorp-
ischen Ge- | rechtsamen und Schrifften. | Uff gnädigsten Befehl Sr. |
Hoch-Fürstl. Durchl. zu Schleßwig | Holstein-Gottorp abgefasset/ und
dem | Druck untergeben | Jm Jahr 1686.

4to. [2], 176 pp.; π1, A-Y⁴. CKB

Place of publication uncertain.

2294 Zwey | Schreiben | von | Jhr. Königl. Majest. zu | Dennemarck Erbunter-
thäni- | gen Stadt Hamburg/ worauf sich die | Königl. der Stadt ertheilte
Decla- | ration beziehet/ | De datis den 6. und 16. Octobr. 1686.

4to. χ⁴. CKB

## 1687

2294A ALETOPHILUS non ALETHOPHILUS | Oder | Continuation | Des |
Aletophilischen | Reise-Gesprächs | Zwischen Jhn | und einen Ham-

burger/ | Da Sie unterwegs ins Wirthshaus | zu anderen Passagirern gekommen. | [rule] | Jm Jahr 1687

4to. 40 pp.; A-E⁴.                                                   CKB; KIEL UL

2295  Vom 3. Januarij Fol. 1. | Altonaische RELATION | Nr. I [woodcut: crowned female figure on lion] 1687

8vo. 8 pp.                                                                     SRL

Caption title. SRL has also: Nr. 7 (pp. 49-56) 24 Jan.; 11 (81-88) 7 Febr.; 32 (249-256) 25 April; 43 (337-344) 6 June; 57 (449-456) 25 July; 65 (513-520) 22 August; 69 (545-552) 5 Sept.; 71 (561-568) 12 Sept.; 73 (577-584) 19 Sept.; 75 (593-600) 26 Sept.; 83 (657-664) 24 Oct.; 89 (705-712) 14 Nov.; 93 (737-744) 28 Nov.; 95 (753-760) 5 Dec.; 99 (785-792) 19 Dec. Stadtbibliothek Hildesheim has Nr. 85 (pp. 673-680) 31 Oct.

2296  An | Jhre Königl. Mayst. | Zu Dännemarck/ Norwegen | allerunter-thänigste | SUPPLICATION | Dero Regierungs-Raths | Herrn Heinrich Pohlmannen/ | Pro Citatione ex L. Diffamari | Wider den Magistrat zu Hamburg/ absonderlich Meurer/ | Scheelen/ Langermann/ Röver/ Uffelman/ Fegesack und | den Fiscalem. | Mit beygefügter | EDICTAL-CITATION | Der Hamburgischen Gerichts-Verwalter | wider ersag-ten | Regierungs-Rath. | Jmgleichen | Die Königl. Gegen-CITATION | ex L. Diffamari | wider | Den Hamburgischen Magistrat, und insonders die ob- | vermeldete sieben Persohnen. | [rule] | Jm Jahr 1687.

4to. A⁴ B².                                                                     CKB

2297  BAUDISSEN, ERNST CHRISTOPH VON *and* WOLF HINRICH VON BAUDISSEN

Glückwünschendes | Ehren-Gedicht/ | Mit welchem/ | Alß | Der Wohl-Edle/ Vest-und Hochgelahrte | Herr M. JOH. GEORGIUS | WAS-MUTH, | Seine Professionem Homileticam vermittelst einer In- | augural Oration, am 17 Martii, des itztlauffenden | 1687 Jahrs/ antrat/ | Jhre Schuldigkeit haben ablegen wollen/ | Desselben beyde Untergebene | Ernst Christoff ⎫ von Baudißen/ | Equites Holsati. | [rule] | KJEL/ | Wolff Hinrich ⎭ Gedruckt bey Joachim Reumann/ Acad. Buchdr.

4to. χ².                                                                     KIEL UL

2298  BESELIN, J. A.

(Trauergedicht über Margarete Morhof, geb. von Degingk). Kiel: Joachim Reumann, 1687.

Folio. χ².                                                                        *

Formerly in Kiel UL (LmC 12-118ª).

2299  BOJE, MICHAEL

Labsahl in Trübsahl/ | Das ist | Die süsse Gottes Gnad— Die tröstet früh'
und spath: | Wormit sich auch zu jeder Zeit/ in Lieb und Leid | Der |
WolEhrenvester/ HochAchtbahrer und Wol- | weiser Herr/ | H. Johann
Gudejohan/ | . . . | Von | MICHAEL/ Bojen Past: . . . | [rule] | Glück-
stadt/ gedruckt bey Reinhard Janßen/ . . . [1687]

4to.  88 pp.; A-L⁴.                                                       CKB

On page 78, added title: *Geistlicher Johanniter-Orden | Bey Christlicher Leich-*
*bestattung | . . . | Herrn Johann Gudejohann/ | . . . | Von | SEBALDO*
*Borndin/ | Diacon. Eccles. Wilstr.*

2300  BOLDICH, ERNST CHRISTIAN

Der glückliche Schritt . . . Abdanckungs Rede über Magdalena Margaretha Hanfmannin. . . . Copenhagen, 1687.

Folio.                                                                    *

*OHM* I, 55.

2301  BRÄMER, CHRISTIAN

Einfältige Catechismus-Fragen. Copenhagen, 1687.

8vo.                                                                      *

*Moller* I, 68; *Bibl. Botsackiana*, 1709, IV, p. 6; *Cat. lib. Masii*, 1713, 8vo Nr. 1017.

2302  (Der Catechismus sampt der Auslegung). Kiel 1687.

8vo.                                                                      *

Formerly in Kiel UL (M 37).

2302A BRÜGGE, ANDREAS VAN DER

(Trauergedicht über Marg. Morhof geb. von Degingk). Kiel: Joachim
Reumann, 1687.

Folio. χ².                                                                *

Formerly in Kiel UL (LmC 12-118).

2303  DENMARK. *Laws, statutes, etc.*

WJR Christian der Fünffte/ von | . . . | . . . Glückstadt den 28. Februarij,
Anno 1687.

Broadside.                                                                CNA

Decree regarding inferior coins.

2304 DENMARK. *Laws, statutes, etc.*

WJR Christian der Fünffte/ von | . . . | . . . Glückstadt . . . 28. Fe- |
bruarij, Anno 1687

Broadside. CNA

Decree regarding coinage in Holstein.

2305 DENMARK. *Laws, statutes, etc.*

Wir Christian der Fünffte/ | . . . | . . . Gottorf den 1 Martii Anno 1687.

Broadside. CKB

Decree against "geringhaltige Müntz-Sorten."

2306 DENMARK. *Laws, statutes, etc.*

WJR Christian der Fünffte/ von | . . . | . . . Glückstadt/ den 7. Aprilis,
Anno 1687.

Broadside. CNA

Decree ordering a day of prayer 22 April.

2307 DENMARK. *Laws, statutes, etc.*

Wir Christian der Fünffte/ | . . . | . . . Gottorff den 30 April. Anno 1687.

Broadside. CNA

Decree against extravagant weddings, baptisms, and burials.

2307A DENMARK. *Laws, statutes, etc.*

Wir Christian der Fünffte/ | von GOttes Gnaden/ König zu Dänne-
marck/ | . . . | . . . Gottorff den | 14 April. Anno 1687.

Broadside. CKB

Decree setting a "Fast-Buß-und Bet-Tag" 22 April.

2308 DENMARK. *Laws, statutes, etc.*

WJR Christian der Fünffte/ von | . . . | . . . Glückstadt/ den 4ten Maij
Anno 1687

Broadside. CNA

Decree against extravagant weddings, baptisms, and burials in Holstein.

2309 DENMARK. *Laws, statutes, etc.*

WJR Christian der Fünffte/ von | . . . | . . . Glückstadt/ den 30. Junij,
Anno 1687

Broadside (two sheets pasted together). CNA

Decree protesting an edict issued in Hamburg against Jacob Heinrich Paulli and treatment received by him.

2310 DENMARK. *Laws, statutes, etc.*

Octroy und Concession | Dem Königl. Commerce Directeurn in Norwegen | Jürgen Thor Möhlen/ ertheilet | Sein Saltz von Saltz mit gewissen Conditionen in das Hertzoghumb [sic] Schleßwig | einzuführen und zu verhandeln. | . . . .

Broadside.                                                           CNA

Decree dated at Copenhagen, 12 July 1687, signed Christian [V].

2311 DENMARK. *Laws, statutes, etc.*

WJR Christian der Fünffte/ von | . . . | . . . Glückstadt/ den 27ten Augusti | Anno 1687.

Broadside.                                                           CNA

Decree ordering thanksgiving 4 September for victory over the Turks.

2311A DENMARK. *Laws, statutes, etc.*

Wir Christian der Fünffte von Gottes Gnaden/ | König zu Dennemarck/ Norwegen/ . . . | . . . | . . . Copenhagen den 15. Septembr. Anno 1687.

Broadside.                                                           CKB

Decree levying a special military tax.

2312 DENMARK. *Laws, statutes, etc.*

WJr Christian der Fünffte/ von Gottes | . . . | . . . Copenhagen den 10. Decembr. | Anno 1687.

Broadside.                                                           CNA

Decree regarding payment of an extraordinary military tax.

2313 DENMARK. *Laws, statutes, etc.*

WJR Christian der Fünffte/ von | . . . | . . . Glückstadt den 31. | Decembris Anno 1687.

Broadside.                                                           CNA

Decree condemning insults to Henrich Pohlmann, "Holsteinischer Regierungs-Rath und Assessor."

2314 FUCHS, JOHANNES

Johannes Fuchsen | Holsteinisches | Ding und Recht | [double rule] | KJEL/ | Bey Johann Sebastian Riechel/ 1687.

4to. 36 pp.; A-D⁴ E².  CKB

Riechel was a Kiel bookseller.

2315  (Gesangbuch der Süder-Dithmarscher). Glückstadt, 1687

12mo.  *

*Bibl. Ehrencron,* 1717, p. 44.

2316  GIESE, JOACHIM

Catechismus-Fragstücke. Kiel, 1687.

8vo.  *

*Moller* I, 210.

2317  GIESE, JOACHIM

Handbüchlein vor Dethlef Gottlieb, einen getauften Mohren, verfertigt.
Kiel, 1687.

8vo.  *

*Moller* I, 210. Formerly in Kiel UL.

2318  GLASS, SALOMON

Biblisches Handbuch. Schleswig, 1687

8vo.  *

*Bibl. Mejeriana,* 1701, 8vo. Nr. 1359.

2318A Hamburgisch | Mordt-THEATRUM | Besprengt mit dem Blute |
HIERONYMI SNITQUER, | Kauffmann und Bürger | zu | HAM-
BURG. | [rule] | Editio tertia correctior. | Mit einer neuen Vorrede/ |
und | APPENDICE. | [rule] | Jm Jahr 1687.

4to. [12], 132 pp.; a⁴ b² A-Q⁴ R².  KIEL UL

On p. 121, separate title: *APPENDIX | Zu dem | Hamburgischen | Mordt-
THEATRO, | Besprengt mit dem Blute | HIERONYMI SNITQUER*

2319  HAMERICH, HENRICH

Väterlicher Seegnen (carmen in nupt. filii). Schleswig, 1687.

Folio.  *

*OHM* I, 232.

2320  LASSENIUS, JOHANNES

Biblischer | Weyrauch | Zum süssen Geruch | Gottseeliger Andachten/ |
Auß H. Schrifft also zusamen [sic] gelesen/ | Das mit des Heiligen

Geistes eige- | nen Worten/ die GOtt-Liebende Seel/ täglich | mit GOtt
in allerhand dero Geistlichen und Leib- | lichen Anliegen reden; Und
zum Christlichen | Leben auch seeligen Todt sich gefast | machen
könne. | Samt | Heilsahmer Vorbereitung | zum Beicht-Stuhl/ | Und
Heiligen Abendmahl. | Mit allerhand neüen/ Morgen und Abend/ |
Buß/ Beicht-und Communion-Liedern/ | und nicht unangenehmen
Kupffern hin und | wieder versehen. | Dem Gecreützigten JEsu allein zu
Ehren/ | Und der/ mit seinem Blut erlöseten heiligen Gemeine GOt- |
tes/ in Copenhagen und Anderswo. | Zu Beförderung ihres Christen-
thums/ angezündet | von | D. Johanne Lassenio, | Mit Königl. Majest.
Allergnädigsten Privilegio. | [rule] | Zu finden bey Johan M. Liebe
Buchhändlern. | Gedruckt bey Jh. Kön. Majest. und der Universit.
Buchdr. | Joh. Phil. Bockenhoffer/ 1687.

8vo. [12], 761, [7] pp.; $\pi^6$, A-V$^8$, W$^8$, X-Vv$^8$, Ww$^8$, Xx-Zz$^8$; 19 plates.  HAB

2321 LASSENIUS, JOHANNES

D. JOHANNIS LASSENII | Heiligen | Perlen-Schatzes | Erster Theil/ |
über den Monath | JANUARIUS, | Also eingerichtet | Daß zu Beforder-
ung des thätigen | und GOtt-wollgefälligen Chri- | stenthums; | Die
GOtt-begierige Seel/ zu ihrer heiligen | Freüde/ Anwachs in der wahren
Gottsee- | ligkeit/ auch Seeligen Gewin/ des | Himlischen Jerusalems. |
Täglich/ mit zweien Christlichen Be- | trachtungen sich erbauen könne. |
Mit Königl. Mayest. Allergnädigsten Privilegio. | Auch vielen erbau-
lichen Kupffer-Stücken. | [rule] | Kopenhagen/ | Gedruckt bey Jh.
Königl. Mayt. und Univ. Buchdr. | Johann Philipp Bockenhoffer/ 1687.

8vo. [6], 208 pp.; $\pi^4$ (−1), A-N$^8$; engraved preliminary title-page, 9 plates.  CKB

Engraved preliminary title (repeated in each part of the 12-volume set, dated 1687-
1689): *D. Johannis Lassenij | Heiliger | Perlen-Schatz.* Cf. also Nos. 2322-8, 2369-
70, 2421-2.

2322 LASSENIUS, JOHANNES

D. JOHANNIS LASSENII | Heiligen | Perlen-Schatzes | Ander Theil/ |
über | den Monath | FEBRUARIUS. | Kopenhagen/ | [rule] | Gedruckt
bey J. Königl. Mayt. und Univ. Buchdr. | Johann Philipp Bockenhoffer.
[1687]

8vo. Pp. [1-2], 229-432, [1-8]; $\pi$1, O-V$^8$, W$^8$, X-Cc$^8$, $\chi^4$; engraved frontispiece, 8
plates.  CKB

Gathering $\chi$ is a *Register der Titul/ Des | Ersten und Andern Theils.*

2323 LASSENIUS, JOHANNES

D. Johannis Lassenii | Heiligen | Perlen-Schatzes | Dritter Theil/ | über

den Monath | MARTIUS. | [rule] | Kopenhagen/ | Gedruckt bey Jh.
Königl. Mayt. und Univ. Buchdr. | Johann Philipp Bockenhoffer/ 1687.

8vo. Pp. [1-2], 433-672, [1-2]; π1, Dd-Ss⁸, χ1; engraved preliminary title, 8 plates.
                                                                                          CKB
Index on χ1.

2324  Lassenius, Johannes

D. Johannis Lassenii | Heiligen | Perlen-Schatzes | Vierdter Theil/ |
über | den Monath | APRILIS. | Kopenhagen/ | [rule] | Gedruckt bey J.
Königl. Mayt. und Univ. Buchdr. | Johann Philipp Bockenhoffer. [1687]

8vo. Pp. [1-2], 673-864, 867-930, [1-2]; π1, Tt-Vv⁸, Ww⁸, Xx-Kkk⁸, χ1; engraved
frontispiece, 8 plates.                                                       CKB
Index on χ1.

2325  Lassenius, Johannes

D. Johannis Lassenii | Heiligen | Perlen-Scha- | tzes | Fünffter Theil/ |
über | den Monath | MAJUS. | Kopenhagen/ | [rule] | Gedruckt bey J.
Königl. Mayt. und Univ. Buchdr. | Johann Philipp Bockenhoffer/ 1687.

8vo. Pp. [1-4], 1-256, 247-262; π², a-r⁸; engraved frontispiece, 8 plates.     CKB
Index on π2.

2326  Lassenius, Johannes

D. Johannis Lassenii | Heiligen | Perlen-Scha- | tzes | Sechster Theil/ |
über | den Monath | JUNIUS. | Kopenhagen/ | [rule] | Gedruckt bey J.
Königl. Mayt. und Univ. Buchdr. | Johann Philipp Bockenhoffer/ 1687.

8vo. Pp. [1-2], 273-528, [1-2]; π1, s-v⁸ w⁸ x-ii⁸, χ1; engraved frontispiece, 8 plates.
                                                                                          CKB
Index on χ1.

2327  Lassenius, Johannes

D. Johannis Lassenii | Heiligen | Perlen-Scha- | tzes | Siebender Theil/ |
über | den Monath | JULIUS | Kopenhagen/ | [rule] | Gedruckt bey J.
Königl. Mayt. und Univ. Buchdr. | Johann Philipp Bockenhoffer/ 1687.

8vo. Pp. [1-2], 529-784, [1-2]; π1, kk-vv⁸ ww⁸ xx-aaa⁸, χ1; engraved preliminary
title-page, 8 plates.                                                         CKB
Index on χ1. See also No. 2322.

2328  Lassenius, Johannes

Lobsingende Andacht, darinn D. Luthers, und anderer Christlicher
Lehrer, alte und neue Lieder sind zusammengebracht zum Behuf eines

Kirchen-Gesang-Buchs vor die teutsche Gemeine zu S. Petri in Kopenhagen: Mit einer Vorrede und Censur von D. Joh. Lassenio mit Fleiße
wieder übersehen, und auf ein merckliches vermehret. Copenhagen,
1687.

12mo.                                                                                                            *

*Moller* II, 452.

2329   MORHOF, DANIEL GEORG

(Ode auf den Abschied Oelgarde Catharina Blomin geb. v. Rantzow,
Wulff Blomen Eheliebste). Kiel, [1687].

Folio.                                                                                                          *

*OHM* III, 472.

2330   MÜLLER, HERMANN

JESVS | Der Weg zum Leben/ | Welchen | GOtt kund gethan | ... |
Frauen Cielke Klüvers/ | ... | von | HERMANNO Müllern/ |
Adsessore des Münsterdörfischen Consisto- | rii und Pastore zu Süderau. |
[rule] | Glückstadt/ Gedruckt bey Reinhard Janssen/ 1687.

4to. [6], 112 pp.; $\pi^4$ (−1), A-O$^4$.                                                          CKB

2331   [PAULLI, JACOB HENRIK]

Abgenötigte | Dritte und letzste | DECLARATION | wegen des ver-
meinten | Hamburgischen | Stadt-Verraths/ | wodurch Endsbenandter |
alle bißhero von Jhm ausgebrachte | grobe Lügen/ und sonsten | so woll
à Senatu, als von anderen | privat-Leuten in Hamburg/ | durch öffent-
lichen Placaten | und | Pasquillen/ | Jhm zugefügte Beschimpfungen |
und injurien/ | Ein- vor allemahl von Sich ablehnet | und auf deren |
Authores retorqviret. | [rule] | Jm Jahr 1687

4to. A$^4$ B$^2$.                                                                                          CKB

2332   [PAULLI, JACOB HENRIK]

Nähere | Declaration | wegen des vermeinten | Verraths | Der | Stadt
Hamburg. | Womit nebst vielen andern/ der annoch | mit-inhafftirter/
und peinlich ange- | klagter | Hr. Nicolaus Silm/ J. U. Lic. | Aus
Entsbenanten aldorth ertapten/ und wieder aller Völ- | cker Recht à
Senatu angehalten/ und mißgebrauchten Schrifften und | Briefen/
fälschlich beschuldiget wird: Wie dessen das eintzige hie- | rin ange-
führte Extract-Schreiben vom 23. Martii 1686. | ein mehr als überflüssiger
Beweiß. | Mit beygefügter præliminairen Retorsion gegen die neulich

außge- | gangene Hamburgische also mit unfug genante | Warhafft
DEDUCTIONS-Schrifft. | [rule] | Glückstadt/ Jm Jahr 1687.

4to. 22 pp.; A-C⁴. CKB; BM

Another issue, with variant title-page (Kiel UL).

2333 [PAULLI, JACOB HENRIK]

Probe | Fälschlicher Über-und | Hinzusetzung | Der | PAULLINIschen |
Brieffschafften/ | Worauff | Cordt Jastram, und | Hieronymus Snitquer |
unschuldig | Zum Tode verurtheilet. | [rule] | Glückstadt/ 1687

4to. χ². CKB

2334 [PAULLI, JACOB HENRIK]

Wolbegründeter | DEFENSIONS-Schrifft | Wieder Bürgermeistere und
Raht | der Stadt | Hamburg | abgedrungene Continuation. | Worinnen/ |
Das aldorth wegen eines vermeinten | Stadt-Verraths | Am 19. Novemb.
1686. publicirte, und öffentlich | affigirt-gewesene | Lügen-Placat, |
Zusampt der nach der Zeit außgegebenen | Hamburgischen | Unwahr-
hafften DEDUCTION-Schrifft/ | Mit wahren ohnwiedersprechlichen |
Umbständen und | Beweißthümen/ von Endsbenandten kürtzlich |
wiederleget worden. | [rule] | Glückstadt/ Jm Jahr 1687.

4to. 62 [2] pp.; A-H⁴ (H4 blank). CKB

Author identified in "Approbatio," p. 62. Originally published 1686 (No. 2275).

2335 POHLMANN, HENRICH

Dero zu Dännemarck/ | Norwegen &c. &c. Kön. Majest. | im Hertzog-
thumb Holstein verordneten Re- | gierungs-Raths/ und Assessoris im |
Pinnenberg-und | Altonauischen Ober-Appellations- | Gerichte/ | Hen-
rich Pohlmannen/ | Wieder | Die von dem Niedern Gerichte zu Ham-
burg/ | uff Getrieb der Meuerschen Faction, außgelas- | sene verleumb-
derische Edictal- | Citation | Höchstabgenötigte | Ehren-Rettung. | Mit |
Beylagen von Lit. A. biß MMM. | inclusivè. | [rule] | Glückstadt/ |
Gedruckt durch Reinhard Janßen/ Königl. bestalten | Buchdrucker/ Jm
Jahr 1687.

4to. 218 pp.; A-Dd⁴, χ1. CKB; HALLE UL; (BM)

2336 Der Römischen Käyserlichen | Majest | EDICTUM | und Schreiben |
an | Jhre zu Dännemarck/ Norwegen &c. &c. | Königl. Majest. | wegen |
Der ohnlängst im Druck ausgegebenen | PAULLINIschen | Defensions-
Schrifften | wieder Bürgermeistere und Rath der | Stadt Hamburg. |

Zusampt dem Königlichen | Gegen-EDICT, und Antwort-Schreiben. | [rule] | Jm Jahr 1687

4to. A-B⁴.                                                                              CKB

2337 Rötscher, Johannes Volcmar

Der mächtige Gnadenschutz | Christi | ... | Hn. Fridrich Jügerts | ... | von | M. Johanne Volcmaro Rötschern | ... | [rule] | KJEL/ | Gedruckt bey Joachim Reumann/ Acad. Buchdr. 1687

4to. 59, [1] pp.; A-G⁴ H².                                                              CKB

Another issue, erroneously dated 1678.

2337A Rohn, Christopher

Alß | Der Wohl-Edle/ Vest und Hochgelahrte | Herr M. JOH. GEORG. | WASMUTH, | Auff der weitberühmten Universität Kiel/ | Die von Ihrer Hochfürstl. Durchl. | ihm gnädigst auffgetragene | Professionem Homileticam, | Zur löblicher Nachfolge seines unvergleichlichen Hn. Vaters/ | Den 17. Martius 1687. öffentlich antrat/ | Wolte seine schuldige Pflicht Glückwünschend abstatten | Christoph: Rohn/ auß Lübeck | Der H. Schrifft Beflissener. | [rule] | KJEL/ | Gedruckt bey Joachim Reumann/ Acad. Buchdr.

Folio. χ².                                                                              SHLB

2338 Schmidt, Joachim

Einer in der Creutz-Schule | ... | Frauen Anna Engelbrechts/ |gebohrnen Schraders/ | ... | Durch | Joachim Schmidt/ Hoff-Predigern daselbst | [woodcut: coffin] | [rule] | PLOEN/ Gedruckt durch Tobias Schmidt. [1687]

Folio. 32 pp.; A-H².                                                                    SHLB

2340 Verboth | Unverarbeitet oder alt Kupffer | und Meßing/ auch neue Kupffer und Mes- | sing-Wahren auß und in das Für- | stenthum Schleßwig | zuführen. | Hafniæ die 8. Martii Anno 1687 | [royal monogram] | [rule] | Gedruckt bey Jhr. Königl. Mayest. und Univ. Buchdr. | Johann Philip Bockenhoffer

4to. χ².                                                                                CNA

2341 Vollständiges | Gesang-Buch/ | Darinnen nicht allein die al- | te/ gewöhnliche | Kirchen-Gesänge/ | Sondern auch viel neue geist- | reiche Lieder zubefinden: | Alle auff bekandte Melo- | deyen/ zu männigliches/ abson- | derlich der Einfältigen desto | bessern Gebrauch. | Deme zu Ende beygefüget ist ein | kurtzes/ aber auff vielerhand Fälle/ | Zeiten und

Anliegen gerich- | tetes | Gebet-Büchlein/ | Nach der vermehrten Edi-
tion | gedrucket/ | und | Zum sechstenmal auffgeleget | [vignette] |
[rule] | PLOEN/ | Druckts und verlegts Tobias | Schmidt/ im 1687sten
Jahr.

12mo. [8], 475, [15], 169, [5] pp.; )(⁴, A-Dd¹² Ee⁸.                          SRL

X6 has separate title: *Kurtzes | Gebet-Büchlein | Doch | Auff vielerhand Fälle
und | Anliegen gerichtet. | [rule] | Plöen/ | Gedruckt durch Tobias Schmidt. | Jm
Jahr 1687.*

2342  WILHELMI, JOHANN CASPAR

Hortus passionalis floridus; Blumenreicher Passionsgarten, darinn
XLVIII. Glaubens-und Lebenslehren, auß der Passions-Historie, unter
dem Bildnisse der Gartengewächse, vorgestellet werden. Mit vorherge-
hender Betrachtung aller Gärten der Heiligen Schrift, und einem Anhange, so wol einer Sinnbilderischen Vorstellung des Grabes Christi, als
drey neüer Passionslieder. Plön, 1687

12mo.                                                                            *

*Moller* I, 732

2343  WILHELMI, JOHANN CASPAR

Jesu Christi Wanderschaft, in XXX. Sonnetten vorgestellt. Plön, 1687.
4to.                                                                             *

*Moller* I, 732.

2344  WILHELMI, JOHANN CASPAR

(Leichpredigt über J. N. Wildhaginn). Plön, 1687.
Folio.                                                                           *

*Moller* I, 732.

2345  WÖRGER, FRANZ

Auserlesene Biblische Kern-und Trostprüche, in XXI. Predigten erkläret.
Copenhagen, 1687.
4to.                                                                             *

*Moller* I, 746.

## 1688

2346  Vom 2. Januarij Fol. 1. | Altonaische RELATION | Nr. I [woodcut:
crowned female figure on lion] 1688

8vo.  8 pp.                                                                     SRL

Caption title. SRL has also Nr. 3 (pp. 17-24) 9 Jan.; 5 (33-40) 16 Jan.; 7 (49-56) 23 Jan.; 9 (65-72) 30 Jan.; 11 (81-88) 6 Feb.; 13 (97-104) 13 Feb.; 17 (129-136) 27 Feb.

2347   AREND, CAI

Gebetlein auf die tröstliche Leidensgeschichte unsres Heylandes, sammt Anhang einer geistlichen Morgen und Abend-Übung. Glückstadt, 1688.

12mo.                                                                                          *

OHM I, 21; *Bibl. Schroedter,* 1724, p. 687 gives date as 1668.

2348   BECMANN, NICOLAUS

(Eine gesegnete Ehe in nupt. Joh. Krebs). Schleswig, 1688.

4to.                                                                                          *

OHM I, 37.

2349   BÜTTNER, DAVID

(Leichpredigt über Hans Sittig von der Oelsnitz). Kopenhagen, 1688.

                                                                                              *

OHM II, 452. *Cat. Lib. Chr. Brämer,* 1701, *Libri Incomp.* 4to, nr. 28, lists "Joh. Lassenius, Leichpredigt über Hans Sittig. Hafn. 1686."

2350   (Confessions-Werk und Solennitæten bey dem Ubergang des Grafen Georg Albrechts zu der Ewangelisch Lutherischen Religion). Schleswig, 1688.

Folio.                                                                                         *

*Thott* V/1, 256.

2351   DAMPIERRE, JACQUES SERCUEIL DE

LE PASSE PAR- | Tout François, | Par | J. S. de Dampierre, | Maitre de langue de la Reine | de Dannemarck, &c. | [three asterisks] | Französ-ischer | Haupt-Schlüssel/ | Durch | J. S. De DAMPIERRE, | Ihro Maj der Königin zu Denne- | marck und Norwegen/ &c. | Sprach Meister. | Troisieme Edition corrigée en plu- | sieurs lieus. | [rule] | KOPENHA-VEN, | verlegts | Johann Justus Erytropilus/ | Anno M DC LXXXVIII.

12mo. [20], 220 pp.; )(1-10, A-J¹², K².                    GREIFSWALD UL

Title in red and black.

2352   DENMARK. *Laws, statutes, etc.*

König Christian IV und Herzog Friedrichs Revidirte Landgerichts-Ordnung von 1636 für Schleswig Holstein . . . Glückstadt, 1688

4to.                                                            *

*Cat. lib. Ancker,* 1789, II, p. 238. Cf. Nos. 1266 and 2451A.

2353 DENMARK. *Laws, statutes, etc.*

WJR Christian der Fünffte/ von | ... | ... Glück- | stadt/ den 9ten Febr:
Anno 1688

Broadside.                                                     CNA

Decree issued jointly with Duke Christian Albrecht of Schleswig-Holstein, ordering
repair of roads and bridges in the vicinity of Oldesloe.

2354 DENMARK. *Laws, statutes, etc.*

WJr Christian der Fünffte/ von Got- | tes ... | ... | ... 24 Julii Anno
1688.

Broadside.                                                     CKB

Decree against dueling.

2355 DENMARK. *Laws, statutes, etc.*

WJR Christian der Fünffte/ von | ... | ... 18ten. Septembr. Anno 1688.

Broadside.                                                     CKB

Decree regarding a victory celebration 29 September.

2356 DENMARK. *Laws, statutes, etc.*

WJr Christian der Fünffte von Got- | tes Gnaden/ ... | ... | ...
Copenhagen den 10. Novembr. Anno 1688.

Broadside.                                                     CNA

Decree regarding payment of a tax on land and contributions of rye and oats.

2357 DORNKRELL VON EBERHERTZ, JACOB

Antecedentium Praxis, | Oder die | Erste Göttliche Predig/ | So nach der
in vorhergehendem Wercklein ange- | wiesener Methode abgefasset/ |
und | Jn der Hauptkirche S. Johannis zu | Lüneburg/ den 8. Sonntag
nach der Heil. Dreiei- | nigkeitfest/ war der 5te tag des Monats Augusti
des 1688. | Jahrs/ in der hohen Missenpredig gehalten | worden/ |
Darinn das 10. Lässtück des H. Lebenswandels | Jesu Christi des
HERRN/ oder die Wahl der Hh. 12. Apostel/ | auch ihre von dem
Weltheilande gegebene Instruction, (wie dieselbi- | ge nach harmon-
ischer bündigkeit/ von den Hh. Evangelisten Matth. | cap. 5.6.7. per tot.
Marc. 3. (13-19) und Luca 6. (12 ad fin. beschrieben/ | und in gemein die

Berg-oder auch Feldpredig genennet wird) | der damahls versamleten
gemeine Gottes öffentlich | vorgetragen ist | Durch | Jakobum Dornkrell
von Eberhertz/ | S.S. Theol. Dd. | [rule of type ornaments] | PLOEN/ |
Gedruckt und verlegt durch Tobias Schmidt/ | Zu finden bei Siegfried
Ripenau/ Buchhändler. [1688]

4to. 64 pp.; A-B⁴, C², D-E⁴, F², G-J⁴.                    SRL; Berlin Staatsbibliothek

On p. 21, separate title: *Antecedentium Praxis,* | *Oder die* | *Zweite Göttliche*
*Predigt/* | *...* | *1689.* On p. 41, separate title: *Antecedentium Praxis,* | *Oder die* |
*Dritte Göttliche Predig/* | *...* | *[1688].*

2358    Dornkrell von Eberhertz, Jacob

JAKOBI DORNKRELII ab Eberhertz/ SS. Theol Dd. | Des Göttlichen
Worts | Kirchen-mangel/ | Und der menschlichen kunst-reden überfluß. |
Das ist: | Unwiedertreiblicher Beweis/ | Daß/ und wie die öffter und
öffentliche ablesung der gantzen hei- | gen [sic] Schrifft/ bei denen kirch-
enversamlungen (als woraus dieselbige eine ge- | raume zeit vermisset ist)
nothwendig wiederum einzuführen: hingegen aber der ü- | berflüßigen
oratoriæ ecclesiasticæ, oder den menschlich-gekünstelten kirchen- |
reden/ wöchentlich so viel stunden zu entziehen sein. | Wobei zugleich
das/ was der öffentlichen Schrifft-ablesung | entgegen zu stehen das
ansehen haben möchte/ abgelehnet: | Und mit einem nöthigen Zuruff |
1. An alle rechtgläubige Reichs-amtleute Gottes auf erden/ | 2. An alle
gewissenhaffte Seelen-wächter/ Hirten und Lehrer/ | Wie auch | 3. An
alle aufmercksame Zuhörer/ und sämtliche Schrifft-liebhabere/ | Darinn
jeder seiner obliegenden schuldigkeit und gebührenden pflicht/ | so ihm
in täglich-und fleißigster handhabung der H. Göttlichen Schrifft oblie-
get/ | recht wahrzunehmen/ hertzlich und wohlmeinend erinnert/ und
demselbigen mit | höchstem fleiß nachzuleben/ angemuntert und be-
schlossen wird. | Aus welchem allen der große mißbrauch der heutigen
kirchen-re- | den erscheinen/ was für ein mannigfältiger unrath in der
Gemeine Gottes da- | her entstanden/ wie demselbigen abzuhelffen/ die
H. Schrifft-ablesung/ und an- | der erbauliche lehr-arten wieder einzu-
führen/ die menschliche vielredenheit aber gehö- | riger massen einzu-
schrencken sei/ gezeiget wird. | [rule] | PLOEN/ | Gedruckt und verlegt
durch Tobias Schmidt/ 1688. | Zu finden/ bei Siegfried Ripenau/
Buchhändl. allhier.

4to. [24], 28, [8], 172 pp.; π1 (=)o(4), )o(⁴ ()o(1 + *⁴, −)o(4), )(−4)(⁴,
5)(², ²*⁴, A-E⁴, F⁴ (F1 + "F3.4"), G-U⁴, X-Y².          Berlin Staatsbibliothek

On two folio leaves signed F3-4, inserted between F1 and F2: "Der Biblische Leß-
Calender."

2359  DORNKRELL VON EBERHERTZ, JACOB

Der | Wenig-bauenden | heutigen | Kirchenlehrart | höchstnöthige
Verbesserung. | Dargewiesen und angepriesen | Durch | Jakobum Dorn-
krellium | von Eberhertz. [1688]

4to. *⁴.                                                       SRL

*Bibl. Kielmans-Egg.*, III, p. 484 Nr. 4259, lists edition with sub-title: *oder
Beweis, daß die Ablesung der H. Schrifft in unsern Kirchen wieder einzuführen
nötig sey*, Plön 1688. SRL copy bound with same author's *Antecedentium Praxis*
(No. 2357).

2360  Friedrich Christian Helm/ | . . . | Klag-und Trost-Schrifft | . . . | Jungf.
Hedwig Maria | Helminn/ | . . . | den 24. Sept. 1688 | [rule] | [Glück-
stadt] Gedruckt bey Reinhard Janßen.

4to. χ⁴.                                                       KIEL UL

2361  GIESE, JOACHIM

Die hiṁlische | ACADEMIE | Des Allerhöchsten/ | . . . | Herr MAT-
THIAS | Wasmuth/ | . . . | M. Joachimus Giese/ Pastor Primar. in Kiel. |
[rule] | KJEL/ Gedruckt durch Joachim Reumann/ Acad. Buchdr.
[1688]

4to. 107, [1] pp.; A-N⁴ O².                                    CKB

2362  GUDE, HENRICH LUDWIG

Circula rerum humanorum oder Abdanckungs-Rede über Daniel Hausmann. . . . Schleswig, 1688.

Folio.                                                           *

*OHM* I, 222; *Fortegn. Bøger*, 1759, p. 110.

2363  HEERFORT, CHRISTOFFER

M. G. ! | Das beliebte Rosenfeld/ | . . . | Jacob Fromm/ | . . . | Else/ geb:
Rosen- | feldin | . . . | Jm Jahr 1688, den 30 Maji | . . . | Christoffer
Heerfort/ | Junior | [rule of type ornaments] | Copenhagen/ Gedruckt
bey Jh. Königl. Majest. und Universit. | Buchdr. Joh. Phil. Bockenhoffer.

Folio. χ².                                                     OSLO UL

2364  JÜRGENS (*i.e.*, IRGENS), JOACHIM

Autoschediasma | De | VITRIOLO | Das ist | Ein im Eyl verfertigter
und | annoch rauher doch in der | Natur woll gegründe- | ter neuer |
Bericht | vom | VITRIOLO | Und dessen Essentz, Natur, | und Eigen-
schafften | Kürtzlich allen Liebhabern der Me- | dicin, der Bergwercke

und Mine- | ralien zu gefallen | Zusammen geschrieben | von | D.
Joachimô Jürgens | Medicô Regiô und Stadtz Physicô | zu Drontheim in
Norwegen. | [rule] | COPENHAGEN/ | Gedruckt bey dero K.M. und
Univ. Buchdr. | Johann Philip Bockenhoffer/ 1688.

8vo. [6], 130, [6] pp.; $\pi^4$ (−1), A-E$^{12}$ F$^8$ (F7-8 blank).            CKB; (BM)

2365    KLOTZ, STEPHAN

Erklärung der Sonntags-Evangelien, da aus einem jedweden Evangelio
die Lehre vom Heiligen Abendmahl angeführet wird, nebst dem Griech-
ischen Text, der Syrischen Version, mit Hebräischen Lettern, wie auch
der Vulgata it. Vers. Gall. Italicâ, Hispanicâ, Anglicâ & Belgicâ &c nebst
angehengtem Fest-Theil über die vornehmste Feste. Glückstadt, 1688.

4to.                                                                     *

*Bibl. Kielmans-Egg.*, II, 459.

2366    KRAMER, MAURITIUS

עמי עשו | Eine | Nöhtig erachtete Christliche | Warnung | für dem
ungeschmakten | Qvaker- | qvarke | An die Christliche Gemeine zur |
Marne in Ditmarschen/ als seine an- | vertrauete liebe Zuhörer/ | getahn |
Von | MAURITIO Kramer/ | Pastore daselbst | [rule] | Glükkstadt/ |
Gedrukkt bey Reinhard Janßen/ | Jm Jahr 1688

8vo. Pp. 1-64, 1-353, 336-350, [1-2]; a-d$^8$, A-Z$^8$, χ1.            KIEL UL

Title in red and black. Kiel UL copy has added t-p. inserted with imprint,
*Hamburg/ | In Verlegung Georg Wulff Buchhändl. in | S. Johannis Kirch/ im Jahr
1688.* χ1 errata sheet.

2367    LASSENIUS, JOHANNES

JOHANNIS LASSENII | Der H. Schrifft Doct. Prof. Publ. und Past. |
an St. Petri Kirchen | Heiligen | Perlen-Schatzes | Erste Vertheilung |
über die Monaht | JANUARIUS, FEBRUARIUS | MARTIUS und
APRILIS. | Jn der Furcht GOttes/ auß dessen geoffen- | bahrten Wort
also eingesamlet/ | Daß zu Beforderung des Thätigen | und GOtt Wolge-
fälligen Christenthums | Die GOtt-begierige Seel/ | Täglich mit Zweyen
Christlichen Betrach- | tungen sich Erbauen könne. | Mit überal hinzuge-
thanen Sin-Bildern. | Unter Königl. Majest. zu Dännemarck/ Norwe-
gen. | Auch Churfl. Durchl. zu Sachsen/ Allergnädigsten Privilegiis. |
[rule] | Copenhagen/ | Gedruckt bey J. Kön. Mayt. und Univ. Buchdr. |
Johan Philip Bockenhoffer/ 1688. | Zu finden bey Joh. Melchior Liebe/
der Universit. | Buchhändlern.

8vo. [14], 930, [14] pp.; )(⁸ [−])(8], A-V⁸, W⁸, X-Vv⁸, Ww⁸, Xx-Lll⁸; engraved frontispiece, 34 plates.　　　　　　　　　　　　　　　　　CKB

Title printed in red and black.

2368　LASSENIUS, JOHANNES

JOHANNIS LASSENII | Der H. Schrifft Doct. Prof. Publ. und Past. | an St. Petri Kirchen | Heiligen | Perlen-Schatzes | Andere Vertheilung | über die Monaht | MAJUS, JUNIUS, | JULIUS, und AUGUSTUS. | Zu Aufferbauung des Algemeinen | Christenthums | Jn der Furcht des HErrn eingesamlet/ | Auch zu mehrer Verständnüß der | heiligen Betrachtungen/ | überal mit nöhtigen Sin-Bilder versehen. | Unter Königl. Majest. zu Dännemarck/ Norwegen/ | Auch Chur-Fürstl. Durchl. zu Sachsen/ | Allergnädigsten Privilegiis. | [rule] | Copenhagen/ | Gedruckt bey J. Kön. Mayt. und Univ. Buchdr. | Johan Philip Bockenhoffer/ 1688. | Zu finden bey Joh. Melchior Liebe/ der Universit. | Buchhändlern.

8vo. [16], 1024, [16] pp.; )(⁸ [−])(8], a-v⁸, w-vv⁸, ww-rrr⁸ (rrr8 blank); frontispiece, 32 plates.　　　　　　　　　　　　　　　　　CKB

Title printed in red and black.

2369　LASSENIUS, JOHANNES

D. Johannis Lassenii | Heiligen | Perlen-Scha- | tzes | Achter Theil/ | über | den Monath | AUGUSTUS | [ornament] | Kopenhagen/ | [rule] | Gedruckt bey J. Kön. Maytt. und Univ. Buchdr. | Johann Philipp Bockenhoffer/ 1688.

8vo. pp. [1-2], 785-1024, [1-2]; π1, bbb-qqq⁸, χ1; engraved preliminary title-page, 8 plates.　　　　　　　　　　　　　　　　　CKB

Index on χ1. For other volumes see Nos. 2321-7, 2370, 2421-2.

2370　LASSENIUS, JOHANNES

D. Johannis Lassenii | Heiligen | Perlen-Scha- | tzes | Neünter Theil/ | über | den Monath | SEPTEMBER. | [ornament] | [rule] | Kopenhagen/ | Gedruckt bey J. Kön. Maytt. und Univ. Buchdr. | Johann Philipp Bockenhoffer/ 1688.

8vo. [4], 272 pp.; π², (A)-(R)⁸; 8 plates.　　　　　　　　　　　CKB

For other volumes see Nos. 2321-7, 2369, 2421-2.

2371　LASSENIUS, JOHANNES

D. Johannis Lassenii | Heiligen | Perlen-Scha- | tzes | Zehnder Theil/ | über | den Monath | OCTOBER. | [ornament] | [rule] | Kopenhagen/ |

Gedruckt bey J. Kön. Maytt. und Univ. Buchdr. | Johann Philipp Bock-
enhoffer/ 1688.

8vo. Pp. [1-4], 273-560; $\pi^2$, (S)-(V)$^8$ (W)$^8$ (X)-(Ll)$^8$; 8 plates.                CKB

2372  LASSENIUS, JOHANNES

D. Johannis Lassenii | Heiligen | Perlen-Scha- | tzes | Eilffter Theil/ |
über | den Monath | NOVEMBER. | [ornament] | [rule] | Kopenha-
gen/ | Gedruckt bey J. Kön. Maytt. und Univ. Buchdr. | Johann Philipp
Bockenhoffer/ 1688.

8vo. [1-4], 561-800; $\pi^2$ (Mm)-(Vv)$^8$ (Ww)$^8$ (Xx)-(Bbb)$^8$; 8 plates.                CKB

2373  MAJOR, JOHANN DANIEL

Kurtzer Vorbericht/ | betreffende | D. Johann-Daniel Majors | Der
Medicin Professoris in Kiel/ wie auch Hoch-Fürstl. | Schleßwig-Holstein-
ischen Leib-Medici, | MVSEVM CIMBRICVM, | oder insgemein so-
genennte | Kunst-Kammer/ | mit darzu-gehörigem | Cimbrischen Con-
ferenz-Saal. | [rule] | Gedruckt zu Plöen/ | durch Tobias Schmidt/ 1688.

4to. 54 pp.; A-G$^4$; 4 plates.                                                 CKB; KIEL UL

G4 lacking, probably blank.

2374  MASIUS, HECTOR GOTTFRIED

Der abgefertigte Jesuit in Frankreich. Copenhagen, 1688.

                                                                                    *

A reissue of *Päbstlicher Sauerteig,* 1688 (No. 2375). *Cf.* Ehrencron-Müller, *Forfatterlexikon* V, 333.

2375  [MASIUS, HECTOR GOTTFRIED]

Päbstlicher | Sauerteig | außgefeget/ | Oder: | Schriftmäßige Wie- |
derlegung | Päbstlicher Lehre | Jn dreyen Puncten: | I. Von der Messe. |
II. Von der Kirchen-Folge/ | III. Von dem rechtmäßigen Be- | ruff der
Evangelischen | Prediger/ | Sampt einer Apologie gegen eine | Frantzös-
ische Schrifft eines Jesuiten. | Hiebevor bey gegebener Gelegenheit in |
Franckreich entworffen von | H.G.M. S.Th D. & P.P. | [rule] | Copen-
hagen/ Gedruckt bey Jhr. Königl. H. Buchtr. | Joachim Schmedtgen/
1688.

8vo. 201, [3] pp.; A-M$^8$ N$^6$.                                                        CKB

Also issued under title: *Dreyfache Anhang nemlich: Eine Beantwortung etlicher
Fragen von der Messe. II. Eine Erinnerung . . . Kirchenfolge. III . . . Rechtmäßiger
Beruf der Evangelischen Prediger.* (Ehrencron-Müller, *Forfatterlexikon* V, 332 f.;
*Cat. lib. Povelson,* 1738, p. 38.)

2376  MOHR, JOHANN

Rechenbuch. Schleswig, 1688.

8vo.                                                                    *

*Cat. lib. Matthiæ Welleji,* 1721, 8vo, 846. CKB has Schleswig, 1696 (No. 2788).

2377  MOLLER, JOHANNES

Schertz Gedicht auf den hochzeitlichen Ehren-Tag Gottfried Neanders.
. . . Schleswig, 1688.

Folio.                                                                 *

*OHM* I, 430-1.

2378  OLDERMANN, SAMUEL

Schuldige | doch | Betrübte Pflicht | Welche | Bey dem Todesfall | Des |
Hoch Ehrwürdigen/ Hoch Edlen/ Vesten | und Hochgelahrten | Herrn
MATTHIÆ | Waßmuths/ | Der Heil. Schrifft hochberühmten Do- |
ctoris, und bey der Kielischen Universität hoch- | verdienten ProfessorIs
Theologiæ, | Mit trauriger Feder abstatten wollen | dessen Schwieger-
licher Freund | Samuel Oldermann. | [rule] | KJEL/ | Gedruckt durch
Joachim Reumann/ Acad. Buchdr. [1688]

4to. χ². KIEL UL; CUL

2379  PROPOSITIONES | Und | POSTULATA | Welche | Jhro Hochfürstl.
Durchleuch- | tigkeit von Hollstein-Gottorff &c. an denen ho- | hen
Käyserl. Königl. Chur-und Fürstlichen/ bey denen | Hollsteinischen
Tractaten in Hamburg anwesenden Respectivé | Herren Ministern
übergeben lassen/ und denn | darauff erfolgte | Jhro Königlichen
Majestät | zu Dennemarck und Norwegen &c. | DECLARATION |
Und | Antwort. | [ornamental rule] | Gedruckt im Jahr 1688.

4to. A-B⁴. CKB

Another edition: A-B⁴ C² (C2 blank), on B1, added title: *DECLARATION | So*
*wegen | Jhr. Königl. Maj | zu Dennemarck und Nor- | wegen &c. | auff Jhro*
*Fürstl. Durchl. zu | Hollstein-Gottorff gethane | POSTULATA | eingegeben*
*worden. | Altona | Den. 5. Januarii Anno 1688.* (CKB; Kiel UL. Altenhof has as
a separate.)

2380  REYHER, SAMUEL

Kurtze Beschreibung der Sechsigtheiligen Rechnung, wie selbige sehr
vortheilhaftig, durch sonderliche Rechenstäblein, kan verrichtet werden.
Kiel, 1688.

8vo.                                                                    *

*Moller* II, 724; *Bibl. Ehrencron,* 1717, p. 359; *Bibl. Brinckmannianae,* 1722, p. 139.

2380A ROHN, CHRISTOPHER

Die wohlabgelegte Rechnung der Zeit/ | . . . | Matthiä Wasmuths/ | S.
S. Theol.Doct. | Und Hochverdienten Prof. P. auff der weitberühmten |
Universität Kiel/ wehmühtigst entworffen/ | den 9 December 1688 |
Christophorus Rohn/ | S.S. Theol. Stud. | [rule] | KJEL/ | Gedruckt
bey Joachim Reumann/ Acad. Buchdr.

4to. χ².                                                    KIEL UL

2381 SCHMIDT, JOACHIM

Seelen Triumph . . . Trost-Predigt über Catharina von Bühlowen, Frantz
von Kramers Wittwe. Plön, 1688.

4to.                                                              *

*OHM* I, 594.

2382 SCHÖLTZ, FRIEDRICH

Weg zur Gottseeligkeit. Glückstadt, 1688.

12mo.                                                            *

*Bibl. Schroedter,* 1724, p. 690.

2383 WASMUTH, MATTHIAS, JR.

Letztes Ehren-Gedächtniß/ | Auff den seeligsten Hintritt | . . . | Herren
Matthiä Waßmuthens/ | . . . | von | Matthiä Waßmuthen/ Med. Stud. |
. . . | KJEL/ | Gedruckt bey Joachim Reumann/ Acad. Buchdr. [1688]

Broadside.                                                  KIEL UL

2384 WILCKENS, JOHANN HERMANN

(Trauer-Gedicht: Georg Hinz). Altona: Chr. Reimers, 1688.

                                                                 *

Formerly in Kiel UL (LmC 44-10).

2385 ZITSCHER, PETER

Henochs | Wall-und Himmelfahrt/ | . . . | Herrn M. HERMANNI |
Erdmanns/ | . . . | Von | P. Zitzschærn/ | Königl. Schloß-Past. zu |
Glückstadt. | [rule] | Glückstadt/ gedruckt bey Reinhard Janßen/ | im
Jahr 1688.

4to. 120 pp.; A-P⁴.                                            CKB

On p. 99, separate title: *Abdanckungs-Rede/* | . . . | *Von* | *M. ANDREA
HÖYERN.* . . . Appended: *Piæ Lacrymæ* | . . . | *Fundebat* | *Amici* | . . . (a-b⁴ c²).

2386  Zitscher, Peter

Die selige Vermählung mit Christo oder Abdanckung über Jfr. Hedwig
Maria Helminn. Glückstadt, 1688.

4to.                                                                                    \*

*OHM* II, 1039.  Formerly in Hamburg Staatsbibliothek.

## 1689

2387  Abdruck │ Der von │ Jhrer Königlichen Majestät │ zu Dennemarck Nor-
wegen │ Zu den Altonaischen Tractaten verordneten │ Herren Ministris │
Endlichen │ DECLARATION │ Welche Sie am 26. May/ st.v. der hohen
Mediation │ übergeben. [1689]

4to. χ². BM

Perhaps published in Altona.

2388  Vom 25. November Fol. 723 │ Die Altonaische RELATION │ No. 87
[woodcut: crowned female figure on lion] 1689

8vo. Pp. 723-730; χ⁴. Deutsch-Nienhof

Caption title.

2389  Altonaischer Vergleich │ zwischen │ Jhr. Königl. Maje- │ stät zu Dennemarck Norwegen &c. │ an einer/ │ Und │ Jhr. Hoch-Fürstlichen │ Durchl.
zu Holstein Gottorff │ anderer Seiten/ │ Durch Sorgfalt/ grosser Mühe
und Arbeit │ Der hohen Herrn Mediatoren │ Vermittelt und zu Altona
geschlossen den 20, 30 Junii │ ANNO 1689. │ [rule] │ Gedruckt im Jahr
1689.

4to. χ². CKB

Another edition: *Der Altonaischen │ Vergleich/ │ De Anno 1689. den 20 Junii,* )(².

2390  Altonaischer Vertrag/ │ zwischen │ Dero Königl. Mayest. │ zu Dennemarck Norwegen &c. &c. │ und │ Jh. Hoch-Fürstl. Durchl. │ zu Hollstein
Gottorff. │ Vermittelt und geschlossen durch die dazu Gevoll- │ mächtigte
hohe Käyserliche/ Chur-Sächsische/ Chur- │ Brandenburgische Herrn
Mediatores und Abge- │ sandten den 20. Junij 1689. │ [rule of type orna-
ments] │ Altona/ Gedruckt im Jahr 1689.

4to. χ². CKB

Same text as *Altonaischer Vergleich* (No. 2389). Another edition, n.p., in BM. Also
published in Hamburg, by Thomas von Wiering.

2391   BECK, JOHANN JOSEPH

Der Berg verliert | Was Phœbus ziert | Das Untergehn | Bringt Aufferstehn | Oder | Traur-und Trost-Gedicht | . . . | Herrn Georg Ernest | Heldbergen/ | . . . | Von | Johan Joseph Becken | . . . | KJEL/ Gedruckt bey Joachim Reumann/ Ac. Buchd. [1689]

4to. χ⁴.                                                                               KIEL UL

2392   BOLDICH, ERNST CHRISTIAN

Schuldigste Thränen | über | Den unverhofften Todesfall | . . . | Hn. | JUSTI VALEN- | TINI Stemanns/ | . . . | M. Ernst Christian Boldich/ | Königl. Schloßpredigern auff Cronenburg und | der Teutschen Gemeine in Helsingör | Pastorn. | [rule] | Gedruckt in der Königl. Veste Glückstadt/ | bey Reinhard Janßen. [1689]

Folio. χ².                                                                              CKB

Verse.

2393   B[URCHARD], P[ETER] A[NTON]

(Hochzeitsgedicht: Georg Becken & Katharina Hagen). Schleswig: Joh. Holweins Erben, 1689.

                                                                                       *

Formerly in Kiel UL (LmC 5-60).

2394   BURCHARD, PETER ANTON

Trostschreiben an das betrübte Hochgräfliche Samsøische Hauß bey Beerdigung Annæ Christianæ Güldenlöw. 1689.

Folio.                                                                                 *

*OHM* I, 82.

2395   [BURCHARD, PETER ANTON]

Verdoppeltes Leidt/ | Durch | Höchstbetrübtes Absterben | Jhrer hohen Gnaden/ | Christiana Gül- | denlöw/ | Vermählten Gräffin | von Ahlefeldt. | Beseüfzet | Bey Deroselben Beysetzung in Kopenhagen | Am 7 November des Jahres 1689.

Folio. χ².                                                                              CKB

Verse.

2396   BURCHARD, PETER ANTON

Der vereinigte Götter-Streit. | Dem | Allerdurchleüchtigsten Großmächtigsten | Könige und Herren | König Christian | dem Fümften/ | Zu

Dennemarck und Norwegen/ der Wenden und Gohten/ Hertzogen zu
Schleß- | wig/ Holstein/ Stormarn und der Dithmar- | schen/ Grafen zu
Oldenburg und | Delmenhorst/ | Wie höchstgedachter Königl. Majest. |
Gebuhrts-Tag/ | Den 15 April, Anno 1689 in Kopenhagen auf dem |
Schloß Amalienburg celebriret ward/ | vorgestellet. | Auffgesetzet
durch | P. A. Burchard. | Und in der Music gebracht durch | P. E.
Schindler. | [rule] | Gedruckt bey J.K.M. und Univ. Buchdr. J. P.
Bockenhoffer.

4to. [8], 22, [2] pp.; )( ⁴, A-C⁴ (C4 blank).                          CKB; (BM)

2397  COPIA | Des an | Jhro Königliche Mayestät | zu Dennemarck Norwegen
      &c. | von denen Ministris der sämbtlichen Herren Mediatoren | zuletzt
      abgelassenen | Schreibens/ | Durch welches und denen darinn enthal-
      tenen | nachdrücklichen Remonstrationen, höchstgemelte Jhro | Königl.
      Mayst. Sich endlich bewegen lassen/ die von | Jhnen in der vorgewesen
      Hoch-Fürstl. Hollsteinischen | Gottorffischen Sache vorgeschlagene
      Friedens- | Conditiones allergnädigst zu placedi- | ren und anzunehmen.
      [1689]

      4to. χ⁴.                                                         CKB

2398  COPIA | Königl. Dännemarck. | Antwort-Schreibens/ | An | HERRN |
      Christian Albrecht zu | Schleßwig/ Hollstein/ Gottorff &c.

      4to. χ⁴.                                                         CKB

      Dated at end *Coppenhagen den | 27. Decemb. 1689.*

2399  DENMARK. *Laws, statutes, etc.*

      WJR Christian der Fünffte/ von | . . . | . . . 21. Jan: Anno 1689.

      Broadside.                                                       CKB

      Decree postponing a meeting of the Holstein "Ober-Amptgericht" until 4 April.

2400  DENMARK. *Laws, statutes, etc.*

      WJr Christian der Fünffte/ von Gottes | . . . | . . . Copenhagen den 16.
      Februarii Anno 1689.

      Broadside.                                                       CNA

      Decree regarding payment of a tax on land.

2401  DENMARK. *Laws, statutes, etc.*

      WJr Christian der Fünffte/ von Gottes Gna- | den . . . | WJr Leopold von
      Gottes Gnaden Erwehlter Römischer | . . . | . . . 22. Februarii Anno 1689.

      Broadside.                                                       CKB

Reissue by King Christian and Duke Christian Albrecht of Schleswig-Holstein of an imperial decree against the sale of horses and munitions outside the empire.

2402  DENMARK. *Laws, statutes, etc.*

WJr Christian der Fünffte/ von Gottes Gna- | den ... | ... | WJr Leopold von Gottes Gnaden Erwehlter Römischer | ... | ... 22. Februarii Anno 1689.

Broadside (two sheets pasted together).                                            CKB

Reissue by King Christian and Duke Christian Albrecht of Schleswig-Holstein of imperial decree forbidding intercourse with France.

2403  DENMARK. *Laws, statutes, etc.*

WJR Christian der Fünffte/ von | ... | ... Glückstadt/ den 15. April. Anno 1689.

Broadside.                                                                          CNA

Decree setting a day of prayer 26 April.

2404  DENMARK. *Laws, statutes, etc.*

WJR Christian der Fünffte/ von | ... | .. Glückstadt ... | ... 27. Maji, Anno 1689.

Broadside.                                                                    CKB; CNA

Decree forbidding trade on Sundays and holidays and the sale of "Brandwein/ Bier oder Wein in den Krügen oder Weinhäusern" before conclusion of divine service in Holstein and Pinneberg.

2405  DENMARK. *Laws, statutes, etc.*

WJr Christian der Fünffte/ von Gottes | ... | ... 3. Septembris Anno 1689

Broadside.                                                                       KIEL UL

Decree issued jointly with Duke Christian Albrecht of Schleswig-Holstein, regarding payment of a tax on land.

2406  DENMARK. *Laws, statutes, etc.*

WJR Christian der Fünffte/ von | ... | ... Glückstadt den 17ten Septembris, Anuo [sic] 1689

Broadside.                                                                          CNA

Decree appointing 22 September as a day of thanksgiving for victory over the Turks "an dem Morava Strohm."

2406A DENMARK. *Laws, statutes, etc.*

WJR Christian der Fünffte/ von | . . . | WIR LEOPOLD von GOttes
Gnaden erwehlter Römischer Käyser . . . | . . . | . . . 1ten. Octobris, Anno
1689.

Broadside (3 sheets pasted together).                                              CKB

Reissue by King Christian & Duke Christian Albrecht of Schleswig-Holstein of an
imperial decree declaring war on France.

2407  DENMARK. *Laws, statutes, etc.*

WJR Christian der Fünffte/ von | . . . | . . . Glückstadt/ den 31ten
Octobris, Anno 1689.

Broadside.                                                                          CNA

Decree issued jointly with Duke Christian Albrecht of Schleswig-Holstein, regarding payment of a land tax to be divided between King and Duke.

2408  DENMARK. *Laws, statutes, etc.*

WJR Christian der Fünffte/ von | . . . | . . . Glückstadt/ den 15ten
Novembris, Anno 1689.

Broadside.                                                                          CNA

Decree regarding the circulation of small foreign coins.

2409  Die Europäische | FAMA [1689]

12mo. $\chi^4$.                                                         DEUTSCH-NIENHOF

Issue No. 98 [sic] "Vom 18. November 1689," and No. 91 [sic] "Vom. 9. December 1689." Caption title. Published in Altona.

2410  Extract-Schreibens | Aus | Coppenhagen/ | Vom 20. April 1689.

4to. $\chi^2$.                                                                      CKB

About the fire at the Amalienborg opera performance.

2411  GIESE, JOACHIM

Des heiligen Geistes | Als | Göttlichen Professoris, | . . . | GEORGII
ERNESTI | Heldbergs/ | . . . | Von | M. Joachimo Giesen/ Pastore Pri-
mario in Kiel. | [rule] | KJEL/ Gedruckt durch Joachim Reumann/
Acad. Buchdr. [1689]

4to. 94 pp.; A-M$^4$.                                                            KIEL UL

M4 lacking, probably blank.

2412  Der glückliche Friedens-Bote/ | welcher mitbringet | Den | Altonaischen
Vergleich | zwischen | Jhr: Königl. Maj. zu Dennemarck Norwegen

&c. | an einer/ | Und | Jhr: Hoch-Fürstl. Durchl. zu Holstein Gottorff |
anderer Seiten | Durch Sorgfalt/ grosser Mühe und Arbeit der hohen |
Herrn Mediatoren | Vermittelt und zu Altona geschlossen den 20. 30.
Junii, | ANNO 1689.

4to. $\chi^2$.                                                                    CKB

2413  HAMERICH, HENRICH

Seliger Tausch Gottes mit | uns Menschen/ | Bey | Frühzeitigen/ doch
höchstseligen Hintritt | Des | Durchleuchtigen und Hochgebohrnen |
Printzen und Herrn/ | Hn: FRIEDRICH | WILHELMS, | Hertzogen
zu Schleßwig Holstein/ Stor- | marn und der Ditmarschen/ Grafen zu |
Oldenburg und Delmenhorst/ | Als derselbe | Den 19 Decemb: des
abgewichenen 1688sten | . . . | Von | H. Hamerich/ | Fürstl: Glücksb:
Hoff-Prediger. | [ornamental rule] | Schleßwig/ gedruckt bey Sel:
Johann Holweins | nachgelassenen Witwe. [1689]

4to. [6], 34 pp.; A$^4$, B-J$^2$.                                               CKB

Title within border of type ornaments.

2414  HARTNACK, DANIEL

Nöhtige Beschneidung des zu weit und ungeziemend außgestreckten
Theils der Mißgunst und Tadelsucht. (Altona?), 1689.

8vo.                                                                               *

*Moller* II, 304.

2415  HARTNACK, DANIEL

Zurückgewiesener Mercurius, oder Retorsion aller, in der allhie heimlich
vertheilten Schmähschrift enthaltenen, Jnjurien, wieder Joh. Melch.
Stengern Jnspectorem zu Wittstock. [1689]

4to.                                                                               *

*Moller* II, 304.

2416  Jhr. Königl. Mayst. | zu | Dännemarck/ Norwegen/ &c. | zu den |
Altonais. Tractaten | verordneten Herren Ministris übergebene | end-
liche | Declaration | Geschehen den 16 May st. v. 1689.

4to. $\chi^2$.                                                                    CKB

2417  Klag-und Trost-Gedicht/ | Bey | Dem frühzeitigen doch sehligen |
Absterben | . . . | Frauen Eleonoren/ | gebohrnen Büttnerin/ | Des |
Woll-Edlen und Vesten Herren/ | Hn: Georg Bocken/ | . . . | Ehe-

Schatzes/ | . . . | Von | Einem guten Freunde. | [rule] | Glückstadt/
gedruckt bey Reinhard Janßen/ 1689.

Folio. χ². CKB

Verse.

2418 Der | Königl. Dänischen Ministrorum | Fernere | DECLARATION, |
Oder | Zum Fundament gesetzte Conditiones | Die | RESTITUTION |
Jhrer Hoch-Fürstlichen Durchl. | zu Holstein Gottorff | betreffend.
[1689?]

4to. χ². CKB

2419 Kurzer Unterricht Von der Frantzösischen Sprache . . . 1689.

*Cf.* No. 2231. *

2420 LASSENIUS, JOHANNES

Biblischer | Weyrauch | Zum süssen Geruch | Gottseeliger Andachten/ |
Auß H. Schrifft also zusamen gelesen | Das mit des heiligen Geistes ei- |
genen Worten/ die GOtt-Liebende | Seel/ täglich mit GOtt reden |
könne. | Samt | Heilsahmer Vorbereitung | zum Beicht-Stuhl/ | Und
Heiligen Abendmahl. | Mit allerhand neüen/ Morgen-und | Abend-Buß-
Beicht-und Communion-Lie- | dern/ auch Kupffern hin und wie- | der
versehen. | Dem Gecreützigten JEsu allein zu Ehren/ | Und der/ mit
seinem Blut erlöseten heiligen Ge- | meine GOttes in Copenhagen und
Anderswo/ | Zur Beförderung ihres Christenthums/ angezündet | von |
D. JOHANNE LASSENIO, | Mit Königl. Majest. zu Denm. und
Churfl. Durchl. | zu Sachsen Allergnädigsten Privilegio. | [rule] |
Gedruckt bey Jh. Kön. Majest. und der Univ. | Buchdr. Joh. Phil.
Bockenhoffer/ 1689. | Zu finden bey Joh. Melch. Liebe der Univer. |
Buchhändler.

12mo. [12], 720, [8] pp.; a⁶, A-Ff¹², Gg⁴; frontispiece, engraved t-p., 19 plates.
CKB

2421 LASSENIUS, JOHANNES

JOHANNIS LASSENII | Der H. Schrifft Doct. Prof. Publ. und Past: |
an St. Petri Kirchen | Heiligen | Perlen-Schatzes | Dritte und letzte
Vertheilung | über die Monaht | SEPTEMBER, OCTOBER, NO- |
VEMBER und DECEMBER. | Zu Aufferbauung des Algemeinen |
Christenthums | Jn der Furcht des HErrn/ auß Göttlichem | Wort
eingesamlet/ | Auch zu richtiger Verständnüß der | heiligen Betrach-
tungen | Uberal mit nöhtigen Sinbildern versehen. | Unter Königl.
Majest. zu Dennemarck/ Norwegen/ | Auch Chur-Fürstl. Durchl. zu

Sachsen/ | Allergnädigsten Privilegiis. | [rule] | Copenhagen/ | Gedruckt
bey J. Königl. Majest. und Universit. Buchdr. | Johan Philip Bocken-
hoffer/ 1689. | Zu finden bey Joh. Melchior Liebe/ der Universit. |
Buchhandlern.

8vo. [14], 1040, [16] pp.; )($^8$ (−1), (A)-(V)$^8$ (W)$^8$ (X)-(Vv)$^8$ (Ww)$^8$ (Xx)-
(Sss)$^8$ (Sss 7-8 blank); engraved t-p., 32 plates.                              CKB

For other volumes see Nos. 2321-7, 2369-70, 2422.

2422  LASSENIUS, JOHANNES

D. Johannis Lassenii | Heiligen | Perlen-Scha | tzes | Zwölffter Theil/ |
über | den Monath | DECEMBER. | [ornament] | [rule] | Kopen-
hagen/ | Gedruckt bey J. Kön. Maytt. und Univ. Buchdr. | Johann
Philipp Bockenhoffer/ 1689.

8vo. pp. [1-4], 801-1040, [1-16]; $\pi^2$, (Ccc)-(Sss)$^8$, (Sss 7-8 blank); 8 plates.   CKB

Cf. No. 2421.

2423  Leich-Cypreß | . . . | Frauen Eleonoren/ | gebohrnen Bütnerin/ | Des |
Woll-Edlen/ Vest-und Woll-weisen | Hn: Georg Bocken/ | . . . | Von |
Nachgesetzten. | [rule] | Glückstadt/ gedruckt bey Reinhard Janßen.
[1689]

Folio. [a]$^2$, b-c$^2$.                                                        CKB

Verse by several hands.

2424  MAGIRUS, KASPAR

(Abdanckung über Hedwig Reimann). Copenhagen: Joach. Schmedtgen, 1689.

4to. 20 pp.                                                                      *

See R. Mende: *Katalog der Leichenpredigten Sammlungen . . . Liegnitz*, 1938, p.
399.

2425  [MORHOF, DANIEL GEORG]

ODE/ | Welche | Bey der Beerdigung | . . . | Herrn Georg Ernest |
Heldbergen/ | . . . | KJEL/ | Gedruckt bey Joachim Reumann/ Ac.
Buchd. [1689]

4to. χ$^2$.                                                                  KIEL UL

Signed: D.G.M.

2426  PETERSEN, JOHANNA ELEONORA (*née* VON MERLAU)

Gespräche | des | Hertzens | mit | GOTT/ | Erster Theil. | Auffgesetzet |
Von | JOHANNA ELEONORA | PETERSEN, | Gebohrne von und zu

Merlau. | [rule of type ornaments] | PLOEN/ | Verlegts Siegfried Ripenau. | Gedruckt durch Tobias Schmidt/ | 1689.

8vo. [24], 295[=303], [1] pp.; )($^4$ ):($^8$ A-K$^8$ L$^8$ (L2+ $^2$)($^4$) M-S$^8$ T$^4$; 2 plates.
                                                                                        HALLE UL; HAB

On $^2$)(1, separate title: *Gespräche* | ... | *Ander Theil.* | .... HAB copy has signature †$^4$ instead of $^2$)($^4$.

2427  RICHTER, JOHANNES HENRICH

Lingva profana, die Lästerhafte Zunge, mit beygedruckten Bedencken hochgelahrter Leute über ein factum. Schleswig, 1689.

8vo.                                                                                                    *

*Moller* I, 544.

2428  RIDEMANN, CHRISTIAN

Die Pfingst-Lust-Weyen | Verwandelt | in Leid-Cypressen | Durch | Den Todt | Des Weil. HochEhrwürdigen/ HochEdlen und | Hochgelahrten | Hn. JUSTI VALEN- | TINI Stemann/ | ... | CHRISTIANI Ridemans/ | Predigers der Christlichen Gemeine | zu Beyenfleth. | [rule] | Glückstadt/ | Gedruckt bey Reinhard Janßen. [1689]

Folio. χ$^2$.                                                                                            CKB

Verse.

2429  SCHIPPING, PETER

Abgenöthigtes | Gespräch/ | Von | Dem Bande der Re- | ligion und Societät/ | Worinnen | D. MASII | INTERESSE PRIN- | CIPUM CIRCA RELIGIO- | NEM EVANGELICAM | Gegen eines neulichen Scribenten | Ernsthaffte Bedancken | verthädiget wird/ | Verfasset | Von | Petro Schipping/ Th. C. | [rule] | Gedruckt im Jahr 1689.

8vo. 71, [1] pp.; A-D$^8$ E$^4$.                                                                         CKB

Ehrencron-Müller, *Forfatterlexikon* V, 333, states Schipping may be a pseudonym of H. G. Masius.

2430  SCHLESWIG-HOLSTEIN-GOTTORFF. *Laws, statutes, etc.*

WJr von Gottes Gnaden Christian | Albrecht/ Erbe zu Norwegen/ POSTULIR | TER COADJUTOR des Stifftes Lübeck/ ... | ... | ... Tremßbüttel/ den 21. Septemb. 1689.

Broadside.                                                                                              CNA

Decree regarding the sale of brass, copper, and other metals.

2431 SCHLESWIG-HOLSTEIN-GOTTORFF. *Laws, statutes, etc.*

Wir Von Gottes Gnaden | Christian Albrecht/ Erbe zu Norwegen |... |
Hertzog zu Schleßwig ... | ... | ... 8. November. Anno 1689

Broadside.                                                                   KIEL UL

Decree forbidding gifts at weddings & baptisms and ostentation at funerals.

2432 SCHRÖDER, JOSIAS HERMANN

Glückwünschender Zuruff . . . womit Herrn Christoff Francken, wie
derselbe zum Pro-Rector eingeführet worden, gehorsamst übergeben von
J. H. Schröder. Kiel, 1689.

Folio.                                                                          *

Formerly in Kiel UL (LmC 18ª-61).

2433 SPECHT, CHRISTIAN

Valet-Predigt/ | Welche | Zu Hannover | Jn der Kirche S. Crucis, bey
christlicher/ sehr | volck-reicher Versamlung/ Anno 1689. am Sontage
Palma- | rum, an welchem zugleich das Fest der Verkündi- | gung Mariæ
zu feyren war/ | Aus den Worten Pauli in der Apostel-Geschicht am
XX. | Cap. im 31. und 32. Versen: | Darumb seyd wacker/ &c. biß
— Wort seiner | Gnaden. | An Stat der ordentlichen Haupt-Predigt
gehalten/ und nun | auff vielfältiges Verlangen und Ansuchen zum |
Druck heraus gegeben hat/ | CHRISTIAN Specht/ | Damahliger Pastor
der Kirche zu S. Crucis in Hannover/ numehro | aber Fürstl. Holst. Jhro
Hochfürstl. Durchl. des Herrn Bischoffs zu | Lübeck/ und Hertzogen zu
Schleßwig-Holstein &c. bestalter | Beicht-Vater/ Hoff-Prediger/ und des
Bi- | schoffthums Lübeck Superin- | tendens. | [rule of type ornaments] |
PLOEN/ Gedruckt und verlegt durch Tobias Schmidt.

4to. [8], 57, [15] pp.; )(⁴, A-J⁴.                                            KIEL UL

2434 STEMANN, JUST DANIEL

Der mit vielen Thränen beklagte Abschied | Des Weil: | HochEhr-
würdigen WohlEdlen und Hochgelahrten Herren/ | Herren Doct. |
Just Valentin Stemans/ | ... | ... | Just Daniel Stemann | Med. Stud. |
[below:] Glückstadt/ | Gedruckt bey Reinhard Janßen/ im Jahr 1689.

Broadside (32 x 25.5 cm).                                                     CKB

2435 TÄNTZER, JOHANN

Der | DIANEN | Hohe und Niedere | Jagt-Geheimnüß | Dritter Theil/ |
Darinnen | Abermahln viel nützliche und nöhtige | Jagt Wissen-

schafften | Gründlich und außführlich zu befinden/ | Welche auch | Mit vielen Kupfer-Stücken erklähret werden: | Mit grosser Arbeit be- schrieben und viel darin | Neu-inventiret | Durch | Johann Täntzern/ | Und seiner Verlegung. | [ornamental rule] | Copenhagen/ | Zu finden bey Johann Jost Erythropilus Buchhändlern/ | 1689.

Folio. Pp. [1-8], 3-132 (including 12 plates counted as 24 pages), [1-2] pp.; $\pi^2$, )($^2$, A-Cc$^2$; engraved frontispiece.                                      CKB; (BM)

Title in red and black. Dedication is dated *Kopenhagen Anno 1687.* At end of work: *Copenhagen den 30 Augusti Anno 1689.* Preliminary title: *Der | Dianen | Hohe und Niedere | Jagt | Geheimniß | Dritter Theil.*

2436   Traur und Trost-Gedicht | Als | Jhrer Hohen Gnaden | Der | Hochge- bohrnen Frauen/ | Frau Christiana Gül- | denlew/ | . . . | Hn. Friderich von Alefelt/ | . . . | Seiner Gottsehligen Frau Gemahlin | Leich- Begängnüß | Den 7 Novembr. Anno 1689 in der Königlichen Residentz Stadt Co- | penhagen gehalten ward. | [ornamental rule] | Gedruckt bey Jhr. Königl. Maj. und Univers. Buchdr. Joh. Phil. Bockenhoffer. [1689]

Folio. χ$^2$.                                                                CKB

2437   WEDDERKOPF, GABRIEL

Das Herlichste und Heilsamste | Christen-Werck/ | bestehend | Jn Geistlichen Gottgefälligen | Betrach- | tungen | Zur Ubung der Gottselig- keit | vorgestellet/ | Von | M. Gabriel Wedderkop/ | Predigern bey der Haupt- | Kirchen in Kiel | [rule] | KJEL | Jn Verlegung Sebastian Richels/ | Buchh. 1689.

8vo. [24], 416 pp.; $^\pi$A$^8$, b$^4$, A-Cc$^8$.                                    CKB

2438   WEDDERKOPF, GABRIEL

Der Kinder GOttes | Heilsamste Arbeit | auff Erden/ | Durch einige Geistliche | Betrachtungen | zur Gottseligkeit | vorgestellet/ | Von | M. Gabriel Wedderkop/ | Predigern bey der Haupt- | Kirchen in Kiel. | [rule of type ornaments] | KJEL/ | Jn Verlegung Sebastian Richels | Buchh. 1689

8vo. [16], 416 pp.; $^\pi$A$^8$, A-Cc$^8$.                                          SRL

2439   WEIS, OTTO

Himmel-Freude | über | Einen zuvor unbekehrten Türck und Heide/ | Nunmehro | Jm fästen Glauben an den einigen wahren GOTT/ und den Er | außgesandt hat seinen Sohn JESUM (Joh: 17.v.3) CHristum/ | durch die Tauffe in ihm angezündet von dem Heiligen | Geist/ | Be- kehrten Christen | Deß | Hoch-Edlen und Wollgebohrnen Hrrn |

HENNJNG UL- | RJCH LUTZOV | Zu Söholt/ | Jhro Königl: Hoheit zu Dennemarck und Norwegen | Hoff-Marschallen/ | ULRJCH | Genant/ | Zu Erinnerung/ daß sein Nahme/ der zuvor auff den schwartzen Brieff | mit dem Griffel der Verdamnuß angezeichnet (Esa: 8. v.1.)/ nun im | Himmel mit den außerwehlten auff dem weißen Stein geschrieben (Apoc: 2.v.17.) durch daß theure seines eintzigen Heylandes | JESU CHristi Verdienst; | Vollenzogen den 27. Jun: Anno 1689. | an welchen Tag | Er auß einen Sünder Gerecht/ | Auß einem Kind des Zorns ein Kind der Gnaden GOttes/ | Und auß einem Erbe der ewigen Verdamnüß ein Erbe deß Ewigen | Lebens geworden/ | Schuldigst darreicht | von | Deß Taufflings | Durch daß Wort GOttes und JEsu Lehre | Leiter zum Himmel | Otto Weis. | [rule of type ornaments] | Kopenhagen/ | Gedruckt bey Christian Wering Universit. Buchdr.

Folio. 7 leaves.                                                        CUL

2440  ZITSCHER, PETER

Die | Gekrönte Priester-Treue | . . . | Hn. JUSTI VALENTINI | STEMANN, | . . . | Von | P. Zitschærn/ | Königl. Schloß-Pastorn zu | Glückstadt. | [rule] | Glückstadt/ gedruckt bey Reinhard Janßen/ | Jm Jahr 1689

4to. 146, [22] pp.; A-X⁴.                                               CKB

On p. 117, separate title: *Der grosse Gewinn* | . . . | *Von* | *M. HENRICO Hahn/ P; on T2, separate title: Schuldigste Thränen* | . . . | *Von Desselben nachgelassenen hochbetrübten* | *Schwieger-Sohn und Kindern;* on U4, separate title: *Ehren-Gedächtniß* | . . . | *Von einigen Vornehmen und Wohlmeinenden* | *Herren und Freunden.*

2441  Die zwischen | Dero Königl. Mayest. | zu Dennemarck Norwegen &c. &c. | und | Jh. Hoch-Fürstl. Durchl. | zu Hollstein geschlossene Friedens- | Puncten.

4to. χ².                                                                DRÜLT

Dated at end, "Altona 20 Junij 1689." Possibly an appendix to another publication.

# 1690

2442  ALARDUS, NICOLAUS

D. NICOLAI ALARDI, | Dero Königl. Majest. zu Dennemarck Nor- | wegen &c. General-Superintendenten, in denen | Graffschafften Olden-burg und Del- | menhorst/ | Theologisches | Bedencken/ | über den |

Von einigen des E. Hamburgischen | MINISTERII | publicirten | Neuen
Religions-Eyd. | [rule] | Gedruckt im Jahr 1690

4to. )(⁴.                                                                CKB

2443  Als die | Weyland Hoch-gebohrne Gräfinn | und Frau/ | Fr. Catarina
Hedewig | Gräfinn zu Rantzau und Löwenholm/ Frau | auff Breiten-
burg/ | ... | ... beygesetzt wurde/ | ... | Ein | Dem gantzem Hoch-
gräflichem Hause | Unterthänig-Verbundenster Diener | [rule] | Glück-
stadt/ | Gedruckt bey Reinhard Janßen [1690]

Folio. [2], 10 pp.; π1, A-C² (−C2).                                 Kiel UL

Intended to be sent to persons who attended funeral. Handwritten note on Kiel
copy identifies author as "Canz. Secretaire Goude."

2444  Alß | TIT: | Hr. Jacob Eschen- | berg | Und | Jfr. Catharina Hed- | wig
Lassenia. | Den 30 Heumonahts 1690 | in Copenhagen. | Jhr Hochzeit-
liches Feyer | begingen | Wolte seine Schuldigkeit hiemit | ablegen |
J.C.G. | Imprimatur, | C. BARTHOLIN. | [rule] | Gedruckt bey Jhr.
Königl. Majest. und Universit. Buchdr. | Johann Philipp Bockenhoffer.

Folio. χ².                                                              CUL

2445  BACHMANN, GEORG FRIEDRICH

Hollsteinische | Freudens-Bezeugung/ | über des | Hochwürdigsten/ |
Durchlauchtigsten/ | Fürsten und Herren/ | Hn. Christian Al- |
brechts/ | Postulirten Coadjutoris des Stiffts Lübeck/ | Erbens zu Norr-
wegen/ Hertzogens zu Schleßwig/ | Holstein/ Stormarn und der Ditt-
marschen/ Grafens zu | Oldenburg und Delmenhorst/ | HochFürstl.
Wiederkunfft | auff dero Residentz Gottorp | Endlich | Jm abgewichenen
1689 Jahr höchst-erfreulich wiederumb erlebet; | Nun aber | Bey Antritt
des 1690 Christ-Jahres/ | Nebst demütigsten Glück-Wunsch | Zum Neuen
Jahr | unterthänigst vorgestellet | Von | Georg Fridrich Bachmann/
Pastorn auff der Jnsul | Arniß/ unter dem Schleßwigischen Thumb-
Capitul. | [rule] | KJEL/ | Gedruckt durch Joachim Reumann.

Folio. [A²] B².                                                        CKB

2446  [BOHSE, AUGUST?]

OLLA PODRIDA, | sonsten | Olle putterie | Von süß und sauren/ |
Von gesaltzen und ungesaltzenem/ | Ohne sonderbahrer Sorgfalt nach-
dem es vorgekommen in der Eile | untermenget | Und an | Des Woll
Ehrenvesten/ Großachtbarn und | Kunstgelarten Herrn/ | Hn: JO-
HANN FRI- | DERICH MAITREN, | Berühmten Musici, und der
Kirchen zu St. Marien in | Flenßburg wohlbestalten Organisten/ | Mit |

Der GroßEhr und Tugendreichen Jungfer/ | Jungfer ANNA | Des Woll
Ehrenvesten und Großachtbahrn Herrn/ | Hn: HANS MELCHIOR, |
Wohlfürnehmen Bürgern und Handelsmann | daselbst/ | Eheleiblichen
Jungfer Tochter/ | Hochzeitlichem Ehren-Tage | Alß den 7 Julij 1690. |
Zum Nach-Essen auffgetragen | Von | TALANDER. | [double rule] |
SCHLESWJG/ | Gedruckt bey seel: Johann Holweins nachgelassenen
Erben.

Folio. χ².                                                          CKB

Verse.

2447  [BOHSE, AUGUST?]

(Hochzeitsgedicht: Friedrich Heldt & Anna Katherina Tyche) Schleswig: Joh. Holweins Erben 1690

Folio. χ².                                                             *

Formerly in Kiel UL (LmC 9-89). Signed "Talander."

2448  BOYE, HENRICH

Bey den früh-zeitigen | jedoch | Höchst-seeligen Hintrit/ | . . . | Hn.
Henrich Schupps | . . . | Henrich Boye. | [below] Gedruckt bey Jhr.
Königl. Mayest. und Universit. Buchdrucker Johann Philip Bockenhoffer. [Copenhagen 1690]

Broadside.                                                          CUL

2449  BRÄMER, CHRISTIAN

Himmels-Gedancken | Verfasset | auf dem Berg | Thabor/ | Und bey der
Erklärung | Der | Verklärung Christi | entdecket. | Auch | Mit einem
allgemeinem Register/ | und vielen Sinn-Bildern/ unter Königl. |
Maytt: zu Dännem: Norwegen/ wie auch | Chur-Fürstl. Durchl. zu
Sachsen/ | allergnädigsten Privilegiis | außgegeben | Durch | M. Chri-
stian Brämer/ Lubec. | [rule] | Copenhagen/ | Auf des Autor. Unkosten |
Bey Johann Jacob Bornheinrich gedruckt/ | 1690.

4to. [40], 880, [8] pp.; π² a-b⁸ c² A-Jjj⁸ Kkk⁴; engr. preliminary t.-p., 25 plates.
                                                                   CKB

Engraved preliminary title: *Himmels Gedancken | verfaßet auf dem Berg |
Thabor. | Und bey der Erklärung | der | Verklärung Christi | entdecket | von | M.
Christian Bræmer Lubec | [rule] | Copenhagen auf des Autor Vnkosten | von
Joachim Schmedgen Jhr | Königl: Hoheit privil: Buch- | drucker gedrucket.* Title
within ornamental border; emblem in each corner of page. *Moller* I, 68, lists an
edition of 1694.

2450    [Brandt, Bonaventura Frederiksen]

Herrn | Mag: GREGORIO | ZIMMER, | ... | ANNÆ CATHARJNÆ |
BRANDT | ... | den 27. Novembr. 1690. | ... | Bonaventura Frid:
Brandt. | [rule of type ornaments] | COPENHAGEN/ Gedruckt bey
Johan Adolph Baxman

Broadside.                                                                         Oslo UL

2451    Crane, Johann

Traur-und Submissionschrifft | Jn | Dervorhin anhängig gemachten
Ambts-Klage | Wieder | Den Feind des Menschlichen Lebens/ | über |
Den abermahligen Hinriß | Des | Hoch-Wollgebohrnen Herrn/ | Herrn
Marqvardi | Guden/ | ... | Von | JOHANN CRANEN, | Ober-Sach-
waltern. | ... | [woodcut: coffin] | ... | [rule] | Glückstadt/ gedruckt
bey Reinhard Janßen/ 1690.

Folio. χ².                                                                         CKB

German and Latin verse.

2451A  Denmark. *Laws, statutes, etc.*

Revidirte | Landgerichts-Ordnung/ | So | Jm Nahmen | Jhr: Königl:
Majest: zu Dennemarck/ | Norwegen/ &c. | Christian des Vierdten/ |
Und | Jhr: Hoch Fürstl: Durchl: | Friederichen/ | Erben zu Norwegen/
beyder Hertzogen zu | Schleßwig/ Holstein/ Stormarn und der Dit-
marschen/ | Graffen zu Oldenburg und Delmenhorst/ &c. Gevettern/ |
Zu beförderung der ordentlichen Justitz und Rechtens in | den Fürsten-
thumben Schleßwig/ Holstein/ und dero in- | corporirten Landen/ |
Verfasset und publiciret Anno 1636. | Jtzo zum Drittenmahl auffgeleget/
und nicht allein mit | unterschiedlichen Constitutionen und Edicten, so
in den Gerichten täg- | lich gebrauchet werden/ vermehret/ sondern auch
von vielen men- | dis corrigirt, in paragraphos eingetheilet/ und mit
kurtzen | marginalibus illustriret, | Benebst angedrückter Landes-
Matricul/ und außführlichem | INDICE, so wol über den Textum, als
die demselben beygedrückte | Edicta und Constitutiones. | [rule] |
Gedruckt in der Königl. Vestung Glückstadt/ durch | Reinhard Janßen/
im Jahr M.DC.XC.

4to. [16], 304 pp.; a-b⁴, A-Pp⁴.                                                   CKB

Title printed in red and black.

2452    Denmark. *Laws, statutes, etc.*

Schiffs- | ARTICUL, | Wornach | Wir CHRISTIAN | der Fünffte ...
[1690]

4to. 48 pp.; A-F⁴.                                                                         CKB

Caption title. Rules for ships engaged in commerce with Guinea, under Nicolaus
Janszen Arff. Dated Copenhagen 1 June 1690.

2453   DENMARK. *Laws, statutes, etc.*

WJR Christian der Fünffte/ von | ... | ... 11ten. Januarij, Anno 1690

Broadside.                                                                              KIEL UL

Decree issued jointly with Duke Christian Albrecht of Schleswig-Holstein, regarding payment of a tax on land.

2454   DENMARK. *Laws, statutes, etc.*

WJR Christian der Fünffte/ von | ... | ... Glückstadt/ den 26. April.
Anno 1690.

Broadside.                                                                                 CNA

Decree calling an annual day of prayer the fourth Friday after Easter.

2455   DENMARK. *Laws, statutes, etc.*

WJR Christian der Fünffte/ von | ... | ... Glückstadt/ den 24. Maij,
Anno 1690.

Broadside.                                                                                 CNA

Decree issued jointly with Duke Christian Albrecht of Schleswig-Holstein, calling a
meeting of the "Quartal-Gericht" at Rendsburg 8 July.

2456   DENMARK. *Laws, statutes, etc.*

WJR Christian der Fünffte/ von | ... | ... 25. Junij Anno 1690.

Broadside.                                                                                 CKB

Decree issued jointly with Duke Christian Albrecht of Schleswig-Holstein, regarding a meeting of the courts at Flensburg 3 September.

2457   FRIESE, DETHLEV MARCUS

Traur-Rede, bey der .. .Beysetzung Fr. Catharinæ Hedwig Brocktorfinn,
Gräfin von Ranzou, ... Glückstadt, 1690.

                                                                                            *

*Moller* I, 199.

2458   Genauer | Unterricht | Jn was Zustand die | Holländische Flotte | Sich
nach der den 30 Junii gehal- | tenen | Battaille | befunden. | [rule] |
Copenhagen/ Gedruckt im Jahr 1690.

χ² (15.8 x 10.6 cm).                                                                       CUL

2459    GILLET DE LA TESSONNERIE

Die Regierkunst oder der kluge Hofmeister ... [transl. Benj. Knobloch].
Schleswig, 1690.

8vo.                                                                      *

*Moller* II, 143. Cf. Nos. 954, 1104.

2460    [HARTNACK, DANIEL]

Dem | BIBLIOTHECARIO | Der | Studirenden Jugend | angehängte |
Vertheidigung | Derer | Weder zur Ungebühr noch ungleich | beyge-
brachten | ALLEGATEN | à pag. 200. usque ad fin. | Wider eine |
Neulichst alhie angelangte Schrifft/ | benühmt | Rettung der Lehr | Ph.
J. Sp. | [ornament] | [double rule] | ALTONA/ | Jn der Königl.
privilegirten Druckerey/ | Anno 1690.

8vo. [16], 112 pp.; )*(⁸, A-G⁸.              NIEDERS. LANDESBIBLIOTHEK HANNOVER

2461    HEERFORT, CHRISTOFFER

Der spielende Cupido | wurde bey dem fröhlichen | Hochzeit-Feste |
Des | Edlen Ehren-Vesten und Kunst- | Erfahrnen | Hn. Johañ Kirch-
hoffs | Königl Mayt. zu Dennemarck und Nor- | wegen privilegirten
Apothecker in Dero | Residentz-Stadt Copenhagen/ | Und der | Viel-
Ehr-und Tugend-Begabten | Jfr. Anna Christina | geb. Westens/ | ... |
von | Dero | Imprimatur, | C. BARTHOLIN | Dienst-verbundenen
Anverwandten | Christophoro Heerfort | Jun: | [rule] | Gedruckt bey
Jhr. Königl. Mayst. und Universit. Buchdr. | Johann Philipp Bockenhof-
fer. [1690]

Folio. χ².                                                              CKB

Verse.

2462    HOYER, ANDREAS

Gratuita peccatorum ... Leichpredigt über Eleonora Büttnerinn Georg
Bocken ... Eheliebste. Glückstadt, 1690.

Folio.                                                                    *

*OHM* I, 266.

2463    KENCKEL, STEPHAN

Helden-Brieff des Herrn Christophori Madewitzen an seine Braut Maria
Elisabeth ... Crusen. Schleswig, 1690.

Folio.                                                                    *

Formerly in Kiel UL (LmC 12-2).

2464    Königl. Dännemärckische | Kirchen-CON- | STITUTION | Jn der |
        Herrschaft Pinnenberg | [ornament] | [ornamental rule] | Altona |
        Gedruckt und verlegt durch Christian Reymers/ | Königl. privilegirten
        Buchdrucker/ im Jahr | 1690.

        4to. 8 pp.; )(⁴.                                                        CKB

        CKB's copy printed and bound with: *Weiland Herrn Otten* | . . . | *Hoff-Gerichts-* |
        *Ordnung* | . . . | *Altona/* | . . . | *1690.* (No. 2491.)

2465    KORTHOLT, CHRISTIAN

        Christian Kortholten/ D. | Christliche Erinnerung | von dem | Bann |
        Unbekandter Sünder. | [rule] | KJEL/ | Gedruckt durch Joachim
        Reumann/ | Jm Jahr 1690.

        8vo. 40 pp.; A-B⁸ C⁴.                                                  CKB

2466    KORTHOLT, CHRISTIAN

        Christian Kortholten/ D. | Christlicher Unterricht | von dem so ge-
        nandten | Bestechen | Beeidigter Personen/ | absonderlich | der Zöllner
        und Licent- | eiñehmer: | Wie auch von anderm Unterschleiff/ so | bey
        der Kauffmanschafft/ der Oberkeit | zum nachtheil/ vorzugehen | pfle-
        get. | [rule of type ornaments] | PLOEN/ | Gedruckt und verlegt durch
        Tobias Schmidt/ | 1690

        8vo. 26 pp.; A-B⁸.                                   LANDESBIBLIOTHEK WEIMAR

        All after B5 lacking, with no apparent loss of text.

2467    KORTHOLT, CHRISTIAN

        Christian Kortholten/ D. | Gezwungener | Communicant. | [rule] |
        KJEL/ | Getruckt durch Joachim Reumann/ | im Jahr 1690.

        8vo. 64 pp.; A-D⁸.                                                     CKB

        Pp. 55-64 are Latin "Notæ."

2468    KORTHOLT, CHRISTIAN

        Trost-Schrifft/ | . . . | Hrn. Simon Henrich | MUSÆUM, D. | . . . | Uber
        den tödtlichen Hintrit | seiner Hertz-liebsten/ | . . . | Fr. Anna Mar-
        gareta/ | gebohrnen Schröderinn/ | mitleidend verfasset | von | Christian
        Kortholten/ D. | [rule] | KJEL/ | Gedruckt durch Joachim Reumann/
        Acad. Buchd. [1690]

        4to. 16 pp.; A-B⁴; 1 plate.                                            CKB

2469    LANGEMACK, MICHAEL

        Catechismus Frag und Antworten darin der Catechismus Lutheri nach
        seinem eigentlichen Verstande erkläret wird etc. Schleswig, 1690.

12mo.                                                                                    *

F. Witt, *Quellen und Bearbeitungen der schleswig-holsteinischen Kirchenge-*
*schichte,* 2. Aufl., Kiel 1913, p. 220. *Thott I/2, 503,* lists an edition of 1697.

2470   [MASIUS, HECTOR GOTTFRIED]

Kurtzer Bericht | von | Dem Unterscheid | Der wahren Evangelischen |
Lutherischen/ und der | Reformirten | Lehre/ | Nebst einem Anhang/
und | Erörterung folgender Fragen: | I. Ob zwischen den Lutheranern
und | Reformirten eine Religions-Einig- | keit und Brüderschafft zu
hoffen? | II. Ob nicht die Reformirten Gewis- | sens halber verbunden
seynd Krafft | ihrer eigenen Lehr-Sätze/ zu uns zu | treten? | Entworffen
von | H.G.M.D. & P.P. | [rule] | Verlegt durch Johann Jost | Erythro-
pilum 1690.

12mo. [24], 408, 82 pp.; a¹², A-R¹², ²A-²C¹² ²D⁶.                          CKB

²D6 lacking, probably blank. ²A1 has title: *Kurtzer Anhang/ | und | Erörterung |*
*Folgender Fragen: | 1. Ob zwischen din* [sic] *Luthe- | ranern und Reformirten*
*eine | Religions-Einigkeit zu hoffen/ | und wie sie zu erhalten? | 2. Ob nicht die*
*Reformir- | ten Gewissens halber verbun- | den sind Krafft ihrer eigenen | Lehr-*
*Sätze zu uns zu | treten?*

2471   [MASIUS, HECTOR GOTTFRIED]

Das | Treue Lutherthumb/ | Entgegen gesetzet | Der Schule Calvini, |
Womit des | Vermummeten Huberti Mosani Be- | richt von der Welt-
lichen Obrigkeit/ so er gegen | D. MASII Interesse Principum neulich
her- | ausgegeben/ | wiederleget wird. | Sampt einem Catalago Errorum
Becman- | nianorum, und eines Reformirten Schrei- | ben an einen guten
Freund/ | Entworffen von | M.D.E.P.P. | [rule] | Gedruckt in Koppen-
hagen/ | Zu finden bey Johann Jost Erythropilum | Anno 1690

4to. [8], 299, 43, [1] pp.; a⁴, A-Oo⁴, Pp², ²A-²E⁴, ²F².               CKB

Author: M[asius] D[octor] e[t] P[rofessor] P[rimarius]. On leaf ²A1, separate
title: *Anhang/ | Worinnen erstlich vorgestellet wird | SPECIMEN | ERRORUM |*
*Becmannianorum, | Als ein Prodromus eines grössern Bewei- | ses daß Herr Joh.*
*Christ. Becman in allen | Wissenschaften sich sehr gröblich versehen/ auch zuwei- |*
*len Päbstliche Hypotheses in seinen Moralibus | angenommen: | Eiligst entworffen |*
*Von | Th. C. R. F. | Dan auch | Eines Reformirten vernünfftiges Urtheil | von*
*Herrn Becmans Vornehmen. | [rule] | COPENHAGEN/ Verlegt durch JOHAN-*
*NEM JUSTUM ERYTHROPILUM, | Im Jahr 1690.*

2472   MOLLER, JOHANNES

Das Meister-Recht im Liebes-Handwerke in nupt. Jo. Fried. Meisteri,
. . . et Annæ, Jo. Melchersens . . . filiæ. Schleswig, 1690.

Folio.                                                                                   *
*OHM* I, 430-1.

2473  MORHOF, DANIEL GEORG

Hochverdienter Nachruhm | Der Weiland | Hochgebohrnen Gräfin und
Frauen/ | Fr. Catharina | Heedwig | Gräfin zu Rantzou und Löwen-
holm/ | Frauen auff Breitenburg/ &c. | Wie dero entseelter Cörper
eingesetzet worden/ | entworffen | Von | D. G. Morhofen/ D.P. | [rule] |
Kjel | Gedruckt durch Joachim Reumann/ Acad. Buchdr. | 1690

Folio.  χ². CKB; KIEL UL

Verse.

2474  MORHOF, DANIEL GEORG

Als | . . . | Herrn Johan Conrad Kiefer/ | . . . Seine Eheliebste | . . . | in
Schleßwig beerdigen ließ/ | schrieb dieses | mitleidend | Daniel Georg
Morhoff. | [rule] | KJEL/ | Gedruckt durch Joachim Reumann/ Acad.
Buchdr. | Jahr 1690

4to.  χ². KIEL UL

2475  MÜLLER, CHRISTIAN RUDOLPH

Die immer siegende Liebe . . . oder Leich-Abdenckung über Dorothea
von Reichau, Hr. Johan Otto von Raben, . . . Eheliebsten. Copenhagen,
1690.

Folio. *

*Bibl. Joannes Grammius*, 1748, p. 102.

2476  MUSAEUS, JOHANN SEBASTIAN

Hochverdienter Nachruhm | der | Hoch-Edlen Frauen | Fr. Anna Mar-
garetha/ | gebohrnen Schröderin/ | Hn. Simon Henrich Museus/ D. |
Professoris und Facult. Juridicæ | Assessoris, | Sehligen Ehe-Frauen/ |
Auß schuldiger Pflicht entworffen | von | Johann Sebastian Musæus |
[ornaments] | Kjel/ | Gedruckt/ durch Joachim Reumann/ Acad.
Buchdr. 1690

4to.  χ². CKB

2477  NEUMARCK, ERNST GOTTLIEB

Enchiridion, oder Historisches Hand-Gebet-Büchlein. Plön, 1690.

12mo. *

*Moller* II, 583; *Bibl. Breitenaviana*, I, 1747, p. 387.

2478  NICOLAI, MARTIN

Geistlicher Adler-Flug oder Abdanckung über Frau Eleonora sl. Georgii
Bocken Eheliebste. Glückstadt, 1690.

Folio. ❋

*OHM* I, 461.

2480 St. Sulpis, Victor de

Richtiger Weg zur Seeligkeit/ | Oder | Dringende Ursachen | Warumb
ein im Pabstum Gebohrner dasselbe | verlassen und die Wahre | Evan-
gelische Lute- | rische RELIGION | Annehmen müsse/ wenn er sich
seiner | Seelen Heil und Seeligkeit vergewissern wil. | Aus H. Göttlicher
Schrifft erweißlich ge- | macht/ und mit unwiedersprechlichen Grün- |
den dargethan. | Von | V. D. S. S. | Einem Piemontesischen von Adel. |
[ornament] | [rule] | Copenhagen/ | Gedruckt bey Johan Adolph Bax-
man | im Jahr 1690

4to. [4], 20 pp.; A-C⁴. CKB

2481 Schirmer, Martin

Martin Schirmers | COMPENDIVM | GEOMETRIÆ, | Oder | Kurtzer/
doch Gründlicher/ | Begriff | Der Geometrie/ | Zum | Feldmessen und
Fortificiren | sehr nützlich | [rule] | Copenhagen/ | Auf Unkosten des
Autoris. | Gedrukkt bey Joh. Jacob Bornheinrich. | 1690.

8vo. [8], 72 pp.; )(⁴, A-D⁸ E⁴. CKB

CKB copy interleaved.

2482 Schmidt, Sebastian

Kurtze Erklärung der | ersten 8 Capittel | Deß | Buchs Josuä | aus deß
Hochwürdig. | Hn. D. Seb. Schmidii | Mscr. in diese kurtze | gebracht |
Von | Hermanno Zimerman. | Prediger zu Marschacht | [ornament] |
Gedrucket in Schleßwig in der | Fürstl. Druckerey Anno 1690.

12mo. [2], 118 pp.; π1, A-E¹². CKB

E12 lacking, probably blank. From leaf E5v, text set in smaller type. CKB copy
bound with Schmidt's *Der XXVII. Psalm . . . Schleßwig . . . 1691* (No. 2535).

2483 Seger, F.

Die warme Winter-Liebe/ | Als | Jungfer Maria Jßings | Mit | Herrn
Joachim Horn | Den 1 Octobr. Anno 1690 in Copenhagen | Jhr Hoch-
zeitliches Feyer begingen/ nebst beygefügtem | Glücks-Wunsche/ darge-
stellet von | . . . | F. Segern | [below:] Gedruckt bey Jhr. Königl. Mayst
und Univ. Buchdr. Joh. Phil. Bockenhoffer.

Broadside (34 x 25 cm). CKB

Verse.

2484   SPENER, PHILIPP JACOB

D. Jacob Philipp Speners/ | Chursächsischen Ober-Hoff-Predigers und |
Kirchen-Raths/ etc. | Erfordertes | Theologisches | Bedencken/ | über
den | Von Einigen des E. Hamburgischen | MINISTERII | publicirten |
Neuen Religions-Eyd. | [ornamental rule] | PLOEN/ | Gedruckt durch
Tobias Schmidt/ 1690.

4to. A-D⁴ E².                                                          CKB

2485   Trauer-Gedancken | Uber | Den gar zu frühzeitigen Hinriß | Des wey-
land | Wohlgebohrnen Herren/ | Herren Marqvard | Guden/ | . . . |
Von | H.L.G. | [rule] | - - - - - Justissimus unus | Hic fuit ex Cimbris &
servantissimus aeqvi, | [rule] | Glückstadt/ | Gedruckt bey Reinhard
Janßen. [1690]

Folio. χ².                                                          CKB

Verse.

2486   TRIBBE, JOHANNES DANIEL

Gedächtnis-Seule bey dem Abschiede Catharina Hedwig Gräfin zu
Rantzou. Glückstadt, 1690.

Folio.                                                                 *

*OHM* I, 689.

2487   TRIBBE, JOHANNES DANIEL

Reminiscere et obliviscere Boccianus oder Leichen Rede über Jungfer
Metta Lucia Bock. Glückstadt, 1690.

4to.                                                                   *

*OHM* I, 689.

2488   TRIBBE, JOHANNES DANIEL

[Hebrew] Die liebliche Rancken Zierde bey der Beerdigung Anna von
Hevern, gebohrne Ranckin. . . . Glückstadt, 1690.

Folio.                                                                 *

*OHM* I, 689.

2489   Trost-Gedichte/ | Uber den früzeitigen jedoch höchstseeligen Abschied |
der Weyland/ | Hoch-Edlen Frauen | Fr. Anna Margaretha/ | ge-
bohrnen Schröderin/ | Des Hoch-Edlen/ Vesten und Hochgelahrten
Herrn | Hn. Simon Henrich Museus/ D. | . . . | von | Des Hn. Dr.
Stryckens gesammten Tischgenossen. | [ornament] | KJEL/ | Gedruckt/
durch Joachim Reumann/ Acad. Buchd. 1690.

4to. $\chi^2$. CKB

2490 Trost-Schrifft | über | den höchstschmertzlichen Hintritt | der | Hoch Edlen Frauen | Fraüen | Anna Margaretha/ | gebohrnen Schröderin/ | Herrn Simon Henrich Musäus/ D. | Professoris und Facult. Juridicæ Assessoris, | sehl. Ehefrauen/ | . . . | auffgesetzet von | Des Herrn Wittwers Tischgenossen. | [below:] Kjel | Gedruckt/ durch Joachim Reumann/ Acad. Buchdrucker [1690]

Broadside (36.5 x 29.4 cm). CKB

Verse.

2491 Weiland Herrn Otten | Grafen zu Hollstein/ Schauenburg und | Stern- berg/ Herrn zu Gehmen und Bergen/ &c. | Hoff-Gerichts- | Ordnung. | Vormahls im Jahre 1640. gedrücket in der | Stadt Rinteln/ itzo bey vielem Nachfragen zum | andernmahl heraus gegeben. | Wobey gefüget | Die Königliche Dännemärckische | Kirchen-CONSTITUTION | Jn der Herrschafft Pinnenberg. | [rule] | ALTONA/ | Gedruckt und Verlegt durch Christian Reymers/ | Königl. privilegirten Buchdrucker/ Jm Jahr | 1690.

4to. [12], 88, [16] pp.; $\pi^2$ ($\pi$1 + )($^4$), A-N$^4$. CKB

CKB copy printed and bound with *Königl. Dännemärckische* | *Kirchen-CON-* | *STITUTION* | . . . | *1690* (No. 2464).

2492 Wiederauffgelegte | PRIVILEGIA | Oder Freyheiten/ | Welche Dero zu Den- | nemarck/ Norwegen etc. Königl: Maytt: | höchstsel: und rühmlichsten Angedenckens/ &c. | Der Portugisischen Nation He- bräischer | Religion, auch ihren Adhærenten und Familien, So | in der Veste Glückstadt anitzo wohnen und in künfftig kommen | möchten/ Allergnädigst hat mitgetheilet und gegeben | den 19. Junij Anno 1630. | Wobey Derer zu Dennemarck/ Norwegen/ etc. | Königl. Königl. Majest. Majest. Allerglorwürdigsten | Andenckens Allergnädigst ertheilte Con- firmation de Anno | 1648. Declaration von Anno 1651. Prolongation auff | zehen Jahr/ de Anno 1655. Anderweitige Declaration von | Anno 1657. Erweiterte Prolongation auff noch Fünff und | Zwantzig Jahr von Anno 1664. Und der itzo Regierenden | Königl. Maytt. Confirmation wie auch Declaration de | Anno 1670. Auch Extensio Privilegij de Anno 1682. Und | Declaration von Anno 1684. Auch Erweiterte Pro- | longation auff noch Fünff und Zwanzig Jahr | in Anno 1686. gefüget. | Præsent: dem Herrn Præsidenten Nicolaus Starck | den 29. Junij. | Publicat in Curia coram Senatu Glückstadt den 30. | Junij Anno 1686. | [rule] | Gedruckt im Jahr 1690.

4to. A-D$^4$. KIEL UL

2493  ZIMMERMAN, JOHANN JACOB

SCRIPTURAS. COPERNIZANS | seu potius | ASTRONOMIA CO-
PERNI- | CO-SCRIPTURARIA | BIPARTITA. | Das ist: | Ein gantz
neu-und sehr curioser | Astronomischer | Beweißthum | Des Coperni-
canischen Welt-Gebäudes | aus Heil. Schrifft/ | Worinnen | I. Bey des der
Sonnen samt anderer Fixsternen räumlicher | Stillstand/ als auch der
Erd-Kugel samt anderer Planeten | natürlicher Umlauff buchstäblich
angewiesen; | II. Die vermeintlich widersprechende Gegen-Sprüche aus |
dem Hebräischen u. Griechischen Text deutlich erörtert werden; | Um/
so wohl die Hoheit/ Fürtrefligkeit und Autorität des H. Prophetischen
Worts/ | wider die heuttägige Verkleinerung der Spinosisten/ Natu-
ralisten und Atheisten/ als auch (bey | gleichwol nothwendiger Hand-
habung des Natur-mässigen Copernicanischen Welt-Gebäudes/) | der
hochheiligen THEOLOGIÆ zur Veneration, den buchstäblichen Ver-
stand der H. Schrifft/ | wider den von bißherigen Copernicanern ange-
schmützten Layen-Verstand/ | best-müglichst zu verwahren; | Nebens
untermengter Erläuterung einiger Carthesianischen uñ Chymischen
Geheim- | nissen/ auch etlicher durch des Lichts Natur poëticè und
sonsten illustrirten Glaubens-Articuln/ | Jn zweyen Theilen einfältig
entworffen/ | Und der Collegior. Curiosorum Judicio untergeben | Von |
JOHANN JACOB Zimmermann/ Philo-Mathematico, | Aus Vayhingen
an der Entz Würtenberger-Lands gebürtig. | [rule] | Jn Verlegung des
Autoris zu Hamburg und Altona/ alda gedruckt von Christian Rey-
mers/ | Königlichen privilegirten Buchdrucker/ Anno 1690

4to. 62, [10] pp.; A-H$^4$ J1, )o(1, χ$^2$.                              KIEL UL

2494  ZITSCHER, PETER

Die Edleste Eitelkeit | . . . | Herrn Marqvard | Guden/ | . . . | Von | P.
Zitzschern/ | Königl. Schloß-Pastorn zu Glückstadt. | [rule] | Gedruckt
bey Reinhard Janßen/ 1690.

Folio. 32 pp.; A-H$^2$.                                                   KIEL UL

## 1691

2495  Vom 5. Januarii Fol. I. | Die Altonaische RELATION. | No. I [woodcut:
crowned female figure on lion] 1691

8vo. 8 pp.                                          NIEDERSÄCHSISCHES STAATSARCHIV

Caption title. Entire volume, nrs. 1-96, paginated; in all, 792 pp. Niedersächsisches
Staatsarchiv, Wolfenbüttel, has also nrs. 3, 5-7, 10-11, 14, 18-27, 31-34, 38-50, 52-65,
67-69, 71-73, 75-83, 86, 88, 90, 96.

2496 ANDREÆ, JOHANNES CHRISTOPHERUS

Daß weisse Ehren-Kleid/ | Jn welchem seinem JESU | Als ein getreuer
Knecht nachzufolgen | Der | Wol-Ehrwürdige/ in GOtt Andächtige |
und Hochgelahrte HERR/ | Herr M. DANIEL | ALBINUS, | ... |
Von | Johanne Christophoro Andreæ, | Pastore zu Cappelln. | [rule] |
Schleßwig/ gedruckt bey Johann Holweins Erben. 1691.

4to. π1, A-B⁴.                                                              CKB

2497 Antwort- | Schreiben | Eines | Freundes auß Holstein/ an | einen andern/
zu Regensburg | anitzo befindlich/ | de dato den 2. Novembr. 1691.

4to. A-B⁴.                                                                  CKB

2498 BOYE, HENRICH

Hochzeitliches Nymphen-Gedicht | Seiner Hertzgeliebtesten | Frau
Mutter | (Tit.) | Fr: Anna Boyen | Und | Neuen | Pflege-Vater | (Tit.) |
Hn: Johann Abroh | Zu sonderbahren Ehren | aus | Kind-verpflichteter
Schuldigkeit | auffgesetzt | von | Heinrich Boyen. | Anno 1691. den 15.
Octobris. | Imprimatur, | C. BARTHOLIN. | [ornamental rule] |
Copenhagen/ Gedruckt bey Jhr. Kön. Majest. und Dero Universit. |
Buchdr. Joh. Phil. Bockenhoffer.

Folio. χ².                                                                  CKB

Verse.

2499 BURCHARD, PETER ANTON

Einem Haffen himmlischer Ruhe . . . der Fr. Mutter Magdalena
Burchardin. Kiel, 1691.

Folio.                                                                        *

*OHM* I, 82.

2500 CORDES, HEINRICH

Der Neü-angelegt- | Historisch-Algebraischer | Garten-Bau/ | Von 26.
Curieusen Historien/ | als zu einem neüen Garten gehöri- | gen Stäm-
men. | Welche aus bewährten Geschicht- | Schreibern extrahiret/
gleichsam Ex- | empels Weise/ in die edle Algebram ver- | fasset/ auffs
deütlichste resolviret/ und allen so | tahner Kunst-und Historien be-
gierigen Gemüh- | tern/ zu sonderbahrem Nutzem und Ergetzung/ |
auff eine vorhin schwerlich versuchte | Ahrt vorgestellet | von | HEIN-
RICH CORDES Lub. | Scholæ German. Hafniens. | p.t. Substitut. | Jn
der Kunst-Rechnungs-liebenden | Societæt | Dem Continuirenden. |
[rule] | Copenhagen/ 1691. | Gedrukt bey Christian Wering Universit.

Buchdr. | Jn Verlegung des Authoris und bey demselben/ wie auch | in Lübeck bey Peter Bökmann/ Buchhändler/ | zu bekommen.

8vo. [32], 173, [3] pp.; a-b⁸, A-L⁸.                                                    CKB

Title printed in red and black. Leaves b4v-b6r contain list of members of the "Kunst-Rechnungs-liebenden Societæt." Leaves b6r-b8v contain verses to Cordes by Franciscus de Hammershaimb, Henricus Vrangel, Joach. Henr. Carstens, and Cordt Danxst.

2502    DANXST, CORDT

Arithmeti-Geometri-Algebrai- | Und Historische Ergetzlichkeiten/ | Erst- und Zweiter Theil/ | Worinnen | Die von verschiedene berühmte Authores | hiebevor in ihren Büchern zwar angeregte; bisher | aber von niemand zur gnüge erklärte | So genandte: | Buchstab-Rechen- | Kunst/ | mit denen 24. Buchstaben im Teut- | schen Alphabet, | Auf Begehr einiger guten Freünde/ gantz | deütlich und klar angewiesen/ | Nebenst | Einem Appendix bestehende | in Resolvirung zwey vormahls Componir- | te Cossisch-oder Algebraische Aufgaben in Zahlen/ | heraußgegeben von | Cordt Danxst. | Buchhalter/ und der Edlen Zahlen- Kunst beflißener/ | Jn der zu Hamburg aufgerichteten Kunst-Rech- | nungs-liebenden Societet, genandt | Dem Denckenden. | [rule] | Copenhagen/ Gedruckt bey Christian Wering Univ. Buchd. | Jn Verlegung des Authoris. im Jahr 1691.

8vo. [32], 31, [3], 80, [2], 56, [4] pp.; a-b⁸, A-L⁸.                                   CKB

Title printed in red and black. Appendix, with separate pagination, begins on leaf H2, which has separate title-page.

2503    DANXST, CORDT

Fruchtbringendes | Gespräch-Spiel/ | Darinnen | Die Eygentliche Be- schaffenheit | von der zu Hamburg Aᴏ: 1690 Vito Julij | aufgerichteten | Kunst-Rechnungs-lieben- | den Societet, | Gesprächsweise beschrieben/ und darge- | than wird/ daß solche nur bloß und allein zur | Ehre GOttes/ Nutz des Nechsten und aufneh- | men der Edlen Zahlen-Kunst gestifftet worden. | Wobey dann auch | Die von einigen Kunsthäßigen Leüten | dagegen außgestreüete Calumnien/ (damit Sie | dieses so wol abgesehene Werck bey GOtt-und | Ehrliebenden Gemüthern/ welche bißhero der | Sachen nicht völlig berichtet sind/ zu verklei- | nern und unterdrücken suchen/) Ernstlich wie- | derlegt worden von | CORDT DANXST | Buchhalter/ und in besagter Societet | genandt DER DENCKENDEN. | [rule of type ornaments] | Gedruckt in Copenhagen bey Christian Wering | Acad. Buchdr. im Jahr 1691.

12mo. [6], 102 pp.; A-D¹² E⁶.                    NIEDERS. LANDESBIBLIOTHEK, HANNOVER

Title printed in red and black.

2504  DANXST, CORDT

Kurtze | Doch | Gründliche INSTRVCTION | Von | Handels-Buch-
halten/ | Und | Was vor Bücher Nothwendig | (Nach dem die Handlung
ist) | Dazu gebraucht werden müssen/ | Dann auch | Wie solche Bücher
ordentlich einzurichten | und zuverwalten/ | Getreulichst angewiesen/
und zum Dienste derer/ so sich seiner Infor- | mation hinführo bedienen
werden/ zum Druck befordert | Von | Cordt Danxst/ | Des so genandten
Jtalienschen Buchhaltens und der Edlen Zahlen- | Kunst Beflissener/ |
Jn der zu Hamburg aufgerichteten Societet | der Kunstvereinigten
Rechen-Meistere | genandt | Dem Denckenden | [ornament] | [rule] |
COPENHAGEN/ | Gedruckt bey Jhr Königl. Hoheit Buchtr. Joachim
Schmedtgen. 1691.

Folio. [4], 23, [1] pp.; π², A-F².                                            CKB

Title printed in red and black.

2505  DENMARK. *Laws, statutes, etc.*

WJR Christian der Fünffte/ von | ... | ... Glückstadt/ den 10ten Martij
1691.

Broadside.                                                                   CNA

Decree issued jointly with Duke Christian Albrecht of Schleswig-Holstein, calling a
meeting of the "Landgericht" at Flensburg 21 April.

2506  DENMARK. *Laws, statutes, etc.*

WJR Christian der Fünffte/ von | ... | ... Glückstadt/ den 6. April.
Anno 1691.

Broadside.                                                                   CNA

Decree calling an annual day of prayer the fourth Friday after Easter.

2507  DENMARK. *Laws, statutes, etc.*

Wir Christian der Fünffte/ von Gottes Gnaden | ... | .... [7. May 1691]

Broadside.                                                                   CKB

Decree issued jointly with Duke Christian Albrecht of Schleswig-Holstein, levying
an extraordinary tax on land.  Date added by hand in CKB copy.

2508  DENMARK. *Laws, statutes, etc.*

WJR Christian der | Fünffte/ von GOttes | Gnaden/ König zu Dänne- |
marck/ Norwegen/ ... | ....

4to. )(².                                                                    CNA

At end: *Glück- | stadt den 14ten Maji, Anno 1691.* Decree regarding rights of in-heritance, the payment of interest, the negotiation of credit, and the registration of "Testamenta nuncupativa."

2509  DENMARK. *Laws, statutes, etc.*

WJR Christian der Fünffte/ von | . . . | . . . Glückstadt den 14ten Maij Anno 1691.

Broadside (2 leaves pasted together).                                           CNA

Decree regarding marriage agreements.

2510  DENMARK. *Laws, statutes, etc.*

WJR Christian der Fünffte/ von | . . . | . . . Glückstadt den 26. Junij Anno 1691

Broadside.                                                                       CNA

Decree protesting a "Copia eines Schreibens aus Hamburg/ vom 11. Maij."

2511  DENMARK. *Laws, statutes, etc.*

Wir Christian der Fünffte/ von Gottes Gnaden | . . . | . . . 1ten Augusti Anno 1691.

Broadside.                                                                       CKB

Decree issued jointly with Duke Christian Albrecht of Schleswig-Holstein, regard-ing a meeting of the "Quartal-Gericht" at Schleswig 15 September.

2512  DENMARK. *Laws, statutes, etc.*

WJR Christian der Fünffte/ von | . . . | . . . Glückstadt/ den 1sten Septembris, Anno 1691.

Broadside.                                                                       CNA

Decree ordering thanksgiving 6 September in Holstein because of an imperial vic-tory over the Turks.

2513  DENMARK. *Laws, statutes, etc.*

Wir Christian der Fünffte/ von Gottes Gnaden/ | König zu Denne-marck/ Norwegen/ der Wenden und Gohten/ | Und von desselben Gnaden/ Wir Christian Albrecht . . . | . . . | . . . Gottorff/ den 16. Sept. Anno 1691.

Broadside.                                                                       CNA

Decree calling a "Landgerichts-Tag" at Gottorff castle 17 November.

2514  DENMARK. *Laws, statutes, etc.*

WJR Christian der Fünffte/ von | . . . | . . . Glückstadt den 28. Decembr. Anno 1691

Broadside (2 leaves pasted together).                                    CNA

Decree, reproducing an imperial decree of 7 October issued by Emperor Leopold, against France.

2515   Die Europäische │ [FAMA]

12mo. One leaf, pp. 353-354.                              Deutsch-Nienhof

Issue No. 41, "Vom 15. Jun. 1691." Fragment. Caption title. Published in Altona.

2516   Fleischer, Philip

Der keuschen Liebe Glückseeligkeit │ . . . │ Hn. Johan Kiesers/ │ Und │ Der Wol-Edlen und Tugendbegabten Jungfer │ J. Elisabeth Öllers/ │ . . . │ Jn glückwünschender Gratulation │ eilfertig erwogen von │ Imprimatur, │ C. Bartholin. │ Philip Fleischer. │ L.L. Studioso. │ [rule] │ Copenhagen/ Gedruckt bey J. P. Bockenhoffer/ Jhr. Kön. Maj. │ und Universit. Buchdr./ 1691.

Folio. $\chi^2$.                                                              CKB

Verse.

2517   Friis, Nicolaus

Der feste Liebes-Grund │ Als dem │ Wollgebohrnen Herrn │ HERRN │ Lorentz de BOSSET │ . . . │ JUNGFER │ Margaretha Elisa- │ beth de STUART, │ Den 6 Januarii itzt lauffenden Jahres mit Hochzeitlicher │ Solemnité beygeleget ward/ │ . . . │ Dehro │ Dienst-ergebenster Knecht │ Imprimatur, │ C. BARTHOLIN. │ NICOLAUS FRIIS. │ [rule] │ Copen-hagen/ Gedruckt bey Joh. P. Bockenhoffer/ Jh. Königl. Maytt. │ und Universit. Buchdr./ 1691

Folio. $\chi^2$.                                                              CKB

Verse.

2518   Giese, Joachim

Schuldigste Observantz, welche an dem Nahmens Tage des Hn. Joachim Giesen. . . . Kiel, 1691.

Folio.                                                                        *

Formerly in Kiel UL (LmC 8-15).

2519   Hahn, Hinrich

Hiobs │ Einiger Trost in Noth │ und Todt. │ Womit nach dessen Exem-pel │ Der weiland HochEhrwürdige/ Wol- │ Edle und Hochgelahrte Herr/ │ Hr. CAJUS Arend/ │ . . . │ Von dessen Successore │ M. HEN-

RICO HAHN. | [rule] | Glückstadt/ | Gedruckt bey Reinhard Janßen. [1691]

4to. 88, 20 pp.; A-L⁴, a-b⁴, c².                                    CKB

On leaf a1r, added title: *Geistreiche Anmerckungen* | *Welche* | *Der weiland* | *HochEhrwürdige/ WolEdle und Hochgelahrte* | *Herr* | *Herr CAJUS Arend/* | *...* | *Als seinen erwehlten Leich-Text, ...* | *... Glückstadt/ gedruckt im Jahr 1691.*

2520 KORTHOLT, CHRISTIAN

Christian Kortholten/ D. | Biblische | Fest-Andacht/ | Gesangs-weise | vorgestellet; | Sammt etlichen andern | Geistlichen Bet-Buß- | Creutz-Trost-Danck-Lob- | und Lehr-Liedern | [double rule] | KJEL/ | Gedruckt durch Joachim Reumann/ | Jm Jahr 1691.

8vo. 104 pp.; A-F⁸ G⁴.                                              CKB

2521 KORTHOLT, CHRISTIAN

Der | im Garten zu Gethse- | mane | Geängstete und | Bludt-schwitz-ende | JESUS/ | andächtig zu betrachten | fürgestellet | Von | Christian Kortholten/ D. | KJEL/ | Gedruckt durch Joachim Reumann/ | Jm Jahr 1691.

8vo. [16] pp., pp. [1-2] 3-184; A⁸ (A1+a⁸) B-L⁸ M⁴.                CKB

Pp. 148-184 are Latin "Notæ."

2522 LUND, THOMAS

Das Geistliche | Königreich | auff Erden/ | Oder | Die so mannigfaltige Herrlich- | keit/ welche wir von Gott gewür- | digten | Geistlichen Könige | hie im Reich der Gnaden | besitzen. | Entworffen | Durch | THOMAM LUNDIUM, | Predigern zu S. Marien in Flens- | burg. | [ornamental rule] | PLOEN/ | Gedruckt und verlegt durch Tobias Schmidt/ | im 1691sten Jahr.

8vo. [2], 18, 1231, [45] pp.; )(⁸, )( )(², A-Kkkk⁸ Lllll⁶.         CKB

Title printed in red and black. On )(2 − 2)(2: dedication, separately paginated.

2523 MAJOR, DETLEV JOHANN

(Hochzeitsgedicht: Wilhelm Huldrich Waldschmidt & Margareta Dorothea Major) Kiel: Joachim Reumann, 1691

                                                                    *

Formerly in Kiel UL (LmC 18-5).

2524 MAJOR, JOHANN DANIEL

Präliminär-Discurs, oder Summarischer Entwurff etlicher Gedancken

von Pasquillen und denjenigen Personen, so daran ein sündliches Ge-
fallen oder auch ein Christ-löblich und genereuses Mißfallen tragen.
Kiel, 1691.

4to.                                                                                 *

CKB: Jus 58515 (lost). Superscript in runes.

2525  MASIUS, HECTOR GOTTFRIED

Als der │ Erfreüliche Geburts-Tag │ Des │ Allerdurchleuchtigsten Groß-
mächtigsten │ Königes und Herrn/ Herrn │ Christian des Fünfften │
Königes zu Dennemarck Norwe- │ gen/ der Wenden und Gothen/
Hertzogs │ zu Schleßwig/ Holstein/ Stormarn und │ der Ditmarschen/
Graffen zu Oldenburg │ und Delmenhorst/ │ Unsers Allergnädigsten
Erb-Königes │ und Herrn/ │ Von der Königlichen Universität │ Höchst-
feirlich begangen ward/ │ Wolte seine Allerunterthänigste Pflicht │ mit
diesen Zeilen abstatten/ │ Dero Königl. Majest. │ Allerunterthänigster/
Allergetreüester und Ergebenster │ Knecht und Vorbitter │ H. G.
MASIUS. │ [ornamental rule] │ Copenhagen/ Gedruckt bey Jhro Königl.
Majest. und dero Universit. Buchdr. │ Johann Philip Bockenhoffer/ im
Jahr 1691/ den 15 April.

Folio. $\chi^2$.                                                                      CKB

2526  MASIUS, HECTOR GOTTFRIED

M. D. E. P. P. │ Erinnerungs- │ Schreiben │ An │ HUBERTUM
MOSANUM │ Wie er die Sache angreiffen müsse/ │ wo er Doct: Masij │
Treues Lutherthum │ beantworten wolle. │ Sampt │ HUBERTI MO-
SANI │ Antwort. │ [rule] │ Franckfurt an der Oder/ im Jahr 1691.

4to. 16 pp.; A-B⁴.                                                                    CKB

That the book was printed in Copenhagen is apparent from the 2 conjugate can-
cellans leaves bound in at end of CKB volume containing the above (as well as
*Huberti Mosani* │ *Fernerer Bericht* │ *von* │ *Der Reformirten Lehre* │ *Von der* │ *Weltl.*
*Obrigkeit* │ . . . *Franckfurt an der Oder/ in Verlegung Jeremiä Schreyen* │ *und*
*Heinrich Johann Meyers Erben* │ *Daselbst druckts Johann Cöpselius/ der löblichen*
*Universität Buchdrucker.*). On [A1] of the cancellans, title reads ". . . *Lutertumb* │
*beantworten wolle* │ [rule] │ *COPENHAGEN/* │ *Gedruckt bey Jhr Königl: H:*
*Buchtr. Joachim Schmedtgen* │ *1691."* The text is the same in both cases but is set
from different types; both dated "Hafnia, è Mus. d. 26. Febr. 1691." Hjelmstjerne
286ᵉ in CKB comprises only the cancellans leaves, containing prefatory note (A1v-
A2v).

2527  [MASIUS, HECTOR GOTTFRIED]

Das │ Gründlich Verthädigte │ Treue Lutherthumb/ │ Entgegen gesetzet │

Der Schule Calvini/ | Jn einer Specialen Wiederlegung des Becman- | nischen Fernern Berichts/ von der Reformir- | ten Lehre/ | Von der Weltlichen Obrigkeit/ | Der Wahrheit zu Steuer und zur Rettung des Sel. | Lutheri und andrer Lutherischen Lehrer/ | Sampt | Der Theolog- ischen Facultät in Copenhagen Ge- | wissenhafften Judicio von dieser Sache. | Zum Druck befordert | Von | M. D. E. P. P. | [ornamental rule] | COPENHAGEN/ | Jn Verlegung Johan Jost Erythropil/ 1691.

4to. [16], 184, [2], 500 pp.; )o(⁴, b⁴, A-Y⁴, χ1, ²A-Rrr⁴, Sss².      CKB

On leaf A1 separate title: *Erster Theil | Des | Gründlich Verthädigten | Treuen Lutherthumbs/ | Darinn | Lutherus und andre Lehrer der Lu- | therischen Kirche | Von | Joh. Christoph. Becmans groben Auf- | lagen und schweren Injurien vin- dici- | ret werden.* | [ornament] | [ornamental rule] | *COPENHAGEN/ | Gedruckt im Jahr Christi 1692;* on χ1, separate title: *Ander Theil | Des Gründlich Verthädig- ten | Treuen Lutherthumbs/ | Darinnen | Die Schule Calvini überzeuget wird/ | Daß ihre vornehmste Lehrer | gefährliche Lehr-Sätze von der Weltlichen | Obrig- keit hegen.* | [ornament] | [rule] | *Copenhagen/ | Gedruckt im Jahr Christi 1692.*

2528   [MASIUS, HECTOR GOTTFRIED]

Unverzögerte | Generale-Wiederlegung | Des | Fernern Berichts/ | Welchen Joh. Christoph. Becman unter dem | Nahmen Huberti Mosani | gegen | MASII Treues Lutherthumb | heraus gegeben/ | Als ein Pro- dromus der Specialen Wiederlegung/ beste- | hend in dreyen Theilen/ | Als/ I. Eine Beantwortung der nichtigen Exceptionen | des Mosani. II. Eine Rettung des theuren Lutheri | und anderer | Lutherischen Lehrer. III. Eine fernere | Uberweisung dessen/ was | die Lutheraner und | in Specie Masius in dieser Controver- | sie behauptet/ unter dem Titul: | Pietas Calviniana erga Summum | Magistratum. | entworffen | Von | M.D.E.P.P. | [rule] | Copenhagen/ Gedruckt im Jahr 1691.

4to. [16], 122 pp.; )⁴, )( )(⁴, A-P⁴ Q1.      CKB

2529   [MASIUS, HECTOR GOTTFRIED]

M.D.E.P.P. | Vernunfft-und Ge- | wissens-Fragen | An | Hr. Johan Christopher Becman, | zu Beantwortung seiner Glossen/ über | D. Masii Erinnerungs-Schrei- | ben an Jhn/ | Wodurch der Leser kürtzlich und gründ- | lich sehen kan/ | Wie sehr gröblich gedachter Becman sich | gegen die Warheit gesetzet/ und seiner hitzigen | Feder gegen alle Christliche Bescheidenheit | den Lauff gelassen/ | Sampt einem curieusen Anhang; | Des berühmten Reformirten Theologi, | Hr. Jurieu, | Offen- hertziges Geständnis/ | Worauß erhellet/ das D. Masius der Reformir- ten | Lehrer Sentiments besser alß Becman ver- | standen habe. | [rule] | Gedruckt im Jahr 1691.

4to. [4], 75, [1] pp.; A-K⁴.      CKB

2530 [MORHOF, DANIEL GEORG]

Ode | Welche | Bey des | Wollgebohnen Herrn/ | Herrn | Balthasar von Alefeld/ | Erbherrn auff Heiligenstät und | Mehlbeck. | Leich-Bestattung abgesungen worden | [ornament] | Kjel | Gedruckt durch Joachim Reumann/ Acad. Buchdr. 1691

Folio. $\chi^2$. CKB

Verse.

2531 MORHOF, DANIEL GEORG

Pindarische Trauer-Ode bey Beerdigung Sophia Ida geb. Gräfin v.d. Nath Haus Ranzau auf Quarnebeck Eheliebste. . . . Kiel, (1691).

Folio. *

*OHM* III, 474.

2532 MORHOF, DANIEL GEORG

Warer Adel | Bey | Des Wollgebornen Herrn/ | Herrn Balthasar | von Alefeld/ | Erbherrn auff Heiligenstät und | Mehlbeck. | Beerdigung/ | Welche den 15. Tag Monats Julii. in Jtzehoe mit Hoch-Adlichen | Gebräuchen geschehen. | Auß dem Leich-Text. Sirach am 1. Cap. v. 11. und folgende. | Vorgestellet | von | D. G. Morhofen/ D. Prof. | [woodcut: coffin] | KJEL/ | Gedruckt durch Joachim Reumann/ Acad. Buchdr. 1691.

Folio. $\chi^2$. CKB

Verse.

2532A [PIPER, ———]

Als | Der Hoch-Edelgebohrne Herr | Ernst Günther | Wardenburg | Jhro Königl: Maytt: zu Dennemarck/ Norwegen | wohlbestalter Regierungs-Rath in Dero Graff- | schafften Oldenburg und Delmenhorst. | Und | Die Hoch-Edle und Tugendreiche | Jungfer | Susanna Gerdraut | Piper/ | Am 28sten Octobr. 1691. Ehelig vertrawet | würden/ | Wolte hiemit seine Schuldigkeit abstatten/ | Piper. | Imprimatur, | C. BARTHOLIN. | [rule] | Gedruckt bey Joh. Phil. Bockenhoffer/ Königl. und Univers. Buchdr.

Folio. $\chi^2$. CKB

Verse.

2533 RELATION | Wegen | Des grossen und erschrecklichen | Brandes |

Zu | Schlaitz | im Voigtlande. | [rule] | Kopenhagen/ | Druckts
Johan Jacob Bornheinrich. | 1691.

4to. )(⁴.                                                                      CKB

2534 RÖTSCHER, JOHANNES VOLCMAR

Gewisser und wolbewährter Trost für | alle Bußfertige Sünder | ... |
Henrici Reinbothen/ | ... | M. Johanne Volcmaro Rötschern/ | ... |
[double rule] | Schleßwig/ gedruckt bey Johann Holweins Erben. [1691]

4to. A-J⁴.                                                                     CKB

2535 SCHMIDT, SEBASTIAN

Der XXVII. Psalm. | Jn | Unterschiedenen Predig- | ten erkläret | Von |
Sebastian Schmidt/ | Der H. Schrifft Doct. und | vornehmsten Profess.
zu Straßburg/ | wie auch des Kirchen-Convents | daselbst Præside. |
[woodcut: angel] | [rule] | Schleßwig/ gedruckt bey Johann | Hol-
weins Erben. Anno 1691.

12mo. 213, [3] pp.; A-J¹².                                                     CKB

2535A SCHWESINGER VON CRONHELM, ANDREAS

Evangelische Sing-Andacht vor alle der wahren apostolischen Lehr zuge-
thanen Christen Darinnen 280 Alte und Neue geistreiche Lieder. Glückstadt: Reinhard Janßen, 1691.

                                                                              *

Emil Brederek, *Geschichte der schleswig-holsteinischen Gesangbücher*, Kiel 1919,
p. 41.

2536 SEGER, F.

Der bitter-süsse Wittiben-Zucker | Bey dem | Hochzeitlichen Ehren-
Feste | ... | Hn: JOHANN | ABROH/ | ... | Fr: ANNA | BODEN/ |
... | von | Deroselben verpflichtesten Diener | Imprimatur, | C.
BARTHOLIN. | F. Segern. | [ornamental rule] | Copenhagen/ Ge-
druckt bey Jh. Königl. Mayest. und Univ. Buchdr. | Johann Philip
Bockenhoffer. [1691]

Folio. χ².                                                                     CKB

Verse.

2537 Verordnung | Wegen | Einrichtung der neüen | Königlichen Academie
in | Copenhagen. | Hafniæ die 26 Septembr. Anno 1691. | [monogram of
Christian V] | [rule] | Gedruckt bey Jh. Königl. Majest. und Dero
Universit. | Buchdr. Johan Philip Bockenhoffer.

4to. χ⁴.                                                                 HERLUFSHOLM

2538   Des | Aller-Durchläuchtigsten/ | Großmächtigsten Königs und |
       HERRN/ | Herrn Christian | Des Fünften/ | Von GOttes Gnaden/
       Königs | zu Dännemarck/ Norwegen/ der Wen- | den und Gothen/
       Hertzogs zu Schleßwig/ | Hollstein/ Stormarn und der Dithmarschen/
       Grafens | zu Oldenburg und Delmenhorst/ | Artickuls-Brief | Und |
       Kriegs-Gerichts- | Instruction | Belangende | Den Krieg zu Lande/ |
       Worauf alle und jede/ Uns mit Kriegs-Pflicht | Verwante/ und zu Lande
       Dienende/ schwehren/ und darnach | in allen Puncten sich schuldiger
       Gebühr bezei- | gen sollen. | Mit Königlichem Privilegio. | [rule] |
       KOPENHAGEN/ | Gedruckt bey Johan Jacob Bornheinrich/ 1692.

   8vo. 148, 4 pp.; A-T⁴.                                              CKB

   On A1, engraved preliminary title: *König Christian | des Fünften | Articuls-Brief |
   und | Kriegs-Gerichts | Instruction | belangende den | Krieg zu | Lande.* Title-page
   identical with that of other edition, same year, with text from a different setting of
   type: 137, [5] pp.; A⁸ (−A8), B-J⁸ (J8 blank). *Bibl. Hartmaniana*, 1720, Appendix, p. 75, Nr. 29, lists an edition in 4to, Glückstadt, 1692.

2538A Vom 25. Januarius Fol: 49 | Die Altonaische RELATION | No. 7
       [woodcut: crowned female figure on lion] 1692.

   8vo. Pp. 49-56.                         NIEDERSÄCHSISCHES STAATSARCHIV

   Caption title. Niedersächsisches Staatsarchiv, Wolfenbüttel, also has nr. 8, 28
   January 1692, pp. 57-64.

2539   Aus den Schrifften des | Hr. SAM. PUFENDORFII | Kurtzer aber |
       Gründlicher Beweiß | Durch Vernunft und | Erfahrung bestätiget/ |
       Daß der Calvinismus mit einer Monarchie | incompatible sey/ | Zu
       Bekräftigung der War- | heit die D. Masius hievon in seinen Schrifften |
       mit grossem Fug und Recht verthädiget | Und zu Joh. Christoph
       Becmans Confusion und Schande/ | daß Er sich einer so unläugbahren
       Warheit entgegen | zusetzen unterstanden. | Zum Druck befordert | von |
       Einem Warheit Liebenden. | [ornamental rule] | Gedruckt Anno 1692

   4to. 18 pp.; A-B⁴ C1.                                              CKB

2540   BECK, JOHANN JOSEPH

   Streit zwischen der Gerechtigkeit und der hertzlichen Barmhertzigkeit
   Gottes über den gefallenen Menschen, da dann der Sohn Gottes ein
   Mittler worden und beyden ein Vergnügung gethan und also durch sein
   Mittler-Ampt die Erlösung auf sich genommen. . . . Kiel, 1692.

   4to.                                                                 *

   *OHM* II, 60.

2541  BECK, JOHANN JOSEPH

Trauergedicht über Anna Musaeus geb. von Deging. . . . Kiel: Joachim
Reumann, 1692.

*

Formerly in Kiel UL (LmC 78-60).

2542  BENTZEN, SIGFRID

(Trauer Oden über Henr. Bloem auß Revenstorf). Kiel, 1692.

Folio.                                                             *

*OHM* I, 39.

2543  BRÄMER, CHRISTIAN

Seeliger Zustand | Der | Verstorbenen Gerechten/ | Bey der am 19ten
Septemb. 1692. angestelten/ Hochansehnlichen | Leichbegängniß/ | Des
Weyland/ | Hoch-Ehrwürdigen/ Hoch-Edlen/ und Hoch-gelahrten
Herrn/ | HERRN | JOHANNIS | LASSENII, | . . . | Von | M. Christian
Brämer, Lubec. | XXXI. Jährigem Prediger daselbst. | [rule] | Kopen-
hagen/ | Verlegt von Johann Jost Erythropilo, Buchhändler. | Gedruckt
bey Conrad Hartwig Neuhoff/ 1692.

4to. [8], 131, [1] pp.; π⁴, A-Q⁴ R².                    CKB; STADTBIBL. NÜRNBERG

On p. 109, added title: *Das Betrhänte* [sic] *Norden* | *Uber den* | *Höchstschmertz-*
*lichsten Verlust* | . . . | *Hn. JOHANNIS* | *LASSENII,* | . . . | *von* | *P.A. Burchard.* |
*Königl. Vice Probsten des Segeberschen Consistorii, und* | *Pastorn zur Heiligen-*
*hausen* | . . . ; on p. 115, added title: *Des* | *Hoch-Ehrwürdigen/ Hoch-Edlen und*
*Hochgelahrten* | *Herrn* | *Hn. JOHANNIS* | *LASSENII* | . . . | *von* | *Piper* | . . . ;
on p. 121, added title: *Die Verwelckte Fürtrefflichkeit* | *wurde Bey der Hoch-*
*schmertzlichen Bestattung* | . . . | *Hr. JOHANNIS* | *LASSENII* | . . . | *von* | *S.*
*DUBRAVIO, Theol. Stud. aus Ungarn* | . . . .

2544  BURCHARD, PETER ANTON

Bitterer Thränen Gruß, damit die Asche Georg Beckens . . . benetzet.
Schleswig, Joh. Holweins Erben, 1692.

Folio.                                                             *

*OHM* I, 81. Formerly in Kiel UL (LmC 5-61).

2545  DANXST, CORDT

Fruchtbringendes | Informations-Gespräch | Anzeigende/ wie über eine
(so genandte) | Winckelier-oder Kleine Handlung/ | da man ordinaire
bey Ellen und Qvartiren/ Lod- | ten und Qvintins/ kurtz/ ins kleine
verkaufft. | Auffs allerkürtzeste und verständlichste/ nach dem | (so zu

tauffen beliebten) | Jtaliänischen-STYLO, | Richtig Buch zu halten; | Also/ daß man ohne vielem Nachsuchen/ in diesem | und jenem Buche/ ex tempore sehen kan/ wie man | in seiner Handlung stehe: | Wobey zugleich/ | Die von einige Buchhalters eine Zeithero | angewiesene gantz unnöhtige | Theoretische Weitläufftigkeit/ | Wie auch | Unterschied- liche/ bey einige des Buchhaltens-Ungeübte | Eingerissene Mißbräuche/ | Notiret/ erkläret und verbessert werden. | Zum höchstnöthigen und nützlichen Unterricht/ al- | len denen/ welche besagter kleinen Hand- lung zugethan | sind; Jnsonderheit aber die/ so sich seiner mündlichen | Information bedienen/ | Aus eigener Erfahrung/ vermittelst eine/ nicht bloß | in Theoria, sondern vielmehr bey allen Begebenheiten/ in | Praxi dienlichen Methode, dermassen comprehendible, kurtz | und verständ- lich/ (wie von keinen jemahls/ biß anhero geschehen ist) | vorgestellet/ und aus Liebe zur Richtigkeit/ in gegenwärtig | beqvemen Format/ wolmeinend verfasset Von | Cordt Danxst/ | Handels-Buchhaltern und Arithmetico | [ornamental rule] | Impr: impensis Autoris Anno 1692.

8vo. [16], 94 pp.; $\pi^8$, A-F$^8$.                                     CKB

On $\pi$8v, poem to the author by Friedrich Christian Cramer. F8 lacking, probably blank.

2546 DANXST, CORDT

Memorial denen Liebhabern der edlen Wissenschaft des Buchhaltens und der unschätzbaren Zahlen-Kunst vorgestellet. Copenhagen, 1692.

4to.                                                                          *

Ehrencron-Müller, *Forfatterlexikon*, II, 322. *Nova literaria maris Balthici 1700*, p. 114.

2547 DANXST, CORDT

Ein | Nach jetz-üblichen Mercatorischen-Stylo | eingerichtetes | Han- dels- | MEMORIAL, | Tractirende |

( I.) Von Einländische ⎱
( II.) — Außländische ⎰ Proper- ⎫
(III.) — Commission — — — — ⎬ Handlung
(IV.) — Einländische ⎱ ins Groß. |
( V.) — Außländische ⎰ Compagnia- ⎭

Männiglich/ Jnsonderheit aber denen/ so sich in der | Un-schätzbahren Scientz des (so genandten) | Jtaliänischen Buchhaltens/ | Informiren zu lassen/ geneigt; | Mit Besondern Fleiß und Sorgfalt/ | Jn Hochteutsch- Dänisch-und Niederländischer Sprache/ | auffs allerkürtzeste und deut- lichste beschrieben/ | Von | Cordt Danxst/ | Handels-Buchhaltern und

Arithmetico. | [ornament] | [rule] | COPENHAGEN/ | Gedruckt bey
Jhro Königl. Hohh. privil. Buchdr. Joachim Schmedtgen/ 1692.

Folio. (a)-(c)², A-K², χ1.                                          CKB

On (a)1v: "Der Author erkennet nicht ein eintzig | Exemplar vor das seine/ ohne
wel- | ches er mit eigener Hand unterge- | zeichnet." χ1: errata leaf. CKB copy is
not signed. Possibly identical with *Memorial zu dem Winckelier-Handel nach
heutigem Mercatorischen Stylo eingerichtet,* listed in Ehrencron-Müller, *Forfatterlexikon,* II, 322.

2548  DANXST, CORDT

Summarien über die im Handels Memorial befindliche Handels-Posten
nebst einer kurtzen Anleitung wie solche zu journalisiren. Copenhagen,
[1692?].

Folio.                                                                *

Ehrencron-Müller, *Forfatterlexikon* II, 321.

2549  DENMARK. *Laws, statutes, etc.*

Neue | PRIVILEGIA, | So | Jhre Königl. Mayest. zu Denne- | marck/
Norwegen/ &c. | Der Stadt und Festung | Rensburg/ | Den 19 April 1692.
allergnädigst ertheilet. | [rule] | COPENHAGEN/ | Gedruckt bey Jhr.
Königl. Mayest. und Univ. Buchdr. | Johann Philip Bockenhoffer.

4to. χ⁴.                                                            CKB

2550  DENMARK. *Laws, statutes, etc.*

PRIVILEGIA, | Welche | CHRISTIANUS IV. Dero zu Dänne- | marck/
Norwegen/ &c. Königl. Majest. Höchstsel: | und Glorwürdigsten An-
denckens &c. der | Neuerbauten Stadt | Glückstadt/ | De Anno 1617.
den. 22 Martij allergnä- | digst ertheilet. | Wie auch ferner denen
Holländern de Anno 1624. | den 14. Febr. Jmgleichen denen Armenian-
ern de Anno | 1624. den 23. Julij. So dann auch nachgehends der ge-
meinen | Bürgerschafft und denen diversen Nationen, die in der Glück- |
stadt wohnen/ und sich daselbst auffhalten/ de Anno 1629. | den 9.
Decembris. | [ornament] | [rule] | Glückstadt/ gedruckt im Jahr 1692.

4to. a-b⁴.                                                          CKB

2551  DENMARK. *Laws, statutes, etc.*

Wieder auffgelegte | PRIVILEGIA | Oder Freyheiten/ | Welche |
CHRISTIANUS 4tus | Dero zu Dennemarck/ Norwegen &c. | Königl.
Majest. Höchstsel: und Rühmlich- | sten Andenckens/ &c. | Der Nieder-
ländischen Nation, auch ih- | ren Adhærenten und Familien, so in der

Veste | Glückstadt anjetzo wohnen/ und ins künfftig kommen | möch-
ten/ allergnädigst hat mitgetheilet/ und gegeben | Anno 1631. den 17.
Octobris auff 25. Jahr. | Wobey denn zugleich FRIDERICI 3tii, Dero zu |
Dännemarck/ Norwegen &c. Königl. Majest. Allerglor- | würdigsten
Andenckens/ Allergnädigste Confirmatio de Anno | 1648. den 28. Julij.
Wie auch die fernere Prolongatio und | Extensio de Anno 1656. den 31.
Januarij auff 20. Jahr. So- | dann anderweitige Confirmatio und Extensio
von CHRI | STIANO 5to, Der itzo Regierenden Königl. Majest. de
Anno | 1670. den 29. Novemb. auff 10. Jahr. Und dann weiter die |
Königl. Renovatio und Extensio de Anno 1686. den | 20. Aprilis auff 20
Jahr. | Præsent: dem Hn: Præsid: Nicolaus Starck den 29. Junij 1686. |
Public: in Curiâ coram Senat: den 30. Junij Anno 1686. | Zum Druck
befodert durch | F.P. und D.V.D.S. | Als jetzige Deputati der Nieder-
ländischen Nation. | [rule] | Gedruckt im Jahr 1692.

4to. A-C⁴ D1.                                                                              CKB

2552  DENMARK. *Laws, statutes, etc.*

WJR Christian der Fünffte/ von | ... | ... Glückstadt/ den 11. April.
Anno 1692.

Broadside.                                                                                  CNA

Decree setting annual day of prayer the fourth Friday after Easter.

2553  DENMARK. *Laws, statutes, etc.*

WJR Christian der Fünffte/ von | ... | ... Glückstadt den 27. Junij,
Anno 1692.

Broadside.                                                                                  CNA

Decree requiring persons who would attend foreign academies to spend a year at
the Royal Academy in Copenhagen first.

2554  DENMARK. *Laws, statutes, etc.*

WJR Christian der Fünffte/ von | ... | ... Glückstadt/ den 10. Aug.
Anno 1692.

Broadside.                                                                                  CNA

Decree issued jointly with Duke Christian Albrecht of Schleswig-Holstein, calling a
meeting of the "Quartal-Gericht" at Rendsburg 14 September.

2555  DENMARK. *Laws, statutes, etc.*

WJR Christian der Fünffte/ von | ... | ... Glückstadt/ den 28.
Septembr. Anno 1692.

Broadside.                                                                                  CNA

Decree issued jointly with Duke Christian Albrecht of Schleswig-Holstein, calling a "Landgerichts-Tag" at Rendsburg 14 November.

2556  DIBBERN, NICOLAUS

Gründliche Beschreibung | des so genanten | Italiänischen-Kauff- | männischen Buchhaltens | über | Ein- und Außländischen-Proper | Handlungen/ | Nebst beygefügten Haupt- und Apart-Büchern vor | allen Kauff-Leuten/ die ins Groß handeln; | Wie auch | Ein Neu/ | Und hiebevor noch niemahln einiger Orten/ nach der | Jtaliänischen Methode eingerichtetes | Buchhalten | Vor Handels-Leuten/ die feine oder grobe Wahren | in Laden oder Buden ins kleine verkauffen | alles | Mit vielen Fragen und Antwort | Nach jetzigen | Kauffmännischen Styl und Usantz so wol denen/ die | Rechnung über Einnahme und Außgabe abzulegen haben/ als | auch denen/ welche zu der Kauffmannschaft Beliebung tragen/ | zum Dienst mit Fleiß eingerichtet und | verfertiget/ | Von | Nicolao Dibbern | Buchhaltern/ | Wie auch der Schreib-und Rechen-Kunst Beflissenen. | Mit Königl. Majest. auch Chur.-Fürstl. Durchl. zu Sachsen Allergnä- | digsten Privilegiis | [rule] | COPEN- HAGEN/ | Jn Verlegung des Authoris, und daselbst bey ihm zu finden. | Gedruckt bey Jhr. Königl. Maj. und Univ. Buchdr. Joh. Phil. Bocken- hoffer/ Anno 1692.

4to. $\pi^2$, )($^4$, A-P$^4$, $\chi^2$, $^2$A-B$^4$ S-V$^4$ W$^2$ X-Bb$^4$-Cc$^2$, $^2$)($^4$, 2)($^4$ (2)(4 blank); 1 plate.
                                                                              CKB
Title printed in red and black.

2557  FÖRTSCH, JOHANNES PHILIPP

Das rechte Leben | Bey der Hoch-Fürstlichen | Beysetzung | Der Wey- land | Durchleuchtigsten Fürstin | Frauen | MARJEN | ELJSABETH/ | . . . | Auffgesetzet von | Johanne Philippo Förtschen/ Med. Lic. | Hochfürstl. Hoff-Medico. | [double rule] | Schleßwig/ gedruckt in der Fürstl. Druckrey | bey Sehl. Johann Holweins Erben. [1692]

4to. )($^4$, $\chi^2$.                                                        CKB

Verse. Duchess Maria Elisabeth died in 1684

2558  GIESE, JOACHIM

Kräfftiges Süßholtz/ | als | Ein bewehrtes Lindholtz/ | Wider das bitter Todten-Wasser im absterben | . . . | Barbara Apollonia/ | Des WolEdlen/ Vesten/ Hochgelahrten | und Hochweisen Herren | OTTONIS NICO- LAI Lindholtzen/ | . . . | von | M. JOACHIMO Giesen/ Past. Prim. in Kiel. | [rule] | KJEL/ Gedruckt durch Joachim Reumann/ Acad. Buchdr. [1692]

4to. 92 pp.; A-L⁴ M². $\qquad$ CKB

On pp. 87-92, "Abdanckung" by Bernhard Burchard, "Prediger an St. Nicolai."

2559 GIESE, JOACHIM

Der Selig Sterbenden | HJMMELS WAGE/ | . . . | Frawen URSULÆ, | gebornen HÖLLERJN/ | Des Weyland | Hoch-Edlen/ Vesten und Hochgelahrten | Hn. MATTHIÆ Clausens/ | . . . | Von | M. JOACH-IMO Giesen/ | Pastore Primario in Kiel. | [rule] | Kiel/ gedruckt bey Joachim Reumann/ Acad. Buchdr. [1692]

4to. [6], 106 pp.; [A]⁴, B-O⁴. $\qquad$ CKB

2560 Glückstädtisches Gesangbuch. 1692

8vo. $\qquad$ *

*Cat. bibl. Pohlmann,* 1723, p. 231. Possibly identical with *Vollständiges Gesang-Buch* (No. 2592).

2561 HARTNACK, DANIEL

Anzeige daß der Autor der unter seinem Nahmen außgegebenen Gratulation an D. Joh. Frid. Mayern ein Ertzcalumniante und Ehrendieb sey. [Schleswig?], 1692.

4to. $\qquad$ *

*Moller* II, 305.

2562 HARTNACK, DANIEL

Weiteres Nachdencken über D. Phil. Jac. Speners Bedencken von denen, durch D. Joh. Wilh. Petersen außgegebenen, Prophezeyungen vom Chiliastischen Reiche. 1692.

4to. $\qquad$ *

*Moller* II, 305.

2563 HÖPKEN, DANIEL NICLAS VON

Die allgemeine Betrübnüß | Uber | Den höchstschmertzlichen Abgang | Der Weyland | Durchl. Fürstin und Frauen | Frauen MARJEN | ELJSABETH/ | Gebohrnen Churprinzessin zu Sach- | sen/ und zu Jülich/ Cleve und Berg/ auch in | Ober und Nieder-Lausnitz/ Erb-Prinzessin | Verwittibter Herzogin | Zu Schleßwig Holstein/ Stormarn und der | Dittmarschen/ Gräffin zu Oldenburg | und Delmenhorst/ | Bey dero Hochfürstl. Beysetzung | Jn dero Hochfürstl. Ruhe-Kamer | Jm Thum zu Schleßwig | So geschehen den 5. Febr. 1692. | Auß Unter-thänigster-Pflicht | Vorgestellet von | Daniel Niclas von Höpken. |

[double rule] | Schleßwig/ gedruckt in der Fürstl. Druckrey | bey Sehl. Johann Holweins Erben.

Folio. χ². CKB

Verse. Cf. No. 2557.

2564  KEIL, CHRISTIAN

Neu Jahrs Wunsch und Gebeth. Kopenhagen, 1692

8vo.                                                                                          *

*Cat. lib. Frid. Rostgaard,* 1712, 8vo, 152; *Cat. lib. Gottsch. Mühlhausen,* 1760, p. 56.

2565  KORTHOLT, CHRISTIAN

Ursachen, warum ein im Pabstthum gebohrner dasselbe verlassen, und die wahre Evangelische Religion annehmen etc. Kopenhagen, 1692

*

*Thott* I/2, 46.

2566  KOPFF, JOHANN PHILIPP

Klag-Gedicht/ | . . . | Fr. Salome Qveisserin/ | Gebohrne Hintzin/ | . . . | Von | Dero gehorsambsten Schwieger-Sohne | und ergebensten Knechts | Johann-Philipp-Kopff. | [rule] | [Glückstadt/ gedruckt bey Reinhard Janßen 1692]

4to. χ². KIEL UL

Appended: *Schmertz-und kläglich-außgestreuete* | *Trauer-Cypreßen* | . . . | *Von* | *Nachberührten.* | [rule] | *Glückstadt/ Gedruckt im Jahr 1692,* 4 leaves; *Die Ruhe ohn Unruh/* | . . . | *Bey Hochansehnlicher Volckreicher Versamlung zu Mün-* | *ster-* | *dorff in nachgesetzter einfältigen Arien vorgestellet* | *und abgesungen.* | [rule] | *Glückstadt/ gedruckt bey Reinhard Janßen,* 2 leaves; *Letzte Ehren-Pflicht* | . . . | *Von Nachgesetzten.* | [rule] | *Glückstadt/ gedruckt bey Reinhard Janßen,* 2 leaves; *Trauer-Gedancken/* | . . . | *von Dero gehorsamsten* | *Nachgesetzten* *Söhnen* | [rule] | *Glückstadt/ gedruckt bey Reinhard Janßen/ 1692,* 2 leaves; *Hochverdienter Nach-Ruhm* | . . . | *von einem* | *Deroselben* | *gantzergebensten* *Diener* | [rule] | *Glückstadt/ gedruckt bey Reinhard Janßen,* 4 leaves.

2567  LASSENIUS, JOHANNES

Das betrübte/ und von GOtt | Reichlich Getröstete | Ephraim/ | Jn | Hundert/ Vier und Achtzig | Seiner | Geistlichen Anfechtungen/ | Wie die in seinem fast 30 Jährigen | öffentlichen Lehr-Amt/ an unter- schiedenen | Orten/ bey Beicht-und Pfarr-Kindern | ihm vorgekommen/ | Und dagegen gesetzten so viel/ | Trost-Reden/ | Auß den süssen Krafft- und Trost-Qvellen der | Heil. Schrifft zusamen getragen | Und anjetzo/ zu Aufferbauung der Kirchen | GOttes/ und Aller Geistlich Ange-

fochte- | nen fernerem heiligen Trost. | Außgegeben | Unter Königl.
Majest. und Churfürstl. Durchl. zu Sachsen | Allergnädigsten Privi-
legiis. | JOHANNES LASSENIUS, | Der Heil. Schrifft D. Prof. Publ.
Consist. Assess. und Pa- | stor an St. Petri Kirche in Kopenhagen. |
[rule] | Kopenhagen/ | Bey Johann Melchior Lieben/ Buchhändl. |
Gedruckt bey Jhr. Königl. Mayt. und Univ. Buchdrucker/ | Johann
Philip Bockenhoffer/ im Jahr 1692.

8vo. Pp. [1-20], 1-669, 680-1306, [1-50]; a⁸ (−a7, 8), )(⁴, A-V⁸ W⁸ X-Vv⁸ Ww⁸ Xx-
Vvv⁸ Www⁸ Xxx-Mmmm⁸ Nnnn1; engraved preliminary title, frontispiece.   CKB

Preliminary title: *Das* | *Von Gott betrubte* | *und reichlich getröstete* | *EPHRAIM.* |
*Durch Mund Hand und* | *Feder* | *D. Iohannis Lassenÿ* | *Kopenhagen. 1692.* Title
printed in red and black. Preface is in Latin, signed by J. Baggerus, D.

2568   LASSENIUS, JOHANNES

Biblischer | Weyrauch | Zum süssen Geruch | Gottseeliger Andachten/ |
Aus H. Schrifft also zusamen gelesen/ | Das mit des Heiligen Geistes
eigenen | Worten/ die Gott-Liebende Seel/ täglich | mit Gott reden
könne. | Samt | Heilsahmer Vorbereitung | zum Beicht-Stuhl/ | Und
Heiligen Abendmahl. | Mit allerhand neuen/ Morgen- und | Abend-Buß-
Beicht-und Communion-Lie- | dern/ auch Kupffern hin und wieder |
versehen. | Dem gecreutzigten JEsu allein zu Ehren/ | Und der/ mit
seinem Blut erlöseten heiligen | Gemeine GOttes in Copenhagen und |
Anderswo/ | Zur Beförderung ihres Christenthums/ ange- | zündet von |
D. JOHANNE LASSENIO. | Mit Königl. Maj. zu Denm. und Ch.
Durchl. | zu Sachsen allergnädigsten Privilegio. | Andere Edition/ aufs
neue übersehen und | vermehret. | [rule] | Copenhagen/ Zu finden bey
Joh. Melch. Liebe | der Kön. Univers. Buchhändl. | Gedruckt bey Joh.
Jacob Bornheinrich/ | Anno 1692.

12mo. [20], 827, [13] pp.; a¹² (−a11, 12), A-V¹² W¹² X-Ll¹² (Ll12 blank); engraved preliminary title, frontispiece, 19 plates.                   CKB

Dedication is dated Ash-Wednesday, 1687.

2569   LASSENIUS, JOHANNES

CASTRUM DOLORIS | HAFNIENSE | Bestehend in | XXIV.
PARENTATIONEN | Oder | Leich-und Ehren-Reden/ | Bey | Hoher
Standes/ auch anderer Fürneh- | men und Christlichen Persohnen/ |
Beerdigung/ | Jn der Teutschen Kirchen zu St. Petri in Copen- | hagen
öffentlich gehalten. | Auch XXIV Andern/ so wol in der Gemeine da- |
selbst geredeten/ als schrifftlich mit-getheilten | Klag-Trost und Ge-
dächtnüß | Reden | über die | Jn der Anno MDCLXXXIX, den XIX
Aprilis | auff SOPHIEN AMALIENBURG, enstandenen kläg- | lichen

Feüers-Brunst/ jämmerlich umbge- | kommene | Theils seine gewesene
Theür-geschätzte Beicht-Kin- | der/ als sonst in dem gecreützigten JEsu
allerwehrteste | Freünde und Freündinnen. | Zu dero unsterblichem
Angedencken/ | Auch kräfftigem Trost/ in dem heiligen Geist/ der
schmertzlich | Bethränten Hinterbliebenen/ | heraußgegeben | von | D.
Johanne Lassenio | SS. Theol. Prof. Publ. Consistor. Asses. und Pastore |
daselbst. | [rule] | Copenhagen | Jn der Bockenhofferischen Druckerey |
1692.

Folio. Title-page only.                                        CKB

No evidence that more was printed or published.

2570   LASSENIUS, JOHANNES

Himmlischer Morgen-Thau der süssen Gnade Gottes, auß verschiedenen
Tröpflein vieler herrlichen Kern-Sprüche der Heiligen Schrifft zur Be-
giessung des Pflantz-Gartens Christi aufgesammlet. Copenhagen, 1692.

8vo.                                                             *

*Moller* II, 453; *Bibl. Botsackiana,* 1709, II, 16.

2571   LASSENIUS, JOHANNES

Lob-singende | Andacht/ | Dazu des theuren Mannes | GOTTES | D.
MARTIN LUTHERS | Und anderer Christlichen Lehrer. | Alte und
Neue Lieder | außerlesen/ zu behuff | Eines Kirchen | Gesangbuchs | Für
die Teutsche Gemeine zu | St. Petri in Kopenhagen. | Samt einem |
Gebet-Büchlein/ | auch Vorrede und Censur | Johannis Lassenii | Der H.
Schrifft Doctoris, P.P. | und Predigers daselbst. | Auch von demselben/
in dieser neuen | Edition, mit Fleiß übersehen/ und | auf ein merckliches
vermehret. | Unter Kön. M. allergnädigsten Privilegio. | [rule] | Kopen-
hagen/ | Zu finden bey Joh. Melchior Lieben/ | Der Königl. Universit.
Buchhändl. | Drukts Joh. Jacob Bornheinrich/ | Anno 1692.

12mo. [12], 689, [15] pp.; 107, [1] pp.; a2-7, A-Ee$^{12}$ Ff1-4 Gg-Kk$^{12}$ Ll$^6$; 12 plates.
                                                                CKB

Title engraving: "Kopenhagner Teutsches Gesang Buch. 1692." On Gg1, separate
title: *D. Johan. Lassenii | Morgen- | Und | Abend-Buß-Beicht | Communion und
an- | dere Zeit- und Noth- | Gebete. | [rule] | Copenhagen/ | Zu finden bey Johan
Melch. Liebe/ | Der Königl. Universit. Buchhändl. | Drukts Joh. Jacob Bornhein-
rich/ | Anno 1692.*

2572   Lebens-Lauff | Des | Berühmten THEOLOGI | Herrn | D. JOHANNIS
       LASSENII. [c. 1692]

8vo. 63, [1] pp. A-D$^8$.                                        CKB

2573  Letzte Ehren-Pflicht/ | ... | Fr. Ursula Clausen/ | gebohrnen Müllerin/ |
... | abgestattet. | [rule] | KJEL/ | Gedruckt bey Joachim Reumann/
Acad. Buchdr. | Anno 1692.

4to. )(⁴, χ².                                   CKB

Verse by Franz Dietrich Kohl, Friedrich Gramm, and Stephan Klotz.

2574  [MAJOR, JOHANN DANIEL]

Bevölckertes | Cimbrien: | oder/ die | zwischen Ost- und West-See
gelegene | halb-Insel | Deutschlandes/ | nebst dero | Ersten Einwohnern/
und ihrer eigendlichen/ durch viel | und grosse Umwege geschehenen
Ankunfft/ | summarischer weise vorgestellet/ von | [monogram] |
[rule] | zu Plön gedruckt | bey Tobias Schmied/ Fürstl. Buchdrucker: |
Anno 1692.

Folio. [4], 162, [2] pp.; )(², A-V² W² X-Rr²; 4 plates.      CKB; (BM)

2575  MALTZAHN, ARNOLD

Richtige Wolfahrt der flüchtigen Wallfahrt, in 50. Betrachtungen der
irdischen Pilgrimschaft vorgestellet. Plön, 1692.

8vo.                                                 *

*Moller* I, 437; *Bibl. Wedderkoppiana*, 1722, p. 256; *Cat. lib. Oksen*, 1738, p. 54; *Cat.
lib. Lehmann* I, 1740, p. 241.

2576  [MASIUS, HECTOR GOTTFRIED]

PALINODIÆ BECMANNIANÆ | SPECIMEN, | Oder | Abgenöhtig-
ter | Wiederruff/ | Welchen | Johan Christopffer Becman/ | Jn seiner
Abfertigungs-Schrifft/ zwar zum | Theil indirectè gethan/ | Aber |
Rechtens wegen directè thun solte/ | Jn | Beantwortung seiner Abfer-
tigung/ | Kürtzlich gezeiget/ und | Durch eine dreyfache Liste/ | Aller
redlichen Reformirten Urtheil | übergeben | Von | M. D. E. P. P. |
[ornamental rule] | Copenhagen/ Gedruckt bey Jhr Königl. Hoh. Bucht.
Joachim | Schmedtgen. 1692.

4to. 132 pp.; A-Q⁴, R²                                     CKB

2577  MASIUS, HECTOR GOTTFRIED

Ander Theil | Des Gründlich Verthädigten | Treuen Lutherthumbs/ |
...

*See* No. 2526.

2578  MOHR, NICOLAUS

Sehnlich Klage | über | ... | HERRN | Georgij Mohrs/ | ... | Von | Des

Seligst-Verschiedenen | Sohne | NICOLAO Mohren/ | Sch. Itzeh.
Alumno. | [rule] | Glückstadt/ gedruckt bey Reinhard Janßen. [1692]

Folio. χ². CKB

Verse.

2579 MOLLER, JOHANNES

Der Hochedlen Freyheit . . . Jn nupt. Bernh. Meinecken et Margaretæ,
Gerh. Reimeri . . . [filiæ]. Schleswig, 1692.

4to. *

*OHM* I, 430-1.

2580 MOLLER, JOHANNES

Jocoseria . . . in nuptiis Jac. Hansenii und Brigitta, Bernh. Strickeri, . . .
filiæ. Schleswig, 1692.

Folio. *

*OHM* I, 430-1.

2581 NAGEL, JOHANN HELFRICH

Englischer Wächter Englische Wacht, aus dem Fest-Michaelis Evang.
Altona, 1692

8vo. *

*Bibl. Schroedter,* 1724, p. 477.

2582 PFENNING, JOHANNES MATTHIAS

Wolverdienter-Nachruhm | . . . | Fr. Ursula | Clausen/ | gebohrnen
Müllerin/ | . . . | Von | Johannes Matthias Pfenning/ | [rule] | KJEL/ |
Gedruckt bey Joachim Reumann/ Acad. Buchdr. [1692]

4to. A⁴. CKB

2583 [REICHENBACH, ELISA SOPHIA VON]

Die | Weißheit | Salomonis. | Der | Durchläuchtigsten Princessin |
Sophia Amalia/ | Gebohrner Herzogin zu Schleß- | wig-Hollstein/ |
Stormarn und | der Dithmarschen/ Gräffinn zu Olden- | burg und
Delmenhorst &c. | Unterthänigst gewidmet | Von | E. S. v. R. | G. v. C. |
[rule] | Schleßwig/ | Gedruckt bey Lorentz Eckstorff/ Hoch-Fürstl. |
Hoff-Buchdrucker/ 1692.

8vo. [6], 290 pp.; A-S⁸ T⁴; engraved frontispiece. CKB

Frontispiece ("Sophia Salomons") is signed by J. Friedlein, Kiel.

2584  Sᴛ. Sᴜʟᴘɪs, Vɪᴄᴛᴏʀ ᴅᴇ

Richtiger Weg zur Seeligkeit/ | Oder | Dringende Ursachen | Warum
ein in Pabstthum gebohrner dasselbe | verlassen und die wahre | Evan-
gelische | Religion | annehmen müsse/ wenn er sich seiner | Seelen Heil
und Seeligkeit verge- | wissern wil. | Auß Heil. Göttlicher Schrifft
erweißlich ge- | macht/ und mit unwiedersprechlichen Grün- | den
dargethan/ | Von | Einem Exulirenden Piemontesischen | von Adel |
[ornamental rule] | Copenhagen/ | Gedruckt bey Johann Adolph Bax-
man im Jahr 1692

4to. [4], 20 pp.; A-C⁴.                                            **CKB**

On A1v, the "Censura" is signed by H. G. Masius.

2585  Sᴀɴᴅʜᴀɢᴇɴ, Cᴀsᴘᴀʀ Hᴇʀᴍᴀɴɴ

Casp. H. Sandhagens/ | der regierenden Hoch-Fürstl. | Durchl. zu
Schleßwig und Holstein/ | General-Super. Consist Rahts/ | Oberhoff-
predigers und | Probstes/ | Erstes Zehen | Theologischer | Send-
schreiben/ | darin unterschiedliche | Oerter der Schrifft | erkläret
werden. | [ornament] | [rule] | Schleßwig/ | Gedruckt bey sel. Johann
Holweins | Erben/ 1692.

12mo. [2], 346 pp.; π1, A-N¹², O1-11, P⁶.                           **CKB**

2586  Sᴀɴᴅʜᴀɢᴇɴ, Cᴀsᴘᴀʀ Hᴇʀᴍᴀɴɴ

Der seel. | Lebens-Beschluß | . . . | Stephani Kenkels/ | . . . | Von |
Caspar Hermann Sandhagen/ | . . . | [rule] | Schleßwig/ | Gedruckt bey
Lorentz Eckstorff/ Hoch-Fürstlichen | Hoff-Buchdrucker. Anno 1692.

4to. 84, [28] pp.; A-O⁴.                                           **CKB**

On pp. 77-84, "Abdanckung" by Joachim Engel; on L4v ff., verse by several hands.

2587  Schertz-Gedichte/ | Auff | Den Hochzeitlichen Ehren-Tag | . . . |
HERRN | Johann Dieterich | Michelsen/ | Medicinæ Doctoris, | Mit der |
Wolgebohrnen Jungfer/ | JUNGFER | Anna Margareta/ | Des |
Wohlgebohrnen Herrn/ | Herrn Hinrich Vohlmans/ | . . . | eintziger
Jungfer Tochter | Wie selbige den 4. Eebr. [sic] 1692. in Glückstadt |
feyerlichst gehalten wurde/ | Ubergeben | Von Guten Freunden. |
[rule] | Glückstadt/ gedruckt bey Reinhard Janßen.

Folio. χ².                                                        **CKB**

Verse.

2588  Sᴄʜɪʀᴍᴇʀ, Mᴀʀᴛɪɴ

Martin Schirmers | Kunst-Mas | des Raums/ | Zur | Geometrie und

Fortification | höchstnötig. | Imprimatur, | C. Bartholin. | [ornamental rule] | Copenhagen/ | Auf Unkosten des Autoris. | [rule] | Drukts Johan Jacob Bornheinrich/ | 1692.

8vo. [4], 44, 24 pp.; $\pi^2$, A-C$^8$(−C7, 8), $^2$A$^8$ $^2$B$^4$.                    CUL

The leaves $^2$A1-$^2$B4 contain remarks on and examples of addition, subtraction, multiplication, division, and progressions.

2589  SCHLESWIG-HOLSTEIN-GOTTORFF. *Laws, statutes, etc.*

Wir Christian Albrecht von | Gottes Gnaden/ Erbe zu Norwegen/ Postu- | lirter Coadjutor des Stiffts Lübeck/ Hertzog . . . | . . . | . . . 2. Martij Anno 1692.

Broadside.                                               KIEL UL

Decree renewing the privileges (specifically: religious freedom) of Friedrichstadt.

2590  Die ungeänderte Augspurgische Confession oder Bekenntniss des Glaubens etlicher Fürsten und Städte überantwortet Kayserlicher Majestät zu Augspurg 1530. Schleswig, 1692.

12mo.                                                       *

*Bibl. Schroedter,* 1724, p. 656; *Cat. lib. Lehmann* I, 1740, p. 87; *Theil Bücher Casp. Herm. Sandhagen,* 1745, p. 166.

2591  VERMEHREN, PAUL

Als der | Höchstglückliche Gebuhrts-Tag | Des | Allerdurchläuchtigsten/ Groß- | mächtigsten Königes und Herrn/ | Herrn | CHRJSTJAN | Des Fünfften/ | Königs zu Dennemarck Norwe- | gen/ der Wenden und Gothen/ Hertzogs | zu Schleßwig/ Holstein/ Stormarn und Ditt- | marschen/ Graffen zu Oldenburg und | Delmenhorst/ | Anno 1692 den 15 April, mit allgemeiner Freü- | den-Bezeugung Höchstfeyerlich begangen ward/ | hat | Jhrer Königlichen Majestät Preißwür- | digste Thaten mit diesen betrachten/ und | Deroselben eine fernere langwierige Regierung | in tieffster Demuth anzuwünschen sich erkühnen wollen | Dero Königlichen Majestät | Allerunterthänigster/ Allergehorsahmster | und devotester Knecht | P. Vermehren. | [rule of type ornaments] | Copenhagen/ Gedruckt bey Jhro Königl. Majest. und Dero Universit. | Buchdr. Johan Philip Bockenhoffer.

Folio. A-B$^4$ C$^2$.                                          CKB

Verse.

2592  Vollständiges Gesang-Buch darinnen nicht allein die alte gewöhnliche

KirchenGesänge sondern auch viele neue geist-reiche Lieder zu befinden. 1692.

    \*

Emil Brederek, *Geschichte der schleswig-holsteinischen Gesangbücher,* Kiel 1919, pp. 3 ff. Seventh edition of Plön hymnal (?). Cf. Nos. 1895, 2122.

2593 [WEBER, IMMANUEL]

Zeitläffige | Staats- | Begebenheiten/ | worinnen vor diesmahl | die | zwischen der | Königl. Majest. zu Dännemarck | und der | Stadt Hamburg | Zeithero obschwebende | Zwistigkeiten und Jrrungen/ | sonderlich den | Glückstädtischen Elb-Zoll | betreffende | mit unpartheyischer Feder | eröffnet werden/ | durch | LEVINUM v. Ambeer | [rule] | verlegts in Altona | Jost Ferdinand Gidschel/ | Anno 1692

4to. a$^4$, A-F$^4$.      CKB; (BM)

Dedication (a2r-a4v) in French.

2595 ZWERG, GOTTHARD JOHANNES

MONUMENTUM HONORIS | . . . | Herrn Hans von Thienen/ | . . . | Durch | Gotthardum Johannem Zwergium, | Predigern und Dienern am Worte Gottes zu Tundern. | [rule] | KJEL/ | Gedruckt bey Joachim Reumann/ Acad. Buchdr. [1692]

4to. [16], 53, [13] pp.; A-H$^4$ J$^4$ (−J4), )(4, )()($^2$.      CKB

)(1 has separate title: [coat of arms] | *Ehren-Gedächtniß* | . . . . Signed "M. J.G.P.P. in K." (i.e., Joachim Giese).

## 1693

2596 Als dem . . . Herrn Christiano Kortholten . . . die Pro-Rectoratswürde . . . auffgetragen ward, wolten hiemit ihre Schuldigkeit abstatten . . . sämtliche Tischgesellschaft. Kiel, 1693.

Folio.     \*

Formerly in Kiel UL (LmC 18$^a$-101).

2597 Als zwischen | . . . | Herrn PETER | PETERSEN | . . . | Jungf. ANNA | LORENTZEN/ | . . . | Das Ehe-Band durch Priesterliche Copula- | tion den [   ] Julii Anno 1693 geknüpffet | wurde/ | . . . | Copenhagen/ Gedruckt bey Jh. Königl. M. und Univers. Buchdr. | Johan Philip Bockenhoffer.

Folio. χ$^2$.      OSLO UL

Verse by Nicolaus Harboe (in Latin) and Nicolaus Lorentzen. Date on t-p. not filled in.

2598  ARNKIEL, TROELS

Christliche | Confirmation | Derer | Catechumenen/ | Von der | Apostel
Zeit an bißher | Aus der Heil. Schrifft und Antiquität | der Kirchen |
Beleuchtiget | Von | M. TROGILLO Arnkiel/ | Probsten und Pastoren
zu Apenrad. | [ornament] | [double rule] | Schleßwig/ | Gedruckt bey
Lorentz Eckstorff/ Hoch-Fürstl. | Hoff-Buchdrucker. Anno 1693

4to. [16], 264, [4] pp.; a-c⁴, A-Hh⁴, Ji², Kk⁴.                        CKB

2599  BOTSAC, BARTHOLD

Abschieds-Rede | Nach Anleitung | Act. XXI. 14. | bey sehr Volckreicher
Versam̄lung | in der Kirchen zum Brüdern/ | Unter unzehlich vergos-
senen | Thränen | DOM: EXAUDI | Nachmittags | Auff Veranlassung
seiner Ampts- | Veränderung/ da die Braunschweigische | Superin-
tendentur, gemäß ordentlichen Beruff/ | Mit dem Pastorat bey der
Teutschen Kirche | St. Petri in Copenhagen/ | auch Theologischen
Profession bey der dasigen Königl. Universität | zu verwechseln/ |
gehalten | durch | BARTOLDUM BOTSACCUM Doct. | [rule] |
Copenhagen/ | Auff Kosten des Autoris Anno 1693.

4to. 40 pp.; A-E⁴.                                                     CKB

2600  CRUSIUS, JOHANNES

Sehet welch ein Mensch ! | Das ist | Eine kurtze Betrachtung | Von dem |
Leyden und Sterben unsers HErrn | und Heylandes | JEsu Christi |
Genommen | Aus denen | Vier Evangelisten/ | Und | Heraus gegeben |
Von | JOHANNE CRUSIO, | J. U. Stud. | [rule] | KJEL/ | Gedruckt
durch Joachim Reumann/ Acad. Buchdr. | Anno 1693

4to. A⁴.                                                              CKB

2601  DANXST, CORDT

Kurtz-gefasste Instruction vom Buchhalten übern Groß-Handel &c. Copenhagen, 1693.

12mo.                                                                   *

*Cat. Matthia Moth,* [1719], p. 8.

2602  DENMARK. *Laws, statutes, etc.*

WJR Christian der Fünffte/ | ... | ... Glückstadt/ den 4. Martij, Anno
1693.

Broadside.                                                            CNA

Decree regarding the circulation of small foreign coins.

2603 DENMARK. *Laws, statutes, etc.*

WJR Christian der Fünffte/ | ... | ... Glückstadt den 16. Augusti, Anno 1693.

Broadside.                CNA

Decree regarding mourning at the death of Queen Ulrica Eleonora of Sweden.

2604 DENMARK. *Laws, statutes, etc.*

WJR Christian der Fünffte/ | ... | ... Gottorff/ den 28ten Augusti Anno 1693.

Broadside.                CNA

Decree issued jointly with Duke Christian Albrecht of Schleswig-Holstein, calling a meeting of the "Quartal-Gericht" at Schleswig 3 October.

2605 DENMARK. *Laws, statutes, etc.*

WJr Christian der Fünffte/ | ... | ... Gottorff den 4. Sept. Ao. 1693

Broadside.             CNA; CKB

Decree issued jointly with Duke Christian Albrecht of Schleswig-Holstein, calling a "Land-Gerichts-Tag" in Kiel 16 November.

2607 DENMARK. *Laws, statutes, etc.*

WJR Christian der Fünffte/ | ... | ... Glückstadt/ den 13ten Novembr. ANNO 1693

Broadside.                CNA

Decree issued jointly with Duke Christian Albrecht of Schleswig-Holstein, forbidding subjects to enter foreign military service.

2608 DENMARK. *Laws, statutes, etc.*

WJR Christian der Fünffte/ | ... | ... Glückstadt/ den 29. Novemb. Anno 1693.

Broadside.                CNA

Decree forbidding inhabitants of Pinneberg and Altona to enter foreign military service.

2609 FREDERIK II, *King of Denmark*

Etzliche | Außerlesene und vornehme | Sprüche | und | Sententzen/ | Aus den Sprüchen Sa- | lomonis und JEsus | Sirach/ | Zusammen gebracht | Durch den | Durchläuchtigsten/ Großmäch- | tigsten und Hochgebohrnen | Fürsten und Herrn/ | Herrn Friderich/ | der Ander | König zu Dännemarcken/ | Norwegen/ der Wen- | den und Gothen/

&c. | Nach dem Seine Königliche Majestät | solche Bücher mit Fleiß selbst hat | durchgelesen. [1693]

12mo. 198 pp.; A-H$^{12}$, J$^4$.       CKB

J3 lacking, probably blank. First published 1583.

2610 [Förtsch, Johannes Philipp]

Musicalisches Lustspiel, am 45ten Geburtstage Fridericæ Amaliæ, Hertzoginn zu Holstein-Gottorf, oder dem 11. April Anno 1693 vorgestellet. Schleswig, 1693.

4to.        *

*Moller* II, 199.

2611 Goldschmid, Peter

Die ewig erquickende Ruhe der Frommen, so da bestehet im seligen Anschauen Gottes, in III. Betrachtungen vorgestellet. Schleswig, 1693.

8vo.        *

*Moller* I, 212.

2612 Die | Klugheit der Gerechten/ | Die Kinder | Nach den wahren Gründen | des Christenthums von der Welt | zum HErrn zu erziehen. | Sambt denen darüber gewechselten | Streit-Schrifften/ | und | E. E. Hochweisen Rahts | der Stadt Hamburg | Protocoll-mässigen Bericht/ | auch was sonsten | Occasione der Horbischen | Sache fürgefallen/ ordentlich zu- | sammen getragen/ | Und denen | Wahrheit-liebenden unpartheyischen | Gemühtern zu beurtheilen öffentlich | fürgeleget. | [rule] | ALTONA/ | Gedruckt und verlegt bey Christian Reymers/ Königl. privil. | Buchdrucker. [1693]

8vo. Pp. [1-32], 1-824, 829-1172; ):($^8$,):( ):($^8$, A-Dddd$^8$.    CKB

Title on verso of first leaf. On ):(1r, added title: *ACTA* | *HAMBUR-* | *GENSIA.*

2613 Knoff, Christopher, *editor*

Etliche | Psalme und Sprüche/ | Welche | Der Durchläuchtigste/ Großmächtigste | Fürst und Herr/ | Hr: Friderich der Ander | Zu Dännemarcken/ Norwegen/ der Wenden und | Gotthen König: Hertzog zu Schleßwig/ Holstein/ Stormarn | und der Dithmarschen: Graff zu Oldenburg und Delmenhorst/ etc. | Selbst | Aus dem Psalter zusammen gezogen/ | Jm Jahr 1586. | Kürtzlich und einfältig erkläret durch Seiner Königl. Majest: Hof-Prediger | M. Christoferum Knoff/ | Denenselben | Das Preißwürdigste Gedächtnüß | Dieses in GOtt Christseligsten Königs | Jn seinem | Leben/ Regierung und Sterben | Jst

beygefüget worden. | Mit Königlicher Majest. zu Dännemarcken und
Norwegen &c. allergnädigst | verliehener sonderbarer Frejheit. | [rule] |
COPENHAVEN gedruckt Jm Jahr CHristi 1693.

4to. Pp. [1-12], 1-766, 777-1017, 1002 [i.e., 1020], 1021-1066; $\pi^6$, A-Rrrrr$^4$

CKB

Title printed in red and black. Rrrrrr4 lacking. Printed and issued with Johann
Lauerentzen, *Das* | *Preißwürdigste Gedächtnüß* | . . . | *Friderich des Andern/* |
. . . [Copenhagen 1693], (No. 2623).

2614  KORTHOLT, CHRISTIAN

Creutz-uñ | Gedult-Spiegel/ | Aus Göttlicher Schrifft und | der alten und
neuen Kirchen- | Historie fürgestellet | Von | Christian Kortholten/ D. |
[rule] | PLOEN/ | Gedruckt und verlegt durch Tobias | Schmidt/ |
Jm 1693sten Jahr.

8vo. Pp. [1-16], 1-64, 67-399, [1-3]; )($^8$, A-Bb$^8$.                  CKB

Leaf )(8 contains Latin poems by Matth. Nicol. Kortholt and Sebastian Kortholt,
of Kiel.

2615  LASSENIUS, JOHANNES

Johan-Lassenii | ARCANA | POLITICO- | ATHEISTICA. | Oder |
Politische | Geheimnüß | Vieler | Hin und wieder versteckten/ |
Unartigen | ATHEISTEN. | Jn | Einigen Gesprächen | entdecket und
verworffen. | [ornament] | Gedruckt im Jahr 1693.

12mo. Pp. 1-161, 164-194; A-H$^{12}$.                                    CKB

Same dedication and text as in 1666 edition, apparently published outside monarchy.

2616  LASSENIUS, JOHANNES

Besiegte | Atheisterey/ | Darinn | Aus heiliger Schrifft behauptet/ |
auch theils | Aus der Natur und gesunden Vernunft | erwiesen/ | Daß
die Heil. Schrifft GOttes Wort/ | warhafftig ein GOtt/ die Seele der
Menschen | unsterblich/ eine allgemeine Auferstehung der Todten zu |
hoffen/ Teufel/ Gespenster/ Himmel/ Höll/ ein Gewissen | und ewiges
Leben sey: Mit gründlicher Beant- | wortung der Gegen-seitigen | Ein-
reden/ | Saṁt unterschiedlichen Anmerckungen/ Und einem Anhang |
vieler hierzu dienenden | Fragen und Antworten/ | Auch einigen Sinn-
Bildern und nöthigen | Registern/ | Zur Ehre GOttes/ und Rettung der |
Evangelischen Warheit/ geschrieben | von | JOHANNE LASSENIO |
der heil. Schrifft D. Prof. Publ. Consist. Assess. | und Pastore an St. Petri
Kirche in Ko- | penhagen. | [rule] | Bey Joh. David Threwner/ | 1693.

8vo.  Pp. [1-30], 1-48, 39-118, 117-970, [1-40]; )(⁸ (−)(8), ):():(⁸, A-Rrr⁸ Sss⁴;
engraved frontispiece, 7 plates.                                                                     CKB

Title printed in red and black.

2617  LASSENIUS, JOHANNES

Das betrübte/ und von GOtt | Reichlich Getröstete | Ephraim/ | Jn |
Hundert Vier und Achtzig | Seiner | Geistlichen Anfechtungen/ | Wie
die in seinem fast 30 Jährigen öffent- | lichen Lehr-Amt/ an unter-
schiedenen Or- | ten/ bey Beicht-und Pfarr-Kindern ihm | vorgekom-
men/ | Und dagegen gesetzten so viel | Trost-Reden/ | Aus den süssen
Krafft-und Trost-Qvellen der | Heil. Schrifft zusammen getragen | Und
anjetzo/ zu Aufferbauung der Kirchen | GOttes/ und aller Geistlich
Angefochtenen | fernerem heiligen Trost. | Außgegeben | Unter Königl.
Majestät und Churfürstl. Durchl. zu Sachsen/ | Allergnädigsten Privi-
legiis. | JOHANNES LASSENIUS. | Der H. Schrifft D.P.P. Consist.
Assess. und Pastor | an St. Petri Kirche in Kopenhagen. | [rule] |
Kopenhagen/ | Bey Johann Melchior Lieben/ Buchhändl. | Gedruckt bey
Johann Jacob Bornheinrich/ Jm Jahr 1693.

8vo.  Pp. [1-12], 1-576, 579-1102, [1-52]; a⁶, A-Cccc⁸; engraved preliminary title, 11
[of 13?] plates.                                                                     CKB

Preliminary title, same as in 1692 edition, including date, 1692. Title printed in red
and black. CKB copy presumably lacking an engraved frontispiece, a portrait of the
author.

2618  LASSENIUS, JOHANNES

Handleitung | Zur | Seligkeit/ | Darin der Heil. Cate- | chismus Lutheri,
von Frag zu | Frag/ nach seinem Geistreichen | Verstande erkläret/ |
Samt beigefügten Morgen und | Abend-Buß-Beicht-Communion | und
andern Gebeten; Auch etzlichen Ge- | wissens/ Fragen/ und kurtzen
Fundament | der Christl. Religion, aus H. Schrift. | Zur Ehre Gottes und
gemeinen Nutzen/ | in der Furcht des HErrn außgefertiget | von | D.
Johanne Lassenio. | [rule] | Zum vierdtenmahl gedruckt | Vor Johann
Jost Erythropilo Buch- | händler in Kopenhagen, 1693.

12mo. [22], 288, [2], 142, 24 pp.; A-N¹², a-g¹².                     KAREN BRAHE

Title printed in red and black. g12 lacking, probably blank. "An dem Leser"
dated "Kopenhaven/ den 10. Octobr. | 1677." On a1, separate title: *Morgen-* |
*Und* | *Abend-Buß-Beicht-* | *Communion und andere* | *Zeit-und Noth* | *Gebet.* |
[rule] | *1693.*

2619  LASSENIUS, JOHANNES

JOHANNIS LASSENII | Der H. Schrifft Doct. Prof. Publ. und Past. |

an St. Petri Kirchen | Heiligen | Perlen-Schatzes | Erste Vertheilung | über die Monath | JANUARIUS, FEBRUARIUS | MARTIUS und APRILIS. | Jn der Furcht GOttes/ aus dessen geoffen- | bahrten Wort also eingesamlet/ | Daß zu Beforderung des Thätigen | und GOtt Wolge- fälligen Christenthums | Die GOtt-begierige Seel/ | Täglich mit Zweyen Christlichen Betrach- | tungen sich erbauen könne. | Mit überal hinzuge- thanen Sin-Bildern. | Unter Königl. Majest. zu Dännemarck/ Norwe- gen/ | Auch | Churfl. Durchl. zu Sachsen/ Allergnädigsten Privilegiis. | Andere Edition/ aufs neue übersehen. | [rule] | Copenhagen/ | Zu finden bey Joh. Melchior Liebe/ der Universität | Buchhändlern. | Druckts Johan Jacob Bornheinrich/ | Anno 1693.

8vo. Pp. [1-14], 1-864, 867-936, [1-14]; )($^8$ (−)(8), A-V$^8$ W$^8$ X-Vv$^8$ Ww$^8$ Xx-Lll$^8$; engraved frontispiece; 32 plates.                                                                         CKB

Title printed in red and black. Lll8 lacking, probably blank. Same plates as in 1688 edition, without engraving of Lassenius.

2620   LASSENIUS, JOHANNES

Johannis Lassenii | Der H. Schrifft Doct. Prof. Publ. und Past. | an St. Petri Kirchen | Heiligen | Perlen-Schatzes | Andere Vertheilung | über die Monath | MAJUS, JUNIUS, | JULIUS und AUGUSTUS | zu Auffer- bauung des Algemeinen | Christenthums | Jn der Furcht des HErrn eingesamlet/ | Auch zu mehrer Verständnüß der | heiligen Betracht- ungen | Uberal mit nöthigen Sin-Bildern versehen. | Unter Königl. Majest. zu Dännemarck/ Norwegen/ | Auch | Churfl. Durchl. zu Sach- sen/ Allergnädigsten Privilegiis, | Andere Edition/ aufs neue übersehen. | [rule] | Copenhagen/ | Zu finden bey Joh. Melchior Liebe/ der Univer- sität | Buchhändlern. | Druckts Johan Jacob Bornheinrich/ | Anno 1693.

8vo. [14], 1024, [14] pp.; )($^8$ (−)(8), a-v$^8$ w$^8$ x-vv$^8$ ww$^8$ xx-rrr$^8$ (rrr8 blank); 33 plates.                                                                                             HAB

Title printed in red and black.

2621   LASSENIUS, JOHANNES

Johannis Lassenii | Der H. Schrifft Doct. Prof. Publ. und Past. | an St. Petri Kirchen | Heiligen | Perlen-Schatzes | Dritte und letzte Ver- theilung | über die Monath | SEPTEMBER, OCTOBER, | NOVEMBER und DECEMBER. | Zu Aufferbauung des Algemeinen | Christenthums | Jn der Furcht des HErrn/ aus Göttlichem | Wort eingesamlet/ | Auch zu richtiger Verständnüß der | heiligen Betrachtungen/ | Uberal mit nöthigen Sinn-Bildern versehen. | Unter Königl. Majest. zu Dänne- marck/ Norwegen/ | Auch | Churfl. Durchl. zu Sachsen/ Allergnädig- sten Privilegiis. | Andere Edition/ aufs neue übersehen. | [rule] | Copen-

hagen/ | Zu finden bey Joh. Melchior Liebe/ der Universität | Buch-
händlern. | Druckts Johan Jacob Bornheinrich/ | Anno 1693.

8vo. [14], 1040, [16] pp.; )(⁸ (−)(8), (A)-(V)⁸ (W)⁸ (X)-(Vv)⁸ (Ww)⁸ (Xx)-
(Sss)⁸ ((Sss 7-8) blank); 32 plates.　　　　　　　　　　　　　HAB

Title printed in red and black.

2622　LASSENIUS, JOHANNES

Joh. Lassenii | Him̄els-Freud | und | Höllen-Leid/ | Erster Theil. | Das
ist/ | Ewigwährender Freu- | den-Saal der Kinder | GOttes. | Darin von
der Freude des ewi- | gen Lebens/ nach Anleitung der H. | Schrifft/
ausführlich gehandelt wird; | mit hinzugethanen 23. Gewissens-Fra- |
gen/ Geistreichen Andachten | und Liedern. | Alles zur Ehre GOttes/
und | Erbauung der Christlichen | Kirchen. | Zum Andernmahl aufgelegt
und mit | Fleiß übersehen. | [rule] | Kopenhagen/ | Druckts Johan Jacob
Bornheinrich/ | Anno 1693.

12mo. [20], 374, [10] pp.; a¹², A-Q¹²; engraved title-page.　KAREN BRAHE

Q12 lacking, probably blank. Preliminary title: *D. Ioh. Lassenii | Himmels
Freüd | und | Höllen-Leid.*

2623　LAVERENTZEN, JOHANNES

Das | Preißwürdigste Gedächtnüß | Des Durchläuchtigsten/ Großmäch-
tigsten/ | und in Gott Christ-Seligsten Königes/ | HERRN | Friderich
des Andern/ | Königs | Zu Dänemarken und Norwegen | der Wenden
und Gotthen/ | Hertzogs | Zu Schleßwig/ Holstein/ Stormarn | und der
Dithmarschen/ | Grafens | Zu Oldenburg und Delmenhorst/ | Jn
seinem | Leben/ Regierung und Absterben/ | Aus verschiedenen alten
Geschriften/ Uhr- | kunden und Kroniken/ | Kürtzest geschehen
möchte/ | Allerunterthänigst zusammen getragen. | Von | JOHANN:
LAUERENTZEN. [1693]

4to. [4], 136 pp.; π², (a)-(r)⁴ (π2 blank).　　　　　　　　　　CKB

Issued together with *Etliche Psalme und Sprüche/ | ... | Hr. Friderich der Ander*
(No. 2613). At end: *COPENHAGEN/ Gedrukt bey Jhr. Königl. Hoh. Buchtr. |
Joachim Schmedtgen.*

2624　Leben und Todt | Des | Weyland Hoch-Ehrwürdigen/ Hoch- | Edlen/
und Hochgelahrten Herrn/ | HERRN | JOHANNIS | LASSENII, |
Der H. Schrift weitberühmten | Doctoris und Professoris Primarii | der
Hoch-löblichen Academie zu Kopen- | hagen/ des Königl. Consistorii
Hoch- | gewürdigten Assessoris, auch ins 17te | Jahr an der Teutschen
Gemeine zu | St. Petri daselbst Hoch-wolver- | dienten Pastoris. | Nach

eingegebener Abfassung in Druck | befördert/ | [ornamental rule] | Jm Jahr 1693.

8vo. A-B⁸ C⁴. CKB

Poem at end is signed: J. M. W.

2625 Letztes Ehren-Gedächtniß/ | . . . | HERRN | Barthold Johann | Brammers/ | . . . | Von | Einigen Gönnern und guten | Freunden. | [skull and crossbones] | [rule] | Glückstadt/ | Gedruckt bey Reinhard Janßen. [1693]

Folio. χ². CKB

Verse in Latin and German by several hands.

2626 MOLLER, JOHANNES

Eilfertige Erklärung der Ehe-Regeln . . . in nupt. Georg Pfeifferi . . . cum Clara Nicol. Mölgards . . . filia. . . . Schleswig, 1693.

Folio. *

*OHM* I, 430-1.

2627 MÜLLER, JOHANN SEBASTIAN

Herrn | Johann Sebastian Müllers/ | in Leipzig | Zeugnüß | der | Wahrheit/ | Herrn Pastoris Horbii unsträfflichen Wandel | betreffend/ auff seinen Reisen/ | wider | die Mönchhausische | Lügen und Läster-Schrifft. | [rule of type ornaments] | Altona/ | Gedruckt bey Christian Reymers/ Königl. privileg. | Buchdrucker/ 1693.

4to. A⁴. CKB; CUL

2628 Der | Regierenden Hoch-Fürstl. Durchl. zu | Schleßwig-Holstein | gnädigste Verordnung | wegen der | Confirmation | derer | Catechumenorum/ | [double rule] | Schleßwig/ | Gedruckt bey Lorentz Eckstorff/ Hoch-Fürstl. | Hoff-Buchdrucker. [1693]

4to. χ². KIEL UL

2629 REPLICA | Auff | Die Antwort eines Sachsen- | lauenburgischen Edelmanns/ an seinen | Vetter in Hollstein/ die/ von der Cron | Dennemarck begehrende Demolition | des Orthes Ratzeburg be- | treffend. [1693]

4to. A-G⁴. CKB

At end, "Ploen den 1. Aug. 1693."

2630 SCHLESWIG-HOLSTEIN-GOTTORFF. *Laws, statutes, etc.*

WJr von Gottes Gnaden Chri- | stian Albrecht/ Erbe zu Norwegen/ . . . | . . . | . . . 13. Mart. Anno 1693.

Broadside.                                                                CKB

Decree forbidding hunting on ducal preserves.

2631  SCHLESWIG-HOLSTEIN-GOTTORFF. *Laws, statutes, etc.*

WJr von GOttes Gnaden | Christian Albrecht/ Erbe zu Norwegen |
POSTULIRTER COADJUTOR des Stiffts | Lübeck/ Hertzog zu
Schleßwig/ Holstein . . . | . . . | . . . Gottorff den 26. Sept. Anno 1693.

Broadside.                                                                CNA

Decree regarding legal claims on the Sollwig estate.

2632  Schmertzensvoller Trauer-Klang bey dem seeligen Abschied des Herrn
Johann Daniel Major . . . entworffen von Herrn Bünemanns Tisch-
Genossen. Kiel, 1693.

Folio.                                                                      *

Formerly in Kiel UL (LmC 12-5).

2633  SEGER, JACOB

Als | Dero zu | Dennemarck/ Norwegen/ Erb- und Cron- | Printzl.
Hoheiten/ Printz | FRJEDRJCHS | Hochbetrauter | Cammer-Diener/ |
Der Edle/ Hoch- und Wolgeachte Herr/ | Hr. JOHANN ABROH/ |
Unter Jhrer Königlichen Hoheiten | Suite, nach rühmlichst geendeter
Reise/ von 1692. | Jahres den 8. Jan: biß den [    ] Aprilis dieses
lauffen- | den 1693. glücklich/ und mit sonderbahren Freu- | den bey den
Seinigen anlangete; | Wolte mit diesem | Schertz-Gedichte/ | Seinem
zuverrichtlichem Patrono, und Hochzueh- | renden Herrn Hospiti
begegnen | Dessen unterdienstlich-ergebenster | Diener | Jacob Seger. |
[ornamental rule] | Jm Jahr 1693.

Folio. )(⁴.                                                              CKB

Verse. Date on title-page not filled in.

2634  Ursachen | Warum | Jhr. Königl. Majest. | zu Dennemarck Norwegen/
&c. die | frembde Kriegs-Völcker/ im Fürstenthum | Nieder-Sachsen/
oder Sachsen-Lauen- | burg/ ingleichen die Befestigung der Stadt |
Ratzeburg/ nicht länger dulden können/ son- | dern darinn Wandel
zuschaffen/ und des- | halber Jhrer Reiche/ Lande und getreü- | er
Untersassen höchstnöthige Sicherheit | ernstlich zu besorgen/ genöthi- |
get worden. | Auff Königlichen Allergnädig- | sten Befehl. | [rule] |
Copenhagen/ im Jahr 1693.

4to. A-B⁴ (15.8 x 10.9 cm).                                            CKB

Another edition, n.p. (15.3 x 11.8 cm); another edition, n.p. (16.5 x 10.5 cm).

2635  VETTE, F.

Bei Dem | Hochzeitlichen Ehren-Tag | . . . | Hn. Eberhardus Vette/ |
Wohl-verordneten Vesper-Predigers | in Sonderborg. | Und . . . | . . . |
Eleonora Christiani/ | Des Wohl-Sehligen Herren | Friderich Christian |
Gewesenen Treüfleißigen Vesper-Predigers | Daselbst/ | Aeltesten Jung-
fer Tochter/ | überreichte zur Glückwünschung | Denen glücklich Ver-
mählten Ehe-Leuten | diese Zeilen | Den 14 Novembr. Anno 1693. |
Imprimatur, | C. BARTHOLIN. | F. Vette. | [ornamental rule] | Copen-
hagen/ Gedruckt bey Jhr. Königl. Majest. und Universit. | Buchdr.
Johann Philip Bockenhoffer.

Folio. $\chi^2$.                                                                                              CKB
Verse.

2636  ZWERG, GOTTHARD JOHANNES

Predigamts-Gedancken | . . . | Leich-Begängniß/ | . . . | Bernhardi
Kenckels/ | . . . | durch | GOTTHARDUM JOHANNEM ZWER-
GIUM, | Dienern am Worte Gottes zu Tundern. | [rule] | Schleßwig/
gedruckt bey Lorentz Eckstorff. [1693]

4to. [16], 144 pp.; A-U⁴.                                                                                     CKB

On p. 101, separate title: *I, N. J.* | *Abdanckung* | . . . | *Durch JOACHIMUM*
*Engeln/ p.t.* | *Past zu Braderup;* on p. 117, separate title: *ULTIMA JUSTA* |
*soluta* | *Desideratissimis Manibus* | . . . . Verse by several hands.

## 1694

2637  AHLEFELD, CHRISTIAN ALBRECHT VON

Gebrauch | Des | PROPORTION[IRTEN] | Zirkels/ | Wie auch des-
sen | Zubereitung/ | Jn der | Arithmetic, Geometrie, | Fortification und
Artillerie, | sehr nützlich/ | Deutlich erkläret | Durch | Christian Al-
brecht von Ahlefeld. | [ornamental rule] | Copenhagen/ | Gedrukkt bey
Johann Jacob Bornheinrich/ | Anno 1694.

4to. [8], 84 pp.; )(⁴, A-K⁴ L².                                                                               CKB

2638  Als | Der Weyland | . . . | Herr | M. JOACHIMUS | Giese/ | . . . | Jn
folgender Trauer-Ode eröffnen | Hn. D. Stryken Tisch-Genossen. |
[rule] | KJEL/ | Gedruckt bey Joachim Reumann/ Acad. Buchdr. |
Anno 1694

Folio. $\chi^2$.                                                                                              CKB

2639 Vom 26. April . . . | Altonaische RELATION | No. 32 [woodcut: crowned female figure on lion] 1694

8vo. Pp. 249-256.                                                    SRL

SRL has also No. 33 (pp. 257-264) 30 April; 34 (265-272) 3 May; 35 (273-300) 7 May; 36 (281-288) 10 May; 37 (289-296) 14 May; 39 (305-312) 24 May; 40 (313-320) 31 May; 42 (329-336) 7 June; 43 (337-344) 11 June; 44 (345-352) 14 June; 45 353-360) 18 June.

2640 An Herrn Andreas Paul von Liliencron . . . wie auch deßen Frau Ehe-Liebste Elisabeth von Liliencron . . . über den Hintritt der Tochter Anna Margarete Liliencronin . . . von H. L. G. Glückstadt, 1694.

Folio.                                                               *

Formerly in Kiel UL (LmC 11-36a).

2641 Christliches | Gesang-Buch/ | Darinn | Die nöhtigste und bekannteste/ | so wol alte/ als neue/ | Geist-reiche | Kirchen-Lieder | gesamlet; | Zur befoderung des öffentlichen | und privat Gottes-dienstes/ | Sonderlich in den Gemeinen | und Schulen | Des | Bischofftums Lübeck/ | nebst angefügten | Gebet-Buch | in den druck gegeben. | [ornament] | PLOEN/ | Gedruckt durch Tobias Schmiedt/ | Fürstl. Buchdrucker. | [rule] | Jm Jahr Christi 1694

12mo. [2], 678, [32], 182 pp.; π1, A-Oo$^{12}$, Pp$^2$.                CUL

Added title on leaf Gg8r: *Kurtzes | Gebet-Buch/ | Aus | Geistreicher Theolo- | gen Schrifften zusam- | men getragen.*

2642 DANXST, CORDT

I. N. D. | Fragen und Antworten/ | Zum Dienste derer/ | welche sich bey Cordt Danxst/ Handels- | Buchhaltern und Arithmetico hieselb-sten/ | Jn dem (so genanten) | Italiänischen Buchhalten | informiren lassen/ außgefertiget [1694]

Folio. 24 pp.; A-F$^2$.                                              CKB

Caption title.

2643 DANXST, CORDT

Arithmetischer | Weg-Weiser/ | Jn Fragen und Antworten/ | Getreu-lichst anzeigende: | (I.) Die Principia der Rechen-Kunst/ in | gantzen und gebrochenen Zahlen. | (II.) Wie die 4. Species das Fundament | sind/ aller vorkoͤmenden Arithmetischen Reguln. | (III.) Wie die Regula de Tri directa das | Haubt aller andern Reguln zu nennen sey. | (IV.) Wie die aus der Regula de Tri dire- | cta entspringende andere Regulas (so weit solche in der | Handlung gebraucht werden) nemblich: (1.)

Regula de Tri Inversa. | (2.) Regula dupli sive duplex. (3.) Regula
Alligationis | und (4.) Regula Zekis geartet und zu verstehen sind. |
(V.) Wie es mit denen in Handels-Rechens- | Büchern/ unter ver-
schiedene Nahmen befindliche | Rechnungen/ als: (1.) Haußhaltungs-
(2.) Allerhand Wahren- | (3.) Thara- (4.) Interesse- (5.) Rabatt- (6.)
Einländische- (7.) Auß- | ländische Wechsel- (8.) Gewin-und Verlust-
(9.) Baratt- oder Stich- | (10) Theilungs- und (11) Factorey-Rech-
nungen; Dann auch | letztlich mit der Reductio Terminorum zu verste-
hen sey. | Zu Dienste und sonderbahren Nutzen derer/ die seiner Infor-
mation anvertrauet sind; | Außgefertiget/ von | Cordt Danxst/ Handels-
Buchhaltern und Arithmetico. | [rule] | Gedruckt im Jahr 1694.

4to. [4], 100, [6] pp.; $\pi^2$, A-N$^4$, $\chi$1.                                              CKB

2644   DENMARK. *Laws, statutes, etc.*

WJR Christian der Fünffte/ | . . . | . . . Glückstadt/ den 1. Martij, | Anno
1694.

Broadside.                                                                                       CNA

Decree issued jointly with Duke Christian Albrecht of Schleswig-Holstein, calling a
meeting of the "Quartal-Gericht" at Rendsburg 13 April.

2644A DENMARK. *Laws, statutes, etc.*

WJR Christian der Fünffte/ | von GOttes Gnaden König zu Dänne-
marck/ . . . | . . . | . . . Glückstadt/ den 12. April. | Anno 1694.

Broadside.                                                                                       CKB

Decree, issued jointly with Duke Christian Albrecht of Schleswig-Holstein, calling
a "Land-Gerichts-Tag" at Rendsburg 31 May.

2645   DENMARK. *Laws, statutes, etc.*

WJR Christian der Fünffte/ | . . . | . . . Glückstadt/ den 22. Novemb.
Anno 1694.

Broadside.                                                                                       CNA

Decree against appeals to "das Pinnenbergische Ober-Appellation-Gericht" in cases
involving less than 50 Rixdollars.

2646   FÖRTSCH, JOHANNES PHILIPP

Kläglicher Nachruff | Und | Die darauff aus der Grufft erschallende |
Antwort/ | Als der | Wohlgebohrne HERR | Herr Otto Rantzau/ | . . . |
Von | JOH. PHILIP. Förtsch/ | Med. Doct. und Hoch-Fürstl. Leib-
Medico | Zu Eutin/ | Und in Music gebracht | Von | GEORG. Oester-
reichen/ | Jhro Hoch-Fürstl. Schleßwig-Holsteinischen Regierenden

Durchl. jetziger Zeit | bestallten Capell-Meister. | [double rule] | Schleß-wig/ | Gedruckt bey Lorentz Eckstorff/ Hoch-Fürstlichem | Hoff-Buchdrucker. [1694]

Folio. χ². CKB

No music.

2646A Der | Glückstädtischen Bürger | Wacht-Ordnung | [rule] | Gedruckt im Jahr 1694.

4to. χ⁴. CKB

2647 [HARTNACK, DANIEL]

Der | von | Hn. DANIEL HARTNACCIO | schon Anno 1689 | Zu einer Disputation nacher Glückstadt | gefoderte | und | biß dato 1694 | ausge-bliebene | JOHANN MELCHIOR | Stenger. | Durch Veranlassung seiner heraus gegebenen | Schand-Schrifft | wider | E. Ehrwürdiges Ministerium zu | Hamburg/ | und in specie wider | Hn. D.J.F. May-erum, | und | Hn. D. Conrad Tiburt. Rangonem, | zum Druck übergeben 1694.

4to. A⁴ B². GÖTTINGEN UL

2648 HARTNACK, DANIEL

Abgeschlagener Sturm Joh. Melch. Stengers. 1694.

4to. *

*Moller* II, 305.

2649 HARTNACK, DANIEL

(Trostschrift über das Absterben Sophia Elisabeth von Reichenbach). Schleswig 1694.

Folio. *

*OHM* II, 305.

2650 HARTNACK, DANIEL

Vindicirung seiner Retorsion wieder Joh. Melch. Stengern. 1694.

4to. *

*Moller* II, 305.

2651 Herzliche Leidklage über den frühzeitigen Hintritt der Jungfrawen Anna Margarethe von Liliencron ... entworffen von F. C. Glückstadt, 1694

Folio. *

Formerly in Kiel UL (LmC 11-36).

2652 HORBIUS, JOHANN HEINRICH

Der gründliche | Wort-Verstand | Des | Kleinen | Catechismi | D.
MARTINI LUTHERI, | Zur Erweckung | Einer | Jnniglichen Glau-
bens-Freudigkeit/ | Und | Unschweren Lebens-Heiligkeit/ | Auff die
herannahende | Trübselige Zeiten | Vorgestellet | Von | Johann Henrich
Horben/ | Pastore zu S. Nicolai in | Hamburg. | Zum vierdten mahl
gedruckt. | [rule] | Altona/ Gedruckt und verlegt Christian Reymers/
Königl. | privilegirten Buchdrucker/ Jm Jahr 1694.

8vo. [10], 163, [3] pp.; A-L⁸ (L8 blank). HALLE UL

2653 HOYER, NICOLAUS

Die | Getreue Freundinn des HErrn Jesu | . . . | Fr. Agatha Sibbers/ |
. . . | Christian Sibbersens/ | . . . | Eheliebsten. | Anno 1694. den 19.
Martio | . . . | Durch | Nicolaum Hoyern/ Past. adj. zu Clixbüll. | [rule] |
Schleßwig/ gedruckt bey Lorentz Eckstorff/ Hochfl. Hoff-Buchdr.

4to. 87, [1] pp.; A-L⁴. CKB

2654 KIEFFER, JOHANN CONRAD

Trost-Schrifft/ | . . . | Hn. Otto Rantzauen | . . . | Von | Johann Conrad
Kieffer | Kirchen-Rath und Hoffprediger. | [rule] | Schleßwig/ | Ge-
druckt bey Lorentz Eckstorff/ Hoch-Fürstlichem | Hoff-Buchdrucker.
[1694]

Folio. π1, A-E². CKB

E2 lacking. *Cf.* No. 2908.

2655 [KORTHOLT, CHRISTIAN]

Wollgemeintes Bedencken/ | über die Gewissens-Scrupel Hn. Eber- |
hardi Zellern. [Kiel? 1694?]

4to. A-C⁴. SRL

Caption title. SRL dates copy 1694 although internal evidence suggests 1688.

2656 KRUSS, JOHANN

Hoch-verdienter | Nach-Ruhm/ | Des Weiland | Wohlgebohrnen |
HERREN/ | Hn. Otto Rantzau/ | . . . | von | Johann Kruß/ | Med.
Doct. Stadt-Physico und Hoff-Medico | zu Gottorff. | [double rule] |
Schleßwig/ | Gedruckt bey Lorentz Eckstorff/ Hoch-Fürstlichen | Hoff-
Buchdrucker. [1694]

Folio. χ². CKB

Verse.

2657 Des Lebens | Beseuffzete Nichtigkeit/ | ... | Hans Heinrich | NÖRCKS |
... | COPENHAGEN | Gedruckt bey Jhro Königl. Majest. und
Universit. Buchdr. | Johann Philip Bockenhoffer. [1694]

Folio. χ².                                                          Oslo UL

Verse by Heinrich Boye & F. Seger.

2658 Lund, Thomas

(Hochzeit-Gedicht in nupt. Nicol. Richtsen). Schleswig, 1694.

Folio.                                                                  *

OHM I, 369.

2659 Moller, Johannes

Wehmüthige Trauer-Klage, der von Gott durch die innerhalb Jahres-
Frist geschehenen tödliche Entreißung der beyden Prediger im Zorn
heimgesuchten Flensburgischen Marien-Kirche, bey Veranlassung der
Leichbegängniß Joh. Lysii. . . . Schleswig, 1694.

Folio.                                                                  *

OHM I, 430-1.

2660 Muhlius, Heinrich

MADRIGALNO | Auff das | Grab | Des | Weyland Wohlgebohrnen
Herrn Marschalls | HERRN | Otto Rantzowen/ | Als solches von | Der
Durchl. Gnädigsten Herrschafft | durch ein höchst trauerliche Leich-
Conduct mit ansehn- | lichsten Gebräuchen und Solennitäten | Dero
Hoch-Fürstlichen Residentz-Stadt Schleßwig | den 14 Decembr. Anno
1694. gnädigst beehret ward. | [rule] | Schleßwig/ | Gedruckt bey
Lorentz Eckstorff/ Hoch-Fürstlichen | Hoff-Buchdrucker

Folio. χ².                                                          CKB

Verse.

2661 Pauli, Christian

Die ungegründete | Hoffnung | Von Christi Reich auf Erden. | Theils |
Jn Vorstellung der gefaßten Meynung/ ob solte | nu bald die Zeit da
seyn/ da Christus vom Himmel auff Er- | den leiblich und sichtbar
kommen/ und Tausend Jahr mit seinen | Heiligen in dieser Welt
regieren werde; | Theils | Jn Erweisung/ daß ausser der letzten Zu-
kunfft | zum Gericht keine andere zu erwarten sey. | Dargethan | Jn einer
Predigt/ gehalten zu Altena/ auß der | Offenbarung Johannis, Capit.
20. v. 1-6. am Sonn- | tage Exaudi, im Jahr 1694. | von | CHRISTIANO

PAULI, | Pastore der Reform. Gemeine daselbst. | [ornamental rule] |
Jm Jahr CHRJSTJ 1694.

4to. A-C⁴.        CKB

2662  Preißwürdiges | Ehren-Gedächtniß/ | Welches | Dem Weyland Wohlge-
bohrnen Herren | HERREN | Otto Rantzauen/ | . . . | [woodcut: cof-
fin] | [rule] | Schleßwig/ | Gedruckt bey Lorentz Eckstorff/ Hoch-Fürst-
lichem | Hoff-Buchdrucker. [1694]

Folio. A-C².        CKB

On C1 added title: *Abdanckung/* | *Dem* | *Wohlgebohnen* [sic] *Herrn* | *HERRN* |
*Otto Rantzauen/* | *. . .* | *Zu Ehren gehalten* | *von* | *H. F. v. D. K.* | *. . . .*

2663  Rötscher, Johannes Volcmar

Seliger Zustand der Gläubigen im Tode/ | . . . | Catharina Petreiä/ |
gebohrnen Witmackin sel. | . . . | . . . von | M. Johanne Volcmaro
Rötschern/ | . . . | [rule] | Schleßwig/ gedruckt bey Lorentz Eckstorff/
Hoch-Fürstl. Hoff- | Buchdrucker/ Anno 1694

4to. 72 pp.; [A]⁴ B-J⁴.        CKB

2664  Röttscher, Christian Albrecht

Vnvergängliches Denckmahl der Tugend, Fräulein Sophiæ Eleonoræ
von Reichenbach aufgerichtet im Nov. 1694. Schleswig, 1694.

Folio. χ⁴.        *

*OHM* I, 557.

2665  [Sandhagen, Caspar Hermann]

Der Gläubigen Trost | wider den Tod | . . . | Sophien Eleonoren | von
Reichenbach/ | . . . | Schleßwig/ | Gedruckt bey Lorentz Eckstorff/
Hoch-Fürstlichem | Hoff-Buchdrucker. [1694]

4to. )(⁴.        SHLB

2666  Sandhagen, Caspar Hermann

Kurtze Auslegung des VI. Capitels des Propheten Michæ, als verordneten Bußtag-Textes (1694-1696). Schleswig, (1694?).

4to.        *

*Moller* II, 757. *Cf.* No. 3098.

2667  Schleswig-Holstein-Gottorff. *Laws, statutes, etc.*

WJr von GOttes Gnaden | Christian Albrecht/ Erbe zu Norwegen/ |
. . . | . . . 8ten Januarii, Anno 1694

Broadside (3 sheets pasted together).                          KIEL UL

Decree regarding the use of stamped paper.

2668   SCHULTZ, CORNELIUS

Eines treuen Knechtes GOttes │ . . . │ JOHANNIS PETREJI, │ . . . │ von │
CORNELIO SCHULTZEN, │ . . . │ Schleßwig/ │ Gedruckt bey Lorentz
Eckstorff/ Hochfürstl. Buchdruckern/ 1694.

4to. [2], 36 pp.; π1, A-D⁴ E².                                 CKB

2669   SCHWARTZ, JOSUA

Rendesburgische │ Kirchhofs-Ein- │ weihung/ │ Geschehen durchs Wort
Jos. cap. V.v.13.14.15. │ Wie auch Gebeth/ │ Jn Vornehmer Volckreicher
Versamlung/ und │ hiemit auff Begehren schrifftlich wiederholet │ Von │
JOSUA Schwartzen/ │ Der Heil. Schrifft Doctore, Königl. General-
Superin- │ tendenten und Consistorial-Raht/ in den Hertzogthümern │
Schleßwig/ Holstein/ als auch Probsten zu Renßburg. │ Sampt einer │
Nach Gelegenheit des Textes/ mit beygefügten │ kurtzen Erörterung/
der sich herfürthuenden │ Neuen Lehre/ │ Von erforderter grösserer
Heiligkeit im Neuen │ als Alten Testament. │ [rule] │ Glückstadt/ ge-
druckt bey Reinhard Janßen/ Königl. Buchd. │ Jm Jahr 1694.

4to. [6], 66 pp.; A-J⁴.                                        CKB

2670   [STÖCKEN, CHRISTIAN VON]

Die vernünftige lautere Milch des Heiligen Catechismi. Glückstadt,
1694.

12mo.                                                              *

*Moller* I, 659.

2671   [STORNING, HINRICH]

Rettung unserer Lehre und Lehrer, daß wir nemblich so wol reine Lehrer
und Prediger, als auch die reine Lehre, haben. Kürtzlich verfasset von
einem Diener Jesu Christi in Holstein. Ploen, 1694.

12mo.                                                              *

*Moller* I, 666; *Bibl. Kielmans-Egg.,* III, 1394; *Thott* I/2, 638, lists under Joh. Wilh.
Petersen.

2672   Traur-Trähnen über den frühzeitigen Hintritt der Anne Margarethe zu
Liliencron . . . vergossen von M. S. G. Glückstadt, 1694.

Folio.                                                             *

Formerly in Kiel UL (LmC 11-36b).

2673 Verordnung | Des | Gestempelten | Papiers | [rule] | Gedruckt in der Hoch-Fürstl. ResidentzStadt | Schleßwig/ Jm Jahr 1694. | Bey | Lorentz Eckstorff/ Hoch-Fürstl. Hoff-Buchdrucker.

4to. KIEL UL

Kiel copy defective; only A⁴ (paginated 1-8) preserved. On p. 8, catchword "Nume-."

2675 WEDDERKOPF, GABRIEL

Der treuen wollverdienten | Lehrer | . . . | M. JOACHIMI | Giesen/ | . . . | Von | M. Gabriel Wedderkop | Predigern an S. Nicolai Kirchen. | [rule] | KJEL/ | Gedruckt bey Joachim Reumann/ Acad. Buchdr. 1694.

4to. [4], 60 pp.; )(², A-G⁴ H². CKB

Appended: three Latin items, each 4 leaves, and nine German occasional poems, each with separate title: *Heinrich Muhlens | Traur-Ode/ | . . . , χ⁴; Wolverdientes | Ehren-Gedächtnis | . . . | M. CONRADUS OPORINUS | . . . , χ²; Als | Der HochEhrwürdige/ Großachtbah- | . . . | Hn. D. CHRISTIANI Kortholten/ | . . . | Tisch-Gesellschaft, χ²; Wol-verdienter Nach-Ruhm/ | . . . | Nachgesetzte Tisch-Genossen,* 1 leaf; *Als | Der Weyland | . . . | Hn. D. Musæi P.P. | Tischgesellschafft, χ²; Die | im Frühling | . . . | Jhro Woll-Ehrwürden Hn. Pastoris Burchardi | Sämptlichen Tischgenossen | . . . | . . . ,* 5 leaves; *Die wolbelohnte Treue | . . . | Von | Friderico Grammio, χ²; Als . . . M. Joachimus | Giese/ | . . . | beweinen helffen | Valent. Heins. jun. Hamburg | SS. Th. Stud, χ²; Der | Zwar glücklich doch traurig | Versetzte Kirchen-Baum | . . . | Von | Henrico Dürkopen Lübecens, χ²; Rechtmässige Ritterschafft | . . . | von | D. J. Major, χ².*

2676 WEDDERKOPF, GABRIEL

Das | Auff Hohenschulen brennend und schei- | nend Lehr-Liecht/ welches auff dem Leuchter der Hoch- | Fürstlichen Holsteinischen Academie zum Kiel | 29 Jahr geleuchtet | . . . | Hn. CHRISTIANO | Kortholten/ | . . . | durch den Druck außgefärtiget | M. Gabriel Wedderkop. | Prediger im Kiel. | [rule] | Gedruckt durch Joachim Reumann/ Acad. Buchdr. 1694.

4to. [7], 92 pp.; )(⁴, A-L⁴, M². CKB

Appended: *Heinrich Muhlens | Traur-Ode/ | . . . , χ⁴; Als | Der | Magnificus, Hoch-Ehrwürdige und Hochgelahrte/ | . . . | Jhro Magnif. Hn. D. Reyhers Tisch-Gesellschafft, χ²; Als | Der | Magnificus, HochEhrwürdige/ HochEdle/ | . . . | Des Hn D. Musæi P.P. Tischgenossen, χ²; Wolverdientes | Ehren-Gedächtniß | . . . | Von | Hn. D. Stryken Tisch-Genossen, χ²; Das | Betrübte Oster-Fest | . . . | Des (Tit.) Hn. Past. Burchardi | sämptlichen Tisch-Genossen, χ²; Höchstbetrübte | Weh-Klage. | . . . | (Tit.) Herrn M. Martini Bützers | Tisch-Gesellschaft, χ²; Der Traurende Helicon, | . . . | Herren Bünemanns sämptliche Tisch- | Genossen, χ²; Als | Der weyland Hoch-Ehrwürdige/ HochAchtbar | . . . | Von zwenen alhier studirenden Liefländern,* $\chi^2$; *Letzte Schuldigkeit* | . . . *Bartholomæus Johannes Otto* | *Hannemann* | *S.S. Theol. Studiosus,* $\chi^2$; *Letzte Pflicht* | . . . | *O. N. Reumann,* $\chi^2$; *Letzter Ehren-und Liebes-Dienst* | . . . | *Nachgesetzte,* $\chi^2$. Also several occasional pamphlets in Latin.

2677 WILCKENS, JOHANNES HERMANN

Elias Himmelfahrt bey der Hinfahrt Jo. Casp. Rist seines Schwieger-vaters. Altona, 1694.

4to. *

*OHM* I, 732.

2678 WOLF, JACOB

Gründliche Abhandlung des ungegründeten Verdachts, darin ein lieb-loser Feind ihn zu bringen getrachtet. Altona, 1694.

4to. *

*Acad. Gryp. Bibl. Cat.,* 1775, II, 968.

2679 ZITSCHER, PETER

Das | Einmühtige Priesterthumb/ | Bey | Solenner Leichbestättigung | . . . | Hn. Mag. REIMARI | STRUVIJ, | . . . | Durch | P. Zitzschærn/ | Königl. Schloß-Pastorn zu Glückstadt. | [ornament] | [rule] | Glück-stadt/ gedruckt bey Reinhard Janßen/ 1694.

4to. 20 pp.; A-B$^4$ C$^2$. CKB

2680 ZITSCHER, PETER

Letzte Rede an die Gott dessen Wort und Priester liebende Glück-städtische Schloß-Gemeine, auß Act. XX. 31. am 25. Oct. A. 1693 ge-halten. Glückstadt, 1694.

4to. *

*Moller* II, 1039. Republished 1696.

## 1695

2680A Alß Daß | Von Gott geknüpfte Eh-verbindniß/ | Des | Edlen und Vesten/ | Herrn Liebhard Vieth/ | . . . | Mit der | Wol-Edlen/ Groß Ehr-und Tugend-begabten | Jfr. Anna-Margaretha | Jungen/ | . . . | wolte hiemit unzertrentes Wolergehn anwünschen | . . . | L.C. | [ornamental rule] | Gedruckt bey Jhr. Königl. Majest. und Universit. Buchdrucker/ | Johann Philip Bockenhoffer. [1695]

Folio. $\chi^2$. CKB

Verse.

2681 Als | Den Weyland Hoch-Wohlgebohrnen und Hoch- | Mannhaften |
HERREN | Hn. Otto Rantzaw | Ein unverhoffter und gar zu früher
Todes-Fall dieser | Sterblichkeit entriß/ | Ward dieses gesetzt | Von |
Des Hoch-Adelichen Sterb-Hauses | Ergebenstem und verbundenstem
Diener | J. F. S. | [rule] | Schleßwig/ | Gedruckt bey Lorentz Eckstorff/
Hoch-Fürstlichem | Hoff-Buchdrucker [c. 1695]

Folio. χ². CKB

2682 Vom 1. Aprilis Fol. 193 | Die Altonaische RELATION. | No. 25
[woodcut: crowned female figure on lion] 1695

8vo. Pp. 193-200. SRL

Caption title. Pp. 195-198 lacking in SRL copy. SRL has also No. 46 (pp. 361-368)
17 June; 77 (593-600) 26 Sept.; 78 (601-608) 30 Sept.; 79 (609-616) 3 Oct.; 81 (625-
632) 10 October; 82 (633-640) 14 October; 83 (641-648) 17 Oct.; 84 (649-656) 21
Oct.; 85 (657-664) 24 Oct.; 86 (665-672) 28 October.

2683 Das Neue | Testament | Unsers Herrn | Jesu Christi/ | Verdeutschet
durch | D. Mart. Luther/ | Mit eines jeden Capitels kur- | tzen Sum-
marien/ und dero | richtigen Abtheilungen; | Auch Bemerckung | Der
Sonn- und Festtägigen | Episteln und Evangelien/ | Für die Christliche
Gemei- | nen und Schulen deß Für- | stenthums Plöen/ | Auff hoher
Landes-Fürstlicher | Verordnung gedrucket/ | [ornament] | [rule] |
PLOEN/ | Durch Tobias Schmidt/ Fürstl. | Buchdrucker/ 1695.

12mo. Pp. [1-2], 1-216, 207-216, 217, 901, [1-21]; π1. A-Pp¹², Qq1-10.
LANDESBIBLIOTHEK STUTTGART

2684 BOLDICH, ERNST CHRISTIAN

[Poem, without title, on the occasion of the marriage of Prince Frederik
of Denmark and Princess Louise] | [below:] Kopenhagen/ | Gedruckt
bey Jhr. Königl. Hoheit Buchdrucker Joachim Schmedtgen 1695

Broadside (45 x 36.5 cm). CKB

2685 BORCH, CHRISTIAN

(Leichpredigt über Andreas Kasimir Thaddaeus von der Wenge-
Lambsdorff. Übersetzt ins Deutsche von Mag. Joh. Foss) Kopenhagen,
(1695?)

4to. 9 leaves, 148 pp. *

Formerly in Kiel UL (4to M 96d 206).

2686 [BOTSAC, BARTHOLD] *editor*

Schrifft-Catechismus/ | Das ist: | Der kleine | Catechismus | Lutheri/ |

Mit Sprüchen der heiligen | Schrifft erläutert. | Nach dem Braun-
schweigischen Exemplar. | [ornamental rule] | Copenhagen/ | Gedruckt
und verlegt durch J. P. Bockenhof- | fer Königl. Maj. und Univer.
Buchdrucher/ | Jm Jahr 1695.

12mo. 164, [12] pp.; A-G¹² H⁴; 1 folding plate. CKB

Plate "Ad pag. 157. Eingesetztes Heil. Nachtmahl."

2687 BROWNRIG, RALPH

RALPH BROWNRIG, | Wyland | Bischoffs zu Exeter | in Engeland |
Geistreiche Schriften | und | Predigten/ | Auff alle Hohe Fest-und Sonn-
tage/ auß son- | derbahren Sprüchen der H. Schrifft erklähret. | Auß den
Englischen in die Hochteutsche Sprache übersetzet | durch | J. L. |
[printer's monogram] | COPENHAGEN/ | Verlegts Johann Jost
Erythropilus | [rule] | HAMBURG/ Gedruckt bey Nicolas Spieringk/
1695.

4to. Pp. [1-8], 1-255, 266-999; [1-3]; 1-552; )(1-3, A-Jiiiii⁴, a-zzz⁴ (Jiiiii4 blank);
engraved frontispiece. HALLE UL

Title in red and black. Frontispiece, on )(4 verso, portrait of the author engraved
by M. Bernigeroht, with inscription in English. See Plate VIII.

2688 CLAUSEN, MARTIN

Musicalische Opera, auf das Absterben Anna Hedewig Wackerbarth.
Altona, 1695

Folio. *

*Bibl. Schroedter,* 1724, p. 100.

2689 CULEMANN, GREGOR

Die | Glücklich Vermiedene | Priester-Bürde | Welche | Wol und klüg-
lich vermieden | Der | Tit: | Weiland WolEdle/ WolEhrenveste | und
Wolgelahrte Herr | M. MARTINUS | OWMANN. | . . . | Von . . . |
GREGORIO CULEMANN. | [woodcut: coffin] | [rule] | Glückstadt/
gedruckt bey Reinhard Janßen. [1695]

Folio. χ². CKB

Verse.

2690 Da | Dero zu Dennemarck Norwegen | Aller-Durchleuchtigsten Königl.
Majestät | König Christian des Fünfften | Hochst-Erfreulicher Geburts-
Tag | Jn diesen 1695 Jahr den 15 April | Hochst-Feyrlich begangen. |
[below:] Copenhagen/ Gedruckt bey Jhre Königl. Majest. und Universit.
Buchdrucker/ Johan Philip Bockenhoffer

Broadside (53.5 x 31.8 cm). CKB

2691 DANXST, CORDT

Richtigste | Doch | Compendiöse | Beschreibung | Der | Müntz- | Wehrungen/ | Welche | An denen vornehmsten | Oertern in Europa gang- | bahr und gültig sind; | Wobey auch anzeige geschicht | in welche Münze man an selbige | Oerter/ Buch und Rechnung | hält. | Gestellet nach dem Alphabet, und aus | Liebe zu denen die seiner Mündlichen | Information geniesen/ in diesem be- | qvemen Format dem Druck | übergegeben | Von | Cordt Danxst | Handels-Buchhaltern und Arithm. | [rule] | COPENHAGEN | Gedruckt bey Jhro Königl. Hoh. Buch- drucker | Joachim Schmedtgen/ | Jm Jahr 1695.

8vo. [8], 72 pp.; $\pi^4$, A-D$^8$ E$^4$. CKB

2692 DANXST, CORDT

Richtigste | Doch | Compendiöse | Beschreibung | Der | Vornehmsten | Wechsel- | Plätze | Jn | EUROPA, | Und wie von dennen/ auff auß- | wärtige Oerter gewechselt wird. | Gestellet nach dem Alphabet, | und aus Liebe zu denen die seiner Münd- | lichen Information im Buchhalten ge- | niessen/ in diesem beqvemen Format | dem Druck übergeben. | Von | Cordt Danxst/ | Handels-Buchhaltern und Arithm. | [rule] | COPENHAGEN/ | Gedruckt bey Jhro Königl. Hoh. Buchdrucker | Joachim Schmedtgen 1695

8vo. [8], 79, [1] pp.; a$^4$, A-E$^8$. CKB

2693 DENMARK. *Laws, statutes, etc.*

WJr Christian der Fünffte/ | . . . | . . . Gottorff/ den 14. Januarij 1695.

Broadside. CNA

Decree issued jointly with Duke Friedrich of Schleswig-Holstein, ordering mourn- ing at the death of Duke Christian Albrecht.

2694 DENMARK. *Laws, statutes, etc.*

WJR Christian der Fünffte/ | . . . | . . . Glückstadt/ den 8. Februarij, Anno 1695.

Broadside. CNA

Decree forbidding the export of wood from western Holstein.

2695 DENMARK. *Laws, statutes, etc.*

WJR Christian der Fünffte/ | . . . | . . . Glückstadt/ den 15. Febr. Anno 1695.

Broadside. CNA

Decree ordering mourning for the late Duke Christian Albrecht of Schleswig-Holstein.

2696   DENMARK. *Laws, statutes, etc.*

WIR Christian der Fünffte/ | ... | ... 3. April Anno 1695.

Broadside.                                                                CKB

Decree forbidding the export of charcoal.

2697   DENMARK. *Laws, statutes, etc.*

WJR Christian der Fünffte/ | ... | ... Glückstadt/ den 4. April Anno 1695.

Broadside.                                                                CNA

Decree setting annual day of prayer the fourth Friday after Easter.

2698   DENMARK. *Laws, statutes, etc.*

WJr Christian der Fünffte/ | ... | ... 5ten Julii Anno 1695.

Broadside.                                                                CKB

Decree issued jointly with Duke Friedrich of Schleswig-Holstein, regarding a "Quartal-Gericht" at Schleswig 29 July.

2699   DENMARK. *Laws, statutes, etc.*

WJr Christian der Fünffte/ | ... | ... Gottorff/ den 15. Julii 1695.

Broadside.                                                                CNA

Decree issued jointly with Duke Friedrich of Schleswig-Holstein, ordering mourning at the death of Prince Christian of Denmark.

2700   DENMARK. *Laws, statutes, etc.*

WJr Christian der Fünffte/ | ... | ... Gottorff den 2. Augusti. Anno 1695.

Broadside.                                                          CKB; CNA

Decree issued jointly with Duke Friedrich of Schleswig-Holstein, calling a "Land-Gerichts-Tag" at Schleswig 16 September.

2701   Des Durchleuchtigsten Fürsten | und HERRN | HERRN | Friederichs/ | Erben zu Norwegen/ Hertzogs | zu Schleßwig/ Holstein/ Stormarn | und der Ditmarßen/ Graffen zu | Oldenburg und Delmen- | horst/ &c. &c. | Verordnung | Wegen | Derjenigen/ so in dero Fürsten- | thumen und Landen zu Kirchen-und | Schul-Bedienungen befordert werden wol- | len/ und was sie in acht zu | nehmen. | Sub dato Gottorp/ den 28.

Febr. 1695. | [rule] | SCHLESWIG | Getruckt bey Lorentz Eckstorff Hochf. Hoffbuchtr.

4to. $\chi^2$.        CKB

2702 Förtsch, Johann Philipp

Getreues Denck-Mahl | Dem Weiland | Hochwürdigsten/ Durchläuchtigsten | Fürsten und Herrn/ | HERRN | Christian Albrecht/ | Erben zu Norwegen/ | POSTULIRTEN COADJUTORI | des Stiffts Lübeck/ | . . . | . . . von | JOHANNE PHILIPPO Förtschen/ D./ Seiner Hoch- | Fürstl. Durchl. wie auch Hochfürstl. Bischöffl. Eutinis. Hoff-und Leib- | Medico. | [rule] | Schleßwig/ gedruckt bey Lorentz Eckstorff/ Hoch- | Fürstl. Hoff-Buchdrucker. [1695]

4to. )(⁴,$\chi^2$.        CKB

On )(4r, added title: *Ode* | . . . .

2703 [woodcut: two angels with motto: SOLI DEO GLORIA] | Freudige | Hertzens-Gedancken/ | Welche/ | Als | Der Edle und Wohlgelahrte | HERR | JOHAN. HEL- | FRICH Nagel/ | Th. Stud. | Am Tage seiner | Beforderung/ | Die bißherige vacante Rector Stelle zu Glückstadt be- | trat und der Schulen daselbst nunmehro würcklich als Rector | vorge- | stellet wurde/ | Aus wohlgesinnetem Gemüth und auffrichtiger | Freund- | schaffts-Pflicht entdecken wolten | innen benante | Freunde. | [orna- | ment: flower basket] | [rule] | Glückstadt/ gedruckt bey Reinhard | Janßen/ | Jm Jahr 1695.

Folio. $\chi^2$.        CKB

Verse in German and Latin by several hands.

2704 Fürstliche | Schleßwig-Holsteinische | Holtz-Ordnung. | [rule] | Schleß- | wig/ | Gedruckt durch den Hoff-Buchdrucker | Lorentz Eckstorff/ Anno 1695.

4to. 23, [1] pp.; A-C⁴.        CKB

2705 Grimberg, Nils

Kurtze Beschreibung | Des | Nieren und Bla- | sen Steins | Das ist | Gründtliches Bedencken | von beyder Natur und Ei- | genschafften/ | deroselben Nahmen/ | Ursachen/ de materiali & efficiente | tàm Diag- | nosticis, qvàm Pathogno- | micis, nicht minder auch von dem | Utero Dulech, und der Cura Pro- | phylactica & Therapeu- | tica, | Gestellet durch | NICOLAUM GRIMBERG Medic: | practic: Helsingörens: |

[ornamental rule] | HAFNIÆ, | Sumptibus Authoris, | Literis Justini
Hög Acad: Typ. | Anno 1695

8vo. [8], 52 pp.; )(⁴, A-C⁸ D².                                              CKB

2706  HAHN, HINRICH

Christliche Altars-Weyhe des aufgerichteten neuen Altars zu Meldorff
über das Evangelium am XX. post Trinit. Glückstadt, 1695.

                                                                              *

J. Hellmann, *Süder-Dithmarsische Kirchen-Historie,* 1735, p. 81; *OHM* II, 271.

2706A Die herschende Venus | Als der | Durchläuchtigste Großmächtigste |
Printz und Herr | FRIDERICH | Erb-und Cron-Printz zu | Dennemarck
Norwegen &c. &c. &c. | Mit Der | Durchläuchtigsten Princeßin | LOVI-
SEN, | Princeßin zu Mecklenburg. | Dero | Hohe Liebes Erfüllung |
Höchsterfreulich erfolgen sahe | Jn unterthänigster Pflicht | erwogen. |
[ornamental rule] | Gedruckt bey Jh. Königl. Majest. und Universit.
Buchdrucker/ | Johann Philipp Bockenhoffer/ 1695.

Folio. χ².                                                                   CKB

Verse.

2707  HÖPPENER, GEORG

(Trauergedicht über Katharina Didrichsen, geb. Hieronymus). Schleswig: Lorentz Eckstorff (1695).

Folio. χ².                                                                    *

Formerly in Kiel UL (LmC 17-11/12).

2708  JÖNSEN, HEINRICH

Allerbeste Wahl eines rechtschaffenen Lehrers und Predigers oder
Leichpredigt über Christoph Langen, Pastor zu Elmeschenhagen. Kiel:
Reumann, 1695.

4to. 74 pp., 6 leaves.                                                        *

*Moller* I, 284; formerly in Kiel UL (LmC 77-5). Appended: Arnold Maltzahn,
*Beschonte Eitelkeit, oder das Edelste unter dem Eiteln . . . Leichenrede über
Christoph Langen . . .* Kiel, 1695. No. 2715 (Cf. *Moller* I, 437).

2709  KIEFFER, JOHANN CONRAD

PER ASPERA AD ASTRA ! | Oder | Der Seeligste | Leid-und Freuden-
Wechsel | Welchen | Der Weyland | Hoch-Würdigste und Durchläuch-
tigste | Fürst und Herr | Christian Albrecht | Erbe zu Norwegen/ |
POSTULIRTER COADJUTOR | des Stiffts Lübeck/ | Hertzog zu

Schleßwig/ Holstein/ Stormarn und | der Ditmarschen/ Graff zu
Oldenburg und Delmen- | horst/ &c. | Glücklich getroffen. | Und | Als
dero den 27sten Decembr. Anno 1694 verblichene Gebeine unter | vielen
Thränen/ und Leidwesen des gantzen Landes | Den 26sten Februari
Anno 1695. | Abends mit gehöriger solenner Procession | Jn das Hoch-
Fürstliche Begräbniß | in der Thum-Kirchen zu Schleßwig | beygesetzet
worden. | Aus Höchst-gedachter | Jhrer Hoch-Fürstlichen Durchl. SYM-
BOLO | Nach Anleitung der Worte Pauli/ | Rom. VIII, 18. | An
demselben Tage in einer Leich-Rede | fürgestellet hat | JOHANN
CONRAD Kieffer/ | Hoch-Fürstl. Kirchen-Rath und Hoff-Prediger |
[rule] | Schleswig/ | Gedruckt bey Lorentz Eckstorff/ Hoch-Fürstl.
Hoff-Buchdruckern. Anno 1695.

Folio. [4], 44 pp.; $\pi^2$, A-L$^2$; engraved frontispiece.                                    CKB

2710  KIRCHHOFF, A. C.

Schuldigste Glückwünschung | Mit welcher | Dem Hoch-Wohl-Ge-
bohrner und Hoch- | Würdigen Herrn/ | HERRN | CHRISTIAN |
Rantzau | Erbherrn auf Raastorf/ Aschberg/ | Cronshagen/ und Bürau |
Und | Des Stiffts Lübeck hochansehnlichen Canonico | Zu bezeugung
seiner gantz verbundenen Pflicht und | Danckbarkeit | Am ersten Tage
des MDCXCVsten Jahres | Seine Dienstbegierigste Aufwartung abstatten
wollen | Dero verbundenster Diener | A. C. Kirchhoff | [double rule] |
Kjel/ | Gedruckt bey Joachim Reumann/ Acad. Buchdr. [1695]

Folio. $\chi^2$.                                                                                                    CKB

2711  KÜRBELIN, JOHANN GEORG

Die | Durch ein GOttes-Geschick | Beglückte Glückstadt/ | Welche | Als
der Edle/ Vor-Achtbare und Wolgelahrte | Herr | JOHAN. HELF-
RICH | Nagel/ St. Ministerij Candidatus | . . . | . . . | Von | Johan
Georg Kürbelin/ S. Th. Stud. Regio-Lothar. Saxone [1695]

Broadside (34 x 25.5 cm).                                                                            CKB

2712  LUND, JOHANNES

JOHANNIS LUNDII, | in seinem Leben getreuen Die- | ners des
Evangelii bey der Christlichen | Gemeine in Tundern/ | Levitischer |
Hoherpriester | und | Priester/ | Darin | Des Hohenpriesters Kleidung/ |
Salbung/ Amt/ Ansehen im Ge- | richt/ Heyrath/ Nachfolge/ Für-
bildung/ | wie auch der andern Priester Amts-Verrichtun- | gen/ als
Reinigunge der Unreinen und Aussätzigen/ | Erlassung des Gelübdes
der Naziräer/ und andere | Amts-Pflichten/ auch endlich der Priester

und | Leviten Einkünffte beschrieben werden. | Den Liebhabern der
jüdischen Altheiten | zum besten herausgegeben. | Zu finden in Ham-
burg bey Gottfried Liebernickel/ | Buchhändler im Dom. | [rule] |
Schleßwig/ gedruckt bey Lorentz Eckstorff/ | Hochfl. Hof-Buch-
drucker/ im Jahr 1695.

8vo. Pp. [1-16], 1-868, 859-886; (a)⁸, a-kkk⁸.                    CKB

2713  LUND, JOHANNES

JOHANNIS LUNDII, | in seinem Leben getreuen Die- | ners des
Evangelii bey der Christlichen | Gemeine in Tundern/ | Offentlicher |
Gottesdienst | Der | alten Hebräer/ | Darinnen fürgestellet wird/ | wie
das tägliche Morgen-und | Abendopffer gebracht/ der Sabbat/ das | Fest
der Neumonden/ nebst den jährlichen Festen | gefeirrt/ was die Priester
beym Leuchter/ Räuch-und | Brannt-Altar täglich dabey verrichtet/ und
wie sie | mit dem Segen die Gemeine gelassen; | Danebst was bey
demselben | Gottesdienst der Leviten Amt gewesen/ | und wie sie mit
den Priestern das Volck so wol | im Tempel/ als in ihren öffentlichen
Schulen in | der göttlichen Warheit unterrichtet. | Den Liebhabern der
jüdischen Altheiten zu | gut nunmehr ans Licht gegeben. | Zu finden in
Hamburg bey Gottfried Liebernickel/ | Buchhändler im Dom. | [rule] |
Schleßwig/ gedruckt bey Lorentz Eckstorff/ | Hochfl. Hof-Buchdrucker/
im Jahr 1695.

8vo. [16], 1424 pp.; (A)⁸, A-Uuuu⁸.                             CKB

Dedication to Friederich, Duke of Schleswig-Holstein, signed by author's son,
Thomas Lund, 5 January 1695.

2714  Die Lust nach gehabter Unlust | Welche | Bey dem Hochzeit Fest | . . . |
Herrn M. Johan | Eler Schmidt/ | Wohlberuffenen Pastor zu St. Petri, |
Mit | Der WolEdlen Hoch-Ehr-und | Tugendbegabten | Jungf. Anna
Ca- | tharina/ | . . . | Herrn Andres Kellinghusen/ | Wolfürnehmen
Bürgers und Handelsman hieselbsten/ | Eheleibliche | J. Tochter/ | . . . |
Von | Einem dem Hochzeit Hause Höchstverbundenen. | Imprimatur, |
C. BARTHOLIN. | [ornamental rule] | Kopenhagen Gedruckt bey Joh.
Philip Bockenhoffer | Königl. Mayest. und Universit. Buchdrucker.
[1695]

Folio. χ².                                                       CKB

Verse.

2715  MALTZAHN, ARNOLD

Das Bild des Todes | . . . | Herrn M. HENRICI | STORNINGS, | . . . |
Von | Arnold Maltzhahn/ Pastor | zu Kirch-Berkau | [type ornaments] |

[rule] | PLOEN/ | Gedruckt durch Tobias Schmidt/ Fürstl. Buchdr. [1695]

4to. 28 pp.; A-C⁴ D².                                    KIEL UL

2716 MARPERGER, PAUL JACOB

Als | Jhrer Königlichen Hoheit | Des | Durchleuchtigsten Fürsten | und Herren/ | Herren | FRIDERICI | Zu Dennemarck und Norwegen Cron- | und Erb-Printzen | Seiner Durchleuchtigsten Braut | Der | Durchleuchtigsten Fürstin | LOUYSE, | Hertzogin von Meckelburg Gustraw | Einzug in Copenhagen | den 5 Decembr. | Hochst-Feyerlich celebrirt worden. | Fügte in allerdemüthigster unterthänigkeit Seine acclamation, | Der allgemeinen in folgenden mit bey | P. J. Marperger. | [ornamental rule] | Gedruckt bey Jh. Königl. Majest. und Universit. Buchdrucker/ | Johann Philipp Bockenhoffer/ 1695.

Folio. χ².                                    CKB

2717 Nach des | Durchläuchtigsten Fürsten und Herren | HERREN | Friede-richs/ | Erben zu Norwegen/ Hertzogen zu Schleßwig- | Holstein/ Stormarn und der Dithmar- | schen/ Grafen zu Oldenburg und | Del-menhorst &c. | Gnädigem Befehl/ | Sol | an dem angesetzeten | Buß-und Bet-Tage/ | So in diesem Jahr 1695. am 19. April, als den Freytag | nach Jubilate und vor Cantate einfallen | wird/ | Jn Jhro Durchl. Fürsten-thümern der | Gottesdienst folgender massen angestellet | werden.

4to. )(⁴.                                    CKB

2718 Nachricht/ | Wegen der/ | Zwischen Jhr. König- | lichen Majestät zu Dennemarck | Norwegen/ &c. &c. | Und | Herrn Hertzogs Friedrichs | zu Schleßwig-Holstein- | Gottorff Durchläuchtigkeit/ | Erwachsenen Jrrungen. | [rule] | Gedruckt im Jahr 1695

4to. [A]⁴ B-E⁴ (E4 blank).                                    CKB

Another edition: same title, A-D⁴; another edition: same title, A-D⁴. Concludes with vignette.

2719 NAGEL, JOHANNES DANIEL

Die | Zwar | Entfernte aber doch Beständige | Bruder-Lieb/ | Als | Der WohlEdle/ Veste und Wohl- | lahrte | Herr JOHAN. | HELFRICH Nagel/ | S.S. Th. & Philol. Stud. | Jn der Königl. Dännemärckischen Stadt und Fe- | stung Glückstadt nach geschehener ordentl. Vocation als Rector | socher [sic] Stadt-Schulen offentlich vorgestellet und | eingefüh-ret wurde/ | Jn einem | Hertzlichen Wunsch | entdecket und aus Hes-sen | übersandt | Von | JOHAN. DANIEL Nagel/ | Qvæst. Battenb. |

[ornament] | [rule] | Glückstadt/ gedruckt bey Reinhard Janßen/ | Jm Jahr 1695.

Folio. χ².                                                                 CKB

2719A Neldelius, Johannes

Hertzlich-gemeynte | Glückwünschung/ | Womit/ | Als der | Durchläuchtigste | Fürst und Herr/ | HERR | FRJDERJCH | Erbe zu Norwegen/ | Regierender Hertzog zu Schleßwig/ | Holstein/ Stormarn und der Ditmarschen/ Graff | zu Oldenburg und Delmenhorst/ &c. | Mit höchster Freude und Frolocken dero/ sämptlichen | Unterthanen | Seine GOtt gebe/ glückliche | Regierung | Anno 1695. antrat/ | Seine unterthänigste Schuldigkeit/ und schuldigsten Gehor- | sam abstatten wollen/ | Seines Gnädigsten Landes-Vaters | unterthänigster Knecht | JOHANNES NELDELIUS, Ditmarsus. | SS. Theol. Stud. | [rule] | Schleßwig/ | Gedruckt bey Lorentz Eckstorff/ Hoch-Fürstlichem | Hoff-Buchdrucker.

Folio. χ².                                                                 CKB

2720 Nicolai, Martin

Die musicalischen Operii eines christ-adelichen Lebens oder Abdanckung über Anna Hedwig Wackenbarth. Altona, 1695.

Folio.                                                                      *

*OHM* I, 461.

2721 Die Ritter | Der | Königlichen Dänischen | Orden/ | Des | Elephanten | Und | Dannebrogs [1695]

12mo. 14 pp.; F⁶, χ1.                                                       CKB

2722 Sandhagen, Caspar Hermann

Der | Freudige Zutritt | Zu dem | Mitleidigen | Hohenpriester JEsu/ | Barmhertzigkeit und Gnade von demselben | zu entfangen; | Als | Der Weiland | Hoch-Würdigste und Durchläuchtigste | Fürst und Herr | Christian Albrecht | Erbe zu Norwegen/ | POSTULIRTER COADJU-TOR | des Stiffts Lübeck/ | Hertzog zu Schleßwig/ Holstein/ Stormarn und | der Ditmarschen/ Graff zu Oldenburg und Delmen- | horst/ &c. | den XXVI. Feb. Anno 1695/ | Zu den Gebeinen seiner Hohen Vor-Väter/ in der | Dom-Kirche zu Schleßwig in das Fürstl. Begräbniß | gesetzet wurd; | Auff Gottorff bey grosser Versammlung | in einer | Traur-Rede | fürgestellet/ | Von | Caspar Hermann Sandhagen/ | General-Superintendent. und Ober-Hoff-Prediger daselbst. | [rule] | Schleswig/ | Gedruckt bey Lorentz Eckstorff/ Hoch-Fürstl. Hoff-Buch-druckers. Anno 1695.

Folio. 40 pp.; )(², B-K²; engraved frontispiece.　　　　　　　CKB

Frontispiece: engraving of Christian Albrecht, "Joh. Friedlein, sculps.; Ludowig Weyandt, pinxit."

2723　SANDHAGEN, CASPAR HERMANN

Zwey Auslegungen des VII. Capittels des Propheten Michæ, als A. 1695 und 1696 verordneten Bußtag-Textes. Schleswig 1695.

　　　　　　　　　　　　　　　　　　　　　　　　　　　　*

*Moller* II, 757, also gives 1696 publication date. *Cf.* No. 3098.

2724　SCHLESWIG-HOLSTEIN-GOTTORFF. *Laws, statutes, etc.*

WJer Friderich von Gottes | Gnaden/ [Erbe] zu Norwegen/ Hertzog zu | Schleßwig/ Holstein/ Stormarn und der Ditmarschen/ | ... | ... 28. Febr. Anno 1695

Broadside.　　　　　　　　　　　　　　　　　　　　　　KIEL UL

Decree requiring approval by the University of Kiel of persons seeking school and church appointments.

2724A　SCHLESWIG-HOLSTEIN-GOTTORFF. *Laws, statutes, etc.*

WJr Friderich von GOttes | Gnaden Erbe zu Norwegen/ Hertzog zu Schleßwig/ | Holstein/ ... | ... | ... Gottorff/ den 12. Julii. Anno 1695.

Broadside.　　　　　　　　　　　　　　　　　　　　　　CKB

Decree encouraging trade with the port of Eckernförde and granting privileges to new settlers there.

2725　SCHLESWIG-HOLSTEIN-GOTTORFF. *Laws, statutes, etc.*

WJr Friderich/ von GOttes | Gnaden/ Erbe zu Norwegen/ Hertzog zu Schleßwig/ | ... | ... Gottorff den 23. Jul. 1695

Broadside.　　　　　　　　　　　　　　　　　　　　　　CNA

Decree forbidding buying and selling beyond the market place in and near the city of Schleswig.

2726　SCHLESWIG-HOLSTEIN-GOTTORFF. *Laws, statutes, etc.*

WJr Friderich/ von GOttes | Gnaden/ Erbe zu Norwegen/ Hertzog zu Schleßwig/ | ... | ... Gottorff den 30. Jul. Anno 1695.

Broadside.　　　　　　　　　　　　　　　　　　　　　　CNA

Decree regarding duties to be paid on goods arriving by ship on the River Schlei.

2727    SCHLESWIG-HOLSTEIN-GOTTORFF. *Laws, statutes, etc.*

WJir Friderich/ von GOttes | Gnaden/ Erbe zu Norwegen/ Hertzog zu
Schleswig/ | . . . | . . . 12. Augusti 1695

Broadside.                                                                                  KIEL UL

Decree reiterating prohibition (of 8 November 1689) against giving and receiving
gifts at weddings and baptisms.

2728    SCHLESWIG-HOLSTEIN-GOTTORFF. *Laws, statutes, etc.*

WJer von GOttes Gnaden | Friderich/ Erbe zu Norwegen Hertzog zu |
Schleßwig/ Holstein/ Stormarn und der Ditmarschen | . . . | . . . 19
Augusti 1695.

Broadside.                                                                                  KIEL UL

Decree forbidding the export of firewood and coal.

2729    SCHLESWIG-HOLSTEIN-GOTTORFF. *Laws, statutes, etc.*

WJer Friderich von GOttes | Gnaden/ Erbe zu Norwegen/ Hertzog zu |
Schleßwig/ Holstein . . . | . . . | . . . Gottorff den 18. Novembr. 1695.

Broadside.                                                                               CKB; CNA

Decree against "Convivien" at public expense.

2731    SCHLESWIG-HOLSTEIN-GOTTORFF. *Laws, statutes, etc.*

WJer Friderich von GOttes | Gnaden/ Erbe zu Norwegen/ Hertzog zu |
. . . | . . . 26. Nov. 1695

Broadside.                                                                                  KIEL UL

Decree against unauthorized hunting and shooting.

2732    SCHLESWIG-HOLSTEIN-GOTTORFF. *Laws, statutes, etc.*

WJer Friderich von GOttes | Gnaden/ Erbe zu Norwegen/ Hertzog zu |
. . . | . . . 27. Novembr. 1695

Broadside.                                                                                  KIEL UL

Decree against the illegal impressing of "reisende Leute, angesessene Bürger und
Haußleute deren Söhne und Knechte" into military service.

2733    Sing-Freuden-Gedichte/ | über den durch Göttl: Gnade Glücklich
erlebten Funfftzigsten | Gebuhrts-Tag | Des Maystätischen Monarchens |
Christiani qvinti | So den 15. April Anno 1695. einfiel und in Höchstged.
Mayst. | Hoher Gegenwart in Kopenhagen Hochfeierlich gehalten ward.

Broadside (30.5 x 29.5 cm).                                                                     CKB

Printed on satin.

2734 UBELACKER, FRIEDRICH

Hochzeit Gedichte/ | Alß | Der Kunst-erfahrne und Manhaffte | Meister Friderich | Ubelacker/ | Bürger und Kunstmahler/ | Sich mit der | Tugendsamen Jungfer | Jngeborg Halvers/ | Allhier in Copenhagen in der Teutschen St. Petri Kirche | den 7 May 1695, hat copuliren lassen. | [emblem] | Zur Lust und aufmunterung der eingeladenen Hochzeit | Gäste/ von dem Bräutigamb in aller einfalt selber | componiret, und auß guter Meinung denselben | überreichet. | Imprimatur, | Joh. Birchero- dius. | [rule] | Gedruckt im Jahr/ 1695.

Folio. $\chi^2$. CKB

Verse.

2736 Verordnung | Wegen des | Brau-Wesens | in Renßburg. | Hafniæ die 19 Februarii Anno 1695 | [monogram] | [rule] | Gedruckt bey Jh. Königl. Maj. und Univ. Buchdrucker | Johan Philip Bockenhoffer.

4to. $\chi^4$. CKB

2738 Verordnung | Wegen | Der Brawer/ Höcker | und Handwercker im | Ambte Renßburg. | Hafniæ die 8. Junii Anno 1695 | [monogram] | [rule] | Gedruckt bey Jhr. Königl. Majest. und Dero Universit. | Buchdr. Joh. Philip Bockenhoffer.

4to. $\chi^2$. CKB

2739 WEDDERKOPF, GABRIEL

Die adeliche Hochzeit in der Tugend . . . bey dem Absterben Christoph Rantzau vorgestellt und übergeben der Wittwen und Brüdern. Kiel 1695.

4to. *

*OHM* I, 713.

2740 ZITSCHER, PETER

Die rühmliche und seelige | Beständigkeit | . . . | Christlicher Beer- digung | . . . | Herrn Friedrich | Jürgenssen | . . . | Von | Petro Zitschar . . . | Schleßwig/ Gedruckt bey Lorentz Eckstorff/ Hoch-Fürstl. Hoff- Buchdr. [1695]

4to. 96 pp.; A-M⁴. CKB

On p. 51, separate title: *Das* | *Verborgene Manna* | *. . .* | *Von* | *GOTTHARD JOHANNE* | *ZVVERGIO,* | *Predigern zu Tundern;* on p. 68, separate title: *Letzste* | *Thränen-Pflicht/* | *. . .* | *Die nachlebende leidtragende Kinder/* | *Anverwandten und Freunde.*

## 1696

2742 Als │ Der HochEdle/ Vest-und Hoch- │ gelahrte Herr/ │ Herr Friede- │
rich │ Korfey/ D. │ ... │ Zum letzten Ehren-Gedächtniß │ Folgende │
Trauer-Zeilen │ gesetzet. │ [woodcut: coffin] │ [rule] │ Glückstadt/ │
gedruckt bey Reinhard Janßen/ im Jahr 1696.

Folio. [a]² b-f².                                                          KIEL UL

Verse by several hands.

2744 Vom 16. Januarius │ Die Altonaische RELATION │ No. 4 [woodcut:
crowned female figure on lion] 1696

12mo. Pp. 25-32; χ⁴.                                           DEUTSCH-NIENHOF

Caption title.

2745 Anmerckungen │ Uber die │ Nachricht/ │ Welche │ Neulichst wegen der │
zwischen │ Jhro Königl. Majest. │ zu Dennemarck Norwegen/ &c. &c. │
Und │ Jhro zu Schleßwig-Hollstein Regierende │ Hoch-Fürstl. Durchl. │
Hn. Hertzog │ Friderichs/ │ Erwachsenen Jrrungen. │ Ans Licht gege- │
ben/ │ Auff gnädigsten Befehl Höchst-gedachter │ Jhrer Hoch-Fürstl. │
Durchl. │ [rule] │ Gedruckt im Jahr 1696

4to. 32, [48] pp.; A-K⁴.                                                        CKB

E-K: "Beylagen." Another edition: 40, [62] pp.; A-E⁴, a-h⁴.

2746 Antwort-Schreiben │ Eines guten Freundes │ Aus Regenspurg/ │ An │
Seinen Correspondenten in Holstein/ │ Darinnen kürtzlich vorgestellet/ │
wie der Autor des │ übelgenandten │ Wahrhafften Berichts/ │ über │ Die │
Nachricht/ │ wegen der │ Zwischen Jhr. Königl. Majest │ zu Dennemarck │
Norwegen &c. │ Und │ Jhro HochFürstl. Durchl. zu Schleß- │ wig Hol- │
stein Gottorff/ │ Erwachsenen Jrrungen/ │ Jn solchen seinem Bericht │
nichts solides, noch auf ge- │ wissen Grund Beständiges vorgebracht/ son- │
dern indehm er darin- │ nen andere einiger Menschlichen Schwachheiten │
zu beschuldigen sich │ anmassen wollen/ dadurch sich selber der gantzen │
Welt/ als einen │ unbescheidenen Diffamanten, prostituiret habe. │
[rule] │ Jm Majo 1696.

4to. A-D⁴ E².                                                                   CKB

Another edition: 36 pp.; A-D⁴ E².

2747 ARIA [1696]

4to. )(⁴.                                                                       CKB

Caption title. Poems entitled "Der Dannemann," "Der Normann," "Der Teutsche,"
and "Der Morian," on occasion of Christian V's fiftieth birthday.

2748 ARNKIEL, TROELS

T. ARNKIEL, | Præpositi & Past. Apenradensis | SOLILOQUIA
BIBLICA, | Biblische | Seelen- | Gespräche | mit GOTT/ | Jn Drey
Theile/ | Gebethe/ Danck-und | Lobsagunge | unterschieden. | Mit
Worten der Heil. | Schrifft verfasset/ | Nach Ordnung des Catechismus |
mit 5 Registern eingerichtet | Dabey angefüget wird | Das Schleßwig-
Hol- | steinsche alte Gesang-Buch von | dem Autoren emendirt, ver-
mehrt und | mit steten Anmerckungen über alle | Gesänge beleuchtiget/ |
Nebst denen Königl. und Fürstl. | Kirchen-Gebethen in diesen Landen |
[rule] | SCHLESWJG/ | druckts und verlegts Lorentz Eckstorff/ |
Hochfl. Hoff. Buchdrucker An. 1696.

12mo. [72], 614, [34], [48], 323, [13] pp.; (a)-(c)$^{12}$, A-Dd$^{12}$, )($^{12}$, )( )($^{12}$, a-o$^{12}$.
GÖTTINGEN UL

Title in red and black. On )(1r and a1r, separate title: *Schleßwig-Hollsteinisches |
Gesangbuch/ | ... | Schleßwig/ | Gedruckt und verlegt durch Lorentz | Eckstorff/
Hoch-Fürstl. Hoff-Buchdr.*

2749 BOLDICH, ERNST CHRISTIAN

Schlechte | Hoffnung | I. Besserer Zeiten der Kirchen/ | so wohl | II.
Einer grossen Bekehrung der Juden/ | als | III Gäntzlichen Unterganges
des Anti- | christischen Babels | Vor dem Jüngsten Tage und Ende | der
Welt in diesen letzten Zeiten/ | Aus GOttes unfehlbaren Worte mit |
deutlichen und gewissen Gründen dargethan/ | und insonderheit Herrn
D. Speners Behauptung der | Hoffnung besserer Zeiten entgegen geset-
zet/ und der | Warheit zu Steuer/ für den Augen der recht | gläubigen
Kirchen dargeleget | von | M. Ernst Christian Boldig/ | Königl.
Schloßpr. auff Cronenb. und der | Teutschen Gemeine zu Helsingör am |
Oresund Pastore. | [rule] | Zu finden in Coppenhagen/ | Bey Johann
Melchior Lieben/ und in Leipzig/ | bey Johann Ludwig Gleditschen/ |
Anno 1696.

12mo. [20], 451 [i.e., 448] pp.; )($^{12}$ (−)(11, 12), A-S$^{12}$ T$^8$.
CKB

Pagination erratic. CKB copy bound with a refutation: *Halcyonia | ecclesiæ certo
futura, | Das ist: | Gewißheit/ | Der durch | Herrn D. Philip Jacob Spenern/ | ... |
Behaupteten | Hoffnung besserer Zeiten/ | Entgegen gesetzet | Der | Schlechten
Hoffnung/ | Hn. M. Ernst Christian Boldigs/ | ... | Von dem | Freunde der
Warheit. | [rule] | Franckfurt am Mayn/ | Jn Verlegung Johann David Zunners/ |
Jm Jahr Christi 1696.*

2750 BRÄMER, CHRISTIAN

Arbeitender | Christ/ | Mit vielen | Geistreichen Materien/ | und einem |
DISCURS, | von der | Kürtze des Mensch- | lichen Lebens/ | ver-

mehret/ | von dem | Am Worte GOttes/ bey der Kopen- | hagischen Teutschen St. Petri Gemeine/ | in die XXXIII. Jahren | Arbeitendem | M. Christian Brämer/ Lubec. | [rule] | Kopenhagen/ | Verlegts Justus Erythropel/ 1696

12mo. [10], 560 pp.; )($^6$ (−)(6), A-Z$^{12}$, Aa$^4$; engraved frontispiece.                    HAB

2751  BRÄMER, CHRISTIAN

Einfältige Catechismus-Fragen. Copenhagen, 1696.

12mo.                                                                                                    *

*Thott* I/2, 503; *Cat. Christ. Brœmer,* 1701, 12mo. incomp. 3. See No. 1944.

2752  CAUSÆ CONJECTIO | Nebst einer | Kurtzen | DEDUCTION | wegen der | Von | Jhro Königl. Majest. | zu Dennemarck Norwegen/ &c. &c. | An | Die zu Schleßwig/ Holstein Regie- | rende Hoch-Fürstl. Durchl. | Hertzog Friederichen/ | Neulich gemachten vier prætensionen | Auff gnädigsten Befehl höchst-gedachter | Jhrer Hochfürstl. Durchl. zum | Druck befordert. | [rule] | Jm Monath Maji Ao. 1696

4to. 45, [3] pp.; A-F$^4$.                                                                            CKB

Another edition: same title, but with date "Anno MDCXCVI," A-C$^4$.

2753  CHRISTIANI, VALENTIN

Wolverdiente Ehren-Seul/ | über | . . . | Fr. Margarethæ Clotzin/ | Gebohrnen Clausin/ | . . . | Auffgerichtet | Von | VALENTINO CHRISTIANI, | Sch: Tönn: R. | [ornament] | [rule] | Glückstadt/ gedruckt bey Reinhard Janßen/ | Jm Jahr 1696.

Folio. $\chi^2$.                                                                                      CKB

Verse.

2754  CLAUSEN, MATTHIAS

Bittere Trähnen | . . . | MARGARETHÆ | Clotzin/ | Gebohrnen Clausin/ | . . . | Von | MATTHIA Clausen. | [woodcut: skull and crossbones] | [rule] | Glückstadt/ gedruckt bey Reinhard Janßen/ 1696.

Folio. $\chi^2$.                                                                                      CKB

Verse.

2755  COLBRAND, NICOLAUS

Dreyfache unpartheyische Rechtsbelehrung wegen einer Holländischen, auf 600000 Gulden sich belaufenden, Erbschaft, pro Anna Müllers, contra Peter von Rheden, samt Specie facti, und Beylagen, von ihm außgegeben. Altona, 1696.

Folio.                                                                    *

*Moller* I, 105.

2756  DAMPIERRE, JACQUES SERCEUIL DE

LE PASSE PAR | Tout François, | Par | J. S. de Dampierre, | Maitre de
langue de la Reine | de Dannemarck &c. | Französischer | Haupt-
Schlüssel/ | Durch | J. S. De DAMPIERRE, | Jhro Maj. der Königin zu
Denne- | marck und Norwegen/ &c. | Sprach-Meister | Troisieme Edition
corrigee en | plusiers lieus. | [rule] | KOPENHAVEN, | verlegts |
Johann Justus Erytropilus/ | Anno MDC XCVI.

12mo. [20], 220 pp.; )($^{12}$ (−)( 11, 12), A-J$^{12}$, K1-2.        CKB

Title printed in red and black.

2757  DENMARK. *Laws, statutes, etc.*

WJR Christian der Fünffte/ | . . . | . . . Glückstadt/ den 12. Martij, Anno
1696.

Broadside.                                                                CNA

Decree condemning a pamphlet entitled "Kurtze Historische Beschreibung der
Uhralten Käyserl. und des Heiligen Römischen Reichs Freyen An-See-Kauff-und
Handels-Stadt Hamburg" by Wolffgang Henrich Adelungk and published by
Conrad Neumann in Hamburg.

2758  DENMARK. *Laws, statutes, etc.*

WJR Christian der Fünffte/ | . . . | . . . Glückstadt/ den 28sten Octobr.
Anno 1696.

Broadside.                                                                CNA

Decree regarding the circulation of foreign coins in the Duchies.

2759  Ehren-Klag-und Trost-Gedicht | . . . | Fr: Margarethen/ | Gebohrnen
Bensen/ | . . . | Hn: Georg Bocken | . . . | Hertzlich-geliebten Ehe-
Schatzes/ | . . . | Von | Nachgesetzten. | [rule] | Glückstadt/ Gedruckt
bey Reinhard Janßen/ Königl. | Buchdrucker. [1696]

Folio. [a]$^2$, b-e$^2$.                                                   CKB

Verse by several hands.

2760  Erklärung der Medaille | So Dero | Königl. Mayst. zu Dännemarck
Norwegen/ | Anno 1696 den 15 April/ als Dero zum Fünfftzigsten Zahl
einge- | fallenen Geburths-Tage überreichet worden. | [below:] Ge-
druckt bey Jhr. Königl. Majest. und Universit. Buchdrucker Joh. Phil.
Bockenhoffer.

Broadside (38 x 31.5 cm). CKB

Verse. Another edition (48 x 33.5 cm).

2761 ESMARCH, MARK

Gläubiger Jungfrauen | . . . | Margaretha Sibbers/ | . . . | von | M. Marco Esmarch/ Pastore Seniore der Clitzbülschen | Gemeine Tunderischen Amts. | [rule] | Schleßwig/ gedruckt bey Lorentz Eckstorff/ Hochfl. Hoff-Buchdr. [1696]

4to. 79, [1] pp.; A-K⁴. CKB

2762 FRANCKE, WOLFGANG CHRISTOPH

Die an Gott stets bleibende Gottes-Kinder/ | . . . | Hn. M. Gabriel | Wedderkops/ | . . . | Von | Wolfgang Christoph Francken/ | Predigern der Gemeine daselbst. [i.e. Kiel] | [rule] | KJEL/ | Gedruckt durch Joachim Reumann/ Acad. Buchdr. | 1696.

4to. 32, [8] pp.; A-D⁴, )(⁴. CKB

2763 [. . . .] | gegründete | Dänische Jubel-Jahr/ | Bey einfall | Des den 11ten Octobris 1696. zum Fünff und Zwantzigsten mahl höchst-feyerlich | begangenen | Geburths-Fests | Jhro Königl. Hoheit des Cron-Printzen | . . . | August Wygand K. D. Rath | [Bockenhoffer]

Broadside (c. 45 x 30 cm). CKB

T-p of CKB copy defective.

2764 GERCKENS, SIMON

Der seelige Tod oder Abdanckung über Herman Gröning . . . Glück-stadt, 1696.

4to. *

*OHM* II, 223.

2765 GRAMM, FRIEDRICH

Sonnen-klarer | Beweißthum/ | Daß | Christoffer Franck/ D. | Anderer seiner grossen Jrrthümer vor diesesmahl | zu geschweigen/ | Jn | Erklärung der Ewigkeit Got- | tes/ ein offenbahrer Socinianer sey; | Der | Gantzen gelahrten Welt/ insonderheit aber | denen Professoribus Academiæ Kiloniensis, denen Su- | perintendenten, Pröbsten und Predigern in den | Fürstenthümern Schleßwig-Holstein/ wie auch de- | nen auf der Kielis. Universitæt Studirenden, | Vorgestellet | Von | M. Friderico Grammio | [rule] | Gedruckt im Jahr 1696

4to. A-F⁴ G². CKB

2766 GRATULATION | Allerdurchleuchtigste Großmächtigste | Königin [1696]

Folio. χ². CKB

Caption title. Verse on occasion of Queen Charlotte Amalie's 46th birthday.

2767 HAHN, HINRICH

Der immer-grünende Palm-Baum/ | . . . | Fr: Margaretha | Clotzin/ | gebohrnen Clausin/ | . . . | Von | M. HENRICO HAHN, | Præp: Austral: Dithmars: & | Past: prim: Meldorff: | [rule] | Glückstadt/ Gedruckt bey Reinhard Janßen/ | Königl. Buchdrucker. [1696]

Folio. [6], 37, [1] pp.; A-L². CKB

2768 HAMERICH, CHRISTIAN

Die Kron der Gerechtigkeit | . . . | Herr Ehrenfried | Amthor/ | . . . | Von | CHRISTIANO Hamerich/ | Eccl. Patr. Past. Prim. | [woodcut: coffin] | [rule] | Glückstadt/ gedruckt bey Reinhard Janßen/ Königl. Buchd. [1696]

Folio. 36 pp.; A-J². CKB

2769 HAMERICH, HENRICH

Vergönnete Priesterehe (in nupt. Pet. Struve). Kiel, 1696

Folio. *

*OHM* I, 233.

2770 Hochbetrübte Schuldigkeit/ | . . . | Daniel Dieterich | von Buchwald/ | . . . | abgeleget und übergeben | S.B.P.S. |[woodcut: coffin] | [ornamental rule] | Glückstadt/ Gedruckt bey Reinhard Janßen. [1696]

Folio. χ². CKB

Verse.

2771 Hoch-Fürstl. | Confirmirtes | Reglement/ | Bey | Oeffentlichen Auff-zuge | Der | Bürgerschafft | Jn der | Stadt-und Vestung | Tönningen. | [type ornaments] | [rule] | Schleßwig/ | Gedruckt bey Lorentz Eck-storff/ Hoch-Fürstl. | Hoff-Buchdrucker/ Anno 1696.

4to. 15, [1] pp.; A-B⁴. CKB

2773 Hochzeits-Gedicht | Und | Geschicht/ | Auf den Eh-verbindlichen Ehren-Tag | . . . | Hr. Johan Ocksen/ | Treufleißiger Seelen-Hirt/ an S. Marien | Kirche in Flensburg/ | Mit seiner Vielgeliebten Braut | Der Wol-Edlen/ Hoch-Ehr-und Tugendgezierten | Jgfr. Anna Peters/ | . . . |

[woodcut: emblem flanked by angels] | Imprimat. Casp. Bartholin. | Zusammen gereimet/ | von | Einem Bruder. | [ornamental rule] | Kopenhagen/ | Gedruckt bey Jhro Königl. Majestäts und Universit. Buchdr. | Joh. Philip Bockenhoffer. [1696]

Folio. χ².                                                        CKB

Verse.

2774   JUSTIFICATI- | ONS-Schrifft | Uber | Die fruchtlose in Stockholm abgegangene | CONFERENZ | Wegen der | Bey der Krohn Schweden vermög | der mit denen Allirten aufgerichteten | Tractaten | Ange-suchten Hülffsleistung/ | Nebst | Beygefügtem Protest und Reservation daselbst ad | Protocollum gegeben | [type ornaments] | [rule] | Gedruckt im Jahr 1696.

4to. )(⁴ (16.5 x 11.7 cm).                               CKB

Place of publication uncertain (possibly Slesvig). Another edition, A-B⁴ (15.7 x 10.5 cm); another edition, A-B⁴ (15.7 x 11.2 cm); both presumably published out-side monarchy.

2775   KING, WILLIAM

Rechtmässige Vertheidigung | Des | Königreichs | Dännemarck/ | Jn welcher | Eine ohnlängst unter dem Titul/ | Dännemarcks Gegenwär-tiger Staat/ | herausgekommene Schrifft | gründlich beantwortet und widerleget/ auch anbey | gewiesen wird/ | Daß der Autor von Königl. Dänischen Staats- | und andern Affairen theils keine zulängliche und gnug- | same Wissenschafft gehabt/ theils aber mit Vorsatz und aus | Passion wider Dännemarck geschrieben habe; | Erstlich in Englischer Sprach gedruckt/ nachgehends ins | Französische übersetzet/ und bey allen und jeden Capiteln | mit nöthigen Zugaben vermehret; | Anjetzo aber zusammen wegen vieler darinnen enthaltenen | Curiosen Particu-laritäten/ welche zu einer vollständigen Nachricht | dessen/ was sowol den Autorem der Relation, als auch den Staat von | Dännemarck und die Holsteinische Affairen betrifft/ sehr | dienlich sind/ in Hochteutscher Sprach | heraus gegeben. | [rule] | Cölln/ bey Pieter Marteau, 1696.

4to. )(⁴ )( )(⁴ (−))( )(4), A-V⁴, χ1.                    CKB

According to CKB catalogue, the book was issued in Copenhagen, with false place of publication. A refutation of Molesworth's *An Account of Denmark*, London, 1694.

2776   KOHL, FRANZ DIETRICH

(Trauergedicht über Ursula Wedderkop, geb. Burchard). Kiel: Reu-mann, (1696?)

Broadside.                                                          (SHLB)

Appended: verse by G. C. Riebe, M. G. Wedderkopf, Fr. Wedderkopf. 2 leaves.

2777   Der Königlichen Stadt und Veste | Glückstadt | Feuer-Ordnung | und
       deren CASSA, | Welche Anfangs mit Vorwissen und Gutbefin- | den der
       Königl. Hochlöblichen Regierung hieselbst/ entworf- | fen/ und folgends
       von Jhr Königl. Majest. zu Dännemarck/ | Norwegen/ &c. Unserm
       Allergnädigsten Könige und Herren/ | zum Besten der Stadt/ doch ohne
       Abbruch hiesiger Stadt | alten Schützen-Gilde/ Allergnädigst confir-
       miret, nnd [sic] von | E. E. Rath hieselbst zu besserer Notitz eines jeden/
       dem | daran gelegen/ zum Druck befordert. | [emblem] | [rule] | Bey
       Reinhard Janßen/ Königl. bestalten Buch- | drucker/ im Jahr 1696.

       4to. A-C⁴.                                                    KIEL UL

       C4 lacking, probably blank.

2778   Kurtz verfassete | SPECIES FACTI | cum | DEDUCTIONE, | Entgegen
       gesetzet | Der | so genannten | CAUSÆ CONJECTIONI, | Betreffend |
       Die | Zwischen | Jhr. Königliche Majestät | zu Dännemarck/ Norwegen/
       &c. | Und | Jhr. Fürstliche Durchläuchtigkeit | zu Schleßwig/ Holstein/
       &c. | Entstandene Jrrungen. | Mit | Königl. allergnädigster Bewilligung |
       gedruckt. | [rule] | Jm Monat October/ | Anno 1696

       4to. 40 pp.; A-E⁴.                                       CKB; KIEL UL

       Headpiece on p. 3 indicates publication by Reumann in Kiel.

2779   Kurtze/ jedoch gründliche | Anzeige/ | Worinnen der Auctor der so
       genandten | Fürstlichen Anmerckungen über | Die Nachricht | Wegen
       der zwischen Jhr. Königl. | Mayst. zu Dennemarck/ Norwegen &c. |
       und | Herrn Hertzogs Friderichs zu Schleß- | wig/ Holstein Gottorff
       Durchl. erwachsenen | Streitigkeiten/ | geirret/ sich selbsten wieder-
       sprochen/ die | angezogene Acta & Documenta zerstümlet allegiret/ |
       folglich/ wie deßen Asserta grösten Theils auff einem nichti- ! gen
       Grund beruhen/ præliminariter, und biß zu einer weit- | läufftigern
       refutation, der unpassionirten Welt zur In- | formation/ mit Königl.
       allergnädigsten | Vorwißen und Approbation | zum Druck befodert. |
       [rule] | Jm Februario Anno 1696.

       4to. 96, [14] pp.; A-B⁴, C1-3, D-M⁴, R1, )(⁴, (b)⁴.       CKB; KIEL UL

       (b)4 lacking, presumably blank. Variant edition with same title: 72, [8] pp.; A-K⁴.
       Variant edition with same title: 72, [12] pp.; A-K⁴ L²; *Nach dem Copenhagenschen*
       *Exemplar, gedruckt zu Altona bey* | *Christian Reimers/ Königl. priviligirten*
       *Buchdrucker/ 1696.* Another edition, same title: 21, [3] pp., pp. 23-96, [1-12];
       A-M⁴, N1, )(⁴, (b)1-3 (C4 blank). BM

2780   LA FOSSE, ESTIENE DE

Die | Allervortrefflichsten Liebes-Zeichen | Jn | Jetzo Regierender |
Königlichen Majestät | Von | Dännemarck Norwegen/ | Bey | Derer den
15ten Aprilis 1696 zum Fünffzigsten mahl glücklichst eingefallenem |
Geburths-Fest | Aus allerunterthänigster Pflicht vorgestellet | von |
Estiene de la Fosse. | [below:] Gedruckt bey Jhr. Königl. Majest. und
Universit. Buchdr. Johan Philip Bockenhoffer.

Broadside (39 x 26.6 cm).                                            CKB

2781   LASSENIUS, JOHANNES *and* HECTOR GOTTFRIED MASIUS

D. JOHANNIS LASSENII | Weyland Prof. P. und Pastoris | bey der
Teutschen Gemeine | Sieben mahl Sieben | Heilige | Passions- | An-
dachten | Für die Frühe-Stunden | Der Sieben Wochen in der Fasten |
Und eben so viel | Für die Abend-Stunden/ | Die durch dessen Todt |
unterbrochen/ | Auf Begehren aber fortgesetzet sind | Von | HECT.
GOTTF. MASIO, | S. S. Th. D. und P. P. | Mit Königl. Majest. auch
Churfürstl. Durchl. zu Sachsen/ | Allergnädigsten Privilegiis. | [rule] |
Copenhagen/ | Bey Johan Melchior Liebe/ der Königl. Universität
Buchh. | Druckts Johan Jacob Bornheinrich/ 1696

8vo. [12], 553, [3] pp.; a1-6, A-V$^8$, W$^8$, X-Kk$^8$, Lll-6 (Ll6 blank); engraved preliminary title-page.                                                 CKB

Preliminary title: *D. LASSENII | Heilige | Passions-An- | dachten.* Engraving of
author, presumably used as frontispiece in second edition, missing in CKB copy.
Second edition identical except for frontispiece, engraved preliminary title-page, and
the title-page. Cf. No. 3000.

2782   LÖHNER, EMANUEL

Des Hoch-Wohlgebohrnen izzo in | GOTT-ruhenden Herrn/ |
HERRN | Daniel Dieterichs | von Buchwald/ | . . . | Von | EMANUEL
LÖHNER, | Diac: Beyenfleth: | [woodcut: skull and crossbones] |
[rule] | Glückstadt/ Gedruckt bey Reinhard Janßen. [1696]

Folio. χ$^2$.                                                        CKB

Verse.

2783   [LÜSCHNER, ERNST GOTTLIEB]

הבל הבלים הכל הבל | Das ist: | Die verachtete Eitelkeit/ |
. . . | Dorothea Benedicta/ | Gräfin zu Rantzou und Löwenholm . . . |
. . . | Von | Einem/ der/ solang als er lebet/ | . . . | [rule] | Glückstadt/
bey Reinhard Janßen/ Königl. Buchdrucker. [1696]

Folio. 20 pp.; A-E². CKB

Dedication initialed E.G.L.; author identified as Lüschner in *OHM* II, 500.

2784 LUND, JOHANN

JOHANNIS LUNDII, | in seinem Leben getreuen Die- | ners des Heil. Evangelii bey der blühen- | den Gemeine Christi in der Stadt | Tundern/ | Ausführliche Beschreibung | Der | Hütte des Stiffts/ | So auff GOttes Befehl in der Ara- | bischen Wüste erbauet/ | wie auch | Des ersten und andern | Tempels | Davon jener zu Jerusalem | durch Salomo; dieser aber | durch Serubabel und den Hohenpriester | Josua nach der Babylonischen Dienst- | barkeit/ erbauet worden/ | Wobey zu finden der Grund-Riß | des Tempels; | Den Liebhabern der Jüdischen Antiquitæt | zu gute ans Liecht gegeben. | [rule] | Schleßwig/ druckts und verlegts Lorentz | Eckstorff/ Hochfl. Hof-Buchdr. im Jahr 1696.

8vo. [2], 1374 pp.; π1, A-Rrrr⁸; 1 folding plate. CKB

Rrrr8 lacking, probably blank. Note to reader signed by author's son, Thomas Lund, and dated 12 January 1696.

2785 LUTHER, MARTIN

Ein schön | Gebet-Büchlein/ | Des seligen und theuren | Mannes GOTTES | D. Martini Lutheri | Aus seinem eigenen Geist/ | Trost und lebendigen Worten | und Tomis gezogen | Durch eine | Hohe Persohn | auffs neue zum Druck befodert | [rule] | KJEL/ | Gedruckt bey Joachim Reumann/ | Acad. Buchdr. 1696

8vo. [10], 728 pp.; π1, )(⁴, A-Yy⁸ Zz⁴. HAB

2786 MASIUS, PETER

Nummophylacium Hudemannianum, oder Leichenrede über Johann Hudemann ... Glückstadt: R. Janßen, 1696

Folio. *

Formerly in Kiel UL (LmC 9-163); *Moller* I, 383; *Bibl. J. M. Krafft,* 1752, p. 22; *Jöcher/ Rotermund,* IV, 925.

2787 MATTHISEN, SØREN

Eine leichte | Arithmetica | oder | Rechen-Kunst | Worinnen | Aller Sorten Außrechnun- | gen/ nicht allein zur Erleichterung | bey dem täglichen Handel im Kauffen | und Verkauffen/ entweder der Waa- | ren-Preiß steigt oder fällt/ sondern auch | dem Volcke von allerley Stande | sehr beqvem und nutzbar/ | wird gefunden/ | Verfertiget und

in Druck | gegeben | durch | Severin Matthison. | [rule] | Kopenhagen/ | Gedruckt/ durch Joh. Jacob Bornhein- | rich/ im Jahr 1696.

12mo. A-H$^{12}$, J$^4$ (J3-4 blank).                    CKB

Dedication to Prince Wilhelm of Denmark. Also published in Danish.

2788    MOHR, JOHANNES

Ein kurtz-abgefasstes | Rechen-Buch/ | Darinnen | Allerhand Haus-und Handels- | Rechnungen: Auch wie man aus ei- | ner vorhabenden Zahl/ Radicem Quadratam, | Cubicam, Zensizensicam, Sursolidam, Zensi- | cubicam, Bsursolidam, Zensizenzensicam und | Cubicubicam extrahiren soll: Nebst an- | gehängten nützlichen Exempeln. | Deßgleichen ab- sonderliche Arithmet- | Astronom-und Geographische Aufgaben/ so | zum Theil durch di Logarithmos solvirt sind. | Seinen Discipulis zu fernerer Aufmunte- | rung/ Erlust-und Belibung der Edlen Mathe- | matischen Künsten/ zum Andernmahl | fürgestellet | Von | JOHANNE Mohren/ Hamburgensi, | der Mathematischen Kunsten Beflissenen/ und | bestaltem Arithmetico an der Schuel | in Husum. | [rule] | Schleß- wig/ gedruckt bei Lorentz Eckstorff/ | Hoch-Fürstl. Hoff-Buchdrucker/ im Jahr 1696. | Jn Verlegung Petri Matthiæ Ministerii Candidati, als | hier in Husum an der Kirchen wohnhafft/ und bei | demselben zu bekommen.

8vo. [8], 208 pp.; A-N$^8$ O$^4$.                                            CKB

2789    MOLLER, JOHANNES

Jungferlicher Tugendschmuck am hochzeitlichen EhrenTage Mich. Jovers und Mariæ Cath. Bremers . . . Schleswig, 1696.

Folio.                                                                         *

*OHM* I, 430-1.

2790    PRÆTORIUS, AUGUST CHRISTIAN

(Trauermusik über Dorothea Benedikte Rantzau). Glückstadt: R. Janßen (1696)

Folio. χ$^4$.                                                                   *

Formerly in Kiel UL (LmC 22).

2791    RAGER, DETTLEFF

Traur-ODE, | . . . | Daniel Dieterich | von Buchwald/ | . . . | Dettleff Rager/ SS. Theol: Stud: | [woodcut: coffin] | [ornamental rule] | Glückstadt/ Gedruckt bey Reinhard Janßen/ 1696.

Folio. $\chi^2$.                                                          CKB

Verse.

2792 RECKEL, SIMON

Die | beständig harrende/ und nach dem himm- | lischen Reiche sich
sehnende/ | und | von GOTT wolvergnügte | Seele/ | . . . | Fr. Catharina |
Des Weiland | . . . | Hrn. BRODERI | BOISENS, | . . . | Hinterlassene
Frau Wittwe | . . . | auff Begehren ausgefertiget von | SIMONE
RECHELIO, Minist. Seniore. | [rule] | Schleßwig/ Gedruckt bey
Lorentz Eckstoroff [sic]/ Hoch-Fürstlichen | Hoff-Buchdrucker/ Anno
1696.

4to. 48, [16] pp.; A-H⁴.                                                  CKB

G1r, added title: *Christliches Andencken* | *beständiger Treue/* | *. . . .* There follows
verse by several hands.

2793 RICHERTZ, GEORG

Ehren-Ruhm | Und | Gnaden-Lohn/ | . . . | Herrn TOBIÆ | FABRI-
CII, | . . . | . . . am 10. Aug. 1696. abgefodert . . . | . . . | Von | GEORGIO
Richertz/ | Past. zu Altona | [rule] | Altona/ gedruckt Christian Rey-
mers/ Königl. privilegirter Buchdr.

4to. [4], 88 pp.; ):(² A-L⁴.                                              CKB

Appended: *Abdanckungs-* | *Rede/* | *Jn* | *Dem Trauer-Hause* | *gehalten* | *von*
*Johann Hermann Wilckens/* | *Pastore zu Wedel.* | [ornamental rule] | *AL-*
*TONA/* | *Gedruckt Christian Reymers/ Königl. privilegirten* | *Buchdrucker 1696.*
a⁴ b².

2794 ROSENBUSCH, J. C.

MARGARITA PRETIOSISSIMA | Oder: | Die köstlichste Perlen-
Zier. | . . . | Fr: Margaretha/ | Gebohrnen Bensin/ | . . . | HERRN | Hn:
Georg Bocken | . . . | Hauß-Perle/ | . . . | Componiret und in voll-
ständiger Music | gebracht | J. C. Rosenbusch/ | t. t. Organ. | Ein der
gantzen GeEhrtesten/ jetzo | Leid-tragenden Familie | Gehorsamst-
verpflichteter Diener. | [rule] | Glückstadt/ Gedruckt bey Reinhard
Janßen/ Königl. Buchdrucker. [1696]

Folio. $\chi^2$.                                                          CKB

Verse.

2795 SANDHAGEN, CASPAR HERMANN

Die | beständige Liebe Christi | . . . | Johannis Wildenheims | . . . | von |

Caspar Hermann Sandhagen/ Gen. Sup. allhie/ | ... | [rule] | Schleß-
wig/ gedruckt bey Lorentz Eckstorff/ Hochfl. Hof-Buchdrucker. [1696]

4to. 70 pp.; A-J⁴.                                                    CKB

J4 lacking, probably blank.

2796    SANDHAGEN, CASPAR HERMANN

Catechismus-Milch. Ploen, 1696.

12mo.                                                                  *

*Moller* II, 757.

2796A SCHLESWIG-HOLSTEIN-GOTTORFF. *Laws, statutes, etc.*

Hoch-Fürstl. | Schleßwig-Hollsteinische | Verordnung/ | Wie die
Cavallerie nnd [sic] Infanterie in den | Quartieren verpfleget werden
soll. [1696]

4to. χ⁴.                                                          KIEL UL

Issued by Duke Friedrich at Gottorff. Kiel UL has another edition without
misprint, 8pp.

2796B SCHLESWIG-HOLSTEIN-GOTTORFF. *Laws, statutes, etc.*

WJer Friderich von GOttes | Gnaden/ Erbe zu Norwegen/ Hertzog zu |
Schleßwig/ Holstein/ ... | ... | ... Gottoff [sic] den 27 July 1696.

Broadside.                                                            CKB

Decree establishing a market at Gottorff on Tuesdays.

2797    Sonnet | Uber | Die höchst- glück und erfreuliche | ALLIANCE | Jhrer
Hohen Excellence der Herrn Generals | Herrn CHRISTIAN | Gulden-
lew | Mit dem | Hochgebohrnen Fräulein/ | Frl. CHARLOTTE
AMELIE | Daneskjold/ | Gräfin zu Laurwigen | Als dieselbe den 27.
Novemb. 1696 höchst-feyerlich vollenzogen ward. | [below:] Kopen-
hagen/ | Gedruckt bey Jhr. Königl. Majest. und Universit. Buchdrucker
Johann Philip Bockenhoffer

Broadside (42.5 x 31.3 cm).                                           CKB

2798    THOMSEN, NICOLAUS

Der Reichthum des herlichen Erbes Gottes ... Leichpredigt über Anna
Maria Sameland. Schleswig, 1696

Folio.                                                                 *

*Moller* I, 682; *cf. Fortegnelse Bøger,* 1759, p. 112: "Anna Maria von Mander."

2799    TRACTAT | Nach Anleitung | Der | Dermahligen Conjuncturen |

Zwischen | Sr. Chur-Fürstl. Durchl. | zu Hannover/ | Und | Sr. Hoch-Fürstl. Durchl. zu | Schleßwig-Holst. | [rule] | Jm Februario 1696

4to. χ⁴ (15.8 x 11.5 cm). CKB

Another edition, presumably published outside monarchy, 16 x 10.7 cm.

2800 Das verjüngte Alter | Welches | Bey der Hochzeit-Feyr | . . . | . . . HERRN | ANDRES | Kellinghusen/ | . . . | FRAU | ABJGAJL/ | (Tit.) | Sel. Hn. Hans Martensen/ | Wollbenamten Handelsmann in Köge/ | Nachgelassenen Witwe/ | . . . | Von | Einem Freünde. | Imprimatur, | C. Bartholin. | [ornamental rule] | Gedruckt bey Jhr. Königl. Mayest. und Universit. Buchdrucker/ | Johann Philip Bockenhoffer. [1696]

Folio. χ². CKB

Verse.

2801 VERMEHREN, PAUL

Reyse Thränen über das Absterben des Grafen Friedrich Christian Danneskiold . . . Kopenhagen (1696)

Folio. *

*Thott* V/1, 347; *OHM* I, 698.

2802 Verordnung wie es am Buß- und Bet-Tage den 8ten May 1696 in dem Fürstenthum soll gehalten werden.

4to. *

*Cat. lib. Lehmann,* I, 1740, p. 111.

2803 VOLKMAR, JOHANNES

MEMORIA | FRIDERICI CORFEYI | . . . | Friedrich Korfey/ | . . . | Von | JOH. Volckmar/ SS. Theol. Licent. | Præpos. und Past. zu Jtzehoe. | [rule] | Glückstadt/ bey Reinhard Janßen/ Königl. | Buchdrucker/ im Jahr 1696.

Folio. 20 pp.; A-E². KIEL UL

2804 Wahrhaffter Bericht | daß | in denen | Fürstl. Anmerckungen | über | Die Nachricht | wegen der | Zwischen | Jhro Königl. Majest. | zu Dennemarck/ Norgewen [sic] &c. | Und | Jhro zu Schleßwig-Holstein Regierenden | Hoch-Fürstl. Durchl. | Herrn Hertzog Friderich | Erwachsenen Jrrungen | Keine Contradictiones und Jrrungen ent- | halten/ die Acta und Documenta, da es nöthig in- | tegra, und unzerstümlet beygeleget/ auch die Argumenta auff | richtigen Grund beruhen; und daß der Schrifftsteller unter dem Titul | (Kurtze jedoch gründliche

Anzeige) nichts reelles/ sondern nur leere | Wörter angeführet/ und seine vielfältige menschliche Schwach- | heiten der Welt zu erkennen gegeben. | Auff Hoch-Fürstl. gnädigsten Befehl gedrückt. | [rule] | Jm Monath Martio Anno 1696.

4to. 80 pp.; A-K⁴.                                          CKB; (KIEL UL)

Kiel copy has: "Norwegen."

2805  WEIGEL, ERHARD

Alß des | Allerdurchläuchtigsten Großmächtigsten | Königs und Herrn/ Herrn | Christian des Fünfften | Königs zu Dennemarck/ und Norwe-gen/ der | Wenden und Gothen/ Hertzogs bu Schleßwig/ Hol- | stein/ Stormarn und der Dittmarschen/ Grafens | zu Oldenburg und Delmen-horst/ &c. | Allerhöchsterfreuligster | Geburths Tag | Den XV. Aprilis Anno M DC XCVI. | Hochfeyerlich begangen wurde; | Wolte | Seine allerunterthänigste Devotion | Mit Vorstellung | Des an solchem Fest alljärlich in besonders merckwürdi- | gen Gegen-Stand und Gang erscheinenden | Heraldischen Himmels | Zu | Einem allergehorsamsten Glückwünsch/ bey per- | sohnlich-allerunterthänigster Aufwartung/ | Jn folgenden Zeilen | Ablegen | Erhard Weigel/ Röm. Kayserl. Maytt: | auch Pfalß Sultzb. Rath/ und Senior | Prof. Publ. zu Jena. | Imprimatur, | C. BARTHOLIN. | [ornamental rule] | Copenhagen/ Gedruckt bey Just Høg/ Academ. Buchdr.

Folio. χ².                                                   CKB

Verse.

2806  WEIGEL, ERHARD

Der geschmückte | Stern-Himmel/ | Welcher/ | den alten Heidnischen Greul an ihm/ | Durch die Wappen | Europæischer Stände | unter-druckt. | Zur Ehre des Alleinigen GOttes/ | Und | Hoher Potentaten in Europa | unsterblichem Nach-Ruhm. | Jnsonderheit zum ersten/ in Gestalt eines Königl. Throns/ dem | nächstes an den Nord-Pol grentz-enden/ und also höchsten | Monarchen/ | Dem | Allerdurchleuchtigsten Großmächtigsten | König und Herrn/ Herrn | Christian dem Fünften/ | König zu Dennemarck Norwe- | gen/ der Wenden und Gothen/ Hertzogen | zu Schleßwig/ Holstein/ Stormarn und | der Ditmarschen/ Graffen zu Oldenburg | und Delmenhorst/ | Seinem Allergnädigsten König und Herrn | Allerunterthänigst offerirt von | Erhard Weigeln/ der Röm. Käys. Majest. wie auch | Pfaltz-Sultzb. Rath/ und Seniore Prof. Publ. zu Jena. | [rule of type ornaments] | Gedruckt im Jahr 1696.

Folio. π², A² (A1+B²).                                       CKB

2807 WESTPHAL, JOHANNES

In JESU regno celebris victoria victi, | . . . | Daniel-Dieterich | von Buchwald/ | . . . | Von | M. JOH. WESTPHAL, Pastore zum | Krummenteich/ und Consistorij Mün- | sterd. Assessore. | [woodcut: coffin] | [ornamental rule] | Gedruckt im Jahr Christi 1696. [Glückstadt: Janßen]

Folio. χ². CKB
Verse.

2808 [WYGAND, AUGUST]

Aus der | Stadt Hamburg | RECESSEN | Und | Verfassungen | Angestellete kurtze Betrachtung | Zwoer Fragen: | I. Ob E. E. Raht berechtiget/ durch sein | Widersprechen/ die von der versamleten | Erbgesessenen Bürgerschafft ordentlich | gemachte Schlüsse zu vernichtigen/ oder | deren Krafft und Wirckung zu hemmen? | 2. Ob die Wahl der Rahts-Personen derge- | stalt/ daß die versammlete Erbgesessene | Bürgerschaft solche auf keinerley weise an | sich nehmen könne/ dem Rahte zustehe? | Nach deren Erörterung denen von E. E. Rahte wider | die Erbgesessene Bürgerschafft neulich erregeten Streitig- | keiten abzuhelffen. | [rule of type ornaments] | Gedruckt im Jahr 1696.

4to. A⁴. CKB

Place of publication uncertain: possibly Altona.

2809 [WYGAND, AUGUST]

Dero Königl. Majestät zu Dänne- | marck Norwegen/ &c. &c. | Bestalten Rahts/ | August Wygands/ | Entsetzter Vortrab/ | Oder | Kurtzer Anfang des künfftigen | Beweises; | Daß alles | Jn ermeltem Vortrab enthalten (I.) die reine/ lautere vor | GOtt und aller Welt bestehende Warheit bleibe; (2.) Darin der jetzo | prædominirenden Parthey des Hamburgischen Rahts nicht der tausendste Theil der | in ihnen zum Be- und Unterdruck der wehrten Bürgerschafft wohnenden Boßheit/ | noch weniger die bey dem gemeinen Gut in Hamburg vorgehende entsetzliche Diebe- | reyen enthalten oder vorgestellet; Und (3.) das von ermelter Rahts-Parthey darwi- | der durch getriebene und publicirte so genannte Warnungs-Edict eine verlogene/ Ehr- | lose/ calumnieuse und mit einem Wort/ Schelmische/ Büttels-feuerswürdige Schand- | Charteque sey/ dergleichen eher von unvernüfftigen Bauerflegeln/ als einem | GOtt- und Ehr-liebenden Magistrat zu vermuhten. | [rule] | Psal. LII, v.3.4.5. 6.10. | . . . | [rule of type ornaments] | Gedruckt in diesem 1696. Jahr.

4to. A-L⁴. CKB

2810   [Wygand, August]

Dero | Königl. Majest. zu | Dännemarck Norwegen &c. &c. | Bestalten
Raths | AUGUST WYGANDS | Unumbgängliche Vorstellung | Daß |
Einige anitzo in Hamburg unter die Leute gebrachte Me- | morial und
Briefe/ so Er respective an Königl. Majest. und einen Grossen Mi- | nister
geschrieben und sich darin die Stadt Hamburg in Königliche Gewalt
zuliefern anhei- | schig gemacht haben solle/ nicht die Seinige/ sondern
ohnzweifentlich von dem Herrn Syndi- | co Bosteln und der ihm an-
hangend prædominirenden Raths-Parthey erfunden und außge- | streuet
worden/ damit der wehrten Bürgerschafft mit dergleichen eingebildeten
Gefahr die | Augen verkleistert und Sie von der sonst zubefürchtenden
Einführung besserer Administrati- | ons-Ordnungen abgewendet/ her-
gegen unter den so lang vom Raht gesuchten Dominat ge- | bracht/ und/
mit einem Wort/ der Bürgerlichen Freyheit entsetzet werden mögen.
Wobey zu- | fällig die Frage erörtert wird: Wie und durch was für
Mittel E. E. Raht/ wenn Er sich wie- | der Ayd und Pflicht der Erbge-
sessenen Bürgerschafft Schlüssen zustimmig zuerklären | weigert/ zu
obliegender Schuldigkeit und Zustimmung anzuweisen | und zubringen
sey? | [rule of type ornaments] | Psalm. 4. v.3. | ... | Psalm. 5. v.9.10.11. |
... | [rule of type ornaments] | Gedruckt im Jahr 1696.

4to. A⁴.                                                                    CKB

2811   [Wygand, August]

Das | Unvergleichlichste Winckel-Rechte | Drey-Eck. | [crown] | [geo-
metrical emblem] | Auff | Jetzo Regierender Königl. Mayestät | zu
Dännemarck Norwegen | CHRISTIANI V. | Den XVten Aprilis 1696.
zum Fünfftzigsten | mahl eingefallenem Geburths-und daher stam-
mendem | Jubel-Feste auß aller unterthänigster Devo- | tion und Erge-
benheit entworffen. | [ornamental rule] | COPENHAGEN/ | Gedruckt
bey Jh. Königl Mayest. und Universit. Buchdrucker/ | Johann Philip
Bockenhoffer.

Folio. [A]-[B]².                                                            CKB

Verse.

2812   [Wygand, August]

Dero Königl. Majest. zu Dänne- | marck Norwegen | Bestalten Raths |
August Wygands | Vortrab/ | Der nach und nach von Jhm zu Ver-
theidigung seiner | Ehre und Unschuld heraus zugebenden Schrifften; Jn
welchem | Nicht nur eine kleine Anzeige geschicht/ daß das liebe |
Hamburg bey seiner eingebildeten Freyheit durch betreiben | Eines

Ehrbaren Raths/ insonderheit durch das Patrocinium und Schutz | so Sie
ungetreuen Verwaltern des Gemeinen Guts leisten/ in den elendesten |
Stand gerathen; sondern auch/ daß die gegen ermeldten Rath Wygand |
den 10ten May 1695. außgesprochene Urthel/ (Richterlichen Ehren
vorbe- | hältlich) eine Wider-Rechtliche/ auf lauter falschen Sätzen und
schändli- | chen Unwarheiten gegründete Sentenz sey; angewiesen; Die
Löbl. Bür- | gerschafft zugleich/ nebst der gantzen Ehrbaren Welt/ von
mehrgedachten | Rath Wygands aufrichtiger und zu nichts als Bestem
und Aufnehmen | der guten Stadt Hamburg abzielenden Intention |
versichert wird. | [rule] | Hiob V. v.11 & seqq. | . . . | [rule of type orna-
ments] | Gedruckt im Jahr 1696.

4to. 21, [3] pp.; A-C⁴ (C4 blank).                                   CKB

2813  ZITSCHER, PETER

Conciones miscellaneæ oder Sonderbahre Predigten über einige außerlesene, so wol Buß- alß andre, Texte der H. Schrift, der Glückstädtischen
Schloß-Gemeine zugeschrieben.  Glückstadt, 1696.

8vo.                                                                 *

*Moller* II, 1039.

2814  ZITSCHER, PETER

Letzte Rede . . . Glückstadt, 1696.

See No. 2680.


## 1697

2815  ANDREÆ, JOHANNES CHRISTOPHERUS

Die tröstende Hoffnung/ | . . . | Frau Margareta Lucia | Zuergin/
gebohrne Martini/ | . . . | von | Joh. Christoph. Andreæ, Pastore zu
Cappeln. | [rule] | Schleßwig gedruckt bey Lorentz Eckstorff/ Hoch-
fürstl. Hoff-Buchdrucker. 1697.

4to. 52 pp.; A-F⁴ G².                                                CKB

2816  ANDREÆ, JOHANNES CHRISTOPHERUS

Der wohlgepaarte Adel (in nupt. Benedikt von Alefeld und Ida Marg.
Rumor).  Schleswig, 1697

Folio.                                                               *

*OHM* I, 19.

2817    BOTSAC, BARTHOLD

Die | Persönliche | Hochzeit | Des | Sohnes Gottes/ | Welche | Nach
Anlaß des ordentlichen Evangelii | Dom. XX. post Trinit: | Seiner
Werthen Gemeine in St. | Petri Kirche versamlet | Jn Gott vorgetragen/ |
Und auff Begehren zum fernern Lesen und andächtigen | Nachsinnen im
Druck überlassen/ | Dero verordneter Pastor | BARTOLDUS BOT-
SACCUS, | SS. Theol. Doct. Ejusdemq; Prof. Regius in Univers: Hafn: |
[rule] | Copenhagen/ Gedruckt bey Jhr: Königl. Hoh. Buchdr: |
Joachim Schmedtgen/ | Verlegts Samuel Garmann/ Buchhändler 1697.

4to. [4], 36 pp.; $\pi^2$, A-D$^4$, E$^2$.                                CKB

Contains marginal notes in Latin.

2818    BRÜGGE, ANDREAS VON DER

Dem | Edlen/ Groß-Achtbahren und Hochbenambten | HERRN/ |
Michael Strüver/ | Weit-berümbten Banquier in der Königl. | Residence
Copenhagen/ | Und der | Edlen/ Viel-Ehr-und Tugend-belobten |
JUNGFER/ | Elsabe Christina | Eggers/ | Als | Vielgeliebten Hoch-
zeitern/ | Beglückwünschete | Jm Jahr 1697 den 12 des Wein-Monats |
aus Brüderlicher Pflicht/ | Andreas von der Brügge/ | J. U. C. | Imprima-
tur, | C. BARTHOLIN. | [rule of type ornaments] | COPENHAGEN/ |
Gedruckt bey Jhr. Kön. Mayst. und Universit. Buchdrucker/ | Johann
Philip Bockenhoffer.

Folio. $\chi^2$.                                                          CKB

Verse.

2819    BURCHARD, PETER ANTON

Bittre Thränen bey der Grabstette seines Bruders M. H. Burchardi. Kiel
1697

Folio.                                                                    *

*OHM* I, 81; formerly in Kiel UL (LmC 5-211).

2820    DENMARK. *Laws, statutes, etc.*

Verordnung | Wegen des Gestempelten Papiers. | . . . 26. Julij, Anno
1667. | [below:] Glückstadt/ Gedruckt bey Reinhard Janßen/ Königl.
Buchdrucker/ Jm Jahr 1697.

Broadside.                                                                 CKB

Decree originally issued by King Frederik III (No. 1337).

2821    DENMARK. *Laws, statutes, etc.*

WJR Christian der Fünffte/ | ... | ... Glückstadt/ den 5. Augusti, Anno 1697.

Broadside.                                                                CNA

Decree calling a meeting of the "Ober-Amptgericht" at Glückstadt 25 October.

2822   Die | Durch das Ehliche Liebes Band | Versüssete Aloë | ... | Michael Friderich | Thombsen/ | ... | Jungfer | Charlotta Amalia | von Hagen/ | ... | Von Dero | Gantz ergebendsten Diener | M. J. J. L. | Imprimatur, | C. Bartholin. | [rule] | Gedruckt bey Jhro Köngl. Maj. und Univ. Buchdr./ Joh. Phil. Bockenhoffer. [1697]

Folio. $\chi^2$.                                                           CKB

Verse.

2823   Einfältige doch Hertzliche | Trauer-und Trost-Zeilen | ... | Sr. Jørgen Berndrups | ... | KOPENHAGEN/ Gedruckt bey Conrad Hartvig Neuhof. [1697]

Folio. $\chi^2$.                                                        Oslo UL

2824   1. | Königliche | POSTULATA, | Welche | Der Hohen MEDIATION | den 24. Aug. 1696. zu Pinneberg | übergeben worden. | 2. | Fürstliche Antwort/ | Auff die | Von Königlicher Seiten den 24. Aug. 1696. | zu Pinneberg übergebene POSTULATA | Welche | Der Hohen MEDIA-TION | zu Pinneberg den 24./14 Septembr. 1696. | insinuiret worden. | 3. | Königl. REPLIQUE | Auff vorgesetzte | Fürstliche Antwort. | [rule] | Gedruckt/ ANNO MDC XCVII.

4to. 46 [2] pp.; A-F⁴ (F4 blank).                                          CKB

Place of publication uncertain.

2825   FRANCKE, WOLFFGANG CHRISTOPH

GOtt/ der Seelen außerwehlter Theil/ | ... | Frau Magdalena/ | Gebohrne Braschin/ | ... | Hn. OTTONIS NICOLAI | Lindholtzens/ | ... | Gewesene Ehe-Liebste/ | Samt dero kleinem Söhnlein/ | DETLEF GEORG, | ... | Von | Wolffgang Christoph Francken/ | Predigern der Gemeine St. Nicolai in Kiel. | [rule] | KJEL/ gedruckt bey Joachim Reumann/ ANNO 1697.

4to. [6], 33, [5] pp.; A-E⁴, F².                                           CKB

2826   FUCHS, GOTTFRIED

Kürtzlich doch Genugsamer | und zu länglicher | Unterricht und An- | weisung/ | Gereichend zum nützlichen Gebrauch | Derjenigen von | mihr | Gottfried Fuchsen. | Königl. Majest. zu Dennemarck und |

Norwegen &c./ Bestelten Brand-Directore | in Coppenhagen/ | Verfertigten Slangen-Brand- | Sprützen und Anbringer/ | Den Liebhabern und Erkauffern derselben/ zum | nöthigen und nützlichen Gebrauch auffgezeichnet | und mitgetheilet vom vor | benahnten. | [rule] | COPPENHAGEN/ | Gedruckt bey Jhr. Königl. Majest. und Universt. Buchdr. | Johan Philip Bockenhoffer/ 1697

4to. 16 pp.; A-B⁴.                                                     CKB

2827  GERKENS, SIMON PETER *and* HERMANN BERNHARD GERKENS

Ehren-Cypressen mit welchen das Grab ihrer Mutter beysteuerten Herm. Bern. und Simon Pet. Gerkens. Glückstadt, 1697.

Folio.                                                                  *

*OHM* II, 223.

2828  Die Himlische Vermählung | . . . | Georgia Göedin/ | . . . | Kürtzlich vorgestellet von | M. J.J.L. | [rule] | Gedruckt im Jahr 1697 [Copenhagen]

4to. χ².                                                                CKB

2829  JACOBI, ELIAS

Davids Gesang | Von | Drey Partheien/ | Das ist: | Eine Auffmunterung | Zur allgemeinen | Danckbarkeit/ | Vormahls in einer Predigt über | Psal: XCV. vers. I. | Dem Parlament von | Engeland vorgestellet/ | Jetzt in die Hochteutsche Spra- | che übersetzet/ und zur Proba | Anderer künfftig zum Druck zu | beforderenden verteutscher Englischer | Buß- und Danck Predigten/ | Auff Begehren zum Druk befordert | Von | ELIA JACOBI, | Teutschen HauptPastoren der Königl: Guarni- | son und der Teutschen Gemeine zu S. Sal- | vatoris auff Christianshafen | [rule] | Copenhagen/ Gedrukt bey Jhro Königl: Hoh: Buchd. | Joachim Schmedtgen 1697.

12mo. [10], 71, [3] pp.; )(⁶, A-C¹² (C12 blank).                        CKB

2830  JÜRGENSEN, D.

Die Verwechselung der Vergänglichen mit der Ewigen Hütten . . . Beerdigung des Herrn Georg Höllmers. Schleswig, 1697.

Folio.                                                                  *

Formerly in Kiel UL (LmC 9-126).

2831  JUNGHANS, M.

Was der Himmel außersehen/ | Jst anjetzo auch geschehen | Durch | Eheliche Vermählung | . . . | Hn. Rabe-Wilhelmen | von Scheel/ |

Erbherrn zu Scheelenburg/ &c. | Mit | Dem Hoch-Wollgebohrnen Fräulein/ | Frl. Amalia Schwartz/ | . . . | [woodcut] | . . . | Verpflichtester Client | M. Junghans. | [ornamental rule] | Kopenhagen/ | Gedruckt bey Jhro Königl. Majestet und Universit. Buchdrucker | Johann Philip Bockenhoffer/ 1697.

Folio. χ². CKB

Verse.

2832 KIEL. *University*

WJr Prorector, Decani und Professores der | Hoch-Fürstl. Hollsteinisch-Kielischen Universität thun kund . . . | . . . | . . . 13. Julii 1697.

Broadside. CKB; KIEL UL

Pronouncement condemning Friedrich Gramm, with decree by Duke Friedrich of Schleswig-Holstein that Gramm's publications be burned by the hangman.

2832A Der | Kirchhoff der erhöhten Welt/ | . . . | DETLEV, | Des Heil. Römischen Reichs Grafen zu Rantzou/ Herrn | . . . | Von | Einem/ | Dem HochGräflichen Leid-tragenden Hause/ | zu devoter Unterwürffigkeit sich schuldig bekennenden | Diener. | [skull & crossbones] | [rule] | Glückstadt/ Gedruckt bey Reinhard Janßen/ Königl. Buchdrucker. [1697]

Folio. χ⁴. SHLB

2833 KLUG, FRANZ ERDMANN CHRISTIAN

Glaubens-Grund oder erläuterter Katechismus Lutheri. Glückstadt, 1697.

12mo. *

*Bibl. Kirchhof,* I, 1746, p. 137.

2834 LANGJAHR, JOHANN JACOB

Kurtzgefaßte | Doch | Gründliche Anleitung | Zu | Leichter Erlernung | der | Teutschen | Sprache/ | Allen derselben Liebhabern | zum besten aufgesetzet/ und auf | Begehren zum Druck | befördert | von | M. Joh. Jacob Langjahr. | Verlegts | Johann Melchior Liebe/ | Buchhändl. in Coppenhagen. | [rule] | EJSLEBEN/ | Gedruckt bey Johann Dietzeln/ 1697.

12mo. A-G¹². HAB

Title printed in red and black.

2835 LASSENIUS, JOHANNES

Des | Umb die Christliche Kirche Hoch- | verdienten Herren | JOHAN-

NIS LASSENII, | Weyland der H. Schrift Hochberühm- | ten Doctoris, Professoris und Pastoris an | der Teutschen St. Petri Kirchen in | Kopenhagen | Angefangener | Biblischer Kern | und Außzug | Der gantzen Heil. Schrifft/ | Jn kurtzgefaßten Fragen mit richtiger | Antwort über jedes Capitel erwogen und beleget/ | nun aber zur Auffmunterung der Gottgeheilig- | ten Jugend continuiret und gantz | außgefertiget | Von | M. JOH. JACOB LANGIAHR. | Mit Königl. und Churfürstl. Privilegien | [rule] | Kopenhagen/ gedruckt bey Conrad Hart- | vig Neuhof/ Anno 1697.

8vo. [8], 503, [1] pp.; $\pi^2$, $^2\pi^2$, A-V$^8$, W$^8$, X-Gg$^8$, Hh$^4$.                 CKB

Title printed in red and black. Engraving of author on $\pi$1 verso.

2836    LASSENIUS, JOHANNES

Lobsingende Andacht, darinn D. Luthers, und anderer Christlicher Lehrer, alte und neue Lieder sind zusammengebracht zum Behuf eines Kirchen-Gesang-Buchs vor die teutsche Gemeine zu S. Petri in Kopenhagen: Mit einer Vorrede und Censur von D. Lassenio mit Fleiße wieder übersehen, und auf ein merckliches vermehret. Copenhagen, 1697.

12mo.                                                                            *

*Moller* II, 452. See No. 2320.

2837    Die letzte Pflicht | ... | Hn. Andres Kellinghusen/ | ... | Hertzgeliebten Söhnleins/ | ... | A. K. | ... | [ornamental rule] | Gedruckt bey Jhr. Kön. Maytt. und Universit. Buchdrucker | Johann Philip Bockenhoffer [1697]

Folio. $\chi^2$.                                                                 CUL

2838    MANUALE, | Oder | Kurtzer Begriff | Der | Schauenburgischen | Hoff-Gerichts- | Ordnung/ | So weit dieselbe jetziger Zeit bey dem | Pinnenberg-und Altonaischen Gericht | Jm vorgehenden | Summarischen Process | zu gebrauchen. | [rule] | Altona/ | Gedruckt bey Christian Reymers/ Königlichen privile- | girten Buchdrucker/ Jm Jahr 1697.

4to. 27, [1] pp.; A-C$^4$ D$^2$.                                                 KIEL UL

Herlufsholm copy: 4to. 20 pp.; A-B$^4$ C$^2$.

2839    MARPERGER, PAUL JACOB

Dero | Zu Dennemarck/ Norwegen/ etc. | Königlichen Majestät/ | Königs | CHRISTIANI V. | Staats/ Kriegs und | Friedens | JOURNAL, | Jn welchem/ | Nach kürtzlicher Erzehlung | Der Königl: Hohen Familie | Seiner Mayst: Preißwürdigste | Thaten/ | Chrono-

logischer Ordnung nach/ | Specificirt, | Und | Der Nachwelt zur ewig-
wehrenden Admi- | ration vor Augen gestellet werden/ | Von | P. J.
Marperger. | [rule] | COPENHAGEN | Gedruckt bey Jhro Königl. Hoh.
Buchdr. | Joachim Schmedtgen 1697.

8vo. 56 pp.; A-C⁸ D⁴. CKB

8vo. 56 pp.; A-C$^8$ D$^4$. CKB

2840 [MASIUS, HECTOR GOTTFRIED]

Kurtzer Bericht | Von | Dem Vnterscheid | Der wahren Evangelischen |
Lutherischen/ und der | Reformirten | Lehre/ | Nebst einem Anhang/
und | Erörterung folgender Fragen: | I. Ob zwischen den Lutheranern |
und Reformirten einige Religions-Einig- | keit und Brüderschafft zu
hoffen? | II. Ob nicht die Reformirten | Gewissens halber verbunden
seynd Krafft | ihrer eigenen Lehr-Sätze zu uns zu treten? | Entworffen
von | H.G.M.D. & P.P. | [rule] | Verlegt durch Johann Jost | Erythro-
pilum 1697.

12mo. [16], 364 pp.; a⁸ A-P¹² Q1-2. GÖTTINGEN UL

12mo. [16], 364 pp.; a$^8$ A-P$^{12}$ Q1-2. GÖTTINGEN UL

All after Q2 lacking, with no apparent loss of text. On p. 305, separate title:
*Kurtzer Anhang/ | und | Erörterung | Folgender Fragen: | . . . .*

2841 MAY, JOHANN BURCHARD

Jo. Burchard May/ | Eloqu. & Hist. Prof. P. | eröffnet | Der sämtlich
allhier studirenden Jugend | Jn Kiel | Seinen Vorschlag | wegen der
künfftig anzustellenden | Gelehrten Unterredungen. [Kiel 1697]

4to. χ⁴. KIEL UL

4to. $\chi^4$. KIEL UL

2842 MOLLER, JOHANNES

Abriß einiger obrigkeitlichen Tugenden, welche an Martin Jensen
Bürgermeistern zu Flensburg . . . nach seinem Tode . . . Schleswig, 1697.

Folio. *

*OHM* I, 430-1.

2843 MOLLER, JOHANNES

Pontisches Quodlibet . . . Hochzeittages Johann ther Straten und Magdal.
Doroth. Sülings. Schleswig, 1697

Folio. *

*OHM* I, 430-1.

2844 MÜLLER, CHRISTIAN RUDOLPH

Die Vortheilhaffte Reise | . . . | Fr: Catharinæ/ | Gebohrnen Fischers |
. . . | Hr. Francisci von Hagen/ | . . . | Ehe-Frauwen/ | . . . | Von | C. R.

Müller | [rule of type ornaments] | Gedruckt bey Jhr. Königl. Majest. und Universit. Buchdr. | Johan Philip Bockenhoffer. [1697]

Folio. χ².                                                                          OSLO UL

2845 NAGEL, JOHANN HELFRICH

Die | GOtt und Menschen | wohlgefällige | Orgel-MUSIC. | ... | Hr: Johan Conrad | Rosenbusch/ | Bey der Jtzehoischen Kirchen wohl-bestalter ORGANIST. | Mit der | Edlen/ Groß-Ehr und Tugendbegab-ten | JUNGFER | Hedwig Margareta | Müllerin/ | ... | Von | JOHAN. HELFRICH NAGEL, Sch. Gl. Rect. | [ornamental rule] | Glückstadt/ Gedruckt bey Reinhard Janßen/ Königl. Buchdrucker. [1697]

Folio. χ².                                                                          CKB

Verse.

2846 NELDELIUS, JOHANNES

Der biß in den Todt getreue Rath ... Arnold Mecklenburgs ... Schles-wig (1697)

Folio.                                                                               *

Formerly in Kiel UL (LmC 12-70).

2847 PFLUG, ERDMANN

Beicht- und Sacraments-Fragen. Glückstadt (1697?)

12mo.                                                                                *

*Moller* I, 495.

2848 PFLUG, ERDMANN

(Catechismus Sermone Germanico editus) Glückstadt, 1697

12mo.                                                                                *

*Moller* I, 495.

2849 RATECKENS, JOHANN PHILIPP

Freuden-Opffer | Bey | Der Höchst-erfreülichsten Gebuhrts-Feyer | Jhrer Königlichen Hoheit | Des | Durchleuchtigsten und Großmächtigsten Printzen und Herren | Herren FRIEDERICH, | ... | So Anno 1697 den 11ten Octobri ... | ... Johan Philip Rateckens. | [below:] Copenhagen/ Gedruckt bey Jhro Königl. Majest. und Dero Universit. Buchdr. Johan Philip Bockenhoffer.

Broadside (33.1 x 38.6 cm).                                                          CKB

2850   No. 199 1697 | [woodcut: courier] | Relations-Courier | Freytagis

12mo.                                                              DEUTSCH-NIENHOF

Single leaf, fragment.

2850A REYHER, SAMUEL

Neu erfundenes Uhrwerck/ nach welchem das Sonnen-Jahr also abge-
messen wird/ daß vermittelst desselben der Calender in einen gewissen
und der Natur gemässen Stand könte gesetzet werden. Kiel, 1697.

4to.                                                                     *

*Nova literaria maris Balthici 1698*, p. 38.

2851   ROGERS, NEHEMIAH

Geistreiche Schriften und Predigten. Copenhagen 1697

4to.                                                                     *

*Cat. lib. Terpager*, 1739, p. 13; *Verzeichnis Hans Christian Holst*, 1758, p. 26;
*Georgi* III, 310.

2852   ROGERS, NEHEMIAH

Spiegel der Barmhertzigkeit in zwei Gleichnissen der bekehrten Sün-
derinn und des barmhertzigen Samariters. Copenhagen, 1697.

4to.                                                                     *

*Cat. lib. Lehmann*, II, 1741, p. 287; *Georgi* III, 310: Copenhagen, 1698.

2853   RÜBKE, JACOB

Das | Grosse Glück | . . . | Jf. Elisabeth Scholten | . . . | Vorgestellet | Von |
JACOBO Rübke/ Pastore bey der | Reformirten Gemeine daselbst |
[rule] | Gedruckt bey Reinhard Janßen/ Königl. Buchd. | [Glückstadt
1697]

4to. 44 pp.; A-E⁴ F².                                                   CKB

2854   RÜDEMANN, JULIUS CONRAD

Die | sich zusammen verbindende | Palmen | . . . | Herrn | Johannis
Böhm/ | Gürtlern allhier/ | Und der | Wohl-Ehr und Tugend-begabten |
Jungfer | Catharinæ Mariæ | Dittmars/ | . . . | Derselben | Dienst-
schuldiger Freund/ | Julius Conrad: Rüdemann. Brunsv. | [ornamental
rule] | Copenhagen/ | Gedruckt bey Jhr. Königl. Mayest. und Univ.
Buchdrucker/ | Johann Philip Bockenhoffer. [1697]

Folio. $\chi^2$.                                                        CKB

Verse.

2855   SANDHAGEN, CASPAR HERMANN

Theologisches Sendschreiben (2. Theil). Schleswig, 1697.

12mo.                                                                                            *

*Cat. lib. Franc. Jul. Lutkonii*, 1723, p. 189; *Cat. univ. designati omn. libr. qui hisce Nundinus* ... (Easter) 1698 (Groß): *Anderes Zehen Theologischer Sendschreiben ... samt einer Vorrede und Continuation Herrn Henrici Muhlii. Schleswig: Lorentz Eckhoff.*

2856   SCHIRMER, MARTIN

Anleitung zur Zahl-Rechnung. Copenhagen, 1697.

8vo.                                                                                             *

*Thott* III/2, 243; *Cat. Kiesbye*, 1759, p. 83.

2857   SCHWARTZ, JOSUA

D. JOSUÆ Schwartzens | Königlichen General-Superintendentens/ und Consistorial- | Rahts/ in den Hertzogthümern Schleßwig-und | Holstein/ als auch Probstens zu Renßburg | Gründliche | Wiederlegung/ | Einer | Fast dem halben Theil des Schleßwig-Holsteinischen | Ministerii, im Majo des 1696. Jahres/ zur Buß-Pre- | digt fürgeschriebenen/ durchgehends aber dem | Chiliasmo dienenden | Außlegung | Des Siebenden Capittels Michæ. | Nachdem solche Wiederlegung/ am ersten Septembr. darauff/ | von E. E. Renßburgischen Synodo der Königl. Pröbste bemel- | ter Hertzogthümer/ zu Beybehaltung richtiger reiner | Lehre im Lande/ öffentlich außzugeben/ für | nöthig erkant war. | Der auch mit angehänget ist eine | Theologische Handlung | Mit Herr H. B. etlicher Chiliastischen Lehren wegen; auch wie/ | und aus was Ursachen/ Er denselben freywillig entsaget | habe. | [rule] | Glückstadt/ Gedruckt bey Reinhard Janßen/ Königl. Buchdrucker/ 1697.

4to. [16], 198, [2] pp.; a-b⁴, A-Bb⁴ (Bb4 blank).                          CKB; (BM)

2858   Der Studirenden in Kiel Musique, als die verwitwete Herzogin Friderica Amalia mit Printzen und Princessin aus dem Emserbad in Kiel wieder glücklich angelanget. Kiel, 1697.

Folio.                                                                                           *

*Thott* V/1, 340.

2859   THOMSEN, SAMUEL

Ein in Gott vergnügter Christ oder Leichpredigt über Martin Jessen, Bürgermeister zu Flensburg.... Altona, 1697

Folio.                                                                                           *

*Moller* I, 682.

2860 Tönning, Henrik

Uhrsachen warum er Lutherisch worden. Copenhagen, 1697

8vo.                                                                                          *

*Bibl. Botsackiana,* III, 1709, p. 103; *Cat. lib. Wandalini,* 1722, 8vo. Nr. 505.

2861 Trauer-Trost-Zeilen, welche bey dem Absterben des Herrn Gerhard Nayen ... überreichen sollte Ph.F. Kopenhagen, 1697.

Folio.                                                                                          *

Formerly in Kiel UL (LmC 13-8).

2862 (Trauergedicht auf Detlev, Reichsgraf zu Rantzau) Glückstadt: R. Janssen (1697)

Folio. $\chi^2$.                                                                                  *

Formerly in Kiel UL (LmC 4-15, 4-14).

2863 Wiederauffgelegte | PRIVILEGIA | Oder | Freyheiten/ | Welche Dero zu Dännemarck/ Nor- | wegen/ &c. Königl. Maj. Höchstsel. und | rühm- lichsten Angedenckens/ &c. | Der | Portugisischen NATION | Hebrä- ischer Religion, anch [sic] ihren Adhærenten und Fa- | milien/ so in der Veste Glückstadt anietzo residiren/ und in künf- | tig kommen möchten/ Allergnädigst hat mitgetheilet und gegeben | den 19. Junii Anno 1630. | Allen und ieden so daran gelegen zur dienstlichen | Nachricht aufs Neue zum Druck | befodert. | [ornament] | [rule] | Gedruckt/ Jm Jahr 1697.

4to. A-B⁴.                                                                                     CKB

2864 Wygand, August

Dero Königlichen Majest. zu | Dännemarck/ Norwegen &c. &c. | Be- stalltem Raht | AUGUST WYGAND | Abgenöhtigte | Vertheidigung/ | Wider die von seinen Hamburgischen | Feinden in aller Welt ausge- geiferte Verläum- | dung: Ob wäre Er Autor der vor einigen Tagen ans | Licht gekommenen kurtzen Vorstellung des zwischen Doct. Gott- | lieb Bürger-hold und Meister Freyheit-lieb gehaltenen | Gesprächs. | Wobey zugleich der Hamburgischen Bürgerschafft die | Gefahr/ worinn Sie sich anitzo/ auff einmahl umb ihre Freyheit | und alle zeitliche Glückselig- keit zu kommen/ befindet/ vorgestellet/ mithin ohnmaß- | geblicher Raht gegeben wird/ wie Sie sich zu dessen Abwend-und Wieder-Fest- | stellung ihrer ehmahligen Grund-Gesetze und daraus zustehenden Frey- heit und | Gerechtigkeiten in bevorstehender und künfftigen Versamm- lungen zu verhalten/ | und sich wider der prædominirenden Rahts-

Parthey intendirte | Unterdrückung handhaben könne. | [rule] | Ge-
druckt/ 1697.

4to.  A-B⁴ C².                                                    CKB

2865   Wygand, August

APOLOGIA WYGANDIANA | TRIPARTITA. | Oder | Dero Königl.
Majest. zu Dännemarck | Norwegen &c. &c. | Bestallten Raths | AU-
GUST WYGANDS | Jn drey Theilen abgefassete | Schutz u. Vertheidi-
gungs-Schrift | gegen E. E. Rath der Stadt Hamburg; | Deren der Erste
nebst einer kurtzen Erzehlung: Alles dessen was mit ihm | biß zu
Anfang des den 27. Octobr. 1693. wieder Jhn verhängten Arrests vor-
gangen/ und wie Er an den | Juden Meyer Marx und den von Selbem
an ihn gethanen Transport des in der Hamburgischen Banco | ver-
handenen Juvvelen-Uberschusses kommen; Zugleich gründlich darthut:
Daß ihm ermeldte | Banco oder dafür hafftende Gemeine Stadt den
transportirten Uberschuß/ so sich auf 792824. | Rthl. beläufft/ allerdings
zu schaffen und zu bezahlen schuldig und gehalten sey. | Der Andere
Theil beläuchtet den wider ermeldten Wygand von E. E. Rath ange-
zettelten | Process, so wol an sich selbst/ als die von dem Fiscali formirte
Beschuldigungen/ und zeiget bey deren Wi- | derleg und möglichst
kurtzer Anführung der so mannigfalt begangenen Iniqvitäten und
Nullitäten | Sonnen-klar: Daß Er in der höchsten Unschuld und ohne
das geringste Verbrechen began- | gen zu haben/ beklaget/ folglich
Nulliter und Wider-Rechtlich verurtheilet; Also E. E. Rath | Straff-bahr
und Jhm so wol nach gemeinen Käyserl. als Hamburgis. Stadt-Rechten
zu | aller gebührenden Satisfaction verbunden und gehalten sey. Worinn
dem geneigten Teutschem | Leser/ absonderlich der werthen Ham-
burgischen Bürgerschafft/ so der Lateinischen Sprache unerfahren/ zu
Gefallen/ | alle Lateinische Oerter und Termini, welche mann sich
anzuführen ohnmöglich entbrechen können/ zugleich ins | Teutsche
übersetzet zu finden. | Jn dem Dritten Theil wird bey Untersuchung:
Woher und wodurch das liebe eh- | mahls so herrlich blühende Hamburg
Zeit-hero in so jämmerlichen Verfall gerathen? gezei- | get: Daß zwar
solches durch eingerissene üble Administration der Heil. Justiz, Ver-
untrauung | Geist-und Weltlicher Güter und andere mehrere Neben-
Ursachen geschehen. Es wird aber zu- | gleich so wol in der Apologie
selbst/ als in der an Käyserl. Majest. vorgesetzten Aller-unterthänigsten |
Zueygnungs-Schrifft/ erwiesen: Daß an solchem und allen anderen
Hamburgischem Unwesen und | Streitigkeiten innsonderheit E. E. Rath/
die Hn. Ober-Alten und Herrn Cämmerey-Bürger | Schuld und Ursach
seyn. Wobey schließlich vor erst etliche wenige Wege und Mittel ange-

wie- | sen werden: Wo durch Hamburg wieder in ehmahlig Florissanten/ ja noch besseren/ Zu- | stand zu bringen sey. | [rule] | Gedruckt im Jahr M DC XCVII.

4to. [40], 284 pp.; a-c⁴, )(⁴, ²)(⁴, A-Mm⁴, Nn².                CKB; (KIEL UL)

2866  WYGAND, AUGUST

Dero Königlichen Majest. zu | Dännemarck/ Norwegen &c. &c. | Bestallten Rahts | AUGUST WYGANDS | Gründliche | Untersuchung/ | Ob die Hamburgische Bürgerschafft | befuegt/ wie Sie in der den 23. Sept. 1697. ge- | haltenen Versammlung gethan/ die ehmalig Schnittger | Jastramsche Sache wieder vorzunehmen/ und ob Sie im Fall E. | E. Rath gemeldte Persohnen keines Verrahts überführen kan/ | wie Er sich gleichwol in seinem den 25. Aug. 1686. angeschlagenem | Mandat anheischig gemacht/ die auf denen Thoren steckkende | Köpffe wieder abnehmen und ehrlich begraben | lassen könne? | Wobey zugleich der nichtig und ungegründete Vorwand | der prædominirenden Raths Parthey und anderer übel infor- | mirten Bürger: Ob hätte bey solcher Herunternehmung der Köpffe der Nie- | der-Sächsische Crays allerhand Unruhe zu befürchten; Nebst anderen Ein- | würffen hinweggeräumet/ der Bürgerschafft aber weiter unmaßgeblicher Rath | ertheilet wird: Wie Sie sich bey jetzig für ihre Freyheit so gefährlichen Zeiten | zu verhalten und endlich zu gewünschter Fest-setzung ihres wahren | Wohlseyns zu gelangen Hoffnung | haben könne? | [rule] | Gedruckt/ im Jahr 1697. [Altona]

4to. A-F⁴.                                                          CKB

F4 lacking, probably blank.

2867  WYGAND, AUGUST

Dero Königl. Maj. zu Dännemarck | Norwegen/ &c. &c. | Bestallten Raths | AUGUST WYGANDS | Unumgängliche/ doch Glimpffliche | Ablehnung | Der | Wie in aller Welt/ so auch insonderheit bey | seinem Allergnädigstem Könige und Herrn/ wieder | ihn angebrachten Beschuldigung: | Ob hätte er durch seine Zeithero wider Einen | Ehrbahren Rath der Stadt Hamburg ans Licht ge- | gebene Schrifften nichts anders als Aufruhr und Tu- | mult unter der Bürgerschafft anzurichten | gesuchet. | Wobey sich/ wie die wahren Absichten seines zeitheri- | gen Schreibens und anderer Unternehmungen | angeführet finden; | So weiter von dem elendem Verfall der lieben Stadt; | Wer daran Ursach? | Und wie der gäntzliche/ sonst nicht | mehr ferne Untergang zu ver-

hüten? | Kurtz/ doch gründlich erwehnet wird. | [rule] | Altona/ Jm
Jahr 1697.

4to. A-E⁴.                                                                    CKB

2868  WYGAND, AUGUST

Die unvergleichlich gleiche Buchstaben Zahl, der die Königlichen
Nahmen Christianus quartus, Fridericus tertius und Christianus quintus
und die von ihnen erwehlten symbola Regna firmat pietas . . . zum 51.
mahl eingefallenen Gebuhrts-Tage J. K. M. Christiani V. . . . entworffen.
1697.

Folio.                                                                         *

*OHM* II, 975.

2869  [Engraving of fire-fighting apparatus at Christiansborg, Copenhagen.
Explanatory text above, in a wreath, and below] [1697]
Text in wreath, "Sehet hier. Stelle | auff den Schloss Platz der Königl.
Residentz statt Copenhagen Jhro Königl. Maytt. | zu Dennemarck Nor-
wegen, meines Aller gnädigsten Erb-Königes und Herrn | vormals
bestalter Fontainier und Kunst Meister, nun aber Wirckl. Brant Direc- |
teur. ich Gottfried Fuchs gantz underdænigst. | der Curieusen Welt für
Augen | Meine von gantz Neü und Doppelter Wirckung erfundenen
Schlangen Spritzen | Welche Ao. 1693 D 14 Augusti in Eigener Gegen-
wart Aller Höchst gedachter | Jhro Königl. Maytt. und dero Ministern
auch Meines Vorwesers, des Sel. Brand | Directoris Herman Gerdings, als
einführers alhier der Holländischen Schlan- | gen Spritzen . . ."

Broadside (43.5 x 54 cm).                                                      CKB

Explanatory text is dated "Kopenhagen den 1 May Anno 1697."

## 1698

2870  Alß der | Durchlauchtigste Fürst und Herr | FRIEDERICH | . . . | Mit
Seiner | Durchlauchtigsten Gemahlin | HEDWIG SOPHIA | . . . | Jm
Kiel glücklichst angelanget/ | Wolten ihre unterthänigst-gehorsamste
Pflicht in einer Music abstatten/ | Die samptliche Studirende | [below:]
KJEL | Gedruckt bey Joachim Reumann/ Acad. Buchdr. 1698

Broadside (48.2 x 32.2 cm).                                                    CKB

2870A  Altonaischer MERCURIUS | N° 51 [woodcut: equestrian Mercury]
Und desselben | RELATION | aus | dem PARNASSO. | ANNO 1698.
den 17. Junii.

8vo. χ⁴. (Hamburg Staatsarchiv)

At end: *Diese Relation ist zu bekommen bey Christian Reymers/ Königl.* | *privilegiirten Buchdrucker in Altona.*

2871 Arnkiel, Troels

Christliche | Confirmation | Derer | Catechumenen/ | Wie die Jugend vor Empfahung des Sacra- | ments/ in der Gemeine GOttes vorgestellet/ aus | dem Heil. Catechismus soll examinirt, und in ihrem | Tauff-Bund und Christenthum confirmirt | werden/ | Von der Apostel Zeit an bißher/ | Aus der Heil. Schrifft/ und Antiquität der | Orientalischen und Occidentalischen Kirchen | N. Test. | Und der Jüdischen Kirchen A. Test. | Und der daher entstandenen Initiation der ehrbah- | ren welt-weisen Heyden/ nebst beygefügtem Bedencken | unserer Theologen/ beleuchtiget/ und recommendirt | Von | M. TROGILLO Arnckiel/ | Probsten und Pastoren zu Apenrad. | Zum andernmahl auffgelegt/ und hin und | wieder vermehrt. | [rule] | Schleßwig/ druckts und verlegts Lorentz Eckstorff/ | Hoch-Fürstl. Hoff-Buchdrucker. [1698]

4to. Pp. [1-24], 9-260, [1-4]; A-Mm⁴. CKB

On Mm3r, separate title: *Der* | *Regierenden Hoch-Fürstl. Durchl. zu* | *Schleßwig-Holstein.* | *gnädigste Verordnung* | *wegen der* | *Confirmation* | *derer* | *Catechu-menorum/* | *[rule]* | *Schleßwig/* | *Gedruckt bey Lorentz Eckstorff/ Hoch-Fürstl.* | *Hoff-Buchdrucker.*

2872 [crown above Charlotte Amalia's initials] | I. | Auff Jhr. Majest. der Königin | Gebuhrts-Jahr und-Tag. [1698']

Folio. χ². CKB

Caption title. Contains text accompanying engravings 1-18 in *Der Sieben und zwantzigste April Oder Erfreulichster Gebuhrts-Tag,* 1698 (No. 2945).

2873 Aufmunterungslied | Welches | Vor gehaltener lob-und glückwün-schungs- | rede | über die Höchsterfreuliche | Vermählung | Seiner Durchl. | Jn volständiger musik | abgesungen worden. [1698]

Folio. χ². SHLB

Occasioned by marriage of Duke Frederik IV of Schleswig-Holstein and Princess Hedwig Sophia of Sweden.

2874 Beselin, Johann Wilhelm

בעזה | Pyramidalische | Traur-und Ehren-Seule/ | ... | Achatius Ma-jus | ... | Von | M. Johann Wilhelm Beselin, Past. Wollerwig. Ton. Cim. | [rule] | Schleßw. gedruckt bey Lorentz Eckstorff/ Fürstl. Buchdr. [1698]

4to. A-C⁴. CKB

2875 BÜTEMEISTER, JOHANN DANIEL

Der Letzte Wille | ... | [ornamental rule] | Frau Christina/ | Hertzoginn
zu Schleßwig/ Hol- | stein/ ... | Von | Johann Daniel Bütemeister/ |
Des Bischoffthums Lübeck Superintend. und Hoff-Prediger | zu Eu-
thien. | [rule] | PLOEN/ | Gedruckt bey Tobias Schmidt/ Fürstl. Hoff-
Buchdrucker/ 1698.

Folio. [4], 72, [40] pp.; )(², A-Ff²; engraved portrait.          CKB

Title engraving of the deceased. On leaf T1, added title: *Die bey hohem Mittage*
*plötzlich untergehende* | *Fürsten-Sonne/* | ... | *Vorgestellet von* | *Christian*
*Specht.* | ... | *Ploen/ Gedruckt bey Tobias Schmidt/ Furstl. Hoff-Buchdrucker;*
on leaf Bb1, added title: *Trauriges Scheiden/* | *Doch* | *Freudiger Wechsel/* | ... |
*Otto Strickern/ Fürstl. Bischöffl. Pagen-Hoffmeister* | *Ploen/ Gedruckt bey Tobias*
*Schmidt ... ;* on leaf Dd1, added title, in Latin: *Memoriæ augustæ* | ... | *Andreas*
*van der Brügge* | *Ploenæ* | ...

2876 BURCHARD, BERNHARD

Das Testament und letzter Wille | des sterbenden JESU | ... | Frauen
Catharina | gebohrnen Clausen | ... | CHRISTOPHORI Francken |
... | hertzgeliebten Hauß-Ehre | ... | Von | BERNHARDO BURCH-
ARDO, | Dienern des Göttl. Wortes daselbst. | [rule] | KJEL/ gedruckt
bey Joachim Reumann/ Acad. Buchdr. [1698]

4to. [4], 37, [39] pp.; π², A-F⁴ [G]⁴ [H]², ²A⁴, [²B]⁴.          CKB; KIEL UL

Added titles on F3 (in Latin); [G1]: *Untergang* | *der* | *Tugend-Sonnen/* | ... |
*Paulo Hey, Phil. & Theol. Stud.;* [G3]: (in Latin); [H]1: *Der angetroffene*
*Frühling/* | ... | *Joach. Köhn* (No. 2909); ²A1 (in Latin) by F. D. Kohlius;
[²B1]: *Uber den seeligen hintrit* | ... | *Von* | G. C. S. (No. 2948); [²B3]: (in
Latin). Last two leaves include poems by several hands. CRL copy bound with a
Latin address from the University of Kiel, (A⁴).

2877 BURCHARD, PETER ANTON

Das bethränte Cimbrien über das Absterben Otto von Qualen auf Siggen
und Windebü. Kiel, 1698.

Folio.                                                                   ✱

*OHM* I, 81.

2878 COPIA | Eines | Schreibens | Jh. Römis. Käyserl. Majest. | An | Jhro
Königliche Majestät | zu Dännemarck und Norwegen/ &c. | Betreffend |
Die obhandene | Käyserl. Commission, | des Hamburgis. Wesens hal-
ber/ | Jmgleichen eine | COPIA des hierauf an dem Königl. Dänischen |
Raht und Præsidenten in Wien/ | Herr Urbich, | ergangenen | König-
lichen Rescripti und Ordre, | Worinn Jh. Königl. Maj. zu Dännemarck

breiter decla- | riren/ daß Sie die intendirte Kayserl. Commission durch-
aus nicht | zugeben könten/ sondern zur Observation ihrer habenden
hohen Rechte | alle darzu dienliche Mittel adhibiren und gebrauchen
wolten. | [rule] | Gedruckt den 20. Maji 1698.

4to. A⁴.

CKB

2879 DENMARK. *Laws, statutes, etc.*

CONSTITUTIO, | Betreffend | Die in den Städten der Hertzogtüh- |
mer Schleßwig und Holstein | verwürckte | Brüch-Gelder/ | Und qvô
ordine dieselbe bey den Concur- | sibus sollen collociret werden. | Sub
dato Glückstadt den 4. Novemb. | Anno 1698.

4to. χ².

CKB

Printed by R. Janssen in Glückstadt.

2880 DENMARK. *Laws, statutes, etc.*

CONSTITUTIO | Wegen der | Pfand-und Schuld- | PROTOCOLLEN |
Jn den Städten des Hertzogthumbs | Schleßwig/ | Als | Flenßburg und
Hadersleben. | Sub dato Glückstadt/ den 20. Septembr: | Anno 1698. |
[ornament] | [rule] | Gedrückt bey Reinhard Janßen/ Königl: | Buchdr.

4to. A-B⁴.

CKB

2881 DENMARK. *Laws, statutes, etc.*

CONSTITUTIO| Wegen der | Schuld-und Pfand- | PROTOCOLLEN |
Jn den Städten des Hertzogthumbs | Holstein/ | Als | Glückstadt/
Rendsburg/ Jtzehoe/ | Oldenschloe/ Crempe/ Wilster/ | Segeberg/
Heiligenhafen und | Lütkenburg. | Sub dato Glückstadt den 20.
Sebtembr: [sic] | Anno 1698 | [ornament] | [rule] | Gedruckt bey Rein-
hard Janßen/ Königl. | Buchdr.

4to. A-B⁴ C².

CKB

2882 DENMARK. *Laws, statutes, etc.*

Jhro Königl. Majest. | zu Dennemarck/ Norwegen &c. | Allergnädigste |
Verordnung | Und | CONFIRMATION, | Wornach sich die Fehr-
Schiffer und | Passagier zwischen hier und Hamburg in | Nehmung
und Gebung der Fracht-Gelder | laut folgenden Auffsatzes allerunter-
thä- | nigst zu verhalten. | Sub dato Copenhagen den 11. Octobris | Anno
1698. | [rule] | Glückstadt/ gedruckt bey Reinhard Janßen. | Königl.
Buchdr.

4to. χ⁴.

CNA

2883   DENMARK. *Laws, statutes, etc.*

WJR Christian der Fünffte/ | von GOttes Gnaden/ König zu Dänne-
marck ... | ... | ... 30. Martij, Anno 1698

Broadside.                                                    KIEL UL

Decree issued jointly with Duke Friedrich of Schleswig-Holstein, regarding the
prosecution of delinquents.

2884   DENMARK. *Laws, statutes, etc.*

WJR Christian der Fünffte/ | ... | ... Glückstadt/ den 31. Maij/ | Anno
1698

Broadside.                                                    CKB; CNA

Decree issued jointly with Duke Friedrich of Schleswig-Holstein, ordering the improvement of "Wege/ Stege und Dämme."

2886   DENMARK. *Laws, statutes, etc.*

WJR Christian der Fünffte/ | ... | ... 6. Junij, Anno 1698

Broadside.                                                    CKB

Decree establishing a reward for capture of the murderer of Christian Albrecht
Rantzau (†29 November 1697).

2887   DENMARK. *Laws, statutes, etc.*

WJR Christian der Fünffte/ | ... | ... 3ten Octobr: Anno 1698.

Broadside.                                                    CKB

Decree forbidding export of wood and taxing peat and charcoal.

2888   DENMARK. *Laws, statutes, etc.*

WJr Christian der Fünffte/ | ... | ... 28. Decemb, Anno 1698

Broadside.                                                    CKB

Decree issued jointly with Duke Friedrich of Schleswig-Holstein, ordering payment
of a "Princessin-Steuer" on the occasion of the marriage of Princess Friderica
Amalia.

2889   Dero Regierend Römisch | Kayserlichen Majestät | Aller-Höchstes |
Hand-Schreiben/ | An Königl. Majest. von Pohlen | de Dato Eberstorff
den 23. Sept. 1698. | Nebst der darauf | An | Allerhöchst ged. Kayserl.
Majest. | Von | Auch Allerhöchst-erwehnter | Königlichen Majest. von
Pohlen | würcklichem Rath und Residenten | im Nieder-Sächsischem
Crayse | AUGUST WYGANDEN | Geschehenen Aller-unterthänig-
sten | Vorstellung/ | de Dato Altona den 15. Octobr. 1698. | [rule] |
Gedruckt/ den 28. Oct. 1698.

4to.  A-E⁴ F².                                                CKB

2890  DUBRAVIUS, STEPHAN

Allerunterthänigstes Opfer │ So an den │ Allerdurchläuchtigsten/ Groß- │ mäch- │ tigsten König und Herrn/ │ Hn. CHRISTIAN │ den Fünften │ Erb-König zu Dennemarck/ Norwegen/ der Wen- │ den und Gothen/ │ Hertzog zu Schleßwig/ Holstein/ Stormarn │ und der Dittmarschen/ │ Grafen zu Oldenburg und Delmenhorst/ │ Am Tage dero Höchst- │ erfreulichen │ Geburths-Feyer Anno 1698. den 15. April. │ Zwar eilfertig/ doch mit tiefster Devotion, mit dero Reuterey │ auß Englischen Diensten kommende/ in Anwünschung einer │ langen und höchstgesegneten Regierung/ zu über- │ reichen sich erkühnet │ Jhrer Königlichen │ MAJESTET │ [ornament] │ Imprimatur, │ C. BARTHOLIN. │ Zu alleruntherthänigsten Gehorsam und eyfrigen │ Gebeth für Deroselben Leben verbun- │ denster Knecht │ S. Dubravius. │ [ornamental rule] │ KOPENHAGEN/ │ Gedruckt bey Johann Jacob Bornheinrich.

Folio. χ². CKB

Verse.

2891  ECCARD, JOHANNES NICOLAUS

Trauer-und Trost Schrifft │ Welche │ . . . │ Frauen ANNÆ, │ gebohrnen Würgerin │ . . . │ Hn. Henrich Bornemann │ . . . │ Frauen Eheliebsten/ │ . . . │ Imprimatur, │ C. BARTHOLIN. │ Johannes Nicolaus Eccardus │ Svinf. Francus. │ Bey denen Kön. Dän. Trouppen/ insonderheit bey Jhrer Mayest. der Königin/ wie auch Jhrer │ Königl. Hochheit des Cron-Printzen Regiment in die 6 Jahre gewesener Feld-Prediger. │ [ornamental rule] │ Gedruckt bey Seel. J. P. Bockenhoffers nachgelassenen Wittwe. [1698]

Folio. χ². CKB

Verse.

2892  ESMARCH, NICOLAUS LUDWIG

Traur-und Trost- │ Ode │ . . . │ Margareta Christiana │ von Waßmer/ │ . . . │ Von │ Nicolao Ludovico Eßmarch/ │ Pastoren zum Hertzhorn. │ [rule] │ Gedruckt bey Reinhard Janßen/ Königl. Buchdr. [1698]

Folio. [5] leaves. CKB

Includes verse signed by L. Wittmann & J. S. P. N.

2892A  FUCHS, JOHANNES

Johannes Fuchsen │ Holsteinisches │ Ding und Recht │ [rule] │ Kjel │ Bey Johann Sebastian Riechel/ 1698

4to. 36 pp.; A-D⁴, E². CKB

An earlier edition was published in 1687 (No. 2314). Riechel was a Kiel bookseller.

2893  Gantz kurtz zusammen gezogene | FACTI SPECIES, | Jn Sachen | WYGAND | Contra | Hamburg/ | Wobey/ nebst einer kurtzen Vor-| rede/ nicht | nur die in solcher Sache vor Wyganden ergangene al-| ler-höchste Käyserl. Cammer-Befehle und Decreta, sondern | auch eine Notarial-Verrichtung und Intimation, so Wy-| gand den 26. Sept. 1698. gegen Einen Hochweisen Raht be-| werckstelligen lassen/ der Ehrbaren Welt com-| municiret werden; | Woraus der geneigte Leser finden wird/ daß erwehn-| ter Raht die gegen Wygand abgesprochene Urthel so wenig | legitimiren oder rechtfertigen kan/ so wenig sie Wyganden eines einzigen | Verbrechens mit bestande Rechtens überführen | können oder wollen/ | Der Warheit zu Steuer/ | Entworffen | Von | Einem Wygand-ischen Freunde. | [rule] | Gedruckt den 27. Sept. 1698. [Altona]

4to. A-D⁴. CKB

2894  Gemeiner Bescheid/ | Betreffend | Die bey einem Zeugen-Verhör zu | formirende und zu übergebende Arti-| culos und Interrogatoria. | Sub dato Glückstadt/ den 8. Octobr. | Anno 1698.

Folio. χ². CNA

Also issued in 4to, χ² (CKB).

2895  GENTZEN, SIEGFRIED

(Trauergedicht über Detlev Rantzau). Glückstadt: R. Janssen, (1698?).

Folio. χ². *

Formerly in Kiel UL (LmC 4-11).

2896  GERKENS, SIMON

MAUSOLEUM CURARUM | . . . | Jungf: Margaretha | Christiana/ | Des HochWollgebohrnen Herrn/ | Herrn CONRAD | von Waßmer/ | . . . | Jungfer Tochter/ | . . . | Von | M. SIMONE Gerkens/ | Sloß-Pastore. | [rule] | Gedruckt bey Reinhard Janßen/ Königl. Buchdr./ im Jahr 1698.

Folio. 28 pp.; A-G². CKB

2897  GOUSSAULT, *Abbé*

Abbildung | eines | Ehrlichen und Tugend-| hafften | MANNS | Seinen | Unterschidlichen [sic] Qvalitä-| ten und hervorleuchtenden Tugen-| den nach/ durch welche Er sich beydes bey | GOtt/ bey der erbarn Welt/ seinen Neben-| Christen und sich selbst in Worten/ Wercken | und

Gedancken/ Mittel und Ende seines Le- | bens/ angenehm/ beliebt und wahrhafftig | glückseelig machen kan/ | betrachtet/ | und aus den entworffenen Frantzösis- [sic] | exemplar des Hn. von Goussault, in die- | sen Teutschen Tractat übersetzt | Von | PAVL JACOB MARPERGER. | [double rule] | COPPENHAGEN | Jn Verlegung Johann Jost Erytropels. | 1698.

12mo. )(⁶ (−)(6), A-H¹² J⁶.  Landesbibliothek Weimar

Title printed in red and black. J6 lacking, probably blank.

2898 Grubeville, J. Henr. de

Defensivum wider die Päbstler. Altona, 1698

4to.                                                            *

*Bibl. Muhliana,* 1735, p. 82.

2899 Gründlicher | Beweis/ | Daß dem von | Jhr. Königl. Majest. | in Pohlen/ | Nunmehro zu dero | Residenten | Jm Nieder-Sächsischen Cräyse/ | Verordnetem Königlichen Dänischen Raht/ | Hn. August Wygand/ | Von E. E. Raht die sichere und freye | Residence und Wohnunge in der Stadt Hamburg/ | nicht anders dann so wol zu allerhöchstgedachter Jh. Königl. | als auch Jhro Käyserl. Majestät selbst eignen Despect, Ver- | acht-und Beleidigung/ und des gemeinen Wesens ohnver- | meidlichen Schaden und Nachtheil verweigert | werden könne. | [rule] | Gedruckt im Jahr 1698.

4to. 19, [1] pp.; A-B⁴, C².                                   CKB

2900 Hamerich, Henrich

Das/ vor/ in/ und nach dem Tode/ | ungetrennete | Fürsten-Paar/ | . . . | Herrn Christians/ | Erben zu Norwegen/ Hertzogen zu Schleß- | wig/ Holstein/ . . . | Frauen | Agnes Hedewig/ | Gebohrnen und vermählten Hertzoginn zu | Schleßwig/ Holstein/ . . . | Von | Henrico Hamerich/ Hochfürstl. Probsten | und Hoff-Predigern daselbst. | [rule] | PLOEN/ Gedruckt durch Tobias Schmidt/ Fürstl. Hoff-Buchdrucker. [1698?]

Folio. 59, [5] pp.; [A]² B-Q².                               CKB

2901 Henningsen, Johann Friedrich

Als | Dem Durchlauchtigsten Fürsten | und Herrn/ | Herrn Friederich/ | Erben zu Norwegen/ | Hertzog zu Schleßwig/ Hollstein/ Stor- | marn und der Dittmarschen/ Grafen zu Olden- | burg und Delmenhorst &c. | Zu der | Anno 1698. den 2. Junii. | in Schweden auff Carlsburg | glücklich vollzognen Vermählung | Mit der | Durchlauchtigsten Princeßin | Hedwig Sophien/ | Der Schweden/ Gothen und Wenden | Erb-Prin-ceßin &c.&c.&c. | Jn einer | ORATIONE SOLENNI | unterthänigst gratulirte/ | Wolte nachfolgendes dabey absingen lassen | Jhrer Ho-heiten/ | Unterthänigst-gehorsamster Knecht | Joh. Fried. Henningsen/ Slesv. | [rule] | SCHLESWJG/ | Gedruckt/ bey Lorentz Eckstorff/ Hoch-Fürstl. Hoff-Buchdrucker.

Folio. χ². KIEL UL

Inserted in Kiel copy, Latin "Orationem panegyricum," χ².

2902  Hertzliche Condolence | Uber | . . . | Margareta Christiana | von Waßmer/ | . . . | Von | J. C. | [rule] | Glückstadt/ gedruckt bey Reinhard Janßen/ Königl. | Buchdr./ im Jahr 1698.

Folio. χ². CKB

On χ², Latin poem by Samuel Meyer.

2903  Jhro | Käyserl. Majestät | Hand-Schreiben/ | An | Königliche Majestät | von Dännemarck/ | Sub dato Eberstorff/ den 30sten Sept. 1698. | Das | Hamburgische | Commissions-Wesen | betreffend. | [rule] | Gedruckt den 19. Octobr. 1698

4to. )(⁴. CKB

Presumably published in Altona.

2904  Jhro | Königliche Majestät | von Dännemarck | RESCRIPT, | An den | Herrn Resident Lincker in Hamburg/ | Sub dato Copenhagen den 11. Octobr. 1698. | Wegen des | Käyserlichen an Jh. Königl. Majest. | den 30. Septembr. 1698. aus Eber- | storff abgelassenen | Hand-Schreibens/ | Welch Rescript der Herr Resident den 17. | Octobr. 98. Mittags um 11. Uhr E.E. Rahts Deputir- | ten Hr. Surlanden und Hr. Paulsen in die Feder dictiret | und mit zu Rahthause gegeben. | [rule] | Gedruckt den 19. Octobr. 1698.

4to. χ². CKB

Countersigned by T. B. von Wessen.

2905  Das in GOtt geheiligte und vergnüglich- | Ehelich-Lieben/ | . . . | Hn: JOHANNIS HIE- | RONYMI von Petkum/ | Hochberühmten S. S. Theologiæ Licentiati, | . . . | JUNGFER | Anna Catharina/ | Des wey-land | Edlen und Hochachtbahren | Herrn Joachim Stemann/ | . . . | Jungf. Tochter/ | Wolte auff ihrem Hochzeitlichen Ehren-Tage am 10. Maij des 1698. Jahrs/ | . . . | Jhro HochEhrwürden | Vorbundenstes |

Jtzehoisches Ministerium. | [rule] | Glückstadt/ druckts Reinhard Janßen/ Königl. Buchdr.

Folio. χ². CKB

Verse.

2907 KIEFFER, JOHANN CONRAD

Die | Von GOtt bestimte und dabey glückliche | Todes-Veränderung. | ... | Herr Otto Johann | von Grothuß | ... | Und | Der Wolgebohrner Herr | Hr. Johan Christoff | von Düring | ... | Johann Conrad Kieffern | Kirchen-Raht und Probsten zu Tundern | [rule] | Schleßwig/ | Gedruckt bey Lorentz Eckstorff/ Hochfürstl Hoff-Buchdr. [1698]

Folio. [2], 80 pp.; π1, A-U². CKB

2908 KIEFFER, JOHANN CONRAD

Sonderbahre | Predigten | So | Zu unterschiedenen Zeiten gehalten/ | Und itzt | Sampt einer vordem verfertigten | Trost-Schrifft | Zum | Druck übergeben worden | Von | JOHANN CONRAD Kieffer/ | Hoch-Fürstl. Kirchen-Rath und Hoff-Prediger. | [rule] | Schleßwig/ | Druckts und verlegts Lorentz Eckstorff/ Hoch-Fürstl. | Hoff-Buchdrucker. Anno 1698.

4to. [2], 178 pp.; π², A-Yy⁴, Zz². CKB

Separate title-page for each sermon. On leaf π2: *Das | Brennende Hertz/ | Der Jünger Christi. | . . . .* On leaf K1: *Der | Fürsichtige Gebrauch | Der Zeit. | . . . | Schleßwig/ | Druckts und Verlegts Lorentz Eckstorff/ | Hoch-Fürstl. Hoff-Buchdrucker;* on leaf Mm3: *Der | Uber Jerusalem | Weinende JEsus/ | . . . ;* on leaf Xx3: *Trost-Schrifft | JOHANN CONRAD Kieffers/ | Damit er | Die | Uber den frühzeitigen Todt/ | Des | Hochwohl-gebohrnen Herrn | Herrn Otto Rantzauen/ | . . . | Zum andermahl gedruckt.* (Cf. No. 2654.)

2909 KÖHN, JOACHIM

Der angetroffene Frühling/ | . . . | Fr. Catharina | Franckin/ gebohrne Clausen/ | den 27. Martii 1698. | . . . | Von | Joach. Köhn | [Kiel: Joach. Reumann, 1698]

4to. χ². KIEL UL

2910 Kurtzer | Jedoch auf festem Grund bestehender | Gegen-Beweis/ | Daß die zwischen | Jhre Königliche Majestät | zu Dännemarck Norwegen/ &c.&c. | Und | Jhre Fürstliche Durchläuchtigkeit | zu Schleswig Holstein/ &c.&c. | Annoch schwebende Differentien | Jnsonderheit was das | Exercitium juris Armorum, Fortalitiorum, | Collectarum & Fœderum | betrifft/ | Durch den Altonaischen Tractat entweder gar | nicht gehoben/

oder doch in demselben nicht vor/ sondern | wider Jhrer Durchl. itzo
führende Intention | decidiret worden; | Dem so genannten | Kurtzen
und gründlichen Beweis | entgegen gesetzet/ | Und auf Königl. aller-
gnädigsten Befehl gedruckt | Jm Monat Novembr. Anno 1698. | [rule] |
Altona/ bey Christian Reymers/ Königl. privileg. Buchdrucker.

4to. A-D⁴.                                                      CKB

2911   Kurtzer und Gründlicher | Beweiß | Daß die | Zwischen Jhrer Königl. |
Majest. zu Dennemarck | Norwegen | Und | Jhr. Regier. Hoch-Fürstl. |
Durchl. zu Schleßwig-Holstein | sich jetzo enthaltende Streitigkeiten
schon | vor und bey denen Altonaischen Tractaten gemachet/ | und
durch den daselbst errichteten Vergleich | decidiret und hingeleget
worden. | Aus denen Königl. Dennemarckischen ge- | druckten und
anderen zu Altonah communicirten | Schrifften genommen und mit
deren | eigenen Worten vorgestellet. | Auff gnädigsten Befehl höchstge- |
dachter Jhrer Hoch-Fürstl. Durchl. | zum Druck befodert. | [rule] | Jm
Monath September Anno 1698.

4to. 20 pp.; A-B⁴, C².                                          CKB

Another edition: 4to, 36 pp., A-D⁴, E², possibly printed in Sweden.

2912   LANGJAHR, JOHANN JACOB

Die Siegende | Ehren-Palme/ | . . . | HERRN | Conrad Biermann | von
Ehren-Schild/ | . . . | abgebildet von | M. Joh. Jac. Langiahr | Imprima-
tur, | C. BARTHOLIN. | [ornamental rule] | Gedruckt in Copenhagen/
bey Seel. Joh. Phil. Bockenhoffers | Nachgelassenen Wittwe. [1698]

Folio. χ².                                                      CUL

2913   LASSENIUS, JOHANNES

Das | Betrübte/ und von GOtt Reichlich | getröstete | Ephraim | Jn |
Hundert Vier und Achtzig | Seiner | Geistlichen Anfechtungen; | Wie
die in seinem fast 30. jährigen öffentlichen | Lehr-Amt/ an unter-
schiedenen Orten/ | bey Beicht-und Pfarr-Kindern ihm | vorgekom-
men/ | Und so viel dagegen gesetzten | Trost-Reden/ | Aus den süssen
Krafft-und Trost-Qvellen der | Heil. Schrifft zusammen getragen/ | und
zu Aufferbauung der Kirchen GOttes/ | und aller geistlich Angefoch-
tenen ferneren | heiligen Trost/ | an das Licht gesetzt hat | JOHANNES
LASSENIUS, | Weiland der Heil. Schrifft D. P. P. Consist. Assess. und |
Pastor an St. Petri Kirche in Kopenhagen. | Unter Kön. Dähnischen und
Churfl. Sächs. allergnäd. Privilegiis. | Zum andernmahl auffgelegt. |
[rule] | Kopenhagen und Leipzig/ | Verlegts Joh. Melchior Liebe/ |
Buchhändl. | Gedruckt bey Christian Scholvien/ im Jahr 1698.

8vo. Pp. [1-14], 1-944, 941-1180, 1081-1216, [1-62]; a$^8$ (−a7, 8),b1, A-Ssss$^8$ (Ssss7, 8 blank); engraved title-page; 16 plates. CKB

Title printed in red and black. The plates are the same as in 1693 edition. Engraved preliminary title same as 1692 edition, including date, 1692, but lacking title engraving of author.

2914 LASSENIUS, JOHANNES

Ewigwährender | Freuden-Saal | Der | Kinder Gottes/ | Darinnen von der Freude des | ewigen Lebens/ nach Anleitung | der H. Schrifft/ ausführlich gehandelt | wird/ mit hinzugethanen 23. Gewis- | sens-Fragen/ Geistreichen An- | dachten und Liedern: | Zur Ehre GOttes und Erbau- | ung der Christlichen Kirchen | heraus gegeben | Von | Hn. Johanne Lassenio, | S.S. Theol. Doct. Profess. P. Colleg. | Consist. Assess. und Pastore der Teutschen | Gemeinde zu St. Petri in Copen- | hagen; nunmehro Seeligen. | [rule] | Copenhagen/ | Zu finden bey Joh. Melchior Lieben | Buchhändler. 1698.

12 mo. [24], 374, [10] pp.; a$^{12}$ (±a1), A-Q$^{12}$ (a12, Q11-12 blank). HAB;
KAREN BRAHE

A reissue of the second edition of Lassenius' *Him*[m]*els-Freud und Höllen-Leid* . . . (1693) (No. 2619). Preliminary title of original, with "und Höllen-Leid" printed over to be illegible, faces new title-page.

2915 MARTINI, GOTTLIEB

Der | Schönheit Krafft | bey Vertrauung | Tit: | Hn. Adolph Georg | Berner/ | . . . | Und der | Tit: Jungfer Jungfer | Anna Margaretha | Bürgerin | Hrn. JOHANNES HENRICI | BÜRGERI, | Gewesener Rector zu Mannheim in der Pfaltz an itzo wolbestalter Col- | lega bey der Lateinischen Schule in Bremen | Ehelichen Jungfer Tochter. | Am 24 Novembr. Anno 1698. | [emblem] | Imprimatur, | P. VINDINGIUS. | gepriesen von | Gottlieb Martini. | [ornamental rule] | Copenhagen/ Gedruckt bey Seel. J. P. Bockenhoffers Nachgelassenen Wittwe.

Folio. χ$^2$. CKB
Verse.

2916 MAY, JOHANN BURCHARD

Jo. Burchard May/ | Eloqu. & Hist. Prof. P. | Eröffnet hiemit | Allen und jeden Liebhabern | Der | Teutschen | Redekunst/ | Eine kurtze und gründliche Anleitung | zu derselben. | Wobey zugleich die bißhero durch | dero verabsäumung heut zu tage | eingeschlichene Fehler kürz- lich | angezeiget werden. | [rule] | KJEL/ | Gedruckt bey Joachim Reumann/ Acad. Buchdr. | 1698.

4to. 20 pp.; A-B$^4$ C$^2$. KIEL UL

2917  MEIER, H. J.

Als | Die Wohlgebohrne Jungfer | Margareta Christia- | na von Waß-
mer | . . . | H. J. Meier LL. Stud. | [rule] | Glückstadt/ gedruckt bey
Reinhard Janßen/ Königl. Buchdr. [1698]

Folio.  χ².                                                                    CKB

Verse.

2918  MOLLER, JOHANNES

Das freye doch Christ-gewidmete Ehe-Leben Christoph Crusii Cantoris
in Flensburg und Agathæ Mollerii . . . Schleswig, 1698

Folio.                                                                          *

*OHM* I, 430-1.

2919  MOLLER, JOHANNES

Die nach dem Schiffbruch abermahl gewagte Schiffarth an der andern
Heyrath Henrich Strickers Statsherrn in Flensburg mit Doroth. Sophia
Christianin vorgestellet.  Schleswig, 1698

Folio.                                                                          *

*OHM* I, 430-1.

2920  MONCK, FRANTZ

Des | Obristen | FRANCISCI MONCK | Medicinalischer | RAMON- |
NEUR. | [rule] | PLOEN/ | Gedruckt durch Tobias Schmidt/ Fürstl. |
Buchdrucker/ 1698.

8vo. 86, [2] pp.; A-E⁸, F⁴ (F4 blank).                                          BM

On A7r, separate title: *Nachricht und Ver-* | *zeichniß* | *Derer elenden Menschlichen
Zu-* | *fälle/ bey welchen mein so ge-* | *nannter* | *RAMONNEUR* | *Sehr offt und viel
hundert* | *mahl/ durch Gottes Segen/ heil-* | *sam appliciret, von hohen/ mittlern/
und* | . . . .

2921  [MUHLIUS, HEINRICH]

(Kurze Anleitung zur Erklärung der Bußtexte. Ps. 2. 12).  Schleswig,
1698

4to.                                                                            *

*Jöcher/Rotermund* V, 170.

2922  NAGEL, JOHANN HELFRICH

Die | gar zu früh verwelckte | MARGARIS, | . . . | MARGARETÆ-
CHRI- | STIANÆ von Waßmer/ | . . . | Von | JOHAN. HELFR.

NAGEL. Sch. Gl. Rect. | [rule] | Glückstadt/ gedruckt bey Reinhard Janßen/ | Königl. Buchd. 1698.

Folio. [A]-[B]².                                                              CKB

With Latin verse by several hands.

2923  OPORINUS, CONRAD

Die süß-tröstende künfftige Herrligkeit | Der Kinder Gottes | . . . | Johann Ellermanns | . . . | Von | M. CONRADO OPORINO | Pastore Primario daselbst. | [rule] | KJEL/ | Gedruckt bey Joachim Reumann/ Acad. Buchdr. [1698]

4to. 86, [10] pp.; A-M⁴.                                                      CKB

2924  Die Passion des Glaubens Cron/ aus den Evangelisten als den allerge-wisseste die Zeugniß können geben von Christi Todt und Leben einfältig betrachtet und in kurze Reimen gebracht/ des Nahme heißt Felsen Freund/ der JEsum hertzlich meynd. Ploen: Tobias Schmidt (1698?)

8vo.                                                                          *

*Cat. univ. designatio omn. libr. qui hisce Nundinus . . . (Easter) 1698 (Groß).*

2925  QVESTEL, CASPAR

Caspar Qvestels/ JCti, | Hochfürstl. Holstein-Plönischen bestalten | Hoff-und Consistorial-Raths | Kurtze/ | doch gründliche | Vorstellung | Eines auch im Tode | getrosten Christen/ | Dessen Ursachen/ | Bey diesen letzten fast glaublosen | Zeiten/ | aus Göttlichem Worte/ | zu nützlichem Unterricht/ | Sonderlich aber denen Schwachgläubi- | gen/ zu er-baulicher Auffmunterung/ | von selbigem wohlmeinende mit | ange-führet werden. | [rule] | PLOEN/ | Gedruckt durch Tobias Schmidt/ Fürstl. Hoff- | Buchdr. Jm Jahr Christi 1698.

8vo. [24], 88 pp.; )(⁸, A-F⁸.                          LANDESBIBLIOTHEK WEIMAR

Title printed in red and black.

2926  QVESTEL, CASPAR

Caspar Qvestels/ JC. | Hochfürstl. Holstein-Plönischen bestalten | Hoff-und Consistorial-Raths | Nützlicher Unterricht | Von | Schuldiger Beob-achtung | Der | Rechtmässigen | Gelübden/ | Derer Beschaffenheit | Vornehmlich aus H. Göttli- | cher Schrifft/ | Und dabey so wol | Aus geist- als weltlichen Rechten | gründlich angezeiget/ | Auch | Mit alten und neuen Exempeln | deutlich erklähret/ | Und/ samt einer kurtzen Vorrede/ in unter- | schiedlichen angezeigten Capiteln | vorgetragen wird. | [rule of type ornaments] | PLOEN/ | Gedruckt und verlegt durch Tobias Schmidten/ | Fürstl. Hoff-Buchdrucker. 1698.

4to. [16], 136 pp.; )($^8$, A-H$^8$ J$^4$.                                    HAB

2927  RACHEL, THEODOR

Traur-und Trost-Zeilen | . . . | Jungfer Margareta | Christiana von Waßmer/ | . . . | Von | THEODORO RACHELIO. | [woodcut: coffin] | [rule] | Glückstadt/ gedruckt bey Reinhard Janßen/ | Königl. Buchd. 1698.

Folio. $\chi^2$.                                                                CKB

Verse.

2928  REYHER, SAMUEL, *editor*

Samuel Reyhers/ JCti, | Bey der Hoch-Fürstl. Holst. Universität | Codic. und Mathematum Prof. | Jn Teutscher Sprache vorgestellter | EU-CLIDES, | Dessen VI. erste Bücher | auf sonderbahre Art/ | Mit Algebraischen Zeichen/ also eingerichtet sind/ | daß man derselben Beweise auch in andern | Sprachen gebrauchen kan. | [double rule] | Kiel/ 1698. | Gedruckt durch Joachim Reumann/ Acad. Buchdr.

4to. [18], 392, [2] pp.; )($^4$, ):():($^4$, ):($^2$, A-Ccc$^4$, $\chi^2$.         CKB

2929  RICHERTZ, ARNOLD

Die Tugend stirbet nicht. | . . . | Jungfer Margareta | Christiana/ | . . . | DE WASMER | . . . | ARNOLD Richertz, Alton. | SS. Th. St. | [rule] | Glückstadt/ gedruckt bey Reinhard Janßen/ Königl. Buchdr. [1698]

Folio. $\chi^2$.                                                                CKB

Verse.

2930  RICHERTZ, G. B.

Der Todt der beste Freywerber/ | . . . | Jungfer Margareta | Christiana/ | . . . | DE WASMER, | . . . | Von | G. B. Richertz, Alton. | [rule] | Glückstadt/ gedruckt bey Reinhard Janßen/ Königl. Buchdr. [1698]

Folio. $\chi^2$.                                                                CKB

Verse.

2931  ROSENBUSCH, JOHANN KONRAD

(Trauermusik durch zwei Chöre vorgestellt [nur Text]) Glückstadt: R. Janssen (1698?)

Folio. 2 leaves.                                                               *

Formerly in Kiel UL (LmC 4-12).

2932 Rüdemann, Julius Conrad

Der | Höchstgeschätzte Braut-Schatz/ | . . . | Herr | ELOVIUS | MANGOR | . . . | Jungfer | JOHANNA | Heerfordtin/ | Des | Sehl. Herrn Christophori Heerfordts | gewesenen Königl. Apotheckers allhier | Nachgelassene Jungfer Tochter | . . . | Der 30ste Tag des Monaths Maji des 1698sten Jahres/ . . . | . . . | Von | Untengezeichneten | Imprimatur, | C. BARTHOLIN. | [ornamental rule] | Gedruckt bey Sehl. Joh. Phil. Bockenhoffers nachgelassenen Wittwe.

Folio. $\chi^2$.                                                                    CKB

Verse.

2933 Schirmer, Martin

PRACTICA | GEOMETRIÆ, | Worinnen enthalten unterschiedliche | PROBLEMATA, | So zur Fortification, wie auch | vielen Mathematischen Wißen- | schafften/ nützlich und höchst- | nötig sind/ | Zu unterthänigsten/ unterthänigen | und gehorsamsten Dienst dererjeni- | gen/ so sich seiner Information | gebrauchen/ | Heraus gegeben | von | Martin Schirmer. | [ornamental rule] | Gedrukkt im Jahr Christi 1698.

8vo. [2], 56 pp.; $\pi$1, A-C$^8$ D$^4$.                                            CKB

Presumably printed in Copenhagen. CKB copy bound with Schirmer's *Compendium geometriæ*, 1690 (No. 2481).

2934 Schleswig-Holstein-Gottorff. *Laws, statutes, etc.*

MANDAT | Wegen | Der Betteler.

4to. $\chi^4$.                                                                      SHLB

Issued by Duke Friedrich of Schleswig-Holstein, dated 21 November 1698.

2935 Schleswig-Holstein-Gottorff. *Laws, statutes, etc.*

MANDAT | Wegen | Der Pferde und anderen | Diebereyen.

4to. )($^4$.                                                                        CKB

Issued by Duke Friedrich of Schleswig-Holstein, dated 21 November 1698.

2936 Schleswig-Holstein-Gottorff. *Laws, statutes, etc.*

Verordnung | Des | Gestempelten | Papiers. | [rule] | Schleßwig/ | Gedruckt bey Lorentz Eckstorff/ Hoch- | Fürstl. Hoff-Buchdrucker.

4to. 16 pp.; A-B$^4$.                                                               Kiel UL

Dated at end, "10 Februar. Anno 1698."

2936A Schleswig-Holstein-Gottorff. *Laws, statutes, etc.*

WJr Friderich von GOttes | Gnaden/ Erbe zu Norwegen/ Hertzog zu |
Schleßwig/ Holstein/ . . . | . . . | . . . Gottorff/ den 1. Februarii An. 1698.

Broadside.                                                                                    CKB

Decree requiring the recording of contractual obligations.

2937 Schleswig-Holstein-Gottorff. *Laws, statutes, etc.*

WJr Friderich von GOttes | Gnaden/ Erbe zu Norwegen/ Hertzog zu |
. . . | . . . 3. Febr. Anno 1698.

Broadside.                                                                                 Kiel UL

Decree requiring penance of women bearing children less than seven months after
marriage.

2938 Schleswig-Holstein-Gottorff. *Laws, statutes, etc.*

WJr Friderich von GOttes | Gnaden/ Erbe zu Norwegen/ Hertzog zu |
. . . | . . . 3. Mart. 1698

Broadside.                                                                                    CKB

Decree regarding the arrest of highwaymen and the lodging of strangers.

2939 Schleswig-Holstein-Gottorff. *Laws, statutes, etc.*

WJr Friderich von GOttes | Gnaden/ Erbe zu Norwegen/ Hertzog zu |
. . . | . . . 17. Septembr. 1698

Broadside.                                                                                 Kiel UL

Decree forbidding the making of brandy.

2939A Schleswig-Holstein-Gottorff. *Laws, ordinances, etc.*

VOn GOTTes Gnaden Wir FRIDE- | RICA AMALIA gebohrne
Königliche Erb- | Princesse zu Dannemarck/ Norwegen/ . . . | . . . | Kiel
den 4. Octobr. Anno 1698.

Broadside.                                                                                 Kiel UL
Decree forbidding the making of brandy.

2940 Schleswig-Holstein-Gottorff. *Laws, statutes, etc.*

WJr Friderich von GOttes | Gnaden/ Erbe zu Norwegen/ Hertzog zu |
. . . | . . . 21 Octobr. 1698

Broadside.                                                                                 Kiel UL

Decree forbidding export of grain and taxing brandy.

2941 Schleswig-Holstein-Gottorff. *Laws, statutes, etc.*

WJr Friderich von GOttes | Gnaden/ Erbe zu Norwegen/ Hertzog zu | ... | ... 21. Novemb. 1698.

Broadside (2 sheets pasted together). KIEL UL

Decree regarding thefts of horses and other livestock, and requiring a certificate of sale for horses to be exported from the Duchies.

2941A SCHLESWIG-HOLSTEIN-GOTTORFF. *Laws, statutes, etc.*

WJr Friderich von GOttes | Gnaden/ Erbe zu Norwegen/ Hertzog zu | Schleßwig/ Holstein/ ... | ... | ... Gottorff den 21. Nov. 1698.

Broadside. CKB

Decree against beggars and holders of false passports. Two leaves pasted together.

2942 SCHLESWIG-HOLSTEIN-GOTTORFF. *Laws, statutes, etc.*

WJr Friderich von GOttes | Gnaden/ Erbe zu Norwegen/ Hertzog zu | ... | ... 4. Dec. 1698.

Broadside. KIEL UL

Decree limiting the number of godparents at a baptism and taxing marriages and baptisms solemnized at home.

2943 Den | Schmertzlichen Hintrit | ... | Margareta Christiana/ | ... von Waßmer/ | ... | S. | S. S. | [woodcut] | [rule] | Glückstadt/ gedruckt bey Reinhard Janßen. [1698]

Folio. χ². CKB

Verse.

2944 SCHWEINITZ, DAVID VON

Die Kleine Bibel/ | Das ist/ | Summarien/ | Uber die H. Bibel/ so wol derer Histori- | schen Texte/ als der vornehmsten Lehren und Ver- | mahnungen/ | jedwedern Capitels. | Jn Teutsche Vers gebracht | Durch | Weil. Hn. David von Schweinitz auf Seyf- | fers-und Petersdorff/ Fürstl. Liegnitz. Rath und Landes- | Hauptman/ | Anjetzt aufs neue mit Fleiß übersehen/ und besonders von | vorigen Druck-Fehlern ge- | säubert. | [ornamental rule] | PLOEN/ Gedruckt bey Tobias Schmidt/ Fürstl. | Hoff-Buchdrucker/ 1698

Oblong 8vo. [48], 550, [10], 1 pp., pp. 12-142; A-Pp⁸, Aaa-Hhh⁸, Jii². HAB

On Pp4r, new pagination starts with separate title: *Vierdter Theil | Der Kleinen Bibel/ | Das ist: | Summarien/ | über das | Neue Testament/ | .... *Text within rule borders. Another edition, identical with that of 1698, dated 1699.

2945 Der | Sieben und zwantzigste April | Oder | Erfreulichster Gebuhrts-Tag | Unser | Allergnädigsten Landes Mutter | Fraw | Charlotte Amelie | Königin zu Dännemarck Norwegen etc. | So Anno 1698 zum dreysigsten

mahl in Dännemarck | celebriret worden | [ornamental rule] | Gedruckt
im Jahr 1698

Folio. $\pi^2$, (a)-(d)$^2$, A-J$^2$, [)(]$^2$, )()($^2$, )()()($^2$; [1], 18 engravings.          CKB

Title printed in red and black. Leaves A1-J2 contain engravings 1-18, and are
printed on recto only. Author is either Johann Bartram Ernst or Georg Friedrich
de Franckenau. *Cf.* No. 2872.

2946   SIVERS, PETER AUGUST

Paßions-Catechismus/ | Oder | Die Historia des bittern | Leidens und
Sterben | Jesu Christi/ | Von den vier Evangelisten ein- | hellig be-
schrieben | Jn Fragen und Antwort der | Jugend und derselben Leh- |
rern zu gut gestellet | Und | Mit vielen nützlichen und Er- | baulichen
Anckungen allenthal- | ben gezieret/ | Von | Einem Verehrern des |
Creutzes Christi | [rule] | Schleßwig/ | Gedruckt und verleget/ | Durch
Lorentz Eckstorff/ Hoch-Fürstl. Hoff- | Buchdr. 1698

8vo. [8], 232 pp.; )($^4$, A-O$^8$, P$^4$.          LUTHERAN THEOLOGICAL SEMINARY,
PHILADELPHIA, PA.

2947   [STÖCKEN, CHRISTIAN VON]

Die vernünfftige lautere Milch des heiligen Catechismi. Gl(ückstadt),
1698

12mo.                                                                                    *

*Bibl. Lehmanianae,* I, 1740, p. 89.

2948   Uber den seeligen hintrit | . . . | Fr. Catharina | Franckin/ | gebohrner
Clausin | . . . | Von | G.C.S. | [Kiel: Joachim Reumann, 1698]

4to. $\chi^2$.          KIEL UL

2950   WALDSCHMIDT, WILHELM HULDERICUS

Anchora Salutis | Pro | Variolosis. | Offenbahrung und Be- | schreibung
eines gewissen Liquoris | oder Medicaments, nicht allein von de- | nen so
genanten Kinder-Pocken oder Blattern und | Masern/ die Kinder damit
zu præserviren/ | sondern auch selbige gantz sicher zu | curiren. | Worbey
zugleich der rechte Grund | der Artzney-Kunst/ aus der so genannten |
Cartesianischen Philosophie gezeiget/ und der Theè- | Tranck von denen
falschen und irrigen impu- | tationibus frey gesprochen wird. | Jtzo zum
andernmahl zum Druck befördert und mit | nöthigen Anmerckungen
vermehret | Von | Wilhelm Huldreich Waldschmiedt/ | der Medicin
Doctore und Professore Ordinario | in Kiel. | [rule] | Gedruckt bey
Joachim Reumann/ Acad. Buchdr. | 1698.

4to. [4], 48 pp.; $\pi^2$, A-F$^4$.          HAB

2951  WILDHAGEN, CASPAR

Die GOtt-geheiligte höchstzulässige | Priester-Ehe/ | Bey dem Göttlichen
Trawungs-Band | Des Hoch Ehrwürdigen/ Andächtigen und Hochge-
lahrten Herrn/ | Herrn JOHANNIS HIERO- | NYMI von PETKUM |
. . . . | Jungf: Anna Catharina Stemann/ | . . . . | CASPARO WILD-
HAGEN | 1698 | [below:] Glückstadt/ gedruckt bey Reinhard Janßen:
Kön. Buchdr.

Broadside (38.5 x 29 cm).                                          CKB

Verse.

2952  WILDHAGEN, CASPAR

Die zwar Früh-zeitig verwelckte/ | Doch woll-zeitig versetzte | Himmels-
Blume: | . . . | Jungf: Margareta | Christiana/ | . . . | von Waßmer/ |
. . . | Von | CASPARO Wildhagen/ | Pastore an der Stadtkirchen zu
Glückstadt/ . . . | . . . Assessore. | [rule] | Glückstadt/ gedruckt bey Rein-
hard Janßen/ 1698.

Folio. 22, [2] pp.; [a]², b-f².                                    CKB

f2 contains a Latin poem by Johs. Fecht. Inserted between last 2 leaves in CKB copy
is a Latin poem, in folio, by Johannes Klein.

2953  WYGAND, AUGUST

Dero | Königl. Majest. in Pohlen | Würcklichen | Rahts und Residentens |
Jm Nieder-Sächsischen Cräyse/ | Mein | AUGUST WYGANDS, | Jns
Kurtze gezogene/ ehemahlige | APOLOGIE, | Wie solches in einer
zwischen Mir/ und einem | redlichen Freunde/ CATO genannt/ vor- |
gefallenen | Unterredung | geschehen: | Wobey zugleich eine aber-
mahlige Notarial-Verrichtung/ | und meine zwar an E. Hochw Rath uñ
die Hrn. Ober-Alten drey- | mahl præsentirte/ aber allemahl wieder
zurückgeschickte Memoriale, so Sie de- | nen anderen Löblichen Collegiis
und endlich der Erbgesessenen Bürgerschafft | selbst/ an Hand zu
bringen/ ersuchet worden/ commu- | niciret werden. | [rule] | Gedruckt
den 10. Octobr. 1698. [Altona]

4to. A-D⁴ ²D⁴.                                                    CKB

²D4 lacking, probably blank.

2954  WYGAND, AUGUST

Jhro | Königl. Majestät | von Pohlen &c. | Würcklichen Raths und
Residen- | tens im Nieder-Sächsischen Crayse | Mein | AUGUST WY-
GANDS | Letzte | Warnung/ | An | Die löbl. Erbgesessene Bürger- |

schafft in Hamburg. | [rule of type ornaments] | Gedruckt/ den 29. Octobr. 1698.

4to. A-B⁴.                                                                    CKB

2955   WYGAND, AUGUST

Die | Wegen des versetzten | Aller-Durchlauchtesten Nahmens/ | Zugleich Aller-vortrefflichste | Buchstabs-Verwechselung/ | Da der | Aller-Durchlauchteste Großmächtigste | Königliche Nahme/ | CRISTI-ANUS | QUINTUS, | DANIÆ, NORWEGIÆ, | VANDALORUM GOTHO- | RUMQUE REX, | Auf dem Anno 1698. den XV. Aprilis abermahls | eingefallenem | Geburths-Tage | Allerhöchstgedachter Jhro Königl. Majest. | dreymahl verwechselt | Jn allerunterthänigster Devotion und Ergebenheit ausgearbeitet | und überreichet worden | Von | Dero Königlichen Majestät | Allerunterthänigstem Knecht | Rath August Wyganden. | [rule] | Altona/ gedruckt bey Christian Reymers/ Königl. privil. Buchdr. | [rule] | ZVr ZeIt aLs ChrIstIan Der FVnffte/ DänIsch NorVVegscher | KönIg Ins ZVVo VnD FVnffzIgste Iahr trat.

4to. χ².                                                                    CKB

Verse in German and Latin.

2956   WYGAND, AUGUST

Die zwischen dem Rahte und Bürgerschaft der Stadt Hamburg A. 1697 gewechselte Schriften, von ihm, mit einigen Zugaben, ausgegeben. (Altona) 1698.

4to.                                                                            *

*Moller* II, 975.

## 1699

2957   BOLDICH, ERNST CHRISTIAN

(Leichpredigt über Andreas Günther). Kopenhagen, 1699.

Folio.                                                                          *

*Bibl. Joannes Grammius*, 1748, p. 102; *Bibl. J. M. Krafft*, 1752, p. 21.

2958   BURCHARD, BERNHARD

(Trauergedicht über Anna Magdalena Musaeus, geb. Musaeus) Kiel: Reuther (1699?)

4to. χ².                                                                        *

Formerly in Kiel UL (LmC 78-58).

2959 CRUSIUS, JOHANNES

Genealogische Beschreibung der Succession oder Erbfolge des König-
reiches Groß-Britannien, wie dieselbe sich von Jacobo I. Stuarto, Könige
von Groß-Britannien, auf alle Blutsverwandte Königliche, Chur- und
Fürstliche, Häuser erstrecket, in zwey Tabellen verfasset. Schleswig,
1699.

4to.                                                                          *

*Moller* II, 158; *Index bibl. And. Höjer,* 1752, p. 146.

2960 DENMARK. *Laws, statutes, etc.*

CONSTITUTION, wegen der | Visitation der Kirchen/ und derselben
Kosten. | Sub dato Glückstadt den 11. Decembr. | Anno 1699.

Broadside. [2] pp.                                                      CKB

Caption title.

2961 DENMARK. *Laws, statutes, etc.*

Königl. Pinnenbergische | CONSTITU- | TION. | [rule] | Gedruckt
ANNO 1699.

4to. A-B⁴.                                                              KIEL UL

2962 DENMARK. *Laws, statutes, etc.*

Königliche | CONSTITU- | TION. | Uber das | Pinnenbergische Schuld-
und | Pfand-PROTOCOLL. | [rule] | Gedruckt im Monat Decembr.
ANNO. 1699.

4to. A-B⁴.                                                              CNA

2963 DENMARK. *Laws, statutes, etc.*

Königs Christians | Des Fünfften/ | Dänsches | Gesetz. | Aus dem
Dänschen ins Teutsche | übersetzet. | Worbey die Gleichstellen/ und
einige | Oerter/ die Verwandtniß mit | einander haben/ | So woll aus
dem Gesetze/ als aus | denen Königlichen Verordnungen/ die | nach
Verkündigung dieses Gesetzbuchs | von A. 1683 biß A. 1698 heraus
gegeben | worden/ am Rande mit ange- | führet seyn. | Durch | H. W. |
[ornamental rule] | COPENHAGEN/ | Gedruckt bey Jhro Königl.
Hoh. Buchdr. Joachim | Schmedtgen/ im Jahr 1699.

8vo. [22], 104, 112, 142, 110, 84, [4] pp.; π⁶, a⁸ (−a1,7,8), A-F⁸ G⁴, ²A-G⁸, ³A-H⁸
J⁸ (−J8), ⁴A-F⁸ G⁸ (−G8), ⁵A-E⁸ F⁴.                                     CKB

Books I, II, III-IV, V, VI are separately paginated. The last page of the second book
is incorrectly numbered 86. Another edition with identical wording: 8vo, [24], 104,

112, 142, 110, 84, [4] pp.; a⁸, A-F⁸, G⁴, ²A-G⁸, ³A-H⁸ J⁸ (−J8), ⁴A-F⁸ G⁸ (−G8), ⁵A-E⁸ F⁴. Editor is Heinrich Weghorst.

2964 DENMARK. *Laws, statutes, etc.*

WJR Christian der Fünffte/ | . . . | . . . Glückstadt den 9. Febr. Anno 1699.

Broadside.                                                                          CNA

Decree against vagabonds and beggars.

2966 DENMARK. *Laws, statutes, etc.*

WJr FRIEDERICH der Vierdte/ | von GOttes Gnaden/ König zu Dännemarck/ Norwegen/ . . . | . . . | . . . Glückstadt/ den 1sten September, Anno 1699.

Broadside.                                                                    CKB; CNA

Decree ordering the ringing of bells as a sign of mourning for King Christian V.

2967 DENMARK. *Laws, statutes, etc.*

WJr Friderich der Vierdte/ | von Gottes Gnaden/ König zu Dennemarck/ | . . . | WJr Friderich/ Erbe zu Norwegen/ | . . . | . . . Gottorff/ | den 20. Sept. Anno 1699.

Broadside.                                                                    CKB; CNA

Decree ordering continued ringing of church bells in mourning for King Christian V.

2969 DENMARK. *Laws statutes, etc.*

WJR Friederich der Vierdte/ von | . . . | . . . Glückstadt den 30. Septemb: Anno 1699

Broadside.                                                                          CNA

Decree issued jointly with Duke Friedrich of Schleswig-Holstein, regarding mourning for King Christian V.

2970 DENMARK. *Laws, statutes, etc.*

Wir Friederich der Vierte/ von GOttes | . . . | . . . 9ten October, Anno 1699

Broadside.                                                                      KIEL UL

Decree ordering mourning for King Christian V.

2971 DENMARK. *Laws, statutes, etc.*

WJR Friederich der Vierdte/ von | GOttes Gnaden/ König zu Dännemarck/ . . . | . . . | . . . Glückstadt/ den 8. Decemb. Anno 1699.

Broadside.                                                                                      CNA

Decree ending mourning for King Christian V.

2972  DENMARK. *Laws, statutes, etc.*

WJR Friederich der Vierdte/ von │ ... │ ... Glückstadt/ den 8ten Dec.
Anno 1699.

Broadside.                                                                                      CNA

Decree issued jointly with Duke Friedrich of Schleswig-Holstein, regarding introduction of the Gregorian calendar. Two editions, with slight variations.

2973  DENMARK. *Laws, statutes, etc.*

WJR Friederich der Vierdte/ von │ GOttes Gnaden/ König zu Dänne-
marck/ Norwegen/ ... │ ... │ ... Glückstadt │ den 11. Decembris, Anno
1699.

Broadside.                                                                                  CKB; CNA

Decree limiting expenditures for church visitations in Pinneberg. Also issued as a
single 4to leaf with caption title: *CONSTITUTION, wegen der* │ *Visitation der*
*Kirchen/ und derselben Kosten* (No. 2960).

2975  Die Europäische │ [FAMA]

12mo. χ⁴. Pp. 369-376.                                                        DEUTSCH-NIENHOF

Issue No. 47, "vom 22. Junius 1699." Caption title. Published in Altona.

2976  FUCHS, JOHANNES

JOHANNIS Fuchsen/ JCti, │ und weil. Bürgermeisters zu Kiel/ │
Vollständiges │ INVENTA- │ RIUM, │ Wie solches nicht nur │ Richtern/
Advocaten/ Notarien/ Actuarien/ │ und andern/ welche in Gerichten
umbgehen/ │ Sondern allen │ Rechnungs-Bedienten/ │ So wohl │ Ampt-
Cam̃er-und andern Schreibern/ │ als │ Verwaltern/ Pensionarien/ Vor-
mündern/ Erben/ Kirchen- │ Waysen-und Armen-Vorstehern/ auch
allen denjenigen/ welche frembde │ Sachen und Güter in Besitz-oder
Verwaltung/ und davon │ Rechnung zu thun schuldig/ zu wissen von- │
nöthen und dienlich/ │ Vormahls in lateinischer Sprache/ nach heutiger
Praxi, aus │ bewehrten Rechts-Lehrern und täglicher Erfahrung deut-
lich │ und ausführlich beschrieben/ │ Anjetzo aber zu sonderbahren
Nutzen und Gebrauch/ der lateinischen Sprach │ unerfahrnen/ in die
teutsche übersetzet/ mit einer nützlichen Anweisung/ wie ein Vor- │
mund sich in Einricht-und Ablegung seiner Rechnung zu verhalten/
auch/ wie │ sonsten eine jede Rechnung wohl und genau zu untersuchen/
vermehret/ │ und mit einem vollkom̃enen Register versehen/ │ Von │ N.

G. S. G. W. | [rule] | PLOEN/ Gedruckt und verlegt durch Tobias Schmidt/ Fürstl. Hoff-Buchdr. 1699

4to. [20], 154, [18] pp.; )(⁴, )( )(⁴, )( )( )(², A-X⁴, Y² (Y2 blank).                    CKB

2977   (Gedichte auf Lucia Margareta Petrejen). Schleswig, 1699.

                                                                                          *

*Gl. kgl. Saml.* 3020, leaf 56v (CKB).

2978   GIESE, AUGUST

Spiegel | Des | Heutigen Christenthums | Jn Betrachtung | Der Almo-sen | Darin klärlich zufinden ihre wahre | Beschaffenheit/ auch Noth-wendigkeit | und Nutzen; | Wie schlecht solche Gebühr in acht ge- | nommen werde | Sambt allerley Vorschläge | Auff was weise der Armen Verpfle- | gung formlicher einzurichten sey/ | Anch [sic] Beantwortung dessen/ was da wie- | der konte gesagt/ auch wol pflegt einge- | wandt zu werden | Auffgesetzt | von | Augusto Giesen/ weyland | Rathsverwanten und Fürstl. | Gerichts-Secret. der Stadt | Husum | [rule of type orna-ments] | SCHLESWJG/ | Druckt und verlegt durch Lorentz Eckstorff/ Hoch-Fürstl. | Hoff-Buchdr. 1699.

8vo. 320+[16] pp.; A1, )(⁸, A2-8, B-V⁸.                                                    CKB

Title printed in red and black. Instruction to binder on p. 320 that gathering )( is to be inserted after title-leaf. In CKB copy it has been bound between gatherings A and B.

2979   GIESE, AUGUST

Der | Weh-schreiende | Stein | Oder | Ausführlicher Bericht | Von | Dem Greuel/ | Daß man | Die Diener der Justiz | nicht zu Grabe tragen/ | Auch | Etlicher Frauen in Kindes-Nöthen | niemand helffen wollen: | Samt Erweisung Christlicher Pflicht in | solchen Noth-und Liebes-Diensten. | Wol-meinend auffgesetzt | von | Augusto Giesen/ weyland | Raths-Verwannten und Fürstl. | Gerichts-Secretario in Husum. | [double rule] | SCHLESWJG/ | Druckt und verlegt durch Lorentz Eckstorff/ Hoch-Fürstl. | Hoff-Buchdr. 1699.

8vo. 78, [4] pp.; A-E⁸ χ1.                                                          MUNICH UL

Colophon: *HAMBURG/ | Jn Verlegung Henrich Heußen/ | bey dem es auch an der BANCO zu bekommen ist.* "Vorrede" bears date 1687, of Hamburg edition.

2980   HAHN, HINRICH

Die aus dem Elend dieses Lebens glücklich gerissene Seele . . . Margarethe Elisabeth Arnds. Glückstadt, 1699

Folio.                                                                                                    *

J. Hellmann, *Süder-Dith. Kirchen-Historie,* 1735, p. 81; *OHM* II, 271; H. Bruhn in *Jb. Ver. Dith. Landesk.* V (1925), p. 92.

2981  HAHN, HINRICH

Der gekröhnte Klotz . . . Abdanckungsrede über Stephan Clotz. Glück-stadt, 1699

Folio.                                                                                                    *

J. Hellmann, *Süder-Dith. Kirchen-Historie,* 1735, p. 81; *OHM* II, 271.

2982  HAHN, HINRICH

Die Großmütige Heldtin | . . . | Anna Catharina | Schultzin/ | Gebohrnen Heldtin/ | . . . | Von | M: HENRICO Hahn/ | Præp: und Past: zu Meld. | [rule] | Glückstadt/ gedruckt bey Reinhard Janßen/ Königl. | Buchdr./ im Jahr 1699.

Folio. 22 pp.; [A]², B-F².                                                                      CKB

F2 lacking, probably blank.

2983  HAHN, HINRICH

Die mühseelige Pilgrimschafft des gegenwärtigen Lebens, in einer Abdanckungsrede . . . Frau Justits-Rähtin C. M. Gudin . . . Glückstadt, 1699

                                                                                                          *

J. Hellmann, *Süder-Dith. Kirchen-Historie,* 1735, p. 81.

2984  HANNEMANN, JOHANN LUDWIG

(Trauergedicht über Anna Magdalena Musaeus, geb. Musaeus). Kiel: Reuther, (1699?)

4to. $\chi^2$.                                                                                          *

Formerly in Kiel UL (LmC 78-57).

2985  Hoch-Fürstl. Holstein-Gottorffische | Declaration, | Die Einhaltung des Schanzen-Baues | betreffend. | Jm Monath October/ 1699.

4to. $\chi^4$.                                                                                          CKB

2986  HOLYK, GEORG

Dreyfaches Garten-Buch. Kiel, 1699

8vo.                                                                                                    *

*Bibl. Lehmanianae,* 1741, p. 70; *Cat. lib. Oksen,* 1738, p. 70.

2988   JACOBI, ELIAS

(Trost-Gedicht . . . Margaretha geb. Rohwerin Gärtner). Copenhagen,
1699.

Folio.                                                                    *

*OHM* II, 218.

2989   JOHANN Fuhrmanns | Türcken- | Calender/ | Auffs 1699 Jahr | Alten
und | Neuen Styli | Schleßwig gedruckt/ bey Lorentz Eckstorff.

16mo. [A]$^{16}$ B$^8$.                                                    CKB

Woodcut of Turk's head centered on title-page. On B1, separate title: *Kleines* |
*PROGNOSTICON* | *ASTROLOGICUM,* | *Auff das Jahr nach der Fru-* | *. . .* |
*1699* | *. . .* | *Von* | *JOHANN Fuhrmann/* | *. . .* | *Schleßwig/* | *Gedruckt bey*
*Lorentz Eckstorff.* CKB copy lacks B7-8. B6v bears catchword "Von."

2990   Königliche | Verordnung | Und | TAXA | Der | Gerichts-Gebühren |
Und | SPORTULEN, | Jn dem | Ambt Pinnenberg. | [rule] | Gedruckt
im Monat Decemb. 1699.

4to. )($^4$.                                                               CKB

Issued in Glückstadt.

2991   KOHL, FRANZ DIETRICH

(TrauerGedicht über Anna Magd. Musaeus geb. Musaeus). Kiel: B.
Reuther, 1699

4to. χ$^2$.                                                                *

Formerly in Kiel UL (LmC 78-56).

2992   KORTHOLT, CHRISTIAN

Christian Kortholten/ | der H. Schrifft D. und bey der | Hoch-Fürstl.
Holstein. Universitet | zum Kiel Profess. Primar. | THAVMATO- |
GRAPHIA, | Oder | Umbständliche Relation/ | was in der Weltberühm-
ten Stadt | Hamburg mit einem | Glüenden | Eisernen Ringe | sich
wundersames und merckwür- | diges zugetragen; | Samt angezeigten
Nutzen/ | wie man dessen wider die Atheisten/ Pa- | pisten/ und bey
angefochtenen Perso- | nen sich zu bedienen habe. | [rule] | Jm Jahr 1699.

8vo. 144 pp.; A-J$^8$; 1 folding plate.                                    CKB

On p. 144, signed "Hamburg/ im Jahr 1677. den 26. | Septembr." by Otto Sperling
and M. Herman v. Petkum, Pastor ad D.Petri. Place of publication uncertain.
First edition published in Kiel, 1677 (No. 1878).

2993   KRAMER, MAURITIUS

Die Wiederbringung | Der Evangelischen | Wahrheit | in Teutschland

und andern Ländern/ | Jnsonderheit | in Ditmarschen/ | in zwo hi-
storischen Bußpredigten/ | Wobey noch zum Anhange/ | Eine Cate-
chismuspredigt/ | Der Christlichen Gemeine zur Marne | vor Augen
geleget | Von | MAURITIO Kramer/ | Pastore daselbst. | [ornament] |
[rule] | Glückstadt/ gedruckt bey Reinhard Janßen/ | Königl. Buchdr.
1699.

8vo. [8], 157, [1] pp.; A-K$^8$ L$^4$.                                 CKB; CUL

Title printed in red and black.

2994   Kurtzer Extract aus den ersten 5. Tomis Lutheri Jenischer Edition. Al-
       tona, 1699

       8vo.                                                                  *

       *Bibl. Muhliana*, 1735, p. 559; *Fortegnelse Bøger*, 15. Feb. 1759, p. 46, has *Kern und
       Safft aus*. . . .

2995   LASSENIUS, JOHANNES

       Des | Umb die Christliche Kirche Hoch- | verdienten Herren | JOHAN-
       NIS LASSENII, | Weyland der H. Schrift Hochberühm- | ten Doctoris,
       Professoris und Pastoris an | der Teutschen St. Petri Kirchen | in Kopen-
       hagen | Angefangener | Biblischer Kern | und Außzug | Der gantzen
       Heil. Schrift/ | Jn kurtz gefaßten Fragen mit richtiger | Antwort über
       jedes Capittel erwogen und beleget/ | nun aber zur Auffmunterung der
       Gottgeheilig- | ten Jugend continuiret und gantz | außgefertiget | Von |
       M. JOH. JACOB. LANGIAHR | Mit Königl. und Churfürstl. Privi-
       legien. | [ornamental rule] | KOPENHAGEN/ | Gedruckt bey Sel.
       Conrad Neuhofs nach- | gelassene Wittwe/ Anno 1699.

       8vo. [6], 519, [1] pp.; π$^4$ (−π4), A-V$^8$ W$^8$ X-Hh$^8$ Jj$^4$; engraved frontispiece. CKB

       Portrait of Lassenius as frontispiece. Title printed in red and black.

2996   LASSENIUS, JOHANNES

       Biblischer | Weyrauch/ | Zum süssen Geruch | Gottseliger Andachten/ |
       Aus H. Schrifft also zusammen gelesen/ | Daß mit des Heiligen Geistes
       eigenen Worten/ die | Gott-liebende Seelen täglich mit GOtt in allerhand
       dero | geistlichen und leiblichen Anliegen reden/ und zum Christlichen |
       Leben auch seligem Tod sich gefast machen können. | Sammt | Heil-
       samer Vorbereitung | Zum Beichtstuhl und heiligem Abendmahl. | Mit
       allerhand neuen Morgen-Abend-Buß-Beicht- | und Communion-Lie-
       dern/ auch Kupffern/ hin und | wieder versehen. | Dem Gecreutzigten
       JEsu allein zu Ehren/ und seiner | heiligen Gemeine Aufferbauung |
       Von | JOHANNE LASSENIO, | Weyland der H. Schrifft Doct. P. P.

Consist. Assess. und Pastore | an St. Petri Kirche in Coppenhagen. | Mit
Königl. Maj. und Churfl. Sächs. Allergnädigsten Privilegiis, | Nach des
sel. Herrn Autoris eigener Revision in diesem beqvemen Format | zum
vierdtenmal auffgeleget. | [rule] | Coppenhagen und Leipzig/ | Verlegts
Johann Melchior Liebe. | Anno 1699

12mo. [36], 1072, [20] pp.; π1, a⁸ (−a8), )(¹², A-Yy¹² Zz⁶.                CKB; (BM)

π1: title printed in red and black on leaf twice the size of the others, folded and
tipped in. Zz6 blank.

2997   LASSENIUS, JOHANNES

Heilsame | Evangelisches | Licht/ | Zum gründlichen Unterricht | GOtt-
begieriger Seelen/ aus dem | Licht des Göttlichen Wortes durch | Fragen
und Antwort ange- | zündet | Von dem seel. Herrn | D. Joh. Lassenio, |
Der Heil. Schrifft hochberühm- | ten Doctore, vormahls gewesenen
Pastore an der | Teutschen Kirchen zu St. Petri, wie auch Professo- | re
auff der Königlichen Universität in Coppen- | hagen/ und nach dessen
tödlichen Hintritt zu from- | mer Christen Nutz und Erbauung her- |
aus gegeben. | [ornamental rule] | Kopenhagen/ | Gedruckt bey Seel.
Conrad Neuhoffs | Nachgelassene Wittewe/ 1699.

8vo. 259, [1] pp.; A-Q⁸, )(²; engraved frontispiece.                      CKB

Author's portrait as frontispiece.

2998   LASSENIUS, JOHANNES

D. JOH. LASSENII | Nach-Predigt | Gehalten den 2 Febr: | 1692. | Jn
der Teutschen Kirchen zu St. Petri | in Kopenhagen/ | über das Evan-
gelium/ | Am Fest-Tage | der Reinigung Marien. | [ornamental rule] |
Kopenhagen/ | Gedruckt bey Sehl. Conrad Neuhoffs | Nachgelassene
Wittewe 1699.

8vo. 16 pp.; A⁸.                                                          CKB

2999   LASSENIUS, JOHANNES

Passions-Andachten. Copenhagen 1699

8vo.                                                                        *

*Moller* II, 453; *Cat. lib. Oksen,* 1738, p. 54. CKB has 1696 edition (No. 2781).

3000   LASSENIUS, JOHANNES *and* HECTOR GOTTFRIED MASIUS

D. JOHANNIS LASSENII | Weyland Prof. P. und Pastoris | bey der
Teutschen Gemeine | Sieben mahl Sieben | Heilige | Passions- | An-
dachten | Für die Frühe-Stunden der | Sieben Wochen in der Fasten/ |
Und eben so viel | Für die Abend-Stunden/ | Die durch dessen Tod

unterbrochen | Auf Begehren aber vortgeseßet sind | von | HECT.
GOTTF. MASIO, | S. S. Theol. D. und P. P. | Mit Königl. Majest. auch
Churfürstl. Durchl. zu Sachsen/ | Allergnädigsten Privilegiis. | Zum
andern mahl auffgelegt und mit Kuffern | hin und wieder versehen. |
COPENHAGEN | Gedruckt bey Sehl. Conradt Neuhoffs | Nachge-
lassene Witwe/ 1699.

8vo. Pp. [1-12], 1-164, 177-553, [1-3]; a⁶, A-K⁸, L², M-V⁸, W⁸, X-Kk⁸, Ll⁶ (Ll6
blank); engraved frontispiece and preliminary title-page.                     CKB

Author's portrait as frontispiece. Text identical with first edition. CKB copy
incorrectly dated by hand, "1696."

3001   LASSENIUS, JOHANNES

D. Johannis Lassenii, | Weyland | Prof. P. und Pastoris bey der Teutschen
Gemeine | Verliebte | Sulamithin/ | Oder | Heilige Betrachtungen |
über 26. außerlesene | Macht-Sprüche | Heiliger Schrifft | Zu Beforderung
der Liebe des | gecreutzigten JESU/ | Jn den himlischen Hertzen und
Gemüthern | seiner Außerwehlten/ | Hiebevor in öffentlichen Predigten
der Ge- | meine Gottes vorgetragen/ | Nachgehends in etwas erweitert/
und mit | so vielen Liebes-Liedern/ auch erbaulichen | Kupfferstücken/ |
Der Kirche Gottes/ und deren heiligen Glie- | dern zur Freude/ Trost
und Erbauung | mitgetheilet. | Mit Königl. und Churfürstlichen Privi-
legien. | [rule] | Copenhagen/ | Druckts Johann Jacob Bornheinrich/
1699.

8vo. [8], 636, [8] pp.; a⁴ A-Rr⁸ Ss1-2; engr. prelim. t.-p., plates I-XXV, [XXVI],
[2] double plates.                                                       KAREN BRAHE

The two double plates in the Karen Brahe copy are inserted before p. 1 and after p.
360. Preliminary title: *Die | Verliebte | Sulamithin | entdecket | von | D. Johan
Lassenjo.* All after Ss2 lacking, with no apparent loss of text.

3002   [LINEKOGEL, JOHANNES CHRISTOPH]

Celeglino. Gute Zeitung vor junge Knaben, wie sie können vortreffliche
Männer werden. Ploen, 1699.

Folio.                                                                              *

*Moller* II, 480. *Nova literaria maris Balthici 1700,* p. 59.

3003   MAGNUS, LAURENTIUS

Meditatio Passionalis, | oder | Seelen Kleinod | Für die so sich das
Verdienst | Christi allezeit zueignen. | Nahdemahl das Verdienst Chri- |
sti ist der Grund und Fundament unser | Seeligkeit/ also gebühret uns

nicht allein | in der Fasten-Zeit sondern auch unsere | gantzen Lebenszeit
auff solch theures Ver- | dienst uns zu verlassen/ sintemahl derjenge |
noch nicht recht fromb ist/ der nicht wün- | schet und begehret alle Tage
frommer | zu werden | Von einem vornehmen D. Th, SS. | wol übersehen
und zum Druck verfertiget | LAURENTIUS MAGNUS.S welcher we- |
gen Augenscheinlich Leibes Gebrechlichkeit | in der Jugend nicht
einiges Handwerck | zugethan hat werden können. | [rule] | COPEN-
HAGEN/ | Gedruckt bey Seel. Conrad Neuhoffs nachge- | lassene
Wittwe. [1699?]

12mo. A-B¹².                                                 CKB

3004  MASIUS, PETER

Eleonoræ Tugendberg . . . Traur- Lob- und DanckRede bey Beerdigung
Eleon. Rhodin geb. von Ahlefeld. Altona, 1699

Folio.                                                         *

*OHM* I, 383; according to *Jöcher/Rotermund,* IV, 925, published in Altenb(urg).

3005  MOLLER, JOHANNES

Gute Gedancken über den Gudischen GesellschaftsNahmen Catharinæ
Mariæ Lobetanzin geb. Gudin . . . Schleswig, 1699

Folio.                                                         *

*OHM* I, 430-1.

3006  [MUHLIUS, HEINRICH]

(Kurze Anleitung zur Erklärung der Bußtexte. Hos. 4. 1-2). Schleswig,
1699

8vo.                                                           *

*Jöcher/Rotermund* V, 170.

3007  Nach gnädigstem Befehl | Deß | Durchläuchtigsten Fürsten | und
Herrn/ | HERRN | Friederichs/ | Erben zu Norwegen/ regieren- | den
Hertzogen zu Schleßwig- | Holstein/ Stormarn und der Dithmar- |
schen/ Grafen zu Oldenburg und | Delmenhorst &c. | sol es | an dem
verordneten | Buß-uñ Bettage/ | so in diesem Jahre 1699. den 5. |
Maji, als den Freytag nach Jubilate | und vor Cantate einfallen wird/ | Jn Jhro
Durchl. Fürstenthü- | mern vorgeschriebener Mas- | sen gehalten
werden. | [rule] | Schleßw. gedruckt bey Lorentz Eckstorff/ | Hoch-
Fürstl. Hoff-Buchdrucker.

8vo. 16 pp.; A⁸.                                             CKB

3008  [Niemann, Sebastian]

Gottgefälliges | Rauch-Opffer | Wie auch | Schatz-Kammer | Geist-
reicher | [rule of type ornaments] | Gebether | Und | Andachten | Jn
Vorbereitungen des Hertzens/ um man- | nigfalte Gnaden-Güter/ zur
Auffmunterung des Glau- | bens und Fortsetzung eines Christlichen
Lebens | Auff alle Wochentliche/ Sonn-und Fest-Tage/ nach | eines
jeden Stand und Begebenheit in Buß und Gebrauch | des heiligen
Nachtmahls/ Creutz und Verfolgung/ auch Dancksagun- | gen auff
Reisen/ in Kranckheiten und endlich Todes- | Nöthen nützlich zu
gebrauchen | Nebst einem auff alle Fälle angehängtem Register/ | Auff
abermahliges gnädigstes Begehren der | Hohen Herrschafft zum Druck
befodert | [rule] | Schleßwig druckts und verlegts Lorentz Eckstorff/
Hochfl. Hoffbuchdr. 1699.

4to. [6], 1088, [16] pp.; )($^4$ (−)(4), A-Zzzzzz$^4$; engraved frontispiece.        HAB

Title printed in red and black.

3009  Paschius, Johannes

Unordentliche | Kirchen-Ord- | nung | Mit | Gevattern | Oder | Tauff-
Zeugen/ | Jn der | Furcht des HErren zu | verbessern | Vorgestellet |
Von | M. JOHANNE PASCHIO; | Hoff-Predigern zu Grafenstein. |
[ornamental rule] | SCHLESWIG/ | Druckts und Verlegts Lorentz |
Eckstorff/ Hochfl. Hoffbuchdr. 1699.

12mo. [24], 367, [1] pp.; )($^{12}$, A-P$^{12}$ Q$^4$.                          CKB

3009A Les Plaisirs des Heros: | Oder | Die IV. Edelsten Passionen; | Als | Jhrer
Mayestät | Unsers Allergnädigsten | Erb-Königes | Allerhöchsterfreu-
lichster | Geburts-Tag | Anno 1699 den 15 Aprilis | Feyerlichst begangen
wurde; | Auf dem Schloß zu Copenhagen in der | Musick vorgestellet |
[rule] | COPENHAGEN/ | Gedrukt in dero Königl. Maj:t und Uni-
vers. | privilegirter Buchdrukkerey.

4to. A-D$^4$.                                                                CKB

Title in red and black. Polyglot text, in German, Low German, French, Italian, and
Danish.

3010  Rechtmäßige | Ursachen/ | Warumb | Jhre Königl. Majest. zu | Denne-
marck und Norwegen/ &c. | des Herrn Hertzogen zu Holstein-Got- |
torff/ Fürstl. Durchl. das unbeschrenckte | freye Exercitium Juris
Armorum, | angemasseter Weise/ zu zustehen/ keines | weges gehalten
seynd. | Mit angehängter Wiederlegung einer | neulichst publiq ge-
machten Fürstl. Hollstein- | Gottorffischen | DECLARATION. | Auff-

gesetzet und zusammen getragen von | einem treuen Holsteinischen Land-Patrioten. | im Monath Novembris Anno 1699.

4to. 47, [1] pp.; A-F⁴.                                                                    CKB

Two other editions, from different settings of type, each 47, [1] pp.; A-F⁴. Places of publication uncertain.

3011  RELATION, | Von der prächtigen Beerdigung | Jhro Königliche Majestät in | Dennemarck/ | CHRISTIANI V. [1699]

4to.                                                                                        CKB

Dated, "Coppenhagen/ vom 4. Novembr. 1699."

3012  REYHER, SAMUEL

Aller-und Unterthänigster | Vorschlag/ | Wie die bißhero gebräuchliche Ca- | lender also vereiniget werden können/ daß/ | so lange die Welt nach GOTtes Willen stehen wird/ | keine Unrichtigkeit/ noch Ver- rückung der Feste in der Christl. | Kirche/ mehr zu befürchten/ | Vorgestellet | von | Samuel Reyhern/ JC. | Cod. & Mathematum Pro- fessore bey der Hoch- | Fürstl. Holstein Universität | [rule] | KJEL/ | Gedruckt durch Joachim Reumann/ Acad. Buchdr. | 1699.

4to. 8 pp.; A⁴.                                                                          KIEL UL

3013  REYHER, SAMUEL, *editor*

Samuel Reyhers/ JCti, | Bey der Hoch-Fürstl. Holst. Universität | Codic. und Mathematum Prof. | Jn Teutscher Sprache vorgestellter | EU- CLIDES, | Dessen VI. erste Bücher | auf sonderbahre und sehr leichte Art/ | Mit Algebraischen/ oder aus der neuesten Löse-Kunst | entleh- neten Zeichen/ also daß man deroselben Beweiß auch | in andern Sprachen gebrauchen kan/ eingerichtet/ | auch des II. Buchs Vorträge nebst der gemei- | nen/ auff Algebraische Ahrt bewiesen sind. | [double rule] | Kiel/ | Druckts Joachim Reumann/ Academischer Buch- drucker/ | bey Johann Sebastian Riecheln/ Academischen Buchführer | daselbst/ und in Leipzig zubekommen/ Jm Jahr 1699

4to. [16], 392, [4] pp.; ):(², ):():(⁴, )(², A-Ccc⁴, [Ddd]².
                                        BAYERISCHE STAATSBIBLIOTHEK; CKB

Title printed in red and black. Leaf [Ddd]2 signed Ji3 and has catchword "Gege-." CKB copy lacks [Ddd]², containing errata.

3014  RICHARDI, PETER

Der, wie eine Blume, im Leben aufgehende und im Tode hinfallende Jüngling, oder Leichpredigt über Georg Boysen ... Schleswig, 1699

4to.                                                                      *

*Moller* I, 543; *Thott* V/2, 560.

3015 ROGERS, NEHEMIAH

Der reiche Thor, oder Erklärung des Gleichnusses Luc. XII, 16. 21. &
Tractätlein die christliche Freundlichkeit oder Pauli letzter Abschied in
zwo Predigten vorgetragen . . . Copenhagen: Johann Just Erytropilus,
1699.

4to.                                                                      *

*Thott* I/2, 247; *Bibl. Lehmanianae,* 1741, p. 287; *Georgi* III, 310. *Nova literaria
maris Balthici 1699,* p. 109.

3016 RÜDEMANN, JULIUS CONRAD

Kurtze Bedancken | von dem | Ende des Gegenwärtigen/ | und von
dem | Anfang des Zukünfftigen | SECULI, | Worin gründlich er-
wiesen/ | Daß Jenes mit dem Außgang | dieses Jahres/ | Dieses aber mit
dem Eintritt | in das Zukünfftige zu machen | sey/ | Ans Licht gestellet |
von | Julio Conrado Rüdemann/ | Brunsvicensi. | Bey dem Auctore zu
finden. | [rule] | Copenhagen/ | Gedruckt bey Sl. Joh. Philip Bockenhof-
fers | Nachgelassene Witwe/ im Jahr 1699.

8vo. [6], 88 pp.; $\pi^4$ ($-\pi4$), A-E$^8$, F$^4$.                     CKB

3017 RUMPEL, JOHANN VALENTIN

(Trauergedicht über Anna Magdalena Musaeus, geb. Musaeus) Kiel:
Reuther (1699?)

4to. $\chi^2$.                                                           *

Formerly in Kiel UL (LmC 8-55).

3019 SCHELLHAMMER, G. C.

(Trauergedicht über Anna Magdalena Musaeus, geb. Musaeus) Kiel:
Reuther (1699?)

                                                                         *

Formerly in Kiel UL (LmC 78-53).

3020 SCHLESWIG-HOLSTEIN-GOTTORFF. *Laws, statutes, etc.*

WJr Friderich/ von GOttes | Gnaden/ Erbe zu Norwegen/ Hertzog zu
Schleßwig | . . . | . . . 31 Marty 1699

Broadside.                                                          KIEL UL

Decree regarding counterfeit four-schilling pieces (dated 1697).

3021  SCHLESWIG-HOLSTEIN-GOTTORFF. *Laws, statutes, etc.*

WJr Friderich/ von GOttes │ Gnaden/ Erbe zu Norwegen/ Hertzog zu
Schleßwig │ ... │ ... 7. Junii Anno 1699.

Broadside.                                                                      KIEL UL

Decree forbidding the misuse of horses and wagons assigned to public offices.

3022  SCHLESWIG-HOLSTEIN-GOTTORFF. *Laws, statutes, etc.*

WJR Friderich von Gottes Gnaden/ │ Erbe zu Norwegen/ Hertzog zu
Schleßwig Holstein/ Stormarn │ ... │ ... Gottorff den 2. Decembris Ao.
1699

Broadside.                                                           CNA; KIEL UL

Decree regarding introduction of the new calendar in February, 1700.

3024  SCHRÖDER, JOSIAS HERMANN

Parentations-Rede ... Jürgen Jungens, eines studirenden Knabens ...
Schleswig, 1699.

Folio.                                                                              *

*Moller* I, 603.

3025  SCHWEINITZ, DAVID VON

Die kleine Bibel ... 1699.

                                                                                HAB

*See* No. 2944: editions are identical except for date.

3026  SIBBERN, NICOLAUS

PIUM REGIS MORIBUNDI │ TESTAMENTUM! │ ... │ Herrn
CHRISTIAN │ des Fünfften/ │ ... │ Durch │ NICOLAUM Sibbern/
Rensburg: │ Evangelischen Stadts-Pastorn in Glückstadt. │ [rule] │
Gedruckt bey seligen Reinhard Janßen/ nachgelassenen Wittiben/ 1699.

4to. [8], 56 pp.; $\pi^4$, A-G$^4$.                                          CKB

3027  STEPHAN, JOHANNES

(Trauergedicht über Anna Magdalena Musaeus, geb. Musaeus) Kiel:
Reuther (1699?)

4to. $\chi^2$.                                                                     *

Formerly in Kiel UL (LmC 78-54).

3028  STEURNAGEL, NICOLAUS GOTTFRIED, *transl.*

Des Deutschen Reiches Staat oder Politische Beschreibung welche unter dem Nahmen Severini de Monzambano, Veronensis, ans Licht kommen, und nachmahls von Samuel, Freyherrn von Pufendorf, Joh. Georg Kulpis, Ulrich Obrecht und Christian Thomasius, mit nützlichen Anmerckungen erläutert worden durch ihn verdeutscht. Ploen, 1699.

8vo.                                                                    *

*Moller* II, 870.

3029 STÖCKEN, CHRISTIAN VON

Erklärung vier außerlesener Advents-, Weinacht-, Passions-, und Ostergesänge. 1. Nun komm der Heyden Heiland; 2. Ein Kindelein so löbelich; 3. Ach wir arme Sünder; 4. Christ lag in Todes Banden. Glückstadt, 1699.

8vo.                                                                    *

*Moller* I, 660.

3030 TÄNTZER, JOHANN

Der | DIANEN | Hohe und Niedere | Jagt-Geheimnüß/ | Darinnen | Die gantze Jagt-Wissenschafft | außführlich zu befinden/ | Und zwar | Jn diesem Ersten Theil/ | Wie die Wälder und Höltzungen müssen versehen | seyn/ daß allerhand Jagt-Lusten darinnen können vor- | gestellet werden; dann von den Thieren/ ihrer Eigenschafft | von deren Jugend an biß ins Alter/ welche in Teutschland | und den angräntzenden Reichen zu befinden. | Nach welchen/ | Das übrige in noch unterschied- lichen | Theilen folget/ | Mit grosser Arbeit inventiret und be- schrieben | von | Johann Täntzern. | [ornament] | [ornamental rule] | KOPPENHAGEN/ | Verlegts Johann Jost Erythropel 1699.

Folio. 16, 72 pp.; )(⁴, πB⁴, A-J⁴; engraved preliminary title-page, folding plates A-K, 38 plates.                                   CKB; (BM)

Title printed in red and black. On p. 72, work is dated: "Kopenhagen . . . den 24. Augusti Anno 1682." Page 16 has catchword "Es," which does not appear on p.1 following. The 38 plates contain illustrations numbered I-CXIII. Engraved pre- liminary title: *Der Dianen* | *Hohe und Niedere* | *Jagt Geheimnüß*. Bound with "Ander Theil," Copenhagen, 1686 and "Dritter Theil," Copenhagen, 1689.

3031 THESTRUP, FRANZ

Hochzeit-Fackeln | von dem Vater des Lichts angezündet/ | den jungen Hochzeit-Leuten | um das Gemüth zu erleuchten/ vorgetragen/ | jetzo aber | damit sie frommen Hertzen desto heller | scheinen mögen/ | auf dem Leuchter gestecket | Von | FRANCISCO THESTRUPIO, | Nack- scoviens. Eccles. P. & vicinar. pr. | Nun zu mehrer Vergnügung aus dem Lateinischen | ins Deutsche übersetzet | von | Georg Kramern. | [emblem] | [rule] | Copenhagen und Leipzig | Verlegts Johann Melchior Liebe/ | der Königl. Universität Buchhändler. 1699.

8vo. [32], 127, [1] pp.; A-K⁸.                                          CKB

Latin testimonials on verso of t-p by T. Kingo and H. Bornemann are dated 18 June 1696 and 4 January 1697 respectively. Dedication is dated "Nackskov den 14. Novemb. 1696."

3032  Vorstellung/ | So Nahmens | Jhr. Kön. Maj. von Schweden | &c. &c. | Wegen Uberlassung einiger Teutschen Trouppen | aus Wißmar und dem Hertzogthum Bremen | An des | Herrn Herzogs zu Hollstein- | Gottorff Hoch-Fürstl. Durchl. | beschiehet. | Nebst | Hoch-Fürstl. Holstein-Gottorffische | DECLARATION | Die Einhaltung des Schantzen-Baues | betreffend. | [1699]

4to. χ⁴.                                                                CKB

Caption title. Another edition, χ².

3033  Voss, MARTIN

Die betrübte Unvollkommenheit menschlicher Sachen, als Fr. Margaretha Johansen geb. Boyen begraben ward. Glückstadt, 1699.

Folio.                                                                  *

J. Hellmann, *Süder-Dith. Kirchen-Historie,* 1735, p. 92; *OHM* I, 707.

3034  Voss, MARTIN

Das liebe Land am Begräbnis-Tage Fr. Margaretha Elisabeth Arends gezeiget. Glückstadt, 1699

Folio.                                                                  *

J. Hellmann, *Süder-Dith. Kirchen-Historie,* 1735, p. 92; *OHM* I, 707.

3035  VOSSBEIN, JOHANN

Abdruck | Eines | PROTESTS, | So | Johann Voßbein | thun lassen/ | Wider ein so genannten | Vergleich/ | Welchen sein SchwiegerVater/ | Gerdt Ritter/ | Jhm unter unbefugten Arrest in Lübeck/ | gütige Persuasionen/ bitten und erbitten lassen/ abge- | zwungen und expracticiret hat/ und doch selber nicht gemey- | net ist/ solchen Vergleich zu halten/ sondern nur unter allerhand Erfin- | dungen seinen Schwieger-Sohn zu berucken/ und mehr | und mehr in Schaden zu setzen/ gesuchet; | Denen jenigen zur Nachricht/ welche diese Personen | kennen/ und von der Sache zuvor Wissenschaft haben. | [rule] | Altona/ den 9. Maji, Ao. 1699.

4to. A-C⁴.                                                              CKB

3036 WILCKENS, JOHANN HERMANN

(Leichpredigt auf Christianum V, König zu Dennemarck) Altona, 1699

Folio.                                                                                    *

*Bibl. Schroedter,* 1724, p. 99; *Bibl. Blockiana,* 1773, p. 12; *Cat. lib. F. C. Sevel,* III, 1781, p. 217.

3037 WYGAND, AUGUST

Der aller-vortrefflichst-Geheimnüß-volle Buchstab-Wechsel, Buchstabs-Zahl-Harmonie der—Nahmen des Römisch-Kayserlichen Erb-Haußes Leopoldes Eleonora Magdalena Theresia . . . Nebst einem auf das Römisch-Königliche Beylager abzielend Sechs-fachem Sinn-bild. (Altona?) 1699.

Folio.                                                                                    *

*OHM* II, 974.

3038 WYGAND, AUGUST

Dero | Königlichen Majestät von Pohlen | Rahts und Residentens im Niedersächs. Crayse | Mein | AUGUST WYGANDS | kurtzer und Warhaffter | In Jure & Facto | Unumbstoßlich gegründeter | Gegen-Bericht/ | Auf | Des Rahts der Stadt Hamburg | Endlich | Ans Licht gekrochene so genannte | SPECIEM FACTI | Oder | Kurtzen Begriff &c: | Worinnen Sonnen-klaar zu Tage geleget wird: Daß in ermeld- | tem des Rahts Kurtzem Begriff nicht die geringste Warheit oder Recht- | licher | Beweiß/ sondern lauter wider Recht und Warheit lauffende Gedichte und Verdrehungen be- | griffen/ folglich ich dadurch so wenig des allergeringst Straff-bahren Betriebs oder Verbrechens überführet/ | so gewiß sich mehr-gedachter Raht durch Herausgebung dergleichen Jrrthumbs-voller Schrifft nicht nur | für aller Welt prostituiret/ sondern auch meine Unschuld und an der Stadt Hamburg | und ihrer BANCO habende rechtmäßige Foderung so viel | fester gegründet. | [rule of type ornaments] | Altona/ gedruckt bey Christian Reymers/ Kön. privil. Bdr. im Monat Decemb. 1699.

4to. 100 pp.; A-M⁴ N².                                                      HAB

*Moller,* II, 975, gives date 1700.

3039 ZWERG, GOTTHARD JOHANNES

Die | Von GOtt wolbelohnte Treue | . . . | Leich-Begängnüß | . . . | Hn. Paul Schabauen/ | . . . | von | GOTTHARD-JOHANNE ZWERGIO, | Predigern zu Tundern. | [ornamental rule] | SCHLESWJG/ | Gedruckt bey Lorentz Eckstorff/ Hoch-Fürstl. Hoff-Buchdr. [1699]

4to. [12], 108 pp.; A-P⁴.                                              CKB

On p. 45, separate title: *Der | Dreyfache | Tugend-Glantz | ... | von NICOLAO HOYER, Past. Clixbül. | [rule] | SCHLESWJG/ | Gedruckt bey Lorentz Eckstorff/ Hochfl. Hoffb.*; on p. 59, separate title: *Klag-und Trost-Zeilen | ... | Anverwandten und Freunden/ | ... SCHLESWJG/ | Gedruckt/ bey Lorentz Eckstorff/ Hochfl. Hoffb.*

## 1700

3040   Actorum | Publicorum | Fasciculus Primus | Einiger | Zu mehrem Begriff und Erläuterung | der gegenwärtigen | Schleßwig-Holsteinischen | Affairen | dienlicher Stücke. | [ornament] | Gedruckt ANNO M DCC.

4to. 36 pp.; A-D⁴ E².                                                  CKB

Bound with fascicles 2-10, each separately paginated, and with added title. Fascicles 5, 6, 8, 9, 10 identical with those of other edition (No. 3041). Fasciculus Secundus, 16 pp.; A-B⁴. Tertius, 84 pp.; A-K⁴, L². Quartus, 126 pp.; A-Q⁴ (Q4 blank). Septimus, 118 pp.; A-P⁴ (P4 blank).

3041   ACTORUM PUBLI- | CORUM | Fasciculus Primus. [Secundus, Tertius, Quartus, Quintus, Sextus, Septimus, Octavus, Nonus, Decimus] | Einiger | Zu mehrem Begriff und Erläuterung | der gegenwärtigen | Schleßwig-Holsteinischen | AFFAIREN | dienlicher Stücke.

4to. 56 pp. [64; 84; 126, (2); 112; 71; 118; 68; 62; 94, (2) pp.]; A-G⁴ [A-H⁴; A-K⁴ L²; A-Q⁴ (Q4 blank); A-O⁴; A-J⁴; A-P⁴ (−P4); A-H⁴ I²; A-H⁴ (−H4); A-M⁴ (M4 blank)].                                            CKB; Kiel UL

Each fascicle with separate title. Fascicles Quintus, Sextus, Octavus, Nonus, and Decimus are identical with fascicles of other edition (No. 3040). On p. 2 of fasc. 2, a note, *Nachdem man bey Außfertigung dieses zweyten Fasciculi die bessere Nachricht erhalten/ daß der ... Frantz. Minister, Conte de Guiscar, den Character von Ambassadeur extraordinaire ... legitimiret, so hat man nothig ... im vorigen ersten Fasciculo num V. und VI. gesetzte rubriquen hierdurch zu corrigiren.*

3042   ÆGIDIUS, Barthold Christian

Ehren-PYRAMIDE, | ... | PETRO | ZITZSCHERO, | ... | von | BARTHOLO CHRISTIANO ÆGIDII | S. S. Theol: Studios: | Imprimatur, | H. G. MASIUS D. | [ornamental rule] | COPENHAGEN/ | Gedruckt in der Königl. und Universit. privilegirten | Buchdruckerey/ Anno 1700.

4to. Pp. 1-64, 66-95; [A]⁴, B-M⁴ (−M4).                                CKB

On pp. 76-95, poems by several hands, in Latin and German.

3043 ALBINUS, JOHANN ADOLF, *and others*

(Trauergedichte über Hinrich Seger). Schleswig: Eckstorff, 1700.

Folio. $\chi^2$.

Formerly in Kiel UL (LmC 16-2).

3044 Des Aller-Durchläuchtigsten und | Großmächtigsten Königs und
Herrn/ | Herrn Friderich | des Vierten/ | Von GOttes Gnaden/ Königs
zu Dännemarck/ | Norwegen/ der Wenden und Gothen/ Hertzogs zu
Schleß- | wig/ Hollstein/ Stormarn und der Dithmarschen/ | Grafen zu
Oldenburg und Delmenhorst/ | Und Dero hertzgeliebten Gemahlin/ |
Der Durchläuchtigsten und Groß- | mächtigsten Königin und Frauen/ |
Fr: LOUISE, | Von GOttes Gnaden/ Königinnen zu Dänne- | marcken/
Norwegen/ der Wenden und Gothen/ Hertzog- | in zu Schleßwig/
Hollstein/ Stormarn und der Dithmarschen/ | Gräfin zu Oldenburg und
Delmenhorst/ gebohrner Hertzogin zu | Mecklenburg/ Fürstin zu
Wenden/ Schwerin und Ratzeburg/ | auch Gräfin zu Schwerin/ der
Lande Rostock und | Starrgardt/ Frauen &c. | Jhrer beyderseits König-
lichen Majestäten | Königliche Salbungs-Fest/ | So in der Schloß-Kirchen
zu Friderichsburg den | 15. April im Jahre 1700. hochfeyrlichst vollen-
zogen. | [rule] | Kopenhagen/ Gedruckt in Dero Königl. Majest. und |
Univers. privileg. Buchdruckerey/ in der Studii-Strassen.

4to. 16 pp.; A-B⁴. CKB

3045 Allgemeines | Kirchen- | Gebeht/ | Welches auff allergnädigsten Befehl |
Des Allerdurchläuchtigsten/ Großmäch- | tigsten Königs und Herrn/ |
Hn: Friederich | des Vierten/ | Erb-Königs zu Dännemarck/ Nor- |
wegen/ der Wenden und Gothen/ Hertzo- | gens zu Schleßwig/ Hol-
stein/ Stormarn | und der Dithmarschen/ Grafens zu | Oldenburg und
Delmen- | horst/ u. s. w. | Allemahl nach der Predigt in Sr. Königl.
Mayest. | Fürstenthümern Schleßwig/ Holstein/ wie auch in | Dero
Graffschafft Pinnenberg/ öffentlich soll ver- | lesen und mit Andacht
gebetet werden. | [rule] | Glückstadt/ Gedruckt bey seligen Reinhard
Janßen/ | nachgelassene Wittibe/ Jm Jahr 1700.

4to. )(⁴. CKB

3046 ["Almanach" or "Calender" for 1700, published by Lorentz Eckstorff,
Schleswig]

12mo. [A]-[B]¹². CKB

Title-page missing. On [B]5, separate title: *JOHANN Fuhrmanns/* | *Kleines* |
*PROGNOSTICON* | *ASTROLOGICUM* | ... | *1700* | ... | *Schleßwig gedruckt/*
*bey Lorentz Eckstorff.*

3046A [AMTHOR, CHRISTOPH HEINRICH]

Der sonderbahre Weg | Zu wahrem Glück und beständiger Ruhe | Bey seeligem Hintritt | ... | Johann Christoph Ludewig | Hannemanns/ | Aus schuldigster Compassion | vorgestellt von | C. H. A. | [rule] | KJEL/ gedruckt bey Barthold Reuther/ Acad. Buchdr. Anno 1700.

Folio. $\chi^2$.                                                              SHLB

3047 BIBLE. *New Testament*

D. Mart. Lutheri Teutsches Neues Testament, von Caspar Hermann Sandhagen außgegeben. Schleswig, 1700

12mo.                                                                           *

*Moller* II, 758; *Cat. univ. designatio omn. libr. qui hisce Nundinus* ... (Easter) 1698 (Groß): *Das neue Testament mit sonderbaren Summarien.*

3048 BINER, TIMOTHEUS HILARIUS

Das ehliche Wohl (in nupt. Henr. Jessen). Schleswig, 1700

Folio.                                                                          *

*OHM* II, 63.

3049 BLECH, PHILIPP

PHILIPP Blechs/ Predigers zu St. Dionys. | im Lüneburgischen/ | Vergewisserung/ | Daß Herrn | Casp. Herm. Sandhagens/ | Weiland vortrefflichen THEOLOGI | und hochverdienten Hochfürstlichen | General-Superintendentens in denen Her- | tzogthümern Schleßwig und Hollstein/ | Dem Minist. Anno 1695. und 96. zur Buß-Predigt | vorge-schriebene | Außlegung des VI. und VII. Capit. Michæ | nicht unrecht sey; dem Chiliasmo nicht diene; und die dagegen | gerichtete Wieder-legung solche nicht vermöge umzustossen: | Daraus E. Wol Ehrw. Renßburgische Synode der Kön: | Herren Pröbste wird zu urtheilen wissen/ ob Sie für nöthig | zu erkennen gehabt/ daß solche Wieder-legung außgegeben würde. | Der Sel. H. Sandhagens Außlegung selbst/ | wie sie Ao. 94. 95. und 96. außgefertiget/ mit angehänget ist/ | sammt einer | Kurtzen Anleitung zur Erklärung des 5ten | Capittels Jesaiä. | Dessen in dieser Schrifft sonst beyläuffig gedacht. | [rule] | Schleßwig/ | Gedruckt bey Lorentz Eckstorff/ Hochfürstl. Hoff-Buchdr. 1700.

4to. (a)-(b)⁴.                                                                CKB

3050 BURCHARD, BERNHARD

Gnädiges Aufsehen Gottes auf seine Außerwählten, oder Leichpredigt

über Anna Margareta Johansen, Henningi Wedderkopfs ... Ehfrau ...
Kiel: Reuther, 1700

4to. 138 pp. *

*Moller* I, 79; *Stolberg* II, 420.

3051 BURCHARD, PETER ANTON

Letzte Pflicht | ... | Hr. ANDREAS | PAUL | von Liliencron/ | ... |
PETRUS ANTONIUS BURCHARDUS, | Vice-Præpositus des Sege-
bergischen Consistorii und Pastor. | [ornament] | [rule] | Glückstadt/
gedruckt bey seel. Reinhard Janßen Wittibe. [1700]

Folio. χ². CKB
Verse.

3052 [BURMANN, FRANCISCUS]

D. F. B. | Curieuser Bericht | vom | Sabbath/ | moderiret, | und/ | nebst
einer Vorrede/ | wie auch | Laconismus marginalibus, | neu heraus gege-
ben | Von | Johann Christoph Linekogel, | Pastorn zu Gikau | [rule] |
PLOEN/ | Gedruckt durch Tobias Schmidt/ | Fürstl. Hoff-Buchdr.
1700.

12mo. [14], 193, [9] pp.; A-J¹². ERLANGEN UL

3053 CRANE, JOHANN

Begleitende Seufftzer | ... | Hr. ANDREAS | PAUL | Freyherrn | von
Liliencron/ | ... | Von | JOHANN CRANEN. | [ornament] | [rule] |
Glückstadt/ gedruckt bey seel. Reinhard Janßen Wittibe. [1700]

Folio. χ². CKB
German and Latin verse.

3054 DANXST, CORDT

Der Hurtige | Handels-Rechner/ | Befassende in diesem | Ersten Theil |
122 Tabellen | Worinnen | gantz accurat und richtig ausgerechnet zu
finden | Was eine oder andere Partey Wahre/ welche bey | Ellen/
Pfundt/ Stück etc: eingekaufft | und bedungen worden/ | Nach dem |
Oben in einer jeglichen Tabelle angesetzten | Preyse | Jn hiesige | Dän-
ische Müntze | austrägt und beläufft. | Zu sonderbahren Nutzen der
Herrn Kaufleuten/ | Krahmern/ Buchhaltern und sonsten jedermännig- |
lich in diesen Reichen/ umb solchen im Laden/ aufm | Contoir, bey Auc-
tionen und anderswo zugebrauchen. | Nebenst einer deutlichen Vorrede
und Anleitung | wie alles zu verstehen | Jn Drey Sprachen | Teutsch/

Dänisch und Holländisch | Sorgfältigst und mit Fleiß ausgefärtiget |
von | CORDT DANXST, | Bürger/ Handels-Buchhaltern und Arithme-
tico &c: | Jn der zu Hamburg aufgerichteten | Kunstrechnungs übenden
und liebenden Societet | genandt | Dem Denckenden. | Mit Jhro Königl:
Majestet zu Dennemarck/ Norwegen | Allergnädigsten Privilegio. |
[ornamental rule] | Kopenhagen/ | Zu finden in hiesige Buchladens und
bey dem Author. | [rule] | Gedruckt bey Johann Jacob Bornheinrich |
Anno 1700

Folio. [a]², b², c² (−c2), d², [e-mm]².                                        CKB

Title printed in red and black.

3056   DENMARK. *Laws, statutes, etc.*

WJr Friderich der Vierte/ von GOttes Gnaden/ König zu | . . . | . . .
Copenhagen den 27. Martii Anno 1700.

Broadside.                                                                    CKB; CNA

Decree levying a monthly tax on land to support the navy because of the war with
the Duke of Schleswig-Holstein-Gottorff.

3058   DENMARK. *Laws, statutes, etc.*

WJr Friderich der Vierte/ von Gottes Gnaden König zu Dennemarck/ |
. . . | . . . 22. Aprilis Anno 1700.

Broadside.                                                                         CKB

Decree levying a tax on land and forbidding payments "zur Fürstlichen Got-
torfischen Kasse."

3059   DENMARK. *Laws, statutes, etc.*

WJr Friderich der Vierte/ von Gottes Gnaden König zu Dennemarck/ |
. . . | . . . Kopenhagen den 8. Maji, Anno 1700.

Broadside.                                                                         CNA

Decree levying a military tax on land and calling men and horses to military service.

3060   DENMARK. *Laws, statutes, etc.*

WJR Friederich der Vierte/ von | . . . | . . . 6. Junii, Anno 1700.

Broadside.                                                                         CKB

Decree forbidding contributions to the Duke of Schleswig-Holstein-Gottorff.

3060A DENMARK. *Laws, statutes, etc.*

WJR Friederich der Vierte/ von | GOttes Gnaden/ König zu Dänne-
marck/ Norwegen/ . . . | . . . | . . . Glückstadt den 6. Aug. 1700.

Broadside.                                                                          CKB

Decree levying a tax to be paid in rye and oats.

3061   DENMARK. *Laws, statutes, etc.*

Wir Friderich der Vierte/ von | Gottes Gnaden/ König zu Dänne- | marck,/ Norwegen/ ... | ... | ... Jägersburg den 16ten | Octobr. Anno 1700.

Broadside.                                                                          CNA

Decree permitting the export of horses from the Duchies.

3062   DENMARK. *Laws, statutes, etc.*

Verordnung | betreffend | Die neue Stempel/ | welche zu dem gestempelten Papier | nach diesem gebrauchet werden sollen. | Copenhagen den 9 Nov. Anno 1700. | [monogram] | [double rule] | Copenhagen/ gedruckt in der Königl. Majest. und Uni- | vers. privilegirten Buchdruckerei.

Broadside (15.8 x 11.8 cm).                                                         CKB

3064   EXTRACT | Der zwischen | Jhr. Kön. Maj. von Dennemarck | Und | Jhr. Hoch.-Fürstl. Durchl. | von Hollstein-Gottorff | geschlossenen | Friedens-Articul; | Abgehandelt und zum Schluß gebracht zu Traven- | thal/ | den 18 Aug. 1700

4to. )o($^4$.                                                                       CKB

3065   Extract-Schreiben | Auß | Copenhagen/ | De dato 24. July 1700, | Wegen | Bombardirung der Flotten.

4to. $\chi^2$.                                                                      CKB

Place of publication uncertain.

3066   Friedens- | TRACTAT, | Zwischen | Jh. Königliche Majestät | zu Dännemarck Norwegen/ &c. | Und | Jh. Hochfürstl. Durchläuchtigk. | zu Schleswig-Holstein/ &c. | Gezeichnet zu Travendahl den 18. August. | ANNO 1700. | Nach dem wahrem Original.

4to. )($^4$.                                                                        CNA

3067   [FRIES, ARNOLD?]

Ohnmaßgebliche | Gedancken/ | Uber | Die Frage: | Ob wir mit dem neulichst angetrettenen Jahr/ da | man nach Christi Geburth 1700. zehlet/ das | achtzehende Jahr-hundert/ oder/ das Se- | culum decimum octavum angefangen? oder/ ob | dießes Jahr noch zu dem Siebenze- | henden | Jahr-hundert/ das ist/ zu dem Seculo decimo | septimo zurechnen sey? | aufgesetzt | von | ORLANDO PACIMONTANO. | Anno 1700.

4to. 8 pp.; )(⁴.                                                                    CKB

Regarding authorship see Ehrencron-Müller, *Forfatterlexikon*, III, 121.

3068  GERKENS, SIMON

Das vor dem Tode wol bestellte Königliche Hauß, oder Leichpredigt über Christianum V., König in Dennemarck aus 1. Reg. II. 1-4. Glück-stadt 1700

Folio.                                                                              *

*Moller* II, 223; *Bibl. Lehmanianae* I, 1740, p. 174; *Bibl. Nic. Fossius*, 1751, p. 72: 1699; *Bibl. Noodt*, 1757, p. 100: 1699.

3069  HAHN, HINRICH

Wahre Christen-Freude bey Beerdigung Frauen Catharina Margaretha von Buchwalden ... Glückstadt, 1700

Folio.                                                                              *

J. Hellmann, *Süder-Dith. Kirchen-Historie*, 1735, p. 81; *OHM* II, 271.

3070  HAMERICH, HENRICH

Frommer Christen sicheres Verlaßen ... Engel Christoph von Reventlou ... Ploen, 1700

Folio.                                                                              *

*OHM* I, 233.

3071  HANNEMANN, JOHANNES LUDWIG

Die von der Ewigkeit geschmückte Tugend | ... | Frn. Anna Margareta | Wedderkops Gebohrner Johansen/ | ... | von | JOHANNE LUDO-VICO HANNEMANN, D. & Philosophiæ Natur. | ... | [rule] | KJEL/ Gedruckt bey Barthol Reuther/ Academ. Buchdrucker. [1700]

4to. χ⁴.                                                                            CKB

3072  HANNEMANN, JOHANNES LUDWIG

Schuldige Ehren-Bezeigung Idæ Christinæ Rumohr. Kiel, 1700

Folio.                                                                              *

*OHM* II, 290.

3073  HILDERMANN, JOHANNES STEPHAN

Jesussprüche, welche, nach Anleitung der Sontäglichen Evangelien, das Erkäntniß Jesu Christi vorstellen. Ploen, 1700.

12mo.                                                                    *

*Moller* I, 254; *Bibl. Muhliana,* 1735, p. 206; *Bibl. Lehmanianae* I, 1740, p. 89.

3074  Höchst-schmertzlichster Abschied | . . . | Hr. ANDREAS | PAUL |
Freyherrn | von Liliencron/ | . . . | Durch diesen schweren Sterbfall
höchst- | bekümmerte | Jüngere Söhne. | [ornament] | [rule] | Glück-
stadt/ gedruckt bey seel. Reinhard Janßen Wittibe. [1700]

Folio. χ².                                           CKB

Verse.

## 3074A HOLYK, GEORG

GEORGII HOLYK, | Vermehrtes | Dreyfaches | Garten-Buch/ | Jn
dem ersten Büchlein wird erkläret/ | und gezeuget die gantz neue/ und
durch GOt- | tes Gnade von mir erfundene Fünfferley Copulation |
Triangulation, wie auch die nützliche Incorporation o- | der Einleibung/
durch welche Weise in zwey Jahren | grosse/ fruchtbahre und gesunde
Bäume können auffer- | zogen werden/ als durch die bekandte Hand-
griffe/ nem- | lich durch Propffen oder Jmpffen durch ablactiren oder |
absaugen/ durch Einpfeiffen/ durch Oculier und durch | Peltzen in die
Krone in zehen oder zwölff Jahren-Jtem | von allerley Kranckheiten
und Zufälle an den | Bäumen/ auch allerhand Ungezieffer | zu ver-
treiben &c. &c. | Jn dem Andern Büchlein wird gehandelt von | Blumen/
besonders in specie von Vergrösse- | rung der Nälcken. | Jn dem Dritten
Büchlein wird gehandelt | von Küchen-Garten-Gewächse/ und Con-
servation | von allerley Ungezieffer/ besonders von Kohl | und Spargel
etc | Alles durch eigene Erfahr- und Probirung | auffgezeichnet/ und
allen Garten-Bau-Liebhabern | zu Nutz und Lust in Druck befördert. |
[rule] | KJEL/ | Gedruckt bey Barth. Reuther/ Ac. Buchdr. | 1700.

8vo. [8], 149, [1] pp.; A⁴ B-K⁸ L⁴ (L4 blank).             KIEL UL

## 3074B HOLSTEIN-SCHAUMBERG. *Ordinances.*

Des | Weyland Herrn OTTEN, | Grafen zu Holstein/ Schaumburg und
Sternberg/ Herrn | zu Gehmen und Bergen/ &c. | Unterm dato Bucken-
burg/ den 8. Novembr: Anno 1639. | publicirte | Hoff-Gerichts- |
Ordnung/ | Welche nach das/ im Jahr 1640. zu Rinteln/ durch |
Petrum Lucium, der Universität daselbst bestalten Buch- | drucker/
gedrucktes Exemplar, | Jetzo von neuen auffgeleget; | Nachdem nicht
allein zufoderst der Contextus, in gewisse | Paragraphos eingetheilet/
und mit kurtzen Marginalibus | illustriret/ | Sondern auch Demselben
verschiedene/ nachgehends in der Herrschafft | Pinnenberg und Stadt
Altona/ | Von | Jhro Königl. Majest. zu Dännemarck und | Norwegen/

&c. | Publicirte Constitutiones, | beygefüget/ | Benebst einen Specialen-Register. | [rule] | Glückstadt/ Gedruckt und verlegt durch seligen Reinhard Janßen/ nach- | gelassene Wittibe/ Jm Jahr 1700.

4to. [16], 206 pp.; $\pi^4$, $)($^4, A-Cc$^4$.                                BM

Cc3-4 lacking, probably blank. Pages 84 and 85 omitted in numbering.

3075   KIRCHHOFF, ALBERT CHRISTOPH

Als | Der weyland Hoch-und Wohlgebohrner | HERR/ | Hr. AN-DREAS | PAUL | Freyherr | von Liliencron/ | . . . | A. C. Kirchhoff/ | Der Leidtragenden Söhne Ephorus. | [ornament] | [rule] | Glückstadt/ gedruckt bey seel. Reinhard Janßen Wittibe. [1700]

Folio. $\chi^2$.                                          CKB

Verse.

3076   K[OHL?], F. D.

Lob- und Dank-Ode wegen des Travendalschen Friedens. Kiel, 1700

Folio.                                                    *

*Thott* V/1, 341.

3077   Königl. Mayst. | zu Dennemarck Norwegen | verordnetes | Buß-Gebet/ | Bey obhandenen | Friedens-TRACTATEN | in den Bet-Stunden zu gebrauchen | [ornamental rule] | Jm Jahr 1700

4to. $)($^4.                                       CKB; KIEL UL

3078   Kurtz gefassete schließliche | Abfertigung | Einer sogenandten noch-mahligen und | endtlichen | Behauptung | Des Schleßwig-Hollstein-Gottorfischen | freyen und unbeschrenckten Exercitii | Juris Armorum, armandiæ, | fœderum & fortalitio- | rum &c: | Darinnen | Die für gedachtes freyes Exercitium beygebrachte | nichtige Rationes abgeführet und wiedergeleget/ | hingegen | Die in den Königl. Scriptis enthaltene unbewegli- | che Grunde/ und von dem Hollsteinischen Land-Patrioten | angeführte rechtmäßige Ursachen weiter bestär- | cket werden. | Allen Gerechtigkeit-und Friede-Liebenden | zur Nachricht | Gedruckt im Monat Martio Anno 1700.

4to. [2], 13, [1] pp.; A-B$^4$.                                  CKB

Variant edition with same title, from different settings of type and different ornaments on p. 13; [2], 13, [1] pp.; A-B$^4$. Places of publication uncertain.

3079   Kurtzer | Jedoch | Warhaffter Bericht/ | Woher die Uneinigkeit zwischen der Crohn | Dennemarck und denen Hertzogen von | Holl-stein-Gottorff entstanden. | [rule] | Heraus gegeben im Jahr 1700.

4to. $\chi^2$. CKB

Place of publication uncertain.

3080 LA SERRE, JEAN PUGET DE

Gedancken | von der | Ewigkeit/ | Des HERRN | DE LA SERRE, |
Aus dem Frantzösischen ins | Hoch-Teutsche überbracht/ | Durch | M.
PETRUS SARTORIUS, | Frantzösisch- und Teutschen Pre- | diger am
Königl. Dänischen | Hoff. | [ornament] | Coppenhagen und Leipzig/ |
Verlegts Johann Melchior Liebe. | [rule] | Druckts Balthasar Pentzoldt. |
ANNO M D CC.

12mo. [20], 240 pp.; A1-11, B-L$^{12}$ (−L12). CKB

L12 presumably blank.

3081 LASSENIUS, JOHANNES

Biblischer | Weÿrauch/ | Zum süssen Geruch | Gottseliger Andachten/ |
Aus H. Schrifft also zusammen gelesen/ | Daß mit des Heiligen Geistes
eigenen Worten/ | die Gott-liebende Seelen täglich mit GOtt in allerhand
de- | ro geistlichen und leiblichen Anliegen reden/ und zum Christli- |
chen Leben auch seligem Tod sich gefast machen können. | Sammt |
Heilsamer Vorbereitung | Zum Beichtstuhl und heiligem Abendmahl. |
Mit allerhand neuen Morgen-Abend-Buß- | Beicht-und Communion-
Liedern/ auch Kupffern/ hin | und wieder versehen. | Dem Gecreutzig-
ten JEsu allein zu Ehren/ und seiner | heiligen Gemeine Aufferbauung/ |
Jn dieser 5ten Edition, auff ein grosses vermehret | Von | JOHANNE
LASSENIO, | Weyland der H. Schrifft Doct. P. P. Consist. Assess. und |
Pastore an St. Petri Kirchen in Coppenhagen. | Hoher Potentaten Aller-
gnädigsten Privilegiis. | [rule] | Coppenhagen und Leipzig/ | Verlegts
Joh. Melchior Liebe/ Buchhändler. | Hildburghausen/ Druckts Balth.
Pentzoldt/ 1700.

8vo. [12], 789, [11], 63, [1] pp.; π1, a$^8$ (−a6-8) A-Ddd$^8$, $^2$A-D$^8$; engr. t.-p., 20
plates. CKB

Title printed in red and black. On $^2$A1, separate title: *Lebens-Lauff* | *Des
Berühmten THEOLOGI HERRN* | *D. JOHANNIS LASSENII.*

3082 LASSENIUS, JOHANNES

D. Johan. Lassenii | Communion- | Andacht/ | Darin enthalten ist | Ein
nützlicher Vorbericht/ | Welcher bestehet | Aus einigen Articuln un- |
sers Christlichen Glaubens/ | allen Communicanten zu wis- | sen dien-
lich/ | auch | Eine nötige Vorbereitung | durch | Andächtige Gebether
und | Gesänge/ | Wañ man zur Beichte und zum | Tisch des HErrn

gehen wil/ | Und | Schuldiger Dancksagung | Nach empfangener Abso-
lution | und genossenem Heiligen | Abendmahl. | Mit Königl. Majest.
auch Churfürstl. | Durchl. zu Sachsen/ allerg. Priv. | [rule] | Kopen-
hagen/ | Druckts Johann Jacob Bornheinrich/ | Anno 1700

12mo. Pp. [1-2], [1-24], 25-304; π1, A-M¹² N⁸; engraved frontispiece.

3083  LASSENIUS, JOHANNES

Das für seinen zeitlichen und ewigen | Untergang treulich gewarnete |
Capernaum/ | Worin | Vermittelst 25 Send-Schrei- | ben an allerhand
Lasterhaffte Persoh- | nen/ des falschen Christenthums unartiger wan- |
del bestrafft/ und der rechte Weg aus H. Schrifft | angewiesen wird.
Wie auch | Daß in mancherley Creutz und Trüb- | sahl verfallene/ aber
von Gottes Geist | und Hand wieder auff gerichtete | Jsrael/ | Darin
durch 24. Trostschreiben über ver- | schiedene menschliche Zufälle/ aus
H. Schrifft be- | trachtet und erleüterte/ betrübte und in Schwermuth |
gerathne getröstet und wieder auffge- | richtet werden. | Zur Ehre Gottes
und Erbauung des Nech- | sten mit dem Wunsch erfolgender Besserung
und | kräfftigen Tröstung geschrieben von | D. JOHAN: LASSENIO,
Und nun von | dessen Erben/ so weit es von eigener Hand und Fe- | der
abgefasset und entworffen gewesen ausgefertiget. | Mit Königl. Majest
auch Churfürstl. Durchl. | zu Sachsen allergnädigsten Privilegiis. |
[rule] | Kopenhagen/ Gedruckt im Jahr 1700.

8vo. π1, A-M⁸.                                                              CKB

M7-8 lacking, probably blank.

3084  LASSENIUS, JOHANNES

Johannis Lassenii | Weiland | Der Heil. Schrifft Doct. Prof. Publ. Con- |
sistor. Assess. und Pastoris an der St. Petri | Kirche zu Kopenhagen |
Himmlisches | Gnaden-Licht | Darinn die Göttliche Kirchen-Histo- |
rie der ersten 1700 Jahre der Welt in | Beantwortung hundert und et- |
licher | Curieuser Fragen | über | Die Schein-duncklen Oerther | Der XI.
Capitel des Ersten Buchs Mosis | Jm Zwölffachen Schein | Schrifftmäßig
und vernünfftlich erläutert/ | Und | Allen Liebhabern der Heil. Schrifft |
die Geheimnüße GOttes desto unan- | stößiger zu begreiffen/ mit ge- |
theilt wird. | [rule] | Kopenhagen/ | Druckts Joh. Jacob Bornheinrich/
Anno 1700.

8vo. [8], 338, [22] pp.; )(⁴, A-Y⁸ Z⁴.                                      CKB

Title printed in red and black.

3085 LILIENCRON, C. F. VON

Wehmühtigste Trähnen | . . . | Hr. ANDREAS | PAUL | Freyherrn | von Liliencron/ | . . . | C. F. von Liliencron. | [rule] | Glückstadt/ gedruckt bey seel. Reinhard Janßen Wittibe. [1700]

Folio. χ².     CKB

Verse.

3086 LINEKOGEL, JOHANN CHRISTOPH

Römisches | Jubel-Jahr/ | Bey Dieses Jetzigen Veran- | lassung/ | Denen | Liebhabern derer Historien/ | zu süßer Lust/ | und | gutem Nutzen beschrieben | Von | Joh. Christoph Linekogel, | Pastorn zu Gikau in Holstein. | [ornament] | [rule] | Ploen/ | Gedruckt und verlegt durch Tobias | Schmidt/ F. Hoff-Buchdr. 1700.

8vo. A-E⁸ F⁴.     CKB

3087 MAJOR, DETLEV JOHANN

Als die | Hoch-Edle/ Hoch-Ehr-und Tugendreiche | FRAU | Frau Anna Margaret | . . . | Hn. Henning Wedderkop | . . . | [von] Dettleff Johann Major. | [ornamental rule] | KJEL/ Gedruckt bey Barthol Reuther/ Academ. Buchdrucker. [1700]

4to. χ⁴.     CKB

3088 MASIUS, HECTOR GOTTFRIED

HECT. GOTFR. MASII | SS. Theol. D. & Prof P. | Heilige | Passions- | Gedancken/ | Oder | Kurtze Betrachtung | Des Bluts Christi/ | So da besser redet als | Das Blut Abels/ | Hiebevor in einigen Passions- | Predigten vorgestellet/ | itzt aber | Auff Hohen Befehl | zum Druck befordert. | [rule] | COPENHAGEN/ | Verlegts Johann Melchior Liebe/ | der Königl. Univers. Buchhändler. | [rule] | Gedruckt bey Seel. Joh. Phil. Bockenhoffers nachge- | lassenen Wittwe/ Jm Jahr 1700

8vo. [22], 496, 93, [1] pp.; (a)⁸ (−(a)8), (b)⁴, A-Hh⁸, a-f⁸; 1 plate.     CKB

Title printed in red and black. On a1r, added title: *Anhang/ | Von den Wunder- | Wercken/ die bey Christi | Leyden und Sterben sich | zugetragen/ | Und | Von Seiner | Begräbniß.* f8 lacking, probably blank.

3089 [MORHOFF, CASPAR DANIEL]

Als | (Tit.) | HERR | Henning von Wedderkop/ | . . . | Seine Hertzlich- geliebte | Eheliebste/ | . . . | zu Kiel beerdigen ließ. | [rule] | Anno MDCC.

4to. χ⁴.     CKB

3090 [MUHLIUS, HEINRICH]

Kurtze Anleitung | zur Erklärung | Derer | Buß-Texte/ | Welche aus
Jes. V. 1.2.3.4.5.6. | Nach gnädigstem Befehl | Des Durchläucht. Fürsten
und Herrn/ | HERRN | Friederichs/ | Erben zu Norwegen/ Regier-
enden Hertzo- | gen zu Schleßwig-Holstein/ Stormarn und der | Dith-
marschen/ Grafen zu Oldenburg und | Delmenhorst &c. | An dem
angesetzten | Buß-und Beth-Tage/ | So in diesem Jahre 1700. den 7.
May/ | als den Freytag nach Jubilate und vor | Cantate, einfallen wird/ |
Jn Jhro Durchlaucht. Fürstenthümern | bey dem öffentl. Gottesdienste
abzuhandeln | verordnet seyn. | [rule] | Schleßwig/ gedruckt bey Lo-
rentz Eckstorff/ Hochfürstl. Hoff-Buchdrucker.

4to. 24 pp.; A-C⁴.                                                        KIEL UL

3091 Nachricht | über die | Streitigkeiten | zwischen | Jhrer Königlichen
Majest. | von Dennemarck &c. | und | Jhr. Hoch-Fürstl. Durchl. | von
Holstein-Gottorff &c. | Enthalten in einem Brief eines Edelmanns an
seinen | guten Freund in Holland/ vom 16/26 Nov. 1699. | [rule] | Aus
dem Frantzösischen übersetzet/ und gedruckt | im Jahre 1700. im
Monath Januario.

4to. 35, [1] pp.; A-D⁴ E².                                                 CKB

3092 NAGEL, JOHANN HELFRICH
Die | Allein in GOtt gesuchte | . . . | Anna van de Wiele | Gebohrne von
Berens | . . . | Von | JOHAN HELFRICH NAGEL, | Schol. Gl. Rect. |
[rule] | Glückstadt/ Gedruckt bey seligen Reinhard Janßen/nachlebende
Wittwe. [1700]

Folio. [A]-[B]².                                                           CKB

3093 NAGEL, JOHANN HELFRICH

Die auf Tugent gegründete | . . . | Hr. ANDREAS | PAUL ! von
Liliencron/ | . . . | Von | JOHAN HELFRICH NAGEL, | Scholæ
Glückst. Rect, | [woodcut: skull and crossbones] | [rule] | Glückstadt/
gedruckt bey seel. Reinhard Janßen Wittibe. [1700]

Folio. χ².                                                                 CKB

Verse in German and Latin

3094 NELDELIUS, JOHANN

Der | Gläubigen | Hertzens- | Gespräch | mit | GOTT/ | Zum Dienst und
Ermunte- | rung derjenigen/ so in ihrem An- | liegen ihr Hertz für
GOTT aus zuschüt- | ten/ und mit ihm vertraulich zu reden | ver-

langen; | Bloß aus denen in Heiliger | Schrifft würcklich enthaltenen Gebe- | tern/ auch vornehmsten Macht-Sprüchen | abgefasset/ | Von | JOH. NELDELIUS, | zu bekommen bey dem Autore. | [rule] | SCHLESWJG/ | gedruckt bey Lorentz Eckstorff/ Jm Jahr 1700.

8vo. [62], 460, [12] pp.; a$^8$ (−a8) b-d$^8$, A-Ff$^8$ Gg$^4$ (Gg4 blank); woodcut front.

SRL

Title printed in red and black.

3095   OPITZ, JOSIAS HEINRICH

Triumph-Ode | Welche | Bey Haltung der Lob-Rede | Uber den | Von Jhro Königl. Majest. von Schweden | CARL des XII. | Wieder die Moskowiter | Den 20. November des 1700 Jahrs | Herrlich befochtenen | Sieg/ | Abgesungen worden. | Auffgesetzt | von | Josias Heinrich Opitz/ | Der Heil. Schrifft beflissenen | [rule] | Kjel/ | Gedruckt bey Barthold Reuther/ Acad. Buchdrucker. [1700?]

Folio. χ$^2$.

CKB

Another issue, with title: *Ode/* | . . . etc.

3096   OTTO, JOHAN GOTTFRIED

[crown] | FELICITER | [ornament with motto: Das Beliebte | Eins für Zwey | in einem Schude] | Bey der Ehe-und Glücklichen | Vermählung | Des | Wohlgebohrnen Herrn/ | HERRN | Detlef von Alefeld/ | mit | Dem Wohlgebohrnen Fräulein | FRAULEJN | Magdalenen Sibyllen/ | von Alefeld/ | . . . | den 30. Decembr. des 1700. Jahrs observiret | von | beyder Wohlgebohrnen Vertrauten | Unterthänigst-gehorsamsten Die- | ner. [1700?]

Folio. χ$^2$.

CKB

Verse in Latin and German.

3097   SANDHAGEN, CASPAR HERMANN

Casp. H. Sandhagens/ | Jhrer | Regierenden Hoch-Fürstl. | Durchl. zu Schleßwig und Hol- | stein/ General-Superintendentens/ Consi- | storial- Raths/ Ober-Hoff- | Predigers und Prob- | stens/ | Anderes Theil/ | Dero | Theologischer | Send-Schreiben/ | Darinnen | Unterschiedliche Oerter | der Heil. Schrifft erkläret | werden. | Auch hin nnd wieder die | nechst wider den Autorem | edirte Schrifft wieder- | leget wird. | [rule] | SCHLESWJG/ | Druckts und verlegts Lorentz Eckstorff/ | Hochfl. Hoff. Buchdrucker An. 1700.

12mo. [2], 406 pp.; π1, A-R$^{12}$.

CKB

R12 lacking, probably blank. CKB copy bound with "Erstes Theil," Schleswig, 1703. *Moller* II, 757, lists an edition of 1699.

3098  SANDHAGEN, CASPAR HERMANN

Gründliche Erklärung | Derer | Buß-Texte/ | Welche an denen allge- | meinen | Buß-und Beth-Tagen | Den XI. Maji des 1694, 95, und | 96sten Jahrs | Aus dem Sechsten und Siebenden | Capittel Michæ | Auff | Der Regierenden Hoch-Fürstl. | Durchl. zu Schleßwig-Holstein &c. | Gnädigste Verordnung | Außgefertiget/ | von | Caspar H. Sandhagen/ | Weiland Hochverdienten Hoch-Fürstl. | General Superintendente in denen Hertzog- | thümern Schleßwig und Holstein. | [rule of type orna- | ments] | SCHLESWJG/ | Druckts und verlegts/ Lorentz Eckstorff/ Hochfl. Hoff-Buchdr. | Anno 1700.

4to. 32 pp.; a-d⁴.                                                   KIEL UL

3099  SCHELLHAMMER, GÜNTHER CHRISTOPH

Die von der Gedult bekröhnte Leiche Ida Christina Rumohrin. Kiel, 1700

Folio.                                                                    *

*OHM* II, 777.

3100  SCHELLHAMMER, GÜNTHER CHRISTOPH

Wohlmeinendliche Trost-Zeilen | . . . | Fr. Anna Margareten | Wedder- | koppin/ | . . . . | von | Günther Christoph Schellhammern/ D. und P. P. | [rule] | KJEL/ Gedruckt bey Barthol Reuther/ Academ. Buchdrucker. [1700]

4to. χ².                                                             CKB

3100A  SCHLESWIG-HOLSTEIN-GOTTORFF. *Laws, statutes, etc.*

WJr Friderich der IV. von GOttes | Gnaden/ Erbe zu Norwegen/ Herzog zu Schleß- | wig . . . | . . . . [1700]

Broadside.                                                          CKB

Decree forbidding contributions to the Royal Danish or "Schleßwig-Holstein-Glück- stättischen Casse."

3101  SCHLESWIG-HOLSTEIN-GOTTORFF. *Laws, statutes, etc.*

WJr Friderich von GOttes | Gnaden/ Erbe zu Norwegen/ Hertzog zu | . . . | . . . Gottorff den 1. Febr. An. 1700.

Broadside.                                                          CNA

Decree forbidding export of horses from the Duchies.

3102 SCHLESWIG-HOLSTEIN-GOTTORFF. *Laws, statutes, etc.*

WJr Friderich von GOttes | Gnaden/ Erbe zu Norwegen/ Hertzog zu | Schleßwig/ Holstein/ . . . | . . . | . . . Gottorff den 12. Febr. Anno 1700

Broadside.                                                                CNA

Decree against acceptance of "Patenta oder Mandata" issued without ducal seal.

3102A SCHLESWIG-HOLSTEIN-GOTTORFF. *Laws, statutes, etc.*

WJr Friderich der IV. von Gottes | Gnaden/ Erbe zu Norwegen/ Hertzog zu | Schleßwig/ Holstein/ . . . | . . . | . . . Pinneberg den 9. Jun. 1700.

Broadside.                                                                CKB

Decree levying monthly military taxes on land.

3103 SCHLESWIG-HOLSTEIN-GOTTORFF. *Laws, statutes, etc.*

WJr Friederich der IV. von GOttes | Gnaden/ Erbe zu Norwegen/ Hertzog zn [sic] Schleß- | wig/ Holstein . . . | . . . | . . . im Haupt-quartier zu Pinnenberg den 11. Junii 1700.

Broadside.                                                                CKB

A warning that all subjects of the Duke should return to their homes within three days.

3104 SCHLESWIG-HOLSTEIN-GOTTORFF. *Laws, statutes, etc.*

WJr Friderich der IV. von GOttes | Gnaden/ Erbe zu Norwegen/ Hertzog zn [sic] Schleß- | wig . . . | . . . | . . . Pinnenberg den 11. Junii 1700.

Broadside.                                                              KIEL UL

Decree threatening destruction of property of persons engaged in "Schnaphahnerey."

3105 SCHLESWIG-HOLSTEIN-GOTTORFF. *Laws, statutes, etc.*

WJr Friederich der IV. von GOttes | Gnaden/ Erbe zu Norwegen/ Hertzog zu Schleß- | wig/ Holstein/ . . . | . . . | . . . Pinnenberg den 12. Jun. 1700.

Broadside.                                                         CNA; KIEL UL

Decree granting to Lorentz Eckstorff the privilege of printing new-style calendars for twenty years. Countersigned: J. A. Grabau.

3107 SCHLESWIG-HOLSTEIN-GOTTORFF. *Laws, statutes, etc.*

JM Nahmen Dero zu Schleßwig | Holstein Regierenden Hoch-Fürstl. Durchl. | . . . | . . . Pinnenberg/ den 14. Junii. 1700.

Broadside.                                                                CNA

Decree ordering subjects to return to their homes. Place of publication uncertain.

3108 SCHLESWIG-HOLSTEIN-GOTTORFF. *Laws, statutes, etc.*

WJr Friederich der IV. von | GOttes Gnaden/ Erbe zu Norwegen/ |
... | ... im Haupt-Quartier zu Oldeslo/ den 7. Julij 1700.

Broadside.                                                                CKB

Decree warning that all subjects "sich bey ihren Häusern und Feld-Bau still und
ruhig ... halten."

3109 SCHLESWIG-HOLSTEIN-GOTTORFF. *Laws, statutes, etc.*

WJr Friderich von Gottes Gnaden | Erbe zu Norwegen/ Hertzog zu
Schleßwig | ... | ... im Haupt-Quartier zu Oldersloh/ den | 23. Julii,
Anno 1700.

Broadside.                                                                CKB

Decree regarding the distribution of flour for the allied army.

3109A SCHLESWIG-HOLSTEIN-GOTTORFF. *Laws, statutes, etc.*

Des Durchlauchtigsten | Fürsten und Herrn/ | HERRN | Friederichs |
des Vierdten/ | Erben zu Norwegen/ regie- | renden Hertzogen zu
Schleßwig- | Holstein/ Stormarn und der Dith- | marschen/ Grafen zu
Oldenburg | und Delmenhorst/ &c. &c. | Gnädigste Verordnung/ | Wie
es an dem wegen verliehe- | nen edelen Friedens auff den XIX. Son- | tag
nach Trinitatis den 17. Octobris | dieses 1700. Jahres an- | gesetztem |
Danckfest | Jn Jhro Durchl. Fürsten- | thümern und Landen soll | ge-
halten werden. | [rule] | SCHLESWJG | Gedruckt/ bey Lorentz Ecks-
torff/ Hochfl. Hoff-Buchdr.

8vo. 32 pp.; A-B⁸.                                                         CKB

3110 SCHLESWIG-HOLSTEIN-GOTTORFF. *Laws, statutes, etc.*

WJr Friederich von Gottes Gnaden | Erbe zu Norwegen/ Hertzog zu
Schleßwig/ Hol- | stein ... | ... | ... 2. Nov. 1700

Broadside.                                                            KIEL UL

Decree regarding postal service. Countersigned: C. Melchenburg.

3111 SCHLESWIG-HOLSTEIN-GOTTORFF. *Laws, statutes, etc.*

WJr Friederich von Gottes Gnaden | Erbe zu Norwegen/ Hertzog zu
Schleßwig/ Hol- | stein ... | ... | ... 13. Novembr. 1700

Broadside.                                                            KIEL UL

Decree regarding postal and passenger service. Countersigned: C. Melchenburg.

3112  Schleswig-Holstein-Gottorff. *Laws, statutes, etc.*

WJr Friederich von Gottes Gnaden/ │ Erbe zu Norwegen/ Hertzog zu
Schleßwig/ Hol- │ stein ... │ ... │ ... 15 Decembr. 1700

Broadside.                                                                                KIEL UL

Decree against "verspielen . . . bey hundert und mehr Personen." Countersigned:
C. Melchenburg.

3112A  Schmidt, Sebastian

Kurtzer Bericht/ von dem Unterschied derer Evangelischen Luther-
ischen/ und der Reformirten Lehr-Sätze/ wornach gründlich zu urtheil-
en/ ob selbige nur etliche Neben-Fragen/ oder den Grund der Seligkeit
betreffen/ und eine Religions-Einigkeit und Brüderschafft verhindern
können. Zur Verantwortung eines gegenseitigen Berichts. Mit einem
doppelten Anhang von Ungewißheit des Calvinischen und Papistischen
Glaubens. Entworffen von Sebastian Schmidt/ weiland hochberühmten
Doctore Theologo, und vornehmsten Professore zu Straßburg/ wie auch
des Kirchen-Convents Præside. Schleßwig bei Lorentz Eckstorff/ 1700.

                                                                                                  *

*Nova literaria maris Balthici 1700, p. 120.*

3113  Spener, Philipp Jacob

D. Phil. Jac. Speners │ Churfürstl. Brandenb. Consistorial- │ Raths und
Probsten zu Berlin │ Warhafftige Erzehlung │ Dessen │ Was wegen des so
genanten Pie- │ tismi in Deutschland vor einiger Zeit │ vorgegangen; aus
Gelegenheit H: Ger- │ hard Crœsi seiner Historiæ Quackerianæ │ ein-
verleibter Historiæ Pietistarum │ und zu dero Verbesserung │ auffge-
setzet. │ Welcher beygefüget eine kurtze Vor- │ rede eines Anonymi, und
was ihn ver- │ anlasset solches Büchlein durch den Druck │ zu publiciren/
zumahlen/ weil es die hohe │ Noth erfordert/ auff daß sich die Ketzer-
ma- │ cher darinn bespiegeln/ und hinführo │ einesbessern besinnen │
mögen; │ Und was mehr dabey zu finden/ ist in │ der Vorrede ange-
zeiget. │ [rule] │ Amsterdam und Altona bey Friedrich │ Wilhelm
Stobwasser. │ [rule] │ Anno Christi 1700.

12mo. [12], 107, [1] pp.; )(⁶, A-D¹² E⁶ ()(6 blank).                          HAB

Printed in Amsterdam.

3114  Sweden. *Laws, statutes, etc.*

Jhro Königl. Maytt. zu Schweden General über der Armee in Teutsch-
land/ │ und in denen Hertzogthümbern Bremen und Veerden verord-

neter General Gouverneur | Jch Niclaus Gyldenstern | ... | ... Altona
den 4. Jun. 1700

Broadside.                                                                              CNA

Decree admonishing the populace to be "stille und ruhig" but to furnish the allied
troops with provisions.

3115   TIEDIUS, JOACHIM

Mond- und Sonnen-Cyklus, nach welchem der Neue Calender eingerichtet. Kiel, 1700

4to.                                                                                    *

*Bibl. Breitenaviana,* V, 1747, p. 652.

3116   Trauergedicht über Anna van der Wiele, geb. von Berens von den
Enkeln der Verstorbenen. Kiel: Reumann (1700?)

Folio. $\chi^2$.                                                                        *

Formerly in Kiel UL (LmC 18-75). According to Josef Benzing, *Die Buchdrucker
des 16. und 17. Jahrhunderts* (1963), p. 216, Reumann left Kiel for Hamburg in
1698.

3117   Trauer Ode | ... | Frau Anna Margaretha | ... | ... Wedderkop | ... |
von | Einen guten Freunde auffgesetzet | [rule] | KJEL/ Gedruckt bey
Barthol Reuther/ Academ. Buchdrucker. [1700]

4to. $\chi^4$.                                                                          CKB

3118   Trauer-Ode | ... | HERRN | Hr. ANDREAS | PAUL | von Liliencron/ |
... | Von | S. B. P. S. | Und in einer geringen Traur-Music durch zwey |
Chöre vorgestellet | Von | Johann Conradt Rosenbusch/ Organ. in
Jtzehoe. | [woodcut: coffin] | [rule] | Glückstadt/ gedruckt bey seel.
Reinhard Janßen Wittibe. [1700]

Folio. $\chi^2$.                                                                        CKB

3119   Travendahlischer | Friede/ | Geschlossen den 18. Augusti | Anno
MDCC. | Nach dem Original.

4to. A-B⁴.                                                                             CKB

Another edition, A-B⁴ (−B4); another edition, A-C⁴ (C4 blank); another edition,
A-C⁴ (−C4), on leaf A2r, engraving.

3120   VERMEHREN, P.

Auf | Jhr. Königl. Majestät | Des | Allerdurchleuchtigsten/ Großmäch-
tigsten | Königes und Herren/ | Königs | FRJDERJCH | des Vierten/ |
Königes zu Dennemarck und | Norwegen/ der Wenden und Gothen/ |

Hertzogs zu Schleswig Holstein/ Stor- | marn und Dittmarschen/ Graf-
fen zu Ol- | denburg und Delmenhorst | Königliche Salbung/ | Als
selbige in dero Königl. Schloß-Kirche zu | Friderichsburg den 15. April
1700. mit gewohnlichen | Solemnitäten höchstfeyerlich verrichtet ward. |
[double rule] | COPENHAGEN/ Gedruckt in der Königl. und
Universit. privilegirten | Druckerey in der Studii-Straßen.

Folio. χ². CKB
Verse.

3122 VOSS, MARTIN

Das liebe Eheband durch den Tod Fr. Catharina Margaretha von Buchwalden zerrissen. Glückstadt, 1700

Folio. *

J. Hellmann, *Süder-Dith. Kirchen-Historie,* 1735, p. 92; *OHM* I, 707.

3123 WILCKENS, JOHANN HERMANN

Die Grab- und Ruhe-Stätte des Etatsrath und Amtsverwalters in Pinneberg, Hinrich Suhm, schuldigst beehret. Altona, 1700

*

J. A. Bolten, *Hist. Kirchen-Nachricht von der Stadt Altona,* II, 1791, p. 270.

3124 Der Wolbelohnte und herlich Gecrönte | Liliencron/ | . . . | Hr.
ANDREAS | PAUL | Freyherr | von Liliencron/ | . . . | Ein dem Hohen
Sterb-Hause | Für allEn höChst verbundener Knecht. | [rule] | Glück-
stadt/ gedruckt bey seel. Reinhard Janßen Wittibe. [1700]

Folio. χ². CKB
Verse.

3125 WOLTERS, JOACHIM

Das Bethränte Cimbrien/ | . . . | Hr. ANDREAS | PAUL | Freyherrn |
von Liliencron/ | . . . | entwerffen | wolte/ | JOACHIM WOLTERS, |
Cancell. Reg. Sectetar. [sic] | [ornament] | [rule] | Glückstadt/ gedruckt
bey seel. Reinhard Janßen Wittibe. [1700]

Folio. χ². CKB
Verse.

3126 Die | Zu Traventhal durch die allerseits hohen Hrn. | Plenipotentiarien
Den 18 Aug. Anno 1700 zu | End gebrachte und unterzeichnete |
Friedens-Puncten: | Zwischen | Jhro Königlichen Majestät | zu Dänne-

marck-Norwegen/ &c. | Und | Jhr. Hochfürstl. Durchl. zu | Schleßwig-Hollstein/ &c. | [rule] | Gedruckt im Jahr 1700. im Monath Augusto.

4to. )(⁴.                                                                              CKB

3127   ZWERG, CHRISTIAN OSWALD

Die Evangelische Wahrheit, der XXI. Lehr-Articul Augspurgischer Confession, vermittelst vier unterschiedlicher Betrachtungen über ieglichen Articul. Ploen, bey Tobias Schmidt, 1700.

8vo.                                                                                        *

*Nova literaria maris Balthici 1700*, p. 153; *Moller* I, 752; *Cat. univ. designatio omn. libr. qui hisce Nundinus* . . . (Easter) 1698 (Groß); *Thott* I/2, 483.


# UNDATED TITLES

3128   [AREND, CAI]

Übung des kleinen Catechismi, durch Frage und Antwort vor die Kinder.

12mo.                                                                                      *

*Moller* I, 21: n.p., n.d. May be identical with No. 1516. J. Hellmann, *Süder-Dith. Kirchen-Historie*, 1735, p. 79, lists Cai Arend, *Communion-Büchlein*, Glückstadt.

3129   BALKEN, HENRIK

(Predigt über Jochim Brandt) Ploen.

                                                                                           *

*Thott* V/2, 561.

3130   DENMARK. *Laws, statutes, etc.*

INDEX | über die | Landgerichts- | Ordnung/ | Und | Deren dabey gedruck- | ten Constitutionen und | Edicten; | Nach der zum Dritten-mahl/ | und zwar in Anno MDCXC | auffgelegten Edition einge- | richtet | [type ornaments] | [rule] | Glückstadt/ | Gedruckt bey Reinhard Janßen.

12mo. 128 pp.; A-E¹² F⁴.                                                                  CKB

Published between 1690 and 1699. *Cf.* No. 2451A.

3131   FRISIUS, MATTHIAS, *and others*

(Hochzeitsgedicht für August Rager und Katharina Petrejus). Kiel: J. Reumann

4to. χ⁴.                                                                                  *

Formerly in Kiel UL (LmC 79-31). Printed between 1665 and 1672.

3132 HELT, ADOLPH

Der christliche Soldatenstand in seiner richtigen Verbindung mit dem Gnadenstand. Glückstadt.

8vo.                                                                                    *

*Index O. H. Moller,* 1797, 273.

3133 MARESCHALL, HEINRICH

Tractätchen/ | Worinnen | Das aufrichtige und veritable Neu- | er-fundene | OLEUMLUNÆ, | Nach seinem Ursprung/ Wirckung und | Tugenden ausführlich beschrieben wird: | Von | Heinrich Mareschall/ | Wohnhafftig in Copenhagen. | Auch kan man in Hamburg bey Hn. Brehmer/ am Thum aufm Speers- | Orte/ Nachricht von ihn haben. | [rule] | Altona/ | Gedruckt bey Christian Reymers/ Königl. privil. Buchdr.

4to. A⁴ B².                                                                          CKB

Description of a panacea. Printed around 1700.

3134 MILITAIR-EYD [CA. 1679]

Broadside.                                                                          CKB

Text begins, "WJr anwesende Officirer und Kri- | gesleute sampt und sonders/ . . . ." On verso, same in Danish: *Militair-Eed.*

3135 MORHOF, DANIEL GEORG

Concert auf M. Gabriel Wedderkopf jüngsten Söhnleins Absterben. Kiel.

Folio.                                                                              *

*OHM* III, 472. Published between 1672 and 1696.

3136 [SCHWARTZ, JOSUA]

D. J. S. | Buß-Gebeth/ | Nach den fürnehmsten | Glaubens-Artickeln | abgefasset.

4to. 8 pp.; χ⁴.                                                                      CKB

In CKB copy "S." is expanded by hand to "Schwartzens."

3137 (Gedicht über Erich Mauritius von den P. Schmidtling'schen Tischge-nossen) Kiel: J. Reumann

Broadside.                                                                          *

Formerly in Kiel UL (LmC 30a-71). Published between 1668 and 1670.

3138    [German poem on occasion of Christian V's birthday]

4to. $\chi^2$.                                                                                    CUL

Poem signed: "Hier/ grosser König/ liegt ein Knecht zu deinen Füssen." CUL
copy has ink drawing in place of a title-page.

3139    [Poem listing the Danish kings. No title. At head of page two angels
bearing motto "Soli Deo gloria." Below them a crown]

Folio. $\chi^2$.                                                                                  CKB

Signed at end: "Antonius Teutomann, Cronenburgensis." Published in the 1690's.

ADELUNGK, Wolffgang Henrich 2757
ÆGIDIUS, Barthold Christian 3042
AHLEFELD, Chr. Albrecht von 2637
ALARDUS, Lambert 269, 659
ALARDUS, Nicolaus 270, 2442
ALARDUS, Wilhelm 218, 287
ALBERT, Heinrich 514
ALBINUS, Johann Adolf 3043
ALBINUS, Michael Nicolaus 816
ALBOLD, W.C. 1497
AMDERSEN, Andreas 546, 1721
AMTHOR, Christoph Heinrich 3046A
ANDERSEN, Andreas 490
ANDERSEN, Jürgen 1430
ANDREÆ, Johannes Christopherus 2177, 2496, 2815-16
APELLES, Matthæus de Loew 1899
AREND, Balthasar 1332-33, 1522-23, 1558, 1609, 1783
AREND, Cai 310, 343, 515, 597, 624, 661A, 894, 1020, 1088-90, 1252-53, 1293, 1332-33, 1382, 1387, 1465, 1524, 1610, 1666-67, 1784, 1852, 2213, 2347, 3128, 3128A
ARND, Peter 1091
ARNKIEL, Troels 1431, 1785, 1853, 2047, 2126, 2178, 2598, 2748, 2871
ASSENS, Johann Jensen 734
AULEANDRUS, Paul 1093 (tr.)

BACHMANN, Georg Friedrich 2445
BACHMANN, Joh. 2111
BADENHAUPT, Hermann 1668
BÄHR, Johan Christian de 1696
BAGGER, Hans 2255, 2567
BALKEN, Henrik 3129
BALKONIUS, Johann 344
BALZLOU, Christopher 2194
BANG, Hans 38
BARBAROSSO, Vitus 289, 291, 433
BARTHOLIN, Caspar 142, 516
BARTHOLIN, Thomas 768
BAUDISSEN, Ernst Christoph von 2297
BAUDISSEN, Wolf Hinrich von 2297
BAUM, Johan Caspar 1021
BECK, Johann Joseph 1466, 2127, 2391, 2540-41
BECKER, Abraham 769
BECKER, Christopher Basilius 272-73
BECKER, Diedrich 1857, 1901
BECKER, Johann Adolph 698
BECMANN, Nicolaus 2348
BEECK, Georg 2256
BEERWALD, Georg Christoph 703
BEHRENS, Johannes 1255
BEITIUS, Martin 1787
BELING, Oswald 363, 547, 1384
BELOW, Maria 189
BENEDICHT, Laurentz 183
BENN, M. 1497
BENNICHIUS, Nicolaus Johannes 517
BEN(N)SEN, Johann 1168, 1239
BENTZ, Benedict 1169
BENTZ, Johann Daniel 704
BENTZEN, Sigfrid 2542
BER(C)KENDAL, Johannes 1022, 1028 (ed., tr.), 1170, 1559-60, 1611, 1669
BERENTS, Johann 1526
BERG, Johan Adam 467
BERGMANN, Johann Friedrich 1858
BERGSTÄDT, Andreas 1882, 1902

BERNIGEROHT, M. 2687 (engr.)
BERING, Vitus 1249
BESELIN, J. A. 2298
BESELIN, Johann Wilhelm 2874
BEWERLIN, Hans 147
BEYRHOLMIUS, Andreas 1724
BÈZE, Théodore de 1093
BIFIELD, Nicholas 1859
BILENBERG, Hinrich 1125
BINER, Timotheus Hilarius 1788, 1943, 3048
BING, JcH. 1654
BIRCHEROD, Jacob 2194
BLECH, Philipp 3049
BLIERSTORP, Anthon 1467
BOHSE, August 2446-47
BOJE, Michael 2179-80, 2299
BOLDICH, Ernst Christian 2181, 2300, 2392, 2684, 2749, 2957
BOLDICH, Johannes 625, 1294, 1434, 1468
BOLTEN, Johannes 1469, 1789, 1860
BORCH, Christian 2685
BORCH, Ole 1996
BORDING, Anders 1249
BORNDIN [i.e., BORDIN], Sebaldus 2299
BORNEMANN, Daniel 735
BORNEMANN, H. 3031
BORNHOL(D)T, Matthias 1988A, 2040, 2215-16
BOTSAC, Barthold 2599, 2686 (ed.), 2817
BOYE, Henrich 2448, 2498, 2657
BRÄMER, Christian 1295, 1435, 1470, 1670, 1723, 1790, 1944, 1997, 2301, 2449, 2543, 2750-51
BRÄMER, Johannes 364, 548, 598-99, 626, 675, 705, 1296-97, 1471, 1904
BRANDT, Bonaventura Frederiksen 2450
BRAND(T), Friederich 1561, 1671-72, 1724, 1905, 2194 (tr.), 2217
BRANDT, Nicolaus 2194
BRAUN, Ludvig 574
BRAWER, Johannes 1334
BROCHMAND, Caspar Erasmus 390, 575, 577
BROWNRIG, Ralph 2687
BRÜGGE, Andreas von der 2302A, 2818, 2875
BRUHN, Christian 1998, 2048
BRUHN, Christoph 1612
BRUMMER, Heinrich 1472
BRUNNER, Martin 1026-27
BUCHNER, Johann Caspar 1140
BUECK, Hieronymus 1220, 1335, 1385-86, 1562
BÜLL, Christian Kai 1906
BÜTEMEISTER, Johann Daniel 2875
BÜT(T)NER, Daniel 1725, 1999
BÜTTNER, David 2349
BULLEN, Nicolaus 207
BURCHARD, Anton 1945
BURCHARD, Bernhard 2558, 2876, 2958, 3050
BURCHARD, Caspar 1945
BURCHARD, Georg Hinrich 600, 1264, 1673, 1861, 2257
BURCHARD, Matthias 627, 676, 1298, 1563-65, 1613-14, 1674-75, 1726-27, 1945
BURCHARD, Peter Anton 2182, 2256, 2393-96, 2499, 2543-44, 2819, 2877, 3051
BURMANN, Franciscus 3052
BUTZBACH, Johannes Lenyngus 53
BYSING, Rasmus 1299

CAESAR, Philipp 54

CÆSARIUS, Cornelius 1899
CARNARIUS, Johannes 70
CARSTENS, Joachim Henrich 2500
CHARISIUS, Peder 909-10
CHEMNITZ, Martin 152
CHRISTIANI, Friedrich, 1820, 2050
CHRISTIANI, Valentin 2753
CHYTRÄUS, Georg 313
CLARCKE, Samuel 1028
CLAUSEN, Adolf 2127A
CLAUSEN, Martin 2688
CLAUSEN, Matthias 2754
CLAUSSEN, Christian Albrecht 2258
CLAUSSØN, Peter 2218
CLIPEUS, Johannes 197 (tr.)
CLOSE, Caspar 336-37
CLÜVER, Michael 662, 677
CLÜVER, Nicolaus 662, 677
COGEL, Friedrich 1947
COLBRAND, Nicolaus 2755
CORDES, Heinrich 2500
CORFINIUS, Johannes 518
CORNUSUS, Johannes 161
CRAMER, Andreas 1388, 1474
CRAMER, Christian Anton 1792, 1983
CRAMER, Friederich Andreas 1389, 1461
CRAMER, Friedrich Christian 2545
CRANE, Johann 2451, 3053
CRÖCHEL, Johannes 549, 576, 601, 628, 736,
 1156, 1256
CRUGER, Johann 1437
CRUGER, Stephan 1793
CRULL, Vincent 1032
CRUSIUS, Johannes 2600, 2959
CRUSIUS, Philipp 508
CULEMANN, Gregor 2689
CUNIGUND, Heinrich 1301
CUNITIUS, Andreas 679
CYPRIAN 933

DAME, Friedrich 292
DAMON 1654
DAMPIERRE, Jacques Serceuil de 2128, 2351,
 2756
DANCKWERT, Friedrich Joh. 749
DANCKWERTH, Caspar 237, 645
DANXST, Cordt 2500, 2502-04, 2545-48, 2601,
 2642-43, 2691-92, 3054
DEL CAMPE 1257
DELVER, Gotth. Chr. 1302
DETHARDING, Georg 1954
DIBBERN, Nicolaus 2556
DIECKHOF, Johannes 1912
DIETERICH, Vitus 1158
DITTENHAMMER, Philip 211
DONAUER, Christoph 55
DORN, Reimar 603
DORNKRELL von Eberhertz, Jacob 2357-59
DREYER, Josias 498-99
DUBRAVIUS, Stephan 2543, 2890
DÜRKOP, Heinrich 2675

EBERS, Johann Daniel 1913
EBIO, Eberhard 1182
ECCARD, J. M. 1812
ECCARD, Johannes Nicolaus 2891
ECCARDUS, Elias 163
EDING, Johannes Wilhelm 193
EGENOW, Johann 142 (tr.)
EGGEBECK, Georg 1229
EICKHOLTZ, Hermann 244

ELERDT, Fromhold von 406, 442, 474, 781
ELVERFELD, Jonas von 30
ENGEL, Joachim 2586, 2636
ENGELBRECHT, Jacob 148
ENGENHAGEN, Henrik 1627
ENICCELIUS, Tobias 713, 1350-51
ERDMANN, Hermann 2194
ERNST, Heinrich 407, 743
ERNST, Johann Bartram 2945
ESMARCH, Mark 2761
ESMARCH, Nicolaus 554
ESMARCH, Nicolaus Ludwig 2198, 2892
EUCLID 2928, 3013

FABER, Albert Otho 1043A
FABRICIUS, Jacob 275, 298, 358
FABRICIUS, Peter 2062
FABRICIUS, Tobias 1805
FECHT, Johannes 2952
FEUSTKING, Johann 1103
FINCK, Abel 787, 1588, 1871
FINCKE, Matthäus 324
FISCHER, Georg 604
FISCHER, Hinrich 1485
FLEISCHER, Philip 2516
FLORUS, Bernhard 605
FÖCLER, Isaac 276, 325, 336
FÖRTSCH, Johann(es) Philipp 2097, 2557, 2610,
 2646, 2702
FOSS, Johann 2685 (tr.)
FRÆRSEN, Eric 1806
FRANCKE, Johannes Mattheus 1328
FRANCKE, Wolfgang Christoph 2762, 2825
FRANCKENAU, Georg Friedrich de 2945
Frederick II, *King of Denmark* 2609, 2613
FRESE, Georg 1946
FRICK, Erhard 245
FRIDERICI, Christoph 1548
FRIDERICUS, Johannes 112
FRIDERICHSEN, Johann 164
FRIEDLEIN, Joh. 2583 (engr.), 2722 (engr.)
FRIES, Arnold 3067
FRIESE, Balthasar 500
FRIESE, Detlev Marcus 2457
FRIESE, Johann Christian 2096
FRIESE, Marcus 501
FRIIS, Laurids 1398, 1486, 2140
FRIIS, Nicolaus 2517
FRISCH, Johann(es) 1304, 1444, 1579, 1736
FRISIUS, Matthias 3131
FROUWE, Emichius 949
FUCHS, Gottfried 2826, 2869
FUCHS, Johannes 2314, 2892A, 2976

GÄRTNER, Magnus 2087
GARP, Peter 475, 502, 555
GENNER, Johannes 32
GENSCH von Breitenau, Christoph 1354, 1399
 1525, 1538, 1633, 1960, 2141, 2190A
GENTZEN, Siegfried 2895
GERDES, Joachim 467, 741, 744
GERKENS, Hermann Bernhard 2827
GER(C)KENS, Simon (Peter) 2764, 2827, 2896,
 3068
GEUSS, Johann Philipp 1873
GIESE, August 2978-79
GIESE, Joachim 1539, 1961, 2005-06, 2011, 2063,
 2098, 2142-44, 2268, 2316-17, 2361, 2411, 2518,
 2558-59, 2595
GILLET de la Tessonnerie 954, 1104, 2459
GLASS, Salomon 2318

GLASSIUS, Jacob (Benedict) 788
GLOXIN, Peter Balthasar 714
GÖDEKE, Andreas 1089, 1105, 1119, 1234-35, 1581, 1994
GOLDBERCH, Caspar 745
GOLDSCHMID, Peter 2611
GOUDE 2443
GOUSSAULT, *Abbé* 2897
GRÄSSEL, Jacob 1687, 1739
GRAM, Ægidius 1488, 1636
GRAMM, Friederich 2573, 2675, 2765
GRANOVIUS, Daniel 1962, 2007
GREFFLINGER, Georg 1046, 1540A, 1688
GREIS, Hans Andreas 516 (engr.)
GRIMBERG, Nils 2705
GROTIUS, Hugo 1423
GROTSCHILLING, Han(n)s 1035, 1047, 1193, 1784, 1915
GROSSMANN, Johann 715
GRUBE, Hermann 1356
GRUBEVILLE, J. Henr. de 2898
GRYPHIUS, Andreas 1661
GUDE, Henrich Ludwig 2362
GUTBROT, Johannes 476, 556, 640, 746

HACKE, Martin 224
HAGER, Christoph Achatius 1809-10
HAHN, Hinrich 2440, 2519, 2706, 2767, 2980-83, 3069
HAMERICH, Christian 2768
HAMERICH, Henrich 763, 1812, 2102, 2192, 2226, 2319, 2413, 2769, 2900, 3070
HAMMERICH, Friedrich 790
HAMMERSHAIMB, Franciscus de 2500
HANENFELDT, Bruno 1729
HANNEMANN, Bartholomæus J. O. 2676
HANNEMANN, Johann(es) Ludwig 2984, 3071-72
HARBOE, Nicolaus 2597
HARDENBECIUS, Ambrosius 330, 350
HARDER, Georg 1300
HARDKOPF, Nicolaus 477
HARSDÖRFFER, G. P. 1066-67
HARSSEN, Momme 75
HARTNACK, Daniel 2414-15, 2460, 2561-62, 2647-50
HARTPRECHT, Johannes 791
HASE, Johannes Conrad 1637
HASSING, Niels Christian 113
HATTEN, Henrik von 246, 1266
HAVEMANN, Michael 225
HECKLAWER, Hans Christian 1811
HEERFORT, Christoffer 2363, 2461
HE(E)RMAN, Johan 1489
HEICKE, Claudius 2194
HEIMREICH, Anton Walther See Walther
HEINS, Christoph 583
HEINS, Valentin 1689, 2675
HEINSIUS, Daniel 1724
HELD, Balthasar 1963
HELD, Christian 2064
HELDVAD, Niels 14, 23-24, 31, 56, 60-61, 184, 443, 1638, 1915A
HELM, Friedrich 615
HELT, Adolph 3132
HENNINGS, Erich 2269
HENNINGS, Simon 326, 350-51, 372, 478
HENNINGSEN, Johann Friedrich 2901
HENSBERGEN, Hieronymus von 1648 (engr.)
HERMSDORFF, Christian 607
HESHUS, Ezard 165

HESSELIUS, Peter 1690, 1740
HESSEN, Johannes Andreas 747
HEUBEL, Heinrich Wendel 263, 277
HEY, Paul 2876
HILDERMANN, Johannes Stephan 3073
HINDSHOLM, Hans Jacobsen 327
HOE, D. 674A
HÖFEL, Kunrath 665, 718
HÖPKEN, Daniel Niclas von 2563
HÖPNER, Mark 373
HÖPPENER, Georg 2707
HOFMANN, Anton 1188
HOHENHOLTZ, Ernst 444, 464, 608
HOHENHOLTZ, Johan Friederich 1514
HOHMAN, Georg 961
HOLCK, Henrich Detleff von 1205, 1249
HOLMER, Martin 1445
HOLST, Johannes 2146, 2227
HOLST, Jürgen I. 213-14, 529
HOLTZMANN, Johannes 174, 185, 194
HOLYK, Georg 2986, 3074A
HONOLD, Jacob 1066-67
HORBIUS, Johann Heinrich 2652
HORN, Hildebrand 1742
HORNBERG, Georg Friedrich 201
HORNBOSTEL, Christian 1743
HORNEMEYER, Johan Theodor 1811A
HOSSOM, Jens Mogensøn 1468
HOYER, Anna Ovena 76
HOYER, Andreas 1108, 1189, 2193, 2385, 2462
HOYER, Nicolaus 2653, 3039
HUDEMANN, Johann(es) 445, 504-05, 1109-10, 1236, 1403, 1490
HÜLSEMANN, Caspar Petrus 2010
HÜTTEMANN, Gerhard 1937
HUNNIUS, Nicolaus 336
HUTHMANN, Henning 1582

ISELBURG, B. 1163 (engr.)
IVERSEN, Volquard 1430

JACOBI, Elias 2829, 2988
JACOBI, Laurentius 16
JACOBI, Johann 175
JAGETEUFFEL, Otto 1111
JEBSEN, Johannes 1237, 1812
JENSEN, Johann(es) Jacob 1640, 1692
Jerome, *St.* 2198
JERSIN, Jens Dinesen 300, 415, 1190
JESSEN, Friederich 1112, 1267, 1308, 1358-59, 1404, 1491-92, 1583-84, 1641, 1693-94, 1744-45
JESSEN, Tycho 687, 748
JÖNSEN, Heinrich 1918, 2708
JOHNSEN, Heinrich 1729
JOLI, Alexander 1541
JÜGERT, Peter Jacob 714, 1432
JÜRGENS (i.e., Irgens), Joachim 2364
JÜRGENSEN, D. 2830
JULICHER, Jan Monjoy 1360
JUNGH, Franciscus de 1067
JUNGHANS, M. 2831
JURGES, Johann 348

KEGEL, Philipp 1919
KEIL, Christian 2564
KELLNER, Thomas 1114
KELNER, Hartwich 585, 609
KENCKEL, Stephan 1309, 1361, 1543, 1695-96, 2463
KESLER, Johann 1147
KIEFFER, Johann Conrad 2654, 2709, 2907-08

KIELMANN, Johan Adolph 508, 1120
KILIAN, Gottfried 850, 1051-52, 1115, 1119, 1148, 1191, 1238, 1268, 1405
KILIAN, Martin 1115
KING, William 2775
KINGO, Thomas 2194, 2229, 3031
KIRCHHOFF, Albert Christoph 2710, 3075
KIRSTENIUS, Michael 516
KLEIN, Johannes 2952
KLETT, Andreas 1688
KLOCKAW, Johann 719
KLÖCKER, Gerhard, 1289
KLOTZ, Stephan 331, 358, 558-59, 667, 1192, 1311, 1493-93A, 1748, 1802, 2365, 2573
KLUG, Christian 2012
KLUG, Franz Erdmann Christian 2833
KNOBLOCH, Benjamin 586, 954 (tr.), 966, 1104 (tr.), 2459 (tr.)
KNOFF, Christopher 2613 (ed.)
KNUTSEN, Matthias 1407
KÖHN, Joachim 2876, 2909
KOGEL, Friedrich 1877
KOHL(IUS), Franz Dietrich 2573, 2776, 2876, 2991, 3076
KOPFF, Johann Philipp 2566
KORTHOLT, Christian 1150, 1408-09, 1446-47, 1643-46, 1815-16, 1878, 1884, 1967-68, 2013, 2103-04, 2148-49, 2194-96, 2207, 2241, 2465-68, 2520-21, 2565, 2614, 2655, 2992
KORTHOLT, Heinrich Christian 2271
KORTHOLT, Matthias Nicolaus 2614
KORTHOLT, Sebastian 2614
KRABBE, Erich 2202 (tr.)
KRAGH, A. C. 2194
KRAHE, Christoph 2064A
KRAKEWITZ, Jonas 38 (tr.)
KRAMER, Mauritius 2150, 2366, 2993
KRAUSE, Johann Georg 720
KREYENKAMP, Hermann 1240
KRÖGER, Meinard 1269, 1363
KRÜKK, Johannes 2065
KRUSS, Johann 2656
KÜKELSOM, Alexander von 202
KÜRBELIN, Johann Georg 2711
KUHN, Valentin 611
KULPIS, Joh. Georg 3028

LA FONTAINE, Andreas de 1056
LA FOSSE, Estiene de 2780
LA MARTINIÈRE, P. M. de 1750
LANG, Johann 1750 (tr.)
LANG, Petrus 2287
LANGE, Balthasar Otto 1970
LANGE, P. 2040
LANGE, Paul 1970
LANGE, Peter 1970
LANGEMACK, Michael 2469
LANGEMAKE, Johannes [I] 168
LANGEMAKE, Johann(es) [II] 688-89, 760, 1410-11, 1545
LANGERHANS, Nicolaus 2015
LANGJAHR, Johann Jacob 2834-35, 2912
LA SERRE, Jean Puget de 3080
LASSÆUS, Bernhard 2152
LASSENIUS, Johannes 1312, 1412, 1648, 1880, 1921-22, 2194, 2198, 2229, 2232, 2272-73, 2320-28, 2349, 2367-72, 2420-22, 2567-71, 2615-22, 2781, 2835-36, 2913-14, 2995-3001, 3081-84
LAUREMBERG, Jacob Sebastian 348
LAUREMBERG, Johannes 215, 283, 642, 668A, 721

LAURENTII, Bernhard 1971
LAURENTII, Nicolaus 1751
LAURENTIUS, Ægidius 2105
LAURENTIUS, Bernhard 1494-96
LAUTERBACH, Andreas 375, 449, 560
LAVERENTZEN, Johannes 2623
LEIKEN, Wolfgang Philipp 2253
LEMKE, Henrik 794
LENTE, Hugo 1524
LESLEUS, Claudius Nicolaus 1151
LEYSER, Michael 643
LIBENBERG, Peter 1153
LIBRAMM, Johannes 1755
LILIENCRON, C. F. von 3085
LINDEMANN, Thomas 376, 669
LINEKOGEL, Johannes Christoph 3002, 3052 (ed.), 3086
LIPPE, Christian von der 264
LOBES, Joachim 750
LÖHNER, Emanuel 2782
LÖSCHER, Samuel 1057-58
LÖW, Johann 1125, 1193, 1289, 1465, 1882
LOHMANN, Georg 1924
LOHMANN, Hartwig 121, 283
LOHRIUS, Georg Christoff 1058A
LONERUS, Andreas 62, 247, 278, 533, 561, 690, 722, 972, 1271
LORENTZEN, Nicolaus 2597
LORENTZEN, Otto 534
LUBBERT, Heinrich 1756
LUCAE, Friedrich 2153
LUDERUS, Johannes 506
LÜCOPPIDAN, Peter Joh. 1468
LÜDERS, Garlef 377
LÜSCHNER, Ernst Gottlieb 2783
LUND, Johann(es) 1543, 1696, 1820, 2712-13, 2784
LUND, Thomas 1819, 2066, 2522, 2658, 2713, 2784
LUTHER, Daniel 1118
LUTHER, Martin 138, 302, 691, 1216 (tr.), 1218-19 (tr.), 1274, 1516, 1553, 2683 (tr.), 2686, 2785, 3047 (tr.)
LYRA, Jacob 1244, 1414-15

MAGINA, Giovanni Antonio 1586A
MAGIRUS, Kaspar 2424
MAGNUS, Laurentius 3003
MAJOR, Detlev Johann 2523, 2675, 3087
MAJOR, Johann(es) Daniel 1365, 1416-17, 1499, 1587, 1698-1700, 1757, 1973-75, 2106, 2154-55, 2234-35, 2373, 2524, 2574
MALTZAHN, Arnold 2575, 2715
MANDELSLO, Johann Albrecht 450, 508, 854, 1418
MARCH, Caspar 1547
MARESCHALL, Heinrich 3133
MARPERGER, Paul Jacob 2716, 2839, 2897 (tr.)
MARTINI, Benedict 644, 692, 723-24, 751-52, 1448-49, 1548, 1588, 1701, 1759-60, 1821, 1883, 2156, 2199
MARTINI, Gottlieb 2950
MASIUS, Hector Gottfried 2374-75, 2429, 2470-71, 2525-29, 2576-77, 2584, 2781, 2840, 3088
MASIUS, Peter 2786, 3004
MATRAS, Daniel 248, 353, 1420, 2016
MATTHIÆ, Christian 249-50
MATTHIÆ, Paulus 573
MATTHIES, Hinrich 573
MATTHISEN, Søren 2787
MAURITIUS, Caspar 855

MAUW, Thomas 1328
MAY, Johann Burchard 2841, 2916
MEGANDER, Christoph Wilhelm 1272
MEHRNER, P. N. 1249
MEIER, Christian 693
MEIER, H. J. 2917
MEIER, Habacuc 265
MEIER, Johannes 333, 354, 451-52, 456, 479, 507, 613, 645, 796
MEILAND, Georg 251, 355, 480
MEINDERS, François de 1650
Meinfreund, Theophilus 660, 699, 702, 733, 766, 892, 973, 1059, 1139, 1167, 1215, 1330, 1365A, 1381
Meinfried See "Meinfreund"
METZELIUS, Heinrich 158
MEUSCHEN, Joachim Christian 1925
MEYER, Hermann 694
MEYER, Reinhold 694
MICHAEL, Gregorius 2038
MODEROW, Georg 741
MÖLLER, Christian Ernst 252
MOHR, Johann(es) 1273, 1761, 2376, 2788
MOHR, Nicolaus 2578
MOLDENIT, Johannes 1491
MOLESWORTH, Robert 2775
MOLLER, Franz Henrich 1581 (composer)
MOLLER, Joachim 453
MOLLER, Johannes 2017-18, 2236, 2377, 2472, 2579-80, 2626, 2659, 2789, 2842-43, 2918-19, 3005
MOLLER, Nicolaus 1313
MOLLER, Olaus 535, 614, 695
MOLTKE, Joachim 674A
MOLTKE, Levin Claus 1120
MONCK, Frantz 2920
MONIGO, Johann Heinrich von 2237
MORHOF, Daniel Georg 1450, 1500, 1589-90, 1627, 1674, 1762-63, 2019, 2067, 2107-10, 2194, 2238, 2329, 2425, 2473-74, 2530-32, 3135
MORHOFF, Caspar Daniel 3089
MOSANUS, Hubertus (pseud. for Joh. Chr. Beckmann) 2526
MOTH, Rudolph 1061-62
MÜLLER, Christian Rudolph 1591, 1926, 2475, 2844
MÜLLER, Henrik 2068-69
MÜLLER, Hermann 2040, 2330
MÜLLER, Johann Sebastian 2627
MÜLLER, Johann(es) 336, 1253, 1784, 1937, 2071
MÜNDEN, Bernhard 689
MÜNDEN, Christian 646
MUHLEN (MUHLIUS), Heinrich 2660, 2675-76, 2855, 2921, 3006, 3090
MUSAEUS, Johann Sebastian 2476
MUSÆUS, Simon Hinrich 1702
MUSELIUS, Andreas 253

NAGEL, Johann Helfrich 2581, 2845, 2922, 3092-93
NAGEL, Johannes Daniel 2719
NASSER, Bartholomæus 1314
NAUMANN, Hans-Ludwig 1421
NEANDER, J. L. 1195
NELDELIUS, Johannes 2719A, 2846, 3094
NERICUS, Caspar 204
NEUBER, Georg 753
NEUMANN, Sebastian 1673
NEUMARCK, Ernst Gottlieb 2477
NICOLAI, Jonas 1154

NICOLAI, Martin 2478, 2720
NICOLAI, Nicolaus 2070, 2157-58
NIELSEN, Jonas 1154
NIEMANN, Joachim 63
NIEMANN, Sebastian 2020, 2021 (ed.), 3008
NIEMANN, Theodor 696, 1196
NISSENUS, Coeso 573
NOLDIUS, Christian 2198
NORMAN(N), Johan(nes) Friedrich 562, 2239
NOTHELFFER, Nicolaus 1928, 2022, 2071, 2204

OBRECHT, Ulrich 3028
OLDEN, H. 1497
OLDERMANN, Samuel 2378
OLEARIUS, Adam 481, 508, 547 (ed.), 587, 647, 697, 754, 798, 819, 854, 933 (tr.), 1065-67, 1120, 1155, 1156 (ed.), 1197-98, 1216, 1274, 1277-78, 1315-17, 1328, 1384 (ed.), 1418, 1422, 1430 (ed.), 1451, 1549, 1704-05, 1716
OLEARIUS, Philip Christian 2023
OLTER, Wilhelm 857, 894, 1068, 1114
OPITZ, Andreas 482
OPITZ, Josias Heinrich 3095
OPORINUS, Conrad 1515, 2111, 2675, 2923
OTTENDORFF, Henricus 625
OTTO, Johan Gottfried 3096
OUWE, Wolfgang 859, 1279, 1453

PASCHASIUS, Henr. 184
PASCHIUS, Johannes 3009
Paulinus, Bishop of Nola 2198
PAULLI, Christian 2661
PAULLI, Daniel 1764
PAULLI, Jacob Henrik 2275-76, 2309, 2331-34
PAULLI, Simon 516, 1593
PAULLIN, Christian Frantz 1502, 1652
PELLICERUS, Joh. Georg 1661
PERSENIUS, Stephan 563
PETERSEN, Henning 1246, 2173
PETERSEN, Johann Wilhelm 2240-41, 2671
PETERSEN, Johanna Eleonora, née von Merlau 2426
PETERS(EN), Matthias (engr.) 613, 645, 1402
PETERS(EN), Nicolaus (engr.) 613, 645
PETERSEN, Nicolaus 1978
PETERSEN, Stephan 563
PETKUM, Herman von 2992
PETRÆUS, Peter 1454, 1824 (ed.), 1825
PETRÆUS, Simon 2194
PETRI, Theodor 648
PFEIFF, Daniel 725
PFENNING, Johannes Matthias 2582
PFISTER, Christoph 2277
PFLUG, Erdmann 2847-48
PFLUG, Johan 860
PILULAND, Elias 1706
PIPER 2532A, 2543
PISTORIUS, Joachim 698
PLECIUS, Martin 7
PLOMAN, Andreas 1752
PLUM, Claudius 478
POHLMANN, Henrich 2313, 2335
POLIANDER 1670
PORTEN, von der 893
PORTNER, Johannes 49-50
POSSIVINUS, Antonius 1673
PRÆTORIUS, August Christian 2790
PRAETORIUS, Johann Albrecht 1503-04
PRENGER, Christian 509, 1157
PUFENDORF, Samuel 2539, 3028
PURRIVUS, Christopher 1159

QUEISSER, Marcus 615
QVESTAL, Caspar 2925-26

RACHEL, Joachim 279, 1332, 1423, 1432, 1661
RACHEL, Samuel 2242A
RACHEL, Theodor 2927
RAGER, Dettleff 2791
RAM, Gerhard 254, 1202, 1550
RAM, Stephan 1035, 1550, 1765, 2024
RAMM, Marquard Balthasar 857
RANTZAU, Heinrich 1455
RANTZOW, Marquardt 232, 256
RASCH, Georg 415 (tr.), 1190 (tr.)
RATECKENS, Johann Philipp 2849
RATENBURG, Broder 1707
RAUSCH, Christian 700
RAVE, Johan 457
RAVIUS, Christian 1505
RECKEL, Simon 2025, 2243-44, 2792
REGIUS, Desiderius 564
REHEFELD, Bonaventura 483-84, 510, 589-90, 616, 756, 1318, 1536
REICH, Christopher 1930A
REICH, Johann Ludwig 1982-83
REICHENBACH, Elisa Sophia von 2583
REIMANN, Balthasar 66
REIMARS, Nicolaus 21
REIMER, Joachim Ludwig 1860
REINBOTH, Johannes 226, 356, 536, 591-92, 649-51, 701, 726-28, 757-58, 800, 861, 1066-67, 1121-22, 1156, 1280-81, 1366
REINCKING, Theodor 280, 334, 357, 670, 801-02, 1072, 1282, 1984
RESEN, Hans Poulsen 302 (tr.)
REUMANN, O. N. 2676
REYHER, Samuel 2380, 2850A, 2928 (ed.), 3012, 3013 (ed.)
RICHARDI, Peter 3014
RICHARDUS, Jacob 1767
RICHERTZ, Arnold 2929
RICHERTZ, G. B. 2930
RICHERTZ, Georg 1594, 2793
RICHTER, Johannes Henrich 2427
RIDEMANN, Christian 2428
RIEBE, G. C. 2776
RIEDEMANN, M. H. 1506
RIEHSE, Basilius Johannes 1515
RIES, Johanner 2205
RIESE, Henricus 1994
RIST, Johannes 195, 266, 282, 335, 378-79, 485, 511, 538, 763, 1066-67, 1124, 1283, 1319, 1424
RIST, Johann(es) Caspar 1833, 2160-61
RITTER, Johann Balthasar 1708
RODATZI, Christopher 1834
RODBERG, Christian 1595
RÖTSCHER, Johannes Volcmar 1548, 1701, 1932, 2206, 2337, 2534, 2663
RÖTTSCHER, Christian Albrecht 2664
ROGERS, Nehemiah 2851-52, 3015
ROHN, Christopher 2337A, 2380A
ROSENBUSCH, Johann Konrad 2794, 2931
ROSENKRANTZ, Gunde 424, 803, 987
ROSENKRANTZ, Holger Georg 227
ROSENKRANTZ, Jørgen 593, 804, 868
ROSMANN, Johann Adolf 2029
ROSSOV, Paul 303-04
ROTHGIESSER, C. 854 (engr.)
ROTLÖBEN, Johannes 336-37, 358-59, 380-82, 459-60, 1507
RÜBKE, Jacob 2853
RÜDEMANN, Julius Conrad 2854, 2932, 3016

RÜHLE, Daniel (von Saltzwedel) 671
RUMPEL, Johann Valentin 3017
RUNGE, Friedrich 1906
RUNGE, Marcus 338

SACHSE, Daniel 1367, 1508
SAGER, Friedrich Heinrich 638
St. SULPIS, Victor de 2480, 2584
SALA, Angelus 122
SALDENUS, Willem 1367
SANDHAGEN, Caspar Hermann 2585-86, 2665-66, 2722-23, 2795-96, 2855, 3047 (ed.), 3097-98
SARTORIUS, Peter 1596, 3080 (tr.)
SASS, Niels 205, 216, 255
SAURIUS, Andreas 1425
SAVONAROLA, Hieronymus 1426
SCHACHT, Friederich Eilhard 1588
SCHAEVE, Heinrich 1688
SCHAFFER, Heinrich 461
SCHALL, John Michael 1365
SCHEEL, Joachim 228
SCHEELE, Peter 653, 1835
SCHELLHAMMER, Gunther Christoph 3019, 3099, 3100
SCHENCK, Arn. 187
SCHERMER, Samuel 1247
SCHILLING, Andreas 336, 462
SCHINDLER, P. E. (composer) 2396
SCHIPPING, Peter 2429
SCHIRMER, Martin 2481, 2588, 2856, 2933
SCHLAPRITZ, Hieronymus 2114
SCHLÜTER, Severinus Walther 2208
SCHMIDT, Bernhard 988
SCHMID(T), Christian Alb. 1792, 1983
SCHMIDT, Hans Heinrich 1461, 1548
SCHMID(T), Joachim 2163-64, 2266, 2338, 2381
SCHMIDT, Sebastian 2482, 2535, 3112A
SCHMIDT von Eisenberg, Johannes 1887
SCHMIDT von Eisenberg, Valentin 1323-24, 1372, 1457-58, 1714
SCHÖLTZ, Friedrich 2382
SCHÖNFELD, G. 1373
SCHOPEN, H. von 1161
SCHOTTEL, Justus Georg 1510
SCHRÖDER, Hinrich 565, 594
SCHRÖDER, Jacob 1511
SCHRÖDER, Josias Hermann 2432, 3024
SCHROEDER, Laurentz 283
SCHRÖDER, Laurentius 1126, 1374
SCHRÖTER, Benedict 223
SCHRÖTER, Elias 1873
SCHULTZ(E), Christian 463, 566, 759-60, 991
SCHULTZ(E), Cornelius 1768, 1933, 2668
SCHULTZ, Theodor 654
SCHUMANN, Johannes 486, 567, 1326, 1459, 2075, 2278
SCHUPP, Johann Balthasar 993-96, 1091
SCHWABE, Theophilus 348
SCHWARTZ, Josua 1934, 2219, 2669, 2857, 3136
SCHWEINITZ, David von 2944, 3025
SCHWESINGER von Cronhelm, Andreas 1988A, 2117A, 2535A
SCHWIEGER, Jacob 1002-1004, 1076-77, 1375
SEGER, F. 2483, 2536, 2657
SEGER, Georg 768 (tr.)
SEGER, Jacob 2633
SEHESTED, Jens Steen 1460, 1889
SEIDEL, Simon 267
SELMER, Christian 1658
SELMER, Conrad 4
SELMER, Cornelius 29, 138, 140

SELNECCER, Nicolaus 284
SEMPER, Balthasar Ernst 2120
SIBBERN, Nicolaus 3026
SIMONIUS, N. 1512
SIVERS, Peter August 2946
SLEDANUS, Christian 68, 78, 168
SOLINUS, Christian 1716
SOLOMON, Abraham 2194
SOTHMANN, Johann 1989
SPANGENBERG, Cyriacus 1551
SPECHT, Christian 2433, 2875
SPENER, Philipp Jacob 2484, 2749, 3113
SPERLING, Otto 2245, 2992
STEGMANN, Josua 268
STEINKUHL, Christoph 2218 (tr.)
STEMANN, Just Daniel 2434
STEMAN(N), Just Valentin 1286, 2166
STEPHAN, Johannes 3027
STEURNAGEL, Nicolaus Gottfried 3028 (tr.)
STEVENS, Cosmus 1598A
STÖCKEN, Christian von 763, 1162, 1287, 1659,
1701, 1717, 1840-42, 1890-91, 1936-37, 1991,
2037-40, 2041 (ed.), 2076-80, 2119, 2167-68,
2207-09, 2279, 2670, 2947, 3029
STÖCKEN, Friedrich Gerhard von 2247
STÖCKEN, G. von 763
STÖCKEN, H(e)inrich von 1877, 2117, 2246-
47, 2280-82
STOLBERG, Johann Christian 764
STOLTZ, Bernhard 1513, 1843, 1938
STORNING, Hinrich 1112, 1358, 1376, 1718,
1892-93, 2081-82, 2210, 2283, 2671
STRAUSS, Christopher 464
STRICKER, Benjamin 1599
STRICKER, Otto 2826
STRICKER, Paul 2284
STRIGELIUS, Joachim 341
STRUVE, Reimar 2120
STUBBE, Jacob 2083
STURM, Joachim 425, 512, 1204
STYLLE, Petrus von der 618
SUETONIUS, Tranquillus Gaius 1205, 1249
SUYDERVLIET, A. V. 122
SVANINGIUS, Johannes 593
SYBELIST, Wendelin 508
Sybille Ursula, *Duchess of Holstein-Glücksburg*
1601
SYLM, Georg 1005, 1127

TÄNTZER, Johann 2121, 2286, 2435, 3030
Talander 2446-47
TAMKE, Bernard 1288
TARNOVIUS, Johannes 807
TAUBE, Jacob 1602, 1769
TETING, Niels 127
THEANDER, Theophil 22
THEILE, Johann 2169
THESSEL, Johann(es) 705, 1299 (tr.)
THESTRUP, Franz 3031
THIDOMAR, Johann Christoph 1116, 1127A-29
Thomas à Kempis 1939
THOMASIUS, Christian 3028
THOMBSEN, Johan 1752
THOMSEN, Johann Christian 1514
THOMSEN, Nicolaus 2798
THOMSEN, Samuel 2859
TIEDIUS, Joachim 3115
TÖNNING, Henrik 2860
TOLLIUS, Nicolaus 1130, 1552
TRAPHAGEN, Johann 1131
TRATZIGER, Adam 217

TREBSDORFF, Balthasar 283, 305
TRENCKNER, Johann Heinrich 2288
TRIBBE, Johannes Daniel 2287, 2289, 2486-88
TSCHERNING, Paul 729, 872
TYCHSEN, Tycho Th. 2105

UBELACKER, Friedrich 2734
UCHTERITZ, Heinrich von 1328
ULICH, Michael 620-21
ULCKEN, Andreas 2210A
ULRICH, Bernhard 542, 568
UPPENDORFF, Johannes 1554-55

VERGIL 384, 547, 1384
VERMEHREN, Paul 2591, 2801, 3120
VETTE, F. 2635
VILLEDIEU, Mme. de 1772
VO!GT, Johann(es) Heinrich 489, 543, 569
VOIGTLÄNDER, Gabriel 285, 360
VOLBRECHT, Ludwig 544
VOLKMAR, Johannes 2803
VOTISCH, Laurentius 1132
VOSS, Martin 3033-34, 3122
VOSSBEIN, Johann 3035
VRANGEL, Henricus 2500

WACKEROW, Jacob 1078
WAGENFÜHRER, Hinrich 570
WAGNER, Georg Friedrich 1660A
WAGNER, Gottschalk 623
WALDSCHMIDT, Wilhelm Huldericus 2950
WALTHER, Anton Heimreich 1306, 1402, 1517,
2171-72
WALTHER, Michael 336
WALTHER, Paul 385
WANDAL, Peder Jensen 571, 595, 656, 730, 874-
75
WANDEL, Bagge 1133
WARNICKE, Melchior 1462, 1518
WASMUTH, Matthias 1505, 2250, 2291
WASMUTH, Matthias jr. 2383
WEBER, Georg Henrich 1134-36
WEBER, Immanuel 2593
WEDDERKOPF, Fr. 2776
WEDDERKOPF, Gabriel 1774, 1896, 2044-45,
2251, 2437-38, 2675-76, 2739, 2776
WEDEGE, Joachim 465
WEGENER, Albert 128
WEGHORST, Paul 1775
WEIDENKOPFF, Friedrich 1548
WEIGBERS, Friederich 2198
WEIGEL, Erhard 2805-06
WEINBERG, Hermann Laur. von 1421
WEIS, Otto 2439
WEISER, Bonaventura 223
WEISSER, Philipp 2173
WEIZIUS, Hieronymus 1117
WENDLER, Johannes 286
WERNER, Adam Friedrich 478, 513, 545, 596,
657, 731-32, 762, 812, 882-83, 1079-80, 1211
WERNER, Christian 2252
WERNER, Friedrich 1137
WERNICKE, Christian 2084
WESTPHAL, Johannes 1463, 2807
WEYANDT, Ludowig 2722 (painter)
WICHMAN, J. 1736 (engr.)
WIESE, Albert 1081
WIESENER, Gottfried 1328
WIGAND, Johan 1556
WILCKENS, Johann(es) Hermann 2384, 2677,
2793, 3036, 3123

WILDE, Paulus 1164, 1497
WILDENHEIN, Johann(es) 1849, 2123
WILDHAGEN, Caspar 2951-52
WILHELM, Samuel 230
WILHELMI, Johann(es) Caspar 1720, 2342-44
WILLER, Jacob 1212-13
WILLIUS, Johann Valentin 1850
WINCKLER, Christian 765
WINTERBERG, Nicolaus 306, 2087
WISMAR, Nicolaus 176
WITTE, Johannes 2253
WITTE, Paul 1112
WITTMANN, L. 2892
WITZLEBEN, Georg 1291, 1691
WÖRGER, Franz 1605, 1661, 1776, 2345
WOLCKE, Johann 1455
WOLDENBERG, Paul 658
WOLF, Christian Sigismund 2046
WOLF, Jacob 2678
WOLFF, Johan Georg 1214

WOLTERS, Joachim 3125
WORDINGHAUSEN, Johannes 1292, 1379
WULFF, Jacob Villedsen 1772 (tr.)
WUNDSCH, Balthasar 1429A
WUNDSCH, Johann(es) 1082-83, 1166
WYGAND, August 2808-12, 2864-68, 2953-56, 3037-38

YVON, Peter 1662-63

ZESEN, Filip von 2233
ZIMMERMAN, Johann Jacob 2493
ZIMMERMAN, Tobias 638
ZINZERLING, Joan Bernhard 689
ZITSCHER, Peter 2385-86, 2440, 2494, 2679-80, 2740, 2813-14
ZWERG, Christian Oswald 3127
ZWERG, Gotthard Johannes 2595, 2636, 2740, 3039
ZWERG, Michael 1017, 1520-21

# Index of Printers and Publishers Named

BAXMAN, Johan Adolph 2450, 2480, 2584
BECKENSTEIN, Simon 1859, 1892
BOCKENHOFFER, Johan Philip 2186, 2198, 2231-
  32, 2239, 2249, 2252, 2255, 2259, 2273, 2290,
  2320-27, 2340, 2363-64, 2367-72, 2396, 2420-
  22, 2436, 2444, 2448, 2461, 2483, 2498, 2516-
  17, 2525, 2532A, 2536-37, 2549, 2556, 2567,
  2569, 2591, 2597, 2635, 2657, 2680A, 2686,
  2690, 2706A, 2714, 2716, 2736, 2738, 2760,
  2763, 2773, 2780, 2797, 2800, 2811, 2818, 2822,
  2826, 2831, 2837, 2844, 2849, 2854; †2891,
  2912, 2915, 2932, 3016, 3088
BÖKMANN, Peter 2500
BORNHEINRICH, Johan Jacob 2237, 2288, 2449,
  2481, 2533, 2538, 2568, 2571, 2588, 2617, 2619,
  2621-22, 2637, 2781, 2787, 2890, 3001, 3054,
  3082, 3084
BOTSAC, Barthold 2599
BRÄMER, Christian 1790, 2449
BRENNER, Walther 13
BÜTNER, Daniel 385, 1595
CARSTEN, Johann 726, 757, 861, 1198
CASSUBE, Christian 514, 661, 1158, 1245, 1790
CÖPSELIUS, Johann 2526
COMMELYN, Casperus 1368
DANXST, Cordt 2502, 2545
DIBBERN, Nicholas 2556
DIETZEL, Johann 2834
DRULLMANN, Johann Georg 2229
ECKSTORFF, Lorentz 2583, 2586, 2598, 2628,
  2636, 2646, 2653-54, 2656, 2660, 2662-63, 2665,
  2668, 2673, 2681, 2701-02, 2704, 2707, 2709,
  2712-13, 2719A, 2722, 2740, 2748, 2761, 2771,
  2784, 2788, 2792, 2795, 2815, 2871, 2874, 2901,
  2907-08, 2936, 2946, 2978-79, 2989, 3007-09,
  3039, 3043, 3046, 3049, 3090, 3094, 3097-98,
  3109A, 3112A
EICHHORN, Daniel 691, 1845; †1965
ERYTROPEL, Johan Just 2194, 2351, 2435, 2470-
  71, 2527, 2543, 2618, 2687, 2750, 2756, 2840,
  2897, 3015, 3030
FRISCH, Johannes 1736
GARMANN, Samuel 2817
GERLACH, Christian 1859, 1892
GERHARD, Christian 1934
GEERTSEN, Christian 1375
GIDSCHEL, Jost Ferdinand 2593
GLEDITSCH, Johann Ludwig 2749
GLOCKEN, Jacob zur 244, 247, 278-79, 286, 298,
  309, 328, 331, 333, 338, 352, 354, 356, 364, 373,
  377, 385, 447, 451, 463-64, 479, 490, 507-08,
  512, 533, 535-36, 546-47, 554, 558, 563, 566,
  571, 586, 591-92, 601, 605, 650-51, 660, 699,
  702
GODICHE, Mathias Jörgensen 1113, 1220, 1593,
  1708
GØDE, Georg Clausen 1527, 1586A, 1607-08, 1650,
  1653, 1665A, 1779, 1782, 1791, 1803, 1828;
  †1830, 1832, 1856, 1862, 1879, 1916
GØDE, Henrik Clausen 1027A, 1133, 1138, 1145,
  1171, 1181, 1184-85, 1194, 1199, 1201, 1206,
  1211, 1229-30, 1243, 1245, 1259, 1265, 1299,
  1324, 1329, 1336, 1346, 1352, 1452, 1527
GÖTZE, Matthias 150
GOLDBECK, David 1761
GRIMBERG, Nils 2705
GUTH, Christian 854, 1418
HAKE (Haake), Peder 330, 348, 350, 372, 376,
  435, 717, 732, 812, 814, 837, 858, 864, 867,

877-78, 883, 904, 968; †913, 916, 919, 936,
  938, 943, 951, 1079
HANSSEN, Hans 227, 324
HANTZSCH, Georg 148, 593, 743
HAUBOLD, Christian 2272-73
HAUBOLD, Peder 618, 768, 1291, 1424, 1661, 1724
HEBER, Hans 459
HEBER, Johann 616, 852
HERBERT, Gotfried 1605
HESSELIUS, Peter 1740
HEUBEN, Henrich 2979
HÖFER, Johan 53-55, 57, 61-63, 66, 68, 70, 75,
  78, 84, 90, 95, 103, 106, 113-115, 118, 174, 185,
  (187), (194)
HØG, Just Jensen 2705, 2805
HOLST, Jürgen (Georg) 214-15, 249-50, 318, 389,
  516, 529
HOLWEIN, Johan 138, 591-92, 601, (625), 627,
  (638), (646-47), (649), 650-51, (667), 690,
  (692), (696), 697, 699, (701), 705, 722-24,
  726-28, 730, 733, 735-36, 748, 751-52, 754, 756-
  60, 763, 766, 800, (816), 819, 854, 859, 861,
  875, 892, 933, 954, 961, 966, 972, 1005, 1066-
  67, 1082, 1087, 1104, 1111-12, 1118, 1120-22,
  1127, 1139, 1155-56, 1167, 1192, 1196-98, 1200,
  1204, 1215-16, 1218-19, 1237, 1240, 1244, 1246,
  1264, 1271, 1274, 1280-81, 1292, 1294, 1306,
  1309, 1315-16, 1321, 1323, 1328, 1330, 1356,
  1361, 1379, 1381, 1384, 1389, 1402, 1414, 1416,
  1418, 1429A, 1430, 1432, 1437, 1445, 1448-49,
  1453, 1457, 1461, 1463, 1468, 1472, 1485, 1495,
  1509, 1517, 1520-21, 1536, 1548-49, 1556, 1588,
  1591, 1595, 1634, 1673, 1696, 1701, 1710, 1714,
  1717, 1721, 1728, 1747, 1759-61, 1793, 1819-
  21, 1824, 1847, 1849, 1853, 1861, 1871, 1873-
  74, 1883, 1887, 1943, 1982, 1998, 2010, 2013,
  2015, 2020-21, 2023, 2025, 2036, 2047-48, 2062,
  2066, 2068, 2118, 2123, 2140, 2152, 2156-58,
  2171-72; †2064A, 2189, 2206, 2219, 2226-27,
  2243-44, 2246, 2256-58, 2287A, 2393, 2413,
  2446-47, 2496, 2534-35, 2544, 2557, 2563, 2585
JANSOHN, Christian 960, 1061-62
JANSON von der Arck, Johan 1368
JANSSEN, Reinhard 2102, 2117, 2117A, 2120, 2153,
  2167, 2180, 2184, 2192, 2204, 2209, 2213, 2215-
  16, 2233, 2247-48, 2287, 2289, 2292, 2299,
  2330, 2335, 2360, 2366, 2385, 2392, 2417, 2423,
  2428, 2434, 2440, 2443, 2451, 2451A, 2485,
  2494, 2519, 2535A, 2566, 2578, 2587, 2625,
  2669, 2679, 2689, 2703, 2719, 2742, 2753-54,
  2759, 2767-68, 2770, 2777, 2782-83, 2786, 2790-
  91, 2794, 2803, 2807, 2820, 2832A, 2845, 2853,
  2857, 2862, 2880-82, 2892, 2895-96, 2902, 2905,
  2917, 2922, 2927, 2929-31, 2943, 2951-52, 2982,
  2993, 3130; †3026, 3045, 3051, 3053, 3074,
  3074B, 3075, 3085, 3092-93, 3118, 3124-25
JOLI, Alexander 1541
JÜRGENSEN, Matthias 1173, 1212-13, 1291, 1375,
  1470, 1562, 1670-71, 1723, 1743, 1850
KILIAN, Gottfried 1405
KOCH, Andreas 193, 217, 222, 230, 246, 253, 267-
  68, 273, 289, 292, 303, 336-37, 358, 378, 380-82,
  384, 433, 445, 459-60, 476, 482, 485, 489, 498-
  504, 506, 509-511, 530-32, 543, 555-56, 559,
  565, 567, 570, 585, 589-90, 594, 609, 615-16,
  619, 640, 652, 659, 661A, 687, 729, 742, 746;
  †852, (879)
KOCH, Melchior 319, 569, 624, 740, 894, 932A,
  949, 950, 965, 970, 1002-04, 1006, 1020, 1026-

27, 1034-35, 1047, 1050-54, 1072, 1076A, 1077, 1088-89, 1092, 1105, 1110, 1114-16, 1124-25A, 1126, 1127A, 1128-30, 1134, 1136, 1140, 1142, 1146, 1157, 1161-63, 1165, 1168-69, 1191, 1193, 1202, 1214, 1232, 1235-36, 1238-39, 1251, 1253, 1255, 1266, 1268, 1282-83, 1289-90, 1332-33, 1337, 1346-49, 1353, 1357, 1362, 1405, 1410, 1412, 1465, 1467, 1469, 1483-84, 1497, 1503-04, 1512-13, 1524, 1550, 1565B, 1585, 1610, 1639, 1648, 1658, 1666, 1737, 1750, 1765, 1769, 1784, 1794, 1852, 1857, 1860, 1880, 1901-02, 1915, 1918, 1926, 1928, 1937-38, 1942, 1978-80, 1988A, 1993; †2071

KÖNING, Samuel 1637
KRETZER, Abraham 21
KRUSE, Heinrich 249, 300, 305, 353, 360, 407, 457, 542
KUHN, Valentin 546, 554, 586, 611
LAMPRECHT, Georg 402, 405-06, 461, 465, 467, 474, 478, 480, 513, 516, 518-19, 548, 573-74, 598-99, 604, 620-21, 626, 628, 643, 669, 671, 674, 679, 686, 703-04, 712, 720, 725, 741, 744, 762, 764, 781, 788, 790, 807, 909, 1037, 1046, 1099, 1195, 1205, 1249, 1286, 1295-97, 1386, 1435, 1471, 1502, 1519
LAMPRECHT, Martin 1510
LAMPRECHT, Wolff 1688
(Lavrentson, Johan, director of "Königl; und Universit. privilegirten Buchdruckerey") 3009A, 3042, 3044, 3062, 3120
Leeu see Löw
LESLEUS, Claudius Nicolaus 1151
LIEBE, Johan Melchior 2272-73, 2367-68, 2420-21, 2567-68, 2571, 2617, 2619-21, 2749, 2781, 2834, 2913-14, 2996, 3031, 3080-81, 3088
LIEBERNICKEL, Gottfried 2712-13
LÖW (Leeu), Victor de 988, 995-96, 1043A, 1091, 1093, 1149, 1234, 1304, 1390, 1444, 1462, 1518, 1541, 1560, 1573, 1575, 1611, 1690, 1740, 1805-06, 1844, 1882, 1946, 2008, 2012, 2042; †2114, 2146, 2160-61
LOHRIUS, Georg Christoff 1058A
LUFT, Korfits 1931, 1948, 1951A, 1959, 1990, (2009); †2026
MARTEAU, Pieter 2775
MARTZAN, Melchior 161, 205, 228, 251-52, 271, 283, 299, 302, 311, 326, 355, 387, 390, 423, 436, 458, 491, 572, 575, 577, 596, 607, 612, 622, 657, 673, 685
MATTHIAS, Peter 2788
MEULEN, Cornelius van der 1662-63
MEYERS, Heinrich Johann †2526
MOHR, Johann 1761
MOLTKE, Joachim 248, 288, 299, 302, 353, 406, 410, 429, 431, 442, 474, 516, 686, 691, 781
MORSING, Peter 721, 765, 769-70, 783, 789, 791, 793, 801-803, 808, 810-11, 823, 827, 841, 845, 848, 852, 882; †830, 844, 846, 849, 851, 865, 873, 881, 886, 900, 903, 915, 920, 924-25, 932, 948, 956, 962, 975, 986, 990, 1007, 1012, 1016, 1023-24, 1031, 1045, 1055, 1070-71, 1073, 1084
MÜLLER, Nicolaj †1790
NAUMANN, Johann 586, 697, 1750
NELDELIUS, Johann 3094
NEUHOF, Conrad Hartwig 2121, 2202, 2543, 2823, 2835; †2995, 2997-98, 3000, 3003
NEUMANN, Conrad 2757
NIELSEN, Tyge 214
NISSEN, Niclos 1904
PAPE, Georg 1809

PAULLI, Daniel 1420, 1557, 1565A, (1574), 1576-78, 1581A, 1586-86A, 1592-93, 1603-04, 1606, 1628-31, 1642, 1651, 1655, 1665B, 1684-85, 1691, 1696A, 1703, 1706, 1718A, 1735, 1758, 1764, 1780, 1807, 1809-10, 1813, 1817-18, 1831, 1850, 1855, 1904, 1921, 1927, 1955, 1957, 1976, 1985-86, 1996, 2016, 2086; †2229
PAUSCHERT, Nicolaus 1155
PENTZOLD, Balthasar 3080-81
RASCH, Georg 300
RAUSCHER, Hieronymus 122
REIMERS, Christian 2275, 2384, (2460), 2464, 2491, 2493, 2612, 2627, 2652, 2779, 2793, 2838, 2870A, 2910, 3038, 3133
REUMANN, Joachim 1267, 1284, 1287, 1298, 1307-08, 1314, 1318, 1325-26, 1331, 1334, 1350-51, 1358-59, 1365, 1372, 1404, 1409, 1425, 1446-47, 1450, 1459, 1466, 1487, 1491-92, 1499-1500, 1505-06, 1511, 1514-15, 1546, 1554, 1563-65, 1582-83, 1598A, 1612-14, 1635, 1641, 1643-46, 1674-75, 1686, 1693-95, 1698-99, 1699A, 1700, 1702, 1707, 1709, 1715, 1718, 1725-27, 1729, 1738, 1742, 1744-45, 1752-55, 1757, 1762-63, 1770, 1774-75, 1812, 1815-16, 1835, 1872, 1878, 1881, 1896, 1906, 1954, 1961, 1963, 1967-68, 1970, 1973, 1987, 1992, 2005, 2011, 2019, 2029, 2044, 2060, 2063-64, 2072, 2084, 2096, 2098-99, 2103-05, 2107-08, 2113, 2126-27, 2142-44, 2148-49, 2166, 2170, 2195, 2225, 2251, 2269, 2271, 2291, 2297-98, 2302A, 2337, 2337A, 2361, 2378, 2380A, 2383, 2391, 2411, 2425, 2445, 2465, 2467-68, 2473-74, 2476, 2489-90, 2520-21, 2523, 2530, 2532, 2541, 2558-59, 2573, 2582, 2595, 2600, 2638, 2675-76, 2708, 2710, 2762, 2776, 2778, 2785, 2825, 2870, 2876, 2909, 2916, 2923, 2928, 2948, 2950, 3012-13, 3116, 3131, 3137
REUTHER, Barthold 2958, 2984, 2991, 3017, 3019, 3027, 3046A, 3050, 3071, 3074A, 3087, 3095, 3100, 3117
RIECHEL, Johann Sebastian 2314, 2892A, 3013
RICHEL, Sebastian 2437-38
RIPENAU, Siegfried 2357-58, 2426
ROSE, Georg Hinrich 1637
RUPFF, Christian 225
SARTORIUS, Salomon 176, 206
SCHALL, Johann Michael 1365
SCHMALHERTZ, Valentin †1921
SCHMEDTGEN, Joachim 2129, 2286, 2375, 2424, 2449, 2504, 2526, 2547, 2576, 2623, 2684, 2691-92, 2817, 2829, 2839, 2963
SCHMIDT, Tobias 932A, 1633, 1697, 1719, 1756, 1773, 1834, 1840-42, 1848, 1876-77, 1890, 1924, 1936, 1939, 1997, 2037-41, 2049-50, 2075, 2078-80, 2173, 2240-41, 2278, 2280, 2338, 2341, 2357-58, 2373, 2426, 2433, 2466, 2484, 2522, 2574, 2614, 2641, 2683, 2715, 2875, 2900, 2920, 2924-26, 2928, 2944, 2976, 3052, 3086, 3127
SCHOLVIEN, Christian 2913
SCHREYEN, Jeremias 2526
SCHROEDER, Laurentz 283
SCHÜRER, Zacharias 150
SCHULTZ, Gottfriedt 1673, 1704
SPIERINGK, Nicolaus 2687
STOBWASSER, Friedrich Wilhelm 3113
TAUBE, Jacob 1769
THOMASON (Thom[e]sen), Michael 750, 1038, 2130
THREWNER, Joh. David 2616

TREBSDORFF, Balthasar 305
VÖLCKERS, Heinrich 1719
WALDKIRCH, Henrich 17, 36, 38-39, 41, 45-47, 94, 97, 124-26, 147, 149, 151, 154, 156; †183
WAGNER, Joh. 52
WALTER, Hans 1, 40
WANDAL, Peder Jensen 730, 875
WEGENER, Arnold 40
WEGENER, Nicolaus 1-2, 2A, 3, (4), 5-7, 9-13,

(14), 15, (16), (18), 19, (20), 21, (22), (23), 24, 27, (28-30), 31, 40
WERING, Christian 1098, 1319, 1455, 1652, 1688, 1691, 1934, 2205, 2439, 2500, 2502-03
WERNER, Heinrich 353
WETTSTEIN, Ulrich 1756
WOLFF (Wulff), Georg 1750, 1880, 2366
WURING, Thomas von 2390
ZUNNER, Johann David 2749

# Index of Titles or (in the Case of Funeral Sermons and Occasional Poetry) Persons Eulogized

f.=funeral sermon; o.=occasional poem

Abbildung eines Ehrlichen und Tugend-hafften Manns 2897
Abdruck Declarationis . . . Marquardt Rantzowen 256
Abdruck der . . . Endlichen Declaration 2387
Abdruck Der Privilligien, Stadt-und Burger-Rechten . . . Altena 1390
Abdruck der von Den Königlichen Schwedischen . . . 623A
Abdruck Der zwischen Jhrer Jhrer Röm: Käyserl: . . . 160
Abdruck Dero zwischen Hr. Ditlef Ranzov . . . 188
Abdruck Des am 21. Septembris 231
Abdruck Des Credentzial Schreibens Herrn Montagu 885
Abdruck des . . . Interims-Recesses 1941
Abdruck Eines Intercipirten Schreibens 307
Abdruck Eines Kön. Schwedischen eygenhändig-subsignirten 886
Abdruck Eines Protests 3035
Abdruck I. Jhr. Königl: Mayt . . . Auss gelassene Patents 361
Abdruck Herzog Augusti . . . Schreibens 172
Abdruck Hochrühmlicher Privilligien 1141
Abdruck Käyserl: Friedens Puncten 151
Abdruck Königlichen Maytt . . . Gnedigster Resolution 97
Abdruck Schreibens 84, 90, 232, 362
Abdruck . . . Schreibens an Die . . . Staten General 177
Abdruck Zweyer . . . antwort Schreiben 233
Abdruck Zweyer Intercipirten Schreiben 308
Abdruck Zweyer Patenten 830
abgefertigte Jesuit, Der 2374
Abgelassene Schreiben 1801, 1865
Abgenöhtigte Vertheidigung 2864
Abgenöthigtes Gespräch 2429
Abgenötigte Beantwortung Der Schrifft 2210A
Abgenötigte Declaration 2276
Abgenötigte Dritte und letzste Declaration 2331
Abgenötigter Wolgegründeter Gegen-Bericht 1251
Abgenötigte Widerlegung 1664
Abgenötigt Rechtmessige Retorsion 698
Abgesante Erhebliche Vrsachen 34
Abgeschlagener Sturm Joh. Melch. Stengers 2648
Abrahams Vorsorge 1367
Abriss kürtze Beschreibung . . . Christian-Stadt 1777
Abroh, Johann (o.) 2498, 2536, 2633
Absags Brieff 403
Abschieds-Rede 2599
Abtruck Derer zwischen Jhrer Königl. Maytt. . . . Schreiben 178

Abtruck Dero zue Dennemarck . . . Erklärung 179
Abtruck Königl: Dennemarckischer Dehortatori 887
Abtruck Schreibens . . . Staten General 180
Academie Soer, Die 868
Accord zwischen Dem . . . Jürgen Reichwein 888
Accords Puncta Wegen der Fürstlichen Residentz Gottorff 815, 889
Accords-Puncta Zwischen . . . Vlrich Fridrich Güldenlöven . . . 1778
Accords-Puncten der Stadt Christianstadt 1898
Accords-Puncten So zwischen Denen hohen Alliirten 1779
Accords-Puncten . . . zur Capitulation 1897
achte entstandene Weyse newe Meyster, Der 890
Acta Hamburgensia 2612
Acta Holsato-Plonensia 1380
Acta Jn Sachen Der Herren Gebrüdern Kielmanns-Egg 1995
Actenmessig und zu Recht vestgegründete Ursachen 1474
Act im Parlament 1106
Actorum Publicorum 3040, 3041
Actus Copulationis 249
Adeliche Rose 1002
Adelinne 1021
älteste Weinacht-Gesang, Der 2167
Agnes Hedewig, Duchess of Schleswig-Holstein-Sonderburg-Glücksburg (f.) 2900
A(h)l(e)feld(t), see Alefeld
Aichelberg, Henrich Hanibal von (f.) 1924
Aken, Magdalena von (f.) 1545
Alardus, Wilhelm (f.) 433
Albinus, Daniel (f.) 2496
Albinus, Severin (f.) 1457
Ahlefeldt, Anna Christiana (f.) (2394), 2395, 2436
Alefeld, Balthasar (f.) 2530, 2532
Alefeld, Benedikt (o.) 2816
Alefeldt, Claus (o.) 1674
Alefeld, Detlev (o.) 3096
Alefeldt, Dettlev (f.) 1359
Alefeld, Friedrich (f.) 1280
Alefeldt, Georg (o.) 356
Ahlfeld, Hedewig (o.) 1709, 1715
Alefeld, Magdalena Sibylla (o.) 3096
Ahlefeld, Margarete, nee Ranzau (f.) 313
Alefeldt, Margareta, nee Ranzou (f.) 498
Aletophilus non Alethophilus 2294A
Alexander, Duke of Schleswig-Holstein-Sonderburg (f.) 165
Alle Evangelia vnde Episteln 309
Allegorische jedoch Schriftmässige Antrits-Predigt 715

Allen und jeden Liebhabern Der Teutschen Rede-kunst 2916
Allergnädigste Verordnung 1942, 2882
Allerhand Oden vnnd Lieder 360
Allerneüeste Post-Zeitung 1086
Allerschuldigiste Dancksagung 359
Aller- und Unterthänigster Vorschlag 3012
Allerunterthänigste Relation 1780, 1781
Allerunterthänigste Relationes Von dem wass ferner 1917
Allerunterthänigste Relationes von Eroberung 1916
Allerunterthänigster Glück und Wilkoms-Wundsch 1889
Allerunterthänigstes Opfer 2890
Allervortrefflichsten Liebes-Zeichen, Die 2780
aller-vortrefflichst-Geheimnüss-volle Buchstab- Wechsel, Der 3037
Allgemeines Kirchen-Gebeht 3045
Allgemeines Recept wider alle Trübsal 1302
Alliantz-Tractaten 1557
A[lmanach] v [nde Practica] 23
Allmanach vnd Practica vp dat Jahr M.DC.IX. 31
Allmanach auff . . . M DC LI 605
Almanach vnde Practica 443
Allmanach vnd Prognosticon 354, 451, 479, 507, 660, 702, 733, 766, 892, 1139, 1167, 1215, 1330, 1381
Alpen, Margarethe (o.) 585
Alss . . . Christian des Fünfften . . . Geburths Tag 2805
Als dem . . . Christiano Kortholten . . . die Pro-Rectoratswürde 2596
Als der Erfreüliche Geburts-Tag . . . Christian des Fünfften 2525
Als der Hochwürdigster . . . Christian Albrecht . . . Abend-music 1331
Als der Höchstglückliche Gebuhrts-Tag Christian . . . Des Fünfften 2591
Alss . . . Friederich . . . Mit . . . Hedwig Sophia 2870, 2901
Als Seine . . . Majestät Friederich der Dritte Victorie in Halland 767
Altonaische Relation 2125, 2176, 2211, 2254, 2295, 2346, 2388, 2495, 2538A, 2639, 2682, 2744
Altonaische Mercurius 2870A
Altonaischer Ordinaire und Extraordinaire Relation 1665
Altonaischer Vergleich 2389
Altonaischer Vertrag 2390
Americanische . . . blühende Aloe 1416
Americanische Schulpe 1417
Amor als ein Dieb 1587
Amthor, Ehrenfried (f.) 2768
An Jhre Königl. Mayest. . . . Supplication . . . Heinrich Pohlmann 2296
Anatomisch-und Medicinisches Bedencken 1593
Anbindung . . . Caspari Försteri 674
Anchora Salutis Pro Variolosis 2950
Ancken, Christian von (f.) 599
Andächtige Gebet Auff alle Tage 1722
Andächtiges Buss-Gebeht 2037
Andächtige Seuftzen, aus dem 51 Psalm Davids 1426
Andächtig Gebetbüchlein 288, 674A
Andenck-Seule 1083
Andere Theil des aussführlichen Beweises, Der 651
Ander Tractätlein nemblich Petri Ärndii . . . Biblia, Das 1091
Anderwertige in Jure & Facto . . . Remonstration 342
Anführung zum Catechismo 1269
Angefangener Biblischer Kern 2835, 2995

Anhang der Ordinaire Post-Zeitung 1607, 1608, 1665A, 1782
Anleitung zum rechten Verstand 386
Anleitung zur Zahl-Rechnung 2856
Anmerckungen über die . . . Beantwortung Der Nachricht 2212
Anmerckungen über die falsche 1538
Anmerckungen Uber die Nachricht 2745
Anna, Duchess of Schleswig-Holstein (f.) 1463
Anna Sophie, Princess of Denmark (o.) 1295
Annotationes 1633
Annua recordatio 1087
Antecedentium Praxis 2357
Anti-Marianus 254
Antwort Schreiben an Den Königlichen Schwedischen Raht 893
Antwort Schreiben Auf das Königliche Dänische Mandat 1837
Antwort-Schreiben Eines Freundes auss Holstein 2497
Antwort-Schreiben Eines guten Freundes 2746
Antwort-Schreiben Ihrer Kön. Mayt. in Dennemarck 805
Anweisung zur Lesung der Heiligen Schrifft 1925
Anzeig und Reformation 1981
Anzeige dass der Author 2561
Apocalypsis Reserata 661
Apologia, Oder Schutz vnd Schirmschreiben 60
Apologia Wygandiana Tripartita 2865
Apostolische Letzung 548
Appendix Extraordinaires Relationen 1629, 1665B
Appendix Zu dem Scripto D. J. D. Majoris 1365
Arbeitender Christ 2750
Arbor Witikindea fertilis 1451
Arcana Politica-Atheistica 2615
Arend, Caius (o.) 2209; (f.) 2519
Arend, Margaretha Elisabeth (f.) 3034
Arends, Maria, nee Braun (f.) 1765
Aria 2747
Arithmet- Geomet- Quadrat- und Cubic-cossische Erquick-Stunden 1467
Arithmetica Mercatoria 1809, 1810
Arithmeti- Geometri- Algebrai- Und Historische Ergetzlichkeiten 2502
Arithmetischer Lustgarten 1273
Arithmetischer Weg-Weiser 2643
Arnd, Margarethe Elisabeth (f.) 2980
Arrien, Cæcilia, nee Hannemann (f.) 1110, 1128
Articuln Der dreyfachen Verbündniss 1383
Articulsbrieff 39, 41, 124, 125, 126
Articuls Brief 257, 402, 435, 1710
Articuls-Brief und Kriegs- Gerichts Instruction 2129, 2130, 2538
Artikel Der Alliantz 1653
Aspern, Dorothea Tho (f.) 1410
Assaphs höchste Freude 269
Astrologische Observation 1133
Auff den Unvermutheten Einfall der Schweden 817
Auff Die Glückliche Ankunfft der Holländischen Schiffs-Armada 818
Auff Herrn Christian Fabricius 311
Auff Jhr. Majest. der Königin Gebuhrts-Jahr 2872
Auf Jhr. Königl. Majestät . . . Königliche Salbung 3120
Auffgedeckte Larve Davidis Georgii 1491
Auffrichtiger Beweiss Dass Johannes Reinboth 726
Auffsatz Der Englischen Commissarien 895
Auffzuge vnd Ritterspiele 819
Auffzug Jhr. Durchl. Der Princessin M. S. Hertzogin zu Sachsen 819

Augusta, Princess of Denmark, Duchess of Schleswig-Holstein-Gottorf (f.) 286
Augusta, Duchess of Schleswig-Holstein-Sonderburg-Augustenburg (o.) 598, 622
August Friederich, Prince-Bishop of Lübeck (o.) 1702, 1842
Auss den Actis und Protocollis 897
Aus den Schrifften des Hr. Sam. Pufendorfii . . . Beweiss 2539
Auss der Dänischen Sprach translatirte Verordnung 271
Aus der Stadt Hamburg Recessen 2808
Aus Lübeck 896
Auserlesene Biblische Kern- und Trostsprüche 2345
Ausserlesene Geistliche Lieder 1824
Ausserlesene Geistreiche Gebete 2021
Auserlesene Lob-Gesänge 1601
Ausführliche Beschreibung Der Hütte 2784
Aussführliche Beschreibung Der Kundbaren Reyse 1197, 1549
Aussführliche Beschreibung Wie Sein Hochheit der Printz vom Oranien 1653
Aussführliche Erzehlung 898
Aussführliche Lehre von dem Kirchen-Regiment 1366
Aussführlicher Bericht Aus Fühnen 901
Aussführlicher Bericht Aus Unterschiedlicher 902
Aussführlicher Bericht Von dem harten Treffen 388
Aussführlicher Bericht welcher massen die Stadt Utrecht 1653
Aussführlicher Beweiss Dass des Jesuiten Theod. Bercken 650
Ausführliche Refutation 1525
Ausführliche Relation Aus Copenhagen vom 16. Augusti 1658 820
Ausführliche Relation der ungemeinen Solennien 1254
Ausführliche Relation Des Combats auff der Jnsul Amack 821
Ausführliche Relation Des hefftigen Seestreits 822
Ausführliche Relation von dem See-Gefecht 1854
Ausführliche Relation Von der Attaque auff Rügen 1900
Ausführliche Relation von der zweyten See-Batallie 1855
Ausführliche Relation von dem Treffen 387
Aussführliche Relation von Eroberung 1813
Ausführliche Relation Wegen Ubergabe 1786
Ausführliche Relation Welchergestalt 1856
Aussführlicher vnd Eigentlicher Bericht 389
Aussführlicher und gründlicher Bericht 903
Auss-Führlicher Verlauff 904
Ausfürlicher Von hoher Hand 905
Ausfürliche und Warhafftige Beschreibung 899
Ausführliche Warhaffte und Gründliche Relation 900
Ausführlich in der Theologie . . . Bedencken 2242A
(Ausslegung über den XXXIV. Psalm) 29
Autoschediasma De Vitriolo 2364

Babylonisches Vorwerck 1605
Backsen, Peter (f.) 1768
Ballet von Unbeständigkeit der weltlichen Dinge 587
Balthische Meer 264
Baltzar, Maria (f.) 1468
Baptzin, Henning von (f.) 1127
Barth, Daniel (f.) 750
Bassevitz, Henning von (f.) 480
Beantwortung auff die Beschuldigung 1154
Bechman, Jacob (o.) 1556

Beck, Georg (o.) 2393, (f.) 2544
Beck, Joh. Jos. (o.) 1763
Becker, Frau (f.) 1561
Bedencken Zwener vornehmer Theologorum 2207
Bedrengtes nun wieder Befreyetes Dennemarck 1061
Befreyung Der Stadt Copenhagen 906
Behrens, Dorothea (o.) 1255
Beicht- und Sacraments-Fragen 2847
Bekentniss Nicolai Tetinge 127
Beling, Oswald (f.) 481
Below, Anna (o.) 734
Bensen, Naaman (f.) 1005
Berahtschlagung Apollinis 2087
Berger, Philipp (o.) 609, 615
Berg-Ordnung 491
Bericht Aus Copenhagen 823, 907
Bericht Dess Frieden-Schlusses 434
Bericht vom Abendmahl 142
Bericht Von der Gestrigen 1023, 1024
Bericht Von gelegenheit vnd vnterscheide 152
Bericht Von General Wrangel 908
Bering, Vitus (o.) 1183
Berndrup, Jørgen (f.) 2823
Berner, Adolph Georg (o.) 2915
Bernhard, Naamann (f.) 1484, 1497, 1503
Beschreibenes LandRecht des Nordstrandes 1517
Beschreibung der Jnsul Rügen 1903
Besiegte Atheisterey 2616
Beste Mittel zur Bekehrung der Juden 2250
Bethlemitische Hirten-Freude 1787
Betrachtungen von der Bethe- Leidens- und Sterbe-Kunst 1984
betrübte Jn Creutz-geübte Hjob, Der 1058A
betrübte und von Gott Reichlich Getröstete Ephriam, Das 2567, 2617, 2913
Bevölckertes Cimbrien 2574
Beweissthumb des letzten Jahrs 1513, 1843
Bey Höchsterfreulicher Wiederkunfft . . . Friedrichs 812
Beyerholm, Andreas Evertzen (o.) 2267
Biblia 1216
Biblische Fest-Andacht 2520
Biblischer Weyrauch 2320, 2420, 2568, 2996, 3081
Biblisches Handbuch 2318
Biermann, see Ehren-Schild
Bi(h)lenberg, Margaretha Dorothea (o.) 1125, 1127A
Birckenbusch, Johannes (f.) 1978, 1988A
Blixen, Sophia Heidwig von (f.) 372
Bloem, Henr. (f.) 2542
Blom, Oelgarde Catharina, nee von Rantzow (f.) 2329
Blume, Hans (o.) 1999
Bock, Agatha Catharina (o.) 1658
Bock, Eleonore, nee Büttner (f.) 2417, 2423, 2462, 2478
Bock, Hans (o.) 164
Bock, Margaretha, nee Bensen (f.) 2759, 2794
Bock, Metta Lucia (f.) 2487
Bödeker, Anna Maria, nee Haubolt (o.) 1115
Böhm, Johannes (o.) 2854
Böhmke, Georg (o.) 585
Boekwold, Hedewig von (f.) 338
Bohnenberg, Gesen (o.) 729
Boisen, Broder (f.) 2243
Boisen, Catharina (f.) 2792
Bornemann, Anna, nee Würger (f.) 2891
Bornemann, Heinrich (o.) 1771
Bornholdt, Matthias (o.) 1165
Bornman, Tyre (o.) 712
Bosset, Lorentz de (o.) 2517

Bougwald, Metta von (f.) 1412
Boye, Anna (o.) 2498
Boysen, Friderich (o.) 2205
Boysen, Georg (f.) 3014
Boysen, Johann (f.) 558, 791
Braems, Anna, nee Bruns (f.) 355
Braems, Cæcilia, nee Bruns (f.) 330, 350
Braems, Gothart (f.) 725
Braems, Johann (f.) 478
Brahe, Axel (f.) 769
Brammer, Barthold Johann (f.) 2625
Brandes, Friderich (o.) 1243
Brandt, Anna Catharina (o.) 2450
Brandt, Joachim (f.) 3129
Brandt, Johann-Friederich (f.) 1671
Brandt, Peter (o.) 1905
Bremers, Maria Catharina (o.) 2789
Brennende Hertz, Das 2908
Brethauer, Anna Maria (o.) 1993
Breviarium Arithmeticum 1912
Brevis Grammatica Gallica 248, 353
Brockenhus, Georg (f.) 1708
Brocktorff, Margareta Lucia (f.) 735
Brockdorff, Margareta (f.) 748
Brocktorff, Margareta, nee Rantzow (f.) 1267
Brocktorff, Marquardt Wolff (f.) 1614
Brüggeman, Peter Eberhard (o.) 1357
Brüggemann, Anna Elisabeth, nee Hahn (f.) 1103
Brummers, Gesche (f.) 341
Brunner, Martin (f.) 1114, 1116
Buccina Schlesvico-Holsatica 1429A
Buchner, Paul (o.) 717
Buchwald, Caspar von (f.) 1450, 1490
Buchwald, Catharina Margaretha von (f.) 3069, 3122
Buchwald, Daniel Dieterich von (f.) 2770, 2782, 2791, 2807
Buchwaldt, Emerentzia von, nee von der Wisch (f.) 1675
Buchwald, Jaspar (o.) 1640
Buchwald, Joachim von (f.) 1913
Buchwald, Magdalena, nee Bruchdorff (f.) 1326
Buchwald, Margareta von, nee Blum (f.) 1584
Buchwald, Mette von (f.) 1411, 1412
Buchwaldt, Mette von, nee von Passberg (f.) 1229
Buchwoldt, Anna von (f.) 168
Bueck, Anna, nee Würger (o.) 1771
Bueck, Hieronymus (f.) 1670
Bühren, Christian von (f.) 444
Bühren, Christophor von (f.) 464
Büll, Anna (f.) 1906
Bülow, Margarita von, nee Rantzow (f.) 1613, 1627
Bündnis-Articulen, Oder Alliance 1027A
Bünow, Anna Sophia von, nee von Rothschütz 574
Bürger, Anna Margaretha (o.) 2915
Buck, Albert (o.) 1356
Bunck, Anna Catharina (o.) 1035
Burchard, Anton (o.) 2269, 2271
Burchard, M. H. (f.) 2819
Burchard, Magdalena (f.) 2499
Burchard, Matthias (f.) 1945, 1961, 1963, 1975, 1987
Buss-Gebeth Nach den fürnehmsten Glaubens-Artickeln 3136
Buss-Stimme 390
Buss- vnd Beicht- Histori 1121
Buss- und Bettags- Predigt 1057
Buss- und Communions Lieder 1436

Calendarium Nordstrandico-Holsaticum 1166
Capitulation Oder Accord 312

Carga von denen Ost-Indischen Wahren 1565A
Cartell Vnd Articull 196
Cassius, Andreas (f.) 78
Cassius, Christian (f.) 1834, 1991
Cassube, Anna, nee Ziemers (f.) 1790
Castrum Doloris . . . Friederichen Erben zu Norwegen 1111
Castrum Doloris Hafniense 2569
Catalogus, Aller . . . Hohen Schulen 2068
Catalogus der General- und Particular Tabulen 796
Catalogus Der vornehmsten Städte und Plätze 2069
Catechismus-Fragstücke 2316
Catechismus Frag und Antworten 2469
Catechissmus Kleinigkeiten 2049
Catechismus Lehre 2178
Catechismus-Milch 2796
Catechismus sampt der Auslegung, Der 2302
Catechismus-Schatz 787
Catechismus-Schole Law Teutsch 1300
(Catechismus Sermone Germanico editus) 2848
Causæ Conjectio 2752
Celeglino 3002
(Charles I, King of England) (o.) 1037, 1038
Charles XII, King of Sweden (o.) 3095
Charlotte Amalia, Queen of Denmark (o.) 2766, 2872, 2945
Choragium Melicum 1668
Christens, Helena (o.) 571
Christian Albrecht, Duke of Schleswig-Holstein (o.) 816, 1331, 1422, 1466 (f.) 2702, 2709, 2722
Christian, Duke of Schleswig-Holstein-Sonderburg-Glücksburg (f.) 2900
Christian IV, King of Denmark (o.) 335, 359, 475, (f.) 555, 566
Christian V, King of Denmark (o.) 704, 721, 819, 1764, 1845, 1889, 2396, 2525, 2591, 2690, 2733, 2760, 2780, 2805, 2806, 2890, 3138 (f.) 3011, 3026, 3036, 3068
Christian, Prince ("der Fünffte") (o.) 214, 249, 529, (f.) 560
Christian Jnn Dennemarck . . . Handschreibens 129
Christina, Duchess of Schleswig-Holstein (o.) 1842, 1876 (f.) 2875
Christiani, Dorothea Sophia (o.) 2919
Christiani, Eleanora (o.) 2635
Christianismus 1151
Christianorum media pacis 860
Christlich Andächtig vnd Bussfertig Gebet, Ein 62
Christliche Altars-Weyhe 2706
Christliche Confirmation 2598, 2871
Christliche Danckseule 2006
Christliche Einfeltige Anweisung 1946
Christliche Einweyhungspredigt 2163
Christliche Entdeckung Calvinischer Betrieglichkeit 2181
Christliche Erinnerung 2465
Christliche Frag-Stück 138
Christliche Freyer und Eheman, Der 2098
Christliche Fried- und Freuden-Predigt 2020
Christliche Gründliche Anmerckungen 1673
Christliche hochnöhtige wiederbestellung 280
Christliche Neuiahrsgedancken 1579
Christliche Predigt, Eine 158
Christliche Predig Wie die Versehung Gottes 325
Christlicher Glaubensunterricht 1423
Christlicher Haussvatter 1393
Christlicher Tugend-Spiegel 1507
Christlicher Unterricht 2466
Christliches Gesang-Buch 2641
Christliches Glaubens-Bekäntniss, Ein 2240
Christliche Soldatenstand, Der 3132

Christlike und nütte Kinderfragen 4
Christliche Valet-Predigt 608
Christlicher Buss-Gebet 401
Christlyke Kercken Ordeninge 1, 40
Christo Duce, Arte Comite 228
Chronologia Oder Zeit-Rechnung 1313
Chronologische Gewisse vnd vnwiderlegliche Bewei-
   sung 21
Cimbrischen Musen Glücklicher Zuruff, Der 1314
Clausen, Anna Catharina (f.) 1989
Clausen, Catharine, nee Steenbech (f.) 2127A, 2140
Clausen, Joh. (f.) 2007
Clausen, Katharina (o.) 1307
Clausen, Ursula, nee Höller (f.) 2559
Clausen, Ursula, nee Müller (f.) 2573, 2582
Claussen, Christina (f.) 1164
Claussen, Matthias (f.) 1725, 1726, 1729, 1752,
   1755, 1762, 1770
Claussen, Sophia (o.) 1582
Closter Jungfraw 267
Clotz, Stephan (f.) 2981
Clotz, Margaretha, nee Clausen (f.) 2753, 2754,
   2767
Cluverus, Joh. (f.) 207
Coler, Anna (f.) 486
Collin, Christina (o.) 742
Collyrium Ethico-Politicum 1029
Comitiv und Palatinat 932A, 1033
Comoedia de Harpyjarum Profligatione 215
Comoedia de Raptu Orithyjæ 215
Communion-Andacht 3082
Communion-Büchlein 3128
Compendium Chronologicum, Oder Jahr Rechnung
   333
Compendium Fortificatorium 1065
Compendium Geometriæ 2481
Conciones miscellaneæ 2813
Confessions-Werck 2350
Consideratio Incendiorum 1595
Constitutio Betreffend Die . . . Brüch-Gelder 2879
Constitution Von Justificir-und Zuschreibung 1627,
   1711
Constitution wegen der Visitation 2960, 2973
Constitutiones von dero zu Dännemarck 1347
Constitutiones . . . von wegen des gestempelten
   Papiers 1320
Constitutio Pacificationis 1653
Constitutio Regia de usuris 678
Constitutio vnd Ordnung 115
Constitutio Wegen des Pfand-und Schuld Protocol-
   len 2880, 2881
Continuatio Der aus Fühnen 911
Continuation Der Aussführlichen Relation 912
Continuation des vorigen Bericht 913
Continuation Des . . . Warhafften Berichts 2259
Continuation was weiter im Hertzogthumb Brehmen
   770
Continuirter Aussführlicher Beweiss 728
Copenhagensche Relation 1791, 1862, 1948
Copia . . . Antwort-Schreibens 45, 46, 234, 2398
Copia Chur-Brandenburgischen Schreibens 914
Copia Dänischer Zeitung aus Kopenhagen 391
Copia, Der Königl. Dennemärckischen zu der Holl-
   steinischen Regierung 826
Copia Dero Königl. Majest: . . . mandati avocatorij
   392
Copia Der Vom . . . Friederich dem Dritten . . .
   Newen Privilegien 1098
Copia Der Vom . . . Friderich Dem Dritten . . .
   Privilegien 1097
Copia Des Recesses 47

Copia Dess Schreibens 105
Copia Des . . . Schreibens . . . Remonstrationen
   2397
Copia des von Corfitz Graff von Vhlfeldt 1094
Copia Des von Herrn Detleff Rantzowen 235
Copia Einer Commission 915
Copia Eines glaubwürdigen Schreibens 393
Copia Eines Königl. Schwedischen Schreibens 827
Copia Eines Schreibens . . . an Churfl. Durchl. zu
   Saxen 208
Copia Eines Schreibens aus Copenhagen 916, 917
Copia eines Schreibens aus Dobran 1907
Copia Eines Schreibens Aus Franckfurt am Mayn
   918
Copia Eines Schreibens Jh. Römis. Käyserl. Majest.
   2878
Copia Eines Schreibens Von den Herren Staten
   Generalen 1031
Copia Eines sehr beweglichen Sendt Schreibens 365
Copia Eines von Königl. Dennemärckischen General
   Auditeur 919
Copia . . . Friederich dem Dritten . . . Newen
   Priviligien 1030
Copia . . . Grafen von Ahlefelds . . . Abgelassenen
   Antwort Schreibens 1949
Copia Graff Corfitz von Vhlfeldt Deprecation 1095
Copia J. Königl. Mayt: . . . Aussgelassenen Mandats
   368
Copiæ Jungst Erfolgter . . . Schreiben 154
Copia Jhrer Excelli Herrn Feldmarschals Linnardt
   Torstensens Mandati 395
Copia Jhr Excellentz Herr Christian Graffen von
   Pentz 394
Copia Jhre Excell. Herrn Feldmarschals Linnardt
   Torstensens Scripti 396
Copia Käyserliche Schreibens 316
Copia Königl: Bescheidts 397
Copia Königl. Dennemarckischen Schreibens 236
Copia Königl. Dennemärckischer Andtwort 317
Copia Königl: May: Zu Dennemarck . . . Schreibens
   an den Herrn Administratoren 130
Copia Königl: May: zu Dennemarcken . . . an Die
   zu Meintz 131
Copia Königl. Maytt. . . . Schreibens An Den
   Churfürsten zu Meyntz 366
Copia Schreibens . . . an die Excell. Herrn Reichs
   Cantzlers 198
Copia Schreibens auss Oldesloh 828
Copia Schreibens Auss Stade Glückstadt vnd Ham-
   burg 398
Copia Schreibens Jhr. Königl. Majestät 319
Copia Schreibens . . . Von Cuhrt von Lutzowen 314
Copia Schreibens . . . wider die Stadt Hamburg 315
Copia Sende-Schreibens 662
Copia vnd Abtruck Dessen Vertrags 367
Copia und Nachricht Einer Schwedischen Ordre 920
Copia Von einem Brief aus Copenhagen 829
Copia Von Friedrichs des Dritten . . . Friderichs-
   Oddes Privilegien 1099
Copia Was zwischen . . . Reichsräthen vnd . . .
   Hamburg 199
Copia Zweyer . . . Abgefertigter Schreiben 921
Copia zweyer Brieffe so der Herr Corfitz Graff von
   Vhlfeld 1172
Copia zweyer Schreiben 123, 153, 922
Cornelius, Johann (f.) 1130
Corvinus, Pet. (f.) 614
Coster, Heinrich (o.) 638
Cramer, Andreas (f.) 1971, 1983
Cramer, Augusta Maria, nee Hecklawer (f.) 1389,
   1449

Cramer, Maria Elisabeth (o.) 1792
Creutz- unn Gedult-Spiegel 2614
Cristallinen-Spiegel 855
Cröger, Anna Maria (f.) 590
Cröger, Gregorius (f.) 2160, 2161
Cröger, Magdalena, nee Goldbach (f.) 1805, 1833
Crusius, Christoph (o.) 2918
Cum bono Jehova Contingentia Nova 452
Cuneus antilogicus 201
Curieuser Bericht 3052

Da . . . Christian des Fünfften . . . Geburts-Tag 2690
Da lassen wir Lönhard für rathen 399
Dänisches Kriegs-Recht vnd Articuls Brieff 400
Dähnisches Piket-Spiel 923
Dänsches Gesetz 2963
Danckbaren Gemüths Anzeig 489
Danck-Gebet 1050
Danck-Lied 924
Danck-Predigt Bey dem Danck-Fest 1056
Dancksagung 1173
Danckwert, Joachim (o.) 237
Daniel Redivivus 1118
Danneskiold, Friederich Christian (f.) 2801
Daneskjold-Laurvig, Charlotte Amalie (o.) 2797
Daphnis 266
Daphnis vnd Sylvia 282
Davids Gesang 2829
Davids-Hirtt Der Seine Schafe 364
Davidische Buss-und Bete-Glokke 1965
Davidisches geistliches Harfenspiel 1581
Davids Ruhe Statt 1488
De boni laboris glorioso fructu 594
Declaration An das Folck von Engelandt 925
Declaration einer Schwedischen Declaration 932
Declaration Für die zur See-Handthierende 931
declaration Nebenst angehengten Vrkunden vnd Beylagen 149
Declaration So wegen . . . Postulata 2379
Declaration Wegen Confiscirten Englischen Fordrungen 1336
Declaration Worauss Allerhöchst gedachter 963
Defension-Schrifft 1438
Defensiv-Alliance Und Bündnüss 1950
Defensivum wider die Päbstler 2898
Degingk, Margareta von, (o.) 1547
Dem Bibliothecario Der Studirenden Jugend angehängte Vertheidigung 2460
Denckmahl 883
Denische Moses, Der 1508
Dennemärckische Commission Handlung 102
Der Clerisey Eheschild 564
Der Dianen Hohe und Niedere Jagtgeheimnüss 2121, 2286, 2435, 3030
Der dreyen allgemeinen Beht-Tage Gebeht und Verlesungen 577
Der Evangelischen Pilgrim 245
Der Gläubigen Hertzens-Gespräch 3094
Der Glückstädtischen Bürger Wacht-Ordnung 2646A
Der Kinder Gottes Heilsamste Arbeit 2438
Der Königlichen Bedienten . . . Privilegia 1951
Der Königl. Dänischen Ministrorum Fernere Declaration 2318
Der Königl. Mayest. . . . Declaration 149
Der Königl. Majestät . . . Friedens-Vortrag 1696A
Der Königl. Mayestät . . . Patent 155
Der Königl: Maytt: und Crohn Schweden 426, 427
Der Königlichen Stadt . . . Glückstadt Feuer-Ordnung 2777
Der Königl. Universität . . . Declaration 1171

Der kopenhagenschen Medicinischen Facultät 448
Der Neuen Stadt . . . Glückstadt . . . Privilegium 71
Der Quäcker Geist 1028
Der Quäcker Hertzensgrund 1170
Der Regierenden Hoch-Fürstl. . . . gnädigste Verordnung 2871
Der Römischen Käyserlichen Majest. Edictum 2336
Der Röm. Kay. Mayt: Privilegium 114
Der Schweden Unheil 997
Der Stadt Husum Fewr-Ordnung 328
Der Stadt Husum Vormünder-Verordnung 446
Der Stadt Schleswig Schiff-Brücken Ordnung 2118
Der Stadt Slesswick Stadtrecht 13
Der Stände Resolution 806
Der Studirenden im Kiel Musique 2858
Der Theologischen Facultet . . . Beantwortung 2149
Der Tunderschen Unsterblichen Sterblichkeit 1721
Der Wenig-bauenden heutigen Kirchenlehrart 2359
Der . . . Zu einer Disputation nacher Glückstadt 2647
Dero Königlichen Majestät . . . Abgelassene Schreiben 1801, 1865
Dero Königlichen Majestät . . . Schreiben 214
Dero . . . offene Versicherung 1180
Dero Regierend Römischen Kayserlicher Majestät . . . Hand-Schreiben 2889
Dero zu Dännemarck . . . Henrich Pohlmann . . . Ehren-Rettung 2335
Dero zu Dennemarck . . . Post-Ordnung 685
Dero zu Dennemarck . . . Resolution 1346
Des Adels Allerunterthänigste Declaration 1181
Des Aller-Durchläuchtigsten . . . Articuls-Brief 2129, 2130, 2538
Des Aller-Durchläuchtigsten . . . Friderich des Vierten . . . Salbungs-Fest 3044
Des Aller-Durchleuchtigsten . . . Herrn Ferdinanden des Dritten 932A
Des alten KirchenLehrers vnd Martyrers Cyprians 933
Des Bedrengten Niederlandes Gedächtnüss-Maal 1573
Des Dähnischen und Schwedischen Krieges Aussgang 1866
Des Deutschen Reiches Staat 3028
Des Edlen Mannhaften Admiral Opdams Brief 836
Des Glaubens Kampff vnd Sieg 300
Des Göttlichen Worts Kirchen-mangel 2358
Des Gründlich Verthädigten Treuen Lutherthumbs 2577
Des Herzogs Christian Albrechts Gedanken 1100
Des Hoch- Fürstl. Hauses Schleswig-Hollstein-Gottorp . . . gerechtsame 2162
Des hochlöblichen Königlichen Dennemärckschen Ritter Ordens 620
Des Höchstberühmten Anatomici 768
Des Nordischen Kriegs Anderer Theil 1976
Des Teuffels Weih-Quast 1661
Des Uthinischen Stadt-Gedächtnisses 1947
Des Weiblichen Geschlechts Preiss vnd Ruhm Ballet 572
Des zu Nimwegen Extraordinari-Abgesandten 1867
Designatio der Wahren 221
Dessin, Lüder (f.) 592
Detleffs, Magdalena (o.) 490
Detleffs, Mette Maria, nee Preuss (f.) 1696
Deutsche Poemata 513
Deutscher Lucianus 993
Diarium Tychopolitanum 473
Dickhof, Margareta (o.) 1763
Didrichsen, Katharina, nee Hieronymus (f.) 2707

Die . . . der Reformirten Religion allergnädigst ertheilte Privilegien 2249
Die Herren Holländischen Gesandten 1049
Dienstliche bezeigung der Götter vnd Creaturen 621
Dieweil vermutlich gar weinige . . . Hamburg 349
Discours Oder Hochnötige Erörtterung 934
Diskours von Antenors Thorheit 994
Dithmarsische Chronick 2171
Dithmarsisches Land-Recht 1347
Dittmar, Catharina Maria (o.) 2854
Dorns, Margareta (f.) 640
Dorns, Reimar (f.) 746
Dorothea Juliana, Duchess of Schleswig-Holstein (f.) 882
Dowen, Marcus (f.) 722
Drey Aussgesonderte Krieges-Predigten 1934
Drey Bet-Tags-Predigten 571
Drey Bücher 1238
Drey Hauptbekenntniss der Kirchen, Die 275
Drey nützliche Tractätlein 22
Drey Vnterschiedliche Predigten 656
Dreyer, Dethlev (f.) 1469
Dreyfache Anhang 2375
Dreyfache unpartheyische Rechtsbelehrung 2755
Dreyfacher Sägens-Wundsch 1295
Dreyfaches Garten-Buch 2986
Dritte Abbildung Anthonette Bourignons 1669
Dritter vnd letzter Theil Des aussführlichen Beweises 861
Dubbing, Cecilia (f.) 648
Due, Albert (f.) 568
Düring, Johan Christoff von (f.) 2907

Eberstein, Wolff Diedrich von (o.) 1047; (f.) 1054
Echersen, Heinrich (o.) 1107
Eck, Marie Catharina (o.) 2099, 2113
Eckerich, Gesa, nee Wolf (f.) 1667
Eckleff, Henning (o.) 1868 (f.) 1874
Edict Jhr. Königl. Maytt. . . . An deroselben Admirale 935
Edict Friedrich dess Dritten 1258
Edle Reit-Kunst 1257
Eggers, Elsabe Christina (o.) 2818
Ehe-Lob . . . Ernst Günther . . . Augusta 598
Ehmbsen, Henning (f.) 1520
Ehren-Gedächtnüs Des Neugebornen Kindleins Jesu 747
Ehren-Schild, Conrad Biermann von (f.) 2912
Ehren-Seule 1076
Ehren-Zeilen An den Herrn Andächtigen 1877
Ehrhorn, Catharina (o.) 1165
Ehrhorn, Johannes (f.) 1126
Eid Und Obligation der Prediger 2189
Eigentlicher Bericht Von den Processionen 1264
Eigentliche Relation von dem was vor der Bokul-Schantze passirt 1868A
Eigentlicher Verstandt der Worte Christi 2210
Eigentliche und sonderbare Vorstellung 1510
Eigentliche undt Warhaffte Relation . . . der Insul Fühnen 36
Eigentlich und warhaffter Bericht 872
Eigentliche Warhaffte Relation . . . Herrn von Eberstein 937
Eylfertiges Sendschreiben 995
Eines Trew-Meinenden Patrioten Treuhertzige Erinnerung 803
Einfältige Catechismus-Fragen 1944, 2301, 2751
Einfältige Handleitung zur täglichen Prüfung 515
XCI Psalm, Der 1252
Eiserne Teutsch-Land, Das 1840
Elegie Oder Neu-Jahres-Gedicht 1083

Eleonora, Duchess of Schleswig-Holstein (f.) 2050
Ellermann, Johann (f.) 2923
Elsswig, Margarete von (f.) 2039
Emblema coniungii 164
Enchiridion 2477
Endliche Declaration 2265A
Engelbrecht, Anna, nee Schrader (f.) 2338
Englische Schildwacht 216
Englischer Wächter Englische Wacht 2581
Englische Schildwacht 216
Entsetzter Vortrab 2809
Entwurf etlicher berichtwürdigen Gesichte 534
Entwurff der Execution . . . Caroli Stuart des I. 1037, 1038
Epistola Amici ad Amicum 1683
Erb-Huldigungs Monumentum 1132
Erdmann, Hermann (f.) 2385
Erfordertes Theologisches Bedencken 2484
erfundene Weg, Der 1315
Erinnerungs-Schreiben An Hubertum Mosanum 2526
Erklärung der Medaille 2760
Erklärung der Sonntags-Evangelien 2365
Erklärung über das 1. und 2. Capitel St. Johannis 187
Erklärung vier ausserlesener Advents-, Weinacht-, Passions-, und Ostergesänge 3029
Erklärung Wegen dess Schwedischen Herolden 404
Erläuterter Adventsgesang 2119
Erläuterter Catechismus 1311, 1493, 1748, 1802
Erläuterter Passionsgesang 2168
Ernewerte Nordfresische Chronick 1402
Ernster und eilfertiger Bericht 1150
Ernst Günther, Duke of Schleswig-Holstein-Sonderburg-Augustenburg (o.) 598, 622
Erörterung warum Gott Evam 658
I. Extraordinaire Relation von Allerley Orten, Die 1628
Erste und Eylfertige Antwort 996
Erster Theil Allerhand Oden vnnd Lieder 360
Erstes Hundert der Arithmetischen Historischen Erqvickstunden 1288
Erstes Zehen Theologischer Sendschreiben 2585
ErtzBischöffliche Bremische abgenötigte Defension 408
Erwiedrigter Bericht 1397
Eschenberg, Jacob (o.) 2444
Esmarch, Clauss (f.) 32
Esmarch, Henr. Christ. (o.) 2284
Esmarch, Johannes (f.) 1309
Essens, Anna von, nee Peters (f.) 351
Ethica Complementoria 1688
Etlicher nothwendige Zeit Gebet 1536
Etliche Psalme und Sprüche 2613
Etlyke Geistliche Leder 49
Etzliche Ausserlesene und vornehme Sprüche 2609
Euclides 2928, 3013
Europäische Fama, Die 2409, 2515, 2975
Europäische Mittwochentliche Zeitung 1102
Europäische Relation 938, 2139, 2190
Europæische Relation Auss Unterschiedlichen fremden Oertern 837
Europæische Samstägige Zeitung 1184
Europäische Wochentliche Zeitung 838, 1039, 1145, 1185, 1230, 1265
Euthanasia Oder Christliche Sterbekunst 356
Evangelischen Pilgrim Güldener Wanderstab, Der 245
Evangelische Sing-Andacht 2535A
Evangelische Wahrheit, Die 3127
ewig erquickende Ruhe, Die 2611

Ewig-grünender Lorbeer-Krantz 1124
Ewigkeit So Erschrecklich Erfreulich Vnendlich 765
Ewigwährender Calender 1689
Ewigwährender Freuden-Saal 2914
Exercitz Ordnung 1615
Extract Aus Copenhagen 1186
Extract Auss den uff einem Hollendischen von Riga kommenden Schiffe 840
Extract Aus den Niederländischen Zeitungen 839
Extract aus der Königl. Verordnung 1221
Extract aus verschiedenen Schreiben 941
Extract Der . . . Friedens-Articul 3064
Extract der Proposition 136
Extract Des Glückstadtischen Protocols 410
Extract Des Herrn General Major Bawrn Schreibens 409
Extract Dreyer Brieffe 942
Extract Einiger . . . Schreiben 841
Extract Etlicher Puncten 1274
Extract etlicher vornehmer Schreiben 212
Extract Schreiben auss Copenhagen 412, 3065
Extract-Schreiben Darinnen alles begriffen 782
Extract Schreibens auss Braunssberg 943
Extract-Schreibens Aus Coppenhagen 2410
Extract Schreibens aus dem Königlichen Dennemärkischen Feldlager 783
Extract-Schreibens Aus . . . Copenhagen 946
Extract Schreibens aus Friedrichsöde 784
Extract Schreibens Aus Mittelfahrt 944
Extract Schreibens Aus Rendesburg 842
Extract Schreibens Aus Seeland 1040
Extract-Schreibens Oder Kurtzer Bericht 1187
Extract-Schreibens Datirt Stettin 947
Extract-Schreibens Des Hn. General Admiral Trompen 1803
Extract Schreibens Eines Vornehmen Dänischen Ministri 843
Extract Schreibens Einiger Vornehmen Hohen Officierer 844
Extract Schreibens sub dato Crempe 785
Extract Schreiben Von der herlichen Victorie 411
Extract Verschiedener Relationen 845
Extract Verschiedener von dem Schwedischen General Auditeurn 945
Extract Zweyer Brieffe aus Copenhagen 1041, 1042, 1043
Extract Zweyer Schreiben von der Königlichen Huldigung 528
Extraordinaire Oeresundische Relation 1869, 1870, 1914
Extraordinaire Relation 1628, 1684, 2061
Extraordinaire Relationes 1574, 1631, 1685, 1735, 1804, 1955
Extraordinaires Sambstägige Relationes 1630
Eygentlicher und dem originâl gleichlautender Abdruck Schreibens 846

Fabricius, Christian (o.) 311
Fabricius, Christina (o.) 1728
Fabricius, Tobias (f.) 2793
Fasciculus cogitationum christianarum rythmicus 161
Fasciculus Concionum 1776
Feld-Posaune 786
Femaria Desolata 1643
Ferdinandi Boldershusii Scharffsinniges Bedencken 226
Fernere Continuation Der aus Fühnen 948
Festtheil 1405
Feüer-Ordnung 1575, (2777)
Feur Predigt 1445

Feustking, Johannes (f.) 1235
Fewrruthe Gottes 247
Finckeltauss, Regina (f.) 644
Fiorten Morgen-oc Aften-Sange 2194
Fischer, Catharina (o.) 1526
Fischer, Marina (o.) 2205
Fleischer, Anna Maria (o.) 643
Fleiss der Gottseligkeit 2266
Foderung des Königs von Franckreich, Die 1653
Förster, Caspar (o.) 674
Folget ein Schreiben 450
Fortsezzung unterschiedlicher Considerationen 1576
Fragen und Antworten 2642
Franck, Albert (f.) 476
Franck, Christopf. (o.) 1307, 2432
Francke, Abel (f.) 556
Francke, Catharina, nee Clausen (f.) 2876, 2909, 2948
Francke, Dorothea, nee Moering (f.) 230
Französische und Italianische Grammatica 1420
Frantzöischer Haupt-Schlüssel 2128
Frantzöischer Sprache Weg-Weiser 586
Franzöisches Journal 1577
Freuden-Opffer . . . Gebuhrts-Feyer . . . Friederich 2849
Frewdiger Apollo 373
Freytag, Elsabeth, nee Beyers (f.) 380
Fricke, Maria (o.) 669
Friderica Amalia, Princess of Denmark, Duchess of Schleswig-Holstein (o.) 572, 2610
Fridericus III alter Salomon 1137
Friedens-Articulen 1044
Friedens-Post im Norden, Der 1891
Friedens-Predigt Wie derselbe zuerlangen 459
Friedens-Puncta 847, 1352, 1578
Friedens Puncten 1956, (2441)
Friedens-Tractat 1957, 3066
Friedens Tractaten 1958
Friedens-Vortrag 1696A
Friedrich II, King of Denmark (f.) 2623
Friedrich III, King of Denmark (o.) 544-45, 704, 721, 767, 812, 1003, 1062, 1079, 1081, 1132, 1137, 1211, (f.) 1471, 1488, 1495, 1501, 1502
Friedrich IV, King of Denmark (o.) 2684, 2706, 2716, 2849, 3044
Friedrich, Prince of Denmark (f.) 657
Friedrich III, Duke of Schleswig-Holstein-Gottorf (o.) 608, (f.) 961, 966, 1087, 1111, 1156
Friedrich IV, Duke of Schleswig-Holstein-Gottorf (o.) 2719A, 2870, 2873, 2901
Friedrich Wilhelm, Duke of Schleswig-Holstein (f.) 2413
Friese, Marcus (f.) 1034, 1109
Friese, Maria (f.) 2096
Friese, Sophia Agnese (f.) 600
Frisius, Marg., nee Dreyer (f.) 505
Frommer Christen Sinn vnd Gewinn 331
Fromm, Jacob (o.) 2363
Fruchtbringendes Gespräch-Spiel 2503
Fruchtbringendes Informations-Gespräch 2545
Frühlings-Mayen 1899
Fuchs, Marg. Oelgard (o.) 2225, 2234, 2238
Fühnisches Interscenium 1045
XXV. Anfechtungen des Teufels 1363
für seinen zeitlichen und ewigen Untergang . . . Capernaum, Das 3083
fürnembsten Psalmen vnnd Lobgesänge, Die 299, 686
fürbittende und dancksagende Delmenhorst, Das 1558
Fürsichtige Gebrauch, Der 2908

Fürsten Spiegel 227
Fürstlicher Ertzbischöfflicher Bremischer Nachtrab 334
Fürstliche Schlesswig-Holsteinische Holtz-Ordnung 2704

Gabel, Anna Margaretha von (o.) 1335
Gärtner, Margaretha, nee Rohwer (f.) 2988
Galenbeck, Margarete (f.) 567
Gantz kurtz zusammen gezogene Facti Species 2893
gar Newes Kriegs-Handbüchlein, Ein 474
Garp, Peter (o.) 482
Gebet-Buch 1274
Gebete vnd Lectiones 519
Gebete und Texte 1959, 2183
Gebeth Bey dem DanckFest 950
Gebeth um den edlen Land-Frieden 413
Gebeth und Lectien auff drey allgemeine Bethtage 1632
Gebetlein auf die tröstliche Leidensgeschichte 2347
Gebet und Texte 2255
Gebet Zu . . . Bet-Stunden 1737
Gebrauch Des Proportionirten Zirkels 2637
Geburtsgedichte 223
Gedancken von der Ewigkeit 3080
Gedenck Daran 385
Gedenck daran Fridrichsberg 1017
Gedicht auf die Hochzeitlichen Freuden bey Joach. Danckwert 237
Gegenbeweisung Dass die Heidelbergische Theologen 54
. . . gegründete Dänische Jubel-Jahr 2763
Geistlich New Jahrs vnd Friedens Geschenck 205
geistliche Anatomi, Eine 1246
Geistliche Apotheck 1131
Geistliche Gedancken 951
Geistliche Kauffmanschafft 478
Geistliche Königreich auff Erden, Das 2522
Geistliche Psalmen Lieder vnd Lobgesänge 74, 183
Geistlicher Amts-Rock 1153
Geistlicher Friede 1522
Geistlicher Krieg 1523
Geistlicher Rosengarten 250
Geistliche Rust-Kammer 336, 337, 358
Geistliche Seelenlust 1068
Geistliche Sinnen-Bilder 1155
Geistliche Tagübung 665
Geistliche Uhr 174
Geistliche vor-Weinacht Parodia 952
Geistliche Wallfahrt 2076
Geistreiche Schriften und Predigten 2687, 2851
gekrönete Frjederjch in einem Freuden-Spiel, Der 1702
Gemeiner Bescheid 2894
Gemeines Kirchen-Gebet 1231
Genealogische Beschreibung der Succession 2959
General Admiral Trompen Relation 1807
Geometrische Tractat 1212
Georgius, Laurentius (f.) 1486, 1496
Genauer Unterricht . . . die Holländische Flotte 2458
geschmückte Stern-Himmel, Der 2806
Gerichts Ordnung vnd Stadt Recht 27
Gerkens, Frau (f.) 2827
Gerstorff, Sophia Amalia (o.) 1421
Gesangbuch der Süder-Dithmarscher 2315
Gespräche des Hertzens mit Gott 2426
Gespräch von der Schwedischen Belägerung, Ein 953
gesuchte erste und letzte herausgebene Poesie, Die 1537

gewöhnlichen Sonn-und Festtages Episteln, Die 1274
Gezeugnis der Waarheit 1637
Gezwingener Communicant 2467
Giese, Joachim (o.) 2518 (f.) 2638, 2675
Gläntzende Tauben-Flügel 1724
Glaubens-Grund oder erläuterter Katechismus 2833
Glaubhaffter Bericht Aus Copenhagen 955
Glaubwürdige Relation Des am dritten negstver-wichnen Oct . . . Gefechtes 789
Glaubwürdige Specification 1577
Gloxin, Balthasar (f.) 714, 719, 723
Gloxin, Friedr. (o.) 1825
Gloxin, Friedrich Hanns (o.) 1792 (f.) 2204
Gloxin, Margareta, nee Jügert (f.) 2156, 2157
Gloxin, Sophia Augusta, nee Schacht (f.) 1666
Glückliche Eroberung 1746
glückliche Friedens-Bote, Der 2412
Glücksburgische Buss- und Beicht-Woche 1601
Glückstädtischer Vergleich 1355
Glückstädtisches Gesangbuch 2560
Glück- und unglückselige Kaufmannschaft 265
Glückwünschender Zuruff . . . Christoff Francken 2432
Glückwünschendes Ehren-Gedächtniss 1635
Glückwünschendes Gedicht . . . Friderich Dem Dritten 1062
Gnädigste Constitution 1626
Gnädigst elucidirte und erleuterte Constitution 1711
Gnädigste Resolution 85, 91
Gnädigste Verordnung . . . Danckfest 3109A
Göde, Georgia (f.) 2828
Goldhaus Christlicher und von Gott gesegneten Ehefrauen 1293
Gottgefälliges Rauch-Opffer 3008
Gottorffische Kunst-Cammer 1316, 1704
Gramm, C. (f.) 1644
Gratulation 2766
Gratulation oder Glückwunsch 185
Gravamina, Civium Hamburgens 349
Gregers, Else (o.) 557
Greiffenfeldischer Inqvisitionis End Urtheil 1808
Grenadische Lusthoff, Der 1772
Gröning, Herman (f.) 2764
Gröning, Jacob (f.) 1596
Gröningsches Diarium 1581A
Grotschilling, Hans (f.) 1239
Grothuss, Otto Johann von (f.) 2907
grosse Hertzensangst, Die 2281
grosse in der kleinen Welt, Die 2101
grosse Post Gottes, Die 375
Grosser Reichthum zusammen gebracht 1974
Gründliche Abhandlung des ungegründeten Ver-dachts 2678
Gründtliche aus den Rechten vnd Historischer war-hafften Bewandnuss . . . Remonstration 357
Gründliche Beschreibung . . . Italiänischen-Kauff-männischen Buchhaltens 2556
Gründlicher Beweis Dass . . . August Wygand 2899
Gründliche Erklärung Derer Buss-Texte 3098
Gründliche Informatio 1388
Gründlicher Bericht . . . über die Stadt Bremen 639
Gründlicher Bericht Von der Juden Sabbath 1291
Grundlicher und umbständlicher Bericht 1048
Gründliche und ausführliche Relation 848
Gründliche vnd Erhebliche Motiven vnd Vrsachen 137
Gründliche und nähere Nachricht 2191
Gründliche und warhaffte Relation 956, 957
Gründliche Untersuchung 2866
Gründliche Wiederlegung . . . Schlesswig-Hol-steinischen Ministerii 2857

Gründliche Wort-Verstand Des Kleinen Catechismi, Der 2652
Gründlich Verthädigte Treue Lutherthumb, Das 2527
Grundrichtige Beschreibung . . . Copenhagen 1400
Grundtlicher Bericht aus der H. Schrifft 53
Gülden Kleinodt 66
gülden Kleinod Pauli, Das 1811A
Gülden-Horn 1639. by Tundern gefunden 2126
Güldenlöw, Anna Christiana (f.) 2394, 2395
Güldenlöw, Christian (o.) 2797
güldenes ABC, Ein 157
Günther, Andreas (f.) 2957
Günther, Dorothea, nee Frölich (f.) 381
Günther, Friederich (f.) 731
Gudejohan, Johann (f.) 2299
Gude, C. M. (f.) 2983
Gude, Magdalena, nee von Schönfeld (o.) 2209
Gude, Marquard (f.) 2451, 2485, 2494
Güldene Glaubens-Kette 2148
Gute Gedancken Uber Catharinæ Mariæ Lobetanzin 3005
Gute Newe Jahrs-Zeitung 968

Hacke, Catharina (f.) 1204
Hagen, Catharina von, nee Fischer (f.) 2844
Hagen, Charlotte (o.) 2822
Hahn, Christopher (f.) 1078
Hahn, Vincentz Joachim (o.) 1672
Hake, Anna Margareta, nee Schilling (f.) 1169
Halcyonia ecclesiæ certo futura 2749
Halvers, Jngeborg (o.) 2734
Hamburgischer Palmen-baum 1690
Hamburgisch Mordt-Theatrum 2318A
Hamerich (o.) 2319
Handbuch der Chirvrgiæ 618
Handbüchlein vor Dethlef Gottlieb 2317
Handgriff Von Musqveten und Picken 1875
Handleitung Zur Seligkeit 1648, 1880, 1921, 2618
Hanfmann, Magdalena Margaretha (f.) 2300
Hannemann, Johann Christoph Ludewig (f.) 3046A
Hansen, Dorothea Catharina, nee Schacht (f.) 1699, 1701, 1717
Hansen, Jac. (o.) 2580
Hansen, Johannes (o.) 1582; (f.) 1693
Hansen, Melchior (f.) 1747, 1759
Hansen, Thomas (f.) 563
Hanses, Anna (f.) 1943
Haus Büchlein 407
Haus Gottes, Eine Christliche Einweihungs Predigt, Das 1294
Hausmann, Daniel (f.) 2362
Hauss-Apoteke 263
Haxthausen, Maria Elisabeth von, nee von Geispitzheim (f.) 1296
Hecklauer, Margarete Agnete, nee Soltow (f.) 1811, 1883
Heclauer, Sophie, nee Lælius (f.) 727
Hecklaurer, Johann (f.) 701
Hedwig Sophia, princess of Brandenburg, Duchess of Magdeburg (f.) 2153
Hedwig Sophia, Princess of Sweden, Duchess of Schleswig-Holstein (o.) 2873, 2901
Heefordt, Johanna (o.) 2932
Hegelund, Dorothea, nee Stahl (f.) 1853
Heider, Johannes Hulderich (f.) 1404, 1406, 1429
Heidtmann, Erasmus (f.) 7
Heilige Andachten 2150
Heilige Beht-Andacht 2041, 2079
Heilige Friedens-Arbeit 1162
Heilige Nachtmahls-Musik 1841

Heilige Passions-Gedancken 3088
Heiligen auss Gottes Wort Verlesungs-Texte, Die 575
Heiligen Perlen-Schatzes 2321-27, 2367-72, 2421-22, 2619-21
Heilsame Evangelisches Licht 2997
Heistermann, Joh. Samuel (o.) 647
Heistermann, Maria Elisabeth (f.) 1277
Held, Nicolaus (f.) 1385
Heldberg, Georg Ernest (f.) 2391, 2411, 2425
Helden-Brieff 2463
Helden-Ruhm . . . Niels Juel 1930A
Heldt, Friedrich (o.) 2447
Heller Arithmetischer Lehrspiegel 1301
Helm, Friederich (f.) 1232; 1610, 1639
Helm, Hedwig Maria (f.) 2360, 2385
Helm, Hermann (f.) 269
Helm, Johann (f.) 1901, 1902, 1915, 1918, 1928, 1938
Hennings, Ambrosius (f.) 348, 376
Hennings, Anna Margareta, nee Mauritius (f.) 2235, 2251
Herlichste und Heilsamste Christen-Werck, Das 2437
Herren Holländischen Gesandten notificiren, Die 1049
Herrlich Moral Lied, Ein 744
herschende Venus, Die 2706A
Hertzfliessende Betrachtungen 1740
Hertzens-Grund 1769
Hertzens Seufftzer 268
Hertzfliessende Betrachtungen 1740
Hertzlich-gemeynte Glückwünschung 2719A
(Hertzog Joh. Adolfs Land-Recht) 28
Hertzwolgemeinte Glückwünschung An . . . Johannes Rotlöben 485
Hess, Dorothea (f.) 1168, 1193
Hesselius, Petrus (f.) 2245
Hestenberg, Wilhelm (o.) 669
Hever, Anna von, nee Ranck (f.) 2488
Heyde, Matthias von der (o.) 1036
Heyden, Catharina (f.) 1546
Hierbey gedrücket Näher Bericht und Appendix 792
Himlische Weinachtgedancken 1431
Himmel-Freude 2439
Himmels-Freud und Höllen-Leid 2622
Himmels-Gedancken 2449
Himmlischer Morgen-Thau 2570
Himmlisches Gnaden-Licht 3084
Hinz, Georg (f.) 2384
Hirtengespräche Volkinnæ und Perez 517
Historia Davidis Georgii 1491
Historia der Passion 1274
Historia des Lebens-Lauffs Jesu Christi 2195A
Historia des Leidens und Sterbens Jesu Christi 255
Historia Vom Leben und Christlichen Abscheid . . . Johannis Calvini 1093
Historie der Cleopatra 1317
Historische Warhaffte und Aussführliche Beschreibung 959
Historischer Tagweiser 1736
Hoch-Fürstl. Confirmirtes Reglement 2771
Hoch-Fürstl. Holstein-Gottorffische Declaration 2985
Hoch-Fürstlich Eh- und Liebes Bette, Das 1842
Hoch-Fürstlicher Liebes-Schall 1876
Hoch-Fürstl. Schlesswig-Hollsteinische Verordnung Wie die Cavallerie 2796A
Hoch-Fürstliche Schleswig-Holsteinische erneuerte Verordnunge 2145
Hoch-Gräfflicher Rantzovischer Erster Freudenblick 1312

Hochzeit-Fackeln 3031
Hochzeitliches Ehren-Geschenck 378
Höchst-Rühmliches Gedichte 960
Høg, Jost (o.) 1519
Höllmer, Georg (f.) 2830
Hölmer, Martin (f.) 2244
Hoff-Gerichts-Ordnung 2491, 3074B
Höveln, Godhard von (f.) 1524, 1540A
Hoier, Andr. (o.) 2018
Holck, Erich (f.) 461
Holk, Friederica Sophia (f.) 1286
Holländer, Elisabeth (f.) 628
Hollsteinische Freudens-Bezeugung 2445
Holst, Johann (o.) 2017
Holsteensche Rüggeloeper, De 414
Holsteinische Chronica 1716
Holsteinisches Ding und Recht 2314, 2892A
Holsteinisches Gesang-Buch 2077
Holsteinisches Turtel-Täublein 1234
Holsten Land-Recht, Dat 550
Holtz-Ordnung 2009
Homagium Bremense 253
Honori et amori . . . 189
Honoris & Amoris Ara 1360
Hoppe, Anna (f.) 483
Horn, Joachim (o.) 2483
Horst, Hans (f.) 501
Hortus passionalis floridus 2342
Hoyer, Andr. (o.) 653
Hudemann, Christina, nee Lange (o.) 949
Hudemann, Johann (f.) 2786
Hudemann, Joh. (f.) 2216
Hudemann, Nicolaus (f.) 1353
Hudemann, Wolber, nee Alardus (f.) 2215
Hübsch, Elias (o.) 2182
Hüegen, Henrich (o.) 1146, 1161
Huid, Christen (o.) 405
Hurtige Handels-Rechner, Der 3054
Hydropicus Gratia 788
Hyphantis Poetische Musen 1135

Idea Pessimi Calumniantis 352
Jhrer Königl. Majest. . . . Admiralen Herrn Niels
    Juelen aussfürliche Relation 1813
Jhr. Königl. Mayst. . . . endliche Declaration 2416
Ihrer Königl. Majestät in Dennemarck Glückliche
    Eroberung 1764
Jhr. König. Maytt. von Schweden 963
Ihrer Königl. Majest. zu Dennemarck . . . Aller-
    unterthänigste Relationes 1916, 1917
J. K. M. zu Schweden Intercipirtes Schreiben 962
Jhro. Käyserl. Majestät Hand-Schreiben 2903
Jhro Königliche Majestät von Dannemarck Rescript
    2904
Jhro Königl Maj. Von Gross-Britannien Allergna-
    digste Rede 1642
im Garten zu Gethsemane, Der 2521
Jm Nahmen der heiligen Dreyfaltigkeit 298
Jm Nahmen dess DreyEinigen Gottes Die Wahre
    und veste Grundlehre 1892
Jm Namen Jesu . . . Danck-Gebet 1050
im Zorn-feuer Gottes Auffgehende Gnaden-Sonne,
    Die 2012
Immanuel Gott mit Uns 1691
Immerwährendes Neu-Jahrs-Geschenck 1542
Jn Jesu Namen. Amen! 1965
Jn Teutscher Sprache vorgestellter Euclides 2928,
    3013
Inaugurations-Predigt 1281
Index über die Landgerichts-Ordnung 3130
[Information von den eigentlichen Ursachen] 166

Jnhalt und Meynung Der Oration 964
Jns Kurtze gezogene ehemahlige Apologie 2953
Institutiones Anatomicæ 516
Instrumentum Pacis 849
Instrumentum Proportionum 377
Instrumentum wegen des Hertzogs . . . Restitution
    1966
Intercipirtes Schreiben 962
Interims-Recess 1941
Jssing, Maria (o.) 2483
Italianische Grammatica 2016
Italiänische Wahr-Sager, Der 1586A

Jacob, Eddonis (f.) 554
Jacob, Numme (f.) 1244
Jacobi, Laur. (f.) 1415
Jacobs, Hinrich (o.) 573
Jährliche Schlesswig-Holsteinische Fast-Buss- und
    Beht-Tag, Der 2078
Jansen, Elisabeth (o.) 2182
Jebsen, Jo. (o.) 538
Jensen, Martin (f.) 2842
Jessen, Friderich (f.) 1881, 1896
Jessen, Friedrich (f.) 1435
Jessen, Henr. (o.) 3048
Iessen, Margareta (f.) 2146
Jessen, Martin (f.) 2842, 2859
Jespers, Barbara (o.) 405
Jesu Christi Wanderschaft 2343
Jesu Mutter-Hertz 760
Jesus Aarons Brustgeschmeide 310
Jesus Christus meine Zuflucht 759
Jesussprüche 3073
Jesus Syrach 447
Jocoseria 2580
Jöns, Catharina (f.) 1812
Johann, Duke of Schleswig-Holstein (f.) 331
Johann Adolph, Duke of Schleswig-Holstein-Gottorf
    (f.) 63
Johann Fuhrmans Kleines Prognosticon Astrolog-
    icum (3046)
Johann Fuhrmanns Türcken-Calender 2989
Johann Georg Adolph, Duke of Schleswig-Holstein
    (f.) 195
Johann Georg, Duke of Saxony (o.) 1295
Johann Rohtens Geistestrieb 1559
Johannes, Duke of Schleswig-Holstein (f.) 113
Johansen, Claus (f.) 661A
Johansen, Margaretha, nee Boye (f.) 3033
Johnsen, Jacob (f.) 561
Jova Trinune Juva! 623
Jovers, Michael (o.) 2789
Jügert, Fridrich (f.) 2337
Jüngste Ordinari Post-Zeitung 1113
Jürgens, Gertrud (o.) 1183
Jürgensen, Dorothea (f.) 1434
Jürgensen, Friederich (o.) 1707
Jürgens(en), Jürgen (f.) 1543, 1555
Jürgensen, Laur. (f.) 1494
Jürgenssen, Friedrich (f.) 2740
Jugerdt, Petrus (f.) 688, 696
Jung, Anna-Margaretha (o.) 2680A
Jung, Jürgen (f.) 3024
Jung bey Jung 666
Jungfer Euphrosinen 1688
Jura Des Hauses vnd Fürstenthumbs Holstein 329
Jus feciale Armatæ Daniæ 801
Justifications-Schrifft 2774

Käyserlich Notifications Decert 1653
Kallisen, Anna (f.) 549

Kalnein, Wolffgang Hennrich von (o.) 1964
Karnarius, Hedwig Magdalena (o.) 1433
Kauff-Contract 584
Kedings, Augusta Maria (o.) 638
Kellinghusen (f.) 2837
Kellinghusen, Andreas (o.) 2800
Kellinghusen, Anna Catharina (o.) 2714
Kenckel, Anna (f.) 1820
Kenckel, Bernhard (f.) 2636
Kenckel, Catharina (o.) 1707
Kenkel, Stephan (f.) 2586
Kern und Safft 2994
Kiefer, Frau (f.) 2474
Kielische Lob-Denck und Danck Predigt 1308
Kielmann, Johann Adolph (o.) 1314
Kielmann, Margareta, nee von Hatten (f.) 798
Kielmann, Marie Elisabeth (o.) 647
Kielmann von Kielmans-Eck, Metta, nee von der
    Wisch (f.) 1741, 1760
Kieser, Johan (o.) 2516
Kilian, Hieronymus (o.) 1115
Kiliani, Gottfried (o.) 742, 1035; (f.) 1053
Kinder-Bibelbüchlein 1182
Kirchen-Gesänge 1599
Kirchhoff, Johann (o.) 2461
Kirchmann, Margarethe Dorothea (o.) 1868
Kirchow, Henrich (o.) 1125, 1127A
Klag-und Trost-Schrifften 2011
Klahre Andeutung Und wahre Anleitung Zur
    Nachfolge Christi 1939
Klauman, Isaac (o.) 643
Kleider- und andere Ordnung 2060
Kleine Bibel, Die 2944, 3025
Kleine Catechismus, Der 1274
Kleine Hauss- und Feld-Apotheck 2277
Kleine (oder kleiner) Catechismus, Der 302, 691
Kleine Reiss- und Hauss-Apotheck 2114
Kleines Holsteinisches Gesang-Buch 2041, 2079
Kleines Prognosticon Astrologicum 2989, 3046
Klingenberg, Elsabe (o.) 1107
Klöcker, Margareta (f.) 576
Klotz, Eva (o.) 538
Klüvers, Cielke (f.) 2330
Klugheit der Gerechten, Die 2612
Knall und Fall . . . Peter Schumachers 1814
Köll, Margaretha (o.) 615
Königliche Constitution Uber das Pinnenbergische
    Schuld- und Pfand-Protocoll 2962
Königliche Dännemarckische Kirchen Constitutio
    1149, 1794
Königl. Dännemarckische Kirchen-Constitution 2464
Königliche Dennemärckische Proposition 332
Königliche Holtz-Ordnung 1527
Königl. Pinnenbergische Constitution 2961
Königliche Postulata 2824
Königliche Qvaliteten und Eigenschafften 1051
Königliche vnd Fürstliche Constitutio und Taxa 182
Königl. und Fürstliche Constitution 1321, 1509
Königliche Verordnung Und Taxa 2990
Königlicher Mayest: . . . Manifest 318
Königlicher Mayestat . . . Schreiben An die Schwe-
    dischen Reichs Rähte 36
Königl. Dänisches Mandat 2185
Königl: Dännemarckisches Avocatorium 831
Königl. Kirchen-Gebeht 2184
Königl. Mayst. . . . verordnetes Buss-Gebet 3077
Königliches Patent 2131
Königliches Schwedisches an den Feldmarschalck
    Douglas abgefertigtes Schreiben 851
(Königs Christian des vierdten Ordnung) 20
Koesfeld, N. (f.) 2075

Kohlblatt, Christina, nee Hennings (f.) 2127, 2142,
    2155, 2166, 2169, 2170
Kolblath, Joachim (f.) 1745, 1775
Kollen, Elisabeth (f.) 1594
Kollen, Margareta (o.) 609, 615
Kollen, Sara, nee Rolandt (f.) 1882
Kong Valdemars Den Andens Jysk Low-Bog 2202
Kordes, Anne Sophie, nee Salomons (f.) 1292
Kordes, Claus (f.) 1379
Korfey, Friederich (f.) 2742, 2803
Korter Bericht Wo sick ein yeder 15
Kortholt, Chr. (o.) 2596 (f.) 2676
Kortholt, Dorothea Elisabeth (f.) 1992
Kortholt, Hinrich Christian (f.) 1325
Krabbe, Katharina (o.) 1519
Krabbe, Mettha (o.) 703
Kräftige Artzney wieder die Melancholey 794
Kram, Henr. Ern. von (f.) 2164
Kramer, Catharina von, nee von Bühlow (f.) 2381
Krause, Catharina (f.) 287
Krebs, Joh. (o.) 2348
Krieges vnd SiegesGesang 128
Krieg-und Liebes-Streit 1136
Kröger, Clauss (f.) 675
Kröger, Magdalena, nee Goldbach (f.) 1805, 1833
Kroneborg, Margaretha (o.) 1036
Kronüngs-Lied Friedrich III 545
Kronhelm, Anna Sophia von, nee Walter (f.) 2040
Kruse, Katharina (f.) 218
Kürtzlich doch Genugsamer . . . Slangen-Brand
    Sprützen 2826
Kunst-Mas des Raums 2588
Kupffer, Martin (f.) 965, 1006
Kurtz-abgefassetes Rechen-Buch, Ein 2788
Kurtzgefassete Recapitulation 1544
Kurtz gefasete schliessliche Abfertigung 3078
Kurtzgefasste Doch Gründlich Anleitung . . . der
    Teutschen Sprache 2834
Kurtz-gefasste Instruction 2601
Kurtz vnvorgreiffliches Bedencken 167
Kurtz verfassete Species Facti 2778
Kurtze Anleitung zur Erklärung . . . Ps. 2. 12. 2921
Kurtze Anleitung zur Erklärung Derer Buss-Texte
    3090
Kurtze Anleitung zur Erklarung . . . Hos. 4. 1-2.
    3006
Kurtze Anzeige und fürstellung 1241
Kurtze Anzeige Was Wegen der . . . 1242
Kurtze Auslegung des VI Capitels . . . Michæ 2666
Kurtze Beantwortung 1538
Kurtze Bedancken von dem Ende des Gegenwär-
    tigen 3016
kurtze Beschreibung, Eine 203
Kurtze Beschreibung . . . Christianstad 1818
Kurtze Beschreibung der Sechsigtheiligen Rechnung
    2380
Kurtze Beschreibung der Stadt Lands-Cron 1817
Kurtze Beschreibung Des Nieren und Blasen Steins
    2705
Kurtze Beschreibung . . . Reise naher Norwegen 530
Kurtze Beschreibung und Erzehlung von einem
    Juden . . . Ahasverus 6
Kurtze Beschreibung Wie es bey der Huldigung 531
Kurtze Deduction und Antwort 1969
Kurtze Doch Gründliche Instruction Von Handels-
    Buchhalten 2504
Kurtze doch gründliche Vorstellung Eines . . .
    Christen 2925
Kurtze doch warhafftige Beschreibung der Silber
    562, 2239

Kurtze Entdeckung der verkrochenen Papistischen Lehre 2082
Kurtze Erklärung der ersten 8 Capittel . . . Josuä 2482
Kurtze Erleuterung des Beschlusses 374
Kurtze Erinnerungen Welche bey Scharmizirung Treffen 324
Kurtze Fürstellung 1650
Kurtze fundamentalische Erläuterung Des von der Stadt Bremen 641
Kurtze jedoch gründliche Anzeige 2779
Kurtze jedoch warhafftige Relation 793
Kurtze Information in Sachen 2230
Kurtze Reise Beschreibung 1328
Kurtze Relation 301
Kurtzer Aber Warhaffter Bericht 1647
Kurtzer Anhang und Erörterung 2470, 2840
Kurtzer aus den Actis und Protocollis gezogener Bericht 852
Kurtzer Begriff Einer Holsteinischen Chronic 1198, 1705
Kurtzer Begriff Uber die Episteln vnd Evangelia 305
Kurtzer Begriff Unterschiedlicher gottloser und irriger Reden 1663
Kurtzer Bericht 532, 967, 1585
Kurtzer Bericht von Dem Unterscheid 2470, 2840, 3112A
Kurtzer Bericht Von Den Englischen Kauffardey-Schiffen 668
Kurtzer Bericht von . . . Prince Georgen Ankunfft 2151
Kurtzer Bericht Was bey dem zu Coppenhagen 1920
Kurtzer Bericht Wie von den Schweden 1879
Kürtzer Bericht Welchergestalt . . . Vlrica Eleonora 2014
Kurtzer Doch Warhaffter Bericht 1749
Kurtzer Einhalt der Augsburgischen Confession 407
Kurtzer Einhalt und Bedeutung des Ballets 202
Kurtzer Entwurf Der Solennitäten 1586
Kurtzer Extract aus den ersten 5. Tomis. Lutheri 2994
Kurtzer Extract Und Jnhalt 968
Kurtzer Jedoch auf festem Grund bestehender-Gegen-Beweis 2910
Kurtzer jedoch Gründlicher Bericht 1364
Kurtzer Jedoch Warhaffter Bericht 3079
Kurtzer jedoch warhaftiger . . . Bericht 612
Kurtzer und Gründlicher Beweiss 2911
Kurtzer vnd Summarischer Begriff 457
Kurtzer vnd Summarischer Bericht der Vrsachen 418
Kurtzer und warhaffter Bericht 1055, 1749
Kurtzer und Warhaffter In Jure & Facto . . . Gegen-Bericht 3038
Kurtzer Unterricht Von der Frantzösischen Sprache 2231, 2419
Kurtzer Unterricht von geistlichen Versuchungen 2196
Kurtzer Vorbericht betreffende . . . Museum Cimbricum 2373
Kurtzes, flüchtiges und mühseliges Leben 1256
Kurtzes Gebet-Buch 2641
Kurtzes Gebet-Büchlein 1697, 1720, 1773, 1848, 2341
Kurtze Summarische Beschreibung . . . Bret-Spiels 416
Kurtze und andächtige Gebetlein 1382
Kurtze und eigentliche Beschreibung Des . . . Hauses Friederichsburg 467
Kurtze vnd einfaltige Beschreibung . . . Schlesswig 14, 1638

Kurtze vnd gebührliche . . . wolgegründete Antwort 757
Kurtze vnd scheinbare Erklärung 417
Kurtze Verzeichnuss der Schäden 186
Kurtz-runde Beantwortung 677

Lambert, Elisabeth (o.) 570
Landgerichts Ordnung 217, (246)
Landhorst, Magdalena Sybilla (f.) 654
Landwehr, Ernst Moritz (o.) 1686
Lange, Christoph (o.) 1287 (f.) 2708
Lange, Hans (f.) 679
Langelott, Joël (f.) 2062, 2067
Lapis Lydius 1462
Lapländische Doctor, Der 969
Lassenius, Catharina Hedwig (o.) 2444
Lassenius, Johannes (f.) 2543, 2572, 2624
Laurentius, Dorothea Margareta (f.) 1398, 1414
Leben der Seelen im Tode, Das 1072
Lebens-Lauff . . . Johannis Lassenii 2572, 3081
Leben und Todt . . . Johanni Lassenii 2624
LeichPredigt über Joh. XVIII. 9. 1932
leichte Arithmetica, Eine 2787
Lengerken, Johannes von (f.) 2063
Lenschen, Thabea (f.) 224
Lent, Fridericus (f.) 1857
Lente, Christian (f.) 1140, 1163
Lente, Friedrich (f.) 1857, 1926, 1937
Lente, Hugo (f.) 2022
Lente, Theodor (f.) 1386
Lepape, Maria (f.) 326
Letzte Rede 2680, 2814
Letzte Warnung 2954
Levitischer Hoherpriester und Priester 2712
Lex Regia 1258A
Leyer Matzs Lustiger Correspondenz Geist 1498
Liebes-Flammende Jesus Rubinen 2288
Lied aus der Königliche Vestung Glückstadt 285
Lieth, Maria Elisabeth (o.) 1357
Liliencron, Anna Margarethe von (f.) 2640, 2651, 2672
Liliencron, Andreas Paul von (f.) 3051, 3053, 3074-75, 3085, 3093, 3118, 3124-25
Lindholtz, Barbara Apollonia (f.) 2558
Lindholtz, Magdalena, nee Brasch (f.) 2825
Lingva profana 2427
Lippe, Daniel (o.) 1487
Lista der zum Kiell embarquirten Völcker 971
Lista Derer unter Bornholm . . . gefangenen Schweden 1923
Lista Von Jhrer Königl: Majest: . . . Flotte 1972
Litania Israelitico-Nordmarsiaca 1082
Literæ Circulares 1505
Lob des Weingottes 1739
Lobetanz, Catharina Maria, nee Gude 3005
Lob-Gedichte Von der Wahl-Huldigung 1079
Lobgesang über den Geburtstag Jesu Christi 1687
Lob-singende Andacht 2273, 2328, 2571, 2836
Lob- und Dank-Ode 3076
Lob-vnd Ehren Reimen 1080
Lobwürdige Cadmus, Der 1211
Loci comm[unes] 1373
Löbliche Fischerampt, Das 1032
Lorentz, Niels, (f.) 2065, 2066
Lorentzen, Anna (o.) 2597
Lorentzen, Catharina (f.) 512
Lorentzen, Hans (f.) 533
Lorentzen, Lucia, (f.) 991
Lorentzen, Sophia (f.) 1026
Louise, Duchess of Mecklenburg, Queen of Denmark (o.) 2684, 2706A, 2716

Ludwig, Landgraf of Hessen-Darmstadt (o.) 587, 608
Lübbes, Eggricht Johann (o.) 729
Lüders, Christian (o.) 2284
Lüders, Garlev (f.) 536
Lüders, Marcus (f.) 601
Lüthken, Anna (f.) 1148
Lütken, Benedict (f.) 1362, 1403
Lüttichau, Siegfried von (f.) 465
Lützow, Dorothea Maria (f.) 625
Lustiger Wort-und leidiger That-Krieg 1117
Lustige Schwedische vnd Dennemärckische Hasen-Jagt 853
Lux Lucens in tenebris 1413
Lysius, Joh. (f.) 2659

M. G. Sicherer Schild 1076A
Maass, Georg (f.) 503
Madewitz, Christophor (o.) 2463
Madrigalon 2019
Magdalena Sybilla, Duchess of Saxony (o.) 214, 249, 529, 790
Magen, Henricus (f.) 289
Major, Johann Daniel (o.) 2011, 2045 (f.) 2632
Major, Margareta Dorothea (o.) 2523
Majus, Achatius (f.) 2874
Mammon 1453
Mandat Wegen Der Betteler 2934
Mandat Wegen Der Pferde 2935
Mande, Anna Maria von (o.) 2798
Mandelslo, Johann Albrecht von (f.) 450, 508, 854
Mangor, Elovius (o.) 2932
Manifest, Auss was Erheblichen Vhrsachen 802
Manifest . . . Betreffend Die Prætensionen 318, 319
Manifest . . . Betreffendt Die Gerechtigkeit 319
Manifest . . . betreffendt die Vrsachen dess vorgenommenen Kriegs 795
Manifest Oder Summarischer Bericht 419
Manifest und angeführte Uhrsachen 1758
Manifest wider Chur-Cöllen 1655
Manuale . . . Schauenburgischen Hoff-Gerichts-Ordnung 2838
March, Kasper (o.) 1872, 2225, 2234, 2238
March, Katharina, nee Schmeid (f.) 1645
March-Ordnung 1862D
Marie Elisabeth, Duchess of Schleswig-Holstein-Gottorf (o.) 373, 375, 587, 608, 1890 (f.) 2557, 2563
Martens, Erasmus (f.) 510
Martin, Nicholaus (o.) 1580, 2110
Martini, Benedict (f.) 2257
Martini, Dorothea (f.) 2206
Martinsen, Abigail (o.) 2800
Martzan, Melchior (o.) 607, 611
Masquarada 1194
Masquerade der vier Jahrs-Zeiten 1419
Mathematischer Abriss 613
mathematisch und hieroglyphisch Present, Ein 647
Mauritius, Erich (f.) 1465, 3137
Mecklenburg, Arnold (f.) 2846
Medicinalischer Ramonneur 2920
Meditatio Passionalis 3003
Meditationes De Tribus Christianorum Artibus 1282
Meier, Elisabeth (f.) 736
Meinard, Nicolaus (f.) 1090, 1105, 1129
Meineck, Bernh. (o.) 2579
Meinke, Lucia (f.) 2227
Meinstorf, Christophor von (f.) 1278
Meister, Jo. Fried. (o.) 2472
Melchersen, Anna (o.) 2472
Melismata Epistolica 1350-51

Memoriael Van de Heere Charisius 909
Memorial An alle Getreue Einwohner 1060
Memorial denen Liebhabern . . . des Buchhaltens 2546
Memorial zu dem Winckelier-Handel 2547
Mercker, Cordt Henrich 1562
Metallische Probier-Kunst 1996
Métode Nouvéle 1541
Metropoleos Daniæ 1159
Meyer, Johann Adolf (f.) 1458
Meyland, Claus (f.) 1324
Michaelsen, Michael (o.) 379
Michelsen, Johann Dieterich (o.) 2587
Militair-Eyd 3134
Mitwochentliche Zeitung 797
Moderations Motiven 55
Mölgard, Clara Nichol. (o.) 2626
Möller, Olaj 2236
Möller, Ursula (f.) 251, 252
Mohr, Georg (f.) 2578
Moldenit, Anna Margarethe, nee Schacht (f.) 745
Moller, Agatha (o.) 2918
Moltken, Elseba (f.) 741
Mond- und Sonnen-Cyklus 3115
Monimentum 463
Morgenländische Reyse-Beschreibung 844, 1418
Morgen- und Abend- und Buss-Beicht-Communion- . . . Gebete 1921, 2272, 2571, 2618
Morgen- und Abend-Lied 1648, 1880
Morhof, Daniel Georg (o.) 1547
Morhof, Margarete, nee von Degingk (f.) 2298, 2302A
Mühlen, Dorothea zur (f.) 504
Mühlen, Wolber zur, nee Alardus (f.) 1247
Müller, Bernhard (f.) 1564
Müller, Johannes (f.) 1591
Münden, Christian (f.) 689, 692, 694, 700
Müntzedict 106
Munck, Anna Dorothea (o.) 1964
Mund, Christian (o.) 570
Musaeus, Anna, nee von Deging 2451
Musaeus, Anna Magdalena, nee Museaus (f.) 2958, 2984, 2991, 3017, 3019, 3027
Musaeus, Anna Margareta, nee Schröder (f.) 2468, 2476, 2489-90
Musaeus, Petrus (o.) 1305, 1540, (f.) 1738, 1742, 1744, 1753, 1754
Musäus, Simon Heinrich (o.) 2100
Musicalischer Dialogus 1751
Musicalisches Lustspiel 2610
Musicalisch Schawspiel 721
Mutzenbecher, Matthias (o.) 2099, 2113

Nachdenckliches Antwort-Schreiben 1653
Nachdenkender Leichgänger 477
Nach des . . . Herren Friderichs . . . Befehl . . . Buss-und Bet-Tage 2717
Nach gnädigstem Befehl . . . Buss- unn Bettage 3007
Nach jetz-üblichen Mercatorischen-Stylo, Ein 2547
Nach-Predigt 2998
Nachricht über die Streitigkeiten 3091
Nachricht und Verzeichniss 2920
Nachricht Wegen der . . . Erwachsenen Jrrungen 2718
Nachricht . . . Wider Des Hn. Hertzogen 2141, 2190A
Nachrichtliche Anzeige 2077
Näher Bericht und Appendix 792
Nähere Alliantz der Cron Spanien 1653
Nähere Declaration Wegen des vermeinten Verraths 2332

Nähere Tractaten 1592
Nähere Verbündnüss 1653
Nagel, Johan Helfrich (o.) 2703, 2711, 2719
Nastortium 1202
Nayen, Gerhard (f.) 2861
Neander, Gottfried (o.) 2377
Negotia Domestica 2201
Nester, Herman (f.) 1609
Neü-angelegt-Historisch-Algebraischer Garten-Bau, Der 2500
New Astronomischer Haupt-Schlüssel 2291
Neu erfundenes Uhrwerck 2850A
Neu Jahrs Wunsch und Gebeth 2564
Neu-Jahrs Wuntsch 1466
Neu Tractat Von Schifbrüchigen Gütern, Ein 2202
Neüdorf, Anthon (o.) 1134
Neüe Hchheilige Katechismus 1319
Neue Privilegia 1142, 2549
Neue Privilegia den Holländern 116
Neue Reise Jn die Nordischen Landschafften 1750
Newe Relation 420
Neue Testament, Das 1219, 2683
Newe Tragico Comoedia De Bello, Eine 197
Newe und sehr nützliche Metode 1541
Neue und sehr seltzame Relation 856
Neue Zeitung aus Hummelburg 1703
Newe Zeitung auss Schweden 37
Newer Dänischer vnd Schwedischer Mercurius 454
Neuer Frantzösischer Syncretismus 1651
Neüer Teütscher Parnass 1424
Newer Teutscher Post-Reuter 452
neuer und schöner Gesang, Ein 194
Newes Kriegs Büchlein, Ein 442
newes Kriges Tractätlein, Ein 406, 781
Neues Kirchen-Handbüchlein, Ein 1245
Newes Liedt, Ein 974
Neues Müntz-Büchlein 1706
Neues Testament 3047
Neues Trenchier-Büchlein 1688
Neugestimmte Davids-Harfe 763
Neujahrs-Schrift 1602
Neutralitäts-Puncta 889
Neve, Rotger (f.) 2280
Neve, Sophia Elisabeth (f.) 2282
Nicolai, Detleff Georg (f.) 2825
Niederstättin, Maria Elisabeth, née Olearius (f.) 1998, 2010, 2013, 2015, 2023, 2046, 2048, 2097, 2106, 2109, 2123
Niels Tochter, Anna (o.) 716, 720
Nieman, Martha Justina, née Förster (f.) 1793, 1821, 1847
Niemann, Sebast. (f.) 2199
Nifanius, Johannes (f.) 1349
Nimwegischer Friedens-Currier 1927
Nissen, Hanss (f.) 2105
Nissen, Truls (o.) 1728
Nochmahl abbildung Anthonette Bourignons 1611
Nöhtige Beschneidung 2414
Nöhtige erachtete Christliche Warnung, Eine 2366
Nörck, Hans Heinrich (f.) 2657
Nohtwendige Vertheidigung Des heiligen Römischen Reichs 150
Noltenn, Margaretha (f.) 659
Nothelffer, Margaretha Dorothea (f.) 2120
Nothwendige und Trewhertzige Formahnungs Missive 975
Nothwendige Wiederholete Erzehlung 1861
Nova Arithmetica 1761
Norburgische Feur-Schaden 1272
Nord-Fresische Chronick 1306
Nordische Bezoar, Der 1850

Nordischer Friedens-Schluss 1063
Nordischer [Merkur] 2159, 2203
Nordisches Denkmahl 1652
Nord-Schwedische Hexerey 1884
Nützlicher Unterricht Von Schuldiger Beobachtung 2926
nützliches Tractätlein Vom Lobe Gottes, Ein 283
Nummel, Monica (o.) 2008
Nunmehr Ausführliche rechtgründliche und Warhafftige Lista 976
Ny Kircke-Haandbog, En 1245
Nye Tüdinge van der Jamerlyken Waterfloth 64
Nye Tydinge Vth Koppenhagen 43

Obersouverainität des Herrn Jesu Christi 2283
Occasus & Regressus 1365
Ocksen, Johannes (o.) 2773
Octroy und Concession 2310
Odensehisch Vertrag 1064
Ode Welche Bey Haltung der Lob-Rede 3095
Öllers, Elisabeth (o.) 2516
Oersundische Relation 1822, 1823, 1955, 1977
Offenbahrung Beyder Königen zu Dennemarck 421
Offene Versicherung 1180
Offentlicher Gottesdienst Der alten Hebräer 2713
Offt begehrte Beschreibung Der Newen Orientalischen Reise 508
Oheimb, Laurentius (f.) 1563
Ohm, Niklaus (f.) 671
Ohnmassgebliche Gedancken 3067
Ohnvorgreiffliches Feder-Gefechte 1929
Oldenburg- und Delmenhorstische Successions-Sache 1538
Oldermann, Bern. (f.) 2070
Oldermann, Elisabeth, nee Andersen (f.) 1271
Olderogge, D. J. (o.) 1433
Olearius, Adam (f.) 2106
Olken, Andreas (o.) 2019
Olla Podrida 2446
Olsede, Balthasar von (f.) 667
Opera Sacra de pace recuperata 2038
Ordinaire Dingstagsche Zeitunge 1199
Ordinarie Post-Zeitung 1329, 1452, 1653
Ordinarie Wochentliche Zeitung auss Hamburg 858
Ordinance . . . Vnsere Hohe vnd Niedrige Kriegs-Officier 436
Ordonnance . . . Artillerie Bedienten zu Verpflegen 1862A
Ordonnance . . . Cavallerie zu Verpflegen 1862B, 2132
Ordonnance . . . Dragoner zu verpflegen 1863A
Ordonnance . . . Infanterie zu verpflegen 1862C, 1953A, 2133
Ordonnance . . . Milice 1862C
Ordonnance . . . Tragouner zu verpflegen 1863B
Ordonnance . . . unsere Dragoner . . . Verpfleget 2274
Ordnung . . . So wir von Kleidung 2, 19, 57
Ordnung Von Vorlöbnussen Kindelbieren Begrebnussen vnd Kleidungen 2A
Ordtnung Betreffend die Gottesfurcht 118
Ordre Welche . . . Feld-Marschalck Schack 977
Orientalische Reise-Beschreibung 1430
Ortho dias promen Das ist: Vortrab 148
Osten, Augusta Maria Elsabeth von der, nee von Winterfeld (f.) 1723
Ottilamor (o.) 1136
Ovis ruminans 1147
Owmann, Martin (f.) 2689

Päbstlicher Sauerteig ausgefeget 2375

Paijnck, Katarine, nee Schreiber (f.) 604
Palinodiæ Becmannianæ Specimen 2576
Papa Schismaticus 1447
Papiren Feyer-Werck 1046
Paradoxon De Morbo Gallico 1043A
Paraphrasis Germanica 730, 874-75
Parvus mundus 2083
Passe Partout François, Le 2351, 2756
Passion des Glaubens Cron, Die 2924
Passions-Andachten 2999
Passions-Catechismus 2946
Patent . . . An die Bürgerschafft Jn Hamburg 369
Patent vnd Freyheiten 155
Paulli, Elisabeth, nee Fabricius (f.) 762, 764, 807
Paulli, Simon (f.) 1997
Paulssen, Christian (f.) 1332
Pechlin, Sophia Magdal. Doroth. (f.) 2158
Pentz, Christian von (o.) 487
Penu filiorum Dei 595
Persianischer Rosenthal 697, 1066, 1067
Persönliche Hochzeit Des Sohnes Gottes, Die 2817
Peters, Maria Agnesa (o.) 1146, 1161
Petersen, Anna (o.) 2773
Petersen, Anna Catharina (o.) 1554
Petersen, Frau (f.) 1279
Petersen, Nicolaus (o.) 1255
Petersen, Peter (f.) 1196
Petersen, Peter (o.) 2597
Petkum, Johannes Hieronymus (o.) 2905, 2951
Petrejus, Catharina, nee Witmack (f.) 2663
Petrejus, Johannes (f.) 2668
Petrejus, Katharina (o.) 3131
Petrejus, Lucia Margareta (f.) 2977
Pezolt, Mich. (f.) 2177
Pfeiffer, Georg (o.) 2626
Pfeiffius, Daniel (f.) 1220
Pflegepredigt 276
Pharmaceutice Davidica 30
Philandersons Discvrs 988
Philidors Erst Entflammte Jugend 1375
Philipp, Duke of Schleswig-Holstein-Sonderburg-Glücksburg (f.) 1246
Philomusen verdeutschter Svetonius 1205, 1249
Pintzier, Ludwich (o.) 949
Piper, Susanna Gerdraut (o.) 2532A
Pium Regis Moribundi Testamentum 3026
Plaisirs des Heros, Les 3009A
Planctus Ecclesiæ 1893
Plesson, Hieron. (f.) 306
Poetisch-Musicalisches Lustwaldlein 514
Pogwisch, Bartram von (f.) 1589, 1590
Pohl, Friedrich (o.) 1891
Policeyordnung 222, 740, 1348, 1483
Politischer Auss Göttlicher . . . Discurs 422
Politischer Discurs 139
Polnsches Triumph-Lied 799
Popp, Hermann (o.) 1092
Postilion 422A, 455
Postilla Sacramentalis 1405
Post-Ordnung 685
Post-Reuter Vnd Lautschallenden Herold 456
Postulats-Lob- und Lustgedicht 569
Postzeitung 169
Powisch, Anna (f.) 1718
Practica Astrologica Vp dat M.DC.VII Jaer 24
Practica Geometriæ 2933
Präliminär-Discurs 2524
Praxis pietatis 1493A
Praxis Testamenti anamneseos Jesu Christi 593
Predigt Stada Exusta 1550

Predigt über das Evangelium vom guten Hirten, Eine 475
(Predigt vom wahren Christenthume) 343
(Predigt von der ewigen Sonnen) 565
Preisswürdigste Gedächtnuss, Das 2623
Preuss, Johann (o.) 490; (f.) 1695
Preussen, Lucas (o.) 1554
Princeps Christianus 68
Privilegia . . . der Neuerbauten Stadt Glückstadt 2550
Privilegia, Entheilet der neuen Stadt . . . Halss 755
Privilegia ertheilet der newen stadt und vestung 588
Privilegia Oder Freyheiten . . . 190, 191
Privilegia, so den Armenianern 117
Privilegia So der Durchleuchtige 171
Privilegien und Freyheiten . . . der Evangelischen alss Reformirten Religion 2242
Probe Fälschlicher Über- und Hinzusetzung 2333
Prognosticon Astrologicum 354, 451, 479, 507, 660, 699, 702, 766, 892, 1139, 1167, 1215, 1330, 1381
Prognosticon Astrologicum oder Practica 65
Project Der neuen Regierungs-Form 1069
Project, Welcher Gestalt . . . Niels Juel 1930
Propheten, Die 1218
Propositio 1979
Propositiones Und Postulata 2379
Proposition So den 26. Sept: 1980
Proposition von Monsieur De Thou 1071
Proposition Welche . . . Otto Krag Und Gosche von Buchwalt 1070
Psalmen-Lieder vnd Lobgesenge 17
Psalter Davids 284, 1200
Psalter des Königlichen Propheten Davids, Der 1158
Publicirtes Vrtheil wieder Graff Corfitz Vhlfeldt 1201
Pudewel, Gregor von (f.) 859
Pyramis 363

Quäcker Geist, Der 1028
Qualen, Otto von (f.) 292; 2877
Qveisser, Salome, née Hintz (f.) 2566
Quistorp, Johannes (f.) 518
Quod felici factum sit augurio 225

Rabe, Catharina (o.) 2267
Rabe, Dorothea, nee von Reichau (f.) 2475
Rachelius, Catharina Ursula, nee Rothschröder (f.) 1334
Rach-Geschrey 978
Rager, August (o.) 3131
Ramel, Heinrich & Otto (f.) 542
Ramm, Johann (f.) 1088
Ramm, Tabea (f.) 624, 857
Rantzau, see Rantzow
Rantzaw, Benedicta (f.) 1459
Rantzow, Bertram (†1652) (f.) 646, 649
Rantzow, Bertram (†1686) (f.) 2278
Rantzow, Burchard (f.) 193
Rantzow, Catarina Hedewig, nee Brocktorf (f.) 2443, 2457, 2473, 2486
Rantzau, Catharina, nee von Qualen (f.) 1774
Rantzou, Christian (†1664) (o.) 1076 (f.) 1236
Rantzau, Christian (Canon in Lübeck) (o.) 2710
Rantzau, Christian Detlev (o.) 1512
Rantzow, Christoffer (f.) 627
Rantzau, Christoph (f.) 2739
Rantzau, Detlev (o.) 1312, 1512, (f.) 2832A, 2862, 2895
Rantzow, Dorothea (f.) 1192

Rantzow, Dorothea, nee Ahlefeldt (f.) 499, 500, 506, 509, 511
Rantzou, Dorothea Benedikte (f.) 2783, 2790
Rantzow, Hans (†1656) (f.) 758
Rantzow, Hans, Major General 1692, 1694, 1720
Rantzow, Heilwig (f.) 687
Rantzow, Jda (f.) 1112
Rantzow, Metta, nee Sehestet (f.) 1492, 1500, 1511
Rantzow, Moritz (o.) 1709, 1715
Rantzow, Otto (f.) 2646, 2654, 2656, 2660, 2662, 2681, 2908
Rantzau, Sophia Amalia (o.) 1312
Rantzau, Sophia Ida, nee v. d. Nath (f.) 2531
Rechenbuch 2376
Rechenschafft des Glaubens 18
rechte Glückstadt, Die 1332
Rechtmässige Beschwerden und Ansprüche 2270
Rechtmässige Ursachen Warumb . . . Exercitium Juris Armorum 3010
Rechtmässige Vertheidigung 2775
Rede bey Gelegenheit der Bloqvirung 1058
Refutation und Klärliche Wiederlegung 1981
Regier-Kunst, Die 954, 1104, 2459
Rehder, Johannes (f) 1860
Rehefeld, Bonaventura (f.) 1634, 1714
Rehefeld, Sophia Elisabeth (o.) 1243
Reich, Georg (f.) 1189, 2183
Reich, Jakob Christoph (f.) 1982
reiche Thor, Der 3015
Reichenbach, Sophie Eleonora (f.) 2664, 2665
Reichenbach, Sophia Elisabeth von (f.) 2649
Reichow, Juliana Elisabeth von (f.) 626
Reimann, Hedwig (f.) 2424
Reimer, Margareta (o.) 2579
Reinboth, Hinrich (f.) 2534
Reinking, Ant. Gunth. von (f.) 1783
Reinking, Catharina, nee Pistor (f.) 1089, 1119
Reinking, Dieterich (o.) 1191 (f.) 1253, 1268, 1283, 1289
Reinking, Dorothea Vieht (f.) 1214
Reise-Buch 1455
Reise-Manual 1691
Reiss-Predigt 204
Relatio Nova De Contributione Rediviva 457A
Relation aus Copenhagen 862, 1074
Relation aus dem Parnasso 2112
Relation auss Kopenhagen 1073
Relation aus Kopenhagen Vnd Stubkioping 981
Relation aus dem Gottorpischen Parnasse 1422
Relation aus dem Königl. Feldtlager 979
Relation Aus Fynen 980
Relation aus Norwegen Vermüge des Zollners 863
Relation Aus Unterschiedlichen frembden Orten 864
Relation Der Zwischen den Dänischen und Schwedischen Wachten 982
Relation, Der zwischen den Vnsrigen 865
Relation dessen so zwischen beyden Nordischen Cronen 1827
Relation Hvorledis Christianstad 1828
Relation Oder Eigentliche Erzehlung auss Gottorff 281
Relations-Courier 2850
Relation Vnd Aussführlicher Bericht 458
Relation Vnd Continuation 866
Relation vnd gewisser Bericht 94
Relation Vom tödtlichen Hintritt (Cromwell) 867
Relation Von dem was zwischen zwey 1985
Relation Von der . . . Bataile bey Lunden 1830
Relation von der den 4. Decembris . . . Bataille 1829
Relation Von Der Erbhuldigung in Norwegen 1123
Relation Von der Krönung 537

Relation von der prächtigen Beerdigung . . . Christiani V 3011
Relation Von des Schwedischen Königs Gespräch 983
Relation von Jhr. Königl. Mayestatt Flota 423
Relation . . . was bei dem . . . Carrousel 2026
Relation was bey . . . Ulrica Eleanor . . . Ankunft 2027
Relation Was Nach Einschiffung der Völcker 984
Relation Was sich mit denen auss Pommern 1931
Relation Wegen Des grossen und erschrecklichen Brandes 2533
Relation Welcher gestalt 985, 1831, 2028
Relation Wie die Stadt Ydstæd 1832
Relation wie es mit der vom Könige in Schweden 986
Remer, Dorothea (o.) 606
Remonstration Worin die von der Statt Hamburg 170
Rendesburgische Kirchhofs-Einweihung 2669
Renovirte Landes-Matricul 652
Renovirte Licent-Rulle 1392
Renovirte Zoll-Rulle 1391
Replica Auff Die Antwort 2629
Repertorium Alphabeticum 12
Resolution 1346
Retorsio Defensiva 1766
Rettung unserer Lehre 2671
Reventlou, Christoph von (f.) 3070
Reventlow, Conrad (o.) 1335
Revidirte Executions Ordnung 229
Revidirte Landgerichts-Ordnung 246, 1266, 2352, 2451A
Revidirter Französischer Syncretismus 1986
Revocation 2237
Rheder, Margareta (f.) 1789
Rhode, Eleonora, née von Ahlefeld (f.) 3004
Richtiger Glaubensweg 415, 1190
Richtiger Weg zur Seeligkeit 2480, 2584
Richtige Wolfahrt der flüchtigen Wallfahrt 2575
Richtigste Doch Compendiöse Beschribung Der Müntz-Wehrungen 2691
Richtigste Doch Compendiöse Beschribung Der Vornehmsten Wechsel-Plätze 2692
Richtsen, Nicol. (o.) 2658
Ridtzer, Georg (o.) 716, 720
Rige, H. G. (o.) 2152
Rist, Jo. Casp. (f.) 2677
Ritter Der Königlichen Dänischen Orden, Die 2721
Rivesell, Peter (f.) 1819
Römisch, Catharina Magdalena (o.) 1356
Römischer Beelzebub 1409
Römisches Jubel-Jahr 3086
Roht in Weiss verkehrte Sieges-Fahne 1743
Rolla des Tonnen-Baken-und Kapen-Geldes 2112A
Rosen, Anna (f.) 535
Rosenfeld, Else (o.) 2363
Rosensparre, Steen (f.) 38
Rosmann, Ursula, nee Faust (f.) 2029
Rossman, Johannes Adolph (f.) 2143
Rossmann, Johannes Philipp (f.) 2005
Rostius, Christopher (o.) 1993
Rothlöben, Johannes (f.) 485, 559
Rothsten, Jens (o.) 1421
Ruhe, Detlev (f.) 2256
Ruhm-Zeilen 1654
Rumohr, Augusta née Schack (f.) 1470
Rumohr, Ida Christina (f.) 3072, 3099
Rumor, Ida Hedewig (o.) 1672
Rumor, Ida Margaretha (o.) 2816
Ruth, Catharina (o.) 717

Sachs, Daniel (f.) 1806, 1844
Sacrificium eucharisticum 453
Saller, Cathar. Marg. von, née Stahl (f.) 1785
Sameland, Anna Maria (f.) 2798
Sartorius, Anna Margareta, née Mohr (f.) 1297, 1310
Satt wonn . . . Herr Michael Watson 1284
Saurbrauer, Balthasar (o.) 970
Schabau, Paul (f.) 3039
Schacht, Anna, née Koch (f.) 1588
Schacht, Eilhard (f.) 1871, 1873
Schade, Augusta Margareta, nee Marschalk (f.) 705
Schade, Offe (f.) 1299
Schauenburg, Christoff (f.) 1852
Schauplatz Barbarischer Schlavereij, Der 1304
Scheel, Rabe-Wilhelm von (o.) 2831
Schepler, Margaretha (f.) 1444
Schiffs-Articul 2452
Schilling, Andre (f.) 1020
Schilling, Anna (f.) 1027
Schippel, Joh. Nicolaus (o.) 1635, 1654, 1660A
Schippel, Johann Stephan 2084
Schlaff, Liborius Henricus (f.) 1333
Schlechte Hoffnung 2749
Schlesswig-Hollsteinischer Actorum Publicorum 1371
Schlesswig-Hollsteinisches Gesangbuch 2748
Schlesswigische Kirchen Historie 2172
Schlesswigische und Holsteinische Kjrchen Buch, Das 1274
Schmid, Anna (f.) 1318
Schmid, Ida, nee Hecklawer (f.) 1548
Schmidt, Johan Eler (o.) 2714
Schmidt von Eisenberg, Christian & Gottfried (f.) 1887
Schmidt von Eisenberg, Valentin (f.) 1887, 2064A
Schneidebacher, Friedrich (f.) 589
Schneider, Gottfried (f.) 1432, 1448
Schneider, Margarete, née Wasmer (f.) 752
Schnell, Anna Esichen (f.) 724
schön Gebet-Büchlein, Ein 2785
schön geistlich Tractätlein Von Der Zahl Drey, Ein 753
Schönbach, Susanna Elisabeth (f.) 1641
Schöne Erinnerung, Eine 1213
schöne Glantz Gottes, Der 2081
Schola Catechitica Eidorea Ecclesia Christi Regia 972
Scholten, Elisabeth (f.) 2853
Schomaker, Wilh. (f.) 1767
Schreiben an die Stadt Bremen 274
Schreiben An Ihre Kön. May. . . . Vom Nieder-Sächsischen Crayss 805
Schreiben Aus Kopenhagen 989
Schreiben Eines Freundes 2117
Schreiben Von deme was bey . . . Willem Nieupoort 990
Schreiben . . . Wegen der Seqvestration 1836, 1888
Schrifft-Catechismus 2686
Schrifft- und Vernunfftmässiger Unterricht 1756
Schrotering, Albert (o.) 2008
Schuldiges Lob- und Danck-Opffer 2165
Schuldiges Lob und Freuden-Gedicht 790
Schuldigste Glückwünschung 2710
Schuldigste Observantz 2518
Schultz, Anna Catharina nee Heldt (f.) 2982
Schultz, Maria Lepape (f.) 326
Schumacher, Hedwig, nee Miller (f.) 583
Schupp, Henrich (f.) 2448
Schutzrede 800
Schwartz, Amalia (o.) 2831
Schwartz, Margaretha Maria (f.) 2217

Schwedische Grillen 999
Schwedischer Meyneyd-Spigel 424
Schwedischer Pickelhering, Der 1075
Schwedischer vnd Dähnischer Discurs, Ein 1000
Schwedischer Völcker Schiff-Bruch 1988
Schwedisches Fastnacht-Spiel 1001
Schwedisches Meineid 870
Schwedisches Piket-Spiel 871
Schwedische Viel-Frass, Der 869
Schwenck, Anna (f.) 278
Schwerdfeger, Johann (f.) 2071
Scripturas Copernizans 2493
Secundæ Editionis des Jüdtschen Lowbokes 12
Seedorff, Heilwig Ursula, nee Gloxin (f.) 1485
See-Farth 1499
See-städt see Sehestet(t)
Seger, Hinrich (f.) 3043
Sehested, Christian (f.) 1195
Sehestedt, Kay (f.) 272
Sehestet, Georg (Jürgen) (f.) 270, 273
Sehestett, Margaretha (f.) 2144, 2154
Sehet hier 2869
Sehet welch ein Mensch! 2600
Sehnliche Klage gläubiger . . . Seelen 693
Sehnlicher Nachklang vnd Hertzliche Glückwünschung 816
Sellmer, Wibke Magdlena (f.) 1835
Send-Schreiben Eines Dennemärckischen Von Adel 1838
Send-Schreiben Worin die verleumbderische Aufflage 2103
Sententiæ Schuppianæ 1091
Seüffzerlein über das Leiden Christi 1387
Sibbers, Margaretha (f.) 2761
Sibbersen, Agatha (f.) 2653
Sicherer Schild 1076A
Sieben böse Geister 1788
Sieben mahl Sieben 2781, 3000
VII Predigten von der Prædestination 1551
Sieben und zwantzigste April, Der 2945
XXVII. Psalm, Der 2535
Sieges-Seüle 1003
Sigwardsøn, Georg Brochenhus (f.) 1708
Sing-Freuden-Gedichte 2733
Sittig von der Oelsnitz, Hans (f.) 2349
Sönnichsen, Peter (f.) 1108
Soli Deo gloria 2703, 3139
Soliloquia Biblica 2748
Sommer, Margaretha Johanna, nee Rheder (f.) 2179, 2180
Sommer, Rebecca (o.) 482
Sonderbahre Predigten 2908
Sonnen-klarer Beweissthum 2765
Sonnet Uber Die höchst-glück und erfreuliche Alliance 2797
Sontags Fragen Von Den Alten Kirchen-Lehrern 743
Sophia, Queen of Denmark (f.) 176
Sophia Amalia, Queen of Denmark (f.) 2228
Species facti 1598
Specification der Reiter und Dragoner 1839
Specification Derer unter Bornholm gestrandeten Schwedischen Trouppen 1935
Specification . . . Kriegs-Schiffe 761
Specification Oder Verzeichnüs 206
Sperling, Anna Catharina (o.) 1287
Sperling, Paul (f.) 1970, 1973
Spiegel Dänischer Trew 987
Spiegel der Barmhertzigkeit 2852
Spiegel Des Heutigen Christenthums 2978
Spiess, Alexander (f.) 1358
Spruch-Catechismus 2241

Staats Kriegs und Friedens Journal 2839
Starcker Schild Gottes 449
Status Controversiæ 1428
Steffens, Paul (o.) 1658
Steinberg, Georg von (f.) 445
Steinmann, Sophie Elisabeth (o.) 1157
Stekken Arons, Der 1936
Stemann, Anna Catharina (o.) 2905, 2951
Stemann, Justus Valentin (o.) 734 (f.) 2392, 2428, 2434, 2440
Stenger, Johann Melchior 2415, 2647, 2650
Stevens, Catharina (f.) 1298
Stevens, Philipp Jacob (f.) 1583, 1598A
Stilstand 1990
Stöcken, Abel Maria von (o.) 1905
Stökken, Christian von (o.) 1877 (f.) 2192, 2213, 2233, 2247-48
Stökken, Margareta von, nee Grave (f.) 2102, 2117A
Stolle, Anna Sophia (f.) 462
Stolle, Jacob (f.) 484
Storning, Hinrich (f.) 2715
Straten, Johann ther (o.) 2843
Strauss, Margaretha (o.) 1092
Streit zwischen der Gerechtigkeit 2540
Strenæ, Dass sindt: Christliche New Jahr Geschencke 163
Stricker, Briggita (o.) 2580
Stricker, Henrich (o.) 2919
Strüver, Michael (o.) 2718
Struve, Peter (o.) 2769
Struve, Reimar (f.) 2679
Stuart, Margaretha Elisabetha de (o.) 2517
Suedisches Piekets Spiel 871
Sülings, Dorothea (o.) 2843
Sültzberger, Georg (f.) 2044
Sültzberger, Sophia, née von Stevens (f.) 1727
Süssbittere Freude 76
Suhm, Anna Catharina (f.) 1994
Suhm, Hinrich (f.) 3123
Sultzberger, Margaretha (f.) 1565
Summarien över de Evangelia 16
Summarien über die . . . Handels-Posten 2548
Summarische Erzehlung 1377
Summarische Information 1600
Summarische Wiederlegung Einer . . . Remonstration 2285
Summarischer Ausszug 1539
Sun theo 1595
Syndica concio 1552
Synodal Predigt 1052

Tagbüchlein 597
Tatter, Michael Gabriel (o.) 606
Taubmann, Friederich (f.) 1724
Tauf-Sermon 2268
Taxa der Gerichts-Sportulen 2031
Tempel Der Danckbarkeit, Ein 1518
Terckel, Severin (f.) 460
Teutsche Gedichte 2107
Teutsches Neues Testament 3047
Thaumatographia 1878, 2992
Theologia Catechetica 616, 756
Theologia teutsch 52
Theologische Betrachtung Des . . . Cometen 2047
Theologische zu Beforderung der Gottseeligkeit . . . Tractätlein 1967, 2195
Theologisches Bedencken 1188, 1816, 2442
Theologisches Sendschreiben (2585) 2855, 3097
Theriaca Caelestis 2042
thewr edel und hochwerthes New Jahr-Geschenck, Ein 304

Thiene, Hans von (f.) 2595
Thoma, Hermann (f.) 850
Thombsen, Michael Friderich (o.) 2822
Thomsen, Andreas (f.) 2226, 2246
Thomsen, Christina (f.) 1361
Thomsen, Elisabeth (o.) 2017
Thomsen, Marina (o.) 2152
Thornedden, Anna Catharina, nee Brügman (o.) 970
Thränen Christi 1407
Tisch-und Leber-reime 1688
Tod, Anna (f.) 2111
Tonningensis Ecclesiae Evangelicae Concordia 690
Topographia Norwegiæ 2218
Topsen, Anna (f.) 695
Tractätchen Worinnen Das . . . Oleumlunæ 3133
Tractat de Marine 1718A
Tractat Einer Defensiv-Alliantz 1327
Tractat Nach Anleitung . . . Conjuncturen 2799
Tractatus Physic-Theologicus 184
Tractat Von Assistenz 1603
Tragauscher Weinacht- und Oster-Freuden 277
Tragoedia Von den Tugenden vnd Lastern 213
Trauermusik durch zwei Chöre vorgestellt 2931
Trauriges Klag-Lied vnd Trost-Gedicht 195
Traur- und Ehrngedicht 502
Travendahlischer Friede 3119
Treue Lutherthumb, Das 2471
Treuhertzige Auffmunterung 1446
Treuhertzige Warnung 1815
Trifolium sacrum 2253
Trifolium strenæ annuæ 1374
Trigæ Peregrinantium 425
Tritaunischer Antritt und Abscheid 2279
Triumph-Altar 1764
Triumph Des Elephanten 1007
Triumphirende Sieges-Fahn 1845
Triumph-Lied 335, 704
Triumph-Ode Welche Bey Haltung der Lob-Rede 3095
Triumph-Thor bey Krönung Friedrich III 544
Trivmphvs Nuptialis Danicus 214, 529
Trolle, Helena (f.) 1152
Trurige Klageledt van dem groten Flode 75
Türcken-Calender 2989
Tugend Weg- und Lasterbahn 619
Tundersche Unsterbliche Sterblichkeit 546
Turibulum Pietatis Sabbatinæ 279
Tyche, Anna Katherina (o.) 2447

Uber Jerusalem Weinende Jesus, Der 2908
Vbergebung der Festung Bremer-Föhrde 808
Ubelacker, Friderich (o.) 2734
Übereinstimmung der Psalmen Davids 344
Übung des kleinen Catechismi 1516, 1553, 3128A
Übung in der Gottseeligkeit 1489
Umständliche Relation Von der . . . Unterredung 1940
ungeänderte Augspurgische Confession, Die 2590
ungegründete Hoffnung, Die 2661
Universal Welches . . . An das Ertz-Stifft Brehmen 809
Unordentliche Kirchen-Ordnung 3009
Vnparteyscher Ansführlicher Bericht 1009
Vnpartheyliche Erwegung 2043
Unschuld Des Antenors 1008
Untadeliche States-Welt-Man, Der 1460
Vnter den zween Frjderejchen . . . Newe Landesbeschreibung 645
Unterricht Von Der Teutschen Sprache 2108
Unterschiedliche Calendar 973, 1059, 1365A

Unterschiedliche Considerationes 1604
Underschiedliche Oracula Jm Ballett 732
Unterschiedlicher Ellen-auch anderer Maass . . . Vergleichung 1706
Unterschideliche zu der Stadt Bremen . . . Beylage 655
Unterthänige Lob-Rede An . . . Herrn Christian 487
Vnterthänigste Erklarung 1206
Unterwiesene Krancken-Wärter, Der 1954
Untreu schläget seinen eigenen Herren 1207
Unumgängliche doch Glimpffliche Ablehnung 2867
Unumgängliche Vorstellung 2810
unvergleichlich gleiche Buchstaben Zahl, Die 2868
Unvergleichlichste Winckel-Rechte Drey-Eck, Das 2811
Unverzögerte Generale-Wiederlegung 2528
Unvorgreiffliches Bedencken 1698
Uppendorff, Johannes (f.) 1514
Vrsachen und Beschaffenheit der Streitigkeiten 1960
Ursachen Warum . . . die frembde Kriegs-Völcker 2634
Ursachen, warum ein im Pabstthum gebohrner 2565
Uhrsachen warum er Lutherisch worden 2860
Vhrsachen Welche Jhre. Königl. Mayt. als Dominum 1894
Uthermarck, Johannes Adolph (f.) 2025, 2036

Väterlicher Seegnen 2319
Valentin, Birgitta, nee Höen (f.) 713
Valet-Predigt Welche Zu Hannover 2433
Valet-Sermon 1208
Van dem Erschrecklicken Gesichte 69
Van dem Landkope 9
Van dem Wunderteken 95
Van Eiden vnd Eidleistungen 10
Van Processen etlycker sunderbaren Vällen 11
Veer Schertz Gedichte 642
Venninghaus, Wilhelm (f.) 1962
Vera Religio 1858
Verboth Unverarbeitet oder alt Kupffer 2340
Verdeutschete Bucolica 1384
Verdeutschete Waldlieder 547
vereinigte Götter Streit, Der 2396
Verführete Schäferin Cynthie, Die 1077
Vergewisserung . . . Casp. Herm. Sandhagens 3049
Vergnüg- und Unvergnügung Ballet . . . Wilhelminen Ernestinen 596
Verheissungen 1859
Verhör des Catechismi 140
Verlachet Venus 1004
Verliebte Sulamithin 3001
Verlohre Zeit und Arbeit Ballet 622
Vermehrte Newe Beschreibung Der Muscowitischen vnd Persischen Reyse 754, 1120
Vermehrtes Dreyfaches Garten-Buch 3074A
Vernünftige lautere Lehre des Heiligen Catechismi 2208
Vernünftige lautere Milch des Catechismi 1659
vernünfftige lautere Milch Des Heiligen Catechismi, Die 2080, 2208, 2670, 2947
Vernunfft- und Gewissens-Fragen 2529
Verordnete Fast- Buss- und Bet-Tags Texte 2219
Verordnetes Buss-Gebet 3077
Verordnung betreffend Die neue Stempel 3062
Verordnung Des Gestempelten Papiers 2673, 2936
Verordnung . . . mit Vormundschafften 3
Verordnung . . . Nordstrandt 103
(Verordnung Nutzbringender Geselschaft) 672
Verordnung Wegen Certificationen 1259
Verordnung Wegen Der Brawer 2738

Verordnung Wegen der Confirmation 2628
Verordnung wegen der Convoye 98
Verordnung Wegen Derjenigen so in dero Fürstenthumen 2701
Verordnung Wegen des Brau-Wesens 2736
Verordnung Wegen des Gestempelten Papiers 1337, 1565B, 2220, 2820
Verordnung Wegen eingebohrner Vnterthanen 1260
Verordnung Wegen Einrichtung der neüen Königlichen Academie 2537
Verordnung wie es am Buss- und Bet-Tage 2802
Verordnung Wie es mit Administration 2186
Verordnung Wormach der Kopff- und Viehe-Schatz 1910A
Vertheidigung Seines . . . Römischer Beelzebub 1408
Vertrag zwischen . . . Friederichen dem Andern . . . 488
Verzeichniss der Gebete, Gesänge und Collecten 1250
Vette, Eberhard (o.) 2635
Viben, Margaretha Catharina (f.) 2198
Victoria Christiana contra Judæos 2064
Vidimirte Copey Eines Schwedischen intercipirten Schreibens 810
Vidimirte Schreiben 873
Vier einfältige Fragen 1010
vier Elementen, Die 673
(Vier Jahreszeiten und derer Gewitterungen) 56
Vier Memorialien 910
Vierzehen Geistreiche Gesänge 2194, 2229
Vieth, Dorothea (o.) 1191
Vieth, Liebhard (o.) 2680A
Vindiciæ Honoris 670
Vindicirung seiner Restorsion 2650
Vivat Fridericus III 1209
Vördraff einer Nothwendigen Assertion 50
Vohlman, Anna Margareta (o.) 2587
Voigt, Clawes Johansen (f.) 894
Volcmarus, Justus Theodorus (o.) 2072
Vollständiges Gesang-Buch 1719, 1773, 1848, 1895, 2122, 2341, 2592
Vollständiges Inventarium 2976
Volnkommene Beschreibung Der Auff Fühnen geführten Bataillie 1011
Von dem Trost der Christen 70
Von etlichen kräfftigen vnd hochbewerthen spagyrischen Medicamenten 122
Vorbereitung zur Ewigkeit 1968
Vorschlag wegen der künfftig anzustellenden Gelehrten Unterredungen 2841
Vorstellung etlicher Kunst- und Naturalien-Kammern 1699A, 1700, 1757
Vorstellung . . . Wegen Uberlassung einiger Teutschen Trouppen 3032
Vorstius, Christian (f.) 1323
Vortrab 2812
Vortrab Vnd Deduction 428

Wackerbarth, Anna Hedwig (f.) 2688, 2720
Wahre Abbildung Anthonette Bourignons 1560
Wahre und eigentliche Abbildung der Ceremonien 211
Wahre und Reine Lehre, Die 1662
Wahre Vorstellung des nähern Succession-Rechtens 1354, 1399
Wahr- und Gewissen-haffter Vnterricht 1012
Wahrhaffter Abdruck Unterschiedener Responsorum Juris 1660
Wahrhaffter Bericht dass in denen Fürstl. Anmerckungen 2804
Waldschmidt, Wilhelm Huldrich (o.) 2523

Walther, Dorothea, nee Heklawer (f.) 1461, 1472
Waltporger, Jochim (o.) 712
Wandel, Bagge (o.) 557
Wandling, Gottfried (f.) 1372
Wardenburg, Ernst Günther (o.) 2532A
Warhaffte Deduction 96
Warhaffter Abdruck . . . Churfürstliche Collegial-Versamblung 146
Warhaffter Bericht 1210
Warhaffter Bericht Von einem besessenen Knaben 1646
Warhafftige Copey 877
Warhafftige Erzehlung Dessen Was wegen . . . Pietismi 3113
Warhafftige gründtliche doch kurtze Relation 61
Warhafftige Historische Relation Vnd erkleringe 5
Warhafftige newe Zeitung . . . Calmar 37A
Warhafftige Relation 429, 876, 878, 1013, 1014
Warhafftige Relation . . . Joachimus Pistorius und Johann Adolph Becker 662
Warhafftige Relation was . . . fürgefallen bey Lauholm 811
Warhaftiger Abtruck 881
Warhafftiger Bericht . . . Hartwig Lohmann 121
Warhafftiger Bericht . . . Hamburgischen Wesen 2290
Warhafftiger Bericht und Abdruck 879
Warhafftiger Discurss 880
Warhafftiger vnd eigentlicher einer vornehmen Person Communicirter Bericht 431
Warhafftige Wiederleg- vnd Beantwortung 430
Was ists? 1991
Wasmuth, Dorothea, nee Tarnow (f.) 1506, 1515
Wasmuth, Joh. Georg (o.) 2297, 2337A
Wasmuth, Matthias (f.) 2361, 2378, 2380A, 2383
Wassmer, Margareta Christiana von (f.) 2892, 2896, 2902, 2917, 2922, 2927, 2929-30, 2943, 2952
Wassmer, Margaretha, nee Bruhn (f.) 1784
Watson, Michael (o.) 1284
Wedderkop, Anna Margareta, nee Johansen (f.) 3050, 3071, 3087, 3089, 3100, 3117
Wedderkop, Gabriel (f.) 2762
Wedderkop, Ursula, nee Burchard (f.) 2776
Wedderkopf (f.) 3135
Weg des Lebens, Der 1368
Weg zur Gottseeligkeit 2382
Wegen des versetzten Aller-Durchlauchtesten Nahmens, Die 2955
Weh-schreiende Stein, Der 2979
Weidenkopf, Anna, nee Brockes (f.) 2258, 2287A
Weidenkopff, Eberhard (f.) 749, 751
Weiblicher Tugend-Spiegel 2104
Weigbe, Sophie Charlotte (f.) 2232
Weissheit, Salomonis, Die 2583
Weiteres Nachdencken 2562
Weitere Verordnung Wegen der Certification 929
Wenge-Lambsdorff, Andreas Kasimir Thaddaeus von der (f.) 2685
Wenig-bauenden heutigen Kirchenlehrart 2359
Westens, Anna Christina (o.) 2461
Wexel-Recht 2085
Weyland König Christiani Tertij 491
widerkehrende Ninive, Das 1636
Wieder Die von dem Niedern Gerichte zu Hamburg 2335
Wiederauffgelegte Privilegia 1290, 2292, 2492, 2551, 2863
Wiederbringung Der Evangelischen Wahrheit, Die 2993

Wiedererlangung der Jnsul Bornholm 1015
Wiederholte Schutz-rede 1122
Wiele, Anna van der, nee von Berend (f.) 3092, 3116
Wietersheim, Friedrich (o.) 244
Wigand, Magdalena (o.) 1556
Wildenheim, Johannes (f.) 2795
Wildhaginn, J. N. (f.) 2344
Wilhelmine Ernestine, Princess of Denmark (o.) 596
Wilthagen, Moritz (f.) 1437
Winckler, Catharina, nee Grefkens (o.) 607, 611
Winckler, Johann Michael (f.) 2287, 2289
Wind, Christian (o.) 703
Wind, Eric (f.) 1612
Winsen, Henr. von (f.) 291
Wisch, Adolph Philip von der (f.) 1425
Wisch, Marg. von der (f.) 676
Wismar (f.) 175, 327
Witte, Johannes 2253
Wittemak, Elsabe, nee Brauhn (f.) 1240
Wittmak, Christina (o.) 1134
Wochentliche Zeitung 814, 1016, 1138
Wördinghusen, Gerhard (f.) 1237
Wohlgegründete Behaubtung 2293
Wohlgemeinte Rettung des Politischen Discurs 141
Wohlgemeinter Vortrag 2252
Wolbegründete Defensions-Schrifft 2275
Wolbegründete Ehrn-Defension 603
Wolbegründeter Defensions-Schrifft 2334
Wolbegründeter Gegenbericht 1378
Wollgemeintes Bedencken 2655
Wolgemeinte Warnung 2024
Worgewitz, Elisabeth Anna von, nee von Kröcher (f.) 2173
Wunder-Brillen-Zeitung 884

Zehen Hirten Gespräche 384
Zehen-Jährige Alliance 1606, 1653
Zeitläffige Staats-Begebenheiten 2593
Zeller, Eberhard 2655
Zeter Geschrey 432
Zeugnüss der Wahrheit 2627
Ziegeldecker, Friederich (f.) 1521
Ziemer, Anna (f.) 1790
Zeitvertreibende und erlustigende Wahrsagungen 2086
Zimbrischer Dank baum 718
Zimmer, Gregor (o.) 2450
Zimmermann, Anna Christina (o.) 2018
Zitscher, Peter (f.) 3042
Zoll-Rolle im Oresund 466
Zu den Altonais. Tractaten . . . Declaration 2416
Zu Traventhal . . . unterzeichnete Friedens-Puncten, Die 3126
Zurückgewiesener Mercurius 2415
Zustossen Rohr, Das 1904
Zwar Entfernte aber doch Beständige Bruder-Lieb, Die 2719
Zweene geistliche Gesäng 112
Zwerg, Magdalena Sibylla (f.) 1454
Zwerg, Margareta Lucia, nee Martini (f.) 2815
Zwey Auslegungen des VII. Capittels . . . Michæ 2723
Zweyfacher Wegweiser 543
Zwey Gebett 147
Zwey Memorialen Von Herren Otto Krach 1084
Zwey Nützliche Tractätlein 1091

Zwey Schreiben . . . Stadt Hamburg 2294
Zwey vnderschiedliche Tractätlein 159
Zwey von Jhren Königl. Majestät . . . Befehl-Brieffe 1851
zwischen dem Rahte und Bürgerschaft . . . gewechselte Schriften, Die 2956

zwischen Dero Königl. Mayest . . . Friedens-Puncten, Die 2441
Zwo Comoedjen 215
Zwo Dancksagungs- Trost- vnd Warnungs-Predigt 382
Zwölf geistliche Andachten 1919
Zwo Konigliche Schwedische Ordren 1018

# UNIVERSITY OF KANSAS PUBLICATIONS
## Library Series
### *Editor*, JAMES HELYAR

1. *University of Kansas: List of Publications.* Compiled by Mary Maud Smelser. 1935. *available on request*

2. *University of Kansas Graduate School Theses, 1888-1947.* Compiled by Bessie E. Wilder. 1949.*

3. *Two Augustan Booksellers: John Dunton and Edmond Curll*, by Peter Murray Hill. 1958.  *

4. *New Adventures Among Old Books: An Essay in Eighteenth Century Bibliography*, by William B. Todd. 1958. *

5. *Catalogues of Rare Books: A Chapter in Bibliographical History*, by Archer Taylor. 1958.  *

6. *What Kind of a Business is This? Reminiscences of the Book Trade and Book Collectors*, by Jacob Zeitlin. 1959. *

7. *The Bibliographical Way*, by Fredson Bowers. 1959. *

8. *A Bibliography of English Imprints of Denmark*, by P. M. Mitchell. 1960. $2.00

9. *In the Burning of His Library* and *On Medical Travel*, by Thomas Bartholin, translated by Charles D. O'Malley. 1961.

10. *A Bibliography of the Frank E. Melvin Collection of Pamphlets of the French Revolution in the University of Kansas Libraries*, by Ambrose Saricks. 1961. 2 vols., $7.50

11. *Observations on Paper as Evidence*, by Allen H. Stevenson. 1961. 85c

12. *University of Kansas Graduate School Theses, 1948-1958.* Compiled by Bessie E. Wilder. 1961. $2.50

13. *Six Variant Readings in the First Folio of Shakespeare*, by Charlton Hinman. 1961. *

14. *A Petition Regarding the Conditions in the C.S.M. Prison at Columbia, S.C., Addressed to the Confederate Authorities by Col. John Fraser.* Edited by George L. Anderson. 1961. $1.50

15. *William Dampier: Seaman-Scientist*, by Joseph C. Shipman. 1962. $1.50

16. *Maps of the 16th to 19th Centuries*, by Thomas R. Smith and Bradford L. Thomas. 1963. $3.50

17. *Looking at an Early Map*, by R. A. Skelton. 1965. *

18. *A Bibliography of James Joyce Studies*, by Robert H. Deming. 1963. $3.00

19. *Maps of Costa Rica*, by Albert H. Palmerlee. 1965. $6.00

20. *A Checklist of Linneana, 1735-1835*, by Terrence Williams. 1964. $1.50

21. *International Bibliography of Vegetation Maps*, edited by A. W. Küchler. Volume 1: North America. 1965. *

22. *Four Centuries of Shakespeare Publication*, by Giles E. Dawson. 1964. $1.00

23. *A Guide to the Ssu Pu Ts'ung K'an*, by Karl Lo. 1965. $1.50

24. *A Classified Bibliography of Korean Materials, 1808-1962*, by Felix Moos. In preparation

25. *Censored: Books and their Right to Live*, by Elmer Gertz. 1965. *

26. *International Bibliography of Vegetation Maps*, edited by A. W. Küchler. Volume 2: Europe. 1966. $10.00

27. *Bibliography and Natural History: Essays presented at a Conference convened in June 1964 by Thomas R. Buckman.* 1966. $5.00

28. *A Bibliography of 17th Century German Imprints in Denmark and the Duchies of Schleswig-Holstein*, compiled by P. M. Mitchell. 1969. $15.00

29. *International Bibliography of Vegetation Maps*, edited by A. W. Küchler. Volume 3: Union of Soviet Socialist Republics, Asia, and Australia. 1969. $7.50

30. *Rilke's last year*, by George C. Schoolfield. 1969. $1.50

31. *The Two Worlds of University Publishing*, by Roger W. Shugg. 1968. $1.00

32. *Bibliographical Contributions*, 1. $2.00

33. *A Bibliographical Catalogue of the Ellis Collection of Ornithological Literature.* Vol. I. In preparation

34. *The Cuban Revolution of Fidel Castro Viewed from Abroad: an Annotated Bibliography*, by Gilberto V. Fort. 1969. $3.00

35. *Growth and Change in the Early English Press*, by Richmond P. Bond. 1969. $1.00

* Titles marked with an asterisk are now in short supply, and are normally only available to complete the files of institutions maintaining exchange agreements with the University of Kansas Libraries.

The Library Series and other University of Kansas Publications are offered to learned societies, colleges and universities and other institutions in exchange for similar publications. All communications regarding exchange should be addressed to the Exchange Librarian, University of Kansas Libraries, Lawrence, Kansas. Communications regarding sales, reviews, and forthcoming publications in the Library Series, should be addressed to the Editor of Library Publications, University of Kansas Libraries, Lawrence, Kansas.